THE
PROVINCES
OF FRANCE

BELGIUM

GERMANY

LUXEMBOURG

CHAMPAGNE

LORRAINE

ALSACE

Moselle

Vosges

Rhine

FRANCHE COMTÉ

Jura

BURGUNDY

ERNAIS

NAIS

LYONNAIS

SWITZERLAND

SAVOIE

ALPS

DAUPHINÉ

ITALY

Rhone

UEDOC

COMTÉ DE
NICE

PROVENCE

COMTAT VENAISSIN

OUSSILLON

HOWS AND WHYS OF
FRENCH COOKING

Hows and Whys of
French Cooking

ALMA LACH

With a Chapter on Wine by
George Rezek

and a Foreword by André Simon

x

The University of Chicago Press
CHICAGO AND LONDON

The University of Chicago Press, Chicago 60637
The University of Chicago Press, Ltd., London
© 1970, 1974 by Alma Lach
All rights reserved. Published 1974
Printed in the United States of America
International Standard Book Number: 0-226-46740-6
Library of Congress Catalog Card Number: 74-123351

to
"THE PROFESSOR"
and
His Educated Palate

CONTENTS

ILLUSTRATIONS

FOREWORD

Vauvenargues had more than his fair share of misfortunes, but he never was bitter. "The world was surely made *pour des êtres intelligents*—for intelligent people," he wrote soon before his death, adding: "it is so full of difficulties." It is very much the same today. There may be more difficulties, but there are also a greater number of *êtres intelligents*.

There are old men well in their nineties, like me, who tell with moist eyes and a dry tongue how much better and cheaper wine and food were years ago! Those were the days! Nonsense! What is best to eat and drink today certainly costs more in modern paper money, but there is ever so much more of it than there was gold in the good old days! Money, of course, is not only necessary; it is indispensable, but it is not—or it ought not to be—an end in itself; it is and should be a means to an end, the end being whatever is good, better, and best at all levels and in everything that makes life worth living, be it books, art, or music, what we wear, eat, or drink. There is a greater demand for pop singing and baked beans on toast than classical music and fine fare, but here is a book which shows that author and publishers believe, as I do myself, that there is still, and that there will always be, a number of civilized people, not a few but many of them, who will welcome such a book, and be grateful to the author for the help she gives to all who take an intelligent interest in fine fare.

Cookery books published in the course of my long life may be beyond count, but very few of them were like this one, beyond praise!

André L. Simon

April, 1970

PREFACE

Haute cuisine is a logical system of cooking that has developed in France, especially Paris, over the past several centuries. Once the "Hows and Whys" of this *system* are learned, the cook becomes an independent and creative worker who makes up recipes by imaginative adaptations of and refinements upon what generations of cooks and chefs have evolved and codified into standard French procedures.

Paris is the world center of gastronomy—the *étoile* toward which all the lesser stars of food are irresistibly attracted. The provinces of France regularly send their best products to Paris, including young, ambitious chefs and native recipes. Some of these country chefs, Escoffier among them, won places for themselves in the great restaurants of the world specializing in *haute cuisine*. Their provincial recipes were often given star billing on the menus of these great restaurants. Paris, too, has its own mode of simpler cooking, or *cuisine bourgeoise,* which persists in the smaller restaurants and in the private homes of the capital. While the provinces contributed much to the evolution of *haute cuisine,* they also preserved and cultivated many local food traditions. In this second edition I have added the section "Provincial Menus and Recipes" to give some idea of these various local traditions.

Most of the great French cookbooks are designed for French cooks and kitchens. In this book all elements of French cuisine, city and country, are adapted to the American kitchen. Since I have lived and cooked in both the United States and France, I have sought in the discussions and recipes which follow to reconcile French food ideas with American eating habits, to adjust techniques wherever necessary to fit our cooking conditions, and to suggest practical substitutes for materials or equipment not readily found in our kitchens.

There are no shortcuts, bright ideas, spectacular recipes, or complicated pieces of equipment that will convert the kitchen amateur into a culinary artist. But, once he is a culinary artist, he will figure out his own shortcuts, and then use modern ways to do the same old things. But it is only when the hows and whys of French cuisine are understood that the same end can be reached by a different route. This book deals in fundamentals.

Certainly the amateur cook can produce an extraordinary dish. But what about the rest of the meal? And with what will he vary his repertory in the future?

The answer to these culinary questions is to be found in the *logical system* of French cooking. It makes the most of every food and blends the various dishes and wines together into a balanced totality called a meal or menu.

The fun of cooking comes in trying to create and prepare *the great meal*. Therefore, think about the total menu. Let it not overtax your budget, your grocer, or your own abilities. Write the menu down. Have it before you. Eat it in your imagination. Match the wines to the dishes and then consume them in your imagination along with their culinary partners. Let your imagination taste the relationship of one course to the other and then be prepared to change what you mentally question. Think about the meal picture. Does it have color, texture, and design, and do the tastes complement one another?

The art of cooking lies in the ability to taste, to reproduce taste, and to create taste.

ACKNOWLEDGMENTS

To my mother, who allowed me to run loose in her farm kitchen at the tender age of six, I owe an incalculable debt. Her patience, encouragement, and soft teachings helped me to win a 4-H prize that gave me more satisfaction as a child than almost anything I did. Even today when I go home for a visit, my mother and I spend the late hours of the evening (after the dishes are done, that is) discussing and swapping recipes.

My good friend Helen Clapesattle Shugg, author of *The Doctors Mayo,* practiced a little surgery on my presentation. But her efforts went far beyond editorial matters, for she herself cooked from the manuscript as it was being written. So too did Susan Philipson, a young friend and author.

I am indebted to Professor Elwood V. Jensen for his technical advice on the chemical composition in some recipes and his analysis of others. To a number of food and drink experts who have regularly contributed to my knowledge I am grateful. Especially to Dr. George Rezek of the Wine and Food Society I extend my deepest thanks for his contribution of "The Marriage of Food and Wine."

The late André L. Simon, the famous London gourmet and oenophile, was more than generous to a fellow Chevalier du Tastevin in consenting to write a brief Foreword to this book.

To my daughter Sandy I give the thanks that every mother owes to a dedicated eater. Much to my gratification, she has shown herself to be an excellent cook for husband Bill. As for my seven-year-old grandson, he regularly gets more than his share of the caviar and prefers it with crème fraîche and onions. In the hope that he will continue in his fancy food ways, I concocted a special dessert for him, one that he likes and the one I have called Soufflé Glacé Guillaume II in his honor.

And most important of all, the "Professor" of the dedication is my husband, Donald F. Lach. He is the Bernadotte E. Schmitt Professor of Modern History at the University of Chicago. And like most professors, he is a hard taskmaster. When we arrived for our first year in Paris, he ordained: "you will go to the Cordon Bleu and learn to make a sauce. I'm tired of country gravy." So I dedicate this book to "my professor" with the fervent hope that it will not give him ulcers or cause him undue embarrassment!

My gratitude is great to all those who have helped in the production of this book, but I alone am responsible for any errors that remain.

Using the Book

That you know how to use a cookbook I am sure—but let me give you my thinking on this book.

The little blue, white, and red ribbons (the national colors of both France and the United States) are designed to be used as recipe markers. I place the blue ribbon in the recipe being made, and use the other two to mark the cross-reference recipes that are sometimes needed to make the blue-ribbon selection.

Most of the main-dish recipes and the country menus list a wine. The selection is the one we feel goes best with the particular recipe or menu. If our wine choice is not available to you, or does not fit into the budget, then use our selection as a guide and choose another wine from the wine charts.

Liquids used in the recipes are usually wine, vermouth, cider, beer, or stock. Avoid water, since it has no flavor. When water is a part of a recipe, it is usually flavored with a chunk of butter, sugar, salt, herbs, spices, or vegetables.

The thickener of my choice is all-purpose flour rather than any of the other thickening agents, such as arrowroot and cornstarch, which have a tendency to break down and lose their thickening power when overheated. If they are used in a hot sauce, they must be incorporated at the very last minute and the dish served immediately. They are best used to thicken sweet acid fruit sauces and desserts that are to be served cold.

Recipe charts for quick consultation have been added to certain chapters. The basic "mother" recipe is given in full and the individual differences in the offspring recipes are clearly indicated. After you have had a bit of practice, a glance at one of these charts should be enough to enable you to prepare the recipe and its variants.

No cookbook is complete without definitions. My explanations of cooking terms, ingredients, and equipment are located in "Information," pp. 597–614.

All recipes, unless otherwise stated, are written in quarter measurements. Since we normally think in even fractions (such as ¼ or ½ hour, or a quarter or half a dollar), I have worked out most of the measurements in this book in even fractions.

Unsalted butter is used in all recipes calling for butter. If you substitute salted butter, then reduce the salt in the recipe.

All recipes are designed to serve six people, unless otherwise stated.

Throughout the book you will notice recipe ingredients listed such as beurre manié, brown food coloring, and crème fraîche. These foods are as essential to French cooking as salt and pepper. But unlike salt and pepper, these foods cannot be bought in the store, and must be made at home. If you make them first, and then store them in their proper place (see recipes), you are ready to start cooking in the French manner. Here are the recipes.

BEURRE MANIÉ

Beurre manié is an uncooked thickening agent of butter and flour. It is mainly used to thicken (and to adjust the thickness of) sauces.

⅛ pound butter   4 tablespoons flour

1. Cream together butter and flour, always using equal amounts. Put this paste into a small jar. Cover and refrigerate or freeze, depending upon how quickly it will be used. Substitute this paste for water-and-flour mixtures in recipes.

2. If this paste is to be frozen it is best to freeze it in tablespoon amounts since it is not possible to measure it when frozen. When needed, simply add the frozen paste directly to the hot liquids and stir-cook until it is dissolved and the sauce thickened to the desired consistency. One tablespoon will thicken about ¾ cup liquid.

NOTE: Store packets of the paste in a plastic bag, or a berry box, and then they will not get lost in the freezer.

BROWN COLORING

Brown coloring for sauces cannot be bought at the supermarket. It is available to cooks in restaurants, and should be made available to homemakers. Until it is, here is how to make it at home.

½ cup sugar	2 tablespoons boiling water
¼ cup water	1 teaspoon vegetable oil
3 drops red food coloring	

Boil sugar and water until sugar caramelizes and turns a very dark, burnt brown (sugar loses its sweetness when it is burnt). Add boiling water, oil, and red coloring. Stir, cool, and then bottle to have ready for use. It will keep indefinitely. It is not necessary to refrigerate. (I pour this coloring into a small plastic bottle with a nozzle. It is easy to add coloring to sauces from a squeeze-type bottle.) You may double or triple this recipe.

NOTE: Hold a lid over the pan while adding the boiling water to the syrup. It will spatter.

Simple brown coloring can be made by mixing commercial food colorings in the following proportions: 3 of red, 4 of yellow, and 1 of green. Mix and bottle ready to use. The first recipe is the best, but the simple one will do until you make your own.

CRÈME FRAÎCHE

If there is a secret to French cooking, it is to be found in crème fraîche. Never be without it.

1 (8-ounce) carton whipping cream	3 tablespoons commercial yoghurt

1. Pour whipping cream into a jar. Add yoghurt. Mix well, then set into a pilot-heated oven for about 8 hours, or overnight. Next morning stir and refrigerate. Once cold, it will thicken (see notes below). If your oven has no pilot light, make crème fraîche during the day and keep warm in water maintained at about 100 degrees.

2. When down to the last 2 or 3 tablespoons crème fraîche, add another 8 ounces whipping cream, stir, keep warm for 8 hours, and then refrigerate. The last few tablespoons of crème fraîche may always become the starter for more.

NOTE: Not all whipping creams will turn into crème fraîche. The percentage of butterfat is the determining factor and that varies from dairy to dairy. Experiment with the creams available to you. The higher the butterfat content, the better and thicker the crème fraîche.

Whipping cream may be substituted for crème fraîche, but *do not* substitute sour cream unless the recipe so states. Sour cream has a butterfat count of 10 to 18 percent, which is not enough to keep it from curdling when added to hot foods. Whipping cream, with its 30 to 37 percent butterfat, will not curdle when added to hot foods; but it lacks the sour taste.

Freeze a few packets of crème fraîche in 3-tablespoon amounts and then you will always have a starter. Just drop it into 8 ounces of whipping cream and let it warm. Stir once starter has dissolved.

To make your own yoghurt scald 1 pint of milk and then cool to lukewarm. Stir in about 6 tablespoons bought yoghurt. Set in a warm place for about 8 hours, or overnight. Refrigerate the next morning. Handle carefully. To shake yoghurt causes it to become watery. When down to about 6 tablespoons of yoghurt, add another pint of warm milk and make another batch of yoghurt. Repeat again when down to the last 6 tablespoons. You can make about 6 batches of yoghurt, and then the home-made yoghurt starter seems to wear out.

FOND DE CUISINE
[*Basic Stock*]

Stock, broth, and *bouillon* are interchangeable names for the same thing, namely, the liquid obtained by cooking meat, bones, and vegetables together. Throughout this book we will use the word *stock* to mean this unclarified liquid, or the liquid resulting from the following recipe.

3 pounds beef bones	½ pound leeks (2 or 3)
1½ pounds lean beef	3 quarts cold water
½ pound carrots (3 or 4)	2 whole yellow onions
½ pound turnips (3 or 4)	2 whole cloves

1. Put bones and meat into a large kettle. Clean carrots and turnips. Cut carrots into eighths, turnips into fourths. Add to kettle. Clean and wash leeks (see p. 607). Fold the green tops down around the white parts and tie into a bundle. Add to soup kettle. Cover with the water and bring to a boil.

2. Clean and peel onions. Cut one in half. Put cut side down on a piece of foil or in an iron skillet (if you use foil there is no cleaning problem). Place foil over very low heat and burn onion to a depth of about 1/16 inch. Burned onion gives the stock a rich brown color. Stick cloves into the other whole onion.

Remove scum that has collected on the soup, then add the onions. Skim the pot regularly as the impurities collect on top of the liquid.

3. Simmer 3 hours, then remove meat and bones, and discard bones. Cook another 3 hours and then strain, cool, and use in soups or sauces. Freeze, in pint or quart containers, what is not used immediately.

NOTE: Basic stocks are never salted. Salt is added to the recipe in which they are used.

Meat from the stock pot has very little flavor. To use it, cut it up, smother in a curry sauce, and serve with flavorful Rice Pilaf (p. 280).

VARIATIONS
CHICKEN STOCK

Substitute 2 (3-pound) fryers for the bones and meat in the above recipe. Any time you buy chickens, cook the giblets, wings, backs, and necks with some parsley, a carrot and an onion and make a small batch of stock to use in the making of a sauce.

CANNED STOCK

When using canned stock, improve its flavor by adding some diced carrots, onions, parsley, and any other vegetables you have on hand, and cook it for about 20 minutes. Strain and use.

Methods of Cooking

To cook is to be a sorcerer. Through the use of heat, raw ingredients are transformed into edible foods. The medium through which this is done is either dry or moist heat. Cooking by dry heat means to bake or roast food in an oven, and to broil or grill food under or over heat. French-fried foods are considered dry cooked, although the foods are cooked in a deep liquid, namely oil. Moist heat cookery is usually done on top of the range and includes braised, poached, and sautéed foods.

The basic methods of cooking are the same for all kinds of foods. You can French-fry an egg just as easily as potatoes. Chicken and beef are often cooked by the braising method: when braised in red wine, one becomes the famous Coq au Vin, the other Boeuf Bourguignonne. Sautéed crabs and sautéed sweetbreads require in general the same basic treatment.

Comprehension of the similarities that exist between the various dishes and preparations will lead you to an understanding of the *system* employed in classical French cooking. It is not the individual recipe that is important, but rather the *total system* of preparation. Once a cook has gained a command of the *system,* the individual recipes become nothing more than variations on the basic preparations.

But, while remaining conscious of the similarities in the preparation of foods, it is necessary to treat each category of food separately for easy consultation. Such separate treatments will naturally stress the preparation differences, particularly in the finishing of each dish. The studious cook will nonetheless understand that the differences are only superficial, and that the fundamentals of cooking remain essentially the same.

BAKE OR ROAST

To bake or roast means to cook by dry heat. The oven temperature should be high enough to keep the moisture evaporated from the oven as it collects, otherwise a steamed roast is the result. But, the temperature should not be so high as to cook the roast too fast and cause it to dry out.

Put a roast into a hot oven (425–475 degrees). Then reduce the heat as the roast warms. The theory in back of this is simple: there is more condensation at the time the cool roast enters the oven than when it becomes warm. As the food warms, the heat is gradually reduced to about 325 degrees. Cooking temperatures are but approximations. You must know your stove and the food you are cooking, and adjust the temperature accordingly.

Small birds and whole fish, which cook in a short time, are cooked at high temperatures (about 425 degrees), so that they will be nicely browned by the time they are done. Large roasts and big birds, which cook a long time, roast at lower temperatures so that they do not become too brown by the time they are done.

Roasts of meat should be placed in a V-shaped roasting rack to let the heat circulate around the meat and to cook it evenly from all sides.

All roasts should be basted periodically during the cooking time with melted unsalted butter or other fat. Nothing else.

A roast is never covered.

When a roast is done, place it on a hot serving platter and let it rest. During this rest period the meat stops cooking and absorbs the juices within the meat tissues. Then when it is carved the juice stays in the meat and does not run onto the platter.

WHEN IS ROAST MEAT DONE?

For all meat cookery a thermometer is the best way to determine doneness. But there are ways to tell without a thermometer.

1. Feel the meat. Let's think about a roast of beef. In its raw state it is very wiggly and soft. As it cooks the outside gets firm and then the meat cooks down to the center. By pushing the meat it is possible to tell to what extent the meat has cooked toward the center. With practice you will be able to feel when meat is rare, medium, and well done by how much the meat gives when it is pressed with a finger or squeezed between finger and thumb. Practice this technique every time you make a roast. Use a thermometer, if you have one, to help train yourself.

2. To determine the doneness of a leg of lamb, run your index finger

down the leg bone into the meat (it will not burn). If the bone is just warm, the meat is medium cooked. If cold, not done. If hot, well done.

3. Insert a kitchen needle or skewer into the thickest muscle of the meat. Leave it there for about 2 minutes. Withdraw the needle and place the end on the inside of your wrist. If the needle feels cold the meat is still raw; if warm the meat is medium cooked; if hot the meat is medium to well done.

4. When withdrawing the needle catch some of the juice on a white plate. If it is red the meat is rare, if pink the meat is medium, and if white and clear the meat is well done.

5. To test the doneness of poultry use the juice-on-the-plate technique.

BRAISE

To braise means to cook in a vegetable-seasoned liquid. The vegetables may be any combination of carrots, celery, onions, shallots, parsley, or mushrooms, or any single one of these.

The liquid used may be wine, stock, water, tomatoes, or the cooking liquids from other foods that complement the food being braised. The liquid used in braising becomes the sauce.

The food may or may not be larded, marinated, or pre-fried depending upon the quality and the type of food being braised. For example, you might sear a rump roast and then put it to braise, but you would not sear fish steaks.

Any food can be braised, and to my way of thinking this is the best of all methods of cooking—food cooked in its own sauce!

BROIL OR GRILL

To broil or grill means to put oiled foods into or onto a preheated very hot broiler or grill that is oiled at the time the food is put on it to cook. To oil it while it heats would but burn the oil onto the broiler and smoke up the kitchen.

If the broiler or grill is not preheated, the food will stick to it and you will tear the food apart when it is turned or removed from the grill. The broiler or grill *must* be preheated to hot.

Generally speaking thick meats and poultry should be cooked further from the heat and at lower temperatures than thin cuts, since they require longer cooking times. Thin cuts of meat and fish fillets are cooked quickly and need *not* be turned. The hot broiler sears and cooks their underside as the top cooks and browns. Always place on serving platter with the browned side up.

FRENCH-FRY

To French-fry means to cook in deep hot fat or oil. Butter is never used since it burns at around 250 degrees. Pork fat or lard burns at around 400 degrees, most vegetable oils at around 500 degrees, and olive oil at about 550 degrees. Olive oil imparts its own particular flavor to foods; therefore, we use tasteless vegetable oil for French-frying.

We also use a thermometer and hope you will. To test the accuracy of your thermometer, immerse 2 inches of the stem in boiling water, normally considered 212 degrees except when altitude or variations in barometric pressure change the boiling point. If the reading on your thermometer is 200, subtract 12 from the temperature given in the recipe. If it registers 230 for boiling, then add 18 to the temperature given in the recipe. In other words, check your thermometer and don't assume it is accurate. A 5-degree variant in deep-fat frying is not serious, but anything more would be. In candy making, even 2 degrees difference could ruin the candy. I point this out here, because some thermometers for fat cooking are also used for candy making.

The temperature used to French-fry foods is dependent upon the thickness and type of food being cooked. Temperature is all important.

Foods that contain water, and that are not coated, are fried first at about 360 degrees to evaporate the water. Then the oil is heated to around 390 degrees, or hot, and they are fried again to make them crisp. Potatoes are an example.

Batter-coated foods and croquettes are cooked only once, at about 390 degrees, or hot, which sets the coating so it will hold the juices and foods within the covering. The coating should not be so thick that you cannot find the food. Also a thick coating absorbs more fat than one that is thin.

Use a French-fryer with separate basket. Lacking this, use a saucepan and long-handled slotted spoon or strainer. Fill container half full of oil and heat.

Do not add more food than the oil can handle. The temperature of the fat will be reduced by about 20 degrees when food is added. The faster the fat returns to the required temperature the better the finished product.

Drain fried foods on paper towels. Never stack and never cover them or they will become soggy. Always serve them on oven-hot plates. Cold plates cause condensation between the coating and the foods, so they become limp and soggy. As you French-fry foods put them on a cooky sheet covered with paper towels. Keep in a hot oven until all food is fried.

Cool cooking oil after use, strain into a jar, and label, for fish, meat, or vegetables. Refrigerate between uses.

Cooking oils do wear out. When foods will no longer acquire a golden brown in the stipulated time, it is time to change the oil.

French-fried foods are seasoned after they are cooked.

CHART OF COATINGS FOR FRENCH-FRIED FOODS

SIMPLE COATINGS

NO. 1

½ cup cake flour   ½ teaspoon baking powder
Light cream

Combine flour and baking powder on sheet of waxed paper. Dip foods first in cream, drain, then coat with flour mixture. Shake off surplus flour and fry.

NO. 2

½ cup flour   1 egg white
Fine bread crumbs

Dip food to be fried in flour to absorb moisture. Whip egg white with a table fork to make foamy. Dip floured foods in froth, then roll in crumbs. Whip egg white back to a froth between dippings. Fry crumb-coated foods.

NO. 3

Melted butter   Fine, dry bread crumbs

Dip foods to be fried first in melted butter, then in crumbs. Shake off surplus crumbs and fry.

NO. 4

1 whole egg   ½ teaspoon sugar
¼ cup milk   Dash of salt
1 tablespoon vegetable oil   ½ cup flour
Fine, dry bread crumbs

Combine egg, milk, oil, sugar, and salt. Mix well. Dip foods to be fried in flour, then egg mixture, and then crumbs. Fry.

NOTE: To remove excess liquid from food, pull the food between your forefinger and middle finger, thus pushing off the surplus. Then dip in the dry coating and fry. (Technique for Simple Coatings Nos. 1 and 3.)

CHART OF COATINGS FOR FRENCH-FRIED FOODS

BATTER COATINGS

NO. 1

1 cup flour	2 tablespoons oil
1 teaspoon sugar	¼ cup beer
½ teaspoon salt	2 tablespoons warm water

2 egg whites, slightly beaten with fork

Combine ingredients in order given. Mix well, but do not beat. Dry foods to be fried on paper towels. Dip into batter and fry. Season after they are cooked.

NO. 2

1 cup flour	1 egg yolk
½ teaspoon salt	½ cup warm milk
1 teaspoon sugar	1 egg white, slightly beaten

Combine ingredients down to egg white. Let rest an hour before using. When ready to use, whip egg white to a froth and stir into batter. Dip dried foods into batter and fry. Drain on paper towels. Season.

NO. 3

1 egg yolk	1 cup sifted cake flour
¾ cup ice water	1 teaspoon baking powder

Mix yolk and ice water. Stir together and *do not* beat. Sift together flour and baking powder. Sprinkle over liquid. Push down into the liquid with a fork, but do not stir. Batter must be lumpy with some dry flour floating on top of the liquid.

Dip foods to be coated down through the dry flour on top and into the liquid, then out through the dry flour. Fry in deep fat and drain on paper towels. Season after foods are fried.

NOTE: This batter will remind you of tempura batter, only it is better. (Similar to Simple Coating No. 1.)

POACH

To poach means to cook foods in a liquid just below the boiling point, or at a simmer. Protein foods tend to become tough when boiled.

Whether foods are cooked in a lot of liquid or very little, we shall refer to the method of cooking protein in liquid as poaching.

The liquid may be seasoned court bouillon, wine court bouillon, milk court bouillon, chicken or beef stock, white or red wine, mushroom broth, milk, cream, tomato juice, or any combination of these, as well as others, such as vermouth, beer, or even water.

Large pieces of protein, such as whole fish, are put to poach in cold liquids, heated rapidly to a boil and then reduced to a simmer. The theory is that these large foods will then heat and cook from the inside out and their exteriors will not be overcooked by the time the center is done. The contrary is true of small pieces of protein, such as fillets of sole. These are submerged in simmering liquids in the hope of searing their outsides to trap the flavor within. To start them cooking in cold liquids would extract their flavor.

The poaching liquid, when not a court bouillon, is usually used for the sauce. It is usually reduced to half, so do not use too much salt or other seasonings, since the reduced liquids will be concentrated and strong in flavor.

POACHING LIQUIDS CHART

MILK COURT BOUILLON

2 cups milk	Dash of white pepper
2 cups water	2 tablespoons honey
1 teaspoon salt	2 tablespoons sherry

Combine all ingredients in a large skillet. Heat to a boil. Add fish fillets or steaks. Bring again to a boil and then reduce heat to a simmer. Poach about 8 minutes. Do not save this liquid.

PLAIN COURT BOUILLON

2 quarts water	6 sprigs parsley
1 teaspoon salt	1 small bay leaf
¼ cup vinegar	8 whole peppercorns
3 carrots, chopped	3 whole cloves
2 onions, sliced	1 tablespoon honey

½ cup sherry

Boil all ingredients but sherry for 20 minutes. Strain, discard vegetables, add sherry, and cool. Use or freeze until needed. After each use, freeze again.

When ready to use again add enough water to make 2 quarts. The cooking of the fish in this court bouillon will maintain and actually improve the flavor. As long as you keep the court bouillon frozen between uses, it will keep almost indefinitely.

WINE COURT BOUILLON

2 cups water	1 carrot, quartered
2 cups white wine	Juice of ½ lemon
Chunk of butter	2 tablespoons sherry
1 teaspoon salt	1 tablespoon honey

Put all ingredients but sherry and honey into large flat skillet. Simmer 10 minutes. Add sherry and honey, then the fish.

Judge poaching time by the thickness of the particular fish. As a rule of thumb, a 1-inch fillet or steak takes about 8 minutes to poach.

NOTE: This court bouillon may also be saved and frozen. However, most of the wine flavor will have been absorbed by the fish, so it is advisable to add about ½ cup of wine each time it is used. Remove the carrots before freezing the liquid.

SAUTÉ

To sauté means to cook in just enough hot fat to keep the food from sticking. Foods sautéed should be tender, quick-cooking foods. A thin steak will turn out better than a 1-inch steak.

Food cooked in fat should never be tightly covered during cooking since the steam would destroy the crisp coating and cause the food to be steamed.

Have the skillet large enough to give the food room to breathe. There should be space around every piece of food so the sides of the food brown.

Coatings stick to the pan and not to the foods when:
1. The fat is not hot enough at the time the foods are added; or
2. The foods are crowded in the pan, causing them to steam themselves and shed their coatings.

Sauté over high heat in a skillet heavy enough to take the heat. Enamel-coated iron skillets and pans are about perfect for every kitchen job.

Use clarified butter (p. 599) or vegetable oil. Butter may be used without being clarified, but when it is, add about 3 tablespoons oil to every ¼ pound of butter and it will not burn so readily.

Sauces

To cook in the French manner is to know your sauces. They are individualistic, logical, and follow a scheme of organization. They should have body, but not thickness.

The leading warm sauces are either light or dark in color; the leading cold sauces only light. Compound butters are light and may be served either hot or cold.

In the warm sauces we discern 5 mother sauces. The light sauces include Béchamel, Velouté, and Hollandaise; the dark sauces, Demi-glace and Tomate. The cold sauces include 2 mother sauces: Mayonnaise, and Oil and Vinegar (see Chapter XVIII, "Buffet Froid"). Compound butters have only one mother—butter.

If you know the mother, you know the background of each of the offspring sauces. Although the descendant sauces are individually quite different, all those belonging to the same family are simply variations on the parent sauce.

The recipe for each mother sauce is followed by a listing of the offspring sauces. Only the most illustrious descendants of each mother appear in these families. But it is my hope that an understanding of sauce lineages will enable the cook to see the intimate relationships which exist between mothers and children, and in certain cases, between members of separate sauce lines who might in a family setting be called cousins. Understanding of these family ties helps the imaginative cook to simplify her planning of menus and enables her to produce a wide range of sauces with the least amount of effort.

The same rule of thumb applies to sauces as to the selection of wines: light sauces with light meats, dark sauces with dark meats—but there are always exceptions.

When necessary, adjust the thickness of sauces. If too thick, thin with cream or stock; if too thin, thicken with beurre manié.

SAUCES BLANCHES
[*Light Warm Sauces*]

Flour-thickened light sauces will remind you of our simple pan gravies. But, as you will see, they are quite different.

American *gravies* are usually made in the same pan in which meats have been cooked. Normally the fat, the burned flour and the hard, brown tidbits are left in the pan and become a part of the gravy.

French *sauces* are not dependent upon meat fat or meat tidbits for flavor. They are independent creations made from butter, flour, milk, bouillon, or wine, and are designed to complement the particular foods they are to accompany.

SAUCE BÉCHAMEL
[*Cream Sauce*]

⅛ pound butter	Dash of nutmeg
4 tablespoons flour	½ teaspoon salt
2 cups cold milk	⅛ teaspoon white pepper

1 teaspoon sugar

1. Melt butter in skillet. Stir in flour. Cook-stir for 3 minutes without browning. This cooks the flour so the sauce will not taste pasty.

2. Add cold milk, nutmeg, salt, pepper, and sugar. Stir-cook until thickened. Makes about 2 cups.

NOTE: If the Béchamel is to be used as a plain sauce, and not in a variation, it must be diluted with cream.

BÉCHAMEL FAMILY NO. I

In this branch of the family, the special ingredients of the offspring recipe are cooked in the ⅛ pound butter listed in the parent and then the mother sauce is completed. The finishing of the sauce is given in the recipe for the offspring sauce.

ALBERT

Simmer 2 minced shallots, 2 tablespoons horseradish, and ½ teaspoon dry mustard in the butter, then proceed with the basic recipe. Flavor with 1 tablespoon each of sherry and vinegar. Finish with a large chunk of butter. For roasted light meats.

CHAMPIGNON

Sauté 1 cup sliced mushroom caps in the ⅛ pound butter, then proceed with the recipe. Finish with liaison of 1 egg yolk and ¼ cup crème fraîche. For vegetables, eggs, fish, etc.

CURRIE

Sauté 1 tablespoon curry powder in the butter, then proceed with the recipe. Finish with 2 tablespoons of sherry and liaison. For fish, eggs and poultry.

DUXELLES

Sauté 2 minced onions in butter for 10 minutes. Add 1 cup minced mushrooms and simmer another 5 minutes. (Basic duxelle mixture.) Proceed with basic sauce recipe. Finish with liaison. Good on sautéed chicken livers! For poultry, vegetables and eggs.

MOUTARDE

Sauté 1 tablespoon dry mustard in butter, then continue with recipe. Finish with 3 tablespoons whipping cream. For vegetables, poultry and eggs.

SOUBISE

Simmer 2 cups minced onions in the butter for 10 minutes. Add 1 teaspoon confectioners' sugar and continue with recipe. Mash through fine sieve and finish with chunk of butter and 2 tablespoons crème fraîche. For roasted white meats.

SOUBISE-AURORE

Add ½ cup tomato paste to above Soubise recipe.

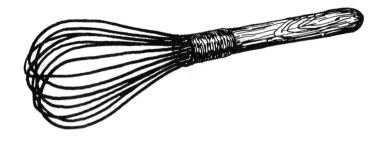

BÉCHAMEL FAMILY NO. II

In this branch of the family, the special ingredients are simply added to the completed mother sauce in its finished form. Read the offspring sauce before making the parent sauce.

AURORE

Add ½ cup tomato purée and 2 tablespoons sherry to Béchamel. For vegetables and eggs.

CHANTILLY

Remove Béchamel sauce from heat. Stir in 1 teaspoon grated fresh lemon rind and 4 tablespoons whipped cream. For vegetables and eggs.

CHAUD-FROID

Soak 1 tablespoon gelatin in ¼ cup cold water. Add soaked gelatin to hot sauce. Stir until dissolved. Stir in ½ cup whipping cream and 2 tablespoons Madeira. Cool and stir until mixture starts to set, and then coat foods. For glazing cold foods.

CHAUD-FROID À LA MOUTARDE

Prepare Moutarde Béchamel and then proceed with Chaud-Froid recipe.

CIBOULETTE

Add 3 tablespoons minced chives and 2 tablespoons whipping cream to basic sauce. Finish with liaison. For poultry, eggs and vegetables.

CRÈME

Add 4 tablespoons crème fraîche to the mother sauce. For poultry, fish, eggs and vegetables.

MORNAY

Finish basic sauce with 2 egg yolks, 4 tablespoons each whipping cream, and grated Parmesan cheese. Heat to melt cheese, but do not let sauce boil, or cheese and eggs both suffer. For eggs and vegetables.

QUENELLE

Combine 2 tablespoons whipping cream with liaison of yolks and crème fraîche. Finish with 2 tablespoons sherry and 2 drops red food coloring, and swirl in a chunk of butter. Add the cooked foods and heat carefully. For quenelles, seafoods, eggs and poultry.

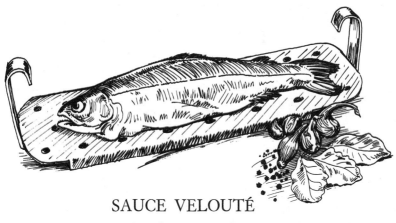

SAUCE VELOUTÉ
[*Velouté Sauce*]

The Velouté sauce is basically a Béchamel sauce made with chicken or fish stock rather than with milk. The offspring sauces in the Béchamel Family are interchangeable with the offspring sauces in the Velouté Family and vice-versa. In other words you can make a Bercy with Béchamel as well as with Velouté.

POULTRY AND WHITE MEAT VELOUTÉ

⅛ pound butter	⅛ teaspoon white pepper
4 tablespoons flour	½ teaspoon sugar
2 cups chicken stock	2 egg yolks
½ teaspoon salt	3 tablespoons crème fraîche

1. Melt butter in skillet and then stir in flour. Stir-cook for a few minutes to release starch in flour. Do not brown. Add cold stock. Stir-cook until thickened.

2. Add seasonings, taste, and adjust. Combine yolks and crème. Add about ½ cup of hot sauce, mix well and then stir this liaison into the Velouté. Heat, but do not boil. When Velouté is turned into other sauces do not add the liaison, unless the particular recipe so indicates.

VARIATION
SEAFOOD VELOUTÉ

If possible get fish heads and bones, then cook these in 2½ cups water seasoned with half an onion, a carrot, and some parsley. Use this liquid in the above sauce in place of the stock. Or, use 1 cup clam juice (bought), and ½ cup each vermouth and chicken stock.

VELOUTÉ FAMILY NO. I

In this branch of the family, the special ingredients of the offspring are cooked in water, wine, or stock, then combined with the mother recipe and finished according to the offspring recipe.

BERCY

Boil 2 minced shallots in ¼ cup white wine until liquid is reduced to nothing. Stir in recipe of Velouté sauce. Flavor with 1 tablespoon lemon juice. Finish with chunk of butter and minced parsley to taste.

BONNEFOY

Boil 4 minced shallots in ½ cup white wine until liquid is reduced to nothing. Add recipe of Velouté sauce. Simmer 10 minutes. Mash through fine sieve. Finish with chunk of butter.

CHAMPIGNON

Boil 1 cup sliced fresh mushrooms in ¼ cup white wine until liquid is reduced to nothing. Add 2 tablespoons Cognac and set ablaze. When flame dies, add Velouté, heat, and finish with liaison of yolks and crème fraîche.

POULETTE

Boil ½ cup sliced mushrooms in ½ cup water for 5 minutes. Strain liquid into Velouté sauce. Finish with liaison, chunk of butter, and 1 teaspoon lemon juice. Sprinkle with minced parsley. Save mushrooms and sauté for steaks, or fold into an omelette.

RAVIGOTE

Boil 3 minced shallots in ¼ cup white wine and 2 tablespoons vinegar. Reduce liquid to nothing. Add Velouté and finish with a chunk of butter. Sprinkle with 1 tablespoon chopped chives and 2 tablespoons fresh tarragon (or ½ teaspoon dried tarragon).

VELOUTÉ FAMILY NO. II

In this branch of the family, the special ingredients are simply added to the completed mother sauce in its finished form. Often the liaison is omitted, and the recipe finished according to the offspring recipe.

BONNE FEMME

To recipe of Velouté add an additional ¼ cup crème fraîche and 1 tablespoon lemon juice.

CURRIE

Soak 1 tablespoon curry powder in 2 tablespoons sherry. Omit liaison. Add 4 tablespoons crème fraîche to Velouté, then stir in flavored sherry. Heat, but do not boil.

SUPRÊME

To Velouté recipe add 2 tablespoons whipping cream and 4 tablespoons crème fraîche. Omit liaison. Finish sauce with chunk of butter.

SUPRÊME-AURORE

To Suprême sauce add 4 tablespoons tomato paste.

SAUCE HOLLANDAISE

In France one would use a heavy tin-lined copper pan to make this sauce. It is specially shaped, very heavy, weighing almost 3 pounds, and in it the sauce is cooked over very low heat. A small, heavy enameled cast-iron pan is a perfect substitute, but, lacking a heavy pan, use a double boiler.

The ingredients that go into a Hollandaise are fairly standard. The methods by which these ingredients may be combined are many. I give you four methods. Try them all, then take the one that works best for you. The hand-whisk method is the way a Hollandaise should be made. For me it is the easiest and fastest method.

Hollandaise-type sauces can never be served more than lukewarm. To reheat them usually causes them to curdle. To maintain their warmth, set the dish containing the sauce in water no hotter than the sauce itself. White wine, vermouth, or clam juice may be substituted for the water when using the Hollandaise with fish.

1½ sticks unsalted butter (¾ cup)	¼ teaspoon salt
4 egg yolks	Dash of white pepper
1 tablespoon cold water	Juice of ¼ lemon, or 1 teaspoon

1. Melt butter in small saucepan. Remove from heat. Skim off foam. Save for seasoning vegetables. Tilt pan to make a well of butter. Impurities will settle to the bottom of the well of butter. (Or pour into a plastic bottle with a nozzle and then stand the bottle upside down in a cup. Impurities will settle into the nozzle. Squirt them out when ready to add butter to the sauce. There will be about 2 tablespoons milky liquid.)

2. Remove from the yolks the thick white piece (called the *core*) that usually adheres to them. Put yolks and water into a heavy copper pan, enameled iron pan, or top part of double boiler. (If using double boiler, put about ½ inch of water in the bottom part of the boiler. Heat to a boil, then reduce to a simmer. Set top part of boiler in the lower part. Check to be sure top part does not touch the water. Lift out the top part; if the bottom is wet, it is touching. Reduce amount of water.)

3. Beat yolks and water continuously with a wire whisk until they have formed a thick custard. (If mixture is cooking too fast remove from heat or boiler and set in cold water to stop the cooking process.)

4. When mixture is thick, gradually add the butter. Spoon (or squeeze from plastic bottle) into custard, drop by drop and then in a fine stream, beating all the while. Leave white residue in bottom of the butter pan. Once butter is added, season with salt, pepper, and lemon juice. Pour sauce into serving dish. Keep it warm in water at same temperature as sauce.

NOTE: *To cure curdled Hollandaise* beat an egg yolk with ¼ teaspoon dry mustard. Then gradually add the curdled mixture to the fresh yolk. The result of such an experience is to end up with a better sauce because of the extra yolk—so don't be too sorry if the sauce curdles.

Hollandaise-type sauces may be made in advance and frozen. Seal the sauce in small boilable bags, then freeze. When sauce is needed, stand boilable bag with frozen sauce in a small pan and let *warm* tap water run over it for about 15 minutes. Cut open the bag and serve.

VARIATIONS
BLENDER HOLLANDAISE

As in master recipe, melt butter and remove impurities; combine yolks with the water and make a thick custard. Set blender container in very hot water to warm. Dry off outside and put custard into container. On low speed add butter drop by drop, then on medium speed add in a fine stream. Finish sauce with salt, pepper, and lemon juice. With a blender and a plastic bottle (see above recipe), Hollandaise is child's play. Blender Hollandaise made on low speed is very good.

MIXER HOLLANDAISE

As in master recipe, melt butter and remove impurities; using 4 yolks and 1 tablespoon water, make a custard. Set mixer bowl into very hot water to warm. Put hot custard into bowl. Add the butter in drops and then in a fine stream while beating with a hand mixer on low speed. Finish with salt, pepper, and lemon juice. The texture of this Hollandaise is finer than that produced by the blender.

SOFTENED-BUTTER HOLLANDAISE

The melted-butter Hollandaise methods are traditional. But the softened-butter method you may find easier. The butter must be completely pliable, but *not* soft to the point of melting.

To the egg-and-water custard of the master recipe add ¼ pound softened butter in six pieces. Beat after each addition until butter is blended with the custard. (Use whisk or hand beater.) Finish with salt, pepper, and lemon juice.

NOTE: If the Hollandaise does not thicken after all of the butter has been added, stir-cook it over very low heat until it does. Don't be worried; it's just that the butter has cooled the custard too quickly, so it must be warmed in order to thicken. But be sure this is done over very low heat, or it will curdle.

Any one of the above methods of making Hollandaise may be used to make any one of the sauces listed in the Hollandaise chart.

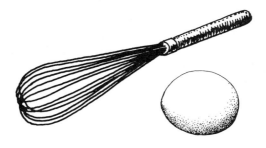

HOLLANDAISE-SABAYON

This is a very special sauce designed to be served on cooked fish. It is made by the softened-butter method of making Hollandaise (see preceding recipe), but the ingredients differ so much I have chosen to list this recipe separately. Employ the same technique as in the making of Hollandaise sauces.

4 egg yolks	2 tablespoons crème fraîche or
2 tablespoons clam juice (bottled) or	whipping cream
white wine	1 tablespoon lemon juice
⅛ pound softened butter	1 tablespoon sherry
Dash of salt, sugar, and white pepper	

1. Put yolks, clam juice, and butter into heavy enameled-iron pan or into top part of double boiler. Cook over low heat, or over hot but not boiling water. Beat continuously with a whisk or hand mixer on low speed until the mixture is the consistency of heavy whipped cream.

2. When thick, remove from heat, set pan on damp cloth to keep it from moving as you beat in the crème, lemon juice, sherry, salt, sugar, and pepper. Pour into a small bowl and serve with Truites Farcies (p. 102), poached sea bass, or other poached fish.

HOLLANDAISE FAMILY NO. I

In this branch of the family, the special ingredients of the offspring are cooked in wine vinegar first and then the mother sauce is made. Finish according to each recipe. For grilled or sautéed meats and fish.

BÉARNAISE

Simmer 2 minced shallots, 3 crushed peppercorns, and 1 tablespoon minced fresh tarragon (or 1 teaspoon dried) with 4 tablespoons wine vinegar. Reduce liquid to about 1 tablespoon. Strain liquid into heavy pan, or top of double boiler. Proceed with Hollandaise recipe, omitting the tablespoon water.

Finish with minced fresh tarragon and chervil, or, lacking these, minced parsley and a few chopped chives.

CHIVRY

Prepare Béarnaise sauce, then finish with enough sieved watercress, spinach, or parsley to make the sauce green in color.

CHORON

Prepare Béarnaise sauce, then finish with enough tomato paste to give it a rich red color.

PALOISE

Substitute 2 tablespoons mint leaves for the tarragon in the Béarnaise recipe and simmer with the shallots. Strain and proceed as for the Béarnaise. Finish with minced mint leaves. Serve with lamb.

HOLLANDAISE FAMILY NO. II

In this branch of the family, the special ingredients of the offspring are simply added to the completed mother sauce. Make the mother sauce first. For vegetables, eggs, fish and white meat of poultry.

ANCHOIS

Add 1 tablespoon anchovy paste to Hollandaise. For fish especially.

CÂPRES

Wash 2 tablespoons capers in cold water. Drain, then blot on paper towels. Stir into Hollandaise recipe. For fish, eggs and poultry.

CHANTILLY

Add 2 tablespoons crème fraîche to Hollandaise. For vegetables.

CITRON

Add 2 tablespoons grated lemon rind to Hollandaise. Great on grilled fish.

DIVINE

Reduce 3 tablespoons sherry to half and then add to recipe of Chantilly sauce. Serve on poached fish or white meat of chicken.

MALTAISE

Add 1 teaspoon grated orange rind and 1 teaspoon thawed frozen orange juice to Hollandaise. Add drop of red coloring. In France they have "blood oranges" and it is their juice that makes the sauce pinkish. Frozen juice is even better for flavor; it doesn't dilute the sauce. Use on asparagus and other cooked green vegetables.

MOUSSELINE

Add 4 tablespoons whipped cream and 1 stiffly beaten egg white to Hollandaise. Adjust seasonings. For vegetables and fish.

MOUTARDE

Add to Hollandaise 2 tablespoons, or to taste, of Dijon-type hot mustard. Good on grilled fish.

NOISETTE

Add ¼ cup ground toasted hazelnuts or almonds to Hollandaise. Especially for vegetables.

SAUCES BRUNES
[*Dark Warm Sauces*]

The grandmother to all brown sauces was the original Espagnole sauce. But she has been replaced by the richer, easier-to-make "mother" Demi-glace and thus her family of sauces continues.

As my father once said after having eaten a bowl of giblet Demi-glace at Christmas dinner: "That's the kind of stuff you wish you could drown in!"

SAUCE DEMI-GLACE
[*Basic Brown Sauce*]

⅛ pound butter	Bouquet garni
2 onions, diced	1 tablespoon tomato paste
2 carrots, diced	½ teaspoon salt
1 tablespoon sugar	⅛ teaspoon pepper
3 tablespoons flour	Red and brown food coloring
3 cups stock	2 tablespoons Cognac
2 cloves garlic, minced	1 tablespoon Madeira

1. Sauté onions and carrots (always in about equal quantities) in the butter for about 30 minutes. Stir in sugar the last 10 minutes of cooking. Increase heat so vegetables will caramelize, but do not let them burn. This gives the rich brown color to the sauce.

2. Stir in flour. Stir-cook for about 3 minutes. Lightly brown flour, then add stock, garlic, bouquet garni, tomato paste, salt, and pepper. Stir until it boils. Reduce heat, set lid askew, and simmer about an hour. Add coloring, if necessary, to make a rich dark brown color, then strain sauce into a clean pan. Finish with Cognac and Madeira. Serve, turn into other sauces, or cool and freeze. (To cool, cover with a lid and set in cold water. Lid prevents tough skin from forming over top of sauce.) If sauce is to be frozen, omit the Cognac and Madeira. Add them at the time the sauce is reheated, and just before serving. Makes about 2 cups.

NOTE: With frozen Demi-glace sauce in your freezer you can quickly make any one of the offspring sauces in the Demi-glace family.

DEMI-GLACE FAMILY NO. I

In this branch of the family, the special ingredients of the offspring are cooked in wine or vinegar, then the cooked mother sauce is added. Finish according to instructions in each recipe.

BIGARADE

Combine 2 tablespoons sugar with 2 tablespoons vinegar. Boil and caramelize. Add Demi-glace.

Remove zest from an orange and a lemon. Cut into julienne strips. Put them into cold water. Bring to a boil, thus blanching them to remove their bitterness. Lift from water and add to sauce. Stir in 2 tablespoons frozen orange juice and 1 teaspoon lemon juice. Simmer 10 minutes.

Finish with Cognac and Madeira from Demi-glace recipe and 2 tablespoons Grand Marnier. Adjust seasonings and thickness of sauce with beurre manié. For fowl.

BORDELAISE

Combine 1 cup red wine and 2 minced shallots. Reduce to ½ cup. Add Demi-glace sauce. Simmer 30 minutes. Strain. Add 1 teaspoon lemon juice and ¼ cup cubed poached beef marrow. Adjust seasonings.

Finish with Cognac and Madeira from Demi-glace recipe and chunk of butter. For grilled meats.

CHATEAUBRIAND

Simmer 3 minced shallots, a pinch of thyme, piece of bay leaf, and 8 minced mushrooms in 1 cup white wine. Reduce to ¼ cup. Add Demi-glace. Simmer 30 minutes. Strain. Adjust seasonings. Add tablespoon of lemon juice, Cognac and Madeira from Demi-glace recipe. Finish with chunk of butter and sprinkle sauced foods with chopped parsley. For grilled steaks.

DIABLE

Simmer 4 sliced shallots in ½ cup white wine and 2 tablespoons vinegar. Reduce liquid to nothing. Add Demi-glace, ¼ cup tomato paste, and dash of cayenne. Simmer 20 minutes. Strain, and adjust seasonings.

Finish with tablespoon lemon juice, Cognac and Madeira from Demi-glace recipe, and swirl in chunk of butter. Sprinkle sauced foods with chopped parsley. For grilled meats and game.

DIANE

Simmer 10 crushed peppercorns in ½ cup vinegar. Reduce to 2 table-spoons. Strain liquid into Demi-glace sauce. Mix bit of hot sauce into ¼ cup crème fraîche, then stir back into sauce.

Cut 1 truffle and the white of one hard-cooked egg into crescent shapes. Use ½-inch pastry tube, a truffle cutter, a small cooky cutter or the "hole" of a doughnut cutter to stamp out crescents. Add to sauce. Adjust seasonings and thickness. Heat and serve. For broiled meats.

DEMI-GLACE FAMILY NO. II

In this branch of the family, the special ingredients of the offspring are sautéed in butter, then reduced in wine or vinegar and the cooked mother recipe added. Finish each sauce according to its own recipe.

CHASSEUR

Sauté 1 cup sliced mushrooms and 2 diced shallots in chunk of butter for a few minutes. Add ¼ cup white wine. Reduce liquid to nothing. Stir in Demi-glace. Add Cognac and Madeira from Demi-glace recipe. Swirl in chunk of butter. Sprinkle sauced foods with minced parsley. For game and poultry.

DUXELLES

Sauté 2 minced onions in chunk of butter for 10 minutes. Add 1 cup minced mushrooms and simmer another 5 minutes. (Basic Duxelles sauce.) Stir in Demi-glace. Add Cognac and Madeira from Demi-glace recipe. Swirl in chunk of butter. Sprinkle sauced foods with chopped parsley. Great on sautéed chicken livers or hard-cooked eggs.

LYONNAISE

Sauté ½ cup minced onions in chunk of butter. Add ¼ cup each white wine and vinegar. Reduce liquid to nothing. Add Demi-glace. Simmer 20 minutes. Add Cognac and Madeira from Demi-glace recipe. Adjust seasonings. Swirl in chunk of butter. For grilled and sautéed meats.

MIROTON

Slice 2 onions thin. Brown in chunk of butter with 2 cloves minced garlic. Add ¼ cup white wine and bouquet garni, and reduce liquids to nothing. Discard bouquet garni, add Demi-glace and 2 tablespoons tomato paste. Heat for 10 minutes. Finish with Cognac and Madeira from Demi-glace recipe and chunk of butter. For roast meats and fowl.

ROBERT

Sauté 2 minced onions in chunk of butter for 5 minutes. Add ¼ cup white wine and 2 tablespoons vinegar. Reduce liquid to nothing. Add Demi-glace. Simmer 30 minutes.

Combine 1 teaspoon dry mustard and 1 teaspoon confectioners' sugar. Moisten with bit of sauce, then stir into the sauce. Adjust seasonings. For grilled chops and steaks.

DEMI-GLACE FAMILY NO. III

In this branch of the family, the special ingredients of the offspring are simply added to the finished mother sauce.

MADÈRE

Boil ½ cup Madeira wine, reducing it to ¼ cup. Stir this into the Demi-glace and add the Cognac from the mother recipe. For grilled meats and fowl. (Adjust thickness of sauce with beurre manié.)

PÉRIGUEUX

To the Sauce Madère add 3 tablespoons chopped black truffles. For grilled steaks.

SAUCE DE TOMATE
[*Tomato Sauce*]

1 onion, minced	4 cups diced fresh tomatoes, or
1 carrot, minced	3 cups canned Italian plum
1 branch celery, chopped	tomatoes
2 cloves garlic, minced	2 teaspoons salt
⅛ pound butter	⅛ teaspoon pepper
3 tablespoons flour	1 tablespoon sugar
1 cup stock	Bouquet garni

1. Simmer onion, carrot, celery, and garlic in butter for 20 minutes in covered skillet. Stir in flour and cook without browning for 3 minutes.

2. Add remainder of ingredients. Simmer for about 2 hours to develop flavor and evaporate some of the liquid. Stir often. If it gets too thick, add more stock.

3. When done remove bouquet garni. Press sauce through food mill, using finest disc. Taste and adjust seasonings. Use, or freeze for later use.

TOMATO SAUCE FAMILY

The tomato sauce family is, for the most part, created through the blending of herbs, spices and seasonings.

ITALIENNE

Add 1 teaspoon orégano and ½ teaspoon sweet basil to sauce. Simmer 10 minutes. Add 2 tablespoons Marsala and some chopped parsley. For pasta.

PORTUGAISE

Take equal parts of Tomato and Demi-glace sauces. Add 2 minced cloves garlic and simmer 30 minutes. Sauté 2 sliced onions in 2 tablespoons olive oil until soft. Garnish sauce with onion rings and chopped parsley. For fish, roasted poultry and grilled meats.

PROVENÇALE

Tie 1 teaspoon dried basil, ½ teaspoon fennel seeds, and ½ teaspoon saffron in a piece of cheesecloth, or cloth. Add to Tomato sauce and simmer 30 minutes. Discard seasonings and add about 3 tablespoons chopped parsley. For fish, eggs, poultry and meats.

SAUCES FROIDES
[*Cold Sauces*]

In addition to the 5 basic warm sauces there are 2 basic cold sauces, or dressings: Mayonnaise, and Oil and Vinegar.

Mayonnaise is a very large sauce family and very versatile. The sauces are used on both hot and cold foods. Oil and Vinegar is a smaller family and limits itself and its relatives to cold foods, mainly vegetables and greens.

Mayonnaise and its various offspring sauces for hot foods are given here. In Chapter XVIII, "Buffet Froid," will be found the Mayonnaise offspring dressings for cold foods. There too will be found the Oil and Vinegar recipes.

MAYONNAISE INFORMATION

Curdled Mayonnaise. See note on how to cure curdled Hollandaise, p. 22.

Failures in making Mayonnaise are attributable chiefly to two factors: (a) using cold ingredients, and (b) adding the oil too fast.

Oil. The oil may be olive oil, other vegetable oil, a blend of these two, or blends of different olive oils. Experiment until you find what you like. I use a mixture of Italian and French olive oils and Spanish when available.

Egg yolks. Rule of thumb: 1 yolk will absorb about 6 tablespoons oil, but 3 yolks will absorb about 1½ cups. Safety in numbers.

MAYONNAISE

3 egg yolks
2 tablespoons vinegar
½ teaspoon salt
⅛ teaspoon white pepper

1½ cups oil
Juice of ½ lemon
1 tablespoon boiling water

1. Have all ingredients at room temperature. For a better sauce remove the hard piece, or core, that clings to each egg yolk. Beat yolks together and then add vinegar, salt, and pepper. Use whisk, hand beater, or mixer.

2. Add oil by drops, then in a fine stream. After every ½ cup stop adding oil and just beat and blend mixture. Use hand mixer on high speed, electric mixer on medium. After ½ cup oil has been added the mixture is thin, but then it starts to thicken with the addition of more oil and will be heavy when finished.

3. After all oil has been added, stir in lemon juice, then water, which will keep it from separating. Spoon or pour into jar and refrigerate. Makes about 1 pint.

NOTE: We recommend making Mayonnaise in a blender. If you do, mix on *low speed* and use a scant 1 cup oil. To add more oil would clog the blender. Add 2 tablespoons boiling water, instead of the 1 in basic recipe.

MAYONNAISE FAMILY

The offspring of this mother sauce are not very different from the parent. They are created merely by adding ingredients to the finished Mayonnaise, except in the case of Aïoli. If you want a full recipe of Aïoli (2 cups), then crush six cloves garlic in the Mayonnaise bowl and make the Mayonnaise with the mashed garlic.

AÏOLI

With mortar and pestle mash 3 cloves of garlic to a pulp. Gradually blend 1 cup Mayonnaise into this essence. For vegetables.

ANDALOUSE

Peel the skin from ¼ each of a red and green pepper (hold over flame to scorch skin, then peel). Cut into julienne strips. Sauté in olive oil. Cool.

Add pepper pieces and 2 tablespoons tomato paste to 1 cup Mayonnaise. Season with ¼ teaspoon sugar, ⅛ clove garlic, mashed, and a dash of salt. For grilled and French-fried foods.

CHANTILLY

Add 1 tablespoon each crème fraîche and lemon juice to 1 cup Mayonnaise, then stir in 4 tablespoons whipped cream. For asparagus and other green vegetables.

MENTHE

Substitute about 10 fresh mint leaves for greens in the Verte sauce, or more, if you like strong mint flavor. For lamb.

NIÇOISE

Add 2 tablespoons each minced pimentos and tomato paste and 1 teaspoon each diced fresh tarragon and chives to 1 cup Mayonnaise. For poached and sautéed fish; eggs and fowl.

NOISETTE

Add ½ cup toasted, ground hazelnuts or almonds to 1 cup Mayonnaise. For green vegetables.

RÉMOULADE

Add 2 sieved egg yolks, 1 tablespoon minced sweet pickles, ¼ teaspoon dry mustard, 1 teaspoon minced parsley, ½ teaspoon anchovy paste, ½ teaspoon each washed capers, dried chervil, and dried tarragon to 1 cup Mayonnaise. For seafoods.

TARTARE

To 1 cup Mayonnaise add: 3 tablespoons minced sweet pickles, 1 minced shallot, 1 minced hard-cooked egg, 2 tablespoons minced parsley and 1 tablespoon chives. For French-fried foods.

VERTE

Drop 4 sprigs parsley, 6 sprigs watercress, 6 spears chives and 2 leaves spinach into boiling water and leave for 2 minutes.

Lift from water with a fork and place in sieve. Wash under cold water, drain, blot on paper towels, then mash through sieve with a spoon. Add to 1 cup Mayonnaise. Taste and adjust seasonings. For poached seafoods and fowl.

VINCENT

Combine equal parts Tartare sauce and Sauce Verte. For seafoods and eggs.

SAUCES AU BEURRE
[*Butter Sauces*]

In addition to the 5 basic warm sauces and the 2 basic cold sauces (see Chapter XVIII), we also have 2 butter sauces, hot and cold, and both are used on hot foods.

Butter sauces are simple creations that can be flavored with almost anything you wish. Maine lobsters become quite special when accompanied with lobster-flavored butter, and grilled steaks take on a new dimension when topped with truffled butter.

When making hot butter sauces, such as Meunière, Currie, or Amandes, it is important and necessary to clarify the butter (see p. 599). If this is not done, the impurities in the butter will burn and give a strange taste to the sauce. However, when crème fraîche or a liaison is added to the butter sauce it is not necessary to clarify the butter, unless the butter is toasted, as in Crème de Beurre.

BEURRES COMPOSÉS
[*Compound Butters*]

HOT

Hot butter sauces must be finished at the last minute. But the toasting of nuts, the cooking of curry, the reducing of wine, and the clarifying of butter may be done in advance.

BEURRE D'AMANDES

¼ pound butter, clarified   1 tablespoon lemon juice
¼ cup sliced almonds   Salt and pepper to taste

Toast nuts in butter. Add lemon juice, salt, and pepper. Pour over grilled or sautéed fish, or cooked green vegetables.

BEURRE BLANC

2 shallots, minced   2 tablespoons crème fraîche
1 cup white wine   ¼ teaspoon salt
¼ pound butter, softened   Dash of white pepper

Combine shallots and wine. Boil, reducing wine to ¼ cup. Remove from heat.

Strain liquid and cool. Whip liquid into the softened butter, a bit at a time, then add crème, salt, and pepper. Beat and warm the sauce by setting bowl into warm water. Do not melt the butter. Serve with poached fish, sautéed chicken, veal, or vegetables.

BEURRE AU CURRIE

¼ pound clarified butter	1 tablespoon sherry
1 tablespoon curry powder	1 tablespoon lemon juice

Salt and pepper to taste

To melted butter add curry powder and cook 3 minutes to release curry flavor. Stir in sherry and lemon juice. Taste and adjust seasonings. Serve with seafoods and poultry.

BEURRE FRIT

Cut ¼ pound frozen butter into 6 large pats. Dip each pat in flour and then in slightly beaten egg white. Roll in fine dry bread crumbs. Dip again in egg white and crumbs. Refrigerate until ready to fry.

At the moment of serving, French-fry in vegetable oil heated to 390 degrees. Done when brown. Serve on poached fish or boiled vegetables. This is a nice way to serve melted butter—encased in a crust.

BEURRE À LA MEUNIÈRE

¼ pound butter, clarified	Salt and pepper to taste
1 teaspoon lemon juice	2 tablespoons chopped parsley

Put clarified butter (p. 599) into heavy skillet. Toast the butter over low heat until it smells nutty. At this point add the lemon juice, salt, and pepper.

Sprinkle the food with parsley and pour the hot butter over both.

BEURRE NOIR

Clarify ¼ pound butter (p. 599) and then toast it over very low heat. Do not let it burn. Takes about 15 minutes. Stir constantly while butter toasts.

BEURRE DE NOISETTE

Make like Beurre d'Amandes, substituting hazelnuts for the almonds. Usually the hazelnuts are minced, not sliced.

CRÈME DE BEURRE

⅛ pound clarified butter
½ cup crème fraîche

⅛ teaspoon salt
Dash of white pepper

Toast butter in small skillet. Remove from heat. Cool, and whisk in crème, salt, and pepper. The trick to this sauce is the coolness of the butter. If butter is too hot, the crème will melt, rather than mix. Err on the side of having the butter too cool. Have crème at room temperature. Serve with poached fish and roasted chicken.

SAUCE AU BEURRE (BÂTARDE)

⅛ pound butter
3 tablespoons flour
2 cups cold water
2 egg yolks

2 tablespoons crème fraîche
Chunk of butter
Juice of 1 lemon
Salt and pepper to taste

Cook flour in butter for about 2 minutes without browning. Stir in cold water. Cook-stir until thickened.

Make liaison of yolks and crème. Stir bit of hot sauce into mixture, then pour into sauce. Remove from heat, whisk in chunk of butter, bit by bit, and add lemon juice. Taste and adjust seasonings.

Use like Hollandaise. It is not as rich, so don't try to pass it off for the real Hollandaise! Serve with poached fish and cooked vegetables.

SAUCE AU BEURRE PERSILÉE

¼ pound butter
3 tablespoons flour
2 cups cold water

½ teaspoon salt
Dash of pepper
Juice of ½ lemon

½ cup minced parsley (lots)

Melt butter in skillet. Stir in flour. Cook a few minutes, then add water, salt, and pepper. Stir until thickened. When ready to serve add lemon juice and parsley. Taste and adjust seasonings.

Serve in separate bowl with Truite au Bleu or Poached Sea Bass.

BEURRES COMPOSÉS

[*Compound Butters*]

COLD

Cold butter sauces may be made well in advance of the time of serving and either refrigerated or frozen.

BEURRE D'AIL

Mash 4 cloves garlic to a pulp in mortar with pestle. Blend in ¼ pound butter. Freeze in small packets ready to use.

BEURRE D'ANCHOIS

¼ pound butter, softened	1 tablespoon sweet sherry
6 anchovy fillets, mashed	1 tablespoon lime juice
Dash of white pepper	

Combine all ingredients. Do not salt; anchovies are salty. Serve with grilled seafoods.

BEURRE DE CHUTNEY

¼ pound butter	1 tablespoon catsup
3 tablespoons chutney	1 tablespoon lime juice
1 teaspoon Worcestershire	1 tablespoon crème fraîche
Salt and pepper to taste	

Put first five ingredients into blender container. Whirl to purée. Pour into dish and stir in crème. Taste and adjust seasonings. Serve with roast lamb, curries, or seafoods.

BEURRE DE CITRON

Blend 1 tablespoon freshly grated lemon rind into ¼ pound butter. Freeze in small packets. Use to flavor sauces, on vegetables, or on grilled fish or poultry.

BEURRE DE HOMARD I

¼ pound softened butter   1 tablespoon sherry
1 (4-ounce) cooked lobster tail, shelled   1 tablespoon lime juice
Salt and pepper to taste

Put all ingredients into blender, or grind lobster through food chopper and then mix. Whirl blender to purée lobster. Correct seasoning. Pack into small dish and chill. Spoon onto hot grilled fish and let it melt. Heat and serve with boiled lobsters.

NOTE: Substitute crab or shrimp to make those flavors.

BEURRE DE HOMARD II

Mash the shell, the little legs, and the creamy parts of a whole cooked lobster in a mortar with pestle, or in a blender. Put into small saucepan. Add ¼ pound butter and heat. Toast butter. Strain butter through a cloth to remove shells and pieces. Pour into small dish and set in ice. When it starts to set, whip with a whisk to make it light and then refrigerate. For grilled whole fish, fillets, or sautéed scallops. Make any time you have lobster shells. Freeze until needed.

BEURRE À LA MAÎTRE D'HÔTEL

¼ pound butter   Dash of white pepper
⅛ teaspoon salt   2 tablespoons lemon juice
4 tablespoons minced parsley

Cream butter and then add salt, pepper, and lemon juice.

Put minced parsley into corner of a towel, twist, and dry. Add to butter mixure. Pack into small dish. Refrigerate.

Spoon onto hot grilled fish, meats, or hot vegetables.

BEURRE MOUSSEUX

Make Sauce au Beurre (p. 37). Cool, then refrigerate until very cold.

When ready to serve stir in 1 cup very stiff whipped cream. Spoon onto poached fish. This might well be called a Mock Chantilly.

BEURRE DE TRUFFES

Blend 1 tablespoon minced truffles into ⅛ pound butter. Freeze in small packets. Serve with grilled steaks or sautéed chicken suprêmes.

Les Soupes
[*Soups*]

All soups in French cooking derive from, or are adaptations of, two basic types: clear and thick soups. A thorough understanding of the preparation of these two categories of soups will help you in making the many variations on them.

In cooking soups, as in cooking all other French dishes, the final product can only be as good as the ingredients used. Do not let the soup kettle become a receptacle for leftovers. Occasionally, yesterday's vegetables may be added, but only if enough fresh vegetables are present in which they can hide.

Soups, when served with a meal, are intended to stimulate the appetite and not to satisfy the hunger. Soup is to a dinner what an overture is to an opera—it prepares us for what is to follow.

CLEAR CONSOMMÉS

The clear soups, called consommés (a word which means a perfectly refined soup), are made from clarified stock.

Crystal-clear consommés are served either hot or chilled. Connoisseurs prefer that they appear on the table unadorned and plain, as perfection in themselves. But they may also quite properly be garnished with simple or elaborate foods.

BASIC CONSOMMÉ

½ cup cold water	6 cups stock
4 egg whites	1 teaspoon salt
2 carrots, minced	⅛ teaspoon pepper
3 tablespoons minced parsley	Red and brown food coloring
1 leek or small onion	2 tablespoons Madeira

1 tablespoon Cognac

1. Put water and egg whites into saucepan. Beat to a froth. Add carrots and parsley. Wash leek (see p. 607), dice and add. Pour in cold stock (never hot, or it will cook the egg whites before they have clarified the stock). Season with salt and pepper.

2. Stir-cook and heat to a boil. When mixture starts to boil, reduce heat, stop stirring, and let simmer for about 10 minutes. Do not let it bubble at all. The egg whites will absorb and hold the impurities from the stock.

3. When done, carefully pour liquids from the coagulated egg-white mixture through a clean damp linen cloth (wet cloth makes a finer strainer than dry cloth because the threads are swollen). Be careful not to break up the cooked egg whites.

4. Once it has been strained, color soup a rich dark brown with food colorings if beef stock is being clarified, but omit the coloring if it is chicken stock.

5. Flavor with Madeira and Cognac. Serve plain, or with garnishings. Consommé may be frozen ready to use, but, when it is, omit the Madeira and Cognac, adding them when it is reheated and ready to serve. To make double-strength consommé, reduce it by half before adding the Madeira and Cognac.

NOTE: If you feel the stock is loaded with impurities, add another egg white or two: the more egg whites the more jewel-like the consommé. However, it should never take more than 1 egg white per cup of stock, and never use fewer than 4 egg whites to 6 cups stock. Nothing is more appealing to sight and taste than a sparkling cup of well-seasoned consommé.

VARIATIONS
JELLIED CONSOMMÉ

Add 1½ tablespoons unflavored gelatin to the cold water and egg whites. Mix well, then continue with recipe. Substitute Port for the Madeira. Pour into a nonmetal bowl, cool, then refrigerate until set. Spoon into ice-server bouillon cups, or cold berry dishes. A clear jellied consommé should be served in glass, not china, to add to its sparkle.

Consommé with gelatin may also be frozen but omit the Port and Cognac. The gelatin freezes into rubbery strips, so the consommé *must* be reheated to dissolve the gelatin. Once gelatin is dissolved, cool, then add the Port and Cognac and refrigerate until set.

GARNISHINGS FOR CONSOMMÉS

Garnishings for consommé may be simple or elaborate.

Simple garnishes are vegetables, pastas, rice, and croutons. Vegetables should be cut as accurately and as uniformly as possible. Make pieces round, or cut into strips diagonally and then into diamonds, or

> Brunoise—¹⁄₁₆-inch cubes
> Chiffonade—Cut into shreds (leafy vegetables)
> Julienne—Strips 2 inches long and about ¹⁄₁₆-inch square
> Paysanne—¼-inch cubes

Vegetable garnishes are always cooked separately in a bit of consommé and then added to the hot consommé in the serving cup.

Pasta garnishings include vermicelli, spaghetti, noodles, or macaroni. These are also cooked separately from the consommé, cut appropriately, and then spooned into the hot consommé. Rice is likewise cooked separately and then added.

Croutons are always passed at the table so they will remain crisp.

In addition to the above simple foods, any food that will give texture, color, and taste may be used, such as cubes of avocados or artichoke hearts.

Elaborate garnishes include egg threads, quenelles, and royales. A few julienne pieces of truffles may join these elegant tidbits providing truffles are not used elsewhere in the meal.

FILS D'OEUFS

[*Egg Threads*]

8 egg yolks	**½ teaspoon salt**
6 cups chicken stock	

1. Whip egg yolks and salt together with a fork. Strain through a sieve to remove hard white particles that adhere to yolks.

2. Heat stock to a simmer.

3. Holding your finger over the opening, fill a very fine funnel with the yolk mixture. The opening should be a little larger than ¹⁄₁₆ inch in di-

ameter. The bigger the opening the bigger the egg threads, and vice versa.

4. Then hold funnel just above the simmering liquid, remove your finger from the opening and move funnel over stock, letting yolks stream into the hot but *not* boiling stock. Cook in small batches, lifting out the cooked threads before adding another batch. Put finger over funnel to close; remove to open.

NOTE: If you can't find a funnel, buy a plastic bottle with nozzle. Fill with yolks and trim the nozzle to the size of the thread you want. Force the yolks from the bottle by squeezing. These bottles are handy kitchen gadgets. Keep some on hand.

In Spain they have a special container designed to hold egg yolks. It looks something like a cow's udder, but with five spigots. Buy one when you go there.

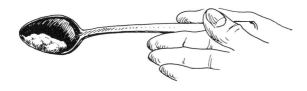

QUENELLES D'OEUF DUR

[*Hard-cooked Egg-yolk Quenelles*]

8 hard-cooked egg yolks	1 teaspoon crème fraîche, or
1 whole raw egg	whipping cream
½ teaspoon salt	1 teaspoon minced parsley
Dash of white pepper	1 teaspoon minced onion

4 cups stock, heated to a simmer

1. Put everything but stock into container of a blender. Whirl to a thick paste. If it seems too soft, add another hard-cooked yolk. It is better to have this too thick than too soft. You can always dilute the mixture with a bit of cream.

2. When of the right consistency the mixture will not fall apart when

cooked (see p. 116). Shape into quenelles, using two teaspoons, and carefully put into simmering stock. Do not let the stock boil. The quenelles float almost instantly. Let them poach about 1 minute, then carefully lift each one from the stock with a table fork and place in ice water to stop the cooking.

3. When they are cool, lift quenelles to a plate. Change the ice water often and have it cold and ready for the next batch of cooked quenelles. Cook in small batches, a dozen at a time. Makes about 4 dozen. Fill soup cups with consommé, then add these quenelles. They are very fragile and very good.

ROYALE

[*Stock Custard*]

1 cup chicken stock or consommé	Dash of white pepper
4 sprigs parsley	1 whole egg
Dash of salt	2 egg yolks

1. Heat stock with parsley, salt, and pepper. Simmer 5 minutes. Remove from heat and set pan in cold water to cool. Remove parsley.

2. Beat egg and yolks together with whisk. Add cooled stock to egg mixture. Strain into an 8-inch buttered casserole. (Custard should be about ¼ inch deep.) Skim foam from top of custard and discard. (Foam gets tough when cooked.)

3. Set casserole in a water bath and bake in 325-degree oven for about 20 minutes. Test by inserting knife into center. If it comes out clean, custard is done. If not, cook another 3 minutes and test again. (This is nothing more than baked custard, but nonsweet and made with stock rather than milk.)

4. When custard is done, let cool in casserole. Then cover and refrigerate until cold. With fancy cutters stamp out pieces of royale, or cut into fancy shapes with a knife. Add to consommé in serving cups. This is very delicate and very delicious.

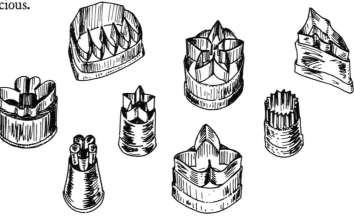

GARNISHED CONSOMMÉS

In classical French cooking, the name of the consommé tells what garnish you may expect to find in the consommé. Here are many variations on the consommé theme:

Brunoise. Add small cubes of cooked vegetables.

aux Cheveux d'Anges. Add fine vermicelli noodles or Egg Threads (p. 42).

Carmen. Add sautéed, peeled tomato cubes and cooked rice.

Chevreuse. Add Chicken Quenelles (p. 149) and juliennes of truffles.

Demidoff. With a small fluted melon-baller, cut out pearls of cooked carrots and turnips and add to consommé.

Julienne. Add julienne-cut vegetables that have been cooked in stock.

aux Profiteroles. Add miniature Profiteroles (p. 360).

aux Quenelles. Add Veal Quenelles (p. 176); Liver Quenelles (p. 152); or Quenelles D'Oeuf Dur (p. 43).

à la Royale. Add pieces of Royale (p. 44).

Rossini. Add Profiteroles (p. 360) stuffed with Truffled Chicken-Liver Pâté (p. 417).

de Madère, Marsala, or Porto. Add 2 tablespoons of the selected wine to each consommé cup.

aux Truffes. Add juliennes of truffles to consommé flavored with 2 tablespoons of Madeira, Marsala, or Port.

HEARTY CONSOMMÉS

These heavy soups the French seem to enjoy eating after the theater, or in the early-morning hours after a night on the town. With them one has plenty of crusty French bread—and it is quite proper to dunk the bread! A fine Burgundy wine goes well with them.

In this country these hearty soups could be enjoyed for Sunday brunch or supper and would be particularly welcome after an evening of cards.

SOUPE À L'OIGNON

[*Onion Soup*]

¼ pound butter	1 teaspoon salt
6 large yellow onions, sliced thin	⅛ teaspoon pepper
2 tablespoons sugar	Chunk of butter
2 tablespoons flour	2 onions, sliced
7 cups chicken stock	6 (½-inch thick) slices French bread

Grated Gruyère or Parmesan cheese

1. Melt butter in saucepan and then add 6 sliced onions. Cover with a lid and simmer for about 30 minutes. Add sugar and flour. Stir-cook a few minutes, then stir in stock, salt (remember Parmesan is salty), and pepper. Simmer for 30 minutes. Taste and adjust the seasonings.

2. Stir-cook 2 sliced onions in chunk of butter until caramelized. Once they are browned and slightly crisp, add to the soup for color and taste.

3. Toast French bread, then place in a warm oven to dry out. Fill individual earthenware bowls with soup. Put toasted bread atop the soup. Let it soak and sink into the soup, then sprinkle with cheese. Broil a few minutes to brown the cheese. Serve with plenty of crusty French bread.

NOTE: Lacking earthenware bowls, pour soup into a casserole, top with toasted bread slices, sprinkle with cheese, and broil. If using a tureen, sprinkle the bread slices with cheese, broil, and then float atop the soup and serve.

Wine: Sancerre

LA PETITE MARMITE

[*Meat Soup in Earthen Pot*]

1 pound lean rump beef, in one piece	4 turnips
1 pound of oxtail, cut up	13 boiling onions (small)
6 marrow bones, or more	2 whole cloves
1 (3-pound) chicken, cleaned	4 leeks
3 quarts water	2 branches celery
1 quart chicken stock	1 tablespoon salt
Giblets and necks from 3 chickens (no livers)	½ teaspoon pepper
	½ small head green cabbage
6 carrots	Toasted French-bread slices

1. Put beef, oxtail pieces, and marrow bones into cheesecloth or a clean cloth. Tie with a string. (Use a napkin or kitchen towel; a double-thick piece of organdy is also perfect.) Remove fat from chicken and tie legs and wings to body (see p. 125). Place meats and chicken in large kettle. Add water and stock. Bring to a boil, then reduce heat and simmer 3 hours. Add giblets and

necks after 2 hours of cooking. Remove scum from the kettle as it collects. Use a slotted spoon, and be careful that the scum does not break apart. Clearness of the liquids is dependent upon careful skimming and slow cooking. Prepare vegetables while meats cook.

2. Peel carrots and cut into 1-inch chunks. Trim off sharp edges, then shape into ovals. Peel, then cut turnips into fourths. Trim like carrots. (Later make a potage from vegetable trimmings and some of the leek tops.) Peel onions. Stick 2 cloves into one. Clean leeks (see p. 607); cut white part into 2-inch chunks; do not use green tops. Peel strings from celery with a potato peeler and then cut into 2-inch pieces. Add these prepared vegetables, salt, and pepper to the kettle at the end of 3 hours. Simmer another hour. Remove scum as it collects and keep sides of kettle wiped clean with damp paper towels.

3. Shred (chiffonade) cabbage. Simmer in 1 cup liquid from the kettle for 5 minutes.

4. When marmite is done, lift meats and poultry to platter. Discard onion with the cloves. Add half cup of ice water to kettle and let stand 10 minutes off the heat. Take meats from cloth. Slice rump beef. Remove marrow from bones and place on small plate. Skin chicken, then remove meat from bones in pieces. Do not slice the chicken; serve in pieces.

5. To serve, ladle liquids into individual hot earthenware or soup bowls. Add an assortment of meats, chicken, and vegetables to each hot bowl. Garnish with cooked cabbage. Spread toasted bread with bone marrow and serve with the marmite. Serves 8.

Wine: Beaujolais

SOUPE AUX CHOUX

[*Cabbage Soup*]

4 (¼-inch thick) slices salt pork	4 cups chicken stock
2 onions, sliced	3 cups water
2 leeks	1 teaspoon salt
1 turnip, diced	⅛ teaspoon pepper
2 carrots, diced	1 tablespoon sugar
2 potatoes, cubed	Grated Gruyère or Parmesan cheese
1 very small head (or ½ pound) green cabbage, shredded	

1. Dice salt pork and place in large kettle. Render fat from it, but do not let it brown. Add onions. Wash leeks (see p. 607). Slice into kettle, using about 2 inches of the green tops. Cover and simmer about 1 hour.

2. Add remainder of ingredients, except cheese. Cover and simmer for 1 hour. Taste and adjust seasonings. Pour into hot soup plates, sprinkle with cheese, and serve with crusty French bread.

Wine: Brouilly

POTAGES
[*Thick Vegetable Soups*]

The thick soups, called *potages* (a word which means garden soup), are made from puréed vegetables. In classical French cuisine the potages are not served cold. Potages may be plain or creamed, and garnished either with pieces of vegetables or pasta. Invariably potages are enriched with butter, cream, or a liaison of yolks and crème fraîche. To my way of thinking a liaison is about the best finish a potage can have.

POTAGE PURÉE DE LÉGUMES
[*Basic Plain Vegetable Potage*]

Plain potages usually include at least one starchy vegetable.

¼ pound butter	⅛ teaspoon pepper
3 leeks	3 medium-sized potatoes, sliced
2 onions, sliced	5 cups cold water
1 carrot, diced	4 tablespoons crème fraîche, or
1 tablespoon salt	whipping cream
1 tablespoon sugar	2 egg yolks

Chopped chives or parsley

1. Melt butter in large saucepan. Wash leeks (see p. 607), slice, and add with the onions, carrot, and salt. Cover and simmer 30 minutes. As vegetables are cooked in butter, their moisture is evaporated and they become saturated with butterfat—a condition that makes them sweet and nutty in flavor. Add the sugar, pepper, potatoes, and water. Cover and cook for about 1 hour.

2. Press soup through food mill and then pour back into saucepan to keep hot. When ready to serve, combine crème and yolks. Ladle some hot potage into the mixture and then stir back into the pan. Heat but do not boil, or yolks may curdle. Garnish with chopped chives or parsley and serve.

VARIATIONS

Many potages may be created from the above basic recipe just by changing the vegetables. Here are a few examples:

POTAGE CRESSONNIÈRE
[*Watercress Potage*]

Wash 2 medium-sized bunches of watercress. Remove tough bottom stems and place tops in blender container. When potage is done, press through a food mill. Then pour 2 cups hot potage into blender container with watercress. Whirl to purée cress. Pour this mixture into the potage. Add liaison of crème and egg yolks, adjust seasonings, and serve. Garnish with a few watercress leaves.

POTAGE DUBARRY
[*Cauliflower Potage*]

Break flowerets from a head of cauliflower to make 3 cups. Add to the saucepan at the same time the potatoes are added. When done, remove 6 cooked flowerets to use later as garnish, then press the potage through a food mill. Finish with liaison of crème fraîche and egg yolks, according to the basic recipe. Garnish with flowerets.

POTAGE D'ÉPINARDS
[*Spinach Potage*]

Remove stems and tough veins from ½ pound fresh spinach, or use 1 package frozen chopped spinach, thawed. Add to basic potage recipe the last 5 minutes of cooking time. Press through food mill, adjust seasonings, and finish with liaison of crème and egg yolks. Garnish with croutons.

POTAGE PORTUGAIS
[*Tomato Potage*]

To basic potage recipe add 3 cups canned Italian plum tomatoes at the time the potatoes are added. When soup is done, press potage through a food mill, then finish with a chunk of butter. *Omit* the liaison of crème fraîche and egg yolks. Adjust seasonings.

NOTE: To make a cream tomato potage, add ½ teaspoon baking soda to the potage and immediately stir in 1 cup whipping cream or crème fraîche. Soda prevents curdling when cream is combined with tomatoes.

POTAGE CULTIVATEUR

[*Farmer Potage*]

3 carrots	2 teaspoons each salt and sugar
2 turnips	Dash of white pepper
½ pound green beans	1 tomato
1 leek	3 medium-sized red potatoes
¼ pound butter	Chunk of butter
6 cups boiling water	Parsley

1. Select long thin carrots. Peel and trim off the fat top part, making the whole carrot nearly the same in diameter from top to bottom. Once carrots are shaped, cut into paper-thin crosswise slices.

2. Peel turnips, then, with an apple corer or a knife, cut as many cylinders as you can from each turnip. Slice them into thin discs like the carrots.

3. Stem the beans and cut into ⅛-inch slices. Select leek about the same diameter as the carrots. Clean (p. 607) and slice it into discs.

4. Melt the butter in a large saucepan. Add the prepared vegetables. Cover and simmer 15 minutes. Add the boiling water, salt, sugar, and pepper.

5. Peel the tomato, cut in half, remove seeds, and squeeze out liquid. Dice onto a plate ready to use.

6. Peel potatoes. With apple corer push out cylinders of potatoes. Then slice them paper thin like the other vegetables. Add to soup and cook 15 minutes.

7. When vegetables are done, carefully whisk in the butter, followed by the diced tomatoes. Pour into soup tureen. Float whole parsley leaves (no stems) over the top. Carefully ladle into soup plates, being careful not to mash the vegetables.

POTAGE NIVERNAISE

[*Carrot Potage of Nevers*]

4 carrots	2 teaspoons salt
2 onions	⅛ teaspoon pepper
2 leeks	2 carrots
¼ pound butter	Chunk of butter
2 potatoes, sliced	2 egg yolks
6 cups water	½ cup crème fraîche

1. Dice 4 carrots, the onions, and washed leeks (see p. 607). Place in saucepan with the butter. Cover and simmer ½ hour. Add potatoes, water, salt, and pepper. Cover and simmer another hour.

2. Peel 2 carrots and cut into lengthwise slices ⅟₁₆ inch thick. Cut these into ⅟₁₆-inch strips and then cut into ⅟₁₆-inch cubes, thus cutting them à la brunoise. Melt chunk of butter in small skillet. Add brunoise-cut carrots. Place a piece of buttered foil on top of the carrots and then cover pan with a lid. Let simmer over very low heat for about 20 minutes.

3. When potage is done, press through food mill. Then pour back into saucepan. Heat. Mix yolks and crème. Add about 1 cup hot potage to this liaison, and then pour into potage. Heat but do not boil. Fill soup tureen with potage and garnish with cooked carrot cubes.

POTAGE DE POIS FRAIS
[*Potage of Fresh Peas*]

¼ pound butter
2 pounds fresh peas, shelled (or
   1 package frozen peas)
1 cup (packed) shredded lettuce
1 onion, diced
2 leeks
2 carrots, diced

6 cups water
2 potatoes, sliced
1 tablespoon sugar
2 teaspoons salt
Chunk of butter
1 cup (about) shredded sorrel
Croutons

1. Put butter, peas, lettuce, onion, sliced leeks (to clean leeks, see p. 607), and carrots into saucepan. Cover and simmer for about 30 minutes. Add water, potatoes, sugar, and salt. Cook another 30 minutes.

2. When done press through food mill. Rinse pan. Put chunk of butter into soup saucepan. Add sorrel and sauté 1 minute. Add puréed soup to sorrel, heat, and serve with croutons (p. 599).

NOTE: If sorrel is not available, leave it out, or substitute spinach leaves, knowing, of course, it will give the color but not the flavor of sorrel.

VARIATIONS
When the sorrel is omitted from the Potage of Fresh Peas and other foods are added, a new potage is created.

POTAGE AMBASSADEURS

Add ½ cup cooked rice to the Potage Fontanges listed below.

POTAGE CAMÉLIA

Omit sorrel from basic recipe and garnish with julienne strips of cooked chicken breast and the white part of a leek. Put the raw breast in the potage when you add the water and potatoes. Simmer 30 minutes, then remove the chicken breast, cool and cut into strips. Leftover chicken may also be used. Sauté strips of leeks in a chunk of butter.

POTAGE FONTANGES

Omit sorrel from basic recipe and garnish with sautéed shredded lettuce seasoned with 1 tablespoon minced fresh chervil, or ½ teaspoon dried chervil. Sauté lettuce in butter 1 or 2 minutes, or until wilted.

POTAGE LONGCHAMP

Omit sorrel from basic recipe and garnish potage with cooked vermicelli noodles.

POTAGE CRÈME D'ASPERGES VERTES
[*Basic Cream of Asparagus Potage*]

Cream potages are normally made from nonstarchy vegetables and thickened with flour. They are best when the vegetables are simmered in butter and the liquids are added after the vegetables are done. The liquid used may be chicken consommé, milk, water, or a combination of these, but seldom water alone. Cream soups are finished with cream, garnished with pasta, pieces of vegetable from which the potage is made, or combinations of these.

2 leeks	1 cup water
2 yellow onions, sliced	2 cups chicken stock
¼ pound butter	3 cups milk
2 pounds fresh asparagus (or 2 packages frozen spears)	2 teaspoons salt
	1 tablespoon sugar
4 tablespoons flour	⅛ teaspoon white pepper
1 cup crème fraîche or whipping cream	

1. Wash leeks (see p. 607). Slice, using about 2 inches of the green tops. Add leeks and onions to saucepan with the butter. Cover and simmer 30 minutes.

2. Wash fresh asparagus. Cut off tough ends of stalks. Cut tips from stalks, or from frozen spears, 1 inch long. Cook tips separately in water seasoned with salt, sugar, and butter. Cook 3 minutes. Put on plate ready to use. Slice stalks. Add stalks to onions and leeks in saucepan and cook covered 10 minutes. Stir in flour and cook a few minutes. Add water, stock, milk, salt, sugar, and pepper. Cook-stir until slightly thickened.

3. Press stalks and potage through food mill. Use liquids to keep pulp moist and it can be pressed through easily.

4. When ready to serve, mix crème and about 1 cup potage, then pour back into saucepan. Heat, but do *not* boil. If mixture is too thick, thin with milk or cream to the consistency of light cream. Pour into soup tureen and garnish with cooked asparagus tips.

VARIATIONS

To change the vegetable in the Cream of Asparagus Potage is to create a different soup.

POTAGE CRÈME DE LAITUES

[*Cream of Lettuce*]

Substitute 2 small heads of Boston or 3 heads of Bibb lettuce for the asparagus. Cut lettuce into shreds (chiffonade). Save some green lettuce shreds for garnishing. When leeks and onions are done (after 30 minutes), add the lettuce and simmer 5 minutes. Add flour, cook a few minutes, then add liquids (except crème), and seasonings. Cook-stir until slightly thickened. Press through food mill. Add crème, heat, pour into tureen and garnish with chiffonade-cut green lettuce, and serve.

POTAGE CRÈME DE CHAMPIGNONS

[*Cream of Mushroom*]

To cooked leeks and onions add 1 pound cleaned and sliced mushrooms, instead of asparagus. Cover and simmer 10 minutes. Add flour, cook a few minutes, then add liquids (except crème), and seasonings. Cook-stir about 10 minutes, then press through food mill. Add crème and serve potage garnished with carved mushrooms (p. 281).

POTAGE CRÈME DE CRÉCY

[*Cream of Carrot*]

Peel and slice 6 carrots very thin. Omit onions, or if leeks are not available use onions, but do not use both onions and leeks. Sauté carrots in the butter along with the leeks for about 30 minutes. Add flour, then liquids (not the crème) and seasonings. Cook-stir 10 minutes, then press through food mill. Finish with crème. Garnish with ½ cup cooked rice.

Oeufs
[*Eggs*]

Eggs are treated with respect in France. They are seldom eaten for breakfast, but they are eaten at almost any other time of the day—when the cook has had time to give them some thought! As Thomas Moore, the Irish poet, wrote in his book on the adventures of the *Fudge Family in Paris:*

> Who can help loving the land that has taught us
> Six hundred and eighty-five ways to dress eggs.

I'm not exactly sure how many different recipes there are for cooking eggs, but I do know that it is vital to cook correctly nature's most nearly perfect food and food package.

Think for a moment about the frail shell that encases the crystal white around a center of golden yellow—think how marvelous is the construction that holds liquids in the form which we call egg-shaped. Think for a moment: is it the hen's skill or the eggs' responsibility? Think, and then master the four basic ways in which eggs are cooked: boiled, poached, in omelettes, and in soufflés. Think if you will, but know that "a hen is only an egg's way of making another egg," or so wrote Samuel Butler.

EGG INFORMATION

For success in egg cookery the eggs must be fresh; this means that they arrive in your kitchen a few days after being laid.

If the white of an egg is watery and the yolk flattens out when the egg is broken into a saucer, it is an old egg. Don't try to poach it in water, but turn it into an omelette and preferably one with a filling. Only fresh eggs can stand alone in hot water and not disintegrate.

Brown eggs and white eggs are of equal value. It is the diet of the hen that determines the flavor of the egg, and not the color of the shell. If you think one brand of eggs is better than another, probably it is. The likelihood is that one hen's diet is better than that of the other.

While eggs are normally served with, or on, a starchy food, it does not always have to be bread or toast. Try eggs in baked potatoes, with noodles or rice, and occasionally on another vegetable high in starch.

If raw eggs get mixed with hard-cooked ones, spin them on a flat surface to determine which is which. The cooked eggs, being solid, spin like a top; the raw eggs, being liquid, turn very slowly.

OEUFS MOLLETS, DURS, ET POCHÉS
[*Soft- and Hard-cooked Eggs*]

A perfectly cooked soft egg has dignity and character. It has a tasty solidified white with a hidden yellow sauce within. A perfectly cooked hard egg is firm, but not rubbery. The white cuts like butter and the yolk crumbles like a moist cake. Both eggs can stand on their own, or become a part of other recipes.

To boil an egg is not to boil it, but to cook it in water just below the boiling point at a temperature of about 210 degrees. This condition we refer to as a *simmer*. I have used the word *boil* to denote cooking eggs in their shell in water brought to a boil and then reduced to a simmer.

Poached eggs are normally cooked in simmering water, but, when we want a poached egg with texture we poach them in simmering hot oil, thus French-fried eggs.

Basic recipes for boiled and poached eggs follow. Then comes a poached-egg chart. Cold egg recipes will be found in Chapter XVIII.

OEUFS BOUILLIS

[Boiled Eggs]

Cook eggs in a pan large enough to hold sufficient water to cover them by 1 inch. Fill the pan half full of cold tap water and then add the cold eggs from the refrigerator. Adjust the water level to 1 inch over eggs. (You're less likely to crack the eggs if water supports them than if you put them directly into a metal pan and then add the water.)

Put the eggs on to cook over high heat. When water comes to a boil, reduce the heat to a simmer and cook to desired doneness as follows:

Very soft. When the water reaches the boiling point, the eggs will be very soft and the yolk hot. About ⅛ inch of the white is coagulated; the rest of the liquid white still clings to the yolk.

Soft. Simmer 1 minute after boiling is reached. The white is almost completely cooked, and the yolk falls from it with no liquid white.

Soft-firm. Simmer 2 minutes after boiling is reached. The white is set and the yolk is just starting to cook. The yolk still falls free from the cooked white.

Firm-soft. Simmer 3 minutes after water boils. Now the yolk is cooked about 1/16 inch in. The yolk does not fall free from the white, but breaks at the point to which the yolk is cooked.

NOTE: We have used large-sized eggs. When using smaller ones, reduce cooking times by ½ minute.

Hard-cooked. Simmer 12 minutes after boiling is reached. Remove from heat and set pan under cold running water. Let cold water run into the pan until the eggs are cold. Once they are cold, refrigerate until ready to use. Do *not* boil eggs and do *not* cook eggs longer than 12 minutes. High heat and overcooking make eggs, as well as all other animal protein, tough.

NOTE: If using medium-sized eggs, reduce cooking time to 11 minutes. For small eggs reduce to 10 minutes.

OEUFS POCHÉS

[Poached Eggs]

Cold water	Fresh eggs (large size)
¼ cup white vinegar	Bowl of cold water
	Salted hot water

1. Fill a 2-quart saucepan with water to a depth of 3 inches. Bring water to a boil. Once it is boiling, add the vinegar and reduce the heat to a simmer.

2. With a spoon stir the water around in the center of the pan to create a whirlpool. Into this water merry-go-round break the eggs, one after the other but no more than 4 at a time. Once all eggs are in the pot, take hold of the handle and turn the pan in the opposite direction to which the water is going. This tends to reverse the motion of the water; it also rolls the eggs so that the white wraps around the yolk. Turn first in one direction and then the other to create a rolling water bath in which the eggs cook.

3. After 3 minutes lift out eggs and put into large bowl filled with cold water. This stops the cooking and washes off the vinegar water. Eggs may remain here for several hours, or until you are ready to reheat them and serve.

4. When ready to serve, cut off streamers of cooked egg white. Put eggs into salted boiling water and heat for 1 minute. Lift eggs out with slotted spoon, blot on paper towels, and serve, or use in other recipes. Cold poached-egg recipes are in Chapter XVIII.

NOTE: Cook the eggs *no longer* than 3 minutes on the first cooking and err on the side of undercooking. Then, when they are reheated, they will be perfectly poached eggs. If you like them softer, cook less time; if harder, cook longer.

If you want to serve the eggs immediately, omit the cold-water step and dunk them directly into a bowl of salted hot tap water to rinse off the vinegar-flavored water, then blot, trim, and serve. The heat of the eggs will continue to cook them, so they too will be poached perfectly.

OEUFS FRITS
[*French-fried Poached Eggs*]

Heat about 1 inch oil in a small saucepan to very hot, or about 360 degrees. Break egg into small dish. When oil is hot, tip pan to one side, making a well of oil. Slide 1 egg at a time into oil. It will foam and bubble. Spoon oil over the top of the egg and cook about 1 minute.

Lift out with pancake turner, drain, then blot on paper towels. Season with salt and pepper. Serve as you would poached eggs. These eggs are crisp on the outside and soft within. A joy to eat.

POACHED-EGG FAMILY

When poached eggs are to be incorporated in other recipes, prepare them beforehand and place in cold water ready to reheat and use.

Sauces for poached eggs are usually from the Béchamel or Hollandaise family. However, equally good are the Demi-glace sauces.

When poached eggs, whether cooked in water or oil, are served with a sauce it is best to place them in tart shells, croustades, tomato halves, or artichoke bottoms. Then the soft-cooked eggs and the sauce will be contained. If using eggs poached in oil, cook them after the sauce is made.

POACHED-EGG CHART NO. I

In this branch of the family we use a sauce from the Béchamel family.

OEUFS POCHÉS À L'AURORE

[*Poached Eggs with Aurore Sauce*]

Poach eggs, 1 per person. Make Aurore sauce (p. 17). Cut fresh tomatoes in half, one half per person. Scoop out seeds and juice. Sauté cut side of tomato in chunk of butter seasoned with 1 minced clove garlic. Cook about 3 minutes. Turn, season tomatoes, and reheat eggs. Place hot egg into each tomato half, set on toast rounds and glaze with Aurore sauce. Sprinkle with grated Parmesan cheese. Brown under broiler.

OEUFS POCHÉS CRÉCY

[*Poached Eggs on Carrots*]

Poach eggs, 1 per person. Make tart shells (p. 355), croustades (p. 599), or toast rounds. Grate 6 carrots into a skillet with a chunk of butter. Season with salt, pepper, and sugar. Cover and simmer without browning until done. Make Crème sauce (p. 18). Spoon cooked carrots into tart shells, top with reheated poached egg and coat with sauce. Garnish with a thin slice of cooked or raw carrot.

OEUFS POCHÉS FLORENTINE

[*Poached Eggs on Spinach*]

Substitute chopped, cooked spinach for the cooked carrots in the preceding recipe. Sprinkle Crème sauce with Parmesan cheese and brown.

OEUFS POCHÉS SUZETTE
[*Poached Eggs in Baked Potatoes*]

Bake 1 potato per person. Prepare poached eggs ready to reheat. Make Mornay sauce (p. 18). When potatoes are done, cut a lid from one side of each potato. Remove ½ the interior of each cooked potato. Then, with a fork, loosen the rest of the cooked potato within the shell. Dot with butter, season with salt and pepper, and spoon some sauce into the potato. Top with a reheated egg, coat with sauce, and sprinkle with Parmesan. Broil to brown tops. (Add interior of cooked potatoes to balance of cream sauce. Pour into small casserole and bake for dinner.)

POACHED-EGG CHART NO. II

In this branch of the family we use a sauce from the Hollandaise family.

OEUFS CÔTE D'AZUR
[*Poached Eggs in Artichoke Bottoms*]

Prepare 1 egg per person and place in cold water ready to reheat. Sauté fresh or canned artichoke bottoms in a chunk of butter. Make Béarnaise sauce (p. 24). Color half the sauce with 1 tablespoon tomato purée and a drop of red food coloring. Add half the quantity of fresh herbs to the remaining Béarnaise sauce. Place Béarnaise sauce in artichoke bottoms, top with hot egg, and glaze with red sauce. Sprinkle with parsley and serve on toast.

OEUFS POCHÉS À LA TOUT PARIS
[*Poached Eggs in Tomatoes on Spinach*]

Substitute Hollandaise sauce (p. 21) for the Béarnaise (above). Instead of artichoke bottoms place poached eggs in sautéed tomato halves, then set on a bed of buttered cooked spinach.

When poached eggs are set on a ham slice and then on a toasted English muffin and topped with red and yellow Hollandaise you'll have Eggs Benedict, in color.

POACHED-EGG CHART NO. III

In this branch of the family we use a sauce from the Demi-glace family.

OEUFS POCHÉS À LA CHARTRES
[*Poached Eggs with Tarragon*]

Make Demi-glace sauce (p. 27). Poach eggs ready to reheat. Place eggs on toast rounds and glaze with sauce. Garnish with fresh tarragon leaves.

OEUFS ROSSINI
[*Poached Eggs with Pâté*]

Make Demi-glace sauce (p. 27). Poach eggs, 1 per person. Cut pâté de foie gras into slices. Place pâté on toast rounds. Top with reheated poached egg. Glaze with sauce and garnish with a slice of truffle.

OMELETTES

The definition of an omelette is scrambled eggs with a shape. Madame Poulard in her restaurant at Mont-Saint-Michel made omelettes famous. I've often thought that maybe what made them so good was the fact that the hens "grazed" on the salty marshes around Mont-Saint-Michel and the eggs got seasoned from within—just like the lambs raised in the salty meadows—but maybe not.

Omelettes may be made any size, but until you master the technique of the 2-3-egg size, don't attempt the 8-10-egg variety. To my way of thinking the small ones are best since no part of them gets overcooked. Also, I prefer to have a whole individual omelette rather than one-half or one-fourth of a large one. Large-sized omelettes are hard to cook, to shape, and to prevent from having at least some small part of them overcooked and dry.

I have worked out a recipe so close to Madame Poulard's that few could tell the difference. The secret is crème fraîche (p. 3). In omelette recipes I use sour cream (it is thicker) as a substitute for crème fraîche and not whipping cream, thus an exception to the general rule.

Following the basic omelette recipe is an omelette chart.

OMELETTE INFORMATION

The skillet. Use a skillet that measures 6 inches across the bottom and 8 inches across the top (approximately) for the 2- to 3-egg omelette (½ cup measured eggs).

Use a skillet that measures 8 inches at the bottom and 10 inches across the top for the 8-10-egg omelette (2 cups measured eggs). The egg mixture should be about ¼ inch deep in the skillet.

Care of the skillet. Often it is said, "Keep the omelette pan for the omelette. Never cook anything else in it and never wash it." If you have such a pan, fine. If not, then buy an enamel-covered iron skillet, properly shaped for omelettes! That is, with the bottom rounded into the sides. This type of skillet can be used for other foods and can be washed, since water does not affect enamel as it does porous iron.

To polish the skillet. Put about one teaspoon each vegetable oil and salt in the skillet. Heat, then remove from the heat and, using paper towels, scour the skillet. Wipe clean with more paper towels and it is ready for omelette making.

OMELETTE

[*Basic Omelette*]

2 large eggs	Salt and pepper to taste
1 tablespoon crème fraîche or sour cream	Softened butter
1 tablespoon butter, or a piece	

1. Break eggs into bowl. Add the crème. Put butter into an omelette skillet. Heat until the butter turns a light brown and gives off a nutty bouquet, but do not let it burn. While this heats, whip the eggs about 30 strokes with a table fork, mashing the crème into the eggs. Do not beat in advance or eggs break down and become watery.

2. Tip and roll the skillet to coat the sides with butter. Pour out butter. Add egg mixture. With a fork pull the cooked edges into the center, letting the uncooked egg mixture run to the bottom. Do not stir, just lift the edges over the middle. When there is no more runny liquid, just soft custard, remove from heat, and sprinkle with salt and pepper. Then, using your left hand, shake the

omelette up the side of the pan toward the handle. With a rubber spatula flip this side over the middle while tipping the pan down, and start the omelette down to the opposite side. With the rubber spatula flip the opposite side over the middle as you tip the skillet back up. Then grasp the handle of the skillet from underneath, tip the skillet up and let the omelette roll out onto a waiting hot plate. The top of the omelette is the middle third, edges underneath. Spread with softened butter and serve. With practice each omelette will take about one minute or less to make. Omelettes should be cooked over high heat.

NOTE: To make a big omelette, use 8 eggs, 4 tablespoons crème fraîche and 4 of butter. Beat 60 strokes and pour into a large buttered omelette skillet. Stir, fold and serve.

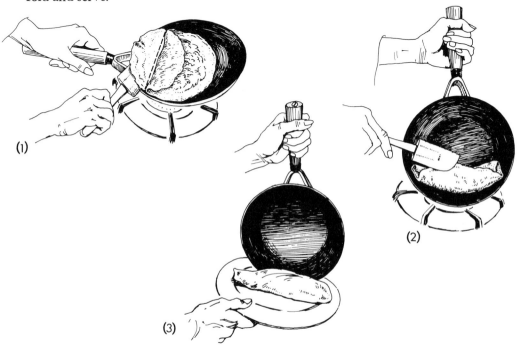

OMELETTE FAMILY

Most vegetables, fowl, and seafoods give excellent flavor to omelettes. Prepare the fillings first and then the omelettes.

OMELETTE CHART NO. I

In this branch of the family the food being folded into the omelette is first sautéed in butter and then seasoned. Fold ¼ of the mixture into each individual omelette. Use the full recipe for a big omelette.

OMELETTE AUX CHAMPIGNONS

[*Omelette with Mushrooms*]

Wash and then slice 1 cup mushrooms. Sauté in a chunk of butter for 2 minutes. Season with salt and pepper. Add 2 tablespoons sherry. Reduce liquid to nothing. Fold into omelettes.

OMELETTE AUX CREVETTES

[*Shrimp Omelette*]

Mince 8 cleaned raw shrimp. Sauté in a chunk of butter seasoned with ½ teaspoon curry powder. Stir-cook about 2 minutes. Add 1 tablespoon crème fraîche and 2 of sherry. Fold into omelettes.

OMELETTE À L'ESPAGNOLE

[*Spanish Omelette*]

Peel and dice 2 tomatoes and 1 onion. Mince ½ green pepper and ½ clove garlic. Sauté all in a chunk of butter. Season with salt, pepper, and sugar. Simmer 20 minutes. Add 2 tablespoons sherry, sprinkle with Parmesan, and remove from heat. Fold into omelettes.

OMELETTE AUX FOIES DE VOLAÍLLE

[*Omelette with Chicken Livers*]

Cut 4 whole chicken livers apart. Roll in flour and sauté in a chunk of butter. Cook about 7 minutes. Season with salt and pepper and sprinkle with dried sweet basil. Pour ¼ cup Cognac over them and set ablaze. Fold into omelettes. Delicious served with a Chasseur sauce (p. 29).

OMELETTE AUX LÉGUMES

[*Vegetable Omelette*]

Sauté any shredded fresh vegetable in butter; season with salt, pepper, and a dash of sugar. Spoon into omelettes and fold.

To make a creamed vegetable omelette, add 2 tablespoons crème fraîche to the sautéed vegetables and then fold into omelettes.

OMELETTE CHART NO. II

In this branch of the omelette family we list a few nonconformists. Each recipe should suggest other possibilities to you. For instance, apple and onion slices can be batter-coated and French-fried as in the Fromage Frit recipe below. Use the chart as an aid in creating your own omelette recipes.

OMELETTE AU CAVIAR

[*Omelette with Caviar*]

Make individual omelettes and place on serving plates. Top with spoonful of crème fraîche and black or red caviar. Domestic black caviar tends to make the omelette look dirty (imported does not), so it is best to put the caviar on top, rather than fold it inside.

OMELETTE AUX FINES HERBES

[*Herbed Omelette*]

Add 2 tablespoons minced parsley and 1 of chives to the recipe. Mix well and cook as in basic omelette.

OMELETTE AU FROMAGE FRIT

[*Omelette with French-Fried Cheese*]

Make batter No. 1 (p. 11). Cut Emmentaler, or Cheddar, into ½-inch-square strips 2 inches long. Dip cheese into batter and French-fry in oil heated to 400 degrees. Lay a strip of cooked cheese in each omelette and then fold. These are delicious! Cheese may also be cooked like Beurre Frit (p. 36).

OMELETTE AUX TRUFFES

[*Truffled Omelette*]

Chop 2 black truffles and marinate in 1 tablespoon Madeira for about 1 hour. Fold a teaspoonful into each omelette.

If using white truffles, substitute Marsala for the Madeira.

SOUFFLÉS

All soufflés are made from a basic cream sauce to which egg yolks and whipped egg whites are added.

The sauce may be made hours in advance of final cooking and the beaten whites folded in just before the soufflé goes into the oven. When the sauce is made in advance, it is always reheated to lukewarm before the egg whites are added.

Cheese-flavored soufflés use an extra egg white. Soufflés containing pieces of food, such as lobster, usually need two extra egg whites to make them light. We have used large-sized eggs. Two whole eggs equal about ½ cup. Two whites measure over ¼ cup. If small eggs are used, all of the recipes will take more yolks as well as more whites. Adjust the number of eggs used in the recipes according to the size of the eggs you are using, knowing that there is a leeway in either direction of about 1 tablespoon.

See also dessert soufflés in Chapter XIV.

SOUFFLÉ INFORMATION

To beat the egg whites. The best equipment in which to beat egg whites is the French hammered-copper, half-moon-shaped bowl with a balloon whisk. As the egg whites inflate, they tend to cling to the hammered dents in the bowl and become the most beautiful whites imaginable. (I've always wondered why some manufacturer didn't dent the metal mixing bowl of his mixer rather than making it so shiny and smooth that it causes the eggs constantly to slip back down as they are whipped.)

But, since very few households have French equipment, here's how to get the best results from your electric mixer.

First, scour the bowl with cleanser to remove any film of oil or grease. Do the same with the beaters. Dry thoroughly. Any trace of oil, water, or egg yolks will prevent the whites from inflating properly. To get maximum volume from whites have them at room temperature.

Start the whites to whip on low speed (No. 3). Whip for about 2 minutes. Then add salt and increase speed to medium (No. 5). Beat another 2 minutes, and then add 1 tablespoon confectioners' sugar. This seems to stabilize the whites while helping them to inflate. Now turn mixer to high speed and beat until stiff.

Using a rubber spatula (previously scrubbed to remove oil), keep whites pushed away from the sides and into the center. Beat until creamy, thick, and glossy, but do not overbeat or whites begin to break down.

Type of dish. Bake soufflés in dishes with straight-up sides, known as soufflé dishes. To use a casserole or charlotte mold with sloping sides is to encourage the soufflé to droop over the sides of the pan rather than to puff up straight and to form what is called a "cap." Soufflé dishes come in all sizes from 1 to 12 cups. To know the size of your dish, simply measure water into it and see how many cups of liquid it holds.

We do not recommend anything larger than a 6-cup size. Smaller, yes—larger no. Large soufflés are apt to fall because of the large surface area. They also require longer cooking, and so too often become overcooked. It is advisable to make two small soufflés rather than a single large one.

If you do not have a soufflé dish, then use whatever casserole you have, but do measure it to know how much it holds.

Preparing the dish. First, butter the soufflé dish and then sprinkle the butter with either Parmesan cheese or flour. The granules up the sides of the dish give the soufflé something to cling to as it creeps up. Once inflated, it has less tendency to fall back down when it has something to hold on to.

Filling the dish. All soufflés must fill the dish *all the way to the top*. Then with a spatula level the batter off smooth and straight. Be sure you have sufficient batter to fill the dish to the brim. Better to have a bit too much than not enough. The dish must be full for the best results.

Once the soufflé dish is full and leveled off, take your thumb and push the batter away from the sides, thus making a groove the width of your thumb around the outside edge. By doing this you start the soufflé in the right direction to puff, and the batter pushes up into a lovely "cap" about 2 inches above the dish—a sight to behold.

To bake the soufflé. Put an oven rack about 6 inches from the floor of the oven and preheat the oven to 400 degrees. Place the soufflé in the center of the rack and bake 10 minutes. Increase the heat to 425 degrees. Bake about 15 minutes. Do not peek, except through the glass door, but that's looking, not peeking.

At the end of the cooking time the cap is not quite pushed out in the center and at that point the soufflé is done. A perfectly cooked soufflé has a slight dent in its cap, which means some of the creamy soufflé mixture at the middle is still uncooked. This uncooked part will become the sauce for the soufflé. If you wait until the cap is completely rounded out, and you may if you wish, there will be no soft custard left in the middle of the soufflé for the sauce.

Sometimes sauce is served on the side; when it is, the soufflé is normally cooked throughout. Needless to say a completely cooked soufflé does not deflate quite as quickly, but it also isn't quite as good. The difference is the same, let us say, as that which distinguishes dry scrambled eggs from creamy, moist ones.

SOUFFLÉ DE CUISINE
[*Basic Soufflé*]

Chunk of butter, grated Parmesan or flour	**Dash of nutmeg**
⅛ pound butter	**⅛ teaspoon white pepper**
4 tablespoons flour	**5 egg yolks**
1 cup light cream	**¼ cup grated Parmesan cheese**
½ teaspoon salt	**6 egg whites**
	2 drops red food coloring

3 drops yellow food coloring

1. Coat a 6-cup soufflé dish, or 6 individual 1-cup dishes, with butter, then sprinkle with Parmesan or flour (see p. 67). Melt ⅛ pound butter in a skillet and then stir in flour. Simmer a few minutes to cook the flour. Do not let it brown. Add cream (always use cold liquids and you'll have no lumps). Add salt, nutmeg, and pepper. (This is a basic Béchamel, only thicker.) Stir-cook until thick.

2. Remove from heat. Stir a bit of hot sauce into yolks. Mix well, then stir yolks into the sauce. Add cheese and mix. Cover with a lid and let sit until you are ready to finish the soufflé. To this point the soufflé can be made hours in advance.

3. When ready to finish soufflé, preheat oven to 400 degrees. Carefully heat the sauce mixture. Start stirring in the center, then, as it heats, gradually work your way to the sides, blending the whole and not breaking it into pieces. Heat to lukewarm, then remove from heat.

4. Beat the egg whites. (Read p. 66 on beating whites.) When the large bubbles in the whites disappear, add the food colorings and then beat until stiff. Color whites to match the yellow sauce, otherwise whites dilute the color of the soufflé. Also, if uncolored whites are not completely blended into the sauce, they will show up as white patches in the baked soufflé.

5. With a whisk stir about a cup of the whites into the sauce. Mix into the custard just as if they weren't beaten whites. This will lighten the custard and make easier the folding in of the balance of the whites. Use a rubber spatula and fold the remaining whites into the custard.

6. Once the soufflé is mixed, pour into prepared dish, *filling full,* then level off with a spatula. With your thumb push the mixture away from the sides (see p. 67). Put into a preheated 400-degree oven. Bake 10 minutes, then increase the heat to 425 degrees. Bake about 15 minutes longer for a large soufflé. For small individual soufflés bake a total of about 12 minutes at 425 degrees. Serve immediately to 4 if it is a large soufflé, or to 6 if individual ones. The large-size soufflé breaks down when cut, so it will not adequately serve 6. The individual soufflés remain puffed and seem like more.

SOUFFLÉ FAMILY

Be sure to read the information on soufflé making given on the preceding pages.

SOUFFLÉ CHART NO. I

In this branch of the family:

a. Vegetables are prepared, then
b. Added to ⅓ of the soufflé recipe, and
c. Spooned into the prepared soufflé dish between 2 layers of plain soufflé.

SOUFFLÉ AUX CHAMPIGNONS
[*Mushroom Soufflé*]

Prepare the basic soufflé recipe to step 3. When ready to continue, mince the caps of raw mushrooms to make 1 cup. Finish the soufflé. Add the mushrooms to ⅓ the soufflé mixture.
Put between 2 layers of plain soufflé and bake.

SOUFFLÉ À LA CRÉCY
[*Carrot Soufflé*]

Peel, slice, and cook 4 carrots in water seasoned with salt, sugar, and butter. When done, drain, purée, and dry off over heat. Add 1 cup puréed carrots to ⅓ of prepared soufflé recipe.
Put between 2 plain layers of soufflé and bake.

SOUFFLÉ AU CRESSON
[*Watercress Soufflé*]

Remove watercress leaves from stems and chop enough to make ½ cup. Add 1 minced shallot to cress, or 1 minced green onion. Combine this with ⅓ of the prepared soufflé recipe.
Put between 2 plain layers of soufflé and bake.

SOUFFLÉ D'ÉPINARDS

[*Spinach Soufflé*]

Remove spinach leaves from the stems. Drop leaves into boiling water for 1 minute to blanch them, then plunge into cold water. Drain, chop, and then blot with paper towels to remove moisture. Squeeze dry in more paper towels or a cloth.

Combine with ⅓ soufflé recipe and spread between two plain layers of soufflé.

SOUFFLÉ CHART NO. II

In this branch of the family:
a. Omit the ¼ cup grated Parmesan cheese, then
b. Increase the egg whites to 7 because of the weight of the pieces of food, and
c. Place the cooled cooked or marinated foods over a layer of soufflé mixture, add a second layer of soufflé, then another layer of the food, ending with a top layer of soufflé. Soufflé Surprise is an exception.

SOUFFLÉ DE CRABE

[*Crab Soufflé*]

Prepare 1½ cups crabmeat. Remove the tissuelike cartilage from the crabmeat. Blot meat dry with paper towels. Put on plate and sprinkle with about 1 tablespoon Madeira. Flake crab with a fork. Layer in the soufflé mixture and bake.

SOUFFLÉ D'ÉCREVISSE

[*Shrimp Soufflé*]

Cut about 10 large cooked cleaned shrimp into 4 thin slices, the long way, thus keeping them in their original crescent shape. Sprinkle with about 1 tablespoon sherry and arrange in layers in the soufflé mixture and bake.

SOUFFLÉ DE HOMARD

[*Lobster Soufflé*]

Prepare about 1½ cups lobster meat. Remove tissuelike cartilage from claws and devein tail. Shred the meat and sprinkle with 1 tablespoon Pernod or sherry. Layer in the soufflé and bake.

If you have cooked a whole lobster, cut in half lengthwise. Remove the meat and clean out the body cavity, then fill about ⅔ full of soufflé mixture. Bake these the last 12 minutes the soufflé bakes and use to decorate platter around the soufflé dish.

SOUFFLÉ DE JAMBON
[*Ham Soufflé*]

Mince ½ pound lean baked ham. Layer in the soufflé mixture and sprinkle each layer with grated orange rind. End with layer of plain soufflé. Serve with prepared Madeira sauce (p. 30).

SOUFFLÉ DE POISSON
[*Fish Soufflé*]

Poach ½ pound fish fillets in 1 cup light cream. Lift out, drain, and flake fish with a fork. Use the poaching cream as the liquid in the basic soufflé recipe. Prepare soufflé.

Layer the fish in the soufflé mixture and sprinkle each layer with grated lemon rind and chopped parsley. Top with plain layer of soufflé.

SOUFFLÉ SURPRISE
[*Poached-Egg Soufflé*]

Poach 4 eggs (p. 56). Blot dry with paper towels, then roll in grated Parmesan cheese.

Fill dish ⅔ full with soufflé mixture. Space the eggs over this layer. Put a dot of soufflé mixture on the outside of the dish in line with each egg to mark its place.

Now cover with remainder of soufflé mixture. Level off top, push away from sides, and then with the back side of a knife cut the top into quarters between the dots of soufflé on the outside. Thus when it is baked you can serve the soufflé knowing where the eggs are located. Let the dots of soufflé bake on the outside to be doubly sure where the eggs lie.

SOUFFLÉ DE VOLAILLE
[*Chicken Soufflé*]

Dice the breast meat of a steamed or baked chicken. Layer in the soufflé. If you have a frozen truffle, mince it, and sprinkle over the chicken layers. Serve with prepared Périgueux sauce (p. 30).

Crustacés and Mollusques
[Shellfish]

Crustaceans and mollusks are nomads of the sea. Wherever they go, their houses go with them—except for the hermit crab. This poor creature of the briny deep has an armored front half like the lobster. From his waist down to the tip of his tail, he lives unprotected until he finds an empty mollusk shell into which he'll fit. Then he backs into it and moves on. Alexandre Dumas said of him: "The Creator, having started to dress him like a lobster, was disturbed or absent-minded during his task and finished him dressed as a slug."

Crustaceans (crabs, crawfish, lobsters, and shrimp) magically change color when cooked. From their protective drab gray-green they transform to an attractive hue of orange-red.

Mollusks (clams, mussels, oysters, scallops, and snails) change not at all in color as they cook. But their shells, impregnable when they are alive, magically open during cooking so that man can find the food treasures within.

Shellfish of all kinds may be cooked by the six basic cooking methods, but they are seldom baked, except in casserole dishes. Shellfish are delicious by themselves, in sauces for one another, or in sauces for fish.

CRUSTACÉS BRAISÉS
[*Braised Crustaceans*]

The French are famous for Bouillabaisse, bisques, and Homard à l'Armoricaine. Legends that come with Homard à l'Armoricaine are many. Some say it was invented by a Parisian chef for one of his wealthy American patrons; others contend it was created in Brittany in the region of Armorica. Personally I find it hard to believe that any chef in France would respect the taste buds of an American sufficiently to create a dish in his honor, especially one with such nuances of flavor.

I think this dish is Mediterranean in origin. In it one finds the foods that are typical of southern France; when these foods appear in other recipes, one refers to the dish as *à la Provençale,* which means using tomatoes, olive oil, garlic, and parsley. But enough of stories. The sauce is also very similar to what we call creole sauce. Shrimp, as well as halibut steaks or other firm-type fish, may be served à l'Armoricaine, or, if you will, à la Provençale.

Bouillabaisse, the ever-popular seafood stew, cannot be exactly duplicated in America any more than can Coq au Vin. Just as our chickens, carrots, and onions have a different flavor, so too do our fish and seafoods.

But differences are not always bad. Our Coq au Vin may even be better and our seafood stews superior to those of the Mediterranean seacoast. Certainly they are not the same, nor is the wine, the water, or the atmosphere in which they are eaten. Give these seafood stews a chance. They are really very good, even if not precisely what you could enjoy in southern France.

HOMARD À L'ARMORICAINE

[*Lobster in Tomato Sauce*]

1 (2-pound) live lobster	1 cup dry red wine
3 tablespoons olive oil	1 teaspoon sugar
(no substitutes)	1 cup chicken stock
2 onions, diced	Salt, pepper, and cayenne
3 shallots, minced	pepper to taste
4 cloves garlic, minced	⅛ pound butter, softened
3 tablespoons Cognac	4 tablespoons flour
2 fresh tomatoes, peeled	2 tablespoons Cognac
and quartered	1 tablespoon Madeira
½ teaspoon saffron shreds	Red food coloring and
1 tablespoon tomato paste	bit of brown
Bouquet garni	Chopped parsley

1. *To kill lobster.* With your left hand grasp the back of the hard body shell (he can't reach you there) and hold the animal firmly on a cutting board. In your right hand (if you're right-handed, of course) have a very heavy, sharp, pointed knife. Insert it at the top of his head between the eyes; cut down between the feelers. His tiny brain rests there, so he is killed instantly. He will wiggle a few minutes. Now cut lobster down through the back and tail, splitting it in half.

2. Remove green tomalley (liver) and the roe. Place on plate to use later in the sauce. Discard the gills and the vein that runs down the back. The vein is translucent before it is cooked, but turns black upon cooking. Rinse out the head part of the lobster, between the eyes. There is a little sac that contains grit in that area which is cut when the lobster is killed. The best way to rid the lobster of it is simply to rinse that part, but not the rest of the lobster. Break large claws from lobster and crack them.

3. Heat olive oil in large skillet. Lay cut sides of lobster in hot oil. Reduce heat and simmer 3 minutes. Turn and cook shell side another 3 minutes. Remove to plate.

4. Add onions, shallots, and garlic to pan. Toss and lightly brown, then lay cut side of lobster down on these vegetables. Pour over 3 tablespoons Cognac and set aflame. When flames die, add ingredients down to the butter. Simmer 10 minutes.

5. Remove lobster from liquid. Extract meat from tail shells by inserting a table fork into the end of the tail and pulling toward the top. The meat comes out easily. Save tail and body shell. Remove meat from leg part of large claws

and then claw meat in one piece, if possible. Discard these shells. Put lobster meat on a plate ready to use. Break small legs from body of lobster ready to use.

6. Boil pan liquids for about 5 minutes to reduce slightly. Remove from heat and stir in tomalley. Discard bouquet garni and strain liquid.

7. Combine butter and flour to make beurre manié. If you have some already made, use it instead of making a new batch. Heat strained liquid, then thicken with beurre manié. Add 2 tablespoons Cognac, Madeira and food colorings to make a rich, red-brown sauce. Add lobster meat and heat.

8. Put lobster tail meat into tail shells and the claw meat into the body part; bend the small legs into V shapes and place around the filled shells to decorate. Coat lobster meat with sauce and sprinkle with parsley. Serve extra sauce on the side. Serves 2.

Wine: Pavillon Châteaux Margaux Blanc

VARIATIONS

CREVETTES À L'ARMORICAINE
[*Shrimp in Tomato Sauce*]

Begin with step 3 in the Homard à l'Armoricaine recipe. Omit lobster. Shell and devein 2 pounds raw shrimp. Add to hot olive oil. Heat and toss for 3 minutes. Pour over the 3 tablespoons Cognac and set aflame. Remove shrimp to a plate. Now add to the pan the onions, shallots, garlic, and remainder of ingredients down to the butter. Simmer 15 minutes, strain liquid and then thicken, step 7. Add Cognac, Madeira, coloring, and shrimp. Heat, and serve on a bed of rice or in coquilles (shells), sprinkled with parsley and accompanied with crusty French bread and a green salad. Serves 6.

Wine: Perrières Meursault

POISSONS À L'ARMORICAINE
[*Fish in Tomato Sauce*]

Begin with step 3 as above, substituting 6 fish fillets or 3 fish steaks for the shrimp, finishing recipe as for shrimp. Serve 1 fillet or ½ steak to each person. Sprinkle with parsley and serve with French bread and a salad. Serves 6.

Wine: Puligny-Montrachet

BOUILLABAISSE
[*Seafood Stew*]

Sauce

5 leeks	1 tablespoon salt
3 large onions, sliced	⅛ teaspoon pepper
½ cup French olive oil	¼ teaspoon saffron shreds
4 cloves garlic, sliced	¼ teaspoon thyme
1 pound fresh tomatoes, diced	1 bay leaf
4 tablespoons tomato paste	6 sprigs parsley
4 tablespoons Cognac	Dash of Tabasco
3 cups white wine (1 bottle)	Beurre manié
4 cups chicken stock	Chopped parsley

Seafoods

1 (2-pound) lobster, cooked	½ pound perch fillets
½ pound red snapper fillets	½ pound mackerel fillets
½ pound sea bass fillets	½ pound swordfish steak
¼ pound eel (if you can get it), sliced	½ pound sole fillets
½ pound cod fillets	

1. Wash leeks (see p. 607). Slice into a large kettle. Add onions and oil, and then brown. Add remainder of ingredients (add saffron directly to the pot) down to the beurre manié. Simmer 30 minutes. To this point this dish can be made and frozen, ready to combine with the rest of the ingredients.

2. Break lobster claws and tail from body. Crack claws and cut tail into 1-inch chunks. (With a wooden pick, remove black vein from pieces. Leave shells on meat.) Wash and cut fillets into 2-inch diagonal pieces.

3. Add lobster, snapper, bass, eel, perch, mackerel and swordfish steak. Cook 5 minutes, then add sole and cod. Cook another 5 minutes. Lift seafoods out as soon as they are done, placing them in a warmed soup tureen.

4. Boil liquid hard for 10 minutes to reduce. Liquid should be the consistency of light cream, but if not, thicken with beurre manié, then cook 3 minutes. Strain liquid through coarse sieve into tureen, mashing through some of the vegetables. Sprinkle with parsley.

5. Serve in flat soup plates, giving each guest an assortment of seafoods. Croutons or toasted French bread is served with the stew. Serves 8–10.

Wine: Fleurie or Mâcon

HOMARD AU COGNAC

[Lobster in Brandy Sauce]

1 (2-pound) live lobster or 2 (9-ounce)
    packages tails
⅛ pound butter
2 tablespoons Cognac
Salt and pepper to taste
1 onion, minced
½ cup Madeira
½ cup white wine
¼ cup Port wine

½ cup sliced mushrooms
Chunk of butter
2 tablespoons flour
½ cup crème fraîche, or
    whipping cream
2 egg yolks
2 tablespoons Cognac
Fine dry bread crumbs
Chopped parsley

1. Kill lobster (p. 74), or use lobster tails. Remove tail and break off large claws. Cut tail, or tails, into 2-inch pieces. Crack claws.

2. Heat ⅛ pound butter in skillet. Add lobster pieces. Simmer for about 5 minutes, then blaze with 2 tablespoons Cognac. When flame dies, add salt, pepper, onion, Madeira, and other wines. Bring to a boil, then simmer 5 minutes. Remove lobster to a plate. Boil liquid 3 minutes, thus reducing it to about 1 cup. Remove from heat. Strain and cool. Take meat from tails and claws. Cut tail meat into ½-inch slices.

3. Simmer mushrooms in chunk of butter for 2 minutes. Add flour. Stir-cook for 1 minute. Add the cool liquid and stir until thickened.

4. Mix crème and yolks. Stir bit of hot mushroom sauce into yolk mixture and then add to the sauce. Add lobster pieces. Heat, but do not boil. Stir in the Cognac. Spoon into 6 coquilles (shells), see p. 611. Sprinkle with fine dry bread crumbs and broil until brown. Sprinkle with parsley and serve as first course.

Wine: Pouilly-Fumé

NOTE: This can be made in advance, refrigerated, and broiled when ready to serve. This recipe will serve 2 as a main course.

BISQUE DE LANGOUSTE
[*Lobster Bisque*]

3 (1½-pound) live lobsters or
   3 pounds lobster tails
3 tablespoons olive oil
Chunk of butter
3 onions, chopped
2 carrots, diced
1 leek, sliced (no green)
4 tablespoons Cognac
1 shallot, minced (omit if you
   don't have them)
2 cloves garlic, mashed and minced
2 cups white wine
3 cups chicken stock
Bouquet garni
Pinch of thyme

2 tablespoons tomato paste
1 branch celery, chopped
Pinch of saffron shreds
2 teaspoons salt
⅛ teaspoon each of pepper and
   Tabasco
Red and brown food coloring
4 tablespoons flour
⅛ pound softened butter
¼ cup Cognac
1 cup whipping cream
½ cup crème fraîche or
   whipping cream
¼ cup sherry
Chunk of butter

1. Kill lobsters (p. 74). If you're sensitive, use lobster tails.

2. Now break off the large claws, leaving the body whole. Heat oil and butter in large kettle. Add claws and lobster bodies, the onions, carrots, and cleaned sliced leek (see p. 607). Cook, but do not brown. When shells have turned red, spoon off the fats, pour over 4 tablespoons Cognac and set aflame.

3. When flames die, add the ingredients down through the salt. Simmer 15 minutes. Discard bouquet garni and remove the lobsters. Cool. Break off little legs and the tail from the body. Cut body shells in half. Discard stomach and gills. Put green tomalley into kettle. Crush bodies. Put little claws and crushed body shells into a blender container. Add some liquids from the pan and whirl to a pulp. Return the pulp to the kettle. Simmer 10 minutes, then strain liquid through a fine sieve into a clean pan. Heat, season with pepper and Tabasco, taste, and adjust seasonings.

4. Color a rich deep red-brown (p. 3). Blend flour with butter (beurre manié). Add enough to thicken the bisque to the consistency of a cream sauce. It must be fairly thick because more liquids will be added. (Freeze remainder of beurre manié.)

5. Remove meat from claws and tail. Devein tail meat, then cut tail into ½-inch-thick slices. Put meat into a skillet. Add ¼ cup Cognac. Heat and set aflame. When flame dies, add to the bisque. Stir in cream, crème fraîche, and sherry. Heat, but do not let it boil. Swirl in chunk of butter and pour into tureen. Serve in soup plates with crusty French bread and a green salad.

Wine: Brouilly

VARIATIONS

BISQUE DE CREVETTES
[*Shrimp Bisque*]

From the preceding recipe omit lobsters, olive oil, and 4 tablespoons Cognac.

Sauté onions, carrots, and leek in butter for 20 minutes. Do not brown. Add 3 pounds frozen shrimp in the shell to the sautéed vegetables. Add remainder of ingredients down through the salt. Bring to a boil, reduce heat, and simmer 3 minutes. Remove from heat. Discard bouquet garni.

Lift out shrimp and place on a plate. Cool shrimp and then shell and devein. Blend shells and some cooking liquid in a blender (or grind shells through a food chopper). Put ground shells and liquids back in cooking liquid. Simmer another 10 minutes. Add pepper, Tabasco, and coloring to make a red-brown sauce. Mix flour and butter to a paste ready to use.

Cut all but 6 shrimp into about 4 pieces. Save the other 6 for garnishing. Put cut shrimp into a skillet. Pour over them ¼ cup Cognac. Heat and set aflame. Let it burn itself out.

Strain cooking liquid through a very fine sieve, or cloth, into a clean pan. Bring liquid to a boil. Thicken with flour-and-butter mixture to the thickness of a cream sauce. Add cream, crème, sherry, and the diced shrimp in Cognac. Heat, but do not boil. Swirl in butter and pour into tureen. Float whole shrimp on top of bisque. Serve in soup plates with crusty French bread and a salad.

Wine: Hermitage

BISQUE DE CREVETTES AUX QUENELLES
[*Shrimp Bisque with Quenelles*]

Peel 7 or 8 of the raw shrimp in the preceding recipe, devein, and set aside. Add the shells to the bisque at the time the unshelled shrimp are added. When these shrimp are done, cool, shell, devein, and freeze to use later. The *cooked shrimp are not used* in this recipe. Follow preceding recipe for completing bisque.

Blot the raw shrimp with paper towels to absorb the moisture. Put into blender container. Add 2 egg whites, 2 tablespoons crème fraîche, 2 tablespoons minced parsley or black truffles, and dash of salt and pepper. Whirl on low speed, then blend to a paste on the highest speed of the blender. This is quenelle mixture. Poach quenelles in chicken broth. See p. 116 for details.

Add the quenelles to the finished bisque, heat and serve in tureen.

Wine: Puligny-Montrachet

NOTE: For special occasions blaze the bisques at the table. Pour ¼ cup heated Cognac into a metal soup ladle, ignite it, and gradually submerge the ladle in the hot bisque, thus floating the blazing Cognac atop the bisque.

CREVETTES AU VIN BLANC
[*Shrimp in White Wine*]

2 shallots, minced	½ teaspoon salt
2 sprigs parsley	Dash of white pepper
1 cup sliced mushrooms (or 5-ounce box)	4 tablespoons flour
	Chunk of butter, softened
⅛ pound butter	3 tablespoons crème fraîche, or
½ cup clam juice (canned)	whipping cream
1 cup white wine	1 egg yolk
1½ pounds cleaned raw frozen shrimp	2 tablespoons Madeira
	2 tablespoons Cognac

Chopped parsley

1. Simmer shallots, parsley sprigs, and mushrooms in butter for about 2 minutes. Add clam juice and wine and bring to a boil. Reduce heat and simmer 5 minutes. Remove parsley sprigs. Add frozen shrimp to liquid. Heat gradually, breaking shrimp apart as they heat. Once to boiling stage, reduce to a simmer and cook for 2 minutes. Season with salt and pepper.

2. Mash flour into butter (beurre manié). Add enough to thicken the sauce. Combine crème and yolk. Stir a bit of hot sauce into it, then stir into hot liquid. Heat, but do not boil. Add Madeira and Cognac. Spoon into coquilles (shells), croustades, or patty shells. Sprinkle with parsley and serve as first course, or as a main dish to 4.

Wine: Beaujolais Blanc

VARIATIONS

CREVETTES À LA CRÈME
[*Creamed Shrimp*]

Substitute whipping cream for the wine in the preceding recipe. Combine clam juice and cream. *Do not reduce* liquids for 5 minutes. Just add the shrimp and continue with the recipe.

Wine: Pouilly-Fuissé

CREVETTES AUX TRUFFES
[*Shrimp in Truffled Sauce*]

Add minced truffles to the sauce in Crevettes à la Crème.

Wine: Château Grillet (Blanc)

CREVETTES AU CURRIE
[*Shrimp in Curry Sauce*]

Simmer 1 tablespoon curry powder in the ⅛ pound butter, then proceed with either the wine or cream-sauce recipe. When curry is cooked in fat, it releases its full flavor.

Wine: Fleurie

FRUITS DE MER
[*Fruits of the Sea*]

Fruits de mer, or fruits of the sea, is a harvest of shellfish. It may contain all of those listed or only some of them, depending upon what you have available, or how expensive you would like to make the dish. Perhaps the one requirement is that it should contain both crustaceans and mollusks, and not just one or the other. This is one of my favorite recipes.

3 raw lobster tails, or 1 pound	½ cup vermouth or white wine
1 pound raw shelled and	2 tablespoons sherry
deveined shrimp	4 tablespoons flour
¼ pound bay scallops, or sea	2 tablespoons crème fraîche, or
scallops, quartered	whipping cream
1 cup small fresh oysters	3 tablespoons sherry
2 cups light cream	1 tablespoon Cognac
¼ pound butter	Salt and white pepper to taste
1 cup sliced mushrooms	Coquilles (shells) or pastry shells
1 clove garlic, minced	

1. Shell lobster tails, remove vein, and cut into slices ½-inch thick. Put on plate ready to use. If shrimp are large, cut in half lengthwise. Add to plate. Wash scallops and oysters in the 2 cups cream. By so doing the liquids from these foods are left in the cream to add flavor to the sauce. Wash them well and then place them on a plate ready to use. Strain cream through dampened cloth into a bowl and have ready to use.

2. Melt butter in enameled skillet or saucepan. Add lobster tails, shrimp, and scallops to butter. Heat. Add mushrooms, garlic, vermouth, and 2 tablespoons sherry. Stir with wooden spoon. Bring to a boil, then reduce to a simmer, and cook 3 minutes. With slotted spoon, lift seafoods out of liquids to plate with oysters.

(continued)

3. Boil liquid, reducing it down to the butter. Stir in flour and cook a few minutes. Add strained light cream and stir until thickened. Add oysters and other seafoods from plate. Heat. Add about ½ cup sauce to crème, then stir into pan. Add 3 tablespoons sherry and Cognac, season, and then taste and adjust the seasonings if necessary. Serve in coquilles (shells) or pastry shells (p. 355).

Wine: Pouilly-Fuissé

CRUSTACÉS POCHÉS

[*Poached Crustaceans*]

Lobsters, crabs, and shrimp may be poached in a court bouillon (p. 13), or by the following recipe.

2 quarts water	6 whole peppercorns
2 teaspoons salt	Juice of 1 lemon and the rinds
1 teaspoon sugar	Chunk of butter

LOBSTERS

For every lobster use 2 quarts water and increase the rest of the ingredients accordingly. Bring water to a boil. Drop the live lobsters in, head first, to kill them instantly. Put the largest lobster in first and then the smaller ones. Pick lobster up by its back and its claws can't reach you. Bring water back to a boil before adding the next lobster.

When all lobsters have been added, reduce heat to a simmer and cook 10 minutes for 1½-pound lobsters, and 15 minutes for those weighing 2 to 2½ pounds. When done, lift out with tongs and place on their backs. Shell holds juice in around the meat. When ready to serve, turn over and cut down through their head and mouth and let drain. When live lobsters are dropped into the water they suck in water. It is this water that drains out when they are cut. If you fail to cut them, they will drain on the plate as they are eaten.

Place drained lobsters, belly side down, on plate. Set dish of clarified butter or other sauce between its claws. One lobster per person.

COLD LOBSTER

Leave lobsters on their backs and chill. When ready to serve, turn them over, cut and drain, then serve on plate with one of the Mayonnaise sauces rather than the melted butter.

SHRIMP IN THEIR SHELLS

Use about 2 quarts cold water for every 2 pounds. Put all ingredients into a large kettle. Add about 2 pounds thawed shrimp. Bring liquid and shrimp to a boil, stirring occasionally. When boil is reached, remove from heat and let stand 5 minutes. Drain, cool in cold running water, shell, and devein. Serve cold with a sauce, or use in recipes.

SHELLED SHRIMP

Shelled and deveined shrimp have no protective coating so must be cooked carefully. Do not cook them in a wine or vinegar court bouillon, but in the above court bouillon for crustaceans. Add about 1½ pounds cleaned frozen shrimp to the 2 quarts seasoned water and bring to a boil. This should take about 6 minutes, and in that length of time shelled shrimp are done. You will notice a color change from translucent to pearl-white. When they become that color, drain immediately and run cold water into the pan to stop their cooking. Refrigerate and serve cold with Seafood Mayonnaise (p. 407). In other recipes use them in their raw state, or add them cooked at the very last moment and heat in the sauce.

CRUSTACÉS SAUTÉS
[*Sautéed Crustaceans*]

Lobsters and shrimp may be sautéed in their shelled, raw state (see Fruits de Mer recipe, step 2, p. 81) and then added to a sauce. But do not sauté them if they are already cooked. To do so would be to cook them a second time, which would cause them to become tough and hard.

Large crabs are usually processed at the point of harvest. We buy frozen "lump" crab from Eastern waters and "king" crab from the West. We need only thaw and remove the tissuelike membrane from these cooked meats and they are ready to serve or add to sauces.

Small soft-shell or blue crabs come whole to market. In season, they arrive fresh at city seafood markets and the surplus of the harvest is frozen for distribution the year round. Usually your fish dealer will clean the fresh ones for you; but, if not, here is how it is done.

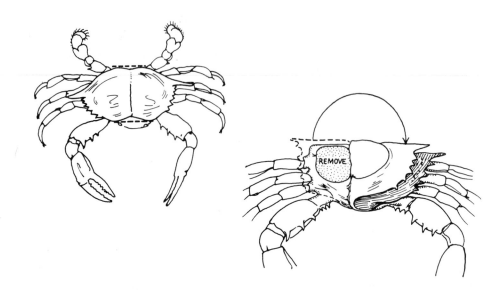

Put the wiggling crab on a cutting board. Hold it with your left hand and with a sharp knife cut off the eyes; this kills the crab instantly. Then cut off the tail. Lift the sides of the shell and underneath will be yellow, puffy gills. Scoop these out, wash the crab, dry on paper towels, and it is ready to cook.

Soft-shells are blue crabs growing up. They have shed their outgrown shells and are in the process of growing new ones when we eat them. They are unknown in France, but treated in the French manner are a fabulous delicacy.

SOFT-SHELLED CRABS À LA MEUNIÈRE

Dip cleaned crabs in cream and then coat with flour. Shake off excess flour and sauté in clarified butter (p. 599). Brown both sides, cooking only a few at a time so they will be crisp. Place on paper towels to drain. Keep in a hot oven while frying the rest.

When all are cooked, pour fat from skillet. Wipe out skillet with paper towels. Add fresh chunk of butter and heat to a nut brown. Put crabs on hot platter and sprinkle with chopped parsley. Add juice of ¼ lemon to hot butter and then pour over crabs and serve. Allow at least 4 soft-shelled crabs per person.

NOTE: If you wonder what you eat of the soft-shelled crab—you eat the whole thing, claws, body, legs, shells, the whole works. If the crabs happen to be quite large, the shell may be a bit tough, in which case you may choose not to eat the claw shells, but they won't hurt you if you do.

Wine: Hermitage Blanc

MOLLUSQUES

The bivalve mollusk family includes oysters, clams, mussels, and scallops. During the R months of the year they are considered to be at their best. A characteristic of the mollusks is that each shell contains but one morsel of food. Scallops are an exception in France, since they are sold in that country with the roe. This is a custom we might well adopt, since these are choice tidbits that we now discard when the scallop is harvested and cleaned. Not only is the roe delicious, but its orange color and its texture add to any dish in which it is used.

Oysters and clams are enjoyed raw as well as cooked, but scallops and mussels are not normally eaten raw.

Mollusks, when cooked, are usually sauced à la Meunière or with a sauce from the Béchamel family.

HUÎTRES ET PALOURDES

[*Oysters and Clams*]

Fish markets will seldom open oysters or clams for you to take home. So that you may enjoy them, here is how it is done.

To open oysters. Buy an oyster knife from your fish dealer, or from a hardware or specialty store. You may pry them open at the hinge, but that is the hard way. Put the oyster, round side down, in your left hand on a towel, the flat side up. You will notice growth rings around the outside of the top shell. At the point where the rings stop, at the edge of the oyster, is the spot to insert the opener to pry up the lid. Once it is open, look for pearls, and then run the opener under the oyster to cut the muscle that attaches the oyster to the lower shell. Serve on the half shell with lemon halves, cocktail sauce, and some fresh horseradish.

To open clams. Buy a clam knife. It has a straight blade, while the oyster knife has a curved blade. Holding the clam in your left hand, the hinge side to your body, put the blade of the knife in the center of the curved side and press between the two shells. As you press to insert the knife the clam seems to clamp the shells tighter. For me, clams are harder to open than oysters. Usually I give up and just pry them open at the hinge, which tears them, but at least I get at the clams. Once they are open, run the knife along the inside of each shell to loosen the clam. Eat as you do raw oysters. Try to open them right, before you break the hinge.

With raw oysters and clams serve a chilled Clos de Vougeot Blanc, Chablis Grand Cru or Pouilly-Fuissé.

HUÎTRES À LA FLORENTINE

[*Oysters Rockefeller*]

24 oysters on the half shell (or 1 pint large oysters)	Dash of nutmeg
	1 teaspoon sugar
Cooked chopped, buttered spinach	½ teaspoon salt
⅛ pound butter	⅛ teaspoon white pepper
4 tablespoons flour	4 tablespoons sherry
2 cups light cream	Grated Parmesan cheese

1. Open oysters. Pour liquid from shells through a damp cloth into a bowl. Cut oysters from shells (p. 85). Check for pieces of shell, then add oysters to bowl. Prepare spinach ready to use.

2. Melt butter in skillet, then stir in flour. Stir-cook a few minutes to cook flour. Add cream, nutmeg, sugar, salt, and pepper. Stir until thickened. Remove from heat. Add sherry.

3. Put 1 tablespoon cream sauce into each shell. Top with a spoonful of spinach, then an oyster, and coat with more sauce. Sprinkle with Parmesan. Heat and brown under broiler for about 5 minutes. Serve 4 to a person as a first course.

NOTE: If you are using oysters by the pint and there are no shells, layer the sauce, spinach, oysters, and more sauce in an ovenproof dish. Broil and serve at the table.

Wine: Côte Rôtie or Fleurie

VARIATIONS

HUÎTRES AUX DUXELLES
[*Oysters in Mushroom-Onion Sauce*]

Simmer 2 minced onions in a chunk of butter for 10 minutes. Then add 1 cup minced mushrooms and simmer another 5 minutes. Use this mixture in place of the spinach and make as you do à la Florentine.
Wine: Pouilly-Fuissé

HUÎTRES AUX TRUFFES
[*Oysters in Truffle Sauce*]

Omit spinach. Lay oysters on a bed of cream sauce, sprinkle with minced truffles, coat with more cream sauce, sprinkle with Parmesan cheese, and broil.
Wine: Côte Rôtie
NOTE: Clams may be substituted for the oysters in the preceding recipes.

QUENELLES D'HUÎTRES
[*Oysters in Sauce with Quenelles*]

Any time quenelles are added to a recipe it becomes something quite special. This one is no exception.

24 small fish quenelles	Dash of nutmeg
1½ cups chicken stock	Salt and pepper to taste
½ cup clam juice (canned)	2 tablespoons sherry
1 pint oysters, or 24 fresh	2 egg yolks
⅛ pound butter	3 tablespoons crème fraîche, or
4 tablespoons flour	whipping cream

Dry bread crumbs

1. Prepare fish quenelles (p. 117). Poach them in a combination of the stock and clam juice. Put on plate ready to use. Take stock from heat. Pour cold oysters into the liquid. Stir to wash and warm oysters. Lift out oysters and place on plate with quenelles. Strain liquid through a damp cloth into a bowl, ready to use. There should be about 2 cups. If not, add stock to make 2 cups.

2. Melt butter in skillet. Stir in flour. Stir-cook for a couple of minutes. Add strained liquid, nutmeg, salt and pepper. Stir until thick. Add sherry, quenelles, and oysters. Make liaison of yolks and crème. Carefully stir into pan, being careful not to damage quenelles. Heat. When hot, spoon into coquilles (shells) or small baking dishes. Sprinkle with crumbs and then broil until tops are brown. Serve as a first course with French bread.
NOTE: For an even more special dish, add a minced truffle to the sauce.
Wine: Montrachet

FRENCH-FRIED OYSTERS OR CLAMS

To make French-fried oysters or clams simply dip them in melted butter, then in fine dry bread crumbs, and fry in vegetable oil heated to 390 degrees. Read pp. 9–10. Drain on paper towels and serve à la Meunière or with Seafood Mayonnaise sauce (p. 407).

Wine: Fleurie

MOULES

[*Mussels*]

Black mussels are one of the joys of being in France. Our rocky Atlantic coasts are covered with these little orange-tan meated bivalves, and it's about time we started to appreciate their succulence.

Mussels cluster on rocks bathed by the tide. At low tide one pulls them in great clumps from the rocks. Once gathered they are pulled apart, the barnacles being scraped off with a dull knife (a clam knife is a perfect tool). They are then scrubbed with a brush, and put to soak.

If a mussel feels light, discard it; the chances are that it is a dead mussel and you want no part of it. If a mussel feels heavy, chances are the shells are filled with sand. Try to open the heavy ones. If they are filled with sand they will come open too easily. Discard them, since you don't want sand in the sauce.

Once the live mussels have been sorted out and their shells cleaned, put them into a bucket of clean fresh water. Let them bubble away for about an hour; then lift them from the bucket to another container. Discard the water. As they drink in the fresh water, they rid themselves of sand and grit. Put mussels back into the bucket, pulling the whiskers from between their shells as you put them into the bucket. Let them drink again for about an hour, then lift out again, rinse out bucket, and cover again with cold water. On this third washing, throw a handful of flour into the water and stir. As the particles of flour fall down through the water, the mussels will suck the flour water in and out and thus cleanse and plump themselves. They love flour, so the water will bubble like crazy and they will make a lot of noise. After about 2 hours of the flour bath, put them into plain water to wash flour from their shells. Now they are ready to cook. This isn't work, for it's really fun to play with them. Always pull the whiskers out when you can.

How to eat mussels. Mussels attach themselves to just one shell. The top shell that opens from them is sometimes broken off and the cooked mussels are served on the half shell they are attached to.

With an empty shell cut between the mussel and the shell, then, using the empty shell, ladle some liquid into the shell and drink and eat the mussel.

MOULES À LA MARINIÈRE

[*Poached Mussels*]

2 quarts mussels (1 quart per person)
Chunk of butter
2 shallots, or 1 onion, minced
½ cup white wine

¼ cup clam juice (canned)
Small bouquet garni
Chopped parsley
Juice of ¼ lemon
Salt and pepper

1. Clean mussels (p. 88). Put butter, shallots, wine, clam juice, and bouquet garni into large kettle. Boil 3 minutes. Discard bouquet garni. Add mussels. Steam 5 minutes. Using both hands, and pot holders, pick the kettle up, holding the lid tight, and shake pan, thus tossing mussels so they cook evenly.

2. When done, they will have opened. Put into flat soup plates, then boil the juices hard to reduce them to half. While this boils, break empty shells from mussels. Sprinkle the mussels in the half shell with parsley. Add lemon juice to pan liquid, taste, and adjust seasonings, then spoon over mussels, leaving grit in bottom of pan. Serves 2. Crusty bread for dunking is a necessary accompaniment.

Wine: Sancerre

MOULES AU BEURRE D'AIL

[*Mussels in Garlic Butter*]

2 quarts mussels, cooked

Beurre d'Ail

½ pound butter, softened
6 slices soft bread
4 cloves garlic, minced

White pepper and salt to season
6 sprigs parsley, chopped
2 shallots, or 1 onion, minced

1. Cook mussels à la Marinière (above). Remove them from the kettle. Break off the empty shells. Loosen mussels from the shell, then arrange shells with mussels on a flat pan. Let them cool while you are making the garlic butter or Beurre d'Ail.

(*continued*)

2. Put butter in mixer bowl. Cut crusts from bread. Tear bread into mixer bowl and add remainder of ingredients. Turn mixer on and it will blend the soft bread into the butter.

3. Cover mussels with the butter-bread mixture, filling the shells. When ready to serve, broil for about 3 minutes, or until bubbly hot and browned. Do not overcook mussels or they become tough. Serves 6 for a first course.

NOTE: This butter-bread mixture may be spread over thawed, raw, cleaned shrimp to make Shrimp de Jonghe. Broil shrimp about 7 minutes.

Wine: Chablis

MOULES À LA CRÈME

[*Mussels in Cream*]

2 quarts mussels (allow 1 quart per person)	2 egg yolks
Chunk of butter	2 tablespoons crème fraîche or whipping cream
2 shallots, or 1 onion, minced	Salt and pepper to taste
½ cup white wine	Chopped parsley

1. Clean mussels (p. 88). Put butter into large kettle with tight lid. Add shallots and wine. Boil hard for 3 minutes. Add mussels, cover, and steam for 5 minutes. Using both hands and pot holders, pick the kettle up, holding the lid tight, and toss the mussels during cooking. Don't remove the lid until 5 minutes are up; then look to see if the shells have opened. If so, they are done; if not, cover, and cook another minute.

2. When done, lift mussels from the kettle to a large bowl. Boil liquids, reducing to half. Remove empty shell from each mussel. Arrange mussels in their half shells on a flat pan. Spoon pan juices from kettle into small saucepan, leaving grit in the kettle. Combine yolks and crème. Stir into juices in saucepan, heat, taste, and adjust seasonings, then pour over mussels in shells. Broil under high heat for about one minute. Put into flat soup plates. Sprinkle with parsley and serve with crusty bread. Serves 2.

Wine: Puligny-Montrachet

COQUILLES SAINT-JACQUES
[*Scallops*]

Scallops are of two kinds. Large sea scallops are found in the ocean and small scallops come from Chesapeake Bay and from off the Eastern Coast.

Sea scallops are processed at the point of harvest, their shells and orange roe being discarded. In France one buys these scallops in their shells and then has the roe to eat and the shells as cooking vessels. It is a real pity that the shells are not packaged with the scallops, just as snail shells are; that we are denied the roe of the scallop to eat is all but a crime.

Chesapeake Bay area scallops, packaged in their own juice, are the choice variety. They reach our better fish markets *au naturel* when in season and the surplus harvest is frozen for year-round enjoyment. Caroline Bay scallops come individually quick frozen. They are without their natural juice, but are more succulent than the sea scallop.

If scallops are frozen, let them thaw before using in a recipe.

COQUILLES SAINT-JACQUES À LA MEUNIÈRE
[*Scallops in Parsley Butter*]

1 pound scallops	3 tablespoons vegetable oil
½ cup flour	Chunk of butter
½ teaspoon baking powder	Chopped parsley
⅛ pound butter	Juice of ¼ lemon

1. Wash scallops in water seasoned with salt. (Use 1 tablespoon per quart of water.) Wash repeatedly in salted water until no dirt particles remain in the bowl. Salt seems to plump the scallops and make them juicier.

2. Once scallops are free of grit, dry on paper towels. If scallops are large, cut in halves, or in fourths, making them bite-sized. Combine flour and baking powder. Coat scallops with this mixture.

3. Heat ⅛ pound butter and oil in heavy skillet. Heat to very hot, then add scallops and brown on all sides. Should take about 3 minutes. Do not crowd the pan.

4. Drain scallops on paper towels, then put on hot platter. Pour fat from skillet and wipe out skillet with paper towels. Add chunk of butter to skillet and toast to a nut brown. Sprinkle scallops heavily with parsley. Add lemon juice to butter and pour over scallops. Serves 4. (Add no salt. Scallops are washed in salted water.)

Wine: Pommard Blanc

COQUILLES SAINT-JACQUES AU VIN D'AIL

[*Scallops in Wine Sauce and Garlic*]

1 pound scallops, sea or bay	⅛ pound butter
¼ cup cream	3 tablespoons oil
½ cup flour	3 cloves garlic, minced
½ teaspoon baking powder	2 teaspoons honey
Dash of white pepper	¼ cup white wine

1. Wash scallops several times in cold water seasoned with salt. (Use 1 tablespoon to 1 quart water.) When they are free of grit, drain, then dry on paper towels.

2. If using sea scallops, cut them in half, or in fourths, making bite-sized scallop pieces. Put scallops into a bowl, add cream, toss, then drain in a sieve. Blot on paper towels and then coat in mixture of flour, baking powder, and pepper. Shake off excess flour.

3. Heat butter and oil, but do not let it brown. Add scallops and garlic. Toss the pan to rotate the scallops. Brown all sides. When brown, spoon fat from pan. Combine honey with wine, pour over scallops, and bring to a boil. Reduce heat and simmer 2 minutes. Spoon into 4 coquilles (shells). Serve with French bread and a Chablis wine. Serves 4.

NOTE: This recipe was given me by French friends living in the Loire Valley, which is also famous for its honey.

COQUILLES SAINT-JACQUES AU GRATIN

[*Scallops in Cream Sauce*]

1½ pounds bay or sea scallops	1 cup sliced fresh mushrooms
1 cup milk	Dash of nutmeg
1 cup cream	½ teaspoon salt
¼ pound butter	Dash of white pepper
1 clove garlic, minced	1 tablespoon Madeira
½ cup dry white wine or vermouth	2 tablespoons Cognac
3 tablespoons flour	Dry bread crumbs

1. When using sea scallops, cut in halves, or in fourths, depending upon their size, but make them bite-sized. Put scallops into large bowl. Pour milk over them. Wash, then lift from the milk to another bowl. Add cream and wash again. Lift to a plate, and have ready to use.

2. Strain milk and cream through a damp cloth. (Fibers swell when the cloth is damp, thus it strains out the very fine particles.) Liquids will be used to make the sauce.

3. Drain all cream from scallops, then blot with paper towels. Melt butter in skillet. Add scallops, garlic, and wine. Bring to a boil, then lift scallops from liquid. Divide among 6 scallop shells, or put into shallow baking dish. Boil pan liquids and reduce them to just the butter. Add flour and stir-cook a couple of minutes. Stir in cream-milk mixture, mushrooms, nutmeg, salt, and pepper. Stir-cook until thickened.

4. Add Madeira and Cognac; taste and adjust seasonings. Spoon into shells, covering the scallops. Sprinkle with bread crumbs. (Crumbs keep a crust from forming and will give texture to the creamy scallops.) These may be made in advance to this point.

5. When ready to serve, place on top shelf of a preheated 425-degree oven and heat for about 10 minutes, or until lightly browned and hot. Serves 6.

Wine: Pouilly-Fuissé

VARIATIONS

COQUILLES SAINT-JACQUES À LA DIEPPOISE

[*Scallops with Shrimp and Mussels*]

With the scallops cook 6 raw shrimp, cleaned and sliced in half the long way. Put two halves into each shell along with 2 poached mussels (p. 89). Fresh mussels should be poached separately to avoid having grit in the pan juices, which become a part of the sauce. Strain mussel juice from the grit in their pan and add to the sauce. If using canned mussels, wash them several times in cold water to remove the grit and the briny taste. Do not use their juice from the can; it is too salty. Coat with the cream sauce and sprinkle with crumbs. Heat when ready to serve, as in above recipe.

Wine: Château Grillet

COQUILLES SAINT-JACQUES À LA OSTENDAISE

[*Scallops with Shrimp and Oysters*]

Make like preceding recipe, substituting 2 small raw oysters for the poached mussels in each shell. Sprinkle with minced truffles and cover with cream sauce. Top with crumbs, heat, and serve.

Wine: Chablis

COQUILLES SAINT-JACQUES À LA FINANCIÈRE

[*Scallops with Quenelles and Truffles*]

To the cream sauce add about 2 dozen fish quenelles (p. 116) and 2 minced truffles. (Financière means expensive and usually includes cocks' combs—but *not* in seafood recipes.) Spoon sauce over filled scallop shells and sprinkle with crumbs. Heat when ready to serve.

Wine: Montrachet

COQUILLES SAINT-JACQUES FRITES

[*French-fried Scallops*]

To French-fry scallops, dip them in melted better, then coat with fine dry bread crumbs and fry in vegetable oil heated to 390 degrees. See p. 9 for details. Serve à la Meunière (p. 36), with Tartare sauce (p. 34), one of the mayonnaise sauces, or with Seafood Mayonnaise (p. 407).

Wine: Fleurie

ESCARGOTS

[Snails]

The snail is also a member of the mollusk family. His house moves with him and, as in most houses, he has but one roof over his head. He is unlike his bivalve brethren with their two shells.

The edible snails of France are unlike the bivalves in that they do not live in or near water, but on land, where they dine upon grape leaves and other greens in the vineyards of southern France. Could it be they are wine-flavored?

Throughout the summer snails gorge themselves, then in a stuffed and lazy condition they hibernate during the winter. After the grape harvest snails are searched for and gathered in their dormant stage and either eaten fresh (in France), or canned for year-round enjoyment. The job of cleaning snails is tedious and long. You will not be confronted with the task since we use the canned variety, just as most of the restaurants do in France.

Snails are packaged 12 or 24 to a can, with an equal number of shells. The shells are clean and ready to use, or they would not be permitted entry into this country. You will need snail pans in which to cook them and forceps to hold onto them while they are eaten, and two-tined small forks with which to pull the snail from the shell. If you do not have this equipment, improvise until you see if you like snails. Then invest in the proper equipment. It may be bought in most specialty kitchenware shops.

To cook snails without the special pans. Set filled snails into collars of foil to support the shells so they do not tip over and spill their juice while cooking. Once they are cooked, put collars and snails onto serving plate. Use wooden picks, or small cocktail forks, to remove the snails from their shells.

Mushroom caps may be used as containers for snails (see p. 285).

ESCARGOTS À LA BOURGUIGNONNE
[*Snails in Garlic Butter*]

Beurre d'Ail:

4 large cloves garlic, mashed	2 shallots or green onions, minced
Dash of salt	2 tablespoons minced parsley
Freshly-ground pepper	1 tube of snails with shells
½ pound butter, creamed	(24 size can)

½ cup white wine or vermouth

1. Mash garlic to a pulp with mortar and pestle. Add salt and pepper and continue to mash. (Snails are salty, so use very little salt.) Blend this garlic pulp into the butter. Add shallots and parsley.

2. Drain snails, then wash them in wine to remove briny taste and to give them flavor.

3. Place about ½ teaspoon of the butter mixture in each dry shell. (Do not wash the shells.) Add the snail, tail, or small end, first, pushing it into the shell. Pack snail in shell with more butter. Place filled shell in snail pans, or set on collar of foil, butter side up.

4. Broil 4 inches from heat for about 5 minutes, or until bubbly and hot with butter slightly browned, and serve at once. Soak up juice with crusty French bread and bathe the palate with a good white Burgundy wine. Serves 4.

Wine: Bâtard Montrachet

GRENOUILLES
[*Frogs' Legs*]

Frogs are amphibians which usually live in quiet fresh waters. In Europe edible frogs are small and abundant; our frogs are larger by two or three times and their legs are correspondingly larger than those ordinarily served in France.

But frogs' legs are good no matter where you find them. Since they have no place of their own, I have chosen to put them with shellfish, even though they have no shells.

For the most part frogs' legs come to us frozen. Rarely is it possible to get them fresh. They come in different sizes, just like shrimp. The young or small legs are better than the large legs. You may wonder if the tidbit you get from small legs is worth bothering with, but once you relish its flavor, you will no longer doubt. Frogs' legs are as versatile in cooking as breast of chicken.

To prepare frogs' legs. Thaw the legs in the refrigerator. Remove the rubber bands that hold them straight, and with a kitchen scissors snip off the tail bone at the top of the legs. Then cut legs apart. They are easier to brown if separated. Wash in cold water, dry on paper towels, and they are ready to cook.

GRENOUILLES À LA PROVENÇALE
[*Frogs' Legs in Tomato Sauce*]

12 pairs of frogs' legs	3 cloves garlic, minced
1 cup vermouth or white wine	6 tablespoons olive oil
3 large ripe fresh tomatoes	(no substitutes)
3 tablespoons chopped parsley	2 teaspoons sugar
Salt and pepper to taste	

1. Prepare frogs' legs as described above. Put into skillet, then pour in vermouth. Bring to a boil, then remove from heat. Lift legs from liquid to a plate.

2. Peel tomatoes, cut in half, and squeeze out seeds and juice. Dice and add to skillet. Add parsley, garlic, oil, sugar, salt, and pepper. Boil liquids 10 minutes to reduce them and concentrate the flavor. Add frogs' legs and simmer 5 minutes. They are done when flesh turns pearl-white. Do not overcook. The size of the legs will determine length of cooking time. Serve as first course in scallop shells, with crusty bread and a light red Burgundy wine. Allow 2 pairs per person; or, if serving as a main dish, serve with rice and a green salad to 2.

Wine: Savigny-les-Beaune

GRENOUILLES AUX FINES HERBES

[*Frogs' Legs with Herbs*]

12 pairs of frogs' legs	Salt and pepper to taste
¼ cup cream	Chunk of butter
½ cup flour	Juice of ¼ lemon
¼ pound butter	3 tablespoons chopped parsley
1 clove garlic, minced	2 tablespoons chopped chives

1. Prepare legs as described on p. 97. Dry on paper towels, dip in cream, drain, then dust with flour.

2. Melt ¼ pound butter. Add garlic, then brown legs on all sides. When done, put onto hot platter. Sprinkle with salt and pepper.

3. Pour fat from skillet and wipe skillet out with paper towels. Toast a chunk of butter in skillet. Then add lemon juice. Sprinkle frogs' legs with parsley and chives and then pour hot butter mixture over them. Serve to 6 as a first course with crusty bread and a white wine.

Wine: Pommard Blanc

GRENOUILLES AU GRATIN

[*Frogs' Legs in Sauce*]

18 pairs of frogs' legs	1 cup white wine
1 cup milk	1 teaspoon sugar
1 cup water	1 cup sliced mushrooms
1 teaspoon salt	2 egg yolks
1 carrot, grated	3 tablespoons crème fraîche, or
1 onion, minced	whipping cream
⅛ pound butter	Fine, dry bread crumbs

1. Prepare frogs' legs as described on p. 97. Put into mixture of milk, water, and salt. Let soak about 30 minutes. Discard liquids.

2. Simmer carrot and onion in butter, with lid on, for about 20 minutes. Add wine, sugar, and frogs' legs. Bring to a boil, then reduce heat to a simmer. Cook 5 minutes. Lift legs from liquid to plate. Mash vegetables and liquid through a food mill and then put back into skillet. Add mushrooms. Simmer a few minutes to cook mushrooms.

3. Remove kernels of meat from frogs' legs. Add to sauce. Combine yolks and crème. Add bit of hot mixture to them, then pour back into skillet. Stir-heat, but do not boil. Spoon into scallop shells, sprinkle with crumbs, and brown under broiler when ready to serve. Serves 6 as first course.

Wine: Hermitage Blanc

Poissons
[*Fish*]

J ust as the French are master sauce makers, they are also unsurpassed when it comes to cooking and saucing seafoods. We cannot duplicate their fish, but we have comparable varieties, plus the mighty salmon of our Northwest.

Fish from cold, clean waters are better tasting than those found in warm, muddy rivers and lakes. Just as eggs taste of the diet the hen has been fed on, fish taste of the waters in which they swam.

In their natural state, fish are tender. They are cooked for only one reason—to improve their flavor. When they are overcooked, they are ruined. Therefore, err on the side of undercooking. Remember, the Japanese eat raw fish—a much tastier dish than overcooked fish!

Fish are cooked by the 6 basic methods of cooking. In what follows you will find the basic recipe for each method, along with recipes of famous dishes.

Baked, broiled, and French-fried fish are usually served with a sauce from the Mayonnaise or Hollandaise family or with one of the hot butter sauces.

Poached and sautéed fish are accompanied by a sauce from the Velouté family, the butter sauces, or Hollandaise. Sometimes the cooking liquids become the sauce.

Braised fish is usually served with a sauce made from the cooking liquids.

POISSONS AU FOUR
[Baked Fish]

To put a whole fish into the oven in its raw state is no trick. But to remove it cooked and whole from the oven to the platter requires a bit of skill. The simplest and easiest way follows.

Cover broiler rack with a sheet of foil. Find the holes in the broiler rack, then punch holes in the foil to match these places. The liquids from the fish as it bakes will drain into the broiler pan through the holes in the foil.

Coat the foil with oil. Set the whole fish belly-side down on the foil. Cover the dorsal and tail fins with foil to reflect the heat and prevent burning. Put a small ball of foil into the mouth of the fish. This keeps the jaws open; then when the fish is done the foil can be replaced with an olive or radish.

When the fish is done, lift the foil from the long sides of the broiler pan up around the cooked fish, making a hammock. Transport baked fish to hot platter. Run a spatula or knife between the fish and the foil to make sure the fish is not stuck. Tear the foil down the middle on each side to underneath the belly of the fish. Pull out the tail half of foil first and then carefully pull out the upper half, depositing the fish in a swimming position on the platter. Remove foil from dorsal and tail fins. Decorate platter and serve.

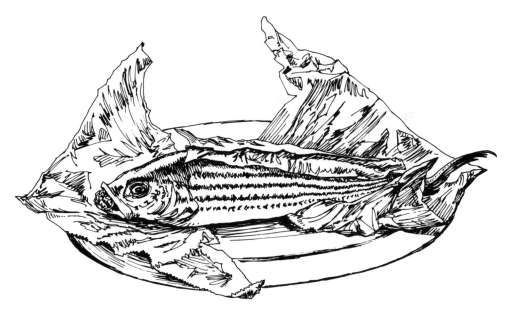

BAKED WHOLE FISH

(Lake trout, pike, pompano, salmon, snapper, whitefish, or other)

1 (3–4-pound) cleaned whole fish	2 cups sliced vegetables
Vegetable oil	4 slices salt pork

Parsley, olives, radishes, watercress

1. Cover broiler rack with foil (see preceding page). Coat with oil. Fill fish cavity with assorted vegetables. (Use carrots, lettuce, parsley, and celery leaves.) Close cavity by sewing with needle and string, or close with skewers.

2. Set stuffed fish on foil, on its belly. Do not use the V-shaped roasting rack that we recommend for roasting meats. Cover fish with salt pork. Wrap dorsal and tail fins with foil and put a small ball of foil into the mouth of the fish.

3. Bake about 50 minutes in a 425-degree oven. Do not reduce the heat. When done, lift foil and fish to heated platter. Tear out foil (see above) and deposit fish in swimming position on platter. Remove slices of pork and the foil from the mouth and fins. Decorate platter with parsley, olives, radishes, and watercress.

4. Skin the fish as it is served. Remove the dorsal fin and bones. Do not serve the stuffing. Vegetables are to give flavor to the fish and to keep the fish in shape. It is not necessary to remove the string or skewers before serving, unless they show. Serve with a sauce from the Hollandaise family (pp. 24–26). Guests season fish at table.

NOTE: If baking whole small fish, lay them on their side on an oiled foil, coat with melted butter and bake a total of 15 minutes in a 425-degree oven.

BAKED WHOLE STUFFED FISH

1 (3–4-pound) whole fish, cleaned
   (pike, salmon, snapper, or other)
2 shallots or 1 onion, minced
1 cup chopped mushrooms
¼ pound butter
2 tablespoons chopped parsley

1 cup bread crumbs
1 cup bay shrimp, or cooked,
   chopped shrimp
Salt and pepper to taste
Melted butter
Flour

1. Wash fish and dry on paper towels. Sauté shallots and mushrooms in ¼ pound butter for 3 minutes. Put parsley, crumbs, and shrimp into large mixing bowl. Add mushroom mixture. Toss, taste, and adjust seasonings, then stuff into dry fish cavity. Sew up cavity with needle and thread, or close with skewers.

2. Cover broiler rack with foil (see p. 100). Coat fish with melted butter and dust with flour. Set fish, belly down, on buttered foil. Cover tail with foil. Bake in 400-degree oven for about 1 hour and 15 minutes. Drizzle with melted butter during baking time. (Butter is better than salt pork when the fish contains stuffing to be eaten.)

3. When done, lift fish and foil to hot platter and tear out foil (p. 101). Remove string or skewers. Be careful not to damage fish. Decorate platter and serve with Champignon sauce (p. 20).

To carve the fish. Cut along the top, or dorsal fin, remove fins, and skin the fish. With a fork carefully pull the fillet away from the backbone. Serve dressing from cavity with each portion.

NOTE: Bay shrimp are the tiny crevette type from the Oregon Bay area. They come vacuum packed. Danish crevettes come canned in brine. Both are cooked, cleaned, and ready to use.

Wine: Montrachet

TRUITES FARCIES

[*Baked Whole Stuffed Trout*]

6 whole trout (about ½ pound
   each)
½ pound sole or pike fillets
1 teaspoon minced chives or green
   onion tops
1 teaspoon chopped parsley
4 egg whites

3 tablespoons crème fraîche or
   whipping cream
½ teaspoon salt
Dash of white pepper
1 tablespoon chopped truffles
Melted butter
Radish roses and watercress

1. Trout must be boned. Use a thin, sharp knife. Put fish on its back. Insert knife at the gills, between the backbone and the flesh. Following the bones, pull the knife up to the end of the bones at the belly incision thus separating flesh from bones. Do each side, then with your fingers pull the backbone and rib-cage out. Some dorsal fin bones will pull out too. Cut this bony belly cage off at the end of the belly incision, leaving the tail bone in the tail meat of the trout. Deboning is not difficult, but it is tricky. Most of all you need a thin, sharp knife. Heat oven and broiler pan to 425 degrees.

2. Blend sole, chives, and parsley in blender container. Add egg whites, 1 at a time, blending after the addition of each. Add crème and seasonings. Put mixture into bowl, then stir in truffles. Lay trout on their sides. Dry cavities of fish with paper towels and then spoon sole mixture into each.

3. Coat hot broiler rack with melted butter. Lay trout, on their sides, on rack. Drizzle with melted butter. Bake in 425-degree oven for about 20 minutes. Do not turn. When done, skin the top side, lift to hot platter, and decorate platter with radish roses and watercress. Serve with Hollandaise-Sabayon sauce (p. 24), or Mousseline sauce (p. 26). Make sauce before cooking trout.

NOTE: If you have no blender, grind sole through food chopper twice and then mix with other ingredients in electric mixer.

Wine: Meursault

POISSONS BRAISÉS
[*Braised Fish*]

Braising should be done in a special pan called a *poissonière*. This pan is oblong in shape, deep, and narrow. It has a rack on which the fish is placed. Then this rack is lowered into the cooking liquid by handles on each end. It works very much like a French-frying basket and makes handling the cooked fish easy.

If you do not have a poissonière, construct a hammock from foil to fit the pan in which the fish will be cooked. Make this hammock from heavy-duty foil, long enough to have foil handles at each end. Punch holes in the bottom of the foil to let the liquids drain through as the fish is lifted. Put fish on the foil and lower into the pan. When fish is done, lift foil and fish to hot platter. Turn foil over, thus rolling the fish off, or tear the foil from under the fish, depositing it onto the platter.

It is usual to braise only whole fish, but salmon and halibut steaks, if thick, may likewise be cooked by this method.

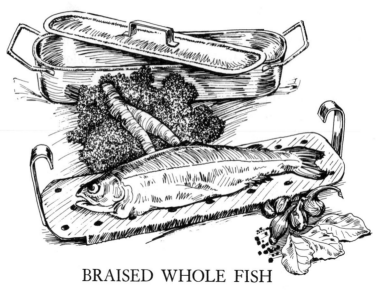

BRAISED WHOLE FISH

[*Whole pike, salmon, snapper, trout, whitefish*]

2 carrots, diced

1 branch celery, diced

2 onions, sliced

⅛ pound butter

1 (3–4-pound) fish, cleaned, head
  and tail removed

1½ cups white wine

1 cup chicken stock

Chunk of butter

4 tablespoons flour

Salt and pepper to taste

2 tablespoons sherry

3 tablespoons crème fraîche or
  whipping cream

Garnishings of parsley and lemon

1. Put vegetables and ⅛ pound butter in bottom of poissonière, or cooking pan. Sauté vegetables 5 minutes. Lay fish on rack, or in foil hammock (p. 103). Set on top the vegetables. Add liquids, bring to a boil, then reduce to a simmer. Set lid askew so liquids can evaporate some. Cook about 40 minutes for large fish. Small whole fish and steaks cook in about 10 minutes. The head and tail are normally removed on braised fish since they would make the sauce too strong in flavor.

2. When done, lift out fish and place on hot platter. Set platter in a warm oven. Put chunk of butter into a skillet. Melt, then add flour and stir-cook for about 2 minutes. Strain cooking liquids, about 2 cups, into the skillet. Stir-cook until thickened. Season, add sherry and crème. Taste. Adjust seasonings and thickness of sauce with beurre manié (p. 2). Heat, but do not boil. Serve sauce in separate dish.

3. Decorate fish platter with nosegay of parsley at the head, and place serrated lemon halves around the fish, with more parsley. If you have a truffle in the freezer, mince it; skin the top side of the fish and sprinkle it with truffle.

Wine: Château Haut-Brion Blanc

POISSONS GRILLÉS
[*Broiled Fish*]

Use whole small fish such as trout, perch, or bass; fish steaks such as halibut, pompano, snapper, salmon, or swordfish; or fish fillets such as sole, cod, flounder, lake trout, sea bass, pike, or whitefish.

4 pounds whole small fish, or 2 pounds of steaks or fillets	**Melted sweet butter**
Vegetable oil	**Salt and pepper to taste**

1. Heat broiler for at least 10 minutes. If the broiler is sizzling hot, it is not necessary to turn the fish. Once the top side is browned the fish is done. It cooks from both sides when the broiler is piping hot.

2. Cut slashes into the skin of a whole fish, a steak or the skin side of fillets. This prevents their curling as the heat contracts the meat.

3. Oil the fish well. Oil the broiler rack at the time the fish is put on it to cook. Do not oil it before, or it will smoke while heating.

4. Put the skin side down, fleshy side up, when broiling fillets. Baste all fish at least once with melted butter and do not turn. Done when top side is browned. When fish is done you will notice a change from translucence to pearly white, or in the case of salmon to a pearly orange. Do not tear fish with a fork to test for doneness. Observe its change in color.

5. Cook whole, 1-inch-thick fish 3 inches from the heat for about 8 minutes.

Cook steaks and 1-inch-thick fillets about 3 inches from heat for about 7 minutes.

Cook other fillets 2 inches from heat for about 4 minutes.

6. Season broiled fish with salt and pepper after it is cooked. Serve with Maître d'Hôtel butter or with one of the butter sauces (p. 39) to complement the particular flavor of the fish.

To cook over charcoal:

Heat a hinged wire grill to very hot. Use any of the fish listed for broiling. Dip fish first into milk, then roll in fine dry crumbs or flour, then dip into melted butter and lay on hot oiled grill. To oil grill dip a pad of paper towels into oil and run it over the hot grill. Close the grill, set over coals, or other heat, and baste often with melted butter as fish cook. Grill each side about 5 minutes for 1-inch-thick fish or steaks. Cook fillets about 3 minutes per side. Fish are delicious cooked over charcoal. Restaurant grills in France are usually heated with charcoal.

Wine: Rully Blanc

GRILLÉ À LA MARINADE
[*Grilled-Marinated Fish Steaks*]

2 pounds of steaks (halibut, salmon,
   or swordfish)
Juice of 1 lemon
½ cup vegetable oil

1 tablespoon chopped parsley
1 teaspoon chopped chives
1 clove garlic, cut in half
1 onion or shallot, minced

1. Put fish in a flat glass dish, just large enough to hold the steaks. Put remainder of ingredients over fish. Marinate about 1 hour. Turn and baste often.

2. When ready to cook, place steaks in hot greased hinged wire grill, or on preheated greased broiler. Grill about 5 minutes per side, or broil a total of about 8 minutes. Baste with marinade as they cook. It is not necessary to turn the steaks being broiled.

Wine: Pouilly-Fuissé

POISSONS FRITS
[*French-fried Fish*]

Fish are normally coated before they are French-fried. This coating may be a simple cream and flour, or a batter-type covering.

4 pounds small whole fish (smelt,
   small bass, etc.), or:
2 pounds fillets (flounder, perch,
   haddock, cod, sole, etc.)

Vegetable oil for frying
Coating of your choice

1. Clean, wash, and then dry the fish on paper towels. If fillets are large, cut them into uniform tapering strips.

2. Heat oil to 390 degrees. Dip fish into coating (p. 10). If using one of the simple coatings, lay the coated fish in the bottom of the fryer basket and lower into the hot fat. If using the batter coating, drop fish as it is dipped directly into the hot fat. Remove each piece as it is done. Do not crowd the pan.

3. When they are done, drain on paper towels and keep warm in a hot oven. Serve with lemon halves, Tartare sauce, or one of the butter sauces (pp. 35–39).

NOTE: Fish float to the top of the oil when done.

Wine: Pommard Blanc

POISSONS POCHÉS
[*Poached Fish*]

To poach means to cook in liquid just below the boiling point—a condition we also refer to as a simmer. See Poaching Liquids Chart, pp. 12–13.

Whole fish are usually poached in a court bouillon acidulated with vinegar or wine. The vinegar-flavored liquid is never used to make the sauce. Poached whole fish are normally sauced with one of the recipes from the Hollandaise (p. 21) or Velouté Vin Blanc (p. 19) families.

Fish steaks are poached in either wine or milk court bouillon. White-fleshed fish become pure white when cooked in milk. Pink-fleshed fish steaks turn a pearly-orange when cooked in wine court bouillon. Milk and wine court bouillons may be used as the liquid of the sauce.

Fish fillets are poached in butter and wine seasoned with shallots, onions, mushrooms, or other vegetables. The liquids usually become the sauce.

When poaching fish and the recipe says, "Cover with a buttered paper," substitute a piece of buttered foil. Too often the paper gives an unpleasant taste to the food being covered, and particularly to fish.

POACHED WHOLE FISH

1 (3–4 pound) lake trout, pike,   Plain court bouillon
    salmon, snapper, or whitefish

1. Prepare the court bouillon (p. 12). Put the whole fish into cold prepared court bouillon. (Never put large whole fish into boiling liquid. It would sear the outside of the fish, overcook it, and not allow the tissues to swell as the fish cooks from the inside out.) Bring the fish and the liquid to a boil and then reduce to a simmer. Cook the required length of time. A poissonière is the perfect pan in which to poach whole fish, but improvise if you haven't one (p. 103).

2. Large whole fish take about 8 minutes per pound, or judge the cooking time by the thickness of the fish. Rule of thumb is, for every inch in thickness allow 8 minutes' cooking time. A round fish 4 inches in diameter takes about 30 minutes to poach; a sole 1 inch in thickness, about 10 minutes.

Wine: Hermitage Blanc

TRUITES AU BLEU

[Poached Whole Trout]

Plain court bouillon
1 cup vinegar

6 (8-ounce) trout (rainbow or brook)

1. Prepare recipe of plain court bouillon (p. 12). Do not handle the trout more than is necessary and do *not* wash trout. It is the slimy film that covers them that reacts with the vinegar to turn them blue. The more film that stays on the fish, the bluer they will be when poached.

2. Thread a kitchen needle with string (Needles, p. 608). Run twine through the base of the tail, where tail fin and flesh meet, then run through the eye sockets, but not through the eye. Pull the twine, shaping the trout into a capital C, or crescent. Tie each trout tight.

3. Have prepared court bouillon boiling. Pour vinegar into deep bowl large enough to hold a trout. Lift trout by the twine, dip in vinegar and then drop into boiling court bouillon. Work quickly, then pour the vinegar into the pan. Poach 5 minutes.

4. Using spatula, lift trout from liquid. Do not lift by string; it will pull out of the cooked fish. Put trout on hot serving platter. Carefully cut string and remove, being careful not to tear the fish. Serve with the traditional Sauce au Beurre Persilée (p. 37) and whole boiled potatoes.

To eat trout. Cut along the dorsal side, peel off skin, remove fins, and with knife lay the fillet off one side, eat it and then fillet the second side by lifting the backbone off the fillet. In this way the trout stays warm, or relatively so.

Wine: Puligny-Montrachet

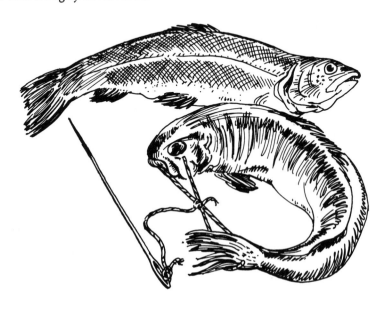

TURBOT BOUILLI À LA MÈRE MARTIN
[*Poached Whole Turbot with Quenelle Stuffing*]

Panade

⅛ pound butter	Salt and pepper to taste
4 tablespoons flour	3 pounds spinach, cooked and
1 cup cold water	buttered

Poaching

1 (5–6-pound) turbot	½ cup white wine
Butter	½ cup water
2 shallots, minced	

Quenelle mixture

½ pound cod fillets	3 or 4 egg whites
½ teaspoon salt	3 tablespoons crème fraîche

3 truffles, minced

Sauce

⅛ pound butter	2 egg yolks
3 tablespoons flour	3 tablespoons crème fraîche
1 cup cream	1 cup cooking liquid

1. Make panade first. Melt butter in a small skillet, and stir in flour. Cook a few minutes without browning the flour, then add water and a dash of salt and pepper. Stir until very thick. Pour into small bowl and set in freezer or refrigerator to get cold. But don't let it freeze. Cook spinach and have ready to use.

2. Wash turbot. Dry on paper towels. Head should be removed. Do not skin, but cut off fins and tail fin with kitchen scissors.

3. With a very sharp, flexible knife, known as a fillet knife, cut down the center of the white side of the fish, along the backbone. (Use white side rather than black side; it will look nicer when served.) Make an incision, perpendicular to the first, 2 inches from the top of the fish and across to each side. The two incisions should make a cross. Carefully, with the fillet knife, cut the flesh from the backbone all the way out to the fins. Lay the fillets back so you can get at the backbone.

4. Now, carefully, with a kitchen scissors cut through the backbone verte-brae, then carefully cut the flesh from the underneath side of the backbone. Do

a one-inch section at a time, lifting out the bone as you go. Be careful not to cut through the underneath skin as you debone the fish for stuffing.

5. Butter a large flat pan. Cut a piece of foil to the shape of the fish, then trim it ½ inch smaller. Butter it, then sprinkle with minced shallots. Lay fish on shallots, cut side up. Add wine and water to pan.

6. Make quenelle mixture. Put cod fillets into blender container. Add cold panade. Blend. Add salt, 2 egg whites, and blend; if mixture looks stiff it will absorb another white, add it, then another if the mixture will hold a fourth. The size of the eggs is a determining factor as well as the moisture in the fish. It may even take 5 egg whites.

7. When egg whites are all added, add crème to make a firm, but moist mixture. Add 1 tablespoon crème at a time and then more if necessary. Test the mixture by poaching ½ teaspoonful in simmering water. If it holds together, add nothing more. Taste the cooked quenelle and adjust the seasonings. If mixture seems heavy, add more crème; if it doesn't hold together, add more egg whites. A quenelle must be light yet creamy and moist. When mixture is perfect, add the truffles.

8. Dry cavity of turbot with paper towels, then fill with quenelle-panade mixture. Close fish, but do not sew. Place foil with fish, filled side up, in pan. Tear a piece of foil to fit inside the pan. Butter the foil and lay it, butter side down, over top of stuffed turbot. Bring liquid to a boil on top of the range, then put into a 425-degree oven. Oven poach about 40 minutes on the lowest shelf of the oven. (One burner under a large pan would not cook the fish evenly, so cook it in the oven.)

9. Start the sauce. Melt butter in skillet, then stir in flour. Stir-cook 2 minutes, but do not brown. Remove from heat. Stir in cold cream to stop the cooking process. Mix together yolks and crème ready to use.

10. When turbot is done the flesh will have lost its translucence and turned a pearl-white. Take from the oven. Discard top sheet of foil. Spoon all liquids from pan. There should be one cup or more. If there is not enough, add white wine to make at least one cup, but do not use more. Pour this into the sauce.

11. Have large serving platter heated and ready to receive the fish. Tip pan on edge of platter and, using the foil under the turbot, slide fish and foil out of the pan onto the platter. Tear foil out from under the fish if it shows, otherwise leave it alone. Set into oven to keep warm while finishing sauce. Oven is off.

12. Heat and stir the sauce until thickened. Finish with mixture of yolks and crème. Heat but do not boil. Remove skin from top side of turbot and surround with well-drained, buttered spinach. Then coat fish with sauce. Pour remainder of sauce into a separate dish to pass at the table. Serve quenelle stuffing with each serving of turbot, along with spinach. Serves 8–10.

To carve. Set blade of carving knife down on fins on one side and pull them away from meat. Put bones on separate plate and send to the kitchen. Cut down middle of turbot lengthwise, then crosswise through stuffing and through bottom fillet. Lift this layered piece of fish and stuffing from the bottom skin and serve. Cut one side, then remove fin bones and carve the other side.

NOTE: Whole sole may be substituted for the turbot. Stuffing will suffice for about 4 sole.

Wine: Montrachet

POACHED FISH STEAKS

Milk court bouillon for	Wine court bouillion for
2 pounds halibut, turbot, and	2 pounds salmon, snapper, swordfish,
other white-fleshed fish	and other pinkish-fleshed fish

1. Prepare the court bouillon for the particular type of fish (p. 12).

2. Add fish steaks to simmering liquid. Bring to a boil, then reduce the heat. Simmer 1-inch steaks about 8 minutes.

3. Lift fish from poaching liquid with a wide spatula to keep from breaking the steak. Blot on paper towels, then place on hot serving platter. Decorate with fancy-cut lemon halves and watercress. Select a positive sauce such as Choron from the Hollandaise family (p. 25).

NOTE: To serve fish steaks cold, poach by the following method. Put steaks into cold milk court bouillon. Bring to a boil, then immediately remove from the heat and let steaks stand in the hot liquid for 10 minutes. Remove from liquids, put into ice water to stop the cooking and to wash off the milky liquid. Drain, blot, and place on a porcelain plate. Cover and refrigerate until cold. Serve with a sauce from the Mayonnaise family (pp. 32 and 407).

FILETS POCHÉS
[*Poached Fish Fillets*]

Some fish markets do not skin thawed Dover sole, fresh flounder, or other flat fish. It is a superior product when it is skinned. This is how it is done.

Lay the fish on paper towels on a counter. With a sharp knife cut down the dorsal fin to the tail and then along the belly. Cut just through the skin and not into the meat. Now hold the tail of the fish with paper towels, then with a knife push the skin up off the tail to get the skin started. (The skin *does* grow down on the tail fin!) Once it is started, take hold of the skin with another paper towel (so the skin won't slip out of your hand) and peel the skin off down to the head. Peel the skin from the other side in the same way. It peels just like a banana. Thawed and fresh fish are easy to skin from the tail up, and not from the gills down (catfish, large-mouth black bass, etc.). The heads of flat fish are normally discarded when the fish is to be poached; they tend to make the meat strong when cooked in liquids.

Once fish is skinned, cut down the center of one side. Then, beginning at the center, cut meat from the bones out to the fins, thus cutting off a fillet, or ¼ of the fish. Do the other fillet and then turn fish over and cut two fillets from the other side.

Fillets may be cooked flat, folded in half, or rolled jelly-roll fashion. If folded, put the skinned side inside, fleshy side out. Roll the fillets with skinned side inside, fleshy side out. With the skinned side on the inside they are less likely to unfold or unroll.

Rolled fillets, just like jelly rolls, taste better when they are filled. Spread fillets with one of the quenelle recipes on pp. 116–18, or with sautéed minced mushrooms. Stand the filled fillets close together in a nonmetal pan and poach in a butter-wine liquid (recipe below). Serve à la bonne femme (p. 21).

NOTE: Dover sole usually arrive in this country frozen. Buy some in their frozen state and keep in your freezer. To skin them when frozen is easier than when they are thawed.

Put frozen sole into a sink of cold water. Once the ice melts from the skin (about 2 minutes), lift sole from water and place on paper towels. With a sharp knife cut around gills and down each side at the fins. Run knife under skin at gills; then, holding fish by the head, grab the skin, using paper towels, and pull it off.

If the skin does not peel off easily, dip the fish in water for another second or two. Peel both sides, then let fish thaw at room temperature and it is ready to fillet or cook whole.

FILETS DE SOLES POCHÉS

[*Poached Sole*]

⅛ pound butter	⅛ pound butter, softened
2 shallots or 1 onion, minced	4 tablespoons flour
1 cup white wine	1 egg yolk
¼ cup clam juice (canned or bottled)	2 tablespoons crème fraîche or whipping cream
6 fillets of sole (¼ pound each)	¼ cup whipping cream
	Salt and pepper to taste

Dash of sugar

1. Melt butter in skillet. Add shallots, wine, and clam juice. Boil 3 minutes. Take from heat. Slash skinned side of fillets several times to prevent warping.

Lay fillets, skinned side down, in hot liquid. Butter a piece of foil and put directly on the fillets. Set a lid down inside the pan on top of the foil. This keeps the foil and fillets down in the liquid. Bring to a boil, then reduce to a simmer. Poach 5 minutes.

2. While fillets poach, blend together softened butter and flour. This is beurre manié. (Many times in this book it has been suggested to keep this mixture on hand for use in thickening. If you have some, use it; if not, make a double batch now and freeze what you don't use.) Stir together the yolk and crème ready to use.

3. When fillets are done, put on hot serving platter. Add ¼ cup whipping cream, salt, pepper and sugar to skillet, heat, then stir in sufficient beurre manié to thicken. Add 1 tablespoon, stir into the sauce, and then add more to thicken. Make the sauce a little too thick to allow for the egg-crème mixture. Remove from heat, stir in liaison of yolk and crème and carefully heat, but do *not* boil. Taste and adjust seasonings, then pour over fillets. Decorate platter with parsley and lemon halves.

Wine: Chablis or Pouilly-Fuissé

VARIATIONS

Recipes for poached fillets of sole are numerous. The name of the dish is derived from the garnish used. You may substitute poached whole sole in any of these recipes, or use any other fillets available to you. Thicken cooking liquids (basically a Seafood Velouté) with beurre manié (p. 2).

FILETS DE SOLES À LA DIEPPOISE
[*Fillets of Sole with Mussels and Shrimp*]

Poach fillets and then make sauce from pan liquid by thickening with beurre manié as in basic recipe above. Add to sauce 1 cup poached fresh mussels (p. 89), or use canned mussels (wash them well), and about ½ cup diced cooked shrimp. Pour over fillets.

Wine: Puligny-Montrachet

FILETS DE SOLES FLORENTINE
[*Fillets of Sole with Spinach*]

Make Mornay sauce (p. 18). Poach fillets as in basic recipe above, and serve on a bed of well-drained, buttered spinach. Coat fillets with Mornay sauce. Sprinkle with Parmesan and broil to brown.

Wine: Pouilly-Fuissé

FILETS DE SOLES MÉDICIS
[*Fillets of Sole with Truffles*]

Poach fillets as in basic recipe above, then make sauce from pan liquid as in step 3 of basic recipe. Mince 2 truffles and add to sauce. Flavor with 2 tablespoons sherry and then spoon over fillets.
Wine: Montrachet

FILETS DE SOLES MONTGOLFIER
[*Fillets of Sole with Lobster, Mushrooms and Truffles*]

Add ½ cup sliced mushrooms to cooking liquids in basic recipe. Poach fillets. Serve with sauce made from pan liquids as in step 3 of basic recipe that has been enriched with ½ cup shredded cooked lobster and 1 julienne-cut truffle, and thickened with beurre manié. Decorate with baked pastry crescents or toast points.
Wine: Château Olivier

FILETS DE SOLES MONTREUIL
[*Fillets of Sole with Shrimp*]

Fold fillets in half, skinned side inside, fleshy side out. Poach according to basic recipe. When done put on round platter, tails to center of plate. Make sauce from pan liquid as in step 3 of basic recipe. Add 1 cup of small cooked, shelled shrimp, or diced cooked shrimp to the sauce. Pour into center of platter and sprinkle with chopped parsley. Serve with miniature whole boiled potatoes.
Wine: Pouilly-Fuissé

FILETS DE SOLES À LA NORMANDE
[*Fillets of Sole with Shrimp and Oysters*]

Add ½ cup sliced mushrooms to cooking liquids in basic recipe. Poach fillets. Thicken pan liquids with beurre manié. Add ½ cup small cooked shrimp and 1 cup raw oysters. Heat until edges of oysters curl. Spoon over poached fillets. Decorate each fillet with a slice of truffle.
Wine: Chablis

FILETS DE SOLES À LA PORTUGAISE
[*Fillets of Sole with Tomatoes*]

Peel 4 fresh tomatoes. Core and dice into a saucepan. Add 8 minced mushrooms (or ½ cup), ½ teaspoon salt, 1 teaspoon sugar, and a dash of pepper. Cook until reduced to a thick pulp. Poach fillets according to basic recipe. Put on hot platter, then make sauce from pan liquids, thicken with beurre manié and season to taste. Surround fillets with tomato pulp and sprinkle with chopped parsley. Glaze fillets with sauce and serve remaining sauce separately.

Wine: Vinho Verde Branco (Portuguese)

FILETS DE SOLES RÉGENCE
[*Fillets of Sole with Quenelles, Oysters, Truffles, and Mushrooms*]

Prepare quenelles (No. 2, p. 117). Cut a large truffle (or use 2 small ones) into 6 pieces. Trim each piece to resemble a small black olive. Dice the trimmings and freeze ready to use in other recipes. Select 12 small mushroom caps. Poach with fillets in basic recipe. Put fillets on hot platter and place in oven to keep warm. Make sauce from pan liquids as in step 3. Add 6 raw oysters, the carved truffles, and 24 quenelles, and heat. Spoon this elegant sauce over the sole fillets. (Although you may substitute other fillets, I would not do so in this recipe.)

Wine: Bienvenue Bâtard Montrachet

FILETS DE SOLES FARCIS
[*Stuffed Fillets of Sole*]

1 (5-ounce) box, or 1 cup, minced fresh mushrooms	4 fillets of sole
Butter	1 tablespoon flour
Salt, pepper, and sugar	¾ cup cream
¼ cup white wine	Dash of nutmeg

1. Wash mushrooms and trim tough bottoms from stems. Mince mushrooms very fine with knife. Sauté them in a chunk of butter for about 2 minutes, then season with salt, pepper, and a bit of sugar. Remove from heat.

2. Melt piece of butter in oval skillet or pan. Add wine. Lay in 2 fillets. Cover with mushrooms. Top with remaining 2 fillets. Cut foil to fit pan. Coat foil with butter and place down in pan over fillets. Poach 5 minutes.

3. While fish cooks make sauce. Melt chunk of butter in small skillet. Add flour, cook 3 minutes, then pour in cream. Add nutmeg, salt, pepper, and a dash of sugar. Stir-cook until thickened (this is a basic Béchamel sauce).

4. Lift cooked fillets to hot oven-proof platter. Strain pan juices into sauce. Stir and then spoon over fillets. Brown under broiler. To serve, cut across middle of each fillet, making 4 servings. Serve with sauce.

Wine: Niersteiner (German)

QUENELLES DE POISSONS POCHÉS
[*Souffléed Fish Dumplings*]

Quenelles are nothing more than souffléed fish dumplings. They are created from ground fillets, made light with egg whites, succulent with whole eggs, cream, or a panade, and kept delicately soft by being poached in seasoned liquid.

The fillets are dried on paper towels to remove as much moisture as possible. Then they are cut into pieces and put into a blender container or put through a food grinder into a small mixer bowl. Egg whites are added one at a time and blended. The amount of moisture in the fish will determine how many whites the fish will absorb. The mixture should be thick, sticky, and smooth.

The only sure way to know if the mixture is the right consistency is to cook one and eat it. If the quenelle is light, airy, succulent, and just a little bit of heaven, it is perfect. But if heavy, chewy, and firm, add more egg whites and test again. You'll know when the mixture is right.

QUENELLES NO. 1
[*Souffléed Fish Dumplings*]

½ pound fillets of flounder, cod, pike, haddock, or sole	3 egg whites
	¼ teaspoon salt
2 whole eggs	Dash of white pepper

1. Dry fillets on paper towels, cut into pieces, and put into blender container. Add whole eggs and blend. Add whites, 1 at a time, and blend. Season with salt and pepper and blend to a thick paste. Test mixture (p. 116).

2. Put mixture from blender into small bowl. Heat about 2 inches of water in medium-sized skillet. Salt the water, using 1 teaspoon salt for each quart of water. Bring water to a boil, then reduce heat to a simmer.

3. Shape fish mixture into quenelles with two teaspoons (see p. 149). Drop quenelles into simmering water. When they rise to the surface they are done. Remove them to a bowl of cold water to stop their cooking. Drain, and they are ready to use in other dishes, or sauce them with Quenelle sauce (p. 18). Makes about 5 dozen, depending upon the size.

Wine: Chablis or Pouilly-Fuissé

QUENELLES NO. 2
[*Souffléed Fish Dumplings*]

½ pound fillets of pike, sole, etc.	Dash of white pepper
3 or 4 egg whites	¼ cup (about) crème fraîche or
½ teaspoon salt	whipping cream

1. Have blender container cold. Chill it by putting into freezer for 10 minutes, or set it in ice cubes until it is cold.

2. Dry fillets on paper towels and then cut into pieces. Put into blender container. Add 3 whites, one at a time, blending after each, then a fourth if mixture does not look wet. Add salt and pepper and blend to a thick paste. Run rubber spatula down sides of blender container to give air to the mixture so it will blend and not just whirl in the middle. (Foods must breathe while they are being blended.)

3. When thick, start adding crème, a tablespoon at a time, on low speed. The amount of moisture in the fish will determine how much crème it will hold. It may be 3 tablespoons, and it may be 5. Too little crème results in dry quenelles; too much causes the quenelles to disintegrate into the water. Test the mixture (p. 116), then adjust the crème, egg whites, or seasonings. If perfect leave it alone.

4. Shape quenelles with two spoons (p. 149). Poach in simmering salted water. Drain and use in sauces or serve with Quenelle sauce (p. 18). Or add ½ cup shredded crab, lobster, or shrimp to the sauce and serve as first course in coquille (shells).

Wine: Pouilly-Fuissé

QUENELLES NO. 3
[Souffléed Fish Dumplings]

⅛ pound butter	2 whole eggs
½ cup water	½ pound pike fillets or others
Salt	4 egg whites
½ cup flour	Dash of pepper

1. Bring butter, water, and ⅛ teaspoon salt to a boil. Remove from heat. Stir in flour to make a thick paste. Set over heat for 1 minute and stir.

2. Remove from heat. Add 1 egg at a time, beating mixture well after each. Pour into a shallow dish and cover with transparent wrap to prevent a crust from forming. Refrigerate until cold. (This is a pâte à choux.)

3. When dough is cold proceed with the recipe. Dry fillets on paper towels, then cut into pieces and blend in blender container. Add all but 2 tablespoons of cold dough. (There should be equal amounts, by weight, of puréed fish and of chilled dough.) Blend well. Add 2 whites, ⅛ teaspoon salt, and pepper. Blend, then add another white and still another if the dough will hold one more. Make and cook quenelles as in Quenelles de Poissons No. 1 (p. 116). Test one, then adjust recipe if necessary. Use in other recipes, or in Quenelle sauce (p. 18). Add 1 minced truffle to the sauce if you wish.

Wine: Montrachet

POISSONS SAUTÉS
[*Sautéed Fish*]

Small whole fish, steaks, and fillets may be sautéed. When the skin of the fish is heavy and tough, it is removed before the fish is sautéed.

Flat fish (sole, turbot, flounder) and *skin fish* (catfish, large-mouth black bass, etc.) have tough skin. They are skinned.

Round-type fish (trout, perch) usually have tender skin. They are scaled and not skinned before they are sautéed. Of course, there are always exceptions.

Before cooking whole fish with the skin on, be sure to slash the skin in several places to allow for contraction as the fish cooks. Failure to do this may cause the fish to crack or its shape to be distorted as it cooks. Also slash the skin that surrounds fish steaks so they will remain flat and not buckle.

Sauté fish in a large pan. There must be space enough around each piece of food so the steam can escape from the pan and not go into the neighboring pieces.

SAUTÉED WHOLE FISH

(Trout, perch, smelt, pan fish, sole, flounder, large-mouth black bass)

4 pounds whole fish

Coatings for fish

¼ pound butter

3 tablespoons vegetable oil

Salt and pepper to taste

1. Dry whole fish thoroughly with paper towels.

2. Whole fish with skin include trout, perch, smelt, and pan fish. Dip these fish in melted butter and fine crumbs to give them a crunchy coating (see Simple Coating No. 3, p. 10). Remember to slash the skin before coating fish so it will remain flat.

3. Whole fish that have been skinned include sole, flounder, and bass. These fish are more delicate so they are dipped in cream, then dusted with flour to which has been added a bit of baking powder (see Simple Coating No. 1, p. 10).

4. Heat butter and oil to very hot. Sauté fish. Brown completely and they are done. Drain on paper towels. Sprinkle with salt and pepper and put on hot serving platter. To put sautéed fish on a cold platter would cause condensation, and thus sogginess. Decorate with lemon halves and parsley. Serve with Beurre à la Meunière (p. 36).

Wine: Hermitage Blanc

VARIATIONS

SOLE AU BEURRE
[*Sole Stuffed with Butter*]

Skin the whole sole (p. 111). Cut down the middle of the backbone, then separate the two fillets from the backbone as in filleting sole, but do not remove fillets. Do just one side. Insert slices of frozen butter. Dip sole in cream and then into flour (p. 10). Lay cut side down in hot fat. Cook 2 minutes, turn and brown the other side for about 3 minutes. Decorate with parsley. This is a kind of fish Kiev.

Wine: Beaujolais Blanc

TRUITES AMANDINE
[*Trout with Almonds*]

Make Beurre d'Amandes (p. 35). Coat 6 whole trout with butter and crumbs. Sauté crisp. Pour sauce over sautéed trout. Garnish with parsley and lemon wedges.

Wine: Sancerre

TRUITES FUMÉES

[Herb-Smoked Trout]

Dip trout in melted butter, then crumbs. Sauté crisp, then lay fish on a wire cake rack.

Now create an herb bonfire. On a piece of foil lay small twigs gathered from the yard, or in the wintertime use bark from fireplace logs, broken into small pieces. Lacking any of these, buy a package of bamboo skewers or wooden picks. Arrange these twigs, Girl Scout fashion, then sprinkle with assorted dried herbs, including rosemary, thyme, basil, tarragon, parsley, or whatever you have.

If you have a cal-rod type broiler, set the foil on the hot cal-rod and put the fish on the grill above it. But, if not, set foil over low heat and put cake rack with fish over foil. Set twigs afire, which will set the herbs to smoking. Finally when everything is hot and burning, sprinkle fish and herbs with warmed Cognac and it should flame. The fish takes on a smoked-herb flavor which is most unusual. Turn the fish so both sides get smoked. Make Béarnaise sauce before sautéing the trout. Serve separately.

NOTE. There are special baskets for smoking sautéed fish. In Paris they may be bought at E. Dehillerin & Cie., 20 Rue Coquillière and 51 Rue J. J. Rousseau. This location is in Les Halles, so plan, when you go there, to eat in one of the famous restaurants in that area. A fish grill will also work, but build the fire up close to the bottom of the basket. Fish grills are available in gourmet-type kitchen shops in our larger cities.

Wine: Pouilly-Fumé

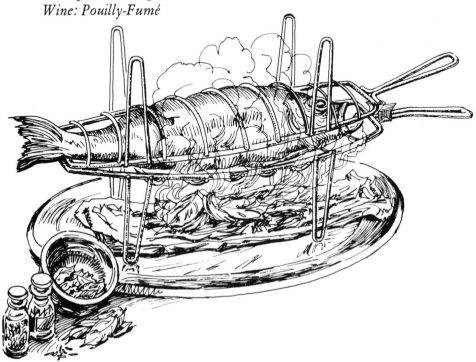

CÔTELETTES DE POISSONS SAUTÉES
[*Sautéed Fish Steaks*]

3 pounds halibut, salmon, swordfish, turbot, snapper or other steaks	¼ pound butter
	3 tablespoons vegetable oil
Coatings for steaks	Salt and pepper to taste

1. Halibut, salmon, and swordfish steaks are usually a slice across the fish. Slash the skin that surrounds the meat. Coat with melted butter and crumbs (No. 3, p. 10) and sauté in hot butter and oil. Cook for about 4 minutes to a side, or until each side is browned. Season and serve with one of the butter sauces (p. 35).

2. Turbot and snapper steaks are usually half a fillet. They may or may not be skinned. In any case, slash the skin side, then dip in cream and coat with flour (No. 1, p. 10). Sauté about 3 minutes per side, or until browned. Season. Serve with a butter sauce (p. 35), or with Hollandaise (p. 21).

Wine: Puligny-Montrachet

FILETS DE POISSONS SAUTÉES
[*Sautéed Fish Fillets*]

3 pounds perch, pan fish, sole, flounder, haddock, or cod	¼ pound butter
	3 tablespoons vegetable oil
Coatings for fillets	Salt and pepper to taste

1. Small fillets of perch or pan fish are usually dipped in melted butter and crumbs to give them a crisp, crunchy coating when sautéed (No. 3, p. 10).

2. The skinned larger fillets of sole, flounder, haddock, and cod are usually treated with cream and flour since they are delicate (No. 1, p. 10).

3. Sauté the coated fillets in hot butter and oil. Drain on paper towels and season. Serve the small, crisp fillets with Tartare sauce (p. 34), the sole fillets with one of the butter sauces (pp. 35–39).

Wine: Erdener Treppchen (German)

FILETS DE SOLES MURAT

[Sautéed Fillets with Vegetables]

6 sole fillets	Butter
Melted butter	3 cooked whole potatoes, cubed
Fine bread crumbs	2 fresh tomatoes
6 cooked artichoke bottoms, fresh	Salt and pepper to taste
or canned	Chopped parsley

Juice of ½ lemon

1. Cut fillets diagonally in half, ready to coat with melted butter and crumbs (No. 3, p. 10). Prepare vegetables before continuing with fish.

2. Sauté artichoke bottoms in chunk of butter until browned. Put on plate ready to use. Keep hot in oven. Add fresh chunk of butter to skillet. Brown potato cubes. Add to plate.

3. Cut tomatoes in slices ½ inch thick. Sprinkle with salt and pepper, dip in crumbs and fry in fresh chunk of butter. Add to plate in oven. Wipe out skillet with paper towels.

4. Coat fillets. Add chunk of butter to skillet. Sauté fish crisp. Place on serving platter. Wipe out skillet. Add ⅛ pound butter to skillet to melt.

5. Put artichoke bottoms around fillets, alternately with piles of potato cubes. Top each artichoke with a tomato slice. Season with salt and pepper and sprinkle the whole with chopped parsley. Add lemon juice to butter and pour over sautéed fish.

Wine: Fleurie

VARIATIONS

FILETS MEUNIÈRE AUX CHAMPIGNONS

[Fillets with Mushrooms]

Sauté fillets crisp. Surround with sautéed sliced mushrooms and serve with Beurre à la Meunière (p. 36).

The name of the dish changes with the garnish—if fried eggplant, *aubergines;* if oysters, *huîtres;* if shrimp, *crevettes,* etc.

Wine: Lacrima Christi (Italian)

FILETS DORIA

[*Fillets with Cucumbers*]

Sauté fillets crisp. Sauté thinly sliced peeled cucumbers in butter seasoned with a bit of sugar and salt. Garnish serving dish with these and sprinkle with chopped parsley.
Wine: Soave (Italian)

FILETS À LA MARÉCHALE

[*Fillets with Truffles*]

Dip fillets in cream and flour. Brown, then sauté 2 minced truffles in a chunk of butter and pour over the fillets. Decorate with parsley. (The French use rougets, or red fish. Our snapper, if fillets are small, make a good substitute for rougets.)
Wine: Liebfraumilch (German)

FILETS À LA MISTRAL

[*Fillets with Tomatoes and Mushrooms*]

Dip fillets in cream then flour, and brown. Sauté 2 peeled, chopped tomatoes, 1 cup sliced mushrooms, a minced clove of garlic, and some chopped parsley in skillet. Boil hard to cook and reduce juice. Season with salt, pepper, and a dash of sherry. Spoon over sautéed fillets.
Wine: Juliénas

FILETS SAINT-GERMAIN

[*Fillets with Potatoes*]

Dip fillets in butter, then crumbs, and sauté crisp. Serve surrounded by browned potato balls sautéed in butter. Béarnaise sauce (p. 24) accompanies this dish.
Wine: Fleurie

Volaille
[*Fowl*]

Chickens are to the cook what a basic black dress is to a wardrobe. As Brillat-Savarin wrote in his *Meditations:*

> . . . poultry is for the cook what canvas is for the painter. . . . It is served up boiled, roasted, fried, hot or cold, whole or in parts, with or without sauce, boned, grilled, stuffed and always with the same success.

But ducks and geese are not so versatile. They require as much thought about their garnishings as a purple dress does. Ducks embellished with oranges or red cherries are delicious; geese have an affinity for the wrinkled prune and the pithy chestnut. These fat birds are best roasted and then sauced.

With turkeys, as with humans, there is something to be said for and against the male and female birds. The tom turkey has a gamier flavor and the meat is coarser. The hen turkey has a milder taste, more breast meat, and is juicier and finer in texture.

Cornish hens and squabs enjoy the same treatment given chickens and may be prepared according to their recipes. The capon has no recipes of its own, but it too may be cooked according to any of the chicken recipes. Coq au vin is especially good when the eunuch capon is substituted for the *Coq.*

RÔTI DE VOLAILLE
[*Roasted Poultry*]

Cooking whole birds with both light and dark meat on them presents a bit of a problem since the white meat becomes tender before the dark. Therefore, cover the white breast meat with a sheet of salt pork to retard cooking and to keep the breast meat from becoming overcooked before the dark meat is tender.

Birds consisting of all dark meat, such as ducks and geese, need no protection from salt pork. Small whole birds, such as Cornish hens and squabs, cook at high temperatures for short periods and likewise require no covering of salt pork. If bird is to be stuffed, do so before it is trussed.

Trussing poultry. A kitchen needle (see p. 608) is a must for this. Thread the needle with about 4 feet of string. Tie one end of the string at the eye of the needle. Stick the needle through the joint where leg and thigh meet, through the body cavity and out through that same joint on the other side. Leave about 6 inches of string on the beginning side. Sew back through the end of the leg, the back, and then out through the end of the other leg. Holding the 6-inch piece of string, pull the legs tight against the body of the bird. Tie tight, then cut string.

Remove tip and second joint of the wings. Leave the "leglike" piece attached to the breast meat. Push the needle through the top of the wing, out at the back to catch the neck skin, then back in and out through the top of the other wing. Pull all but 6 inches of string through to the other side. Now sew back through the end of the wing, through the ribs and out to catch the end of the other wing. Tie tight with the piece of string. Never run the string across the top of the bird—it would leave marks on the breast meat.

There are two schools of thought about what temperature at which to roast meats and fowl. One school says "325 degrees throughout the cooking time." Using this method does not require the cook to be on hand after the roast is in the oven.

The other school of thought says "sear the roast at a high temperature and then reduce the heat as the meat cooks." This latter method is employed in French cooking and I somehow feel it gives better results, so I have worked out a chart of how many minutes to cook at different temperatures. But regardless of which method you employ to cook fowl, the average cooking time comes out to 18–20 minutes per pound for large birds. Small, whole birds (Cornish hens and squabs) require about 1 hour per pound.

ROASTING CHART FOR FOWL

Type of Fowl	*Weight*	MINUTES TO COOK AT DIFFERENT TEMPERATURES: *Begin at 425° for*	*Then at 375° for*	*Then at 325° for*	*and at 425° to brown for*	*Minutes to Rest*	*Number Served*
Capon	6–7 lbs.	40	20	40	20	15	6
Chicken	4–5 lbs.	40		20	20	15	4
Cornish Hen	12 oz.	45				10	1
	16 oz.	60				10	2
	20 oz.	80				10	2
Squab under	1 lb.	45				5	1
Turkey	10–14 lbs.	40	60	2 hrs.	30	20	8
	14–18 lbs.	40	60	2 hrs.	60	20	10
Duck	3–4 lbs.	60				10	2
	6–7 lbs.	40		1 hr.	20	10	4
Goose	10–14 lbs.	40	60	2 hrs.	20	15	6

NOTE: If fowl is filled with a stuffing, increase the cooking time 5 minutes per pound. Add the additional time to the 325-degree cooking period.

POULARDE RÔTIE

[*Roast Chicken*]

1 whole roasting chicken, capon, or turkey, or 6 (12-ounce) Cornish hens, or 6 squabs under 1 pound each
1 onion, sliced
1 carrot, diced
4 sprigs parsley
Salt and pepper
Chunk of butter
Melted butter
½ pound salt pork

1. Remove neck and giblets from the body of the bird. Cut off wing tips and second joints of wings. Cook giblets, wing pieces, and neck in water seasoned with onion, carrot, parsley, and 1 teaspoon salt. Cook until done, then use in a sauce.

2. Sprinkle cavity of bird with salt and pepper. Add a chunk of butter and truss according to instructions (p. 125). If bird is to be stuffed, omit the seasonings and butter. (Stuff all poultry before trussing and just before placing into the oven.)

3. Brush bird with melted butter. Cover white meat with thin sheets of salt pork. Loosely tie in place with string. Place large birds on one side on an oiled broiler rack. Cook according to chart (opposite).

4. Turn large birds from one side to the other about every half hour and baste with butter. Use several layers of paper towels (paper is a poor conductor of heat) to lift and turn heavy birds.

5. During the last half hour of cooking time set a heavy bird on its back, remove salt pork, brush with butter, increase heat to 425 degrees and brown the breast meat.

6. When done, take bird from the oven. Remove trussing strings and let meat rest for amount of time stated in the roasting chart. If a sauce is to be served, prepare it while the bird roasts. Select a sauce from the Demi-glace family (pp. 28–30), or one of the Velouté sauces (pp. 20–21). Chop the giblets and neck meat. Add to the sauce. Taste and adjust the seasonings. Serve sauce separately.

Wine: Puligny-Montrachet

VARIATIONS

In the following recipes, as in the preceding one, roasted chicken, capon, turkey, or Cornish hens may be used. Make the specified sauce while the fowl cooks.

POULARDE ALEXANDRA

[*Chicken with Artichokes*]

Make a Suprême sauce (p. 21). Sauté fresh or canned artichoke bottoms in a chunk of butter. Fill them with the sauce and sprinkle with chopped black truffles. Arrange on platter around roasted fowl.

Wine: Corton Charlemagne

POULARDE À L'ASTURIENNE

[*Chicken Stuffed with Chicken Livers*]

Sauté 1 pound chicken livers in ⅛ pound butter for 5 minutes. Sprinkle them with ½ teaspoon sweet basil. Pour ¼ cup Cognac over the livers. Heat to volatilize some of the alcohol and then set aflame. Remove from heat. Season with salt and pepper. Add 1 cup julienne-cut strips of ham. Mix and then fill cavity of a 5–7-pound bird or divide among small birds. Truss (p. 125) and roast according to chart (p. 126). Prepare Sauce Diable (p. 28). Make garnish for platter. Peel and cook 24 small white boiling onions in seasoned water for 5 minutes. Drain, rinse, and sauté onions in a chunk of butter for 20 minutes, or until tender. Mash bulk sausage meat into pieces in a skillet. Brown and then use to fill canned artichoke bottoms. Sauté the filled artichokes in butter. Add 18 unpeeled cherry tomatoes to onions in skillet. Sauté 2 minutes. Arrange these garnishings on platter around the fowl. Serve sauce separately.

Wine: Château Beychevelle

POULARDE AUX CHAMPIGNONS

[*Chicken with Mushroom Stuffing*]

Season cavity of bird with salt and pepper. Stuff large birds with about 24 large mushroom caps, smaller birds with fewer. Place a chunk of butter in the middle of the mushrooms. Serve with Champignon sauce (p. 20).

Wine: Lacrima Christi (Italian)

POULARDE DEMIDOFF

[*Chicken with Carved Vegetables*]

Peel and cut 8 carrots and 4 turnips into chunks and then carve off the edges, shaping them into uniform oval pieces. (Make a simple potage from vegetable trimmings.) Simmer these carved vegetables in water seasoned with a chunk of butter, salt, and 1 teaspoon of sugar. When done, glaze them in butter. Arrange in neat piles around the roasted fowl. Put slices of truffle on the fowl for decoration. Serve with a Madeira sauce (p. 30).

Wine: Valdepeñas Tinto (Spanish)

POULARDE À L'ESTRAGON

[*Chicken Stuffed with Fresh Tarragon*]

Sprinkle cavity of bird with salt and pepper. Fill with branches of fresh tarragon. Put a large chunk of butter in the middle of the tarragon. Truss and bake according to chart p. 126.

Boil several tarragon leaves in ½ cup of water for about 1 minute. Lift the leaves out with a fork, reserving the ½ cup water, and plunge them into cold water to stop their cooking. When fowl is done, pour the ½ cup tarragon water into roasting pan. Scrape pan juices from the pan and boil the liquids, reducing them to ¼ cup. Skim fat from liquids, then strain essence of tarragon into a recipe of prepared Suprême sauce (p. 21). Adjust seasonings and then thicken sauce with beurre manié, if necessary. Decorate breast of cooked fowl with the blanched tarragon leaves. Fold leaves in half, or leave them long. Serve with sauce. (Grow tarragon in your garden or window box!)

Wine: Château d'Issan

POULARDE AUX HUÎTRES

[*Chicken with Oyster Sauce*]

Prepare Sauce Suprême (p. 21). When ready to serve, add about 24 raw oysters to the sauce. Heat until the edges of the oysters curl, but do not let the sauce boil. Season, and serve separately with roasted chicken.

Wine: Chevalier Montrachet

POULARDE AUX OEUFS

[*Chicken Stuffed with Eggs*]

This creation is a lot of fun for youngsters. Cook about 6 eggs to firm-soft stage (p. 56). Carefully shell them and then roll in chopped parsley. Sprinkle cavity of bird with salt and pepper. Fill with the eggs, which will finish cooking to hard-cooked within the fowl. Serve with Bonne Femme sauce (p. 21). Size of the bird will determine how many eggs the cavity will hold. You should have one egg for each person being served.

Wine: Pouilly-Fuissé

POULARDE TRUFFÉE

[*Chicken with Truffles*]

Slip slices of truffle between the skin and breast meat and between the skin and leg meat. Refrigerate for about 24 hours and then roast. Truffles will give flavor to the meat. Serve with Sauce Périgueux (p. 30).

Wine: Côte Rôtie

POULET À LA DOCTEUR

[*Chicken with Liver Sauce*]

Prepare recipe of Demi-glace (p. 27). Sauté ¼ pound chicken livers in a chunk of butter for 5 minutes. Grind them through a food chopper, or mash into pieces with a fork. Add to the sauce. Heat, taste, and adjust seasonings. Serve sauce separately with roasted fowl.

Wine: Clos Arlot

CANETON RÔTI
[*Roast Duck*]

Fowl that are swimmers have heavier wishbones than their land-bound relatives. To make carving of these birds easier, the wishbone is removed before roasting.

To remove wishbone. Put the bird on its back. Pull the neck skin down over the breast meat. With a small sharp knife reach into the neck cavity and cut through the meat around the wishbone. Once the meat is cut, remove the knife, then with your fingers pull the wishbone from the meat, break it off, and discard.

Stuff ducks (and geese) with dried fruits and/or fresh oranges or apples. Never use bread or rice. Starchy foods soak up fat until they are unfit to eat.

Truss like chicken (p. 125). Do not cover breast with salt pork. Stand duck in sink on his legs and then scald with boiling water. Hot water swells the skin and opens the pores so the fat drains out during cooking. Roast on a rack. Cook according to chart on p. 126.

Baste ducks with a mixture of honey and water, using twice as much water as honey. Baste during the last half hour of cooking. When done, remove trussing strings, let the bird rest, and then carve. The French pre-carve ducks in the kitchen and then put the meat back into place on the frame. This is very wise since there is so little meat on a duck.

To carve ducks. Cut completely around the body of the duck at the top of the legs and wings. Carefully remove breast fillets. Remove legs at the body. Separate thighs from legs. Cut off wing pieces. Place breast fillets on cutting board. Slice thin and then put back in place upon the breast bones. Arrange the thighs, legs, and wings where they belong on the carcass. Press meat to the carcass with your hands. Put into very hot oven to rewarm. (Use oven-proof platter for serving.)

CANETON AUX CERISES
[*Duck with Cherries*]

1 (6–7-pound) duck	1 cup white wine
Salt and pepper	Kirsch
Recipe of Madeira sauce	¼ cup sugar
1 cup pitted fresh cherries, or	Cherry Heering
canned Bing cherries	

1. Remove giblets and neck from duck. Cook to make stock. Clean duck, remove wishbone, sprinkle cavity with salt and pepper, truss and scald (above). Roast according to chart on p. 126. Make Madeira sauce (p. 30), using stock.

2. Put cherries, wine, ¼ cup Kirsch, and sugar into saucepan. Bring to a boil and immediately remove from heat. If the cherries are fresh, let them stand until cool. If canned cherries are used, lift them from the syrup and put them on a plate. After removing the cherries, whether fresh or canned, boil the liquid, reducing it to about ¼ cup, or to a thick syrup.

3. Add this syrup to the cooked Madeira sauce. Taste and adjust the seasonings. Put cherries into small saucepan. Add ½ cup sauce. Heat, then add a dash of Kirsch and of Cherry Heering. Pre-carve the roasted duck (opposite page), and arrange on serving platter. Pour cherry sauce around duck. Serve the plain sauce separately. Serves 2 or 3.

Wine: Fleurie

CANARD À L'ORANGE

[*Duck with Orange Sauce*]

1 (6–7-pound) duck	Recipe of Bigarade sauce
Salt and pepper	2 tablespoons Cognac

2 oranges

1. Clean duck and remove giblets. Remove wishbone (opposite page). Sprinkle cavity with salt and pepper, truss and scald as for Caneton Rôti. Cook giblets and neck to make stock, but do not use the livers in any sauce; they are strong in flavor. Roast duck according to chart on p. 126.

2. Make Bigarade sauce (p. 28), using stock but add the blanched orange and lemon rinds to only ⅔ of the finished sauce. Peel the inner white layer of skin from the orange. Cut out the orange sections. Put these sections into a small skillet. Add 2 tablespoons Cognac, heat, and set aflame. When

flame dies, add the remaining ⅓ of plain sauce. Make orange baskets (see below) and fill with the sauced orange sections. Use to garnish platter. Pre-carve duck (p. 130). Lift some of the shredded rinds from the sauce and strew over the carved duck. Serve remainder of sauce separately. One duck will serve no more than 2 or 3.

Orange baskets. Make two cuts ¼ inch apart from the top of the orange down to the middle. This will form the handle of the basket. Then with a pointed knife make 2-sided triangular cuts from the end of one handle to the other side, cutting through to the middle of the orange, thus cutting it in half at the same time it is being cut in serrated design. Lift off this piece of orange from one side of the handle. Cut the other side of the orange, being sure not to cut through the bottom of the handle. Cut the ¼ inch of orange meat from under the handle after both sides have been removed. Remove the flesh of the orange from the basket part. It is not used in the recipe. A teaspoon is a good tool for this job. Fill baskets with orange-section sauce and place on platter.

NOTE: Baskets can be cut into scallops, reverse scallops, and other designs.
Wine: Saint-Émilion

VARIATIONS
CANETON À LA BIGARADE
[*Simplified Duck with Orange Sauce*]

Prepare Bigarade sauce (p. 28). Glaze roasted duck with some of the sauce. Cut an unpeeled orange into rounds, then cut slices in half. Garnish serving platter with these. Serve sauce separately.

Duck may be prepared according to the chicken recipes that use a dark sauce. See listing under Oie (Goose) variations. In the recipes that use livers, be sure to use chicken or goose livers, but not those of ducks, which are too strong. Duck may also be prepared according to the recipes for goose, but goose with orange or cherry sauce is not too appealing.
Wine: Brouilly

OIE RÔTIE
[*Roast Goose*]

Prepare goose for roasting just as you would duck. That is, remove the wish-bone, truss, scald, and during roasting baste with honey and water. If possible roast goose in a V-shaped rack so that the fat drains from the meat. Roast according to chart on p. 126. Serve with a Demi-glace sauce to which has been added the diced cooked giblets. Or cook and serve in one of the following ways.

OIE AUX MARRONS

[*Goose with Chestnuts*] •

1 (10–14-pound) goose
Salt and pepper
Recipe of chestnuts
Chunk of butter

Crème fraîche or whipping cream
4 apples, quartered
Recipe of Madeira sauce
Watercress

1. Remove neck and giblets from goose. Sprinkle cavity with salt and pepper. Cook the neck and gizzard and make stock. Boil chestnuts (p. 273). Once chestnuts are peeled, dice half of them; slice the remaining half, and put both on plates ready to use.

2. Sauté goose liver in a chunk of butter for about 10 minutes. Chop and then combine with the diced chestnuts. Add sufficient crème to bind the two. Stuff mixture into neck cavity of goose. Fill body cavity with quartered apples. Truss, scald as for roast duck, and roast according to chart (p. 126).

3. While goose cooks, prepare Madeira sauce (p. 30). Add sliced chestnuts to the sauce when it is done, taste, and adjust seasonings. Serve separately. Remove trussing strings from goose, decorate platter with watercress, and serve to 6 or 8. Be sure to serve neck stuffing!

Wine: Valpolicella (Italian)

OIE AUX PRUNEAUX

[*Goose with Prunes*]

1 (10–14-pound) goose
Salt and pepper
20 large prunes

Madeira wine
Butter
Recipe of Miroton sauce

Watercress

1. Remove neck and giblets from goose. Sprinkle cavity with salt and pepper. Cook neck and gizzard to make stock.

2. Simmer goose liver and prunes in water for about 15 minutes. Drain. Put liver into small dish. Cover with Madeira and let it marinate.

3. When prunes are cool enough to handle, pit them. Cut Madeira-flavored liver into as many pieces as there are prunes. Stuff each prune with a piece of liver and a piece of butter.

4. Fill goose cavity with stuffed prunes. Truss, scald (p. 130), and roast according to chart (p. 126). While goose roasts, make Miroton sauce (p. 30) using stock. Serve sauce separately. Decorate platter with bunches of watercress. Serves 6 to 8.

Wine: Morgon

VARIATIONS

OIE À L'ALSACIENNE

[*Goose with Sauerkraut*]

Prepare recipe of Choucroute (p. 194), omitting the garnishes. Roast goose.
Serve on bed of choucroute.
Wine: Hochheimer (German)

OIE À L'ASTURIENNE

[*Goose Stuffed with Livers*]

See Poularde à l'Asturienne (p. 127).
Wine: Château Beychevelle

OIE DEMIDOFF

[*Goose with Vegetables*]

See Poularde Demidoff (p. 128).
Wine: Valdepēnas Tinto (Spanish)

OIE À LA DOCTEUR

[*Goose with Liver Sauce*]

See chicken recipe of the same name (p. 129).
Wine: Château d'Issan

OIE À LA PORTUGAISE

[*Goose with Tomato Sauce*]

Stuff goose with a small bunch of parsley and 2 quartered apples. Truss
and roast according to chart on p. 126. Make Portugaise sauce (p. 31) while
goose roasts.
Wine: Fleurie

OIE TRUFFÉE

[*Goose with Truffles*]

See chicken recipe by the same name (p. 129).
Wine: Côte Rôtie

POULET BRAISÉ
[*Braised Chicken*]

Braised fowl may be cooked on top of the range in a covered casserole, or in the oven. Originally this method of cooking was designed to give flavor to tough birds and to make them tender.

From our modern-day hen houses it is practically impossible to get an old, tough bird, or a bird with old-fashioned flavor. This new breed of pampered fowl, raised under controlled conditions, lends itself well to the braising method of cooking. These birds have very little to lose and lots to gain, especially when braised in wine.

The first step in braising fowl, as well as meats, is to brown in oil, or to sauté them. One always questions whether sautéing and braising should not become one category, but I have kept them separate. Braised fowl is usually sautéed first, but sautéed fowl is not always braised. Braised-fowl recipes are some of the best the French have to offer.

Turkeys, capons, and Cornish hens may be substituted for chicken in the following recipes. But do not use geese and ducks; they are too fat.

POULET BIARRITZ
[*Chicken in White Wine*]

2 (3-pound) fryers	Bouquet garni
¼ cup olive oil	¼ teaspoon dried tarragon
⅛ pound butter	1 tablespoon tomato paste
¼ pound Bayonne or Prosciutto	½ cup chicken stock
ham (in the piece)	2 cups white wine
4 carrots	2 teaspoons sugar
20 small white boiling onions,	1 teaspoon salt
cleaned	⅛ teaspoon pepper
2 cloves garlic, diced	Beurre manié
¼ teaspoon thyme	1 tablespoon Madeira

3 tablespoons Cognac

1. Cut fryers into serving pieces. Brown in olive oil in skillet. When brown, drain off oil and add butter.

2. Cut ham into ¼-inch strips. Peel carrots, cut into chunks, and carve into round balls about the same size as the small boiling onions. Add ham and vegetables to the browned chicken.

(*continued*)

3. Add remaining ingredients down to the beurre manié. Simmer for 1 hour. Remove bouquet garni and thicken liquids with beurre manié. Stir in Madeira. Float Cognac over the top, set ablaze and serve.

Wine: Pomerol

POULET AU CHAMPAGNE
[*Chicken in Champagne*]

2 (3-pound) fryers, cut up	½ cup chicken stock
Flour	2 cups champagne (or vermouth)
¼ pound butter	2 teaspoons sugar
¼ cup Cognac	Beurre manié
1 teaspoon salt	2 tablespoons crème fraîche
¼ teaspoon pepper	1 egg yolk

1 tablespoon Cognac

1. Lightly coat chicken pieces with flour. (Omit the wings and bony pieces.) Sauté in butter until golden, but do not brown. Pour fat from skillet, then add ¼ cup Cognac and set aflame. When flame dies, add salt, pepper, stock, champagne, and sugar. Simmer about 40 minutes, or until done. Put chicken on hot platter. Thicken liquids with beurre manié.

2. Combine crème and yolk. Add about ½ cup of hot sauce to this liaison, mix and then pour back into sauce. Heat but do not boil. Add 1 tablespoon Cognac. Pour sauce through sieve over chicken.

Wine: Champagne or Château Grillet

COQ AU VIN
[*Chicken in Red Wine*]

When poultry and meats are braised in red Burgundy wine they are cooked "à la Bourguignonne."

2 (3–4-pound) chickens, cut up	½ cup vegetable oil

Bourguignonne Sauce

4 tablespoons flour	1 tablespoon tomato paste
¼ cup Cognac	⅛ teaspoon thyme
3 onions, quartered	Bouquet garni
2 cloves garlic, diced	1 teaspoon salt
3 cups red Burgundy wine	⅛ teaspoon pepper
(or 1 bottle)	1 tablespoon sugar

Garnishings and Finish

1 pint mushrooms	1 teaspoon sugar
Butter	Red and brown food coloring
¼ pound salt pork	3 tablespoons Cognac
½ pound small white boiling	1 tablespoon Madeira
onions	Chopped parsley

1. Brown chicken pieces in hot oil. When brown, pour off oil. Sprinkle with flour. Stir pieces with a wooden spoon until flour is absorbed. Pour ¼ cup Cognac over chicken and set aflame. Let flame burn out.

2. Add quartered onions, garlic, wine, tomato paste, thyme, bouquet garni, salt, pepper, and sugar. Stir until mixture starts to boil and then reduce heat and simmer for about an hour.

3. Wash the mushrooms. If caps are small, leave them whole; if large, cut into quarters. Sauté in a chunk of butter for two minutes. Put on a plate ready to use.

4. Cut salt pork into ¼-inch slices and then cut the slices into ¼-inch pieces. Fry crisp, drain and put on plate ready to use.

5. Skin whole boiling onions. Put on to cook in cold water. When water reaches the boil, drain. Rinse onions in cold water and drain again. Add a chunk of butter to the pan. Sprinkle with 1 teaspoon sugar and sauté 10 minutes to caramelize onions. Put on plate ready to use.

6. When ready to serve the chicken, discard the bouquet garni and color the sauce (see p. 3). Add the salt pork and prepared vegetables, and heat. Then add Cognac and Madeira. Taste and adjust the seasonings. Serve in skillet if you have a fancy one or put on hot serving platter, or in fancy casserole. Sprinkle with chopped parsley.

NOTE: The customary French meal includes also whole boiled potatoes and buttered whole green beans. Drink the same red Burgundy that has been used in the preparation of the Coq au Vin. In France it would be a Chambertin. Pommard is a good substitute.

VARIATION
COQ AU VIN BLANC
[*Chicken in White Wine*]

Make according to the Coq au Vin recipe, substituting a white Burgundy for the red. Omit the tomato paste and the food coloring. Finish the sauce with 2 tablespoons crème fraîche or whipping cream. Serve with the same white Burgundy used in the sauce.

Wine: Pommard Blanc

POULET AU CURRIE

[Curried Chicken]

2 (3-pound) fryers, cut up	Dash of pepper
¼ pound butter	4 firm apples
3 large onions	2 tablespoons flour
4 garlic cloves, minced	⅛ pound butter
1 tablespoon curry powder	2 tablespoons sugar
4 tablespoons flour	4 tablespoons crème fraîche or
1 cup white wine	whipping cream
2 cups chicken stock	Beurre manié
Bouquet garni	3 tablespoons Cognac
⅛ teaspoon dried thyme	2 tablespoons sherry
Salt	Chopped parsley

1. Sauté chicken in ¼ pound butter until browned. Place on a platter. Peel and cut each onion into 12 wedges, letting the root core hold the onion layers together. Add to pan and cook about 5 minutes. Add garlic and immediately stir in the curry powder and then the 4 tablespoons flour. (To brown garlic causes it to become bitter.)

2. Add the wine, stock, bouquet garni, thyme, 1 teaspoon salt, and pepper. Stir-cook until mixture starts to boil. Reduce heat. Add dark meat pieces. Simmer 20 minutes. Then add white meat and cook another 30 minutes, or until done.

3. Core apples (do not peel). Cut into large diced pieces. Coat with 2 tablespoons flour. Brown in skillet with ⅛ pound butter. Sprinkle with sugar and 1 teaspoon salt. Cook until browned on all sides.

4. Put chicken on hot serving platter when done. Discard bouquet garni. Add crème to sauce. Adjust thickness of sauce with beurre manié. Put browned apples over the chicken. Stir Cognac and sherry into sauce and pour over the apples and chicken. Sprinkle with parsley and serve.

Wine: Rioja Blanco (Spanish)

POULET EN CROÛTE

[*Chicken Pie*]

Recipe of puff pastry, or Pâte Brisée
2 (3-pound) fryers, cut up
¼ pound butter
2 onions, quartered
2 shallots, diced
3 cloves garlic, minced
4 tablespoons flour
¼ cup Cognac
2 cups white wine
½ cup chicken stock
1 teaspoon tomato paste

Bouquet garni
⅛ teaspoon thyme
Salt and pepper to taste
4 lamb kidneys
Butter
4 (¼-inch thick) slices salt pork,
    diced, or ¼ pound
1 pint mushrooms
3 hard-cooked eggs
Beurre manié
1 egg yolk

1 tablespoon water

1. This is a basic chicken-pie recipe. It can be served in a casserole, in a casserole with a pastry lid, in a deep pan or dish lined with pastry as we would make a cobbler, or in a vol-au-vent made of puff pastry. We will make the casserole with a puff-pastry lid.

2. Make the puff pastry (p. 345). While it chills, prepare the filling.

3. Brown chicken in butter, skin side first and then the fleshy side. In this way the juices are sealed in the chicken, and the skin side, which is served up, has a clean skillet in which to brown. Omit bony pieces of chicken.

4. When both sides are browned, pour off butter (save for other cooking). Add onions, shallots, and garlic. Stir in flour with a wooden spoon. Pour Cognac over and set aflame. When flame dies, add wine, stock, tomato paste, bouquet garni, thyme, salt, and pepper. Simmer 30 minutes. Give puff pastry a turn according to its recipe.

5. Remove outside skin of kidneys. Cut in half, then in chunks. Cook-toss in a chunk of butter for 5 minutes. Drain (see p. 180). Put on plate ready to use. Wipe out skillet with paper towels. Fry salt pork to a crisp. Drain and add to plate. Wash mushrooms. Quarter large ones; leave small ones whole. Sauté in piece of butter for 3 minutes. Add to plate. Give puff pastry a turn. Boil eggs.

6. When chicken is done, arrange pieces in an 8–10-cup casserole. Adjust thickness of sauce with beurre manié, then strain sauce into casserole. Add the crisp salt pork, kidneys, and mushrooms. Shell eggs and cut in half. Add to casserole.

7. Take dough from refrigerator. Give it one last turn, then roll to ⅛-inch thickness on the fourth rolling.

(*continued*)

8. Press a sheet of foil over the top of the casserole to make a pattern. Cut out the pattern and lay it on the dough. Cut out a lid of dough. Cut a ring of dough ¼ inch wide from the dough adjoining where the lid was. Wet the lip of the casserole. Lay this ¼-inch strip on the dampened edge. You won't use it all. Press tight. Dampen strip. Place crust on top of the wet strip. Press, then flute the edge like a pie crust.

9. Now decorate the crust with pastry cut-outs of flowers, leaves, or whatever you wish. Brush the entire crust and decorations with a mixture of 1 egg yolk and 1 tablespoon water. Use a paint brush for this job. Make a ¼-inch hole in the middle of the crust. Insert a small chimney of foil into the hole. This is a vent through which the steam escapes so that the crust will not rise from the edges of the casserole. Put into a 400-degree oven for about 30 minutes to heat contents of casserole and brown crust. Serves 6.

Wine: Volnay les Santenots

POULARDE SAINTE HÉLÈNE
[*Chicken with Quenelles*]

1 (5–6 pound) chicken or capon	½ pound ground veal
Recipe Bourguignonne Sauce	¼ teaspoon salt
⅛ pound butter	Dash of white pepper
½ cup water	3 egg whites
⅛ teaspoon salt	1 whole egg
½ cup flour	6 cups chicken stock
2 whole eggs	Cognac
1 pint fresh mushrooms	Madeira
2 cups water	½ pound pâté de foie gras
Chunk of butter	(bought or made)
Juice of ½ lemon	Flour
Salt	Butter
	2 truffles, julienne-cut

1. Remove as much fat from the fowl as you can. Truss (p. 125) and braise it in Bourguignonne sauce (see Coq au Vin recipe, p. 136). Reduce oil to 2 tablespoons, brown whole chicken and do not pour off oil. Add the flour and continue with the Bourguignonne sauce recipe. Cook covered for about 2 hours or until done. Turn fowl from side to side in the sauce as it cooks.

2. While bird cooks prepare the panade. Heat ⅛ pound butter, ½ cup water, and ⅛ teaspoon salt. When water is boiling, add flour all at once, remove from heat and stir until dough forms a ball in the center of the pan. Add 2 eggs, one at a time, beating after the addition of each. Put mixture into a

shallow pan, cover with transparent wrap, and refrigerate until cold. (This is a panade for the quenelles.)

3. Wash mushrooms. Cut stems off even with the cap. (Save stems and use at another time.) Put caps into 2 cups water seasoned with a chunk of butter, juice of ½ lemon, and some salt. Simmer 2 minutes and then remove from heat ready to use.

4. Put veal and an equal amount of the cold flour mixture (panade) into blender container or small mixer bowl. It will take all but about 2 tablespoons of the panade. Add ¼ teaspoon salt, white pepper, and 2 egg whites. Blend. Add third egg white. Mix well, then add 1 whole egg. Heat chicken stock to boiling, then reduce to a simmer. Shape quenelle mixture according to instructions (p. 149), only make them twice the size. Poach quenelles for about 3 minutes. Lift from stock to a bowl of cold water to stop their cooking. When cool, put quenelles on a plate ready to use.

5. When fowl is done, put on serving platter to rest. Strain the sauce into a clean pan. Skim off fat. Add 2 tablespoons each of Cognac and Madeira. Adjust seasonings and thickness of sauce.

6. Cut pâté into ¼-inch slices. Coat with flour and quickly sauté in butter. Cut whole breasts from each side of fowl. Place on cutting board. Cut diagonally across into ¼-inch slices. Alternate breast meat slices with the pâté and rearrange back in place on each side of the breast bone. Extend the sliced breast meat and pâté down toward the tail, letting the legs support the slices. Glaze with Bourguignonne sauce.

7. Drain the mushrooms. Put them into a medium-sized skillet. Add quenelles. Sprinkle mushrooms and quenelles with Madeira, pour 1 cup sauce into the skillet, and heat. Pour quenelle-mushroom sauce around fowl on platter. Sprinkle with strips of truffle. Serve remainder of sauce separately.

8. Serve a slice of breast meat and of foie gras with a few quenelles and mushrooms to each guest.

NOTE: I often substitute an 8-pound turkey breast for the whole bird. Trim the rib bones from the turkey breast bone to make it sit firmly on the platter. Since this takes a lot of pâté you may wish to make the chicken-liver pâté recipe (p. 416).

Wine: Romanée-Saint-Vivant

POULET GRILLÉ

[*Grilled or Broiled Poultry*]

Broiling is not one of the best methods by which to cook poultry. Too often the meat is scorched, bitter, or dried out by the time it is done. However, with care and constant basting it is possible to prepare a tasty bird by this method.

Chickens and Cornish hens when grilled "whole" are good. But one does not actually leave them whole as a rule. Ordinarily they are cut down the back and flattened to a thickness of no more than that of a 1-inch steak. The leg and wing pieces are tucked into the skin and the whole fowl cooks as one continuous flat piece of meat. After it is cooked, cut it into quarters or pieces.

To grill "whole" poultry out-of-doors, lay a sheet of foil over the top of the bird to reflect the heat and help cook the top side. Turn and baste often, replacing the foil after each turn.

POULET GRILLÉ À LA DIABLE

[*Broiled Chicken with Diable Sauce*]

Diable sauce	Melted butter
2 (2-pound) chickens, or (20-ounce)	Pepper to taste
Cornish hens	Dry bread crumbs

1. Make Diable sauce (p. 28). Preheat broiler for 10 minutes. Put fowl on its back on a cutting board. Insert a heavy butcher knife into the cavity and split the bird open down one side of the backbone. (Kitchen scissors may be used instead of a knife.) Turn the bird breast down. Push open like a book. Cut off the backbone. Cut the tissue around the middle of the breast and remove the main bone that divides the breast meat.

2. Cut holes in the skin between the thigh and the breast meat. Cross the legs and push each end through the cut in the opposite side. Pull leg ends to the inside of the bird. Cut first and second joints from wings. Make small holes in the skin at the ribs. Pull the wing ends through.

3. Brush fowl completely with melted butter. Sprinkle inside of chicken with pepper and crumbs. Grease hot broiler. Put crumb-coated side down on broiler. Broil 5 inches from the heat for about 20 minutes (15 for Cornish hens). Brush with butter about every 5 minutes. Control the heat so skin does not burn and blister.

4. At the end of 15 to 20 minutes, turn bird. Cook fleshy side for about 10 minutes then turn skin side up again. Coat with butter and sprinkle with crumbs. Brown. Cut into halves or quarters and serve to 4. Salt at the table. Serve sauce separately.

NOTE: *To test for doneness.* Stick thigh and catch juices that run out on a white plate. They will be clear and not pink when done. (See p. 7.)
Wine: Clos-des-Mouches

VARIATIONS

As is true in other French recipes, the sauce or garnish gives the name to the dish. Poultry is no exception.

POULET À LA BÉARNAISE
[*Chicken with Béarnaise Sauce*]

Grill or broil chickens and then garnish platter with artichoke bottoms filled with Béarnaise sauce (p. 24).
Wine: Château Grillet

POULET À LA TARTARE
[*Chicken with Tartare Sauce*]

Grill chickens and serve with Tartare sauce (p. 34) in lettuce cups.
Wine: Pouilly-Fumé

POULET GRILLÉ AUX CHAMPIGNONS
[*Chicken with Mushrooms*]

Broil chickens. Cut 3 onions into quarters. Wash and stem ½ pound mushrooms. Sauté onions for 10 minutes in a chunk of butter. Add mushrooms and cook another 5 minutes. Season with salt, pepper, and a dash of sugar. Pour 2 tablespoons Cognac over vegetables and blaze. Arrange in neat piles on serving platter around cooked chickens.
Wine: Frascati (Italian)

POULET GRILLÉ AUX TOMATES

[*Grilled Chicken with Tomatoes*]

Broil chickens. Stem 4 tomatoes. Brush with melted butter. Sprinkle with salt and pepper. Fifteen minutes before chicken is done, set on broiler rack with chicken and broil. Broil also 8 slices of lean bacon. When ready to serve, cut chickens in half. Cross 2 slices bacon over each piece. Garnish platter with broiled tomatoes and decorate with bunches of watercress.

Wine: Niersteiner (German)

POULET FRIT
[*French-fried Poultry*]

Small broilers under two pounds are best for French-frying. Cook in oil heated to a lower temperature than is normally recommended for French-frying. This prevents the outside from being overcooked before the flesh around the bones is done.

| 2 small broilers (under 2 pounds) | Simple coating |
| or Cornish hens | Vegetable oil |

Salt and pepper to taste

1. Cut the broilers into pieces. Cut breast in half. Remove the center bone. Separate legs from thighs. Cut off wing tips. Cook the backs, ribs, and wing tips in seasoned water and make stock to use at another time. (These pieces are too bony to fry.) When these bony pieces are done, remove the meat from the bones. Make Currie sauce (p. 16). Add meat to sauce.

2. Dry the fleshy pieces well on paper towels. Dip them into a Simple Coating, either No. 1 or No. 4 (p. 10). Heat oil to 360 degrees. Add coated chicken pieces, a few at a time, and cook about 5–8 minutes. When done, they will rise to the surface of the oil. Do not crowd the pan. Lift out pieces as they are cooked. Drain on paper towels. Keep warm in a hot oven while frying the remaining pieces of chicken. Season after cooking. Fry parsley (p. 259) for a garnish. Serve with curry sauce. Tartare (p. 34) or Béarnaise (p. 24) sauce may also be served with French-fried chicken.

Wine: Rully Blanc

POULET SAUTÉ
[*Sautéed Poultry*]

Fryers no heavier than 3 pounds are best for sautéing. The leg meat is tougher and requires longer cooking to make it tender. Therefore, put the dark meat in to cook first and then add the breast or white meat. In this way the pieces will all be done at the same time.

Chicken is sautéed "white," which means without being browned; "golden," which means lightly browned; and "brown," which means *really* browned. In French cooking the color of the chicken should match the color of the sauce that accompanies it.

2 (3-pound) fryers, cut up	⅛ teaspoon pepper
½ cup flour	⅛ pound butter
½ teaspoon salt	2 tablespoons vegetable oil

1. Dry pieces of chicken on paper towels. Separate legs from thighs. Cut off the wing tips. Cook the necks, giblets, and wing tips in water seasoned with salt, an onion, a carrot, and a few sprigs of parsley. Remove livers after 5 minutes of cooking. When necks and giblets are done, chop the meat. Make a Demi-glace sauce (p. 27) in advance of cooking the chicken.

2. Combine flour, salt, and pepper in a paper or plastic bag. Add chicken pieces. Shake bag to flour. Heat butter and oil. Sauté chicken legs, thighs, and backs for 20 minutes and then add the other pieces. Cook about 30 minutes longer, or until brown and done. Add diced giblets and neck meat to sauce. Heat and serve with sautéed chicken.

Wine: Beaujolais

SUPRÊMES DE VOLAILLE SAUTÉS
[*Deboned Breast Meat*]

One of the joys of chicken is the *suprême*. To create it, remove the center breast bone that divides the breast meat. Cut the breast in half. With kitchen scissors cut between the ribs and the long, flat, thin bones in the breast meat. Remove the first two joints of the wing. Leave the "leg" joint attached to each piece of breast meat. I remove the thin, flat bones after the suprême is cooked, although it may be removed now simply by running your finger down between the meat and the long bones and then cutting off the bones. Skin the meat from the top down, it is easier.

Sauté suprêmes just like white meat of chicken, but cook a shorter time. Sauté each side about 10 minutes. Do not overcook, but be sure the chicken is done. After suprême is cooked, remove the long, thin, flat bones from the underneath side. They are left in to prevent the muscles from contracting and making the meat tight.

FILETS DE SUPRÊMES SAUTÉS
[*Chicken Fillets*]

To find these choice white-meat tidbits, completely debone the breast meat. Here is how it is done.

Remove the skin. Then, from the inside, make cuts along the breast bone. Into these cuts insert your thumbs and follow the bone to the tip, pushing the meat from the breast bone as your thumbs move. Break out the center bone. Stand the breast up on its wishbone-like big bones and run your thumbs down the breast, pushing the meat from the wishbone and the other bones. Run your thumb, or forefinger, out to the ends of the flat bones, thus removing the meat. This is very easy. Practice any time you have a chicken breast. It takes about 2 minutes to do the job. This is also the easy way to get suprêmes. Leave wing piece attached.

Once the meat is deboned, the little fillet, called the mignon, will separate itself from the main piece of breast meat. Remove it. At the top of it you will notice a big white tendon. Take hold of it with your left hand, and with a knife in your right, push the meat off it while pulling. If your hand slips off the tendon, use paper towels to hold it tight. This must be removed because it is too tough to eat and ruins the precious little mignon if left in. Get a chicken breast and practice this whole technique; it is basically very easy.

There are but two mignons to a chicken, and it will take at least 12 for two people. I freeze them until I have sufficient to serve 2 or more. However, you can serve them along with the chicken breast pieces, but cut the main piece of breast meat into strips similar in size to the small mignon. Lightly coat these *suprême filets* with flour, sauté a total of about 5 minutes and season after they are cooked. The flesh turns a pearl-white when they are done.

When they are done, pour over 2 tablespoons Cognac and set ablaze. When the flame dies, add ¼ cup crème fraîche and 2 tablespoons sherry. Heat, season, and serve with crusty French bread and a salad. The sauce can be thickened slightly with a bit of beurre manié if you wish.

Chicken fillet mignons may be served with practically any sauce. Substitute them in any of the fillet of sole or veal recipes, or prepare them like snails, with garlic butter. They are delicious.

VARIATIONS

Sautéed-chicken recipes could be a book unto themselves. In the recipes that follow use 2 (3-pound) cut-up chickens, 6 whole suprêmes, or 8 suprêmes with the fillet mignons removed (save for later use) and suprêmes cut into fillet pieces. Adjust the cooking time according to the types of chicken pieces being used. Be very careful not to overcook white meat of chicken or it becomes threadlike and tough. Basic sauté recipe (p. 145).

POULET SAUTÉ ARCHIDUC

[*Chicken in Suprême Sauce*]

Make Sauce Suprême (p. 21). Sauté chicken pieces to a "white" color. When chicken is done, put on hot platter. Deglaze pan with ¼ cup Madeira. Strain into Sauce Suprême. Add 1 minced truffle. Spoon sauce over chicken to glaze pieces. Serve remainder of sauce separately.

Wine: Pouilly-Fuissé

POULET SAUTÉ BAZARD

[*Chicken Sautéed with Vegetables*]

Prepare Demi-glace sauce (p. 27). Sauté 2 cut-up chickens to a "brown" color. Deglaze pan with Madeira. Strain into Demi-glace sauce. Quarter 4 fresh or canned artichoke bottoms. Add to sauce and stir in 1 cup sliced fresh mushrooms. Simmer 5 minutes. Pour over chicken on platter. Garnish with blanched, pitted green olives (see p. 598 for blanching) and whole boiled potatoes.

Wine: Moulin-à-Vent

POULET SAUTÉ BRETONNE

[*Suprêmes with Mushroom Sauce*]

Sauté 8 suprêmes to a "golden" color. Put on hot platter. Remove flat bones. Wipe out skillet with paper towels. Add chunk of butter to skillet. Sauté 1 small minced leek, 1 minced onion, and ½ cup minced mushrooms for about 5 minutes. Add 2 tablespoons crème fraîche or whipping cream. Add recipe of Sauce Suprême (p. 21), made in advance. Pour hot sauce over chicken suprêmes. Sprinkle with chopped parsley and serve.

Wine: Piesporter Goldtroepfchen (German)

POULET SAUTÉ À LA CRÈME

[*Chicken in Cream Sauce*]

Sauté 2 cut-up chickens in ¼ pound butter until "golden" in color. Add 1 minced onion and 1 cup sliced mushrooms. Cook 15 minutes. Remove chicken pieces. Stir in 4 tablespoons flour. Add 2 cups cream. Stir until thickened. Add 2 tablespoons Cognac and 1 tablespoon Madeira. Place chicken back in sauce. Cover and simmer 20 minutes.

NOTE: Chicken quenelles make a delicious contribution to the sauce.
Wine: Chablis

POULET SAUTÉ FÉDORA

[*Suprêmes in Sauce*]

Make Sauce Suprême (p. 21). Chop 2 raw shrimp in their shells and cook in 6 tablespoons water. Reduce liquids to about 2 tablespoons. Strain into Sauce Suprême. Discard, or shell and eat shrimp. Add 1 tablespoon lemon juice. Cut 1 truffle into julienne strips. Add to sauce. Cut 8 suprêmes into fillets (see p. 146). Sauté to a "golden" color. Put on platter. Deglaze pan with 2 tablespoons crème fraîche. Strain into sauce. Add dash of cayenne pepper. Glaze suprême fillets with sauce and serve remainder of sauce separately.
Wine: Musigny Blanc

POULET SAUTÉ AUX FINES HERBES

[*Chicken with Herbs*]

Sauté chicken suprêmes to a "brown" color. Put on plate. Remove flat bones. Sprinkle with chopped parsley and chives. With paper towels, wipe out the skillet in which the suprêmes were sautéed. Add chunk of butter. Cook butter to a nut brown and then pour over herbs and suprêmes.
Wine: Hermitage Blanc

POULET SAUTÉ AUX HUÎTRES

[*Chicken with Oysters*]

Sauté chicken fillets cut from 8 suprêmes to a "golden" color. Prepare Suprême sauce (p. 21). Enrich the sauce with 2 dozen oysters. Cook sauce until edges of oysters curl. Spoon over sautéed fillets of suprêmes.
Wine: Bienvenue Bâtard Montrachet

POULET SAUTÉ À LA MARENGO
[*Chicken with Eggs*]

Make Portugaise sauce (p. 31). "Brown" 2 cut-up chickens in olive oil. Put on hot platter and keep warm. Pour oil from skillet. Add 1 cup mushroom caps and ½ cup white wine. Boil and deglaze pan. Add prepared Portugaise sauce and 1 chopped truffle and heat. Pour sauce over cooked chicken. Garnish with toast points and 6 French-fried eggs (p. 57). Sprinkle with minced parsley and serve.

Wine: Vinho Verde Tinto (Portuguese)

QUENELLES DE VOLAILLE
[*Simple Chicken Quenelles*]

4 cups chicken stock for poaching	3 egg whites
1 pound raw chicken breasts (or about ¼ pound skinned and deboned white meat)	3 tablespoons crème fraîche, or 2 tablespoons whipping cream
	¼ teaspoon salt

Dash of white pepper

1. Heat stock ready to use. Skin, debone, and dice breast meat. Put into blender container. Add raw egg whites and blend on highest speed. Reduce speed to medium, and add remainder of ingredients. Put mixture into shallow bowl. Reduce heat so that stock does not boil. Keep it at a simmer.

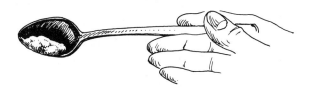

2. With 2 teaspoons mold quenelles. Fill a cup with cold tap water. Dip spoon into it, shake off water, then cut through mixture with the long side of the spoon, filling it about ¼ full, and making a quenelle in the shape of an ellipse. With the other wet spoon push the quenelle out of the spoon and into the hot stock. The quenelles will double in size, so keep them small. Repeat process until all are made.

3. Quenelles are done when they rise to the top. Lift them out, and put into cold stock or water to stop the cooking process. Keep scum removed as it collects on surface of stock. This recipe makes about 4 dozen. These can be refrigerated in stock, ready to use.

(continued)

NOTE: For variety, oil tiny molds, the 1-inch size, then fill with quenelle mixture and drop into hot stock. When done they will float themselves from the mold. To make these molded quenelles different, lay a piece of truffle in the bottom of the mold and then add the mixture, thus a truffled quenelle. Pieces of cooked carrot, raw avocado, mushroom, or parsley may also be used in place of the truffle.

FOIES DE VOLAILLE
[Chicken Livers]

We ordinarily give very little thought to chicken livers. One liver comes with every chicken, and it goes into the stock pot along with the neck and giblets. The liver usually cooks as long as the gizzard and then we decide chicken livers are a pretty dry, cottonlike thing and somehow hope they will taste otherwise when they get into the sauce. But they never do when prepared in this fashion.

However, when properly cooked chicken livers will add to your repertory of delicious dishes. Chicken livers may be served under a sauce as a main course, or as a first course. They can be used in omelettes and other foods. Chicken-liver quenelles are a discovery that will please me for as long as I eat.

FOIES DE VOLAILLE SAUTÉS
[*Sautéed Chicken Livers*]

1 pound chicken livers	**¼ pound butter**
Flour	**Salt and pepper to taste**

1. Fresh livers are best. If using frozen ones, let them thaw. Cut the livers in half, then they will cook more evenly. Remove all fat and white tissue. Check each liver as you cut them apart to be sure the green bile sac is removed.

2. Roll livers in flour, then shake off the surplus. You want just a thin film of flour.

3. Heat butter in a heavy skillet to hot. Add livers. Brown and toss-cook, which means to toss the food in the skillet to turn it over rather than run the risk of puncturing the food with a fork and letting the juices drain out into the skillet. When livers are browned, they are done. They are best served pink or medium, and never well done to the point of being dry. One pound is sufficient for 6 as the first course, but will serve only 3 as the main course. Season after they are cooked.

Wine: Beaujolais

VARIATIONS

FOIES DE VOLAILLE À LA BÉARNAISE

[*Livers with Béarnaise Sauce*]

Make Béarnaise sauce (p. 24). Serve with 1 pound sautéed chicken livers as a first course to 6.

Wine: Pouilly-Fumé

FOIES DE VOLAILLE À LA BORDELAISE

[*Livers with Bordelaise Sauce*]

Make Bordelaise sauce (p. 28). You may also use any of the sauces from the Demi-glace chart (pp. 28–30). Serve with 1 pound sautéed livers as a first course to 6. The dish takes the name of the sauce.

Wine: Givry

FOIES DE VOLAILLE À LA HOLLANDAISE

[*Livers with Hollandaise Sauce*]

Make Hollandaise sauce (p. 21). To finished sauce add 1 tablespoon crème fraîche or whipping cream. Spoon over 1 pound sautéed chicken livers and decorate with minced truffles. Serve as a first course to 6 or, along with grilled tomatoes, to 3 for Sunday brunch.

Wine: Chassagne-Montrachet

FOIES DE VOLAILLE AU MADÈRE

[*Livers with Madeira Sauce*]

Sauté 1 pound livers. Combine 4 tablespoons Madeira and 2 tablespoons Cognac in a cup. Grind fresh pepper over livers. Pour over the wine and Cognac. Heat to volatilize some of the alcohol, then set aflame. When flame dies, stir in

3 tablespoons crème fraîche or whipping cream. Season. Spoon livers onto small hot serving plates. Sprinkle with parsley and serve with toast points and a salad to 3 for Sunday brunch.

NOTE: Substitute sherry or Port for the Madeira and you'll have an entirely different dish. This dish takes the name of the wine.

Wine: Beaujolais

FOIES DE VOLAILLE À LA MEUNIÈRE

[*Livers in Meunière Sauce*]

Sauté 1 pound chicken livers. Sprinkle with parsley and pour over some melted butter seasoned with lemon juice. If you add chopped chives to the parsley you'll have Foies de Volaille aux Fines Herbes. Serves 6 as a first course.

Wine: Pouilly-Fumé

NOTE: In addition to the above recipes, any of the hot butter sauces (pp. 35–37) are delicious served over sautéed chicken livers. Sautéed onions, carrots, artichokes, or spinach may also be served with sautéed livers. Again the name of the dish takes the name of the vegetable. Example: *Foies de Volaille aux Oignons,* etc. Also, any sauce from the Tomato sauce family is good with chicken livers.

QUENELLES DE FOIES DE VOLAILLE ANDRÉ SIMON

[*Chicken-liver Quenelles*]

½ pound chicken livers	1 egg white
1 shallot, minced	Dash of salt and pepper to taste
6 cups chicken stock for poaching	

1. Cut each liver in two. Remove all fat and white tissue. Put raw livers, shallot, egg white, salt, and pepper into blender container. (If you have no blender, grind livers twice through food chopper, then mix with other ingredients.) Whirl blender to blend ingredients. The mixture will be the color and consistency of chocolate pudding and on the thin side.

2. Pour mixture into shallow bowl or dish. Using wet spoons shape the quenelles and drop them into simmering stock. Do not let stock boil. (See p. 149 for details on quenelle making.) Poach quenelles about a minute, then turn them over and poach another minute. These float before they are done. Carefully lift each quenelle from the stock with a fork and place in cold stock to stop cooking. Quenelles may be made a day in advance of using. Leave in the stock and refrigerate. Do not freeze. Quenelles toughen when frozen. Makes about 36 small quenelles. Serve as a garnish to any of the sauced chicken recipes, in any one of the braised-chicken dishes, or in one of the following recipes.

VARIATIONS

QUENELLES DE FOIES DE VOLAILLE BÉARNAISE

[*Chicken-liver Quenelles with Béarnaise Sauce*]

Make Béarnaise sauce (p. 24). Drain, then dry cold quenelles on paper towels. Roll in flour, then dip in slightly beaten egg white and then in fine dry bread crumbs. French-fry in deep fat, heated to 390 degrees, for a few seconds, or until crisp and brown. Serve with Béarnaise sauce as a first course to 6.
Wine: Pouilly-Fuissé

QUENELLES DE FOIES DE VOLAILLE HOLLANDAISE

[*Chicken-liver Quenelles with Hollandaise Sauce*]

Make Hollandaise sauce (p. 21). Spoon over poached quenelles. Serve as first course to 6.
Wine: Chablis

QUENELLES DE FOIES DE VOLAILLE FROIDES

[*Chicken-liver Quenelles Served Cold*]

Make Béarnaise sauce (p. 24). Pour into a dish and refrigerate. Make quenelles and refrigerate. Fill artichoke bottoms with Béarnaise sauce. Cover with liver quenelles. Serve as first course to 6.
NOTE: Toast rounds or tomato slices may be substituted for the artichokes.
Wine: Liebfraumilch (German)

Veau
[*Veal*]

True veal is as hard to find in this country as wishbones in cut-up chickens. The flesh of veal should be a mother-of-pearl pinkish color and should come from a baby calf two to three months of age. It is slaughtered at the time it is weaned from its mother and before it goes on a diet of grass and grain. It is a milk-fed calf. When the calf starts to eat solids, it develops muscles and they begin to turn red. The longer a calf lives, the darker the meat becomes.

French butchers are artists when it comes to cutting meat. They strip the individual muscles from both veal and beef and then tie in roasts or cut individual steaks or medallions of meat across the grain of the meat. We cut veal as we cut beef, but it is not the technique for veal steaks. The connective tissues in a young calf are not strong enough to hold the different leg muscles together. In a slice of veal the various muscles fall apart. Therefore, the only sensible thing to do with a slice of veal is to cut the connective tissues from around the individual muscles and cook the small pieces of veal.

VEAU BRAISÉ
[*Braised Veal*]

Veal is a delicately flavored meat, much like the breast of chicken. Just as we can do more to chicken than fry it, we can do more to veal than bread it. Substitute it in any of the chicken recipes and in most of the sole fillet recipes.

Cognac is seldom used in sauces created for veal. When it is, completely burn off the Cognac leaving only bouquet. Because veal is a lean meat, it is best braised or sautéed.

Since salt tends to toughen protein, all meats should be salted only after they are cooked. When meats are served in or with a sauce, the seasonings in the sauce are usually sufficient for the meat too.

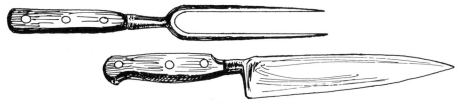

CARRÉ DE VEAU BRAISÉ

[*Braised Veal*]

1 (3–4-pound) piece of veal	Butter
2 carrots, sliced	1 cup chicken stock (or more)
1 onion, sliced	Salt and pepper to taste
Several parsley sprigs	2 tablespoons Madeira

1. If possible have the butcher cut a 4-pound standing veal roast (like beef), which is the back or the loin of veal. If this is not possible, then use a rump roast and have it tied.

2. Put a layer of carrots, onion, and parsley on bottom of roasting pan. Set meat on top of the vegetables. Coat roast with butter.

3. Put in a 425-degree oven. Brown for 25 minutes, then reduce heat to 325 degrees. Add stock and cover pan with a sheet of foil, leaving a small opening on one side for steam to escape. Cook about 25 minutes per pound or about 1½ hours. Baste often. Add more stock if necessary.

4. When done, place roast on platter to rest. Serve plain with the following sauce, or use in other recipes. Strain the pan liquid into a small skillet. Add stock to the pan to make about 1 cup. Heat, then flavor with Madeira. Taste, season, and serve sauce separately. Spoon juice over slices as they are served.

Wine: Beaujolais or Beaune

There are many parts to the following veal recipes. Make the parts while the veal cooks, then the final assembling of the recipes will be easy and quick. These are all delicious and well worth the time and effort they take.

The advantage to these recipes is that the veal is precarved and ready to serve when presented at the table.

CARRÉ DE VEAU À L'ORIENTALE
[Braised Veal with Soubise]

1 (4-pound) veal roast

Step 1: Soubise au Ris
4 onions, sliced
Chunk of butter
¼ cup rice
½ cup water
½ teaspoon salt
Dash of pepper
Cream

Step 2: Pilaf
2 onions, minced
3 mushrooms, diced
Chunk of butter
1½ cups rice
3 cups water
1 teaspoon salt

3 large tomatoes
Salt and pepper to taste
3 tablespoons olive oil

Step 3: Béchamel au Currie
⅛ pound butter
1 tablespoon curry powder
4 tablespoons flour
2 cups milk
Salt and pepper to taste
2 tablespoons Madeira
2 egg yolks
6 tablespoons crème fraîche or
   whipping cream

To finish recipe
Grated Parmesan cheese
Chopped parsley

1. A loin roast is best for this, one that resembles a standing rib roast. But settle for something else if the loin is not available. Braise according to basic recipe (p. 155).

2. Make Soubise. Sauté sliced onions in a chunk of butter for 5 minutes. Add rice, water, and salt. Stir, cover, and cook about 20 minutes, or until rice is tender. Press through a food mill. Put purée back into pan. Add pepper and cream to make it the consistency of mashed potatoes. Set aside ready to use.

3. Make Pilaf. Sauté onions and mushrooms in butter for a few minutes. Stir in the rice. Cook a few minutes and then add the water and 1 teaspoon salt. Boil 2 minutes, then cover and simmer about 15 minutes, or until rice is done and dry. Stir with fork and set aside. Cut tomatoes in half. (Do not skin.) Remove seeds and squeeze out juice. Sprinkle with salt and pepper. Put olive oil into skillet. Lay tomatoes, cut side down, in oil ready to heat.

4. Make Béchamel. Melt butter; stir in curry powder. Cook 1 minute, then stir in flour, and cook a few minutes more. Add milk, salt, and pepper. Stir-cook until thickened. Add Madeira. Combine yolks and crème. Spoon about ½ cup of sauce into this liaison and then stir back into the sauce. Remove from heat, cover with a lid, and set aside until ready to use.

5. *To serve roast.* When roast is done, cut the meat into ¼-inch slices. Coat each slice with Soubise and then stand slices back in place. Thus the roast

is back in its original shape. Carefully rewarm Currie sauce. Coat veal with sauce and sprinkle with Parmesan. Set into a 475-degree oven for about 10 minutes to heat and brown cheese.

6. Sauté tomatoes in oil, cooking each side about 2 minutes. Cover and re-heat Pilaf while tomatoes cook. Fill tomatoes with hot Pilaf and sprinkle them with parsley. Serve roast garnished with the filled tomatoes. Extra sauce is served separately.

NOTE: This recipe is made up of four basic recipes found elsewhere in this book: Roast Veal (below); Soubise au Ris (p. 235); Pilaf (p. 280); and Béchamel au Currie (p. 16). The recipes given here are somewhat different, but the basic ones could also have been used.

Wine: Châteauneuf-du-Pape

NOIX DE VEAU BRAISÉE
[*Braised Roast Veal*]

2 tablespoons vegetable oil	1 cup white wine
Chunk of butter	1 cup chicken stock
1 (3–4-pound) veal roast	1 tablespoon tomato paste
3 carrots, minced	1 teaspoon salt
3 onions, diced	⅛ teaspoon pepper
3 cloves garlic, minced	Bouquet garni
2 tablespoons flour	⅛ teaspoon thyme
2 tablespoons Madeira	

1. Heat oil and butter in a Dutch oven or other heavy pan. Brown roast on all sides. Remove roast from pan. Add carrots and onions. Cover and cook 20 minutes. Add garlic and stir in flour. Cook a few minutes, and then add liquids and all other ingredients except Madeira. Stir until mixture starts to boil. Add roast and put into a 350-degree oven. Allow 25 minutes per pound for braising.

2. When done, put roast on hot platter. Remove strings, if it is tied, and let rest. Strain sauce into clean pan. Add Madeira. Taste and adjust seasonings and thicken with beurre manié if necessary. Serve sauce separately. (This sauce is basically a Demi-glace.) Pre-slice meat and arrange on platter. Decorate platter with bunches of watercress.

Wine: Morgon or Moulin-à-Vent

VARIATIONS
NOIX DE VEAU VICHY
[*Roast Veal with Carrots*]

Vichy, France, is considered a health spa. Carrots are considered a health food, and this recipe is a *spécialité* of Vichy. The carrots may be left whole, or carved into miniature carrots, but our chef made the dish in the following fashion, and I think I prefer it done so.

Prepare Noix de Veau Braisée. Cut about 8 carrots into ⅟16-inch cubes (à la Brunoise). To do this cut carrots into ⅟16-inch lengthwise slices, then cut into strips the same thickness and then into cubes. Tedious, but not hard. Put these little pieces into a skillet with ¼ pound butter, ¼ cup water, ½ teaspoon salt, 1 tablespoon sugar, and a dash of white pepper. Cut a circle of foil to fit inside the pan, butter it, and lay it on top of the carrots. Cover with a lid. Simmer for about 30 minutes over very low heat. Check periodically to be sure the carrots do not burn.

Spoon around precarved roast. Sprinkle with minced parsley and serve. Strain braising liquid, season, and serve separately.

Wine: Les Bonnes Mares

NOIX DE VEAU À LA CHARTREUSE
[*Roast Veal Garnished with Vegetables*]

Prepare Noix de Veau Braisée. Prepare vegetables while meat cooks. Peel 6 carrots. Cut them into 1-inch pieces. Trim and shape each piece to look like a large olive. Cook them in water seasoned with a chunk of butter and a teaspoon each of salt and sugar. Cut 6 turnips into fourths. Shape and cook like the carrots. Cut ½ pound fresh beans into 1-inch lengths. Cook in seasoned water. Cook 1 pound shelled peas in seasoned water. When vegetables are done, butter them, ready to reheat and use. Make recipe of Château potatoes (p. 237). (Make potage from vegetable trimmings.)

When veal is done, precarve and place on serving platter. Garnish with piles of vegetables on the ends of the platter and with potatoes along the sides. Strain sauce and serve separately.

Wine: Beaujolais

NOIX DE VEAU ORLOFF

[*Braised Veal with Mornay Sauce*]

1 (4-pound) veal rump roast

Duxelles

¼ pound butter

4 onions, minced

1 pound fresh mushrooms, minced

½ teaspoon salt

Dash of pepper

½ teaspoon confectioners' sugar

Mornay Sauce

⅛ pound butter

4 tablespoons flour

2 cups light cream

Dash of nutmeg

½ teaspoon salt

⅛ teaspoon white pepper

1 teaspoon sugar

2 egg yolks

¼ cup crème fraîche or

   whipping cream

¼ cup Parmesan cheese

1. Braise veal according to basic recipe on p. 155. Try to get a solid piece of meat, that is, a piece with just one big muscle, rather than a rolled roast.

2. Make Duxelles. Sauté onions in ¼ pound butter for 10 minutes. Do not brown. Add mushrooms and seasonings and cook 5 minutes. Put onto a plate ready to use.

3. This Mornay sauce uses cream, not milk. Melt ⅛ pound butter in skillet. Stir in the flour. Cook a few minutes, but do not let it brown. Add cream. Stir-cook until thickened. Add nutmeg, salt, pepper, and sugar. Cover with lid and remove from heat. It is ready to finish and use.

4. When veal is done put it on a hot platter. Let it rest a few minutes. Combine yolks and crème. Stir into the cooled sauce and then reheat. Do not let it boil.

5. If meat is tied, remove strings. Cut veal into ¼-inch slices. Coat each slice with Duxelles. Place slices on oven-proof platter. Arrange in the form of the uncut veal roast. Coat with Mornay sauce, sprinkle with Parmesan and set into a 400-degree oven for about 20 minutes to heat and brown. Thin remainder of sauce with additional cream, season, and serve separately.

Wine: Pommard Blanc

SELLE DE VEAU À LA NELSON
[*Souffléed Veal Orloff*]

1 (4-pound) rump roast	Madeira
Recipe of Duxelles sauce	Salt and pepper to season

Cheese Soufflé

⅛ pound butter	Dash of nutmeg
4 tablespoons flour	⅛ teaspoon pepper
1 cup light cream	4 egg yolks
½ teaspoon salt	½ cup Parmesan cheese

5 egg whites

1. Braise veal according to basic instructions (p. 155). Make Duxelles sauce from preceding Orloff recipe.

2. While veal cooks, make the cream sauce for the soufflé: Melt butter in skillet. Stir in flour and add cream, salt, nutmeg, and pepper. Stir-cook until very thick. Remove from heat. Add a couple of tablespoons of hot sauce to yolks. Mix, then stir back into sauce. Add cheese. Warm, then take from heat, cover with a lid and set aside until ready to use.

3. When veal is done, take from pan and let it rest for a few minutes. Strain pan juices into a skillet, adding stock to make 1 cup liquid. Flavor with 1 tablespoon Madeira and season. Carve roast. Coat slices with Duxelles as is done in the preceding Orloff recipe. Arrange coated slices in the form of the uncut roast on oven-proof platter.

4. Make a foil collar to encompass the veal, letting it come to about 1 inch above the roast. Grease and flour the collar and stand it on the platter. Fit collar *tight* around roast and then pin the ends of the foil tight together. If there is a trick to this recipe, it is containing the soufflé. The warm roast tends to melt the soufflé.

5. Beat the egg whites stiff. Stir-fold into the thick cream sauce. When mixed, pour into foil collar to cover the roast. Bake in a 450-degree oven for about 20 minutes, or until browned and puffed. This should be sufficient time, since the roast is warm. If not, cook another 5 minutes. The soufflé must be firm enough to hold by itself once the collar is removed.

6. When done, carefully unpin and remove the foil collar. Serve slices of meat with some soufflé. Pan juices served separately.

Wine: Clos de Vougeot Blanc

POITRINE DE VEAU
[*Breast of Veal*]

2 onions, minced
Chunk of butter
1 (5-ounce) box mushrooms,
   minced, or 1 cup
1 pound ground pork
1 teaspoon salt
Dash of nutmeg
⅛ teaspoon pepper
4 sprigs parsley, chopped

2 tablespoons Madeira
2 whole eggs
1 breast of veal with pocket
2 tablespoons vegetable oil
Chunk of butter
1 carrot, sliced
1 onion, sliced
1 cup vermouth or white wine
¼ cup Madeira

1. Sauté onions in chunk of butter for 5 minutes. Remove from heat. Add mushrooms and pork. Add salt, nutmeg, pepper, parsley, and 2 tablespoons Madeira. Mix well and then stir in eggs. Stuff mixture into veal pocket. Close opening with needle and thread, or fasten with skewers.

2. Put oil and chunk of butter into roasting pan. Heat, then brown, the stuffed veal on both sides. Lift out, add sliced carrot and onion to the pan. Set veal back on vegetables. Add vermouth, cover, and braise in a 325-degree oven for 30 minutes per pound. If necessary add more wine during cooking time.

3. When done, place on hot serving platter. Remove skewers or string. Pour ¼ cup Madeira into pan and boil 5 minutes. Strain liquid and serve separately. Decorate platter with bunches of watercress. Carve across the pocket so that the layers of meat and filling show in each slice.

Wine: Les Bonnes Mares

BLANQUETTE DE VEAU
[*Veal Stew*]

"Blanquette" is the name for "white stews." They are made from white meats and are accompanied by a white sauce. The sauce has the depth of velvet and the smoothness of satin.

2 pounds veal, cubed	1 quart cold water

Sauce

3 carrots	1 teaspoon each sugar and salt
2 leeks	Bouquet garni
2 onions	¼ teaspoon thyme
1 clove garlic	1 pound fresh mushrooms, sliced
1 cup water	1 tablespoon lemon juice
1 cup white wine	Beurre manié
2 cups chicken stock	2 tablespoons Madeira
6 whole peppercorns	2 egg yolks

½ cup crème fraîche

1. Put the veal into cold water and bring to a boil. Cook 3 minutes. Discard water and rinse meat in cold water to stop the cooking and to wash off the scum.

2. Cut carrots lengthwise into quarters. Clean leeks (see p. 607). Split lengthwise. Fold over and tie in a bundle. Quarter the onions and cut the garlic in half.

3. Put vegetables and other ingredients down to the mushrooms into saucepan. Add the blanched veal. Bring to a boil, cover, and simmer about 1½ hours. Skim and discard scum as it collects on the surface. Veal, being immature meat, releases more impurities than any other meat as it cooks.

4. Take meat from liquid when done. Discard vegetables and bouquet garni. Strain liquid through a damp cloth. There should be no more than 2 cups. If more, reduce by boiling.

5. Add sliced mushrooms and lemon juice to liquid. Boil 3 minutes. Make beurre manié by mashing together a large chunk of softened butter and 4 tablespoons flour. Stir half into the liquid and then add more to thicken the sauce. It will not take it all. Add the cooked veal and Madeira.

6. Mix together the yolks and crème. Add some hot liquid to them, then stir back into the veal. Heat to thicken, but do not boil. Taste and adjust the seasonings. Serve with rice or boiled noodles.

NOTE: If canned chicken stock is used, little or no salt will be needed, since canned stocks are seasoned.

Wine: Muscadet

VARIATIONS

Leftover roasted chicken given the "blanquette" treatment is a featherbed of goodness. Omit veal from the recipe. Boil the vegetables and liquid about 1½ hours, reducing liquid to 2 cups. Strain and make the sauce with the mushrooms in step 5 (opposite page).

Debone cooked chicken and put meat chunks into a skillet. Add ¼ cup Cognac, heat, and set aflame. When flame dies, add sauce. Add liaison of yolks and cream. Pour onto serving platter. Sprinkle with grated Parmesan cheese and broil to brown the cheese. Serve with rice.

Suprêmes of chicken are equally good under a "blanquette." Omit veal from recipe and make the sauce, as in the above recipe. Sauté the suprêmes in butter (p. 145). Put into shallow baking dish. Pour sauce over, sprinkle with Parmesan cheese and broil. Serve with Gaufrette baskets (p. 240), filled with buttered peas.

CÔTELETTES DE VEAU À LA BONNE FEMME
[*Veal Cutlets in White Wine*]

6 slices bacon, diced
⅛ pound butter
12 small white boiling onions,
    cleaned
1 (8-ounce) box mushrooms
6 veal cutlets
2 turnips
2 tablespoons flour

1 cup white wine
½ cup chicken stock
¼ cup Madeira
1 teaspoon salt
½ teaspoon sugar
Dash of freshly-ground pepper
1 clove garlic, minced
4 potatoes

Chopped parsley

1. Fry bacon crisp. Put into an oven-proof casserole. Pour fat from skillet, wipe out with paper towels, and add the butter. Blanch onions (p. 231), then sauté 5 minutes. Wash mushrooms and remove stems. Add caps to skillet. Cook 5 minutes. Add onions and mushrooms to the casserole. Brown cutlets in the skillet and then place meat on top of the vegetables.

2. Peel turnips. Cut each into 8 wedges. Put on top of veal. Stir flour into skillet. Stir-cook a few minutes, then add white wine, stock, and Madeira. Stir until thickened. Add salt, sugar, pepper, and garlic. Pour over veal. Cover and bake in a 350-degree oven for about 45 minutes.

3. Peel potatoes. Cut into fourths or eighths, and then carve miniature potatoes from them. Add these to the casserole. Cook another 40 minutes, or until potatoes are done. (Cook trimmings from potatoes in seasoned water, drain, and turn into hashed-brown potatoes for another meal.) When done, sprinkle with parsley and serve.

Wine: Montrachet or Meursault

PAUPIETTES DE VEAU
[*Veal Rolls in Red Wine*]

Butter	1 tablespoon tomato paste
2 carrots, diced	½ teaspoon salt
1 onion, diced	⅛ teaspoon pepper
2 onions, minced	Bouquet garni
1 (5-ounce) box of mushrooms, minced, about 1 cup	Pinch of thyme
	24 small pitted green olives
6 veal chops or slices	10 large fresh mushrooms, quartered
Flour	
2 cloves garlic, minced	2 tablespoons Madeira
2 cups red wine	Red and brown food coloring
1 cup chicken stock	Chopped parsley

1. Put ⅛ pound butter into a saucepan. Add carrots and 1 diced onion. Cover and let simmer about 30 minutes.

2. Sauté 2 minced onions in a chunk of butter for 10 minutes and then add the minced mushrooms. Cook an additional 5 minutes, then cool ready to use. This is a Duxelles.

3. If possible, buy slices of veal cut from one muscle, or buy veal chops and remove the meat from the bones. (This may seem wasteful, but you never eat the bones anyway.) Remove any fat, then put each piece of meat on a wet cutting board and pound thin with a wooden kitchen mallet, or with rolling pin or bottom of a heavy pan. Dip mallet into water and it will not stick to the meat. Usually these mallets have a metal end, so use it for the pounding of meat. Flatten all pieces in this fashion. Spread meat with Duxelles mixture. Roll up, jelly-roll fashion. Tie in neat packages. Coat with flour and sauté in a chunk of butter in a skillet to brown all sides.

4. Add 2 tablespoons flour and garlic to the carrot-onion mixture in saucepan. Cook a few minutes, then add remainder of ingredients down to the olives. Once mixture is boiling, reduce heat to a simmer. Add the veal rolls. Set lid askew and simmer about 1½ hours.

5. Put olives into cold water and bring to a boil. Drain and rinse. (This blanches the olives and removes some of the salt.) Sauté quartered mushrooms in a chunk of butter for a few minutes and then add olives. Remove from heat.

6. When veal is done, put it on a hot serving plate. Strain sauce into a clean pan. Heat and then flavor with Madeira. Color a rich brown (p. 3). Spoon about ½ cup sauce into the mushrooms and olives. Heat.

7. Cut strings from veal packages. Glaze veal with some sauce and sprinkle with parsley. Garnish platter with olives and mushrooms. Serve sauce.

Wine: Beaune or Corton

VARIATIONS

PAUPIETTES DE VEAU AUX PRIMEURS

[*Veal Rolls with Spring Vegetables*]

Make Paupiettes de Veau. Leave bouquet garni and thyme out of the sauce. Omit garnish of olives and mushrooms and make the following garnish. Carefully cut assorted vegetables into 1-inch-long strips. Use carrots, green beans, new green onions, turnips, and cucumbers. Cook each separately in seasoned water until done and then glaze vegetables with butter. Arrange in neat piles around the veal. Serve sauce separately.

Wine: Beaune

PAUPIETTES DE VEAU CÔTE D'AZUR

[*Sausage-stuffed Veal Rolls*]

Omit filling of onions and mushrooms in basic Paupiettes de Veau recipe, and substitute the following. Cut crusts from 2 slices bread. Soak in cream and then squeeze dry. Combine with ½ pound lean ground pork, ¼ teaspoon salt, dash of pepper, 1 minced onion, 1 tablespoon chopped parsley, 1 egg white, 1 minced clove garlic, and 2 tablespoons Madeira. Coat veal slices with this mixture, roll, tie, and cook like Paupiettes de Veau (p. 165). Garnish sauce with blanched, pitted green olives, and sautéed whole mushrooms. Serve over veal rolls.

Wine: Château Giscours

PAUPIETTES DE VEAU MARIE-LOUISE

[*Veal Rolls with Sautéed Artichokes*]

Make Paupiettes Côte d'Azur, but omit olive and mushroom garnish. Fill 6 sautéed artichoke bottoms with Duxelles (p. 286). Top artichokes with cooked paupiettes, glaze with sauce, and sprinkle with parsley. Serve remainder of sauce separately.

Wine: Mercurey

PAUPIETTES DE VEAU RICHELIEU

[*Veal Rolls with Sautéed Tomatoes*]

Make Paupiettes Côte d'Azur. When ready to serve, cut 3 large unpeeled tomatoes in half. Squeeze out seeds and water. Sauté in butter seasoned with 1 minced clove garlic, salt, and pepper. Cook cut side down for about 3 minutes, then turn and heat a few minutes. To serve, set cooked paupiettes into each tomato half. Top with a slice of truffle and glaze with sauce. Add blanched green olives to remainder of the sauce and serve separately. Omit mushrooms.

NOTE: Paupiettes may also be made from thin slices of pounded pork, beef, or chicken suprêmes. If using chicken, stuff with Duxelles, and simmer 1 hour. Omit olive garnish, but add the mushrooms.

Wine: *Château Lascombes*

VEAU SAUTÉ
[*Sautéed Veal*]

Veal is easy to sauté, but the garnishings take time. The recipes that follow are traditional and famous. Their garnishings are many, so do them first and then sauté the veal.

CÔTE DE VEAU À LA PROVENÇALE
[*Veal Cutlets Provençale*]

6 veal cutlets, or steaks cut from	Flour
one muscle	¼ cup Madeira
4 onions	¼ cup white wine
4 tablespoons olive oil	¼ cup chicken stock
4 tomatoes, peeled and diced	Salt and pepper to taste
3 cloves garlic, minced	6 slices lemon
Butter	Minced parsley

1. If possible, buy thin slices of veal cut from one muscle. If not possible, then buy veal chops and remove the meat from the bones. Pound veal to ⅛-inch thickness (step 3, p. 165).

2. Peel onions. Cut down in thin wedges. Sauté in skillet with 2 tablespoons olive oil. Cover and cook about ½ hour. Put tomatoes into another skillet with remainder of olive oil. Cook tomatoes about 20 minutes and then pour into strainer and let juices drain out.

3. Put drained tomatoes and garlic into skillet with a chunk of butter. Bring to a boil and then simmer while veal is cooking.

4. Coat pounded veal slices with flour. Heat chunk of butter in skillet. Add veal slices. Sauté each side about 5 minutes.

5. Put veal down the middle of a hot serving platter. Add Madeira, white wine, and stock to skillet. Boil to reduce the liquid to half. Season with salt and pepper. Taste and adjust seasonings.

(continued)

6. Put a tablespoon of tomatoes on every other end of each veal steak, and put a tablespoon of onions on the alternating ends. Strain pan liquid down the middle and decorate each steak with a slice of lemon sprinkled with minced parsley.

Wine: Hermitage or Chianti (Italian)

ESCALOPES DE VEAU À LA VIENNOISE
[*Breaded Veal Cutlets*]

6 thin veal slices (cut from	1 teaspoon vegetable oil
rump roast)	½ cup flour
1 egg white	1 cup fine dry bread crumbs
½ teaspoon salt	⅛ pound butter
⅛ teaspoon pepper	2 tablespoons vegetable oil

Garnishings

2 hard-cooked eggs	6 rolled anchovies
6 slices lemon	12 pitted green olives

Minced parsley

1. Pound veal slices with a mallet, rolling pin, or the bottom of a heavy pan to ⅛-inch thickness. Sprinkle the steaks with water and the pounder will not stick, or dip pounder in water.

2. Combine egg white, salt, pepper, and 1 teaspoon oil on a dinner plate. Put flour on another plate, crumbs on still another. Put butter and 2 tablespoons oil into large skillet ready to heat.

3. Prepare garnishings. Mash yolks of eggs through a sieve. Chop the whites. Put on separate plates. Cut each lemon slice almost in half, keeping rind intact. Remove the fruit sections from one half and wrap the empty rind around an anchovy. Put on plate ready to use. Cut olives in half. Put into cold water and bring to a boil. Once water is boiling, drain and run cold water into the pan. Drain and put olives on plate ready to use. Mince parsley ready to use.

4. Heat butter and oil to hot. Whip the egg white mixture with a table fork, creating a froth on top. Dip the veal steaks in flour, then in the frothy egg white, and then in the crumbs. Pat crumbs into the veal steaks. Sauté in hot fat. Brown both sides, then put steaks down middle of a hot platter.

5. Place lemon half cuddling anchovy in center of each steak. On each end of the platter put rows of egg white, parsley, egg yolk, and then a row of halved olives. Serve some of each garnish with each veal steak. This is very pretty.

Wine: Beaune or Bardolino (Italian)

MÉDAILLONS DE VEAU ST. FIACRE

[*Tournedos of Veal*]

The garnishings for this dish are ambitious. Do them first.

Garnishings

6 fried bread rounds	Cassolette cups
Butter	6 veal tournedos
Potatoes Parisienne	2 tablespoons vegetable oil
6 artichoke bottoms	½ cup chicken stock
Assorted diced spring vegetables	½ cup Madeira
Salt and sugar	Beurre manié

1. Cut 2-inch rounds of bread from firm-type bread. Butter, then fry in skillet. When brown, put on a cooky sheet and set in 250-degree oven to keep warm and to dry out.

2. Prepare ½ recipe of Potatoes Parisienne (p. 237). If using fresh artichokes, see p. 263 for preparation. If using canned, wash them in cold water and sauté in a chunk of butter.

3. Dice vegetables uniformly. Use carrots, green beans, peas and turnips. Cook together in water seasoned with a chunk of butter, salt, and 1 teaspoon sugar. When done, drain, sauté in butter, and keep warm. These will be spooned into cassolette cups or spooned onto the platter. If you have a cassolette iron, make the cups now (p. 367).

4. Veal tournedos may be bought at fancy food shops, or ordered from fancy packers. However, if you can't get them, buy 6 (¾-inch-thick) cutlets, and de-bone them. Sauté these medallions in oil and a chunk of butter. Lightly brown, then cook about 10 minutes on each side. Serve these medium-well done, or pinkish. Put on hot platter when done.

5. Add stock and Madeira to skillet. Boil 5 minutes, then thicken with beurre manié. Slide toast rounds under each veal medallion.

6. Top each with an artichoke bottom. Fill with potatoes and spoon sauce over potatoes.

7. Put vegetables into cassolette cups and set on platter, or spoon them around the veal.

Wine: Fleurie

CÔTE DE VEAU POJARSKI
[*Ground-veal Cutlets*]

2 pounds veal, ground twice	Flour
1 teaspoon salt	3 tablespoons vegetable oil
⅛ teaspoon pepper	Chunk of butter
½ cup crème fraîche, or sour cream	¼ cup Madeira

Pojarski Sauce

⅛ pound butter	Salt and pepper to season
1 cup sliced mushrooms	½ cup crème fraîche, or
½ cup Madeira	whipping cream
¼ cup white wine or vermouth	Beurre manié
½ teaspoon sugar	Minced parsley

1. Have all fat and tendons removed from veal before it is ground. If you have an electric meat grinder, grind the meat yourself.

2. Put veal, salt, pepper, and crème into large mixer bowl. Blend ingredients together. Remove beaters and use a wooden spoon to mash the ingredients against the side of the bowl and to make a thick paste of the veal and crème.

3. Divide the mixture into 8 portions. With the spoon, put a portion on a floured marble slab (it's cold) or a plate. Using the spoon, shape the meat into an elongated hamburger. Flour both sides and then pinch one end into the shape of a cutlet. (Try not to use hands to mold the meat for their warmth mats the meat and causes it to be heavy.) Repeat for each portion.

4. Heat oil and chunk of butter in a skillet. Add floured cutlets. Do not crowd the pan. Sauté each side about 7 minutes, or until browned and done. Add ¼ cup Madeira and heat for 3 minutes. Lift cutlets from the skillet to a hot platter. Keep warm.

5. Add ⅛ pound butter, mushrooms, ½ cup Madeira, ¼ cup white wine, sugar, salt, and pepper to skillet. Boil hard, reducing liquids to about ½ cup. Stir in ½ cup crème. Heat and thicken with bit of beurre manié. Spoon over each cutlet and serve. Sprinkle with minced parsley.

NOTE: Ground breast of chicken or pork may be substituted for the veal. Shape like chicken breasts or like chops. Mushrooms may be omitted from the sauce, the sauce served plain, or minced truffles added.

Wine: Hermitage Blanc or Brouilly

VARIATION

The traditional Pojarski recipe is very delicate. For a change, add some minced green onion tops, minced parsley, and 2 egg whites to the veal. The result will be something like a souffléed burger, juicy and delicious, though not very French. Serve with the plain sauce.

FOIE DE VEAU
[*Calf's Liver*]

Calf's liver, like kidneys, is best when sautéed or broiled. Serve it medium or rare, but never well done or it will resemble rubber. Peel the tissuelike skin from the outside of the liver, otherwise it will contract when cooked and the slices will be warped.

Liver may be served with any of the Rognon sauces (pp. 181–82), with vegetables, or crisp bacon. The garnish gives the name to the dish when there is a garnish.

FOIE DE VEAU GRILLÉ
[*Broiled Calf's Liver*]

6 (½-inch-thick) slices calf's liver	Melted butter
Salt and pepper to taste	

1. Preheat broiler for 10 minutes. Peel skin from liver slices. Dip each slice in melted butter. Lay slices on hot broiler. Cook 3 inches from the heat for 3 minutes. Do not turn. (Heat of broiler cooks the slices on the underneath side.) Season when done. Place on hot serving platter.

2. Serve broiled liver with crisp bacon, sautéed onions, with Chutney or Maître d'Hôtel butter (p. 39).

Wine: Fleurie

FOIE DE VEAU SAUTÉ

[*Sautéed Calf's Liver*]

6 (½-inch-thick) slices calf's liver	¼ pound butter
Flour	2 tablespoons vegetable oil

Salt and pepper to taste

Remove thin skin from around liver slices. Coat liver with flour. Heat butter and oil to hot. Add floured liver slices. Brown both sides and they are done, about 3 minutes per side. Do not overcook. Season after liver is on the serving platter.
Wine: Volnay

VARIATIONS

FOIE DE VEAU AU BEURRE BLANC

[*Sautéed Liver with Beurre Blanc Sauce*]

Prepare sauce (p. 35) and then sauté 6 liver slices. Serve sauce separately.
Wine: Château Carbonnieux

FOIE DE VEAU SAUTÉ AUX FINES HERBES

[*Sautéed Liver with Herbs*]

Cut 6 slices of liver into ½-inch strips across the slices. Flour and sauté for about 4 minutes. Put on hot platter. Melt chunk of butter in clean skillet. Add juice of ½ lemon. Heat. Sprinkle minced parsley and chopped chives over liver. Pour over hot lemon-seasoned butter. Sprinkle with salt and freshly-ground pepper.
Wine: Pomerol

FOIE DE VEAU FLAMBÉ

[*Flamed Liver*]

Cut 6 liver slices into ½-inch strips, flour, and sauté in butter for about 3 minutes. Sprinkle with about 1 teaspoon sweet basil, pour over ½ cup Cognac, heat to volatilize some of the alcohol, and then set aflame. Stir in 4 tablespoons crème fraîche, season, and serve.
Wine: Moulin-à-Vent

FOIE DE VEAU À LA LYONNAISE
[*Calf's Liver with Onions*]

Slice 3 large onions into rings. Simmer in a chunk of butter, covered, for about 30 minutes. Sprinkle with salt and pepper. Add about 1 teaspoon sugar during the last 10 minutes of cooking and let onions caramelize. Don't let them burn. Add juice of ¼ lemon. Cut 6 liver slices into strips, flour, and sauté in a chunk of butter for 4 minutes. Put on hot serving plate and spoon onions over the top. Sprinkle with minced parsley, season, and serve.

Wine: Chianti (Italian)

RIS DE VEAU
[*Sweetbreads*]

The sweetbread, or thymus gland, consists of two parts. The "heart" or round gland is superior in quality to the elongated "throat" gland. In French cooking the "throat" would be used in braised dishes, while the "heart" would be used to sauté or grill. But we do not make a distinction. Unlike most delicate meats, sweetbreads improve in flavor when cooked a long time. They are at their best when braised, but they may also be broiled or sautéed. In French cooking sweetbreads are always blanched before they are used in recipes. This parboiling firms the flesh and helps keep the meat from falling apart as it cooks. Some nationalities do not believe in blanching sweetbreads. They feel some flavor is lost in the process. This may be true, but in my opinion sweetbreads are a superior product when blanched.

Select sweetbreads as white and as free of bloodstains as possible. Let stand under cold running water for about an hour; then they are ready to be blanched.

To blanch them, put sweetbreads into a saucepan and cover with cold water. Add 1 teaspoon salt, bring to a boil and then immediately drain and run cold water into the pan to cool them. When cool, remove the thin outer skin and cut away all cartilage, tubes, and connective tissue. They are then ready to use in recipes.

RIS DE VEAU BRAISÉS À LA SAUCE MADÈRE

[Braised Sweetbreads in Madeira Sauce]

4 pairs veal sweetbreads or	Small bouquet garni
6 pairs of lamb sweetbreads	Pinch of thyme
2 onions, diced	½ teaspoon salt
2 carrots, diced	Dash of pepper
⅛ pound butter	1 cup Madeira
4 tablespoons flour	2 tablespoons Cognac
1 clove garlic, minced	Red and brown food coloring
2 cups chicken stock	Beurre manié

1. Wash sweetbreads, blanch, and trim according to preceding instructions. Sauté onions and carrots in butter for about 20 minutes. Stir in flour. Cook a few minutes and then add garlic and stock. Stir until thickened. Add remainder of ingredients down to the Madeira. Add the throat, or large, sweetbreads. Cook 10 minutes and then add the heart, or smaller, sweetbreads. Set lid askew and cook 30 minutes.

2. Boil Madeira, reducing it by half. When sweetbreads are done, remove them from the sauce and slice or cut into chunks. Strain sauce. Stir in reduced Madeira and Cognac and color sauce a rich dark brown (p. 3). Adjust seasonings and thickness of sauce with beurre manié. Add sweetbreads. Heat and serve with whole boiled potatoes. Or omit potatoes and serve under glass.

Wine: Beaujolais

VARIATIONS

RIS DE VEAU DEMIDOFF

[Sweetbreads with Vegetables]

Blanch sweetbreads and braise as in preceding recipe. Thinly slice 6 carrots, cook in seasoned water and then sauté in butter. Peel 6 turnips. Cut into fourths and then trim each piece round like a carrot. Slice these turnip rounds the same thickness as the carrots. Cook in seasoned water and then sauté in butter. Sauté 2 sliced onions in butter. When sweetbreads are done, remove from sauce and slice, or cut into chunks. Strain sauce. Stir in reduced Madeira and Cognac, and color sauce. Arrange sweetbreads on serving platter. To sauce add cooked vegetables and 2 minced truffles. Heat. Pour over sweetbreads and serve.

Wine: Clos des Lambrays

RIS DE VEAU À LA FLORENTINE
[*Sweetbreads with Spinach*]

Blanch sweetbreads and braise as in preceding recipes. Cook 2 pounds fresh spinach (see p. 256), or 2 packages frozen spinach, in seasoned water. When done, drain and sauté in butter. Make Mornay sauce (p. 18). Arrange a bed of spinach on oven-proof platter. Slice sweetbreads, or cut into chunks, and arrange over the spinach. Coat with Mornay sauce, sprinkle with grated Parmesan cheese and broil to brown the cheese and sauce. Thin the remaining Mornay sauce with cream and serve separately. (Strain the braising sauce and freeze to use at another time. It is basically a Demi-glace sauce. Add reduced Madeira, Cognac, and coloring at the time it is to be used.)

Wine: Beaune

RIS DE VEAU DES GOURMANDS
[*Sweetbreads with Pâté and Truffle Sauce*]

Blanch sweetbreads and braise as in above recipes. Cook asparagus spears (p. 247). Drain and butter, ready to reheat and serve. Slice sweetbreads when done. Flour, then sauté them in butter. Strain braising liquids. Add reduced Madeira, Cognac, and 2 minced truffles, and color the sauce. Sauté slices of pâté de foie gras. Put sweetbread slices around hot buttered asparagus spears. Top sweetbread slices with sautéed pâté and glaze with sauce. Extra sauce is served separately.

Wine: Echézeaux

RIS DE VEAU À LA FINANCIÈRE
[*Sweetbreads in a Crust*]

4 pairs veal sweetbreads or 6 pairs
of lamb sweetbreads

Veal Quenelles

⅛ pound butter

4 tablespoons flour

½ teaspoon salt

Dash of pepper and of paprika

Drop of red food coloring

1 cup cold water

½ pound veal, ground twice

5 large egg whites

6 cups chicken stock

1 cup water

Garnishings and Finish

½ pound mushrooms, quartered

Chunk of butter

20 pitted green olives

6 cocks' combs (canned)

2 tablespoons Cognac

6 tablespoons Madeira

Red and brown food coloring

3 truffles, sliced

Beurre manié

Prepared vol-au-vent

1. Blanch sweetbreads and braise as in Madère recipe (p. 174).

2. To make quenelles, melt ⅛ pound butter in small skillet. Stir in flour. Cook 3 minutes without browning. Add salt, pepper, paprika, and a drop of red food coloring to 1 cup water. Stir into butter-flour mixture. Stir-cook until very thick. Pour onto plate, cover with foil and refrigerate until cold. This is a panade and it should be pinkish in color so it does not dilute the color of the veal.

3. Put veal and an equal amount of the cold panade into a blender container or small mixer bowl. Add 1 egg white at a time and blend. Mixture will hold 4 or 5 egg whites. Poach quenelles in a combination of stock and 1 cup water. See p. 116 for details on cooking quenelles. This recipe makes about 6 dozen small quenelles. Put about 3 dozen quenelles on plate ready to use. Refrigerate remaining quenelles in stock and use in a day or so.

4. Sauté mushrooms in butter for 2 minutes. Add to plate. Put olives and cocks' combs in cold water and bring to a boil to blanch them. Drain, rinse in cold water, and then drain again. Put on plate, ready to use. (Cocks' combs are difficult to acquire. They are an essential part of the garnish for this dish, but not an essential food. The dish will not be ruined if omitted, but it will not be as pretty.)

5. When sweetbreads are done, cut in halves and then in chunks. Put into a large skillet. Add the quenelles, mushrooms, Cognac, and 6 tablespoons Madeira. Heat to perfume contents of the pan and blaze.

6. Strain sauce in which sweetbreads were cooked. Add the reduced Madeira from the Madère recipe. Color sauce a rich red brown. Spoon half the sauce over the sweetbreads. Use just enough sauce to coat ingredients, but do not swim the foods in sauce. Stir in the blanched olives and sliced truffles. Taste and adjust the seasonings. Heat and adjust thickness of sauce with beurre manié.

7. Fill prepared vol-au-vent (p. 351) just before serving. (It can be made days in advance.) Place the cocks' combs on top. Serve the extra sauce separately.

NOTE: When serving a vol-au-vent give each guest a piece of the crust. Break it carefully around the top and then gradually get to the bottom.

Wine: Romanée-Conti

RIS DE VEAU GRILLÉS ET SAUTÉS
[*Broiled and Sautéed Sweetbreads*]

Sweetbreads require special treatment before they are broiled or sautéed. As in all sweetbread recipes they are first blanched, but then they are cooked before they are broiled or sautéed. The second cooking may be done in Madeira sauce, in chicken stock, or by the following recipe.

RIS DE VEAU POCHÉS
[*Poached Sweetbreads*]

4 pairs veal sweetbreads or 6 pairs of lamb sweetbreads

Seasoned water

4 cups water	2 sprigs parsley
1 carrot, diced	½ teaspoon salt
1 onion, minced	½ teaspoon sugar

1. Blanch and trim sweetbreads (p. 173). Boil water with vegetables and seasonings for 15 minutes, then add the blanched sweetbreads. Simmer for about 15 minutes.

2. Drain and cool. Normally, in French cooking the cooled sweetbreads would be placed between two plates, weighted down and refrigerated. I find wrapping them tightly in foil or transparent wrap an easier method of pressing them tight. Once cold and firm the sweetbreads are ready to slice and broil or sauté. Cook according to one of the following recipes.

VARIATIONS

RIS DE VEAU GRILLÉS

[*Broiled Sweetbreads*]

Prepare sweetbreads for broiling as in preceding recipe. Preheat broiler 10 minutes. Dip sliced sweetbreads into melted butter and then lay them on a hot broiler. Cook each side about 5 minutes at 2 inches from the heat. Baste each side once with melted butter during cooking time. Serve broiled sweetbreads with one of the following hot butter sauces: Beurre Blanc, Currie, or Meunière (pp. 35–37); or as follows.
Wine: Clos de Tart

RIS DE VEAU À LA BÉARNAISE

[*Sweetbreads with Béarnaise*]

Broiled sweetbreads with Béarnaise sauce (p. 24).
Wine: Echézeaux

RIS DE VEAU À L'ITALIENNE

[*Sweetbreads in Tomato Sauce*]

Broiled sweetbreads with Sauce Italienne (p. 31).
Wine: Valpolicella (Italian)

RIS DE VEAU PORTUGAISE

[*Sweetbreads in Portugaise Sauce*]

Broiled sweetbreads with Portugaise sauce (p. 31).
Wine: Fleurie

RIS DE VEAU ROSSINI

[*Sweetbreads with Pâté*]

Broil sweetbreads and top with pâté as in the Tournedos Rossini recipe (p. 222).
Wine: Chambertin

RIS DE VEAU SAUTÉS

[*Sautéed Sweetbreads*]

Prepare sweetbreads for sautéing as in recipe on p. 177. Dust slices with flour, dip into one slightly beaten egg white, and then into dry bread crumbs. Sauté in ⅛ pound butter and 2 tablespoons oil. Cook each side about 5 minutes. Serve with lemon wedges or one of the hot butter sauces (pp.35–37). See possibilities under Ris de Veau Grillés. The sauce gives its name to the dish.

Wine: Volnay

RIS DE VEAU À LA BONNE FEMME

[*Sweetbreads in Cream Sauce*]

Sautéed sweetbreads served with Bonne Femme sauce (p. 21).
Wine: Pommard Blanc

RIS DE VEAU À LA CRÈME

[*Sweetbreads in Cream*]

Prepare sweetbreads for sautéing as in recipe on p. 177, then sauté. Wipe browned bits from skillet with paper towels. Add 2 tablespoons Cognac. Heat and set ablaze. When flame dies, add 4 tablespoons Madeira and 4 tablespoons crème fraîche or whipping cream. Heat, and pour over sweetbreads. Decorate with carved mushrooms (p. 281). (Carve the mushrooms and cook 3 minutes with the sweetbreads when they are poached. Lift out and cool in cold water ready to use.)

Wine: Meursault

RIS DE VEAU AUX CHAMPIGNONS
[*Sweetbreads in Mushroom Sauce*]

Serve sautéed sweetbread slices with mushroom sauce (p. 20).
Wine: Puligny-Montrachet

RIS DE VEAU À LA MADÈRE

[*Sweetbreads in Madeira Sauce*]

Serve sautéed sweetbreads with Sauce Madère (p. 30).
Wine: Côte Rôtie

RIS DE VEAU À LA PÉRIGUEUX

[*Sweetbreads in Truffle Sauce*]

Sautéed sweetbreads served with Sauce Périgueux (p. 30).
Wine: Les Bonnes Mares

ROGNONS DE VEAU
[*Kidneys*]

In the cooking of sweetbreads they are usually braised in a sauce before they are sautéed. In the cooking of kidneys the reverse is true. They are usually sautéed or broiled and then added to a sauce.

Unlike sweetbreads, kidneys toughen to the consistency of leather if cooked for a long time. They are best when sautéed or grilled.

ROGNONS DE VEAU SAUTÉS

[*Sautéed Kidneys*]

6 veal kidneys or 10 lamb kidneys
⅛ pound butter

2 tablespoons vegetable oil
Salt and pepper to taste

1. Remove the skin and fat from the kidneys. Cut in half the long way and then cut in ⅛-inch-thick slices.

2. Heat butter and oil in a heavy skillet to very hot, but not smoking. Add the kidneys. Stir-cook for no longer than 5 minutes. They are done when they are hot. Sprinkle with salt and pepper.

3. Pour contents of pan into a strainer in the sink. Let kidneys drain. Never use juice from the kidneys. It has an ammonia odor. Kidneys are now ready to be added to a prepared sauce, to be flamed, or to be tossed in butter. They are not cooked again, only reheated.

VARIATIONS

ROGNONS DE VEAU AUX CHAMPIGNONS

[*Kidneys in Mushroom Sauce*]

Sauté kidneys and let them drain. Put chunk of butter into skillet. Add 2 minced shallots (or 1 onion), 2 cups sliced mushrooms, and 1 cup white wine. Boil, reducing liquid to half. Season with salt and pepper. Add liaison of 2 egg yolks and 3 tablespoons crème fraîche or whipping cream. Add sautéed kidneys. Stir-cook until hot, but do not boil. Taste and adjust seasonings. Serve on toast or in croustades as first course.

Wine: Gevrey-Chambertin

ROGNONS DE VEAU À LA MADÈRE

[*Kidneys in Madeira Sauce*]

Prepare Madeira sauce (p. 30). Sauté kidneys and let them drain. When ready to serve, add kidneys to sauce and heat. Serve sprinkled with minced parsley.

Wine: Côte Rôtie

ROGNONS FLAMBÉS

[*Flamed Kidneys*]

Cut the kidneys into pieces the size of quartered mushrooms. Sauté and then drain. Quarter 1 dozen fresh mushrooms. Sauté in a chunk of butter. Stir in ½ teaspoon flour. Add the sautéed kidneys. Grind fresh pepper over kidneys and sprinkle with salt. Add ¼ cup cognac and set aflame. When flame dies add ½ cup crème fraîche or whipping cream. Heat, but do not boil. Serve in croustades sprinkled with parsley. Serve as first course.

Wine: Echézeaux

ROGNONS DE VEAU GRILLÉS
[*Broiled Kidneys*]

6 veal kidneys or 10 lamb kidneys   **⅛ pound butter, melted**
Salt and pepper to taste

1. Remove skin and fat from kidneys. Cut them lengthwise in half. Run skewers through them lengthwise to prevent their curling as they cook. If they are small, put 2 or 3 halves on each skewer. Brush all surfaces with melted butter.

2. Heat broiler for 10 minutes. Put kidneys, rounded side down, on broiler. Cook 3 inches from heat for about 5 minutes. Do not turn. If grilling over hot coals, cook each side about 3 minutes. Baste often with melted butter. Sprinkle with salt and pepper when done. Serve according to one of the following recipes. The sauce gives the name to the dish.

VARIATIONS
ROGNONS DE VEAU À LA MEUNIÈRE
[*Kidneys with Parsley Butter*]

Heat ¼ pound butter and juice of ½ lemon in a skillet. Put broiled kidneys on hot serving platter, sprinkle with minced parsley, salt, and pepper, and then pour over hot butter-lemon mixture.
Wine: Moulin-à-Vent

ROGNONS DE VEAU HENRI IV
[*Kidneys with Béarnaise Sauce*]

Serve broiled kidneys with Béarnaise sauce (p. 24). Make the sauce before broiling the kidneys.
Wine: Châteauneuf-du-Pape

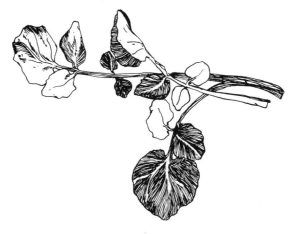

Porc

[*Pork*]

Pig is the only critter on God's green earth that goes whole hog for mankind. From tail to snout he is edible; his bristles become brushes; and only his squeal is wasted. As Charles Lamb admonished in his "Dissertation on Roast Pig":

> Pig, let me speak your praise . . .
> > Your sauce should be considered
> Therefore, banish dear cook, I beseech you,
> > The whole onion tribe and
> Barbecue your hog . . . with
> > Plantations of the rank and guilty garlic.

RÔTI DE PORC

[*Roast Pork*]

And, like Charles Lamb, I too prefer pork with garlic. In the Loire Valley, where honey is a specialty, one enjoys roast pork flavored with garlic and glazed with honey.

Pork is not considered company fare, and is usually not featured on menus in the better French restaurants. Consequently, not many pork recipes come to us from France.

If it weren't for the fact that the French need pigs for hams, pâté, sausage, and truffle hunting, I doubt that they would even bother to raise them. Our hams are not the least bit like French hams, but they are superb when treated in the French manner.

Pork must be cooked well done. Allow 30 minutes per pound or a thermometer reading of 180 degrees. Well done does not mean overcooked.

From my friends in the Loire Valley I learned this recipe. It continues to be one of our favorites.

CARRÉ DE PORC À L'AIL
[*Roast Pork with Garlic*]

1 (4-pound) center-cut pork loin
2 cloves garlic, sliced thin
6 tablespoons honey

¼ cup Madeira
1 cup stock
Salt and pepper

Recipe of whole boiled potatoes

1. To make carving easier, have butcher saw backbone of roast down to, and through, the chop bones, but do not completely cut it off. The skin will hold it in place.

2. Put some slices of garlic between backbone and meat. Using a pointed knife, make pockets in the covering of fat on top. Into each of these gashes place a slice of garlic.

3. Put roast in shallow roasting pan. Roast in a preheated 450-degree oven for 30 minutes. Reduce temperature to 350 degrees. Coat with honey. Cook another 30 minutes, then reduce heat to 325 degrees. Coat again with honey and cook at this temperature for 1 hour, or until done. Cook potatoes (p. 236).

4. Thirty minutes before the roast is done, add the Madeira and stock. The honey will have caramelized in the pan to give good color to the sauce. Add boiled potatoes to the pan. Turn to color all surfaces. When meat is done, put on hot platter. Remove the backbone from the roast. Add potatoes to platter.

5. Skim fat from pan liquid, season, and serve this thin sauce separately. Sautéed tomatoes (p. 271) make the perfect vegetable accompaniment.

Wine: Beaujolais or Valpolicella (Italian)

VARIATIONS
FILET DE PORC RÔTI
[*Pork Fillets with Garlic*]

Have butcher tie two pork tenderloins together, head to tail, thus making a roast of uniform thickness. Stuff slices of garlic between the two pieces of meat and then place in a V-shaped roasting rack. Coat with butter. Lay slices of salt pork over the top. Put into a 450-degree oven and immediately reduce heat to 350 degrees. Roast about 1¼ hours, or until done. For the last 20 minutes of cooking, remove salt pork and coat pork twice with honey. When done, remove strings and garnish with whole boiled potatoes.
Wine: Château Petrus

CARRÉ DE PORC À L'ALSACIENNE
[*Pork Roast with Sauerkraut*]

Make choucroute (p. 194), then roast either a loin or fillets of pork. Surround roast with sauerkraut and garnish with boiled potatoes.
Wine: Liebfraumilch (German)

PORC BRAISÉ
[*Braised Pork*]

Pork loins, fillets, or hams may be substituted in any one of the braised-veal recipes, or simply cooked by the following recipe. If you are using the veal recipes, omit the flour in the sauce recipes and thicken with beurre manié after the sauce has been strained and skimmed of fat. Pork is especially good when braised in a sauce from the Demi-glace family.

CARRÉ DE PORC BRAISÉ
[*Braised Pork Loin*]

1 (3–4-pound) pork loin	Bouquet garni
3 carrots, quartered lengthwise	2 cups white wine or vermouth
2 onions, cut into wedges	Salt and pepper to taste
Several sprigs of parsley	2 tablespoons Madeira
2 cloves garlic, halved	Beurre manié

1. Have butcher saw backbone from roast, but do not cut it off. The bone will hold the roast in shape, and the skin will hold the bone to the roast.

2. Put vegetables, parsley and garlic into a roasting pan. Add roast. Put into 425-degree oven. Brown 30 minutes, then reduce heat to 325 degrees. Add bouquet garni, white wine or vermouth and roast 30 minutes per pound, or a total of 1½ hours at 325 degrees.

3. When done, place roast on platter to rest for 10 minutes. Remove backbone from the meat. Strain liquid into saucepan. Skim fat from liquid. Season with salt and pepper. Add Madeira, heat, and thicken with a bit of beurre manié. Keep sauce on the thin side. Spoon sauce over sliced meat as it is served.

Wine: Beaune or Beaujolais

VARIATIONS

FILET DE PORC BRAISÉ

[*Braised Tenderloins of Pork*]

Substitute 2 tenderloins (tied together) for the loin of pork. Lay tenderloins on top of the vegetables and roast about 1 hour, or until done. Remove strings and serve with thickened sauce.

Wine: Frascati (Italian)

BLANQUETTE DE PORC

[*Pork in White Sauce*]

Make like Veal Blanquette (p. 162), but do not blanch the pork pieces in water. Add them directly to the sauce.

Wine: Grillet

PORC SAUTÉ

[*Sautéed Pork*]

Fried pork chops are as common in the Midwest as fried chicken. Usually a country gravy made with milk accompanies these skillet-fried foods. But for a change treat pork chops to a French sauce from the Demi-glace family.

CÔTES DE PORC SAUTÉES
[*Sautéed Pork Chops*]

6 (¾-inch-thick) pork chops or medallions of tenderloin	Chunk of butter
	2 tablespoons vegetable oil
Flour	Salt and pepper to taste

Flour chops. Heat butter and oil in skillet. Add chops when skillet is hot. Brown and cook each side about 15 minutes. Season with salt and pepper when done.

Wine: Erdener Treppchen (German)

VARIATIONS
CARBONNADES DE PORC À LA PROVENÇALE
[*Pork with Onions and Tomatoes*]

Make like Côte de Veau à la Provençale (p. 167). Buy butterfly-cut pork chops. Dip chops in melted butter and then fine, dry bread crumbs. Sauté in butter and oil. Garnish with sautéed onions and tomatoes like the veal.

Wine: Chianti (Italian)

CÔTES DE PORC À LA BAYONNAISE
[*Marinated Chops*]

In a nonmetal shallow dish put 1 sliced clove garlic, ⅛ teaspoon thyme, 1 bay leaf, 2 tablespoons vegetable oil, 2 tablespoons vinegar, dash of sugar, salt, and pepper. Add 6 pork chops. Turn often and let marinate for about 2 hours.

Dice 2 slices bacon and place in skillet. Fry crisp, then remove from skillet. Save. Blot chops and brown on both sides in bacon fat. Add 2 cups quartered mushrooms. Cover and simmer over low heat for 10 minutes. Add bacon and cook another 10 minutes. Put on serving platter and sprinkle with minced parsley.

Wine: Sancerre

CÔTES DE PORC AUX CHAMPIGNONS
[*Pork Chops with Mushrooms*]

Sauté chops on one side. Cut 2 onions into thin wedges. Turn chops. Add onions to skillet. Cover and cook 10 minutes. Add 2 cups quartered mushrooms. Cover and simmer 10 minutes. Put chops and vegetables on serving platter and sprinkle with minced parsley.

Wine: Muscadet

CÔTES DE PORC À LA SAUCE CHARCUTIÈRE

[*Chops with Pickle Sauce*]

Prepare Sauce Robert (p. 30). Add 3 tablespoons chopped gherkin pickles to sauce and serve with sautéed pork chops.

Wine: Châteauneuf-du-Pape

CÔTELETTES DE PORC À LA BONNE FEMME

[*Pork Chops in White Wine Sauce*]

Make like Côtelettes de Veau à la Bonne Femme (p. 164). Trim fat from pork chops and substitute them for the veal cutlets.

Wine: Vouvray

PAUPIETTES DE PORC

[*Pork Rolls in Red Wine*]

Make like Paupiettes de Veau (p. 165). Variations, see p. 166.

Wine: Château Lagrange or Valpolicella (Italian)

MÉDAILLONS DE PORC SAUTÉS

[*Pork Tenderloins Sautéed*]

3 whole pork tenderloins	2 tablespoons Cognac
Melted butter	3 tablespoons Madeira
Fine dry bread crumbs	2 egg yolks
Chunk of butter	6 tablespoons crème fraîche, or
3 tablespoons vegetable oil	whipping cream
Salt and pepper to taste	Minced parsley

1. Cut ½-inch-thick medallions of pork from the large end of each tenderloin. You should be able to get 4 from each. Reserve tail ends for another meal.

2. Dip the medallions into melted butter and then into crumbs. Heat a chunk of butter and the oil to very hot. Sauté the pork for about 10 minutes on each side. Season with salt and pepper and place on hot serving platter. Wipe out skillet with paper towels. Add Cognac and Madeira. Boil for 2 minutes, then take from heat.

3. Mix yolks and crème in a bowl. Stir, all at once, into skillet. Heat until thickened, but do not boil. Spoon onto each medallion. Sprinkle with minced parsley. Two per serving.

Wine: Riesling (German)

QUENELLES DE PORC
[*Pork Quenelles*]

Ground pork has many uses, but it is at its best in quenelles and in sauced dishes.

6 cups chicken stock	Dash of nutmeg and pepper
½ pound lean pork, ground twice	¼ teaspoon salt
1 shallot, minced	Melted butter
1 whole egg	Bread crumbs
2 egg whites	Chunk of butter
1 tablespoon crème fraîche	2 tablespoons oil

1. Heat chicken stock ready to use in poaching quenelles. Put ground pork, shallot, whole egg, and whites into a blender container, or mixer. Mix well, blending all ingredients together. Keep mixture pushed to the center of the container. Mix in crème, nutmeg, pepper, and salt.

2. Put mixture into a shallow bowl. Read instructions for shaping quenelles (p. 149), but make these quenelles a full teaspoon, then level off the top and push them from the spoon with another wet spoon and into the hot stock. Simmer about 5 minutes. When done, put into bowl of cold water to stop the cooking. They will be about the size of a half dollar.

3. Use these in sauces, or blot them with paper towels, dip in melted butter, then crumbs, and sauté in a chunk of butter and oil. Sauté crisp on both sides and serve with a Béarnaise sauce (p. 24) to 2. This dish is named *Quenelles de Porc à la Béarnaise*.

Wine: Liebfraumilch (German)

VARIATIONS
CÔTES DE PORC POJARSKI
[*Ground Pork Cutlets*]

Prepare according to recipe for Veal Pojarski (p. 170), substituting lean ground pork for the veal. Cook well done.

Wine: Pouilly-Fuissé

FRICADELLES DE PORC
[*Ground Pork Balls*]

Substitute ground pork in the Fricadelles de Boeuf (p. 226). Cook well done.

Wine: Beaujolais

PORC HACHÉ AU VIN ROUGE

[*Ground Pork Burgers in Red Wine Sauce*]

Substitute ground pork in the Bifteck au Vin Rouge (p. 225). Cook well done.

Wine: Chinon

JAMBON
[*Ham*]

Almost every region of France has its own home-cured hams, the most famous being the *jambon* of Bayonne and Toulouse. These hams are cured and usually eaten as hors d'oeuvres.

For cooking purposes the York ham is usually used, and any one of our cured hams can be substituted for it in the recipes that follow. The cold ham found in France that resembles our boiled ham is the famous *jambon de Paris*. It is sold by pork butchers, or at the charcuterie and crémerie shops, under the name of *jambon glacé*.

JAMBON EN CROÛTE
[*Ham in Crust*]

1 whole ham, baked	½ pound butter or margarine
Madère sauce	2 whole eggs
5 cups flour	Ice water
2 teaspoons salt	1 egg yolk

1. Use a whole ham with the bone left in. Bake it, then let it stand at room temperature for about 30 minutes to cool the outside. Prepare the Madère sauce (p. 30) and let it cook while the ham bakes.

2. Blend flour, salt, and butter as for pastry. Add 2 eggs and sufficient water to make a dough. Roll on a floured surface to a thickness of about ⅛ inch and large enough to encase the ham.

3. Trim fat from ham. Carve ham the French way. That is, put ham flat, as it was baked. Cut wedge at shank end and then cut slices off the top of the ham at an angle. Put slices back in place.

4. Cut a piece of foil to fit over slices. Hold the slices in place with the foil and turn ham top side down onto rolled pastry. Leave foil and bring sides of dough up around the ham. Let the shank bone stick out of dough. Trim the dough to fit. Mix yolk and 1 tablespoon water. Coat all edges of dough to be

sealed with egg-water mixture. Seal. Lift ham, turn it over, and place sealed edges down on a buttered cooky sheet.

5. Take some of the trimmed dough and with your hands make a rope of dough about 1 yard long and ¼ inch thick. (Make in 2 pieces and it will be easier to handle.) Arrange this on top of the crust to make a frame above where you believe the cut slices to be. Coat crust and rope with egg-water mixture.

6. Roll some of the trimmed dough pieces to ⅛-inch thickness. With a biscuit cutter, cut out 2-inch circles. Then, using the back of a French chopping knife or a butcher knife, rotate the knife from one position and make marks on the dough to look like a fan, or like a sea shell. Arrange these fans attractively over the dough within the rope frame. Coat with egg-water mixture.

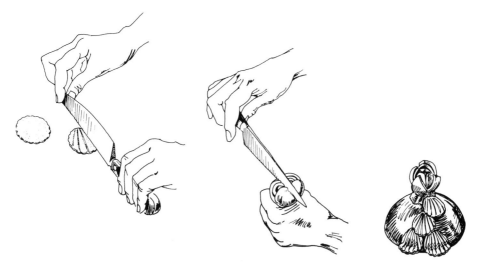

7. Now make a knob with which to lift the dough lid: Roll dough trimmings to ⅟₁₆ inch thick. Cut four 3-inch circles of dough. Coat both sides heavily with flour. Stack these up, then lift them up and push your middle finger up through the middle of the stack, making a kind of balloon about ¾ inch across the top. Squeeze it tight around the bottom with your forefinger and thumb. Then, with a sharp, thin knife, cut a cross in the dough balloon, cutting through all 4 layers of dough, thus making a flower with 16 pie-shaped petals, big petals on the outside and smaller ones at the center. Cut off the dough at the base of the flower. Make a hole in the middle of the lid. Brush crust and base of knob with egg-water mixture and then insert the bottom of the flower knob in the crust. Push the bottom petals down on the dough and open petals. Touch the tips of the petals with egg-water mixture. Give the rest of the crust another coating of egg-water mixture. Bake in a preheated 400-degree oven for about 1 hour. Do not let it get too brown.

(continued)

8. Take ham from oven. Put on serving plate. With a very sharp, thin, knife, cut out the dough at the inside edge of the rope at an angle so that the crust can be replaced and not fall through. Carefully lift out the dough lid, using a spatula: insert spatula under the dough lid and foil, and then use the foil to help lift the lid without breaking it.

9. Once lid is removed, discard foil. Spoon over Madeira sauce to glaze the ham. Replace lid. Lift off lid and serve the ham at the table. Remainder of sauce is served separately.

Wine: Château Margaux

JAMBON À LA MORVANDELLE

[*Ham with Cream Sauce*]

I ate Jambon à la Morvandelle for the first time in the Clos de Vougeot when I was knighted with a grape root and inducted into the noble order of the Confrérie du Tastevin. The festival of the "Trois Glorieuses" that followed the induction ceremonies was a memorable occasion, with wild boar the pièce de résistance. Knowing wild boar is difficult to acquire, I concerned myself with learning the secrets of the ham recipe. If possible, drink a Volnay les Santenots with the ham and thereby enjoy two Burgundian specialties of the village of Nuits-Saint-Georges.

2 shallots, minced	2 teaspoons sugar
2 teaspoons crushed juniper berries	Dash of pepper and of salt
¼ cup red wine	¼ cup Madeira
¼ cup wine vinegar	2 egg yolks
¼ cup chicken stock	4 tablespoons crème fraîche or
Chunk of butter	whipping cream
4 tablespoons flour	8 slices baked ham
1½ cups chicken stock	Grated Gruyère or Parmesan cheese

Chopped parsley

1. Simmer shallots, juniper berries, wine, vinegar, and ¼ cup stock until reduced to ¼ cup. Set aside.

2. Melt butter, and stir in flour. Cook 2 minutes. Add 1½ cups stock, sugar, pepper, and salt. (Remember, the ham is salty.) Stir-cook until thickened.

3. Strain reduced liquid into sauce. Add ¼ cup Madeira. Mix together yolks and crème. Add about ½ cup sauce to yolk mixture. Mix, then stir into the sauce. Heat to thicken, but do not boil. Arrange ham slices in oven-proof dish. Spoon sauce over ham. Sprinkle with grated cheese. Brown under broiler. Serve sprinkled with parsley.

Wine: Volnay les Santenots

PANNEQUETS DE JAMBON

[*Ham Soufflé in Pancakes*]

⅛ pound butter	2 cups ground ham
4 tablespoons flour	1 minced shallot, or small onion
1 cup light cream	1 tablespoon minced parsley
Salt and pepper to taste	2 tablespoons Madeira
Dash of nutmeg	Recipe for crêpes (use 12)
2 egg yolks	Recipe of Champignon sauce

4 egg whites, beaten stiff

1. Melt butter in skillet. Stir in flour. Cook a few minutes. Stir in cream, salt (careful, ham is salty), pepper, and nutmeg. Stir-cook until very thick. Remove from heat. Add a couple of tablespoons sauce to yolks and then stir back into sauce. Add ham, shallot, parsley, and Madeira. To this point the recipe can be made in advance. Cover with a lid and leave until ready to finish recipe.

2. Prepare pannequets or crêpes (p. 365). Freeze what are not used. Make Champignon sauce (p. 16).

3. When ready to serve, beat egg whites. Stir a "gob" into ham mixture and then fold in the rest of the whites. Put about 2 tablespoons ham soufflé down the middle of each crêpe. Bring the sides of the crêpe up over the ham mixture, overlapping them. Put overlapped edge down in a greased oven-proof dish.

4. Put into a 425-degree oven, on the lowest shelf, and bake for about 15 minutes, or until puffed and souffléed.

Serve 2 per person with mushroom sauce spooned over the top. Especially good as luncheon dish accompanied with a tossed salad and dessert.

Wine: Montrachet or Fleurie

CHOUCROUTE GARNIE

[*Sauerkraut Garnished with Ham and Sausages*]

The Germans may have created sauerkraut, but it was certainly the French who made it delectable.

Choucroute

2 No. 2½ cans sauerkraut or	2 cups white wine
3 pounds bulk kraut	2 tablespoons sugar
½ pound lean bacon in one piece	½ teaspoon salt
2 onions	10 whole peppercorns
2 whole cloves	4 sprigs parsley
2 carrots, quartered	1 very small bay leaf, or piece of a
20 juniper berries	big one
2 cups chicken stock	

Garniture

Assorted cooked smoked sausages,	6 smoked pork chops
such as knackwurst, thuringer,	Boiled potatoes
Smokie links, or frankfurters	6 slices boiled ham

1. Put kraut into large kettle and wash in cold water. Drain through colander and put into fresh cold water. Soak about 5 minutes and drain again. Add more water and let stand about 20 minutes. Drain and it is ready to use. Sauerkraut, when cooked in wine, must be washed until it no longer tastes sour with brine.

2. Cut bacon into ¼-inch-thick slices, then cut into ½-inch pieces. Put pieces into cold water and bring to a boil. Drain through sieve. Put into kettle. Cut onions in half. Slice onions down into wedges. Add to bacon. Sauté bacon and onions for about 10 minutes.

3. Squeeze kraut between the palms of your hands to remove the moisture. Add to kettle. Insert cloves into 2 of the carrot pieces, then add carrots, juniper berries (½ cup gin may be substituted for the berries), stock, wine, sugar, and salt. Tie peppercorns, parsley, and bay leaf in cheesecloth or small piece of clean cloth. Add to kettle. Bring to a boil, then cover and bake in a 325-degree oven for about 4 hours.

4. The kraut should be moist, but not wet. Taste and adjust seasonings. It may need salt, depending upon how well the kraut was washed. Discard the carrots and cloth seasoning bag. Usually the juniper berries are not removed, but you may pick them out if you wish.

5. In the last hour of cooking, or after 3 hours, bury the assorted sausages and pork chops in the kraut. Make recipe of boiled potatoes (p. 236). Add ham slices to the kraut the last 10 minutes. Put kraut on large serving platter. Garnish with the sausages and potatoes and fold the ham slices in half and place on the kraut.

Serve with French bread and Alsatian beer and you'll think you're at the Brasserie Lipp, the famous Paris café near the church of St. Germain-des-Prés. If you prefer, drink a German wine.

NOTE: Choucroute is delicious when served with roast duck or goose instead of ham and sausages.

Agneau
[*Lamb*]

Practically every region of France has its own special way of cooking the lambs that frolic in the meadows or graze on the hillsides.

From the picturesque town of Le Puy, in the central plateau region close to the headwaters of the Loire River, we learn that the Auvergne homemaker slips bits of garlic under the skin of lamb and then cooks it.

In the hilly country facing the Pyrénées, the swashbuckling Gascons contentedly herd their sheep and patiently wait for the day when they can enjoy the heartiest of dishes, stuffed shoulder of lamb.

And from the marshy lands around the old fortress of Mont-Saint-Michel, where one hears the beating of waves and the bleating of sheep, we get the famous recipe for agneau près de salée, or lamb from the salty meadows.

In France, the regions and the lamb dishes are many. In America, where the "melting pot" boils, we make a specialty of enjoying the foods of all regions and peoples.

RÔTI D'AGNEAU
[*Roast Lamb*]

Roast lamb is normally garnished with buttered vegetables and Château potatoes. The vegetables are not glazed with the sauce since lamb flavor does not complement vegetables. When rice is served, it goes to the table in a separate dish.

Lamb, like veal, must come from a young animal. But, unlike veal, lamb is a red meat. It should never be served well done, nor should it be served rare. It is best cooked to a delicate pink. Leg of lamb and rolled roasts may be roasted, braised, or cooked on a spit.

Lamb with bone in should cook:

13 minutes per pound for medium, or 155 degrees on thermometer

16 minutes per pound for medium well done, or 165 degrees

Lamb that is deboned and rolled should cook:

25 minutes per pound for medium, or 155 degrees

30 minutes per pound for medium well, or 165 degrees

In France one enjoys a cut of lamb known as *baron,* which is the back half of the lamb. It includes the two legs and both racks of lamb, and usually weighs about 15 pounds. If it is possible to acquire such a cut in your locality tie the legs together and cook it according to the Gigot Rôti or on a spit. Baste with butter. Wrap the top part of the baron (the racks) with foil to retard cooking. Unwrap after 2 hours and then cook to desired doneness.

GIGOT D'AGNEAU RÔTI
[*Roast Leg of Lamb*]

1 (5–6-pound) leg of lamb	Salt and pepper to taste
2 onions, chopped	3 tablespoons Cognac
3 cloves garlic, quartered	1 cup chicken stock
⅛ pound butter	2 tablespoons Madeira

1. Put leg of lamb in a shallow roasting pan. Add onions and garlic to the pan: they should not touch the lamb. Coat lamb with butter and put into a preheated 475-degree oven. Roast 20 minutes and then reduce heat to 350 degrees. Cook 1¼ hours, then test for doneness. Run your finger down into the lamb, along the leg bone. (It won't burn.) If the middle is just warm, the lamb is done. See p. 7 for other ways to test for doneness, or use a thermometer.

2. Place roast, when done, on hot platter and sprinkle with salt and pepper. Add Cognac to pan and heat. Set Cognac aflame. When flame dies, add stock, heat, and scrape brown glaze from pan. Boil a few minutes. Add Madeira. Strain sauce into serving bowl. Skim fat from sauce and serve. Garnish roast as desired, or serve plain.

Wine: Les Bonnes Mares

GIGOT D'AGNEAU PRÉ-SALÉ

[*Salty Roast Leg of Lamb*]

The grass that grows on the meadows around Mont-Saint-Michel is salty because these fields are frequently flooded by the sea. The lambs that graze on these salty meadows have a unique flavor. Legend has it that the meat is seasoned from within because of the salty grass the lambs have eaten.

French chefs are very clever in duplicating the taste of these salt-seasoned lambs. Here is their recipe for making an imitation of the lamb of Mont-Saint-Michel.

1 (5–6-pound) leg of lamb	1 tablespoon boiling water
1 teaspoon salt (sea salt, if possible)	2 carrots, sliced
2 onions, sliced	

1. Run your finger down the leg bone and push the meat away. Dissolve salt in water. Pour this saturated solution down alongside the bone and let it seep into the meat.

2. Put carrots and onions into a shallow roasting pan. Set leg of lamb on top of these vegetables. Roast for ½ hour at 425 degrees, then reduce heat to 350 degrees and cook about 1¼ hours. Test for doneness by running finger down along bone (step 1, p. 197), or use meat thermometer. Serve with thin sauce (Rôti recipe), or with a sauce from the Demi-glace family (pp. 28–30).

Wine: Saint-Émilion

VARIATIONS

As with other roasts of meat, the garnish gives its name to the dish. Roast of lamb may be substituted for the roast beef in its recipes (pp. 210–12), and vice versa. While the roast cooks, prepare the garnish.

GIGOT D'AGNEAU À LA CLAMART

[*Lamb with French Peas*]

Fill tart shells or croustades with Petits Pois à la Français (p. 278). Arrange around roast with fried mashed-potato cakes. Serve with pan sauce from Gigot Rôti (p. 197).

Wine: Beaujolais

GIGOT D'AGNEAU À LA DUBARRY

[*Lamb with Cauliflower*]

Prepare cauliflower balls (p. 266). Arrange around lamb roast. Spoon butter over cauliflower and sprinkle with parsley. Serve with pan sauce (p. 197).
Wine: Morgon

GIGOT D'AGNEAU À LA JARDINIÈRE

[*Lamb with Spring Vegetables*]

With a fluted potato-ball cutter shape carrots and turnips into small balls. Cook these vegetables in chicken stock. Make round potato balls and sauté in butter. Cook peas and butter. Cut green beans into ½-inch lengths. Cook, butter, and arrange vegetables around the lamb, alternating the colors. Serve with Demi-glace sauce (p. 27).
Wine: Nuits-Saint-Georges

GIGOT D'AGNEAU À LA NIVERNAISE

[*Lamb with Carrots*]

Carve carrots in the shape of large olives. Cook them in chicken stock. Drain; add chunk of butter and sprinkle with sugar. Glaze the carrots. Arrange around roasted lamb. Serve with pan sauce (see Gigot Rôti recipe, p. 197).
Wine: Beaujolais

GIGOT D'AGNEAU À LA PORTUGAISE

[*Lamb with Tomatoes*]

Prepare Tomatoes Sauté à la Provençale (p. 271) and Château potatoes (p. 237). Arrange around lamb and serve with Portugaise sauce (p. 31).
Wine: Châteauneuf-du-Pape

AGNEAU BRAISÉ
[*Braised Lamb*]

Shoulder, neck, and breast of lamb are usually braised and used in stew dishes, such as blanquettes, fricassees, and ragouts.

ÉPAULE D'AGNEAU FARCIE

[*Stuffed Shoulder of Lamb*]

1 (3–5-pound) shoulder of lamb, boned   Chunk of butter

Stuffing

½ pound ground pork   ½ teaspoon salt
¼ pound lean ground veal   ⅛ teaspoon pepper
1 shallot or onion, minced   1 egg
2 tablespoons chopped parsley   ¼ cup white wine
1 cup minced mushrooms   2 tablespoons Cognac

Sauce

2 carrots, sliced   ⅛ teaspoon thyme
2 onions, diced   2 cups dry red wine
1 teaspoon sugar   1 cup chicken stock
2 cloves garlic, minced   Beurre manié
1 bay leaf   2 tablespoons Madeira

Chopped parsley

1. If deboning the lamb yourself, remove blade bone first and then the leg bones. Spread meat out on counter, fleshy side up.

2. Mix stuffing ingredients. Blend well. Spread over lamb and roll up like jelly roll. Tie at 1-inch intervals with string and around the meat the long way, making a tight package. Brown lamb roll in butter in roasting pan on top of the range.

3. When roll is brown, remove, and add carrots and onions to pan. Sprinkle sugar over vegetables. Heat to caramelize the vegetables. When they are brown, set lamb on top and add remainder of sauce ingredients, down to beurre manié. Bake in 350-degree oven for about 2½ hours, or until done.

4. When done, put lamb on hot platter and remove strings. Thicken sauce with beurre manié. Add Madeira and strain into sauce boat. Sprinkle lamb with parsley and serve. Garnish platter with browned whole potatoes (p. 237), and glazed whole carrots (p. 229). Degrease sauce and serve.

Wine: Hermitage

AGNEAU NAVARIN
[*Lamb Stew*]

2 pounds cubed lamb	Bouquet garni
2 tablespoons vegetable oil	⅛ teaspoon thyme
Chunk of butter	24 small white boiling onions
1 teaspoon sugar	10 carrots
4 cloves garlic, minced	6 turnips
3 tablespoons flour	6 potatoes
3 cups chicken stock	1 pound green beans
1 teaspoon salt	1 pound fresh peas or 1 package
⅛ teaspoon pepper	frozen peas
1 tablespoon tomato paste	2 tablespoons Madeira

1. In a large skillet, brown lamb in oil and butter. Add sugar to pan and let it caramelize. Spoon off fat. Add garlic and stir in flour. Add stock, salt, pepper, tomato paste, bouquet garni, and thyme. Simmer for about 1 hour.

2. Peel onions and add. Cut carrots and turnips into château shapes (peel, cut in fourths and trim to the size of large olives; see p. 228). Add to lamb.

3. Peel and cut potatoes into château shapes. Add to lamb. Cook another ½ hour or until done. Clean beans and cut into 1-inch lengths. Boil in seasoned water until tender. Cook peas separately in seasoned water until tender. Add green vegetables to lamb the last 5 minutes of cooking time. Remove bouquet garni. Stir in Madeira, taste, adjust seasonings, and serve.

Wine: Pommard

VARIATIONS
AGNEAU À LA BOURGUIGNONNE
[*Lamb in Red Wine Sauce*]

Make according to Beef Bourguignonne (p. 217). Cook 2 hours.
Wine: Gevrey Chambertin

AGNEAU AU CURRIE
[*Curried Lamb*]

To the Navarin recipe add 2 tablespoons curry powder at the time the lamb is added and do not spoon off the fat. Flavor with sherry instead of Madeira.
Wine: Château Grillet

CASSOULET
[*Lamb-Bean Casserole*]

There are three standard varieties of the cassoulet. They are called Castelnaudary, Toulouse, and Carcassonne. Anatole France, the great French literary figure of the nineteenth century, was a devotee of the Castelnaudary. But I prefer the type prepared in Carcassonne. It has everything the others have plus a substantial slab of lamb. It is a real meal in a dish!

3 cups white navy beans	Boiling water
3 pints cold water	4 slices bacon
¼ pound salt pork, sliced	1 pound pork tenderloin
½ pound rind from salt pork	1 pound breast of lamb
2 onions	Salt and pepper to taste
2 cloves	2 onions, diced
2 carrots, cut in chunks	1 clove garlic, minced
6 sprigs of parsley	½ cup tomato paste
1 small bay leaf	1 cup chicken stock
4 cloves garlic, cut in half	6 pork sausages
½ branch celery, diced	¼ roast goose
⅛ teaspoon thyme	Coarse bread crumbs
1 teaspoon salt	Butter

1. Soak the beans overnight in cold water. Drain off liquid the next morning and save. Put beans in large enamel kettle. Add salt pork. Cut the rind into strips and add. Peel onions and stick with cloves. Add onions and carrots. Tie parsley, bay leaf, garlic, celery, and thyme in a piece of cheesecloth. Add to kettle. Add salt and cover with boiling water. Cover with lid and simmer 2 hours.

2. Render fat from bacon slices in a large skillet. Remove bacon and cut into pieces. Cut tenderloin into 6 medallions. Slice breast of lamb into 6 pieces and brown both in bacon fat. Spoon fat from pan. Sprinkle meats with salt and pepper and then add diced onions, minced garlic, tomato paste, and stock. Cover and simmer about ½ hour; then add sausages and cook 15 minutes. If necessary, add stock as it cooks down.

3. Remove carrot chunks, the whole onions, and the bag of seasonings from the beans. Into 6 individual 2-cup cassoulets, or casseroles, put some of the bacon, rind, beans, meats, and goose. Fill with cooking liquid from the beans. Sprinkle each casserole with crumbs and dot with butter. Set casseroles on a cooky sheet.

4. Cover each casserole with foil and bake about 2 hours in a 300-degree oven. (Taste liquids in one casserole, then adjust seasonings by adding them to the bean-soaking liquid.) Keep the casseroles filled with liquid, using the bean-soaking liquid. (You will need most of it.) Serve with a green salad and crusty bread.

NOTE: May be cooked in one large casserole rather than individual ones. When cassoulet is cooked in one pot, it is easier to control the seasonings.

Wine: Châteauneuf-du-Pape

AGNEAU GRILLÉ
[*Broiled or Grilled Lamb*]

Whether for warmth or cooking, heat has always been a problem to France.

Broiled foods as we know them are not common in French households. Steaks and chops are pan-broiled on top of the stove in a skillet that has a grill-like bottom, or they are simply sautéed in a skillet. Restaurants normally use a charcoal grill for broiling steaks and chops.

Lamb chops are at their best grilled over charcoal and next best broiled. Rack of lamb may be grilled, broiled, or cooked on a spit. If you are broiling under heat, care must be taken to prevent charring to the point where the outside of the meat becomes bitter.

Lamb chops may be garnished with any of the garnishes given for broiled steaks, except those glazed with pan sauce. Vegetables that accompany grilled lamb are usually glazed with butter.

BROILING CHART FOR LAMB CHOPS

THICKNESS OF CHOP	DONENESS	INCHES FROM HEAT	MINUTES TO COOK	
			1st Side	*2nd Side*
¾ inch	Medium	3	3	2
	Medium Well		3	3
1 inch	Medium	3	3	3
	Medium Well		4	3
1½ inches	Medium	3	4	4
	Medium Well		5	4
2 inches	Medium	4	6	4
	Medium Well		7	5
2½ inches	Medium	4	7	5
	Medium Well		8	6

1. For well-done chops add 1 minute to medium-well cooking times.

2. Preheat broiler for 10 minutes, then add chops. A solid metal rack, which most broilers now have, is not as good for broiling as the wire racks. The solid metal does not allow the heat to circulate around the meat. When a chop is placed on the metal, it sautés one side, then as rack cools under the chop, the rack tends to steam the chop. If possible, get a wire rack to use when broiling chops.

3. Have chops at room temperature. Oil chops on both sides, then place on hot grill. Score fat to keep chops flat.

4. For out-of-doors cooking and cold chops, add about 1 minute to cooking times. Air circulation around chops reduces the intensity of the heat. Cold chops take longer.

5. Salt and pepper chops *after* they are cooked.

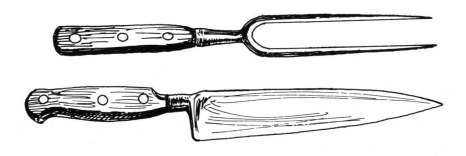

CARRÉ D'AGNEAU GRILLÉ
[*Broiled Rack of Lamb*]

2 racks of lamb	1 tablespoon boiling water
1 teaspoon salt	Melted butter
	Watercress

1. If there is a heavy layer of fat on the lamb, trim it to ⅛ inch. Dissolve salt in boiling water. (I have a hypodermic needle and simply make injections of salt water into the meat along the bone.) With a kitchen fork make holes along the bones and pour the salt solution into the meat, but not on the outside. This salts the meat from the inside and it tastes like the lamb of Mont-Saint-Michel. Of course, you don't have to bother to do this.

2. Preheat broiler 10 minutes. Coat lamb with butter. Broil about 6 inches from heat. Cook top side for about ½ hour. Turn and cook bone side about 20 minutes. Insert thermometer into meat. Its reading should be 155 degrees for medium and 165 for medium well done. When done, sprinkle with pepper (salt too if meat has not been given the salt-bath treatment). Decorate platter with bunches of watercress. Serve with shoestring potatoes and grilled tomatoes.

Wine: Nuits-Saint-Georges

VARIATIONS
CARRÉ D'AGNEAU À LA BÉARNAISE
[*Rack of Lamb with Béarnaise Sauce*]

Put fresh or canned artichoke bottoms in skillet with melted butter. Make Béarnaise sauce (p. 24). Fill artichokes with the sauce. Cover with a lid and set aside. Broil the racks of lamb according to the above recipe. When done, heat artichokes, which will warm the sauce. Surround lamb with Béarnaise-filled artichokes.

Wine: Corton or Beaujolais

CARRÉ D'AGNEAU À LA MAÎTRE D'HÔTEL
[*Rack of Lamb with Maître d'Hôtel Butter*]

Prepare Maître d'Hôtel butter (p. 39). Serve butter in Bibb-lettuce cups surrounding the lamb.

NOTE: Chutney butter (p. 38) is also very good.

Wine: Aloxe-Corton

AGNEAU SAUTÉ
[*Sautéed Lamb*]

The following sautéed lamb recipes may also be made with broiled chops.

CÔTELETTES D'AGNEAU À LA NELSON
[*Lamb Chops with Soubise*]

6 (1-inch-thick) rib lamb chops	Chunk of butter
Recipe of Soubise au Ris	Dry bread crumbs
2 tablespoons oil	Milk

1. Trim heavy fat from chops. Make Soubise au Ris (p. 235).
2. Sauté chops in oil and a chunk of butter. When done, coat top side of each chop with Soubise and sprinkle with bread crumbs. Broil to brown crumbs.
3. Add sufficient milk to the remaining Soubise to make a thin sauce. Heat, season, and serve separately.
Wine: Fleurie

CÔTELETTES D'AGNEAU À LA PORTUGAISE
[*Lamb Chops in Tomato Sauce*]

Chunk of butter	4 tablespoons chicken stock
2 tablespoons vegetable oil	1 teaspoon sugar
6 (1-inch-thick) rib chops	1 tablespoon tomato paste
18 green pitted olives	1 tomato, peeled and diced
3 tablespoons Cognac	Beurre manié
4 tablespoons Madeira	Chopped parsley

1. Heat butter and oil in skillet. Add chops and sauté each side about 3 minutes. Put olives in cold water and bring to a boil. Drain and rinse.
2. Arrange cooked chops on hot platter, overlapping the tails. Keep warm in hot oven. Discard fat. Add Cognac, Madeira, stock, sugar, and tomato paste to skillet. Boil for 2 minutes. Add diced tomato and olives to skillet. Cook 3 minutes. Thicken with a bit of beurre manié. Taste and correct the seasonings. (Seasonings are not listed because of salt in olives and seasonings in tomato paste.) Spoon sauce over chops and sprinkle with parsley. Serve with rice.
Wine: Saint-Julien

CÔTELETTES D'AGNEAU À LA PROVENÇALE

[*Lamb Chops Provençale*]

6 (1-inch-thick) loin lamb chops

6 large mushroom caps

6 pitted green olives

6 flat anchovies

Chunk of butter

2 tablespoons olive oil

Sauce

Chunk of butter

2 tablespoons flour

1 small clove garlic, minced

1 cup cream

½ teaspoon salt

½ teaspoon sugar

Dash of pepper

3 egg yolks

Cream

Madeira

1. Roll tail of chop up close to chop. Tie with kitchen string.

2. Wipe mushrooms with a damp towel. Break stems from inside the caps. Use later in potage or slice and sauté. Put olives into cold water and bring to a boil. Drain, rinse, and drain again, ready for use. Drain anchovies and blot on paper towels. Wrap an anchovy around each olive. Set aside ready to use.

3. Sauté chops 5 minutes in chunk of butter and oil. Turn chops, add mushrooms, and sauté another 5 minutes.

4. Make sauce: Melt chunk of butter and stir in flour. Add garlic, cream, salt, sugar, and pepper. Stir-cook until very thick. Add 4 tablespoons sauce to yolks. Mix and then stir back into sauce. Heat, but do not boil.

5. Put chops on serving platter. Put a spoonful of sauce on each chop. Top with a mushroom cap, cavity up, and let it hold an anchovy-wrapped olive. Thin remainder of sauce with cream and heat. Flavor with Madeira and adjust seasonings. Serve separately.

Wine: Moulin-à-Vent

CÔTELETTES D'AGNEAU EN PAPILLOTES
[*Packaged Chops*]

The French seem to like meats done *en papillotes,* or wrapped in paper. As for me, I think it's too bad to take a beautiful loin lamb chop, brown it nicely, smother it in Duxelles sauce and then wrap it tight and steam-cook it in the oven. However, here's their recipe.

2 onions, minced	6 (¾-inch) thick loin lamb chops
Chunk of butter	Salt and pepper to taste
1 cup minced mushrooms	3 slices boiled ham
3 tablespoons vegetable oil	Parchment (freezer) paper, or foil

1. Sauté onions in butter for 5 minutes. Add mushrooms and cook another 5 minutes. (Duxelles mixture.)

2. Heat oil in a skillet. Add chops and brown each side. Do not cook longer. At this point they must be rare.

3. Take skillets from heat. Salt and pepper both vegetables and chops. Cut ham slices into fourths.

4. Cut out 6 heart or kidney-shaped pieces of waxed, freezer, or parchment paper. Oil each paper. Lay ¼ piece ham on one side of the heart. Top with chop and 1 tablespoon Duxelles mixture and then another ¼ of ham.

5. Fold the other half of the heart over this stack of food, matching the edges. Begin at the crevice, or top of the heart, and make ½-inch overlapping folds around the edge. By folding the folds, one makes the package air-tight.

6. Place packages on a greased cooky-sheet. Bake in a preheated 475-degree oven for about 10 minutes if using parchment paper and 15 minutes if using foil. (Foil repels heat.) Paper inflates as the food within warms because the steam cannot escape. Serve in paper and let guests open their own surprise packages. Place extra plates on the side for the wrapping paper.

Wine: Mazoyères-Chambertin

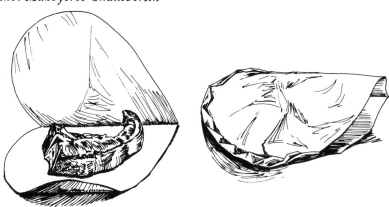

XII

Boeuf

[Beef]

Beef in France is different from ours, chiefly because cattle are not "corn-fed." The meat is not marbled like ours and therefore is usually larded before it is cooked. Since our meat is "larded" on the hoof, it is not necessary to marble it with strips of fat. In French cooking, roasts are usually prepared according to the braising method, since the meat is less tender than our marbled beef.

One of the few cuts of beef common to both America and France is the tenderloin of beef from which we get tournedos, fillets, and châteaubriands. Roasts, such as standing rib and rolled roasts, are not common in France, but they are improved when given the French treatment.

Beef should never be served well done, and this presents a problem since some people do prefer a steak cooked beyond recognition. The best solution is not to offer the possibility of a well-done steak or roast.

Glaze all roasts and steaks with a bit of sauce or melted butter to make them shine. Red meats, unlike light meats, cannot be interchanged in recipes without qualifications.

RÔTI DE BOEUF
[*Roast Beef*]

Spit cooking is perhaps the oldest and best method of roasting meats since the heat hits all sides of the meat as it turns, thus cooking evenly from the outside toward the center while meat juices constantly roll around the meat, keeping the meat basted with its own juices.

Roasts cooked in the oven should be turned often and basted frequently; thus the meat gets the same treatment as it would if it were on a spit. It is not possible to turn very large roasts, but smaller ones present no problem. Several layers of paper towels make it easy to lift and turn the roast with your hands.

The fancy French names that attach themselves to roast-beef dishes come from the way the recipe is garnished. The garnish lends its name to the dish.

CÔTE DE BOEUF RÔTIE
[*Standing Rib Roast*]

1 (5–6-pound) standing rib roast	1 cup red wine
1 onion, quartered	2 tablespoons Madeira
1 carrot, sliced	Chunk of butter
3 tablespoons Cognac	Salt and pepper to taste

1. Score the layer of fat that covers the roast. This prevents the fat from contracting and drawing the meat tight as it cooks. Stand roast on its bony side in roasting pan.

2. Preheat oven to 475 degrees. Cook roast for 20 minutes at this temperature. Then reduce heat to 350 degrees and cook 18 minutes per pound for rare, 20 minutes for medium, and 22 minutes for medium well done. For rolled roasts add 5 minutes to each per-pound cooking time. A meat thermometer will read 140 for rare, 150 for medium, and 160 for medium-well done. At best, cooking times are but guides. What I call rare, you might call raw.

3. Add onion and carrot the last half hour of cooking time. They will give color and flavor to the pan juices.

4. When roast is done, place on platter to rest for 20 minutes. Skim fat from pan juices. Add Cognac and set ablaze to burn off the remaining fat. Add the wine. Stir-cook over high heat, scraping the pan to get all the flavor. Reduce to half the quantity. Finish sauce with Madeira and swirl in a chunk of butter. Season to taste. Strain and serve separately, a spoonful to each serving. You may prefer to prepare a Bordelaise sauce (p. 28) since there is never much pan sauce. Serve with Château potatoes (p. 237) and glazed carrots (p. 229).

Wine: Chambertin

FILET DE BOEUF RÔTI

[Roast Tenderloin of Beef]

1 (3–4-pound) tenderloin of beef	3 tablespoons Madeira
Sheet of fat	Watercress
2 tablespoons Cognac	Cherry tomatoes

Chunk of butter

1. Preheat oven to 475 degrees. Cut the tail end from the tenderloin. (Use it at a later date to make Stroganoff.) Encase tenderloin in sheets of fat (ask butcher to cut fat for larding a roast). Tie them in place.

2. Set roast in a V-shaped roasting rack, then place on broiler pan and in a hot oven. Reduce heat to 350 degrees. Cook 40 minutes, then remove strings and fat from roast. Increase heat to 425 degrees and cook for about 30 minutes to brown the outside of the meat. Brush meat many times during the browning period with a mixture of Cognac and Madeira. Roasting time allows for basting.

3. When meat is done, remove to hot platter. Let rest 15 minutes. Garnish platter with watercress and peeled cherry tomatoes. (Drop tomatoes into boiling water and leave for a count of 15. Drain and cool in cold, running water. Peel off skins, leaving the green stem attached to the tomato.) Run chunk of butter over hot meat to make it shine. Serve with a sauce from the Demi-glace family (pp. 28–30). (Prepare sauce before roasting the fillet.)

Wine: Château Latour

VARIATIONS

FILET DE BOEUF AUX CHAMPIGNONS

[Tenderloin with Mushrooms]

Garnish roasted tenderloin with sautéed mushroom caps (p. 282). Serve with Madeira sauce (p. 30), made in advance of roasting meat.

Wine: Beaune

FILET DE BOEUF DUBARRY

[Tenderloin Garnished with Cauliflower]

Roast the tenderloin according to the master recipe. Prepare cauliflower balls (p. 266) and Mornay sauce (p. 18). Make recipe of Château potatoes (p. 237). When roast is done, coat cauliflower balls with Mornay sauce and broil them until brown. Arrange them and the potatoes around the roast and serve.

Wine: Aloxe-Corton

FILET DE BOEUF FINANCIÈRE

[Tenderloin Garnished Financière]

Prepare Périgueux sauce (p. 30). Make Veal Quenelles (steps 2–3, p. 176). Roast the fillet. Blanch about 2 dozen pitted green olives by putting them into cold water and bringing to a boil. Drain, rinse, and drain again. Carve about 1 dozen mushrooms (p. 281). Cook them in water seasoned with a chunk of butter and a teaspoon of lemon juice. Buy a bottle of cocks' combs (you may omit them) and blanch them at the same time as the olives. Heat these garnishings in about ½ cup sauce, then arrange them around the fillet. Serve remainder of sauce separately.

Wine: Côte Rôtie

FILET DE BOEUF HONGROISE

[Tenderloin Garnished with Caramelized Onions]

Prepare recipe of Demi-glace sauce (p. 27). To the butter, carrots, and onions, in the Demi-glace recipe, add about 1 tablespoon paprika and then proceed with the recipe. Cook about 2 dozen small onions and then caramelize them in butter and sugar. When fillet is done, glaze with sauce and garnish with the onions. Serve the remainder of sauce separately.

Wine: Chinon

FILET DE BOEUF JARDINIÈRE

[Tenderloin with Spring Vegetables]

Garnish roasted fillet with heaps of assorted vegetables, which have been cut into fancy shapes and cooked in stock, alternating their colors around the roast. For the cauliflower and broccoli, if used, serve a dish of Hollandaise sauce (p. 21); for the roast, serve a Demi-glace sauce (p. 27).

Wine: Pomerol

FILET DE BOEUF RENAISSANCE

[Tenderloin with Vegetables]

Make like Jardinière and add small new boiled potatoes to the vegetable garnish. Serve with Périgueux sauce (p. 30).

Wine: Côte Rôtie

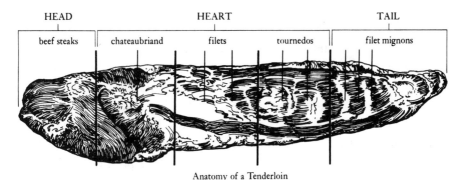

HEAD   HEART   TAIL

beef steaks   chateaubriand   filets   tournedos   filet mignons

Anatomy of a Tenderloin

FILET DE BOEUF PRINCE-DE-GALLES (OR ALBERT)

[*Tenderloin Stuffed with Pâté*]

1 whole tenderloin of beef
  (3–4 pounds)
Périgueux sauce
½ pound chicken livers
⅛ pound butter
¼ teaspoon sweet basil
Dash of pepper and of nutmeg
½ teaspoon salt
½ teaspoon anchovy paste
1 (2-ounce) can black truffles
2 tablespoons Madeira

Butter
2 carrots, minced
1 onion, minced
3 parsley sprigs
1 cup red wine
Larding fat
½ pound small fresh mushrooms
2 tablespoons Madeira
Beurre manié
Watercress

1. Trim fat and cut off tail of fillet at the fillet-mignon section. Slice 2 (1-inch) steaks from the head, making the heart or fillet uniform in thickness. Use tail and steaks for other meals. Make Périgueux sauce (p. 30).

2. Make chicken liver pâté. Cut chicken livers apart. Remove white tissue and fat. Sauté livers in ⅛ pound butter for 5 minutes. Add basil, pepper, nutmeg, salt, and anchovy paste. Grind through food chopper or blend in blender to make a paste. Put into small dish. (You may use canned pâté de foie gras instead of making chicken-liver pâté.)

3. Slice 2 truffles very thin. Soak slices in 2 tablespoons Madeira. Put chunk of butter into shallow roasting pan. Add carrots, onion, parsley, and red wine. Simmer 5 minutes.

4. Remove truffle slices from Madeira. Add Madeira to ground chicken livers and mix. Cut a lengthwise pocket in the fillet from the flat side. Cut to ½ inch of the top side and to within ½ inch of each end of the fillet. Coat this cavity with liver pâté. Insert sliced truffles in the pâté and along the full length of the fillet. Push opening to close it. Tie at 2-inch intervals, beginning at the middle. Lay slices of fat over the opening. Set roast, cut side up, in pan with vegetables and wine.

(continued)

5. Put into preheated 475-degree oven. Roast 30 minutes, then remove fat. Roast another 20 minutes at 350 degrees, or until done.

6. Remove stems from mushrooms. Wash, then sauté caps in a chunk of butter. Save stems for use at another time. Cut remaining whole truffles into fourths. Trim off the sharp edges. Dice the trimmings. Add pieces to Périgueux sauce. Add carved oval truffles to mushroom caps. Heat, but do not cook.

7. Place roast on hot platter. Let rest 15 minutes. Remove strings. Turn cut side down. Add 2 tablespoons Madeira to roasting pan. Heat, skim off fat, and then strain liquid into Périgueux sauce. Thicken with beurre manié if necessary. Serve sauce separately. Place mushroom caps and truffles around roast along with bunches of watercress.

Wine: Côte Rôtie

VARIATIONS

Since tenderloin of beef has so little fat of its own, it takes well to *en Chemise,* or dough-wrapped, cooking. The pastry protects the tender meat and keeps the juices within.

These recipes are luxurious, lengthy, yet easy to make. All of them can be prepared in advance of dinner. Prepare the master recipe through the wrapping of the meat in the pastry, and then cover with a damp towel until time to cook. Of course, the shorter the wait, the better the result.

To test the doneness of a dough-wrapped whole tenderloin insert meat thermometer through the crust under one of the pastry decorations and then the hole left by the thermometer will not be so obvious. Insert the thermometer on the slant and keep it in the middle of the roast.

FILET DE BOEUF PRINCE-DE-GALLES EN CHEMISE
[*Stuffed Tenderloin in a Crust*]

Prepare recipe of pastry (p. 353). Make fillet as for Prince-de-Galles. Tie. Do not cover with larding fat. Brush with Cognac and then melted butter. Roast in a 475-degree oven for 25 minutes. It should be about half cooked. Take from oven, and let cool. Remove strings. Roll pastry to ⅛-inch thickness. Set roast on rolled pastry. Fold dough around meat, trim dough and then brush the edges with mixture of 1 egg yolk and 1 tablespoon water. Seal edges. Place sealed side down on a greased cooky sheet.

Make fancy cutouts from the leftover dough. Decorate the smooth top surface. Give full rein to your imagination and think of the dough as putty in your hands. Brush the dough with the egg-water mixture. Bake in 375-degree oven for about 30 minutes. Do not let dough get too brown before the meat is hot and done.

Let roast stand 10 minutes before carving. Decorate platter with watercress. Serve with Périgueux sauce (p. 30). Make sauce before roasting meat.

Wine: Saint-Émilion

FILET DE BOEUF DUXELLES EN CHEMISE
[*Tenderloin with Duxelles in Crust*]

Prepare dough (p. 353), and Duxelles mixture (p. 286). Sprinkle tenderloin of beef with Cognac and then coat with melted butter. Roast in preheated 475-degree oven for 25 minutes. Take out and let cool. Coat roast with Duxelles mixture. Wrap in dough, decorate and bake as in the preceding recipe. Serve with Chasseur sauce (p. 29), made in advance.

Wine: Château Ausone

FILET DE BOEUF MATIGNON EN CHEMISE
[*Tenderloin with Vegetables in Crust*]

Prepare dough (p. 353). Mince 2 leeks, 2 carrots, 2 turnips, 2 onions, and 2 cloves of garlic. Place vegetables in ¼ pound butter in skillet, cover and sauté for about 25 minutes. Season with salt and pepper when done. Cool vegetables. Roast the fillet as in the above recipes. Cool, then coat with vegetables, wrap in dough, decorate and bake as in the preceding recipes. Serve with a Demi-glace sauce (p. 27); make in advance of roasting the meat.

Wine: Saint Estèphe

BOEUF BRAISÉ
[*Braised Beef*]

The working muscles of the beef have more flavor and texture than non-working muscles like the tenderloin. Since working muscles are strong they require longer cooking times to make them tender. They are usually cooked by braising. Here are some of the best foods I know.

BOEUF À LA MODE

[*Beef in Red Wine*]

1 (4-pound) rump roast	3 cups red wine
¼-inch thick sheet of larding fat	¼ cup stock
Madeira	Flour
1 teaspoon salt	3 tablespoons vegetable oil
¼ teaspoon pepper	Cognac
Dash of nutmeg	2 cloves garlic, minced
2 onions, diced	3 celery tops, diced
1 carrot, diced	1 tablespoon sugar
⅛ teaspoon thyme	2 beef knuckles, split
2 whole cloves	8 carrots
1 large bay leaf	18 small white boiling onions,
¼ teaspoon dried tarragon	cleaned
6 crushed peppercorns	1 pound fresh mushrooms
3 tablespoons wine vinegar	Beurre manié

1. Rump roasts are usually not well-marbled, therefore it is wise to lard them. Cut fat into ¼-inch strips. Sprinkle with Madeira. Then, using a larding needle, insert them into the grain of the meat at 1-inch intervals. Once meat is larded put it into a bowl a little larger than its own size.

2. To the bowl add the ingredients down to the flour. Refrigerate and marinate for about 2 days.

3. Take from marinade, dry on paper towels, roll in flour and brown in oil. Use an enamel-coated Dutch oven if you have one. When meat is brown, spoon off fat, add 3 tablespoons Cognac, and set aflame. When flame dies out, strain the marinade into the roasting pan. Add the garlic, celery, sugar, and split beef knuckles. Cover and braise in 325-degree oven for about 3 hours.

4. Clean carrots and carve into olive shapes. (Cook trimmings and make a potage; see Chapter IV, "Les Soupes.") Add carrots and onions and braise 1 hour more. Add cleaned whole mushroom caps the last 15 minutes of cooking. (Use the stems of the mushrooms for soup, perhaps combined with the carrots.)

5. When meat is done, put on hot serving platter. Let rest 15 minutes. Lift vegetables from sauce and place around meat. Keep warm. Discard knuckles. Strain sauce into a clean pan. Heat, then thicken with beurre manié. Flavor with 4 tablespoons Madeira and 2 tablespoons Cognac. Adjust seasonings and serve sauce separately. Cut meat across the grain into slices and serve to 8.

NOTE: See p. 398 for Boeuf à la Mode en Gelée.

Wine: Châteauneuf-du-Pape

PIÈCE DE BOEUF À LA BOURGEOISE
[*Beef in White Wine*]

Substitute white wine for the red wine in the à la Mode recipe and it becomes a dish with a different name.

Wine: Montrachet

BOEUF BOURGUIGNONNE
[*Beef in Red Wine Sauce*]

¼ pound butter	2 teaspoons salt
3 tablespoons vegetable oil	½ teaspoon pepper
3 pounds cubed beef	12 carrots
Flour	18 small white boiling onions
2 cloves garlic, minced	½ pound fresh mushrooms,
3 cups red Burgundy wine	quartered
⅛ teaspoon thyme	Beurre manié, if needed
Bouquet garni	4 tablespoons Madeira
2 tablespoons tomato paste	2 tablespoons Cognac

Chopped parsley

1. Heat butter and oil in large skillet. Roll beef cubes in flour and then brown in fat. When they are brown, add garlic, wine, and thyme. Add bouquet garni to skillet along with tomato paste, salt, and pepper. Simmer about 3 hours, or cook in a 325-degree oven. Remove bouquet garni after 2 hours.

2. Peel carrots. Cut into chunks and then trim into large olive shapes. Add carrots and cleaned onions to skillet the last hour of cooking. Add mushrooms the last 15 minutes. When done, taste and adjust seasonings and thickness. Use beurre manié if sauce needs thickening. Stir in Madeira and Cognac. Serve sprinkled with parsley.

Wine: Pommard

FILET SAUTÉ STROGANOFF
[*Beef Stroganoff*]

Although this dish is Russian in origin, the chefs of France have a trick or two the Russians would do well to adopt when it comes to making Stroganoff. And now that you know how to make crème fraîche, it is possible to enjoy this dish without having the sour cream curdle. Also, it is a good way to use up the tails of beef tenderloin.

(continued)

½ cup white wine or vermouth
Madeira
½ cup chicken stock
3 cups sliced mushrooms
Chunk of butter
3 onions
2 cloves garlic, minced
Salt and pepper to taste

1 teaspoon sugar
⅛ pound butter
2 tablespoons vegetable oil
2 pounds tenderloin tails
3 tablespoons Cognac
Beurre manié
1 cup crème fraîche, or whipping cream

Minced parsley

1. Combine white wine, ½ cup Madeira, and stock in saucepan. Reduce, by boiling, to about ¾ cup. Remove stems from mushrooms. (Save the stems to use later.) Wash mushrooms, and slice caps. Add mushrooms to reduced wines and remove from the heat.

2. Melt chunk of butter in skillet. Peel onions and slice into thin wedges. Add onions and garlic to skillet. Sauté 10 minutes. Season with salt, pepper, and sugar. Remove from skillet and add to the wine-mushroom mixture.

3. Put ⅛ pound butter and oil in skillet. Cut tenderloin into ¼-inch-thick slices. Add to skillet. Heat and stir with a wooden spoon. Cook about 2 minutes. The meat should heat just long enough to turn gray and still be rare within.

4. Pour Cognac over meat. Heat and then set aflame. Add 2 tablespoons Madeira and the wine-mushroom mixture. Bring to a boil and thicken with beurre manié (p. 2). Stir in crème. Heat, taste, and adjust both seasonings and thickness if necessary. Pour into hot serving dish. Sprinkle with minced parsley and serve with buttered noodles and a green salad.

NOTE: Keep packets of beurre manié frozen and ready to use.

Wine: Romanée-Conti La Tache

BIFTECK
[*Steak*]

Red meats are usually served with dark sauces and red wines. But contrary to this general principle, steaks are often presented with a light Béarnaise sauce. This famous dish is usually called Tournedos Henry IV, an indication of the fact that it was created to soothe the palate of the great Bourbon king from Béarn.

Debates have long raged among culinary historians as to whether or not the Béarnaise sauce really originated in the province of Béarn. Some have pointed out that Béarn does not specialize in beef and that in most of its specialties, oil rather than butter is used as a base. Such circumstantial evidence leads the protagonists of this school of thought to seek elsewhere for the origins of Tournedos Henry IV.

It is often asserted, though without supporting data, that this sauce was created at the royal Château of Saint Germain-en-Laye and served there for the first time to a party held in the pavilion named for Henry IV. It is also alleged that from the beginning the sauce was made from butter, the staple fat of northern France, and not from the oil usually associated with the cooking of Béarn. The name of the sauce, it is assumed, was derived from the fact that it was first served in the pavilion of Henry IV, the greatest of the Béarnaise.

Whatever the historical facts may be, there can be no doubt that the imaginative cook who first thought to serve steak with a light sauce was really responsible for creating a dish worthy of one of France's greatest kings.

Tournedos of beef are also called *medallions, noisettes,* or *mignonnettes.* They are considered choice in French cuisine and are usually sautéed because of their lack of fat. However, when they contain marbling they are excellent broiled or grilled.

BIFTECK GRILLÉ
[*Broiled Steaks*]

For our American taste French steaks always seem to be undercooked. In restaurants this can happen if you do not ask for what you want in terms the waiter understands.

In the broiling of steaks in French restaurants there are 5 categories of doneness.

Au bleu is practically raw, with only the outside heated. The meat is still "blue," or raw, and often not even warm within.

Saignant is really blood red, rare, and the center is warm.

À point is rare with the blood coagulated. It is hot at the center.

Bien is what we would call medium.

Bien cuit, well-done, but it is not possible for a sensitive French cook to char a steak. This is actually medium well, and still slightly pink. If you want it less pink, send it back and repeat: "Bien, très bien, cuit." You might then be successful in getting a well-done steak, but don't bank on it.

Broiled and grilled steaks may be served with any sauce from the Demi-glace family (pp. 28–30), with a sauce from the Béarnaise branch of the Hollan-daise family (p. 24), or with Maître d'Hôtel butter (p. 39). The sauce gives its name to the steak.

BROILING CHART FOR STEAKS

THICKNESS OF INDIVIDUAL STEAKS	DONENESS	INCHES FROM HEAT	MINUTES TO COOK	
			1st Side	*2nd Side*
¾ inch	Rare	2	3	2
	Medium		4	2
	Medium Well		4	3
1 inch	Rare	3	5	3
	Medium		6	3
	Medium Well		6	4
1½ inch	Rare	3	7	4
	Medium		8	4
	Medium Well		8	5
2 inch	Rare	4	8	6
	Medium		9	6
	Medium Well		9	7
2½ inch	Rare	5	9	7
	Medium		10	7
	Medium Well		10	8

1. Preheat broiler for 10 minutes, then add steaks. A solid metal rack, which most broilers now have, is not good for broiling. It does not allow the heat to circulate around the meat. When a steak is placed on the metal it sautés one side, then as the rack cools under the steak, the rack tends to steam the steak. If possible, get a wire rack to use when broiling steaks.

2. Oil steaks on both sides, then place on grill. Score fat to keep steak flat.

3. In out-of-doors grill cooking and for cold steaks, add 1 minute to cooking times. Air circulation around steaks out-of-doors reduces the intensity of the heat. Season after steaks are done.

4. For whole steaks weighing about 2 pounds add 1 minute to each cooking time. Increase cooking time 1 minute for each additional pound. Let whole steaks rest 5 minutes before carving. Season after they are cooked.

TOURNEDOS HENRI IV
[*Broiled Tournedos with Béarnaise Sauce*]

Béarnaise sauce	Oil
6 (1-inch-thick) tournedos	Toast rounds
(well-marbled)	Pont-Neuf potatoes

Watercress

1. Prepare the Béarnaise sauce (p. 24). Pour it into a small porcelain serving dish and set in warm water no hotter than the sauce. Cover with transparent wrap to prevent crust from forming. Preheat broiler.

2. Oil the steaks. Place on broiler and cook according to chart (opposite).

3. When done, set steaks on toast rounds. Garnish platter with Pont-Neuf potatoes (p. 238) and decorate with watercress. Serve with spoonful of sauce atop each steak.

NOTE: Toast absorbs red juices as steaks are cut and keeps juice from running over the plate and into other foods.

Wine: Savigny-les-Beaune

VARIATIONS
TOURNEDOS À L'AMBASSADE
[*Tournedos with Choron Sauce*]

Prepare Choron sauce (p. 25). Sauté 6 artichoke bottoms (fresh or canned) in a chunk of butter. Fill with sautéed diced cucumbers and set atop 6 broiled steaks. Place on toast rounds. Serve Choron sauce separately.

Wine: Clos de Tart

TOURNEDOS BELLE-HÉLÈNE
[*Tournedos with Tomato Sauce*]

Prepare Tomato Fondue (p. 272). Stem 6 large mushroom caps. Use a melon baller or teaspoon to remove brown underneath part (gills) of mushroom caps. Fill with hot Tomato Fondue. Sprinkle with bread crumbs, dot with butter, and broil until brown. Set 6 broiled steaks on toast rounds and top with broiled mushroom caps. Decorate plate with watercress.

Wine: Valpolicella (Italian)

TOURNEDOS À LA BERCY

[*Tournedos with Bercy Sauce*]

Prepare Bercy sauce (p. 20). Broil 6 tournedos, glaze with sauce, and serve remainder of sauce separately.

Wine: Rully Rouge

TOURNEDOS À LA BORDELAISE

[*Tournedos with Bordelaise Sauce*]

Prepare Bordelaise sauce (p. 28). Poach 6 marrow bones. Remove marrow from bones and set atop 6 broiled steaks. Glaze with sauce and set steaks on toast rounds. Serve remainder of sauce separately.

Wine: Château Margaux

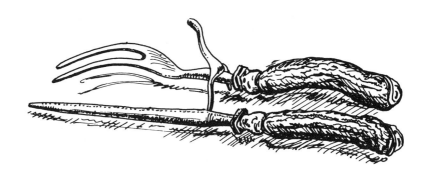

TOURNEDOS ROSSINI

[*Tournedos with Pâté*]

The name "Rossini" in a recipe means that the food is garnished with the two aristocrats of the food world, pâté de foie gras and truffles.

In 1868, following the five hundredth performance of his *William Tell* in the Paris Opera House, Gioacchino Rossini was made an associate of the Institute of France and an officer of the Legion of Honor, and his name, like that of Chateaubriand, was elevated to immortality in the annals of French cuisine.

Prepare recipe of Périgueux sauce (p. 30). Broil tournedos to desired doneness. Cut ½-inch-thick slices of pâté de foie gras from a block of pâté. Slice the same number as there are steaks. Dust with flour and sauté quickly in hot butter. Place a slice of pâté on top of each cooked tournedo, then set tournedos on toast rounds. Top with a slice of truffle and glaze with a spoonful of sauce. Decorate platter with bunches of watercress. Serve remainder of sauce separately.

Wine: Château Lafite Rothschild

SAUTÉS DE TOURNEDOS AU POIVRE
[*Pepper Steaks*]

6 (2-inch-thick) tournedos or fillets	Salt to taste
Whole peppercorns, about ¼ cup	6 tablespoons crème fraîche,
Chunk of butter	or whipping cream
3 tablespoons Cognac	Beurre manié

Chopped parsley

1. Be sure tournedos are of uniform thickness. Mash peppercorns with a mallet or heavy iron skillet. The pepper must be crushed and not ground in a peppermill.

2. Press each side of each steak into the crushed peppercorns. Let them stand about an hour to absorb the pepper flavor.

3. Heat butter in large skillet. Add pepper-coated tournedos and sauté about 8 minutes per side for rare, 10 for medium, and 12 for medium well done.

4. When steaks are done, pour Cognac over them. Heat a second to volatilize the alcohol and then set ablaze. Put steaks on hot serving platter. Boil liquid a minute and then stir in salt and crème. Thicken slightly with beurre manié, and pour over steaks. Sprinkle with parsley and serve.

NOTE: You may prefer to scrape off some of the peppercorns before pouring on sauce—they are quite hot. The sauce may also be strained over the steaks to remove the peppercorns. Serve with French-fried potatoes.

Wine: Châteauneuf-du-Pape

VARIATIONS
TOURNEDOS À LA MAÎTRE D'HÔTEL
[*Tournedos with Maître d'Hôtel Butter*]

Sauté steaks in garlic butter as in Portugaise recipe below and serve with Maître d'Hôtel butter (p. 39). Simple and good!

Wine: Mazoyères-Chambertin

TOURNEDOS À LA PORTUGAISE
[*Tournedos with Tomato Sauce*]

Prepare Portugaise sauce (p. 31). Cut about 6 cloves of garlic in half. Sauté in chunk of butter and 2 tablespoons òil, but do not let the garlic take on color. Heat-stir for about 5 minutes. Discard garlic and sauté the tournedos to desired doneness. (See Tournedos au Poivre for cooking times.) Serve these steaks with Portugaise sauce.

Wine: Valpolicella (Italian)

BIFTECK ORDINAIRE

[*Simple Steak*]

A simple steak and Pommes Frites Pont-Neuf are one of the joys of eating in France. They are available in almost any bistro, or any fine restaurant.

Unfortunately we do not have a steak to equal those of France. But either a rump steak or a round steak, when properly treated, responds similarly.

BIFTECK SAUTÉ

[*Sautéed Steak*]

1 (2-pound) slice of round steak, or rump steak cut ⅜-inch thick	Butter Salt and pepper

1. Separate the muscles of a round steak. To do this, follow the connective tissue in the slice of steak. There will be about 5 pieces, some bigger than others.

2. Heat an iron skillet to very hot. When hot, coat with melted butter and add the steaks. Do not crowd the pan. Sear one side, then turn and sear the other. These steaks must not be served more than medium. To eat them one slices across the grain of the steak. Salt and pepper when ready to eat.

Wine: Pomerol

VARIATIONS

CARBONADES DE BOEUF

[*Breaded Steaks*]

Separate muscles of round steak as in Bifteck Sauté recipe. With a very sharp knife, score the steak on both sides (bought cubed steaks may be used). Dip steak in melted butter and then in fine, dry bread crumbs. Sauté quickly in 2 tablespoons oil and a chunk of butter. Serve with wedges of lemon or Maître d'Hôtel butter (p. 39). Salt and pepper at the time of eating.

Wine: Saint-Émilion

PAUPIETTES DE BOEUF

[*Beef Rolls*]

Have round steak cut ¼ inch thick. Separate muscles of steak as in Bifteck Sauté recipe. Pound thin and then stuff, roll, tie, and cook according to Paupiettes de Veau recipes, pp. 165–166.

Wine: Beaujolais

PAUPIETTES DE BOEUF SAUTÉS
[*Fried Beef Rolls*]

Prepare preceding recipe. When paupiettes of beef are done, lift them from the cooking liquids. Remove the strings. Roll in fine, dry, bread crumbs. Drizzle with melted butter. Roll again in crumbs. Sauté in 2 tablespoons vegetable oil and a chunk of butter. Fry crisp on all sides. When brown, drain on paper towels and serve with a Béarnaise sauce, p. 24 (make while paupiettes cook).
Wine: Pommard

BIFTECK HACHÉ
[*Ground Beef*]

While chuck and other cuts of beef may be used in ground-beef recipes, I think ground round steak is best. It has taste and is lean, which allows the cook to add crème fraîche, butter, eggs, or soaked bread to give the meat richness and flavor.

BIFTECK AU VIN ROUGE
[*Hamburgers in Red Wine*]

2 pounds round ground	2 tablespoons vegetable oil
2 egg whites, not beaten	1 minced onion
2 tablespoons crème fraîche, or	½ cup red wine
sour cream	¼ cup Madeira
2 shallots, minced	1 cup minced mushrooms
1 teaspoon salt	Dash of salt, pepper, and sugar
⅛ teaspoon pepper	2 tablespoons crème fraîche, or
¼ cup flour	whipping cream
Chunk of butter	Minced parsley

1. Put ingredients down through the ⅛ teaspoon pepper into mixing bowl. Mix well. Shape into 8 large patties. Coat with flour. Sauté in butter and oil. Brown both sides. Cook a total of about 5 minutes. They should be medium to rare at this point.

2. Remove hamburgers from skillet. Add onion. Sauté 5 minutes. Add red wine and Madeira. Boil 5 minutes. Stir in mushrooms and cook to reduce wines to about ¼ cup. Season and stir in crème. Add hamburgers and heat. Put on platter. Sprinkle with minced parsley and serve.
Wine: Bardolino (Italian)

FRICADELLES DE BOEUF
[*Ground Meat Patties*]

2 pounds ground round

4 slices bread

Light cream

1 large onion, minced

½ cup minced parsley

Butter

1 teaspoon salt

⅛ teaspoon pepper

2 whole eggs

Flour

2 tablespoons vegetable oil

1. Put meat into mixing bowl. Cut crusts from bread slices. Soak in about ½ cup cream, or enough to moisten. Squeeze dry, and add to meat. Fry onion and parsley in chunk of butter for about 2 minutes. Add to meat. Season with salt and pepper and add the eggs. Mix well, mashing the bread into the meat.

2. Shape meat into 8 patties, coat with flour, and fry in mixture of a chunk of butter and oil. Brown both sides and serve. Do not cook well done, but rare to medium.

Wine: Valpolicella (Italian)

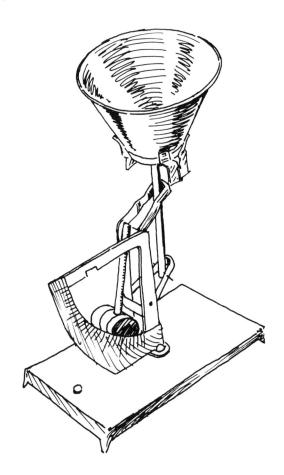

XIII

Légumes
[*Vegetables*]

Vegetables are perhaps the most abused of all the foods we cook. Too often they are served as a sodden mass of disorganized fibers with both color and flavor destroyed in the cooking process. But, when properly treated, their jewel-like characteristics improve with cooking.

The French method of preparing vegetables differs sharply from ours. But if you have eaten vegetables in France, you will gladly switch to the French method of cooking nature's most colorful foods.

All vegetables with chlorophyll fall into six main groups, each of which can be compared to the parts of a plant; that is, root, stem, leaf, flower, fruit, and seed. Categorizing vegetables in this way will help you in their proper preparation because each category should be cooked according to its own particular characteristics. Some vegetables fall into more than one category, but I list them in only one.

Non-chlorophyll vegetables, such as mushrooms and truffles, are fungi and do not fall into these categories. But fungi are considered plants, so their recipes are included in this vegetable chapter.

Root vegetables include carrots, turnips, beets, potatoes, onions, leeks, garlic, and others. These large members of the root family are best when put on to cook in cold water so that they heat and cook from the inside out as the water heats.

Stem vegetables include asparagus, broccoli, and celery. Since they all have *heads*, one might also classify them with flowers, but since the other flower vegetables do not have edible main stems, I have chosen not to list them with flower vegetables. These stalky vegetables should all be peeled. You will enjoy them served with a Hollandaise sauce.

Leafy vegetables include spinach, endive, lettuce, cabbage, watercress, parsley, and others. This family of vegetables is usually green. All are at their best in salads, but all may be cooked.

Flower vegetables include artichokes, Brussels sprouts, and cauliflower. The flower family really blossoms when served with melted butter, but other white sauces may also be served with them.

Fruit vegetables include eggplant, tomatoes, and squashes. These whole fruits are delicious stuffed or cooked in a sauce made from their family member, the tomato.

Seed vegetables include beans, peas, and corn. They are eaten both fresh and dried. Because rice is also a dried seed, I will treat it as a vegetable rather than as a cereal. Green seed vegetables, like green stem and green flower vegetables, are first blanched, then cooked and sauced. Dried seed vegetables are usually soaked overnight. Many Chinese wash rice and let it stand wet overnight, then steam it the next day. Dried seed vegetables are usually served as a substantial part of the meal.

ROOT VEGETABLES

Root vegetables are best when put on to cook in cold water seasoned with salt, sugar, and a chunk of butter. Starting them to cook in cold water lets them heat from the inside out as the water warms. Cooked in this way their outside area is not overcooked before they are done in the middle. All parts are done at the same time.

Vegetables that are grown underground are usually round and fat, or round and long. They may be cooked whole, but in French cooking they are usually cut into quarters, eighths or pieces, then trimmed to an exact shape, and cooked. These shapes are:

Château means each piece trimmed to the size of a large olive.

Fondantes are ovals twice the size of an olive.

Parisienne are small balls of vegetables made with a melon baller.

CAROTTES
[*Carrots*]

Carrots play an important role in French cuisine. They are a basic vegetable and almost always appear in such elaborate garnishes as Jardinière,

Primeur, Chartreuse, Renaissance, and others. Whether served plain or as a garnish, they are cooked in the following manner:

CAROTTES GLACÉES
[*Glazed Carrots*]

12 carrots of uniform size	1 tablespoon sugar
1 teaspoon salt	⅛ pound butter

2 cups water

1. To peel whole carrots, without damaging fingernails and polish, first peel one half and then turn carrot upside down and peel the other end. Trim off the tops. If carrots are fat all the way down, cut into 1-inch chunks and then trim into Château shapes, like large olives. If the carrots are thin and tapering, cut them in half after they are peeled and then shape each half to look like a miniature carrot.

2. Put trimmed carrots into saucepan. Add remainder of ingredients. Carrots should be covered with water. If 2 cups will not cover them, add more water and increase the other ingredients too.

3. Bring carrots to a boil, then simmer until done. Do not cover. Liquids should evaporate down to a thick syrup, the glaze for the carrots. Toss the carrots in the pan occasionally to coat them with the sauce. Serve or use as a garnish. Tuck sprigs of parsley into the tops of the half carrots that have been carved and they will look like small whole carrots.

VARIATIONS
CAROTTES À LA CRÈME
[*Creamed Carrots*]

Cook carrots as in Glacées. When done, add about 4 tablespoons crème fraîche or whipping cream and heat. Taste and adjust seasonings.

CAROTTES À LA VICHY
[*Glazed Sliced Carrots*]

Peel, then cut carrots into ¹⁄₁₆-inch slices. Cook as in Glacées recipe. When done, pour into serving dish and sprinkle with minced parsley.

CAROTTES AUX FINES HERBES
[*Glazed Carrots with Herbs*]

Make recipe of Carottes Glacées. Pour into serving dish and sprinkle with minced parsley and chopped chives.

PAIN DE CAROTTES
[*Carrot Timbale*]

Cook 2 pounds chunked or sliced carrots as in Glacées. When done, press through a food mill and dry off. There should be about 2 cups. Substitute puréed carrots for the spinach in Pain d'Epinards (p. 257).

PANNEQUETS AUX CAROTTES
[*Pancakes Stuffed with Puréed Carrots*]

Stuff prepared Crêpes (p. 365), with Pain de Carottes mixture. Place crêpes in a single layer on a buttered baking platter. Glaze with butter and sprinkle with grated Parmesan cheese. Bake in 375-degree oven for about 20 minutes, or until puffed. Serve with a sauce from the Béchamel family (pp. 16–19).

NAVET
[*Turnips*]

Turnips are cooked like carrots. Select round, flat young turnips. Peel. Then cut them into fourths and trim to Château, or olive, shapes.

VARIATIONS

NAVETS GLACÉS
[*Glazed Turnips*]

Make like Carottes Glacées (p. 229).

NAVETS À LA CRÈME
[*Creamed Turnips*]

Trim turnips into olive shapes, cooked in seasoned water like Carottes Glacées. When done, add 4 tablespoons crème fraîche. Toss, taste, season and serve.

NAVETS AUX FINES HERBES
[*Herbed Turnips*]

Peel and dice turnips. Cook in seasoned water until tender. Drain. Toss in butter. Sprinkle with sugar and brown. Add minced parsley and chives and serve.

NOTE: For a change, add ½ cup crème fraîche, toss, and serve.

OIGNONS
[*Onions*]

Whole onions are blanched before they are used in recipes. Peel onions and then cut a cross into the root end of each one. This lets the onion expand as it cooks so it will not push out the top.

24 whole boiling onions   3 quarts cold water

Peel onions. Cut cross in the root end. Put into about 3 quarts cold water and bring to a boil. Once boiling, drain, rinse, and then cook by one of the following recipes.

OIGNONS GLACÉS
[*Glazed Onions*]

24 whole boiling onions   1 tablespoon sugar
1 teaspoon salt   ⅛ pound butter
2 cups water

Blanch onions in cold water as described above. Put them into a skillet with the rest of the ingredients. Bring to a boil, then simmer about 30 minutes, or until done. Do not cover with a lid during cooking. Liquids should evaporate down to the thick syrup which will glaze the onions. Toss the onions in the pan occasionally to coat them with the sauce. Serve plain, as a garnish to a dish, or in one of the following recipes.

OIGNONS À LA BÉCHAMEL

[*Onions in Béchamel Sauce*]

Prepare recipe of Béchamel sauce (p. 15). Prepare Oignons Glacés. Put onions into a buttered baking dish. Cover with Béchamel sauce, sprinkle with grated Parmesan cheese or fine dry bread crumbs, dot with butter, and brown under broiler.

OIGNONS À LA CRÈME

[*Creamed Onions*]

Prepare Oignons Glacés. When done add ½ cup crème fraîche, or whipping cream, to the skillet. Heat, then sprinkle with Parmesan cheese and broil. Serve in individual dishes.

OIGNONS AUX FINES HERBES

[*Onions with Herbs*]

Prepare Oignons Glacés. Sprinkle with lots of minced parsley and cut chives. Oignons à la Béchamel are delicious when given the same chive treatment.

OIGNONS FRITS

[*French-fried Onions*]

3 large flat onions	1 teaspoon baking powder
½ cup flour	Vegetable oil for French-frying

1. Peel onions. Cut into ⅛-inch-thick slices. Separate slices into rings. Place in ice water for 10 minutes. Remove and dry rings on paper towels.

2. Combine flour and baking powder in a plastic bag. Heat oil in French-fryer. Put 6 rings into the bag at a time to coat evenly with flour. Drop into oil heated to 390 degrees. When brown, lift out and drain on paper towels. Serve with sautéed calf's liver.

OIGNONS EN FRITOTS

[*Batter-fried Onion Rings*]

Peel and slice onions into ⅛-inch-thick slices. Separate into rings. Dip into batter coating No. 3 (p. 11). Fry in oil heated to 390 degrees. Drain on paper towels and serve.

OIGNONS SAUTÉS

[*Sautéed Onions*]

6–8 onions	1 teaspoon salt
¼ pound butter	⅛ teaspoon pepper

1 teaspoon confectioners' sugar

Peel onions and slice very thin. Put into skillet with butter. Cover and cook for about 20 minutes. Add salt, freshly-ground pepper, and sugar. Stir-cook for about 10 minutes. Serve as a garnish to other foods.

PISSALADIÈRE

[*Onion Pizza*]

2 tablespoons olive oil	1 teaspoon salt
¼ pound butter	Dash of pepper
8 large onions, sliced	1 (8-inch) pie shell or tartelettes
2 cloves garlic, minced	Grated Parmesan cheese
¼ teaspoon thyme	3 large fresh tomatoes
1 bay leaf	1 (2-ounce) can flat anchovies

12 small Greek-type black olives

1. Combine olive oil and butter in large skillet. Add onions, garlic, thyme, bay leaf, salt, and pepper. Cover and cook over low heat for about 30 minutes, or until onions are translucent and golden. Discard bay leaf. Pour onions into a sieve to drain off the butter. Save butter to cook with.

2. Make pie shell or tartelettes from Brisée dough (p. 353). Stick the bottom of the pie shell in several places with the point of a knife. (This keeps pie shell from bulging.) Sprinkle crust with Parmesan.

3. Peel and core tomatoes. Slice paper thin. In pie shell place a layer of cooked onions and then a layer of sliced tomatoes. Repeat layers until both are used. (Cheese *only* on the crust, and *not* layered in the tomatoes and onions.)

4. Drain anchovies. Cut them in half, lengthwise. Arrange over the top of the filled pie shell. Place olives in the filling, submerge halfway. Bake tart on low shelf of a preheated 425-degree oven for about 40 minutes, or until brown and hot. Serve hot with a green salad for Sunday brunch, or as a first course.

Wine: Beaujolais

QUICHE PAYSANNE

[*Onion-Bacon Custard Pie*]

4 large onions, sliced	½ teaspoon salt
⅛ pound butter	Dash of pepper and of nutmeg
1 (8-inch) pie shell	1 cup cream
6 slices bacon	1 cup milk
2 teaspoons cornstarch	3 whole eggs

1 egg yolk

1. Sauté onions in butter for 20 minutes. When done, pour into a sieve to drain off butter. (Catch butter and use for cooking—it will be onion flavored.)

2. Make pie shell from Brisée dough (p. 353). Partially bake according to the tarte recipe (p. 355), through step 4.

3. Cut bacon into ½-inch pieces. Fry crisp. Drain on paper towels.

4. Put cornstarch, salt, pepper, and nutmeg in mixing bowl. Add enough cream to make a paste. Add remainder of cream, the milk, eggs, and yolk. Thoroughly mix together with a whisk, but do not beat.

5. Put bacon pieces into prebaked pie shell. Top with sautéed onions. Strain egg-milk mixture into shell. With a spoon, skim the foam from the surface (foam toughens when baked). Bake in a preheated 350-degree oven for about 20 minutes, then reduce heat to 325 degrees and bake about 10 minutes, or until set like custard. Serve warm with a green salad for Sunday brunch or supper. May also be served as a first course, but only when the meal is not heavy.

Wine: Pouilly-Fuissé

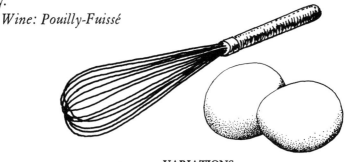

VARIATIONS

QUICHE LORRAINE

[*Cheese-Bacon-Onion Custard Pie*]

Sauté 2 onions in a chunk of butter. Substitute ½ pound sliced Gruyère or Swiss cheese for the 4 large onions sautéed in ⅛ pound butter. Proceed with the Paysanne recipe, adding the sautéed onions to the bacon and cheese strips in the pie shell. Strain milk mixture into crust.

Wine: Fleurie

QUICHE TOURANGELLE
[*Onion-Ham Custard Pie*]

Substitute 1 cup diced cooked ham for the bacon in the Paysanne recipe, then proceed with the recipe.

Wine: Saint-Émilion

SOUBISE
[*Onion Stuffing*]

4 medium-sized onions	½ cup crème fraîche, or
Water	whipping cream
⅛ pound butter	Dash of nutmeg and of pepper
2 tablespoons flour	½ teaspoon salt
1 teaspoon confectioners' sugar	

1. Peel onions and cut in half. Slice into thin wedges. Cover with cold water, bring to a boil, drain, and rinse in cold water and drain again. Sauté these blanched wedges in ⅛ pound butter until soft. Add 2 tablespoons flour. Stir-cook 2 minutes. Add crème, nutmeg, pepper, salt, and sugar. Stir-cook until thick.

2. Put mixture into a blender and whirl; press through a food mill; or mash through a sieve. (This is a kind of Béchamel paste.) This mixture, for the most part, is used in other recipes, as a farci, or stuffing. To use it as a sauce, dilute it with cream and adjust the seasonings.

VARIATIONS

SOUBISE AU RIZ
[*Onion and Rice Stuffing*]

Add ½ cup raw rice to the blanched onions and butter. Sauté 3 minutes. Add 1 cup chicken stock and cook until rice is done and dry. *Omit flour.* Add crème and season as in Soubise recipe. Press through food mill, or blend in blender. Use as a stuffing, or dilute with cream, season, and use as a sauce.

SOUBISE-AURORE
[*Tomato-flavored Soubise*]

Add ½ cup tomato paste to either of the above Soubise recipes. Adjust seasonings.

POMMES DE TERRE
[*Potatoes*]

There are many ways of preparing potatoes, and from the French we get a wide range of exotic and palatable recipes. These include Pommes Frites, Soufflées, Duchesse, Pommes de Terre Anna, and a host of others. But of all these the real challenge, even for a chef, is the souffléed potato. Its preparation, like all the rest, follows exact rules.

Regardless of the recipe selected, be sure the potatoes are of uniform size and shape when they are put on to cook. When making simple boiled potatoes, don't peel potatoes of just any size and unthinkingly plunge them into water. Potatoes of different sizes, and certainly those of different varieties, will require different cooking times.

Let's think, first of all, about plain boiled potatoes. Normally in this country they are peeled, cut into fourths, and dropped into boiling salted water. The sharp edges of a quartered potato are thin. The edges cook in a matter of minutes, and then become soggy and disintegrate into the water. Since the quarters are all of different sizes, the only sure way to know when the potatoes are done is to stab them to death with a fork. The fully cooked ones usually break apart, and the pot of quartered potatoes ends up being water-soaked, with most of the vitamins and minerals lost to the water. But here's how the French make a simple boiled spud.

POMMES DE TERRE BOUILLIES
[*Simple Boiled Potatoes*]

7 Irish potatoes	1 teaspoon salt
Water	1 teaspoon sugar
Piece of butter	

1. Select potatoes of uniform size. Peel, then cut into fourths. Trim each quarter to resemble a small whole potato. Put little potatoes into cold water as they are carved. Put trimmings into another pan of water and turn them into a potage.

2. When potato quarters are all shaped into small potatoes, drain and cover with fresh cold water. Add salt, sugar, and butter to the water. Bring to a boil and simmer about 7 minutes.

3. Test for doneness. Stick just one potato with a two-pronged fork or ice pick. If it is tender, all the potatoes will be done, since they are all the same size. Drain and dry off the potatoes over heat. Serve plain or turn into the following recipes. These will be the best-tasting potatoes you have ever eaten. Enjoy a potato for itself.

POMMES DE TERRE À LA CRÈME
[*Boiled Creamed Potatoes*]

Prepare recipe of boiled potatoes. Dry off potatoes, then add 1 cup cream and simmer until cream is reduced by about one-half. Season with salt, pepper, and nutmeg. (A thinned Béchamel sauce may also be used as a cream sauce, p. 15, but do not reduce it.)

POMMES DE TERRE CHÂTEAU
[*Sautéed Boiled Potatoes*]

Peel potatoes and cut into eighths. Trim each piece to the size of a large olive. Put on to cook in cold water seasoned with salt, sugar, and a chunk of butter. Once potatoes come to a boil, drain and dry off. Heat a chunk of butter and 2 tablespoons oil in a skillet. Add the potatoes. Sauté to a golden color. Serve sprinkled with chopped parsley.

POMMES DE TERRE FONDANTES
[*Sautéed Boiled Potatoes*]

Shape quartered potatoes. Cook as in the boiled-potato recipe and then sauté in butter and oil. Serve plain or sprinkle with parsley.

POMMES DE TERRE À LA PARISIENNE
[*Boiled Potato Balls*]

Peel potatoes. Using a melon baller, cut balls from the potatoes and start them to cook in cold water seasoned with salt, sugar, and butter. Bring just to a boil, drain, and dry off. Sauté in butter and oil like Château potatoes and then sprinkle with parsley.

POMMES FRITES PONT-NEUF

[*French-fried Potatoes*]

Good French-fried potatoes must be blanched or precooked in hot oil before they are browned. In the blanching process the potato pieces are cooked and the water evaporated from them. After blanching they are drained, cooled, and ready for the final last-minute cooking in oil to make them crisp and brown. This blanching can be done hours in advance of the final frying. Idaho potatoes are best to use in all French-fried-potato recipes.

6 Idaho potatoes	**Vegetable oil for frying**
Salt	

1. Peel potatoes. Put them into cold water as they are peeled. Square off the round potato. Cut into ¼-inch, or slightly thicker, slices; then cut these slices into strips the same width as the slice is thick. Make uniform. Soak the strips in cold water for 10 minutes. Dry on a terrycloth towel. (Water washes off the starch and firms the potatoes.) Cook in oil heated to 340 degrees for about 3 minutes. Do not brown. Lift potatoes from oil and drain on paper towels. (Make potage or Duchesse potatoes from trimmings.)

2. When ready to serve, heat oil to 390 degrees (a cube of bread will brown at this temperature in about 30 seconds). Cook only small batches of the potatoes at one time. Cook until crisp and brown. Drain on paper towels, then put potatoes on a wire cake rack, set rack on cooky sheet and into a hot oven while rest of potatoes are being cooked. Salt after they are cooked.

POMMES DE TERRE SOUFFLÉES
[*Souffléed Potatoes*]

Souffléed potatoes are one of the joys of the kitchen. They seem simple, but are tricky to make. Mellow, old Idaho potatoes uniformly cut are the first requirement. Then be careful that the fat on the first frying does not heat above 270 degrees. On this first frying potatoes are blanched or precooked to evaporate the water from them. They must not get brown. Potatoes that are brown will not puff when dunked into hot fat on the second frying. But there will always be duds, or potatoes that do not feel like puffing. If three-fourths of them inflate, you are good. Serve the ones that don't puff as potato chips. Nothing is lost.

6 Idaho potatoes   Salt
Vegetable oil for frying, or rendered beef suet

1. Peel potatoes. Place in cold water as they are peeled. Trim round sides to make a square potato. Round off the corners (make potage from trimmings), then cut into uniform slices about 3/16 inch thick, or a little less than 1/4 inch. Slice with the grain, or the flat way of the potato. The French use a special slicing board called a *mandoline* for this job. It is worthwhile to invest in one. However, they can be cut with a very sharp knife, but keep the thickness even. Soak slices in ice water for about 30 minutes.

2. Heat oil to 260 degrees. Dry six potato slices on a terrycloth towel. Add slices to the oil. Shake the pan to agitate the oil and to keep the potatoes moving. Maintain the temperature of the oil and be sure it doesn't go over 270 degrees. Cook potatoes about 4 minutes. They will remain on the bottom of the pan. Cook in small batches. Then drain on paper towels. Put them on a plate to cool for at least 10 minutes.

3. For the second frying, heat the oil to 320 degrees. Cook a few potatoes at a time. Shake the pan and use a long-handled wire strainer to keep the potatoes submerged in the oil. They should puff and come popping to the top. Once they are puffed, lift out and drain on paper towels. Cook all potatoes a second time, but don't brown. Some will not puff. Let potatoes cool another 10 minutes, or until you are ready to cook and serve them.

4. On the third frying, heat oil to 390 degrees. Add a small batch of potatoes, puffed ones first, and let them brown. Agitate the pan to keep them moving. Add the unpuffed slices and see if they will inflate. If not, brown and serve as chips. Salt after the third frying. Serve in Gaufrette Baskets (p. 240) for an elegant dinner party.

NOTE: Some people omit the second frying. Try each way. Maybe one will work better than the other for you.

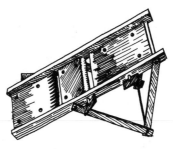

POMMES DE TERRE GAUFRETTES

[French-fried Waffled Chips]

6 Idaho potatoes   **Vegetable oil**

Salt

1. Peel potatoes and put into cold water as they are peeled. Cut the potatoes on a French mandoline cutter, or with a special knife that makes waffle
slices. Cut one slice, then turn potato ¼ way around and cut another slice.
Repeat to make a checkerboard effect in each slice.

2. Put slices into ice water for 10 minutes. Dry on terrycloth towels and
fry in oil heated to 320 degrees for 4 minutes. Drain on paper towels and then
fry a second time in oil heated to 390 degrees. Brown on the second cooking.
Drain on paper towels and sprinkle with salt.

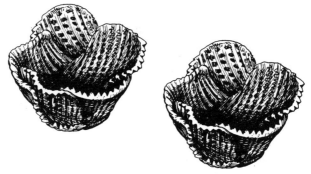

VARIATION

PANIERS DE POMMES DE TERRE GAUFRETTES

[Waffled Potato Baskets]

Cut the potatoes in waffle style on either a mandoline or a special cutter.
The French have a special wire nest in which they make potato baskets. Two
different-sized tea strainers may be substituted. In the big wire nest overlap
about 6 slices of gaufrette-cut potatoes. Then set the smaller basket into it to
hold the slices in place. French-fry twice. Blanch, or precook at 340 degrees for
about 4 minutes to evaporate the moisture from the slices. Lift out, but leave in
basket while oil heats to 380 degrees. Fry baskets a second time. Cook until
brown. (See note below.)

After the potato basket is browned, remove the inside wire basket, turn the big basket upside down, give it a tap on the bottom with the little inside basket and knock the cooked potato basket out onto paper towels. Salt, and let cool. Make the next basket. Fill the baskets with Pommes de Terre Soufflées (p. 239), Pommes Parisienne (p. 237), cooked peas, carrots, or other vegetables.

These baskets can be made weeks ahead of time, so long as they are kept dry. I make about a dozen each time and keep what I don't use on a metal pan in the oven. Pilot-lighted ovens are a perfect place in which to store crisp, dry foods.

NOTE: Baskets are best if cooked twice, but they may be cooked only once at 360 degrees.

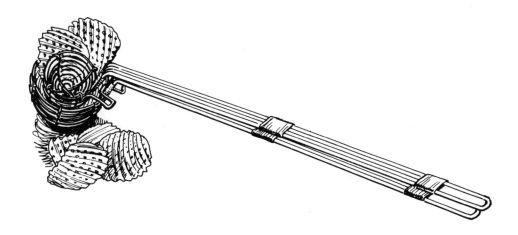

POMMES DE TERRE DUCHESSE

[*Duchesse Potatoes*]

When puréed or riced potatoes are made with eggs instead of milk, they are called Duchesse potatoes. Eggs give potatoes strength and lightness that cause them to puff. They make an attractive garnish to casseroles and meat platters.

6 large red potatoes	1 whole egg
1 teaspoon salt	2 egg yolks
1 teaspoon sugar	Salt and white pepper to taste
Butter	Dash of nutmeg

1. Peel potatoes. Cut each into quarters. Put on to cook in water seasoned with salt, sugar, and a chunk of butter. Boil until potatoes are done. Drain and dry off. Shake pan to be sure the potatoes are completely dry.

(*continued*)

2. Press through a food mill or put through a potato ricer. There should be about 6 cups of riced potatoes. It is a good idea to measure how many you have, then adjust the ingredients accordingly. (The mixture should be soft enough to squeeze through a pastry nozzle, yet firm enough to hold its shape.) Add a chunk of butter and mix well. Mix together egg and yolks, then add them to the potatoes. Mix well and then season with salt, pepper, and nutmeg. If the mixture seems dry, add an egg white; then if it needs more, add the yolk.

3. These potatoes are used in other recipes or to garnish foods. Put them into a pastry bag with star nozzle. Squeeze potato mixture onto a greased and floured cooky sheet: make mounds, designs in the shape of a figure 8, make several 8's on top of one another, or make circles several layers high. When mixture is all used, brown the potato creations in a 475-degree oven. Remove from cooky sheet with pancake turner, and place on platter to garnish foods.

4. These potatoes may be piped around the edge of casseroles or platters and then browned in a hot oven or under a broiler.

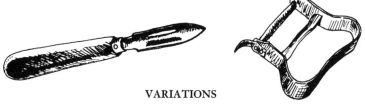

VARIATIONS

In addition to being a garnish for other foods, Duchesse potatoes are at the base of the following recipes.

CROQUETTES DE POMMES DE TERRE

[*Potato Croquettes*]

Make Duchesse potatoes and refrigerate about 2 hours. When they are cold, put on a floured surface. Roll pieces of the potato dough into ropes, 1 inch in diameter. Cut 2-inch pieces from the rope, dip into slightly beaten egg white and then into fine, dry bread crumbs. French-fry in 390-degree oil until brown. These look like corks when they are fried. They can be made any shape.

TARTELETTES AUX POMMES DE TERRE

[*Potato Shells*]

Refrigerate Duchesse potato mixture until cold. Roll on a floured surface to about ¼-inch thickness. Cut out circles and line buttered and floured tart pans. Brush dough with beaten egg. Bake in 400-degree oven until lightly puffed and brown. Remove from pans. Fill with creamed chicken, mushrooms, quenelles, or vegetables.

POMMES DE TERRE MONT-DORE
[*Golden Potatoes*]

Add sufficient cream to a recipe of hot Duchesse potatoes to make them like mashed potatoes. Add ½ cup grated Parmesan cheese and mix. Put on round oven-proof serving platter. Shape like a cone or a mountain. Once shaped, take a fork and make ridges up and down the mountain of potatoes. Coat with melted butter, and sprinkle with grated Parmesan cheese. Heat the potato mountain in a 350-degree oven for about 20 minutes, or until browned and hot.

CROUSTADES EN POMMES DE TERRE DUCHESSE
[*Potato Crusts*]

Chill Duchesse potatoes for about 2 hours. Pat out mixture on a floured surface to 1-inch thickness. Cut out circles with a 2½-inch biscuit cutter. Dip in frothy egg white and then in fine, dry bread crumbs. With the hole part of a doughnut cutter, mark a 1-inch circle in the middle of the potato biscuit to about ½ inch in depth. French-fry in 390-degree oil. When brown, drain on paper towels. Lift out the little circle and carefully remove some of the inside soft potatoes to make room for a filling. Fill with creamed diced chicken, mushrooms, quenelles, or vegetables. Remove the soft potato mixture from the little round circles and set them back over the filling. Serve as a first course, or luncheon dish. These are very pretty.

GNOCCHI DE POMMES DE TERRE
[*Potato Pasta*]

The following recipe is a kind of potato quenelle, but it's called gnocchi. Quenelle ordinarily applies to protein mixtures. I love gnocchi, although they are Italian or Austro-Hungarian in origin. Usually gnocchi are served as a first course with a thinned sauce from the Demi-glace or Béchamel family, or with the simple sauce given with the recipe. Like the preceding recipes, gnocchi are created from a variation on Duchesse potatoes.

6 large red potatoes	2 whole eggs
Chunk of butter	1 egg yolk
1 cup flour	Salt, white pepper, and nutmeg to taste

Sauce

¼ pound butter	½ cup water
Grated Parmesan cheese	

(*continued*)

1. Cook potatoes in seasoned water as in Duchesse potato recipe (p. 241), then drain, dry off and grind potatoes through a food mill. Add a chunk of butter and the flour to the potatoes. Blend well. Add eggs one at a time and beat. Add the yolk, some salt, pepper, and nutmeg. Mix well, taste, and adjust the seasonings.

2. Put mixture into a pastry bag with ½-inch round nozzle tube. Squeeze out about 1 inch of mixture and cut it off with a knife into simmering salted water. Poach gnocchi about 5 minutes, then lift out and put into cold water to stop their cooking. These inflate as they cook.

3. When all gnocchi are cooked, place in a shallow oven-proof dish. Bring ¼ pound butter and ½ cup water to a boil. Pour over gnocchi and sprinkle with Parmesan. Heat and brown on top shelf of a 450-degree oven.

POMMES DE TERRE DAUPHINE

[*Fried Potato Puffs*]

Duchesse Potatoes

3 large potatoes	1 small egg
Salt	1 egg yolk
Sugar	Pepper to taste
Butter	Dash of nutmeg

Pâte à Chou

½ cup water	½ cup flour
⅛ pound butter	2 eggs
⅛ teaspoon salt	Oil for French frying

1. Peel and quarter potatoes. Cook in water seasoned with 1 teaspoon of salt, of sugar, and a chunk of butter. When done, drain, dry off and press through food mill or mash through a ricer. Blend with a piece of butter. Mix in egg and yolk. Season with pepper and nutmeg. (This is a half batch of Duchesse potatoes.) Cover, ready to use.

2. Heat water, butter, and salt. Once mixture is boiling, stir in flour all at once, and continue to stir until a ball forms around the spoon. Remove from heat. Add the eggs, one at a time, beating the mixture well after each is added. (This is a half recipe of Pâte à Chou.)

3. There should be equal amounts of potatoes and dough. Err on the side of more potatoes than dough, and have both about the same temperature. Mix together.

4. Heat vegetable oil to 360 degrees. Using a teaspoon, drop the batter into the hot oil and brown. Drain on paper towels and serve.

NOTE: Mixture may be rolled in fine crumbs and formed into fancy shapes and then fried.

VARIATION
POMMES DE TERRE LORETTE
[Potato Puffs with Cheese]

To the Pommes de Terre Dauphine recipe add about ¼ cup grated Parmesan cheese. Using a tablespoon, drop potato batter into 360-degree oil. When brown, drain and serve.

POMMES DE TERRE ANNA
[Sliced Sautéed Potatoes]

6–8 medium-sized red potatoes   **½ pound melted butter**
Salt and pepper

1. Peel potatoes and put into cold water. Slice each potato on a slicer of some kind, or uniformly slice by hand. These should be very thin, about ¹⁄₁₆ inch.

2. The French have a special pan with straight-up sides and overlapping lid so that the pan can be turned over to brown the top. Such a pan is not necessary. Use an 8-inch, oven-proof skillet, casserole, or cake pan with sides 2 inches high. Coat with melted butter. Select the most perfect slices for the sides and bottom of the pan. Arrange them neatly, overlapping each slice around the sides, then in spiral fashion from the center out over the bottom of the pan. Coat with melted butter. Add another layer of potatoes. Coat with butter, then sprinkle with salt and pepper. Fill pan, coating each layer with butter, and sprinkling with salt and pepper. Use all the butter. Press potatoes down tight, cover with foil, and bake on lowest rack in a 400-degree oven for about 1 hour. After 40 minutes, check to be sure potatoes aren't getting too brown. If they are, slip a sheet of foil under the pan. If they aren't browning, increase the heat to 450 degrees.

3. When potatoes are done, drain off butter. To do this punch a hole in the foil, at the edge, then place a pot holder on the foil and with one hand hold the potatoes in the pan while pouring the butter from the pan. Save butter and use for sautéing. Remove foil. Run a knife around the inside of the pan to be sure the potatoes are loose from the sides. Then put serving plate over the potatoes and invert. Thus the bottom of the casserole becomes the top. Cut like a pie to serve.

NOTE: To make for 2 people, use only 3 potatoes. Arrange the slices in a small enameled-iron skillet, season each layer with melted butter, salt, and pepper, then cover with foil and a lid. Cook over very low heat on top of the range. If potatoes seem too brown before they are soft and translucent, set skillet on an asbestos pad. Top-of-the-range cooking works only with a small quantity of potatoes and in a heavy skillet.

PETITES POMMES DE TERRE ANNA

[*Miniature Potato Tarts*]

Use about 4 very large potatoes. Peel and cut each into fourths. Trim each fourth into a long skinny potato shape. (Make potage from trimmings.) Slice potatoes thin and arrange in buttered tart pans. Season with melted butter, salt, and pepper. Cover with foil, set onto the lowest rack of the oven and bake at 400 degrees for about 40 minutes. When done invert and serve around a roast, or with steaks or chops.

POMMES DE TERRE À LA BOULANGÈRE

[*Potatoes with Onions*]

Thinly slice 5–6 potatoes and 3 onions. Alternate layers of potatoes and onions. Season and make according to Pommes de Terre Anna.

POMMES DE TERRE À LA SARLADAISE

[*Potatoes with Truffles*]

Make like Boulangère, using 6 potatoes and substituting 4 thinly sliced truffles for the onions. (Since truffles are so expensive I suggest you cut 2 truffles into julienne strips and sprinkle them over the middle layer.) Season and make according to Pommes de Terre Anna.

POMMES DE TERRE À LA VICHY

[*Potatoes with Carrots*]

Slice about 6 carrots, or enough to make at least 2 layers, and 5–6 potatoes. Alternate layers of potatoes and carrots. Season and make according to Pommes de Terre Anna.

STEM VEGETABLES

Stalk or stem vegetables, like root vegetables, may be cooked with the skin on; but they are better when peeled. If stalk vegetables are garden fresh, like young asparagus, do not strip them of their protective covering. But garden fresh vegetables are pretty uncommon. Therefore, I recommend that all stem vegetables, asparagus, broccoli, and celery, be peeled before they are cooked.

ASPERGE
[*Asparagus*]

When I'm presented with a plateful of *peeled* shafts of asparagus I recall the sentiments of Uncle Remus and so "all by my own-alone self" I'm happy. "Hit look lak sparrer-grass, hit feel like sparrer-grass, hit tas'e lak sparrer-grass, en I bless ef 'taint sparrer-grass."

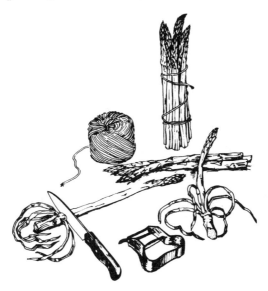

ASPERGES BOUILLIES
[*Boiled Asparagus*]

24 fat stalks of asparagus	Salt
4 quarts water	1 tablespoon sugar
Chunk of butter	

1. Wash asparagus. Rest the tip of the asparagus stalk on the counter. Then, using a potato peeler, start peeling down 2 inches from the tip. Rotate the stalk by the tough base as you peel. At the point where the peeler becomes hard to pull, the stalk becomes tough and inedible. Completely peel the stalk, then cut off the peel and end of the stalk.

2. When all stalks are peeled, divide and tie in three bundles. Put stalks in your left hand, tap on the counter, making the bottom stems all even. With heavy string (a thin string would cut into the asparagus once it is cooked) wrap twice around the bottom, then wrap around the top, and then back to the middle of the bundle. Pick up the other end of the string and tie in the middle. The string is for lifting the cooked asparagus from the water. When peeled, stalks and tips cook in about the same length of time.

(continued)

3. Put about 4 quarts water into a large kettle. Add 2 tablespoons salt. Bring to a boil. Add asparagus bundles and cook 4 minutes. Skinny asparagus cooks in about 2 minutes. (If asparagus is to be served immediately, add 1 minute to cooking time and season water with sugar and butter. Omit steps 4 and 5, but drain on cloth.)

4. At the end of cooking time run fork under string in the middle of the bundle and lift out. Put into sink filled with cold water. Do not wash in running water; it might damage the tender tips. When cool, drain on kitchen towel ready to reheat.

5. When ready to serve, put into kettle of boiling water (about 3 quarts), seasoned with 1 teaspoon salt, 1 tablespoon sugar, and a chunk of butter. As soon as the water returns to a boil, lift out the asparagus by the string and drain on a cloth towel.

6. Once it has been drained, lift by string to hot serving plate. Cut and remove strings. Serve plain with melted butter, or by one of the following recipes. Make the sauce before cooking the asparagus the final time.

NOTE: Asparagus is delicious when chilled and served with a Vinaigrette dressing or Fines Herbes Mayonnaise. (See Chapter XVIII, "Buffet Froid.")

VARIATIONS
ASPERGES AU BEURRE NOISETTE
[*Asparagus in Browned Butter*]

Clarify ⅛ pound butter (p. 599), then heat to a nut brown. Pour sizzling hot over drained, cooked asparagus, and serve immediately.

ASPERGES À LA CHANTILLY
[*Asparagus with Chantilly Sauce*]

Cook asparagus. Make Chantilly sauce (p. 25). Reheat asparagus, and serve with the sauce.

ASPERGES À LA CRÈME
[*Asparagus in Cream*]

Once asparagus is cooled and drained, cut 2-inch tips from stalks and cut stalks into 1-inch pieces. Heat together a chunk of butter and ½ cup crème fraîche, or whipping cream, in a skillet. Season with salt, pepper, and a bit of lemon juice. Add cut asparagus stalks. Heat for about 1 minute, or until hot, then pour into serving dish. Reheat tips in boiling water for a second, then drain, and arrange tips over the top of the creamed asparagus.

ASPERGES À LA HOLLANDAISE

[*Asparagus with Hollandaise Sauce*]

Cooked asparagus served with Hollandaise sauce (p. 21). When asparagus is served with a sauce from the Hollandaise family let the asparagus cool slightly, or it will melt the sauce.

ASPERGES À LA MALTAISE

[*Asparagus with Orange-flavored Hollandaise*]

Cooked asparagus served with Maltaise sauce (p. 26). The orange flavor of the sauce does wonderful things for asparagus, especially the green variety.

ASPERGES À LA MOUSSELINE

[*Asparagus with a Light Hollandaise*]

Asparagus served with Mousseline sauce (p. 26). The lightness of this sauce makes it especially good on asparagus.

ASPERGES À LA POLONAISE

[*Asparagus with Toasted Crumbs*]

Cook asparagus. Arrange spears on serving plate. Sprinkle with sieved hard-cooked egg yolk and minced parsley. Tear 1 slice firm-type bread into fine crumbs. Add crumbs to ⅛ pound clarified butter. Toast bread and butter to a nut brown. Spoon over yolks and parsley.

PAIN D'ASPERGES

[*Asparagus Timbale*]

Substitute finely sliced cooked asparagus for the spinach in the Pain d'Épinards recipe (p. 257).

CHOUX BROCOLIS

[*Broccoli*]

Broccoli, when peeled, becomes far more than a common member of the cabbage family. The peeled stalks are emerald green and translucent when cooked, and they are as different from ordinary broccoli as champagne is from beer.

CHOUX BROCOLIS BOUILLIS

[Boiled Broccoli]

2–3 pounds broccoli	Salt
4 quarts water	1 tablespoon sugar

Butter

1. If possible select broccoli with stalks no bigger than your thumb; but if stalks are larger, cut them in halves or in quarters. Allow 2 thumb-size stalks per serving.

2. Wash broccoli, then peel. Beginning at the bottom of each stalk, insert paring knife under the skin and pull it off in strips down to the head. Discard the leaves and tiny buds that come off with the skin. They are strong in flavor. Make clean, neat peeled stalks with just the heads remaining on the stalks.

3. Tie in handful-size bundles. Bring water and 2 tablespoons salt to a boil. Add broccoli bundles and blanch for 2 minutes after water returns to a boil. Cool by letting cold water run gently down the inside of the pan to displace the hot water. Lift broccoli from cold water, drain, blot on layers of paper towels, and set aside. Use in other recipes, or reheat when ready to serve.

4. When ready to serve, put into kettle of boiling water (about 3 quarts), seasoned with 1 teaspoon salt, sugar, and a chunk of butter. As soon as the water returns to a boil cook 1 to 2 minutes or until just tender. Lift out the broccoli by the string, and drain on layers of paper towels. Once it has drained, place on serving plate. Remove strings. Serve with melted butter, or in one of the following recipes. Make the sauce before cooking the broccoli the final time.

NOTE: Broccoli is delicious when served cold. (See Chapter XVIII, "Buffet Froid.")

CHOUX BROCOLIS EN FRITOTS

[French-fried Broccoli]

Substitute blanched broccoli (use just the flowerets and two inches of the stem) for the cauliflower in the Chou-Fleur en Fritots recipe (p. 267).

VARIATIONS

CHOUX BROCOLIS À LA MILANAISE

[*Broccoli with Parmesan Cheese*]

Place blanched broccoli in buttered casserole. Remove strings. Sprinkle with grated Parmesan cheese. Pour over ⅛ pound melted butter. Bake in 400-degree oven for about 10 minutes. At the moment of serving spoon over ⅛ pound Noisette butter (p. 37).

PAIN DE CHOUX BROCOLIS

[*Broccoli Timbale*]

Dice cooked broccoli to make 2 cups. Substitute broccoli for spinach in the Pain d'Épinards recipe (p. 257).

In addition to the above recipes, broccoli may be prepared by the following recipes for asparagus (pp. 247–249):

Choux Brocolis au Beurre Noisette   Choux Brocolis à la Maltaise
Choux Brocolis à la Crème   Choux Brocolis à la Polonaise
Choux Brocolis à l'Hollandaise

CÉLERI EN BRANCHES

[*Celery*]

Celery is one of the most misunderstood of all vegetables. We gnaw at it and think of it as rabbit food. We toss it into soups for flavor, but seldom do we regard it as a vegetable to be cooked and served with dignity. Experiment seriously with this sturdy member of the parsley family.

CÉLERIS BOUILLIS

[*Boiled Celery*]

6 celery hearts (1½ inches in   4 quarts water
diameter)   1 tablespoon salt

1. Select celery hearts of uniform size. Peel the outside branches with a potato peeler to remove the skin and fiberlike strings. Discard these. Cut off the upper part of the celery stalks at the joints. Save for other use. Run cold water down into the celery hearts to remove any grit that might be trapped within the branches. Tie each stalk around the top of the branches.

(continued)

2. Heat water and salt to a boil. Add celery hearts. Simmer for 10 minutes. Cool by letting cold tap water run into the pan to displace the hot water. When stalks are cool, drain, and then blot on a terrycloth towel or layers of paper towels. Once the celery is blanched in this fashion, it is then ready to be used in other recipes.

CÉLERIS BRAISÉS
[*Braised Celery*]

Tie, then blanch celery (see preceding recipe), cool, and drain. Remove strings. Cut hearts in half lengthwise. Trim bottom ends. Put into skillet with ⅛ pound melted butter. Add 2 cups chicken stock, juice of ½ lemon, 1 table-spoon sugar, and dash of salt. (Easy on the salt; celery has been cooked in salted water and the stock, if canned, is seasoned.) Simmer about 30 minutes over low heat. Do not cover. Put celery cut side down into serving dish and sprinkle with freshly ground pepper and minced parsley. If there is more than ½ cup liquid in the pan, boil to reduce, then pour over the celery.

VARIATIONS
CÉLERIS À LA BÉCHAMEL
[*Celery in Béchamel Sauce*]

Prepare Céleris Braisés. While celery cooks, make the Béchamel sauce (p. 15). Place the braised celery, cut side down, in a buttered baking dish. Add the ½ cup of pan liquids to the Béchamel. Pour over celery and sprinkle with grated Parmesan cheese. Bake in 400-degree oven for about 15 minutes, or until browned and hot.

CÉLERIS À LA CRÈME
[*Creamed Celery*]

Prepare Céleris Braisés. When done, heat 1 cup crème fraîche or whipping cream. Add 1 tablespoon Madeira, and pour over celery. Sprinkle with minced parsley and serve on separate plates.

CÉLERIS AU BEURRE NOISETTE
[*Celery with Browned Butter*]

Make Céleris Braisés. Put into serving dish and spoon over pan liquids. Toast ⅛ pound clarified butter to a nut brown. Pour sizzling hot over the celery at the moment of serving.

CÉLERIS À LA POLONAISE
[*Celery with Toasted Crumbs*]

Make Céleris Braisés, but put celery, cut side *up,* on serving plate. Spoon over liquids. (The curved branches will hold the liquids and garnish.) Sprinkle with sieved hard-cooked egg yolks and minced parsley. Tear 1 slice firm-type bread into fine crumbs and add to ⅛ pound melted butter in skillet. Brown butter and bread. Pour over the yolks, parsley, and celery. Serve sizzling hot. Delicious!

LEAF VEGETABLES

Leafy vegetables usually end up in the salad bowl, although all may be cooked, even lettuce. Methods of cooking leafy vegetables are both simple and involved. Spinach, when properly boiled, can be more succulent than early June peas. Lettuce, when stuffed and braised, becomes something quite different from its normal crisp self. Parsley, when fried, is unusually good and becomes a conversation piece at the table.

CHOUX VERTS
[*Green Cabbage*]

Cut a 2-pound head of cabbage in half. Place flat side down on cutting board and, beginning at the top of the head, cut in fine shreds across the cabbage. Put shreds into a vegetable basket or colander and submerge in boiling salted water. Cook about 3 minutes after water returns to a boil. Lift out, drain and toss with ⅛ pound melted butter. Serve sprinkled with freshly-ground pepper and chopped parsley.

VARIATIONS
CHOU VERT À LA CRÈME
[*Cabbage in Cream*]

Add about ½ cup crème fraîche or whipping cream to melted butter and then toss with cooked cabbage. Season and serve.

CHOU VERT FARCI
[Stuffed Cabbage]

Trim a small head of cabbage of its heavy outer leaves. Blanch head in salted water for 10 minutes. Remove from heat, cool under cold running water, and then drain. Pull leaves down and remove the inside of the cabbage. Dice fine. Make stuffing as in recipe for Endives Farcies which follows. Substitute the diced cabbage for the endive hearts. Fill cabbage cavity. Pull leaves up around filling and tie. Cook in Demi-glace sauce according to Endives Farcies recipe. Set cooked cabbage into a round serving dish, remove strings, and pour sauce around base of the cabbage. Cut into wedges and serve with the sauce.

ENDIVE
[Endive]

Innocent-looking, short, and fat, stalks of endive might be expected to taste soft and sweet. But they are quite the opposite. Somewhat bitter in taste, they are tough enough to require a knife for cutting even when cooked. But it is just these challenging qualities that devotees of endive love.

The plants of the endive are cultivated in total darkness so that they do not develop into a green leafy plant. This pearl-white vegetable, like the truly leafy and green vegetables, is good both in salads and when cooked.

ENDIVES FARCIES
[Stuffed Endive]

12 stalks Belgian endive	3 quarts water
	1 tablespoon salt

Stuffing

Endive centers	1 egg
1 pound ground pork	2 tablespoons Madeira
½ teaspoon salt	Chunk of butter
Dash of pepper	Demi-glace sauce
1 minced shallot	Beurre manié
2 tablespoons chopped parsley	Chopped parsley

1. Blanch endives in boiling salted water for 5 minutes. Drain and cool under cold running water. Carefully pull the outside leaves back and cut out the centers. Dice the centers.

2. Combine diced endive, pork, ½ teaspoon salt, pepper, shallot, parsley, egg, and Madeira. Mix well and then stuff into center of each endive. Tie with string to keep leaves in place and to hold the stuffing within the stalk. Brown in a chunk of butter. Make Demi-glace sauce (p. 27). Sauté carrots and onions in Demi-glace recipe for 10 minutes, then add balance of sauce ingredients, except Cognac and Madeira. Add the browned endive. Simmer about 1 hour. Lift endive from sauce and remove strings. Strain the sauce. Heat, taste, and thicken sauce with beurre manié if necessary. Flavor with Cognac and Madeira from Demi-glace recipe, and glaze endive on serving plate. Sprinkle with chopped parsley. Serve remainder of sauce separately. Always freeze what sauce remains for another meal. Degrease sauce before serving.

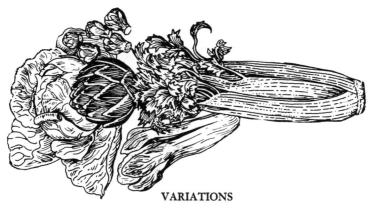

VARIATIONS

ENDIVES BRAISÉES

[*Braised Endive*]

Blanch 12 endive in salted water for about 5 minutes. Cool under cold running water and drain. Cook the blanched stalks in ⅛ pound butter, juice of ½ lemon, 1 cup chicken stock, and 1 tablespoon sugar. Cover and simmer about 1 hour. Turn endive during cooking. If liquid remains, boil away and caramelize the stalks. Serve sprinkled with freshly ground pepper and minced parsley.

ENDIVES À LA CRÈME

[*Endive in Cream*]

Braise endive as above. Lift the braised endive to a hot platter. Stir about 4 tablespoons crème fraîche or whipping cream into the pan. Heat and pour over stalks. Sprinkle with freshly ground pepper and serve.

ÉPINARDS BOUILLIS
[*Boiled Spinach*]

3 pounds fresh spinach, about 3 cups	6 quarts water
	2 tablespoons salt

1. Wash spinach in lots of water. Strip each leaf of its stem and the heavy vein that runs through the middle. Bring water and salt to a boil. Add spinach, bring water back to a boil, and cook 1 minute.

2. Lift spinach from the water with a long-handled strainer. By lifting the spinach from the water, you leave the grit in the water. Put spinach into basin of cold water to stop its cooking. When cool, put in colander to drain. Then squeeze spinach between the palms of your hands to extract the water. It is now ready to be heated and served by one of the following recipes.

VARIATIONS
CROQUETTES AUX ÉPINARDS
[*Spinach Croquettes*]

Drain and dry off 2 cups chopped cooked spinach (2 pounds uncooked) and combine with 1 cup Duchesse potatoes (p. 241). Shape and cook according to Croquettes de Pommes de Terre (p. 242).

ÉPINARDS À L'ANGLAISE
[*Spinach with Melted Butter*]

Cooked spinach served with individual dishes of melted butter. Guests dunk each bite into their own butter pots.

ÉPINARDS AU BEURRE
[*Buttered Spinach*]

Put drained spinach into a large skillet. Heat to dry off spinach. Pour over ¼ pound melted butter. Heat and toss spinach to coat all leaves. Taste and adjust seasonings.

ÉPINARDS À LA CRÈME
[*Spinach in Cream*]

To buttered spinach add 1 cup crème fraîche. Heat, adjust seasonings, and add 1 tablespoon Madeira. If whipping cream is substituted for the crème fraîche, thicken with a bit of beurre manié.

ÉPINARDS AU BEURRE NOISETTE

[*Spinach in Browned Butter*]

Clarify ⅛ pound butter, then toast to a nut brown. Sprinkle spinach with freshly ground pepper, nutmeg, and some minced parsley. Pour sizzling butter over the top.

PAIN D'ÉPINARDS

[*Spinach Mold*]

2 pounds fresh spinach, or	⅛ teaspoon pepper
3 pounds if with roots	1½ teaspoons sugar
3 slices soft bread	3 egg yolks
⅛ pound butter	4 tablespoons grated
1 onion, minced	Parmesan cheese
4 tablespoons flour	3 tablespoons Madeira
1½ cups chilled cream	3 egg whites
⅛ teaspoon nutmeg	½ teaspoon salt
½ teaspoon salt	1 teaspoon sugar

1. Cook spinach (Épinards Bouillis, p. 256). Drain, dry off, and then chop fine. There should be about 2 cups spinach. Be sure it is as dry as possible. Cut crusts from bread, then cut bread into small cubes. There should be about 1 cup cubes. Combine spinach with bread cubes. Mix well.

2. Melt butter in skillet. Sauté onion. Add flour and cook a few minutes. Add cream, nutmeg, ½ teaspoon salt, pepper, and 1½ teaspoons sugar. Stir-cook until thickened. Add about half the hot sauce to the yolks. Mix well and then stir into the sauce. Stir in Parmesan and Madeira. Remove from heat.

3. Add sauce to spinach to make creamed spinach mixture. Beat whites to a froth. Add ½ teaspoon salt. Beat until almost stiff. Add 1 teaspoon sugar and beat to a firm stiffness. Fold into spinach mixture. Butter a 5- or 6-cup charlotte mold. Fill to the top. Put a 2-inch buttered foil collar (step 1, p. 336, for instructions on making collars) around the top of the mold. Tie in place around the pan and hold the top together with a paper clip or pin. Add rest of spinach mixture. Set in a hot-water bath (p. 614) and bake about 1½ hours in a 325-degree oven, or until puffed and set like custard.

4. When the spinach mold is done, carefully remove the foil collar. Set mold in round serving dish, tie a napkin around the mold as a chef does around his neck, and serve at the table. Serve plain or with a Mornay (p. 18) or Champignon sauce (p. 20). Make sauce while spinach bakes.

(continued)

NOTES: If spinach mold is served with Blanquette de Veau or other meat dish with creamy sauce the sauce from the meat is sufficient for the spinach.

If using a heavy porcelain or enamel-coated soufflé dish, do not cook in a water bath, and reduce the cooking time to about 40 minutes, or until mold is puffed and browned.

To determine the size of the casserole, simply measure water into it before it is buttered.

This recipe yields about 6 cups uncooked spinach mixture.

If a larger cooking dish is used, say 8 cups, a foil collar is not necessary since the spinach mixture will not rise above the pan. But the mold will also not be as pretty to serve since it will not rise above its container or stand at attention when served.

VARIATIONS
PAIN D'ÉPINARDS FRITS
[*Fried Spinach Mold*]

Cut leftover spinach mold into slices, coat with flour and sauté in butter.

PANNEQUETS D'ÉPINARDS
[*Spinach-stuffed Pancakes*]

Make crêpes (p. 365). Prepare Pain d'Épinards down to placing in mold. Stuff each crêpe with mixture. Place stuffed crêpes on a buttered baking platter. Glaze with butter, sprinkle with grated Parmesan, and bake in a preheated 375-degree oven for about 20 minutes, or until puffed. Serve with a sauce from the Béchamel family (pp. 16–19).

LAITUE
[*Lettuce*]

In this country lettuce is normally used just in salads, but try cooking it for a change.

LAITUES BRAISÉES
[*Braised Lettuce*]

Use Boston-type head lettuce or large Bibb lettuce in Endives Braisés recipe. Allow ½ head per serving. Blanch lettuce, cool, and drain. Press each head between the palms of your hands to extract the water. Cut heads in half;

cut out and discard core. Roll core end up into the top leaves. Tie with string. Braise according to the Endives Braisés recipe. Do not cover, and cook for only 20 minutes. Do not caramelize the lettuce; to do so makes lettuce as tough as parchment paper. When done, put lettuce on serving platter and remove strings. Serve with pan liquids and sprinkle with freshly ground pepper and minced parsley.

LAITUES À LA CRÈME
[*Lettuce in Cream*]

Blanch lettuce, then follow recipe for Endives à la Crème. Remove the strings before pouring the cream sauce over the lettuce.

LAITUES FARCIES
[*Stuffed Lettuce*]

Blanch, cool, and drain 3 heads Boston lettuce. Cut in half; then cut out cores. Remove center lettuce leaves and dice. Then follow recipe for Endives Farcies, using diced lettuce in place of the endive centers in the stuffing. Divide the stuffing among the 6 halves of lettuce. Roll, tie, and braise in sauce according to Endive recipe. Simmer for about 45 minutes. Pork filling must be well done. When done, place on platter and remove strings. Thicken sauce, add Madeira and Cognac, and glaze lettuce bundles. Sprinkle with minced parsley. Serve remaining sauce separately. Skim fat from surface of the sauce before serving.

PERSIL FRIT
[*French-fried Parsley*]

The taste of French-fried parsley will surprise and delight you. Break small branches of parsley from the stalk. Wash and dry. Put into wire basket and submerge in oil heated to 360 degrees. Fry for about 5 seconds, then remove and drain on paper towels. Use as a garnish.

When using any of the batters on pp. 10–11 to coat food, dip some dry, clean parsley into the batter and fry until brown and crisp. Use as a garnish for the particular food being batter fried.

FLOWER VEGETABLES

Flower vegetables have many petals which grow like a blossom on a central stalk. The group is made up of the "head" vegetables.

The artichoke is a bloom of elegance. This flower with its prickly leaves is one of the rare delicacies of the vegetable world. To eat it is an adventure, for no thistle ever grew that so easily puts aside its spiny exterior to let the ravenous eater get directly at its heart.

Artichokes are eaten for themselves and are used as containers in which to display other foods. We find them filled with Béarnaise or Provençale sauce. And, when other vegetables need a platform on which to stand, artichokes may support them.

Cauliflower, in its natural state, is arranged in nosegay fashion. Green leaves encircle its snowball head. With care cauliflower can be cooked and presented in its natural state. That Mark Twain should have described it as "cabbage with a college education" gave it a dubious reputation. But, since he did, let us give it a postgraduate course.

Thomas Wolfe in his writings seemed to feel that Brussels sprouts tasted as if they had soaked up the "wet, woolen air" of England. But that's not true when they are properly cooked.

In this section we will do our best to keep vegetable flowers from looking like the last roses of summer.

ARTICHAUT
[Artichokes]

Artichokes, to be eaten, must be understood. Each has a heart (or bottom), a choke, a cone, a stem, and petals. At the base of each petal is a tiny kernel of meat. To get this nugget off, pull the base of the cooked petal between the teeth and strip it out. Discard the petal and break off another petal, dunk, and eat. Once all the petals have been removed, one is confronted with a cone of tissue-like purplish petals that look good enough to eat, but one normally does not. The base is tender, but the tip is a thorn. This inverted cone lifts off to reveal a cushion of down which is *not* edible. This is the choke. With a teaspoon, scoop it from the firm meaty base which is the edible artichoke bottom. Once the choke is removed, cut the bottom into wedges and eat. The elegance of artichokes is unrivaled.

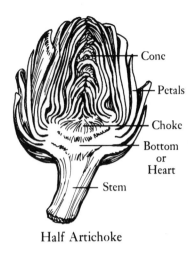

Cone

Petals

Choke

Bottom
or
Heart

Stem

Half Artichoke

ARTICHAUTS BOUILLIS

[Boiled Artichokes]

6 artichokes   **6 quarts water**

3 tablespoons salt

1. The preparation of whole artichokes is always the same. Hold the flower by the stem and plunge it up and down in a basin of cold water to remove the dirt particles trapped in the petals. Do not soak artichokes or they become tough. Break off the stems at the base of the flower and the small base petals. With a knife, cut ¾ inch off the top. With a scissors snip ½ inch from the top of each petal to remove the thorny tip. Place, base down, in boiling, salted water. Boil about 45 minutes, or until the base, where the stem was, sticks tender.

2. When artichokes are done, lift from the water, and stand on their heads to drain. Then turn right side up and carefully open the petals. Pull out the "cone" and set aside. With a teaspoon, reach inside and scoop out the choke, leaving the artichoke bottom. Push the petals back tight. Turn the cone up, point down, into the artichoke and fill cone with Hollandaise (p. 21).

3. Pull off each petal, beginning at the bottom, dunk its base in the sauce, then pull between the teeth to extract the kernel. Discard petals as they are eaten. Once petals have all been eaten, discard the cone. Cut the heart or bottom into wedges and enjoy with more sauce.

ARTICHAUTS BARIGOULE

[*Stuffed Artichokes*]

Boil artichokes, drain, and remove chokes. While artichokes cook, make a double recipe of pork filling from stuffed endive recipe (p. 254). (Omit the diced endive centers.) Fill artichokes, place a square of salt pork over the filling and tie with string into neat packages. Cook in a Demi-glace sauce (p. 27) just like stuffed endive. When done, remove strings and spoon sauce over each artichoke. Serve remaining sauce separately in individual dishes to accompany each artichoke. Dip petals into sauce and eat the kernels. Then eat stuffing with the artichoke bottom. These are nice for Sunday brunch on a cold winter's day.

ARTICHAUTS AU BEURRE

[*Artichokes with Butter*]

Boil artichokes, drain, and remove cones and chokes. Fill inverted cones with minced parsley and put back inside. Serve each artichoke with a small dish of hot melted butter. Dunk the base of each petal and eat. Then eat the heart or artichoke bottom.

ARTICHAUTS FARCIS AUX ARTICHAUTS

[*Artichokes Stuffed with Artichokes*]

This recipe is one I created for our "Tired Old Wine Society." We're a group of eight who pamper ourselves by drinking ancient wines (often of the nineteenth century) with the foods of today. It is nice to have the kernels removed from the petals of an artichoke, buttered, and then packed into the artichoke bottom ready to eat. I think the French of the olden days would approve.

Boil artichokes and drain. Remove petals from each and scoop out the chokes. Trim artichoke bottoms on the outside, making them neat. Rub with a cut half lemon. Set into a skillet with melted, cool butter. Remove the kernel from each petal. Hold the petal on a plate, and using a silver fork mash out the kernel. Blend this pulp into a chunk of softened butter to which a large pinch of Fruit Fresh (see p. 605) has been added. Have the butter right on the plate and mash each kernel into it. Once all kernels are removed and blended with the butter, fill the artichoke bottom. Shape the filling to a point and coat with melted butter from the skillet. Treat each artichoke in the same way. When ready to serve, cover skillet with a lid and heat until hot.

NOTE: This is a time-consuming job, but can be done in advance.

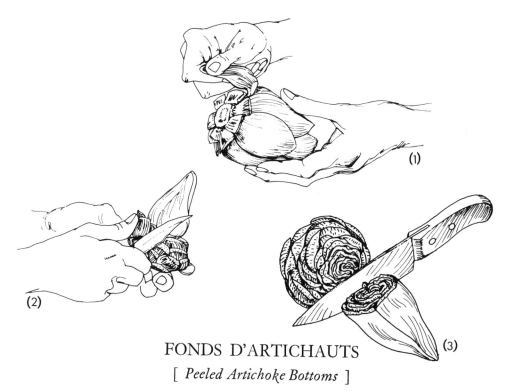

(1)

(2)

(3)

FONDS D'ARTICHAUTS

[Peeled Artichoke Bottoms]

6 large artichokes	6 tablespoons flour
1 lemon, cut in half	6 cups cold water
1 teaspoon salt	Melted butter

1. Wash artichokes by plunging them up and down in cold water. Break off stem at base of flower. Then break off each petal, beginning at the base and going around in a circle. Break off the petals when the artichoke is raw. This leaves the kernel, which is at the base of the leaf, attached to the heart, or bottom, of the artichoke. In other words, the exterior of the artichoke bottom holds the kernels. Remove all the petals, up to the cone, or to where there are no more kernels on the leaves. At this point trim off the ragged outside edges, making the base neat, and then cut straight across the top of the artichoke bottom. Rub with a cut lemon half, and put into bowl of water acidulated with lemon juice. Treat each artichoke in the same way.

2. Put salt and flour into enamel or nonaluminum saucepan. Add enough water to make a paste; then add the rest of the water. Stir-cook and bring to a boil. Add the prepared artichoke bottoms. Simmer about 45 minutes. When done, remove the choke with a teaspoon and you have an artichoke bottom. Rub with cut lemon and coat with melted butter.

3. Artichoke bottoms, or hearts, are usually used as containers for other foods. They may carry potatoes Parisienne (p. 237), or other carved, cooked vegetables, and then be used to garnish meat dishes. When filled with quenelles or poached eggs and topped with a sauce they become an elegant first course. These carriers of food are unlimited in possibilities.

FONDS D'ARTICHAUTS À LA DUXELLES

[*Artichokes with Duxelles*]

Stuff artichoke bottoms with Duxelles (p. 286), sprinkle with Parmesan, and brown under broiler. Any of the Duxelles variants may also be used as a filling.

FONDS D'ARTICHAUTS À LA FLORENTINE

[*Artichokes with Spinach*]

Fill artichoke bottoms with Pain d'Épinards (p. 257), and sprinkle with Parmesan cheese. Melt ⅛ pound butter in shallow baking dish. Add filled artichokes. Bake in preheated 400-degree oven for 15 minutes, or until puffed and browned. Serve with butter from the dish, which should become slightly browned during baking.

For a simpler version fill with buttered, cooked spinach, glaze with Mornay sauce (p. 18), sprinkle with Parmesan, and broil.

FONDS D'ARTICHAUTS À LA HOLLANDAISE

[*Artichokes with Hollandaise*]

Fill cooked artichoke bottoms with Sauce Hollandaise (p. 21), sprinkle with minced parsley, and serve as a first course, or with poached or sautéed fish.

FONDS D'ARTICHAUTS À LA NIÇOISE

[*Artichokes with Tomato Sauce*]

Make Tomato Fondue (p. 272). Fill artichokes, sprinkle with dry bread crumbs and broil.

CHOUX DE BRUXELLES

[*Brussels Sprouts*]

Nothing is sadder than a Brussels sprout that has been cooked to death! Save the Brussels sprout from this horrible fate by following carefully this recipe.

CHOUX DE BRUXELLES BOUILLIS
[*Boiled Brussels Sprouts*]

1½ pounds Brussels sprouts	**Salt**
3 quarts water	**Butter**
1 tablespoon sugar	

1. Remove tough and yellow bottom leaves from each sprout. Cut each stem even with base of sprout. Cut a cross in the stem end. This lets the sprout expand and the center cook. Add 1 tablespoon salt to water. Bring to a boil then add sprouts. Cook about 6 minutes to blanch them. Remove from heat and let cold water run into the pan to displace the hot water. Drain when cool.

2. When ready to serve, reheat the blanched sprouts for about 3 minutes in 3 quarts fresh boiling water seasoned with 1 teaspoon salt, chunk butter and sugar. Drain, pour into serving dish and spoon melted butter over the sprouts.

NOTE: Sprouts may be cooked a total of 10 minutes, drained, and buttered, but they are a superior product when blanched and then reheated in fresh seasoned water.

VARIATIONS
CHOUX DE BRUXELLES À LA CRÈME
[*Brussels Sprouts in Cream*]

Melt ⅛ pound butter in skillet. Stir in 1 tablespoon flour, then add 1 cup crème fraîche or whipping cream. Stir until slightly thickened. Season with salt, pepper, sugar, and a dash of nutmeg. Add blanched sprouts. Simmer for about 4 minutes.

CHOUX DE BRUXELLES À LA MILANAISE
[*Brussels Sprouts with Parmesan*]

Butter a baking dish and dust with grated Parmesan cheese. Add blanched Brussels sprouts, sprinkle with more cheese and drizzle with melted butter. Bake in 400-degree oven for about 15 minutes. Toast clarified butter to a nut brown, spoon over sprouts and serve.

CHOUX DE BRUXELLES À LA POLONAISE
[*Brussels Sprouts with Toasted Crumbs*]

Blanch sprouts, cool, and then reheat in boiling water, drain and butter. Put into serving dish, sprinkle with sieved hard-cooked egg yolk and minced parsley. Tear 1 slice firm-type bread into fine crumbs. Toast in ⅛ pound clarified butter. Spoon over sprouts and serve.

CHOUX-FLEURS
[*Cauliflower*]

The big white bloom of the cauliflower as it comes is pallid, stiff, and uninteresting. But, when removed from its frame of greenery, separated into individual flowerets, cooked and rearranged back into its greenhouse, the cauliflower qualifies as a glamour food.

CHOU-FLEUR AU BEURRE
[*Buttered Cauliflower*]

1 large head cauliflower	1 tablespoon salt
3 quarts water	Melted butter

1. Select a cauliflower of purest white surrounded by the greenest greens.

2. Carefully cut the entire white head from the green leaves. Trim the bottom of the outer green leaves so that it will sit straight. Cook this outer part in boiling salted water for 2 minutes. Lift out and cool in cold water, drain, and dry on towels ready to use. Cut the individual flowerets from the main stem. With a paring knife, peel the stem of each floweret. Begin at the end of the stem, strip the skin from the little stalks down to the flower. It is very easy.

3. Once all flowerets are peeled, put them into a vegetable basket or colander and submerge in the boiling salted water. Cook about 5 minutes, or until quite done, depending upon the size of the flowerets. When stems stick tender, remove.

4. Set kettle under cold running water and displace some of the hot water, but keep cauliflower warm. Running water will not damage the tender, cooked vegetables as much as draining them.

5. When flowerets can be handled, mold them like this. Put a clean linen towel over your left hand. Into it place about 3 flowerets, buds in your hand, stems up. Cup your hand around the flowerets and then turn your hand down. With your right hand, grasp the towel tight at the base of the flowerets, the stems being caught in the towel. Gently twist the towel tight. Towel molds the 3 flowerets into 1, cuts off the cooked stems and squeezes out the water. Do this over a sink.

6. Untwist towel and place molded cauliflower balls in a skillet with melted butter. Keep warm over low heat. When all are molded, arrange them in the blanched green outer leaves. Spoon hot melted butter over them and serve.

VARIATIONS
CHOU-FLEUR EN FRITOTS
[*French-fried Cauliflower*]

Cook flowerets in salted water, drain and cool. Dip in batter coating No. 3 (p. 11). French-fry in vegetable oil heated to 390 degrees. Drain on paper towels. Serve plain or with Béarnaise sauce (p. 24). Fry some parsley (p. 259), to serve with the fried cauliflower.

CHOU-FLEUR MORNAY
[*Cauliflower with Mornay Sauce*]

Prepare recipe of Mornay sauce (p. 18). Cover and keep warm until ready to use. Cook cauliflower and mold into balls. Place them on an oven-proof serving platter. Coat with Mornay sauce and sprinkle with grated Parmesan cheese. Heat in a 450-degree oven for about 15 minutes, or until browned. Serve extra sauce separately.

CHOU-FLEUR À LA POLONAISE
[*Cauliflower with Toasted Crumbs*]

Put cauliflower balls into outer green leaves, sprinkle with sieved hard-cooked egg yolks and minced parsley. Toast fine bread crumbs in ⅛ pound clarified butter and pour over flowerets.

FRUIT VEGETABLES

The fruits of the vegetable patch include eggplant, tomatoes, cucumbers, and squashes.

Eggplant arrived in this country early in the nineteenth century, while tomatoes appeared on our tables late in that century. Even though it arrived late, the tomato quickly made a vital place for itself in our culinary repertoire. The purple eggplant remains a stranger to many American tables, and the white ones are complete foreigners.

Squashes too are neglected. This seems particularly strange since we learned about them from the American Indian. It is even thought that the word "squash" is an abbreviated form of the Narragansett word "askuta*squash*," which means uncooked produce. There are practically no French recipes for squash, but this all-American food responds well to French cooking techniques.

In France, pumpkins are served as a vegetable and are usually boiled and buttered. In the markets of Paris one buys a piece of pumpkin, never the whole fruit. Jack-o'-lanterns are unheard of. Pumpkins are to eat, not to have fun with.

AUBERGINE
[*Eggplant*]

Botanically the purple eggplant is related to deadly nightshade or belladonna. It was popularly thought, even in the enlightened days of Dr. Samuel Johnson, to produce raging insanity in those who dared to eat it. "Mad apple" was the misnomer Englishmen of the eighteenth century gave the innocent eggplant.

AUBERGINES FRITES
[*Fried Eggplant*]

Cut 2 eggplants into ½-inch slices. Peel each slice and sprinkle with salt. Stack the slices on a plate. The salt draws out the water. Let them drain for about 30 minutes. Rinse in cold water and dry on paper towels. Cut into ½-inch strips. Roll in flour and French-fry or fry in a skillet in ½-inch-deep hot fat. Drain on paper towels and serve like French-fried potatoes. Taste before salting.

AUBERGINES À LA MEUNIÈRE
[*Fried Eggplant with Parsley Butter*]

Fry eggplant, drain, sprinkle with minced parsley, and pour over hot melted butter seasoned with lemon juice.

AUBERGINES À LA MIREILLE
[*Fried Eggplant in Tomato Sauce*]

Make sauce from Artichauts à la Mirelle recipe (p. 413), but omit the artichokes. While sauce cooks, prepare the eggplant and fry as in the preceding recipe. Put eggplant into a shallow casserole. Discard bouquet garni and celery tops from sauce, then pour sauce over eggplant. Sprinkle with grated Parmesan and bake in a 450-degree oven for about 15 minutes, or until hot. Sprinkle with minced parsley. Serve hot.

AUBERGINES FARCIES
[*Stuffed Eggplants*]

3 skinny, long eggplants	1½ cups cream
3 tablespoons vegetable oil	½ teaspoon salt
2 onions, minced	Dash of pepper and of nutmeg
Chunk of butter	2 cloves garlic, minced
2 tablespoons olive oil	2 tablespoons Madeira
1 cup minced mushrooms	3 tablespoons minced parsley
3 tablespoons flour	Dry bread crumbs

1. Cut eggplants in half lengthwise. Make crosswise slashes through the flesh. Heat oil in skillet. Place cut side of eggplant down in skillet. Sauté cut side about 10 minutes, turn, and cook skin side about 5 minutes. Cook until meat can be easily pulled from the skin.

2. When done, carefully remove the pulpy flesh from the skins. Be sure to leave the skins intact. Put the pulp into a bowl.

3. Sauté onions in butter and olive oil for 5 minutes. Add the mushrooms and cook 2 minutes (Duxelles mixture). Stir in the flour, then add cream, salt, pepper, and nutmeg. Stir-cook until thickened. Add to eggplant pulp, then add garlic, Madeira, and parsley. Mix well, then fill eggplant skins. Sprinkle with crumbs. Bake in 400-degree oven for about 20 minutes. One-half stuffed eggplant per person.

VARIATIONS

AUBERGINES À LA DUXELLES

[*Eggplant Soufflé*]

Cut eggplants in half, fry and remove pulp from the skins, as in step 1 in Farcies recipe. Make Duxelles mixture (p. 286). Add the Duxelles to the pulp in mixing bowl. Season with 1 teaspoon sugar, ½ teaspoon salt, and dash of pepper. Stir in 2 tablespoons minced parsley, 2 tablespoons flour, 2 tablespoons crème fraîche, 2 egg yolks, and 2 tablespoons Madeira. Whip 2 egg whites very stiff and then fold into the eggplant mixture. Fill the eggplant skins with mixture. Sprinkle with Parmesan and set on a cooky sheet. Bake in 400-degree oven for about 20 minutes, or until puffed and browned.

AUBERGINES À LA PORTUGAISE

[*Eggplants in Tomato Sauce*]

Cut eggplants in half, fry and remove pulp as in step 1 in Farcies recipe. Put pulp from eggplants into a bowl. Peel and dice 3 tomatoes. Sauté tomatoes in 2 tablespoons olive oil. Add 2 minced cloves garlic, 3 tablespoons minced parsley, 1 teaspoon sugar, ½ teaspoon salt, and dash of pepper. Add pulp from eggplants. Mix well and stuff into skins of the eggplants. Sprinkle with crumbs. Bake in 400-degree oven for about 20 minutes, or until hot.

COURGE

[*Squash*]

We have two categories of squash: the winter, or hard-skin type, and the summer, or soft-skin type. Winter squash include acorn, hubbard, and turban. Their meat is orange in color, and they are hard to cut and clean. I suggest baking them whole. Once they are cooked, cut them, discard the seeds, and scoop the pulp from the rind. Use the pulp as a vegetable or in such dessert favorites as squash pie and pudding.

Soft-skinned squash include yellow summer, green zucchini, and the white "pattypan." They are eaten in their entirety. They may be cooked according to any one of the eggplant recipes or one of the six basic methods of cooking meats. Serve them buttered or with a sauce. Particularly good are sautéed zucchini with Hollandaise sauce and fried pattypan with Portugaise sauce.

Cucumbers may be cooked like summer squash; pumpkin, like winter squash.

TOMATE
[*Tomatoes*]

Perhaps you have wondered why tomatoes are called fruit when we eat them as a vegetable. There is no mystery—like the other fruits in this section, they are simply the fruit of the plant.

In France, England, and this country, tomatoes were often referred to as "apples of love" (or pommes d'amour); in Italy, as "apples of gold" (or pomodori); and in Germany, as "apples of paradise" (or Paradiesapfel).

To peel a fresh, ripe tomato it is not necessary to heat water to a boil. Simply put the tomato in the sink and let very hot tap water run over it. Count to 20 and then peel. If, however, you do use boiling water, count only to about 12 and then peel. Tomatoes are not normally peeled when they are cooked and served whole. They need the skin to hold them in shape.

TOMATES SAUTÉES À LA PROVENÇALE
[*Sautéed Tomatoes with Garlic*]

3 large tomatoes	3 large cloves garlic, minced
2 tablespoons vegetable oil	Salt, pepper, and sugar to taste
1 tablespoon olive oil	Minced parsley

1. Remove stems if still attached; then cut tomatoes in half. Shake out liquid and seeds. Put cut side down on paper towels to drain.

2. Heat oils to very hot in skillet. Slip the cut side of the tomatoes down the side of the pan. These snap a lot and the oil may ignite. If so, cover with lid to smother flame. Fry about 1 minute, then turn and fry 1 minute. Put into a baking dish, cut side up.

3. Sprinkle each cut side with garlic, salt, pepper, and sugar. Broil about 3 minutes and then serve sprinkled with parsley. Delicious with all grilled meats, fish, and poultry.

VARIATIONS
TOMATES FARCIES À LA DUXELLES
[*Duxelles Stuffed Tomatoes*]

Sauté 1 cup minced onions for 5 minutes in a chunk of butter. Add 2 cups minced mushrooms and sauté another 5 minutes. Season with salt, pepper, and sugar. Remove seeds from sautéed tomato halves. Stuff with mixture. Coat with crumbs and broil about 3 minutes, or until tops are brown. Serve sprinkled with parsley.

TOMATES SAUTÉES AUX FINES HERBES
[*Tomatoes Stuffed with Herbs*]

Sprinkle fried tomato halves with salt, pepper, sugar, minced parsley, chives, and dry bread crumbs. Dot with butter and brown under broiler.

FONDUE DE TOMATES
[*Tomato Fondue*]

4 fresh tomatoes or 2 cups canned whole, Italian plum tomatoes	2 cloves garlic, minced
2 shallots or 1 onion, minced	Dash of pepper
1 teaspoon salt	Chunk of butter
2 teaspoons sugar	2 tablespoons Madeira wine
	3 tablespoons minced parsley

Remove cores from fresh tomatoes. Dice and place in enamel skillet or saucepan. Add remaining ingredients and simmer about 40 minutes. Put through food mill to mash and remove skin and seeds. Taste and adjust seasonings. Use, or freeze in small packets ready to use.

NOTES: This seasoned tomato purée is used as a garnish. It may be served in artichoke bottoms or in mushroom caps, or spooned onto steaks or chops.

Minced black truffles or mushrooms may be added for flavor and color. Make this recipe a staple in your freezer.

SEED VEGETABLES

Vegetables that fall into the seed category usually grow in pods or husks. These include beans, peas, corn, rice, and chestnuts.

All may be grown to maturity and then harvested and cooked from a dry state. But we love fresh new peas and young green beans. French chefs wax happy over their treatment of green beans and certainly they can hold their own when it comes to peas. But about limas and corn they are not really knowledgeable. They seem to prefer rice pilaf to plain boiled rice, and their famous cassoulet, made from dried beans and meats, is in the lamb section.

From the street vendors of Paris I learned how to deal with chestnuts. If shivering old men can roast chestnuts over charcoal in a cold drizzle on the Champs Élysées, we should be able to cook chestnuts in our warm, modern kitchens.

MARRON
[*Chestnuts*]

Whether fruit or seed, the chestnut is tricky to open. Buy a pound of the largest chestnuts available. Then, with a sharp serrated knife, slash the rounded side of each chestnut through outer shell and inner brown skin. Put them in a metal baking pan and heat 10 minutes in a 500-degree oven. Sprinkle with about ½ cup cold water and bake another 10 minutes. The shells will partially open. Remove from the oven and, as soon as the chestnuts can be handled, peel off the outer shell and the inner brown skin. If you have trouble doing this, drop the chestnuts into cold water, bring to a boil and simmer 10 minutes. Cool under cold running water and then peel them. The first method is the better one, for no flavor is lost to the water. Once they are peeled, use the chestnuts in the following recipes, or in Chestnut Soufflé (p. 310).

VARIATIONS
MARRONS À LA SAUCE BIGARADE
[*Braised Chestnuts in Bigarade Sauce*]

Prepare Bigarade sauce (p. 28). Make the recipe below of Marrons Braisés. Reduce the cooking liquid to ¼ cup. Substitute 2 tablespoons Grand Marnier for the Madeira. Break up chestnuts with a fork. Add chestnuts and their sauce to the Bigarade sauce. Adjust seasonings and thickness. Serve with roast duck, goose, or capon.

MARRONS BOUILLIS
[*Boiled Chestnuts*]

Put about 1 pound peeled chestnuts into 2 cups water seasoned with a chunk of butter, 1 teaspoon salt, and 1 teaspoon of sugar. Boil about 40 minutes, or until tender. Serve as a vegetable with roast fowl.

MARRONS BRAISÉS

[Braised Chestnuts]

Put 1 pound peeled chestnuts into a skillet. Add 1 cup chicken stock and 1 cup white wine. Make a small bouquet garni with parsley, 1 bay leaf, and a 4-inch piece of celery. Add to liquids in skillet. Add a chunk of butter, 1 teaspoon sugar, ½ teaspoon salt, and a dash of pepper. Simmer 40 minutes, or until chestnuts are tender and liquid reduced to less than half. Add 2 tablespoons Madeira. Thicken slightly with a bit of beurre manié. Serve as a garnish to roasted red meats.

MARRONS GLACÉS

[Glazed Chestnuts]

Put about 1 pound peeled chestnuts into 2 cups water seasoned with a chunk of butter, dash of salt, 2 tablespoons each of sugar, Madeira, and Grand Marnier. Simmer 40 minutes, or until chestnuts are tender and glazed, and liquid syrupy. Add water if necessary and do not let liquid burn.

MARRONS GRILLÉS

[Roast Chestnuts]

To roast chestnuts, cut them on their rounded sides and then put them into a special chestnut skillet and toast over coals in a fireplace. (The bottom of a chestnut skillet is full of ½-inch holes which allow the heat to hit the chestnuts directly. Or substitute a wire popcorn popper for the skillet.) To roast chestnuts in the oven, slash them on rounded sides, place on a cooky sheet, and roast in a 400-degree oven for about 1 hour. Sprinkle them often with water as they roast. Shell and eat one to test. They will be mealy throughout when done.

PURÉE DE MARRONS

[Puréed Chestnuts]

Peel and then boil chestnuts in water until done. Drain. Purée in a food mill, food chopper, blender, or ricer. Mash completely, then add a chunk of butter and crème fraîche or whipping cream. Whip to the consistency of whipped potatoes. Season with salt, sugar, and dash of pepper. Serve like whipped potatoes.

HARICOTS VERTS BOUILLIS
[*Boiled Green Beans*]

1½ pounds green beans
3 quarts water

Salt
Chunk butter

1 teaspoon sugar

1. Remove the ends and string the beans if necessary. If beans are uniform in size and young, they may be cooked whole. If not, cut them into 1-inch pieces or French-cut them lengthwise.

2. Bring water to a boil and add 1 tablespoon salt. Put beans into a vegetable basket, or drop into the water. Cook whole beans about 5 minutes, cut beans about 4 minutes, and French-cut beans about 2 minutes. Eat a bean to test for doneness. They should be tender but firm. Lift from the water, or pour into colander. Submerge in cold water to stop their cooking. Drain when cool.

3. When ready to serve, reheat the blanched beans for about 1 minute in 3 quarts fresh boiling water seasoned with 1 teaspoon salt, chunk butter and sugar. Drain, pour into serving dish, butter, or use in one of the following recipes.

VARIATIONS
HARICOTS VERTS AMANDINE
[*Green Beans with Almonds*]

Toast ½ cup sliced almonds in ¼ pound clarified butter. Reheat blanched French-cut beans in seasoned water for 1 minute. Drain, then put into serving dish. Pour toasted butter and almonds over them.

HARICOTS VERTS À L'ANGLAISE
[*Green Beans with Melted Butter*]

Boil whole young beans, cool, and drain. When ready to serve reheat for 1 minute in boiling seasoned water. Drain. Serve with individual bowls of melted, clarified butter. Guests dunk, or spoon the butter over the beans, and eat them.

HARICOTS VERTS AU BEURRE

[*Buttered Green Beans*]

Heat about ⅛ pound butter in skillet. Add the blanched beans. Cook-toss until all beans are coated with butter and are hot.

HARICOTS VERTS AU BEURRE NOISETTE

[*Green Beans in Toasted Butter*]

Toast ⅛ pound clarified butter to a nut brown. Reheat blanched beans for 1 minute in seasoned water, drain, and put into serving dish. Sprinkle with parsley. Pour sizzling butter over beans and serve.

HARICOTS VERTS À LA CRÈME

[*Creamed Green Beans*]

Heat about 1 cup crème fraîche or whipping cream in a skillet. Thicken slightly with a bit of beurre manié. Season to taste. Add reheated blanched beans. Mix, then pour into serving dish. Sprinkle with minced parsley and serve.

HARICOTS VERTS À LA POLONAISE

[*Green Beans with Toasted Crumbs*]

Toast ⅛ pound clarified butter and 1 slice bread torn into fine crumbs. Reheat blanched beans, drain, and put into serving dish. Sprinkle with parsley and the sieved yolk of 1 hard-cooked egg. Pour over the hot butter-bread mixture and serve sizzling hot.

PETITS POIS BOUILLIS

[*Boiled Fresh Peas*]

4–5 pounds peas in the pod	**Salt**
4 quarts water	**1 tablespoon sugar**
Chunk of butter	

1. It will take between 4 and 5 pounds of peas in the pod to serve 6 persons. Shell the peas and put them into a strainer or colander that will fit into a kettle of water. Bring water and 2 tablespoons salt to a boil. Submerge the peas. Blanch for about 3 minutes.

2. To test for doneness, eat one of the largest peas. Peas should be firm-soft. When done, submerge peas in cold water to stop their cooking. Drain. When ready to serve, reheat in fresh boiling water seasoned with 1 teaspoon salt, the sugar, and butter. Heat 1 minute, drain, and serve plain, or by one of the following recipes.

VARIATIONS
PETITS POIS AU BEURRE
[*Buttered Peas*]

Melt ⅛ pound butter in large skillet. Reheat cooked peas, drain, and then add to skillet. Toss peas to coat with butter and pour into serving dish.

PETITS POIS AU BEURRE NOISETTE
[*Peas with Toasted Butter*]

Toast ⅛ pound clarified butter to a nut brown. Pour over reheated cooked peas in serving dish. Serve sizzling hot.

PETITS POIS À LA CRÈME
[*Peas in Cream*]

Heat ½ cup crème fraîche or whipping cream. Add 1 teaspoon sugar and the blanched peas. Heat for 1 minute. Serve in small dishes. Eat with a spoon.

PETITS POIS AU FENOUIL
[*Peas with Fennel*]

Fennel is available in many supermarkets and most Italian groceries. When it is in season treat yourself to this recipe. Cut the ferny tops and part of the stalks from a fresh fennel bulb. Tie into a bundle. Add to the water at the time the peas are blanched. Remove three branches from the fennel bulb. Cut them into thin slices. Sauté in ⅛ pound melted butter, just for a second, and then add the peas, a dash of sugar and 1 teaspoon Anisette liqueur. Heat, toss, and serve.

PETITS POIS AU JAMBON
[Peas with Ham]

Blanch peas and drain. Cut 3 slices boiled ham into julienne strips. Dice 1 onion and place in skillet with ⅛ pound butter. Add 1 teaspoon sugar. Stir-cook 5 minutes. Add ham. Heat for a minute, then stir in blanched peas and 4 tablespoons crème fraîche. Heat, season, and toss. Serve in individual dishes.

PETITS POIS À LA FRANÇAISE
[Sautéed Peas]

This is a most famous dish. Normally fresh peas are used, but it seems a shame to destroy the succulent goodness of new peas by cooking them so long. Therefore, I suggest using frozen peas in this recipe.

18 small white, boiling onions	1 tablespoon sugar
6 lettuce leaves, shredded	1 teaspoon salt
⅛ pound butter	½ cup cold water
2 (10-ounce) packages frozen peas	

1. Peel, then blanch onions (put into cold water, bring to a boil, and drain; rinse in cold water and drain again).

2. Put onions and remainder of ingredients into a skillet. Add peas in their frozen state. Cover with lid and bring to a boil. Simmer about 30 minutes. Stir occasionally to mix the ingredients.

3. When done, there should be about ½ cup liquid left. If not, add some water. Thicken liquids with a bit of beurre manié, or leave juice thin. Serve in individual small bowls and eat with a spoon.

NOTE: This recipe is even better when finished with about 4 tablespoons crème fraîche.

RIZ
[Rice]

Whenever possible, buy rice in bulk from one of the nationality stores that exist in our larger cities. Chinese, Japanese, Italian, Greek, and Indian grocers all carry many varieties and grades of rice. Experiment with the different types available. Almost all of them have better flavor, and are much less expensive, than the fancy converted rice on the supermarket shelves. If, however, you are using converted rice, washing is not necessary.

RIZ AU BLANC
[*Boiled Rice*]

1½ cups long-grain rice　　　　　2½ cups boiling water

1 teaspoon salt

1. Put rice into saucepan. Run warm water into pan. Wash rice between the palms of your hands to rub off the starch. Drain water. Wash two more times. Drain, cover with lid, and set aside.

2. Add boiling water and salt. (The easiest and safest way to get measured boiling water is to put 2½ cups cold water into a pan and bring it to a boil.) Stir, and boil 2 minutes. Reduce heat, cover, and simmer about 15 minutes, or until done. All water should be evaporated and rice dry. Little holes appear on the surface of the rice when it is done.

3. If rice must be held for any length of time, set lid askew and keep over very low heat, or put into a casserole with lid askew and place in 275-degree oven.

VARIATIONS
RIZ ARLEQUIN
[*Colored Rice*]

Put ¼ cup cooked rice into ½ cup hot water that has been colored with about 10 drops yellow food coloring. Let stand 5 minutes. Drain, blot, and dry off over low heat. (These dyed grains of rice should be quite dry, so they will not tint the white rice.) Toss with cooked rice just before serving.

RIZ AUX CHAMPIGNONS
[*Rice with Mushrooms*]

Sauté 1½ cups sliced mushrooms in ⅛ pound butter. Add to cooked rice and toss.

RIZ AU PERSIL
[*Parsleyed Rice*]

Toss ¼ cup minced parsley with cooked rice. Use plain boiled, or Arlequin rice.

RIZ PILAF

[Pilaf]

1 onion minced	1½ cups rice
Chunk of butter	2 cups chicken stock
1 tablespoon vegetable oil	½ cup water

Sauté onion in butter and oil. Stir-cook until toasted, but do not burn. Add rice. (It is not necessary to wash rice when it is blanched in butter and oil.) Stir-cook until grains turn white. Add boiling stock and water. (Canned stock is seasoned, so add no salt. If using homemade stock, which is not salted when it is made, then add 1 teaspoon salt.) Bring to a boil, then reduce heat, cover, and cook over very low heat about 15 minutes, or until done. Toss rice with a fork or chopsticks (a spoon mats the grains together), and serve.

NOTE: Do not remove lid during cooking unless necessary to add more liquids. To do so causes a loss of steam.

FUNGI

[Plants without Chlorophyll]

Edible fungi are mushrooms and truffles. Their nutritional value is little, but their flavor value is great. Both grow from underground spores. Mushrooms pop through the ground and are harvested by man. Truffles grow underground and must be searched for and dug out by man and beast. Sows are used in France and dogs in Italy.

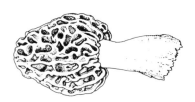

CHAMPIGNONS

[Mushrooms]

There are many edible mushrooms. Of the wild variety the morel is the best. Its flesh looks like a sponge and it grows in a cone shape. You cannot mistake the morel. They are one of the joys that come with living in the Midwest. They are found in April and May. (Buy a wild-mushroom guide before hunting.)

Since they grow wild, they are usually quite dirty. Wash them many times in cold water. It is advisable to cut them in half and wash out their hollow inside. Once they are clean, dry and sauté in butter. Then serve à la Maître d'Hôtel (p. 39). Or they may be served in cream sauce, dipped in batter and French-fried, or dipped in a simple coating and sautéed in butter. Look for morels every spring. Where you find them one year you will usually find them the next year. Keep their hiding place your secret. They like to grow in damp areas around rotting logs, but not on them. Cultivated mushrooms are not the delicacy that morels are.

Always wash mushrooms just before they are to be cooked. Put them into a bowl of cold water. Wash them between the palms of your hands, just like washing your hands. Repeat washings until mushrooms are clean.

Mushrooms of varying sizes will cook in the same length of time and will not be overcooked if: large mushroom caps are cut into quarters; medium-sized caps in half; and small caps left whole.

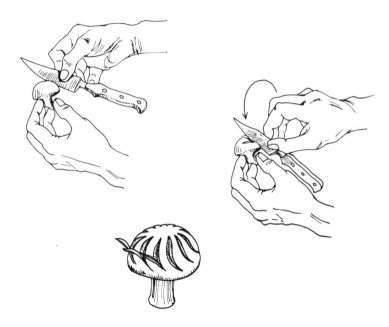

HOW TO CARVE MUSHROOMS

Carved mushrooms are used to decorate foods. Select firm, medium-sized mushrooms as white and as perfect as possible. Wipe with a damp cloth, being careful not to damage the thin skin that covers the cap. It is this thin skin that gives color contrast to the cut mushrooms.

Sharpen a 4-inch paring knife. Hold the knife at a point just below the handle, on the blade, so that the weight of the knife will be in the handle.

(*continued*)

Carefully and quickly slip the blade in at the center of the mushroom at a 45-degree angle and let the weight of the handle roll the blade down the mushroom to cut out a thin wedge. Turn mushroom by stem, and space the cuts close and even around the cap. (Practice on mushrooms before slicing or dicing them.)

Roll a lemon on the counter to make it soft and pliable; then it will release its juice. Cut in half. Using one half, squeeze juice and at the same time rub the little wedge pieces of mushroom off the cap. Put cap, head first, into cold water in a pan. When all mushrooms are carved, squeeze the juice from the remaining half lemon into the water. Add a chunk of butter, bring to a boil and then remove from the heat and let stand until ready to be used. Trim stems even with the caps. Place caps on the foods to be decorated. Save stems to use later.

CHAMPIGNONS BOUILLIS
[*Boiled Mushrooms*]

In French cooking mushrooms are almost always precooked in seasoned water, as are the carved mushrooms, and then incorporated into recipes.

This method is fine for carved mushrooms since that is the only cooking they get. But to precook mushrooms for other recipes means a loss of both flavor and texture.

Therefore, you will find I sauté mushrooms in the butter at the beginning of some recipes, while in others I cook mushrooms in the wine, or simply add them to the sauce at the end of the cooking time. The result I want from the mushrooms depends upon how they will be treated. Also I do not like the wilted, slimy texture of mushrooms cooked in seasoned water.

CHAMPIGNONS SAUTÉS
[*Sautéed Mushrooms*]

1 pound mushrooms	½ teaspoon salt
¼ pound butter	⅛ teaspoon pepper
½ teaspoon confectioners' sugar	

Wash mushrooms, drain, and dry. Cut stems even with caps; then cut mushrooms into quarters or halves to make them uniform in size (p. 281). Save stems and use later. Sauté caps in butter for 3 minutes. Sprinkle with salt, pepper, and sugar. Toss to coat all mushrooms. Use as a garnish to a dish, or in other recipes.

CHAMPIGNONS FARCIS

[*Stuffed Mushrooms*]

Remove stems from 1 pound large mushrooms. With a melon baller cut out the gills from the underneath side and some of the meat from the caps. Make a Duxelles from the stems, meat from the caps, and onions (p. 286). Sauté the caps for 2 minutes in an oven-proof skillet. Dilute Duxelles with 2 tablespoons crème fraîche. Fill caps, sprinkle with grated Parmesan cheese, dot with butter, and, when ready to serve, broil 3 minutes. Serve with grilled steaks or as a first course.

CHAMPIGNONS AUX FINES HERBES

[*Mushrooms with Herbs*]

Sauté 1 pound mushroom caps in butter. Sprinkle with parsley and minced chives. Serve on buttered toast, or as a garnish to a meat dish.

CHAMPIGNONS À LA HOLLANDAISE

[*Mushrooms with Hollandaise Sauce*]

Make Hollandaise sauce (p. 21). Break off stems from mushrooms down in the caps. With a melon baller cut out some of the mushroom, making the cavity larger. Use the largest caps from the box. Sauté 2 caps per person in a chunk of butter, season, and then fill with Hollandaise. Use to garnish poached fish or sautéed chicken fillets. Mushroom caps may also be filled with Béarnaise sauce (p. 24) and served with grilled steaks.

CHAMPIGNONS AU MADÈRE

[*Mushrooms in Madeira Sauce*]

Sauté 1 pound mushroom caps (stems removed) according to Champignons Sautés. Add 4 tablespoons Cognac, heat, and then set aflame. When flame dies, add 4 tablespoons Madeira. Heat, then stir in 1 cup crème fraîche. Season, heat, and thicken with bit of beurre manié. Good over sautéed suprêmes of chicken.

CHAMPIGNONS À LA PROVENÇALE

[*Mushrooms in Tomato Sauce*]

Make Provençale sauce (p. 31). Buy 1 pound large mushrooms, cut stems even with caps, and then quarter them. Sauté in butter and then season. Add to Provençale sauce and serve as a first course in croustades, in hollowed-out hard rolls, or on toast.

CROÛTE AUX CHAMPIGNONS
[*Creamed Mushrooms with Herbs*]

Prepare Champignons aux Fines Herbes, above. When done, stir in 1 cup crème fraîche or whipping cream. Adjust seasonings. Heat and thicken with a bit of beurre manié. Serve in croustades or on toast. Serve as first course or as a luncheon dish accompanied with salad and dessert.

CHAMPIGNONS SOUS CLOCHE
[*Mushrooms under a Glass Bell*]

Remove stems from 24 medium-sized mushrooms. With a melon baller cut out the gills and curved edges from the underneath side of the mushrooms, making the cavity larger. Fry small rounds of bread (see p. 599) to fit under each mushroom. Butter the special porcelain dishes that fit under the glass bells, then coat them with crème fraîche or sour cream.

Coat mushroom cavities with crème or sour cream and then heap with Maître d'Hôtel butter (p. 39) or butter mixture from the snail recipe (p. 96), or stuff with other foods and dot with butter. Arrange bread rounds in dishes. Set each stuffed mushroom cap on a bread round. Cover each dish with a glass bell and bake in 350-degree oven for about 20 minutes, or until hot and mushrooms are cooked. Serve as a first course. These may be baked in a tightly covered casserole and served at the table, but they lose their glamour.

VARIATIONS
CHAMPIGNONS-BROCOLIS SOUS CLOCHE
[*Caps Stuffed with Cooked Broccoli*]

Cook small stalks of broccoli (p. 250). When done, cut off the buds. Serve stalks as a vegetable for dinner. Fill hollowed-out mushroom caps with Beurre d'Ail (p. 89). Top with broccoli bud and coat with more Beurre d'Ail. Set caps on bread rounds. Put into buttered and crème-coated dish. Sprinkle with fine, dry bread crumbs. Bake under glass bell as in master recipe. These taste like oysters.

CHAMPIGNONS AUX CHAMPIGNONS SOUS CLOCHE

[Caps Stuffed with Mushrooms]

Break stems from caps. With melon baller remove gills and trim underneath side of caps. Mince stems, gills, and trimmings. Sauté in a chunk of butter. Stuff into hollowed-out caps. Top with butter, set on bread rounds and into buttered and crème-coated dish, cover with bell, and bake.

CHAMPIGNONS-ESCARGOTS SOUS CLOCHE

[Snails in Mushroom Caps]

Remove stems of large mushrooms and hollow out the cavity of the mushrooms with a melon baller. Coat with lots of Beurre d'Ail (p. 96), add snails, and cover with more snail butter. Set on fried bread rounds, put into buttered dish (no crème), sprinkle with dry crumbs, cover with bell, and bake about 20 minutes.

CHAMPIGNONS-POULET SOUS CLOCHE

[Mushroom Caps with Chicken]

Dice raw white meat of chicken fine. Mix chicken with sufficient Beurre d'Ail (p. 89), to coat the pieces. Fill hollowed-out caps. Set on buttered toast rounds and into a buttered and crème-coated dish. Cover with bell and bake about 20 minutes.

CHAMPIGNONS-QUENELLES SOUS CLOCHE

[Caps with Shrimp Quenelles]

Shape shrimp quenelles round, rather than long (p. 79). Prepare mushrooms as in above recipes. Fill each cap with Maître d'Hôtel Butter (p. 39), top with a quenelle, and dot with more butter. Bake in dish covered with bell for 20 minutes.

NOTES: Under glass is the sure way to have hot food. Remove the bell at the table when the food is served.

Beurre d'Ail recipes are several. They may be made and then frozen ready to use. Let these recipes become freezer staples.

DUXELLES

[Sautéed Mushrooms and Onions]

Duxelles as such is not a sauce, but a mixture. It is added to sauces and used as a farci, or filling. Duxelle usually lends its name to the dish in which it is being used, or becomes a part of the name.

½ cup minced onions	2 cups minced mushrooms
⅛ pound butter	½ teaspoon salt
1 minced shallot (if available)	Dash of freshly-ground pepper

½ teaspoon confectioners' sugar

Sauté onions in butter for 5 minutes. Add shallot and simmer another 5 minutes. Add mushrooms. Stir-cook 5 minutes. Season, and mixture is ready to use in other recipes.

VARIATIONS

DUXELLES À LA CRÈME

Add 2 tablespoons Madeira and 1 cup crème fraîche to Duxelles mixture. Thicken with bit of beurre manié, season, and serve with sautéed chicken suprêmes or fish.

DUXELLES AUX FINES HERBES

Add minced parsley and chives to the cooked Duxelles, or to the Duxelles à la Crème. Serve with omelettes, poached fish, or chicken suprêmes.

TRUFFLES

Truffles are both black and white, and each type is expensive. We use them as we do mushrooms, but not so frequently because of their cost. In one 4-ounce can there are five or six truffles, depending upon their size. Use what is called for in the recipe and add the juice to the sauce. Freeze the remaining truffles in individual packages in Madeira wine. Then, when using these frozen truffles, slice, dice, or cut them into the desired pieces. Use the truffles for garnish, or in a sauce to which you add the wine. Frozen truffles will keep indefinitely. (High heat and long cooking toughens truffles.)

In France sows are trained to smell out and root up the underground truffles, while in Italy dogs are taught to find them. Dogs are less of a problem than sows because they do not like truffles to eat. Sows must be smacked across the snout and the truffles snatched away. In return for finding the truffle, the sow gets a handful of corn. A dog carries the truffle to its master and is rewarded with a chunk of bread. Both animals are kept hungry during truffle season to make them hunt the hidden fungi and thereby win a meal for themselves.

VARIATIONS

TARTELETTES FARCIES AUX TRUFFES
[*Béchamel Tarts with Truffles*]

Make miniature tartelettes (p. 356), fill with Béchamel sauce (p. 15), and coat with minced truffles. Serve as a first course.

TARTELETTES FARCIES AUX DUXELLES À LA CRÈME
[*Duxelles-Filled Tarts with Truffles*]

Fill tartelettes with Duxelles à la Crème (p. 286) and top with minced truffles.

See also the recipes for Omelette aux Truffes (p. 64), Pâté aux Truffes (p. 417), and Pommes de Terre à la Sarladaise (p. 246).

Entremets

[Sweets]

For the most part the sweets in this chapter are creations made of eggs and milk. In general they are derived from two basic dessert sauces: Crème à l'Anglaise and Crème Pâtissière. Independent desserts, such as sweet omelettes and the famous Sauce Sabayon, are exceptions to the rule.

Crème à l'Anglaise is a thin cream sauce, thickened only with egg yolks. It is the master recipe for ice creams, Bavarois, and mousse desserts. Ice creams are shown off best when presented as a bombe, a Comtesse-Marie, or a Lady Melba. The Bavarois, given body with gelatin and lightness with whipped cream, ordinarily takes the form of a charlotte or a Marquise Alice. When stiffly beaten egg whites are added to the Bavarois, it becomes a mousse. But not all mousses are made from Bavarois. A few of the mousses are creations entirely to themselves.

Crème Pâtissière is flour-thickened Crème à l'Anglaise. It is the filling for most pastries and the foundation of dessert soufflés.

CRÈME À L'ANGLAISE
[*Thin Sweet Cream Sauce*]

2 cups milk	½ teaspoon salt
8 egg yolks	6 tablespoons whipping cream
10 tablespoons sugar	1 teaspoon vanilla or 2-inch piece vanilla bean

1. Scald milk in saucepan. (If using vanilla bean, split it lengthwise, then add it to the milk. It will release its tiny black seeds for flavor.) Beat yolks in a saucepan and then add sugar and salt. Mix well.

2. Set pan on a damp dishcloth and it will not move about as you stir in the milk. Add half the hot milk. Stir and then add the rest.

3. Stir-cook sauce over very low heat until custard becomes as thick as whipping cream, or until it coats the back of a spoon. The foam on top will disappear as the custard becomes cooked. Also there is a color change. *Never boil* or the sauce will curdle. When it has thickened, set immediately into cold water to stop its cooking. Stir until cool. Add cream and vanilla, if using the liquid variety. If vanilla bean has been used, remove it, rinse, let it dry, and tuck it into a jar of granulated sugar to give the sugar flavor.

4. Strain sauce into a clean dish or bowl. It is necessary to strain the sauce because some egg white always clings to the yolks and it is cooked when hot milk is added. If not strained out, the cooked white will remain as little lumps in the sauce. Chill sauce and serve, or use in other recipes.

GLACES
[*Ice Creams*]

Homemade ice cream was a joy of my childhood. Every Sunday I would sit beneath the box-elder tree and hand-turn the ice-packed freezer until the paddle would no longer move through the frozen custard. Then came the reward of "licking the paddle," and my job was finished for another Sunday.

Mother would pack the ice cream down tight in the container and admonish, "Now it must age for two hours." Always she said the same thing, but her disappointment would have been great had we not sneaked a few tastes during the aging process.

An old-fashioned hand-turned freezer will give youngsters of today a taste of early Americana, but from start to finish you can make a batch of ice cream in an hour with an electrical machine. As the novelist Stendhal said while molding his mouth around a teaspoon of homemade ice cream: "What a pity this isn't a sin."

GLACE À LA VANILLE

[*Vanilla Ice Cream*]

Recipe of Crème à l'Anglaise　　　　　**Crushed ice**
Rock salt

1. Make Crème à l'Anglaise (p. 289) and cool. When cold, pour into a 1-quart freezer container. Cover with lid. Put container into the bucket and fasten the turning device.

2. Put a 2-inch layer of ice in the bucket around the container. Sprinkle with salt. Add more ice and salt. Tromp down tight with the handle of a wooden spoon. Repeat layers until bucket is filled to the edge of the lid.

3. Turn the crank slowly at first; then, when you begin to feel a pull, increase the turning speed, but don't whip the liquid out the top. (If using electric freezer, follow its instructions.)

4. Keep the ice poked away from the drain hole in the bucket so that the water can escape.

5. When the paddle becomes too difficult to move through the frozen ice cream, it is time to stop. (Electric freezer takes about 20 minutes to churn custard into ice cream.) Remove the turning mechanism and wipe off the lid with paper towels. Tip the bucket, drain off most of the water, and then remove the lid.

6. Slip two fingers under the top of the paddle, and while pushing the ice cream from it, pull out the paddle and give it to a deserving crankster.

7. Pack the ice cream down tight in the container. Put a cork into the hole in the lid and cover container. Pack bucket with ice and salt. Cover with newspapers, then a rug or bath towels. Let ice cream age for at least 2 hours. Should serve 6.

NOTE: Ice cream may be packed in molds and aged in the freezer compartment, but the ice cream is better when aged in ice and salt.

To make richer ice cream, use half cream. If freezing ice cream in a half-gallon freezer, double the recipe.

VARIATIONS
GLACE AU CAFÉ
[*Coffee Ice Cream*]

Heat 2 teaspoons instant coffee and ¼ cup coffee beans (espresso coffee beans, if possible) in the milk. Remove from heat, cover, and let stand about 5 minutes. Strain liquids into a clean pan. Beat into the yolk-sugar mixture in the Anglaise recipe and then cook according to that recipe. Freeze ice cream and then pack into a fancy, 3-cup mold. Put into a zero-degree freezer. Unmold and serve decorated with rosettes of whipped cream and candied violets.

GLACE AU CITRON
[*Lemon Ice Cream*]

Add 2 tablespoons grated lemon rind to the hot Crème à l'Anglaise. Omit vanilla and flavor with ½ teaspoon lemon extract and 1 tablespoon Kirsch, and add 2 tablespoons crème fraîche. Add yellow food coloring to make sauce a dark lemon color. (Color will fade with freezing, so make it darker than it should be.) Freeze ice cream, and then pack in a square 3-cup mold. Unmold the ice cream when ready to serve, and decorate each corner with a rosette of whipped cream.

GLACE AUX NOIX
[*Walnut Ice Cream*]

Grind 1 cup walnuts through finest blade of food chopper. Add to the hot milk in the Anglaise recipe, then stir half into yolk-sugar mixture and proceed with recipe. Do not strain the custard. Cool, then flavor with 2 tablespoons crushed praline, p. 343 (you may use bought praline, or it may be omitted), 2 tablespoons crème fraîche, and 1 tablespoon Kirsch. Freeze ice cream and then pack in a square 3-cup mold. When serving, decorate each corner with a rosette of whipped cream and a walnut half.

BOMBES GLACÉES
[*Molded Ice Cream*]

A bombe is a mold of 2 or more flavors of ice cream, sherbet, ice, fruit, or a combination of these. Its shape is always fancy and the recipe takes the name of the mold when the mold has a special name.

The only trick to making a bombe is to let each layer harden before adding the next flavor, or layer. Make them as varied as you wish. Practice on bought ice creams and then make them from the homemade variety. They can be made in advance, frozen, unmolded, frozen again, and then wrapped ready to serve.

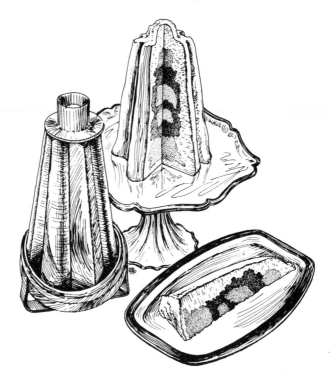

BOMBE COMTESSE-MARIE

[*Mold of Vanilla Ice Cream and Strawberries*]

This bombe is made of vanilla ice cream and fresh strawberries. It gets its name from the square Comtesse-Marie mold in which it is shaped.

Recipe of Crème à l'Anglaise	½ cup sugar
2 tablespoons crème fraîche	3 tablespoons Kirsch
1 quart strawberries	Whipped cream

1. Put a Comtesse-Marie mold (square container with a lid) into the freezer to get cold.

2. Make Crème à l'Anglaise (p. 289) and cool. Stir in crème fraîche and freeze into ice cream in a freezer.

3. When frozen, remove paddle. Coat the entire square mold with a 1-inch layer of vanilla ice cream. Press a sheet of foil against the ice cream to hold it in place and then fill foil with rice or dried beans. Put back in freezer compartment to harden the ice cream. Pack remaining ice cream in freezer container, or in another container and put into the electric freezer compartment.

4. Stem berries. Save the 4 most nearly perfect ones for the garnish. Cut the rest into lengthwise slices. Put into a bowl. Add sugar and Kirsch. Refrigerate and let marinate.

5. When ice cream in mold has hardened, remove, empty out the beans and lift foil from ice cream. Drain berries, reserving liquid, then pack berries into ice-cream mold. Fill to ½ inch of the top of the ice cream. Cover with foil and the lid and freeze hard. When berries are frozen, remove lid and foil and cover with vanilla ice cream from freezer. Re-cover with foil and lid. Put into freezer compartment to age for at least 8 hours. Mash remaining cut berries with a fork. Then add to the reserved marinade from the berries. Refrigerate until ready to serve.

6. To unmold, remove lid and foil. Dip container in cool water, dry off mold, invert on serving plate, run knife into edge of mold to break the suction. It should drop out onto the plate.

7. Smooth off the sides. Make rosettes of whipped cream on each corner. Top each with a whole berry. Serve with the strawberry sauce.

VARIATIONS

BOMBE AÏDA

[*Lemon Sherbet and Kirsch Soufflé Glacé*]

Line a square mold with 1 inch of Glace au Citron (p. 291) or sherbet. Freeze according to Comtesse-Marie recipe. Fill center with vanilla ice cream, or Kirsch-flavored Soufflé Glacé (p. 336). Freeze. Decorate each corner of the ice cream when unmolded with rosettes of whipped cream and top with miniature lemon-peel roses. To make roses cut the skin from a lemon, making it paper thin. Cut the peel into 3-inch lengths and taper each end. Wrap each piece of peel in a spiral to create a rose. Set into each rosette of whipped cream. Or, to make life simple, grate a bit of lemon peel and sprinkle in center of each rosette of whipped cream. (See Lemons, p. 385.)

BOMBE DORIA

[*Nut Ice Cream and Chestnut Mold*]

Line a mold with Glace aux Noix (p. 291). Freeze according to Comtesse-Marie recipe, then fill center with vanilla ice cream or Soufflé Glacé (p. 336) to which has been added ¼ cup chopped Marrons Glacés (p. 274). Flavor chestnuts with 2 tablespoons Curaçao. Freeze. Decorate with rosettes of whipped cream and whole glazed chestnuts.

NOTE: When making a tall bombe, arrange the different layers of ice creams or flavors lengthwise of the mold. Serve it standing up tall and straight and slice it across so that each serving has all flavors.

CHARLOTTE GLACÉE
[*Ice-Cream-Filled Charlotte Mold*]

When ice creams are fenced in with ladyfingers and shaped in a charlotte mold the dessert takes the name of the mold and the particular flavor of ice cream it is created from.

Line charlotte mold with ladyfingers and then pack with ice cream. The name of the ice cream gives its name to the dish: Charlotte Glacée au Café (with Coffee Ice Cream, p. 290), Charlotte Glacée aux Noix (with Walnut Ice Cream, p. 291), Charlotte Glacée à la Vanille (with Vanilla Ice Cream, p. 290).

NOTE: If you want to make life simple, buy ladyfingers and ice cream and make a Charlotte Glacée.

MELBAS GLACÉES
[*Fruit Sundaes*]

These rich ice-cream desserts are named for the lady of operatic fame. They are considered glamour desserts by the French, but in reality they are nothing more than fruit sundaes drizzled with a red fruit syrup and decorated with whipped cream. But they are far better than anything concocted at the corner drugstore.

FRAISES MELBA
[*Strawberries with Vanilla Ice Cream*]

Dissolve ½ cup sugar in ½ cup Grand Marnier and 2 tablespoons Kirsch. Stem 1 quart whole ripe strawberries. Pick out the 12 least desirable berries for use in a sauce. Add rest of the berries to the liqueurs and refrigerate for about 2 hours. Lift berries from liquid. Boil liquid and reduce to a syrup. Remove from the heat. Cool. Mash the 12 berries through a strainer and into the syrup. Half fill a crystal bowl with 1 quart vanilla ice cream. Stand the liqueur-flavored berries over the top. Drizzle with strawberry sauce. Dot with rosettes of whipped cream between the berries. Serve at the table on chilled plates.

PÊCHES MELBA

[*Vanilla Ice Cream with Peaches*]

Cook 2 cups sugar, 1 cup water, ½ teaspoon Fruit Fresh (see p. 605) and 1 tablespoon Kirsch for about 5 minutes to make a syrup. Peel 3 large, ripe peaches, cut in half, remove pits and add to syrup. Cook about 10 minutes, or until peaches are just tender. Lift from syrup. Cool syrup, then put peaches back into it and refrigerate. When ready to serve, put 1 quart of vanilla ice cream into a crystal bowl. Drain peach halves, and lay rounded side up, over the ice cream. Drizzle with Raspberry Glaze (see below), and dot with whipped cream between the halves.

POIRES MELBA

[*Vanilla Ice Cream with Pear Halves*]

With a sharp knife and a melon baller, core 6 whole pears from the blossom end. Once cores are removed, then peel pears. Leave the stems attached. Cook in syrup like Pêches Melba. Cool and refrigerate in the syrup. When ready to serve, paint a slight "blush" on the cheek of each whole pear. (Dilute red food coloring with water and paint it on the pear with a small brush.) Set pears over 1 quart vanilla ice cream in crystal bowl, drizzle with Raspberry Glaze and dot with rosettes of whipped cream.

NOTE: *Glace aux Framboises* (Raspberry Glaze): Add 2 tablespoons Kirsch and 1 tablespoon Grand Marnier to an 8-ounce jar of raspberry jelly. Heat to melt the jelly. Cool pan in ice water and then spoon between the halves of fruit. Prepare in advance and have ready to use.

CRÈME RENVERSÉE

[*Baked Caramel Custard*]

When whole eggs are substituted for the yolks in the Crème à l'Anglaise recipe, and the custard is baked, this famous French dessert is created. To make it by the Anglaise recipe, with yolks only, would be to create a Spanish flan, which is heavier. Try both and see which you prefer.

4 tablespoons sugar	¾ cup sugar
4 tablespoons water	Dash of salt
2 cups milk	1 teaspoon vanilla or 2-inch piece
4 whole eggs	vanilla bean

1. Put 4 tablespoons sugar and water into a 4-cup charlotte mold, or pan. Heat until sugar caramelizes and turns a dark brown. Remove pan from heat. Set into cold water to stop its cooking. Lift from water and twist pan

around to allow liquid caramel to coat the sides. If the syrup hardens before the pan is completely coated, heat again.

2. If using vanilla bean, add it to the milk and heat to a boil. Beat eggs with a whisk. Add ¾ cup sugar and salt. Mix. Pour half the hot milk into the egg-sugar mixture. Stir and then add the rest of the milk. Add vanilla if the bean has not been used. Mix well. Strain sauce into the caramel-coated pan. (There are always pieces of egg white that get cooked by the hot milk. Strain them out to make a better custard.) Now skim the foam from the top of the custard; it becomes tough when baked.

3. Set mold, or pan, in a hot-water bath. Bake on lowest shelf of a pre-heated 325-degree oven for about 50 minutes, or until done. To test for done-ness, gently shake the pan. If custard has a flabby wiggle, bake another 5 minutes and test again. When it has a firm wiggle, it is done. You will be able to tell. Start testing after 40 minutes of baking and every 5 minutes so that you will learn the different wiggles in a custard. (But don't shake it to pieces; easy does it!) There will also be a change in color as the custard bakes toward the middle. Remember, it will go on baking after it is removed from the heat, so don't overcook it to the point of being dry and firm.

4. Cool on wire cake rack and then cover and refrigerate until very cold. When ready to serve, run a knife around the top of the custard to loosen it from the pan, then set mold over low heat for a second to melt the caramel. Put serving plate over the mold and quickly invert. If there is still caramel in the mold, heat it again and then pour it around the custard. Remove custard from pan just before serving. Custards have a tendency to crack if made to wait too long out of the mold.

BAVAROIS À LA CRÈME

[*Bavarian Cream*]

The classic shape of the Bavarois is that of the charlotte mold, but any mold may be used.

2 envelopes unflavored gelatin	Recipe of Crème à l'Anglaise
½ cup cold water	1 cup whipping cream
4 tablespoons confectioners' sugar	

1. Stir gelatin into water. Let soak. Make Crème à l'Anglaise (p. 289). Add soaked gelatin to hot sauce. Stir until gelatin dissolves and then cool in cold water. Prepare a mixing bowl with ice cubes and cold water. Set Anglaise into it. Stir continuously until it starts to thicken. Remove.

2. Whip cream in a chilled bowl. Set into ice water and whip. It is better to have cream wait than the Anglaise. Once cream is fluffy and stiff, add confectioners' sugar. Quickly stir into syrupy Anglaise. Do not overwhip cream!

3. Rinse a 5–6-cup mold with cold water. Check how much the mold holds by measuring water into it. Pour Bavarois into mold. Cover with transparent wrap. Refrigerate about 8 hours, or until firm.

4. When ready to serve, dip mold into warm water, dry off, put serving plate over top, and invert. The mold will drop out onto the plate. Decorate with whipped-cream rosettes (using a pastry bag with star nozzle) or serve plain.

NOTE: When Bavarois recipes are to be molded in individual serving dishes or goblets, the gelatin may be reduced to 1 envelope.

If Anglaise sets before the whipped cream is added, set Anglaise in warm water and stir until it is liquid again and then repeat the ice-water treatment.

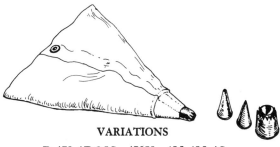

VARIATIONS

BAVAROIS AUX ANANAS

[*Pineapple Bavarian Cream*]

Drain 1 cup crushed canned pineapple. Put into small dish. Add 2 tablespoons Kirsch and let marinate. Make Bavarois. When starting to set, fold in the whipped cream and then the marinated pineapple. Pour into a rinsed 6-cup mold, or individual dishes. Refrigerate at least 8 hours. Unmold and decorate with rosettes of sweetened whipped cream.

BAVAROIS À L'ORANGE

[*Orange Bavarian Cream*]

Make Anglaise. Grate the rind of 2 oranges into the milk in the Crème à l'Anglaise recipe (p. 289). Bring milk to a boil and then strain milk through a fine sieve to remove the orange pieces. Cook Anglaise, then proceed with the Bavarois à la Crème recipe. Substitute ½ cup orange juice (from the oranges) for the water. Add 2 envelopes gelatin and let soak. Add soaked gelatin to the hot Anglaise. Stir until dissolved. Cool, then refrigerate. When starting to set, stir in sweetened whipped cream from Bavarois recipe. Rinse a 6-cup mold with cold water and then fill with Bavarois. Cover with transparent wrap and refrigerate at least 8 hours. Unmold and decorate with rosettes of whipped cream and candied violets.

BAVAROIS AU CHOCOLAT

[*Chocolate Bavarian Cream*]

Make Bavarois. After the gelatin has dissolved in the hot Crème à l'Anglaise, add 4 ounces of chopped bittersweet chocolate. Cover pan and let stand about 10 minutes, or until chocolate is melted. Stir chocolate into the sauce and then cool. When starting to set, fold in the whipped cream and pour the whole into a rinsed 6-cup mold. Refrigerate at least 8 hours. Unmold and decorate with sweetened whipped cream. Make fancy with chocolate curls, or grated chocolate.

NOTE: *To make chocolate curls:* Peel slices from a bar of chocolate with a potato peeler. To prevent the curls from breaking, wrap the chocolate in a plastic bag and place it in lukewarm water for about 2 minutes, but do not let it get soft.

BAVAROIS AUX FRAISES

[*Strawberry Bavarian Cream*]

Slice 1 pint fresh ripe strawberries into a bowl. Cut them the long way, rather than across; they are prettier. Sprinkle with ¼ cup sugar and 2 tablespoons Kirsch. Let marinate. Make the Bavarois and let cool. Rinse a 6-cup charlotte mold with cold water. Lift choice berry slices from marinating liquids. Blot on paper towels and then stand wide end of berry on bottom of mold, pointed end up the side. When Bavarois is cold and starting to set, spoon a 1-inch layer into the mold against the berries. Refrigerate. Mash remaining berries and drain in a sieve. Stir them into the remainder of the Bavarois crème. Spoon crème into the mold. Refrigerate at least 8 hours. Unmold and decorate with sweetened whipped cream piped onto the top through a star nozzle.

BAVAROIS AUX PÊCHES

[*Peach Bavarian Cream*]

Substitute 3 sliced ripe peaches for the strawberries in Bavarois aux Fraises and marinate. Make Bavarois. Put some curved slices of peaches around the bottom of a rinsed 6-cup charlotte mold. Then stand slices into each "peach joint" and lean them up the sides of the mold. Fill mold with 1 inch chilled Bavarois cream. Put in freezer, on top of other foods, for about 5 minutes to set the cream. Check to see that the peach slices have held their places. Mash remaining peach slices, drain, and then add to the remaining Bavarois crème. Fill mold. Refrigerate at least 8 hours. Unmold and decorate with sweetened whipped cream piped through a star nozzle, or leave plain.

CHARLOTTE À LA RUSSE

[*Bavarian Cream with Ladyfingers*]

When the name Charlotte Russe appears, you may be sure of two things: the dessert has been shaped in a charlotte mold, and the mold has been lined with ladyfingers.

| **Recipe of ladyfingers** | **Bavarois à la Crème** |

1. Make ladyfingers (p. 323) and Bavarois crème (p. 296). Line an 8-cup charlotte mold with the ladyfingers. To do this, turn the mold upside down. Then cut the ladyfingers in half and taper the cut ends to a point, making wedges or petals from the halves. Fit these onto the bottom of the pan, then turn pan right side up and fit them tight into the bottom, rounded side down. Cut a small round piece for the center of the petals. Force it into the center.

2. Now trim one end from enough ladyfingers to line the sides of the mold. Stand these tight together around the inside. When Bavarois is starting to thicken, add the whipped cream and fill the lined mold. Cover and refrigerate for at least 8 hours.

3. When ready to serve, trim ladyfingers off even with the custard (sometimes they stick above a little) and then invert on a serving plate. Refrigerate until ready to serve. Cut between the ladyfingers to serve.

VARIATIONS

CHARLOTTE À L'ORANGE

[*Orange Charlotte Russe*]

Line the mold with ladyfingers and then fill with Bavarois à l'Orange mixture (p. 297).

Any of the Bavarois variations may be used. Omit the whole fruits that decorate the mold in the peach and strawberry recipes and mash all the fruit to flavor the Bavarian cream. The dish takes the name of the particular filling: Charlotte aux Ananas (Pineapple Charlotte Russe), Charlotte au Chocolat (Chocolate Charlotte Russe), Charlotte aux Fraises (Strawberry Charlotte Russe).

CHARLOTTE ESTIVALE

[*Cake-Bavarian Cream Mold*]

This charlotte illustrates the way by which French cuisine makes new dishes through combinations. Three basic recipes are combined to make a new creation.

Biscuit Roulé	Bavarois à la Crème
Butter and Chocolate Glace	½ pint whipping cream

1 tablespoon confectioners' sugar

1. Make Biscuit Roulé (p. 322) to step 6. Make icings (p. 339) while cake bakes. When cake is cool, cut it as follows.

2. Press a 6-inch-wide piece of waxed paper around half the outside of the charlotte mold (from handle to handle). Let the paper take the shape of the mold. Cut out this pattern on the marks made by the mold. Make another piece like it, then place them inside the mold and trim them to fit. Do not let them overlap. Trace bottom of mold on waxed paper. Cut out circle.

3. Place patterns on cake. Cut out 2 sides and the bottom from the cake. (Save the patterns.) Cut the bottom circle of cake in half. Place the cake pieces on a wire cake rack. Pour warm butter frosting over 1 semicircle and 1 side piece. Ice the other 2 pieces with Chocolate frosting. Let the icing set while making the Bavarois (p. 296). Let Bavarois cool.

4. Brush paper patterns, sides and bottom, on one side with vegetable oil and then place in mold, dry side to mold. Cut the cake pieces as follows. Cut each side strip into 4 matching pieces. When the strips are cut the same size, they will *interchange* and fit together. Line the mold with them. Place iced side against the oiled-paper lining, and alternate the colors. (These can be iced any color you choose.)

5. Whip cream from Bavarois recipe and add to Bavarois when it starts to thicken. Fill lined mold. Refrigerate for at least 8 hours, or until firm. When ready to serve, place plate over top of mold and invert. Shake pan and mold will drop out. Remove waxed paper from bottom and sides. Put semicircles of iced cake back into their original circle, icing side up. Cut evenly, make 4 wedges on each side, or each color. Lay these wedges in alternating colors over the top of the Charlotte. Refrigerate until ready to serve.

6. Whip cream and sweeten. Put into a pastry bag with a small star nozzle. Pipe cream over the cracks, around the top and around the bottom. Set a big red strawberry or cherry in the center of the top. (The whipped cream is to cover up the imperfections in fitting the pieces together. If you've done a masterful job, then don't cover up the edges. I might add, at this point, that half of cooking is knowing how to correct the imperfections!)

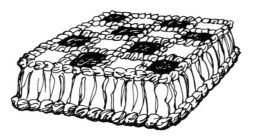

MARQUISE ALICE

[*Checkerboard Bavarois Cake*]

This aristocratic Bavarois lady is a "square" of the dessert world. Her checkerboard dress is child's play to create.

Recipe of ladyfingers	Kirsch
¼ cup mashed praline	1½ cups whipping cream
(may be omitted)	4 tablespoons confectioners' sugar
Bavarois à la Crème	1 cup strawberry jelly (or other
2 tablespoons Grand Marnier	red jelly)

1. Make ladyfingers from the Biscuit Roulé (pp. 322–323). Make praline (p. 343); cool and crush fine. Make Bavarois (p. 296), but flavor with Grand Marnier. Add whipped cream from Bavarois recipe when starting to set. When ladyfingers are cool, turn about 12 upside down on a plate. Sprinkle generously with Kirsch, but do not dissolve them. Let them stand. Rinse an 8 x 8-inch cake pan with cold water.

2. Pour about half the cold Bavarois into the pan. (If it is too cold it may set, in which case just finish the recipe.) Refrigerate until set. With a pancake turner, place the ladyfingers over the set Bavarois. Add praline to remaining Bavarois. Pour over the ladyfingers. Cover with transparent wrap and refrigerate at least 12 hours, or until firm.

3. Once Bavarois is firm, dip pan into warm water, dry off, place a chilled serving plate over pan, and invert. Refrigerate while beating the cream.

4. Whip cream. Once it has thickened add confectioners' sugar and beat until stiff. Frost entire dessert with whipped cream, making it smooth and even. Put the remaining cream into a pastry bag with a star nozzle. Using a ruler, mark lines every 2 inches in both directions across the whipped-cream coating. Then pipe whipped cream around the top edge of the cake and on each line, making squares.

5. Heat the jelly with 2 tablespoons Kirsch and then cool. Fill every other square with the cold red liquid jelly, leaving the alternate squares white, thus a checkerboard cake. Serves 8.

NOTE: This technique may be applied to any square cake.

MOUSSES D'ENTREMETS

[*Sweet Mousses*]

A mousse differs from a Bavarois in that it usually contains stiffly beaten egg whites. Any Bavarois can be turned into a mousse, but the reverse is not true.

Recipe of Bavarois à la Crème	**Dash of salt**
3 egg whites	**6 tablespoons sugar**

1. Make Bavarois (p. 296). At the time the whipping cream is added to the partially set Bavarois, whip the egg whites and salt until starting to get stiff. Then sprinkle in the sugar and beat until whites are very stiff. Fold into the Bavarois mixture alternately with the whipped cream.

2. Pour mixture into a rinsed 8-cup mold. Cover with transparent wrap and refrigerate 8 hours, or overnight.

3. To unmold, dip container into warm water, dry off mold, place serving plate over the top and invert. Mold should drop out. If not, lift up an edge of the mold and run a knife down the inside of the mold to break the suction. The mousse will drop out, but if it does not, pick plate and mold up and turn both over. Dip again in warm water, dry mold, and again invert. Decorate mold with whipped-cream rosettes, or serve plain. Serves 6 to 8.

VARIATIONS

MOUSSE AU CAFÉ

[*Coffee Mousse*]

Make Bavarois à la Crème (p. 296). To the milk in the Anglaise recipe add 4 tablespoons instant coffee (espresso gives the best flavor) and then proceed to make the Anglaise into a Bavarois and then into a Mousse by adding the beaten and sweetened egg whites at the time the whipped cream is added to the Bavarois. Pour into mold and refrigerate. Decorate with whipped cream, bought candy coffee beans, or serve plain.

MOUSSE AU CHOCOLAT NO. 1

[*Chocolate Bavarian Mousse*]

Make Bavarois au Chocolat (p. 298). Fold the 3 stiffly beaten and sweetened egg whites into the Bavarian cream at the time the whipped cream is added. Proceed with the Mousse recipe. Unmold and decorate with Crème Chantilly (p. 332) or chocolate curls.

MOUSSE AUX FRAISES NO. 1

[*Strawberry Bavarian Mousse*]

Make Bavarois aux Fraises (p. 298); mash all of the berries into the Bavarois. Add the beaten and sweetened egg whites at the time the whipped cream is added to the Bavarois. Proceed with the Mousse recipe. Unmold and decorate with rosettes of whipped cream and strawberries.

MOUSSE À L'ORANGE

[*Orange Bavarian Mousse*]

Make Bavarois à l'Orange (p. 297). At the time the whipped cream is added, also fold in the beaten and sweetened egg whites and proceed with the Mousse recipe.

MOUSSE AUX PÊCHES

[*Peach Bavarian Mousse*]

Make Bavarois aux Pêches (p. 298). At the time the whipped cream is folded into the mixture also add the sweetened and stiffly beaten egg whites. Proceed with the Mousse recipe. Unmold and decorate with rosettes of whipped cream and candied (bought) violets.

At the beginning of this section I said that the Bavarois recipes could all be turned into Mousse recipes, but that the reverse was not true.

Here are three examples of what I mean. They are individualistic, and they are all unlike the Bavarois-Mousse recipes in that they use no milk.

MOUSSE AU CHOCOLAT NO. 2

[*Chocolate Mousse*]

4 ounces bittersweet or German sweet chocolate	1 teaspoon vanilla
4 egg yolks	½ teaspoon pure peppermint flavoring
⅛ pound butter	4 egg whites
Dash of salt	6 tablespoons sugar

1. Put chocolate into a saucepan. Cover with two inches of very hot tap water. Cover with a lid. Let stand about 5 minutes. When you can stick your finger through the chocolate it is soft enough to complete the recipe. (If water cools, carefully drain it from the chocolate and replace with more hot tap water.)

(*continued*)

2. When chocolate is soft (but not dissolved), drain off the water. (Don't worry that some water clings to the chocolate.) Add the yolks. Stir with a whisk and cook over very low heat until thick. Remove from heat. Add the butter, salt, vanilla, and peppermint. Mix well. Cool, but do not let it get cold.

3. Beat egg whites. When big bubbles give way to little ones, start adding the sugar. Beat until stiff. Beat a "gob" of whites into the chocolate, mixing it in well. Fold remainder of the whites into the chocolate. Pour into individual serving dishes. Cover with transparent wrap. Refrigerate until ready to serve. Decorate with whipped cream or serve plain with crisp cookies.

NOTE: This is a 5-minute dessert and one you may well serve more often than any other.

MOUSSE AUX FRAISES NO. 2

[Strawberry Mousse]

2 envelopes unflavored gelatin
½ cup cold water
1 pint fresh ripe strawberries
½ cup confectioners' sugar
4 tablespoons Kirsch
2 egg whites
Dash of salt

6 tablespoons sugar
Red food coloring
1 cup whipping cream
4 tablespoons confectioners' sugar
Whipped cream and berries for decorating

1. Put gelatin and water into small saucepan. Let soak. Wash and hull 1 pint strawberries. Mash through a food mill or sieve into a bowl. Add ½ cup confectioners' sugar and Kirsch. Dissolve gelatin by heating, and then stir it into strawberries. Refrigerate until mixture starts to set.

2. Beat egg whites and salt until stiff. Add sugar gradually and beat very stiff. Add red coloring to make the same color as the berries. Whip cream and dye red. Stir in 4 tablespoons confectioners' sugar.

3. Add whites and cream alternately to the thickened berries. Pour into a cut-glass bowl or fancy dish. Refrigerate until set. When ready to serve, decorate the top with rosettes of whipped cream (do not dye red) and a few choice berries.

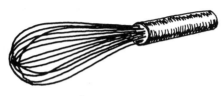

ORANGE À LA CYRANO
[*Orange Rum Mousse*]

This recipe is as unusual and as entertaining as the original Cyrano de Bergerac.

6 large oranges	½ cup cold water
1 cup orange juice	¾ cup dark rum
¼ cup lemon juice	1 tablespoon grated orange rind
1 cup sugar	1 cup crème fraîche
Dash of salt	1 cup whipping cream
2 envelopes unflavored gelatin	Whipped cream for decorating

Candied violets (bought)

1. Cut tops from oranges 1 inch down and in zigzag fashion. Squeeze juice from oranges by sticking a fork into the orange meat and use the fork as a squeezer. Do not damage the skins. They will be used as a serving dish. Once most of the juice has been extracted, remove pulp of orange. A teaspoon is the best implement with which to do this. Strain juice, using only 1 cup.

2. Put juices, sugar, and salt into nonmetal bowl. Stir and let sugar dissolve. Soak gelatin in water. Put rum into small pan. Grate the zest from the orange tops to make 1 tablespoon. Add to the rum. Heat rum to a simmer. Do not let it get too hot, or boil, or it may ignite itself. Remove from heat. Add softened gelatin and stir until dissolved. Cool, and then stir into juices and sugar. Refrigerate until mixture starts to set.

3. When syrupy and thickened, stir in the crème fraîche. Refrigerate again until mixture starts to set. (If you have no crème fraîche made [see p. 3], increase whipping cream to 1½ cups.) Whip the cream and then fold into the thickened orange mixture. Fill orange shells. Pour rest of mixture into a buttered mold or dish. (Size of oranges will determine how much Cyrano will be left.) Cover oranges and dish with transparent wrap. Refrigerate until set. This dessert should be made in individual servings. It is not stiff enough to hold together in a big mold.

4. When ready to serve, decorate with rosettes of sweetened whipped cream and top each with a candied violet.

NOTE: Frozen concentrated orange juice may be substituted for the fresh orange juice. Use ¾ cup concentrated juice and dilute it with ¼ cup water. Mold in goblets since there will be no empty orange shells.

CRÈME PÂTISSIÈRE
[*Thick Sweet Cream Sauce*]

10 tablespoons sugar or ½ cup plus	5 egg yolks
2 tablespoons	2 cups whole milk
8 tablespoons flour	1 (2-inch) piece vanilla bean or
¼ teaspoon salt	1 teaspoon vanilla

1. Put sugar, flour, and salt into a saucepan. Stir together with a whisk. Add yolks and enough milk to make a paste. Add remainder of milk and vanilla bean. Stir-cook over very low heat until thick. Remove from heat, remove vanilla bean, or add vanilla if bean has not been used.

2. Set pan in cold water. Stir until cool, then use in one of the following recipes.

NOTE: If sauce is to be used as a dessert sauce, it *must* be diluted with cream, liqueur, or a combination of the two. Thin it to the consistency of heavy whipping cream.

VARIATIONS
CRÈME PÂTISSIÈRE AU CHOCOLAT
[*Fillings for Éclairs and Profiteroles*]

To milk in master recipe add 4 ounces bitter chocolate and proceed with sauce. Cool, and then add 3 stiffly beaten egg whites sweetened with 6 tablespoons sugar.

CRÈME PÂTISSIÈRE AUX LIQUEURS
[*Filling for Fruit Tarts*]

To the cooled basic Crème Pâtissière add 2 tablespoons each of crème fraîche, Kirsch, and Grand Marnier. The combination of these two liqueurs gives a persimmon flavor to the sauce.

NOTE: To make Poires à la Crème Pâtissière aux Liqueurs, sauté fresh pears, then lightly caramelize them with sugar and serve the pears hot with the cold sauce.

CRÈME PÂTISSIÈRE À LA VANILLE
[*Filling for Cream Puffs*]

To the cooled basic Crème Pâtissière add 3 stiffly beaten egg whites sweetened with 6 tablespoons sugar.

CRÈME SAINT-HONORÉ

[*Filling for Savarin, Paris-Brest, Croquembouche and La Religieuse*]

Soak 1 envelope unflavored gelatin in ¼ cup cold water. Make Crème Pâtissière. Stir soaked gelatin into hot sauce. Stir until dissolved. Add 4 tablespoons crème fraîche or whipping cream. Set in cold water and stir until cool. Add dash of salt to 3 egg whites and whip. Gradually add ½ cup sugar when whites start to stiffen, and beat until very stiff. Fold into the cooled sauce.

VARIATIONS ON CRÈME SAINT-HONORÉ
CRÈME SAINT-HONORÉ AU CAFÉ

[*Coffee Flavored*]

Dissolve 4 teaspoons instant coffee in 1 tablespoon hot coffee or boiling water. Stir into hot Pâtissière sauce at the time the gelatin is added in Saint-Honoré recipe. Stir until dissolved and then continue with the Saint-Honoré recipe.

CRÈME SAINT-HONORÉ AU CHOCOLAT

[*Chocolate Flavored*]

Add 4 ounces bittersweet chocolate to the Crème Pâtissière at the time the soaked gelatin is added. Cover and let stand until chocolate is soft, then proceed with the Crème Saint-Honoré recipe.

SOUFFLÉS D'ENTREMETS

[*Sweet Soufflés*]

Dessert soufflés are nothing more than a heavy Crème Pâtissière made light with beaten egg whites. Dessert soufflés ordinarily contain no butter and are therefore lighter than main-dish soufflés.

BASIC DESSERT SOUFFLÉ RECIPE

½ cup sugar	Chunk of butter
½ cup flour	Granulated sugar
½ teaspoon salt	6 egg whites
1½ cups light cream	2 tablespoons sugar
5 egg yolks	Red and yellow food coloring
1 teaspoon vanilla	Confectioners' sugar

(continued)

1. Read general soufflé information (pp. 66–67). Stir sugar, flour, and salt together in a saucepan with a whisk. Add cream. Stir-cook over low heat. Custard will be very thick.

2. Remove from heat. Mix some hot sauce into yolks and then pour back into sauce and blend. Add vanilla. Cover and let sauce cool until you are ready to finish the soufflé. To this point, soufflé can be made in advance. Coat a 6-cup soufflé dish with butter and then sprinkle with sugar. (See general information on soufflés if you have questions.)

3. When ready to bake the soufflé, rewarm the custard if it is refrigerator cold. It should be room temperature. To the egg whites add one drop of red and two of yellow food coloring. Whip the whites. When big bubbles give way to tiny ones and whites start to stiffen, gradually add the sugar and beat until stiff. (Whites are colored to match the yellow custard so they will not dilute the color. Also, even if the whites are not completely mixed into the custard, there will be no telltale patches of white.)

4. With whisk, stir about 1 cup whipped whites into the cooled sauce to lighten it. Remove whisk and with rubber spatula or spoon fold rest of whites into mixture.

5. Pour into prepared soufflé dish, filling dish, level off with spatula, and push away from sides with your thumb. Put into a preheated 400-degree oven. Bake 10 minutes. Increase heat to 425 degrees. Bake about 15 minutes more and then carefully slide rack from oven and sprinkle the top with confectioners' sugar. (This step can be omitted until confidence is gained.) Push back into oven and let soufflé glaze for about 2 minutes. Serve immediately to 4 or 6.

NOTE: To make a checkerboard top, do not level off even with the top. Instead, with the spatula make waves over the top and then carefully make waves or dents across these waves in the opposite direction. Remove the soufflé mixture from the spatula as it collects. Once the pattern has been made, push the soufflé away from the sides with your thumb. The raised squares puff higher than the indented areas and the design so created is quite effective. With the spatula, diamonds or swirls may also be created over the top.

VARIATIONS

SOUFFLÉ ARLEQUIN

[*Two-colored Soufflé*]

Make the basic soufflé custard. Divide it in half. To one half of hot custard add 2 ounces bitter chocolate. Cover, and let the hot custard soften the chocolate. Stir chocolate into the custard when it is melted. Cover both custards and let them cool.

When ready to bake soufflé, whip the whites. Stir a "gob" into each batch of custard; then fold in remainder of the whites, adding about one-half cup more whites to the chocolate mixture than to the vanilla. (Chocolate is heavier; therefore, it takes more whites to inflate that part and keep it even with the vanilla soufflé as it bakes.)

Make a divider for the soufflé dish from foil. Stand the wall across the middle of a prepared 6-cup soufflé dish. Put half the chocolate into its side, and then pour the vanilla into its half of the dish. Once vanilla is in, add the rest of the chocolate. Level off the top of each with the spatula and then carefully pull out the wall of foil while pushing the mixture from it. Let the two soufflés bump together in the middle. The chocolate soufflé should be about ¼ inch higher than the vanilla. Once baked they will be about even. Push soufflé away from sides with your thumb. But be careful not to push one color into the other. Bake according to basic soufflé instructions. The resulting soufflé should remind you of Harlequin's costume.

SOUFFLÉ AU CHOCOLAT

[*Chocolate Soufflé*]

To hot soufflé custard add 4 ounces bitter chocolate. Cover pan. Let chocolate soften and then stir into the custard. Finish soufflé according to basic recipe, increasing the egg whites to 7.

SOUFFLÉ AUX FRAISES

[*Strawberry Soufflé*]

Cut strawberries into quarters to make 1 cup. Marinate in ¼ cup Kirsch and 2 tablespoons sugar. Make basic soufflé custard. Increase egg whites to 7, and finish soufflé mixture when ready to bake. Drain berries and then layer them in the soufflé mixture as it is added to the soufflé dish. Bake according to basic instructions.

SOUFFLÉ AU GRAND MARNIER

[*Grand Marnier Soufflé*]

To the custard add the grated zest of an orange, 2 tablespoons Cognac, and 2 tablespoons Grand Marnier. When ready to bake, finish the soufflé with 6 beaten egg whites and bake according to basic recipe.

SOUFFLÉ AUX MARRONS

[*Chestnut Soufflé*]

Prepare glazed chestnuts (p. 274). When done, crumble about 15 chestnuts and then soak them in 2 tablespoons Grand Marnier. Make basic soufflé recipe, increasing the whites to 7. Layer chestnuts in the soufflé mixture as it is added to the prepared dish. Bake according to basic instructions. This is a rich soufflé.

SOUFFLÉ ROTHSCHILD

[*Rich Fruit Soufflé*]

Marinate ½ cup assorted diced candied fruits in 2 tablespoons Kirsch for about 2 hours. Make basic soufflé recipe, increasing the whites to 7. Layer fruits in the soufflé mixture as it is added to the dish. Bake according to basic recipe.

OMELETTE SOUFFLÉE

[*Quick Soufflé*]

Omelette Soufflé is a wonderful quick delicacy. It is light as a feather and may be spiked with the liqueur of your choice.

5 egg yolks	**¾ cup sugar**
¼ teaspoon salt	**Red and yellow food coloring**
10 tablespoons sugar	**Grated zest from an orange**
6 egg whites	**1 tablespoon Grand Marnier**
Confectioners' sugar	

1. Put yolks, salt, and 10 tablespoons sugar into mixing bowl. (Use 2 tablespoons sugar per yolk and 2 tablespoons sugar per white. You can make these any size from 3 to 7 yolks.) Beat with electric beater on high speed for about 10 minutes, or until yolks are thick and light in color. They should almost hold a peak.

2. Beat whites in a clean bowl with an electric or hand beater. When big bubbles give way to tiny ones, add 2 tablespoons sugar (this stabilizes whites). Add remaining sugar as whites are beaten very stiff. Color with red and yellow to match the yolk mixture.

3. Add zest and Grand Marnier to yolks. With a whisk fold yolks into the beaten whites. Butter a very large oval oven-proof platter. Put mixture onto platter, all but about 2 cups. With a spatula, shape the soufflé into a boat or half a football shape. Now, still using the spatula, make waves around the outside of the boat.

4. Put the 2 cups of mixture into a pastry bag with a star nozzle. Make fancy decorations over the top ridge and around the edges that join the platter.

5. Put confectioners' sugar into a fine sieve. Shake sugar over the soufflé. Wipe off edge of platter. Put into a 400-degree oven. Bake about 10 minutes. Increase heat to 425 degrees; bake another 5 minutes, or until soufflé is puffed and high spots are browned. If it has not browned after 5 minutes, increase heat to 450 and bake another 5 minutes. Serves 4 adequately. It will seem like a lot, but it goes down fast.

OMELETTE AU SUCRE
[*Sweet Omelette*]

An Omelette au Sucre is like a breakfast omelette. It is custardy in texture and may be filled with slices of marinated fresh fruit or vanilla ice cream. When the eggs, sugar, and flavorings are on hand this dessert can be made in minutes.

OMELETTE AU GRAND MARNIER
[*Basic Dessert Omelette*]

2 eggs per person	Dash of salt
1 tablespoon sugar	Chunk of butter
1 tablespoon crème fraîche or	Granulated sugar
sour cream	1 tablespoon Cognac
1 tablespoon Grand Marnier	2 tablespoons Grand Marnier

1. This recipe is for one omelette. Double, triple, or quadruple it, but keep the same proportions. Big omelettes are hard to handle.

2. Put eggs, sugar, crème, Grand Marnier, and salt into bowl ready to beat. (Add salt now; it's not possible to salt a dessert omelette after it is cooked.)

(continued)

3. Toast butter in scoured omelette pan, but do not let it burn. Beat egg mixture 40 strokes with a fork and then pour into pan. Lift edges to center as it cooks. (See p. 61 for details on omelette making.) When ready to fold, add fillings if they are being used, if not fold and roll omelette out onto serving plate.

4. Sprinkle with sugar. Heat the back side of an old butcher knife on burner of range. Sear sugar diagonally, each way, thus making diamonds. Do this quickly. Have knife heating while omelette cooks.

5. Pour Cognac and Grand Marnier around omelette and set aflame. Serve blazing hot. Serves 1.

VARIATIONS

OMELETTE ALASKA

[*Ice Cream Omelette*]

Make omelette according to basic recipe. When ready to fold, put about 2 teaspoons vanilla ice cream down the middle and then fold and finish according to basic recipe. Flame and serve. Work quickly. Do not attempt this recipe the first time you make omelettes.

OMELETTE AUX FRAISES

[*Strawberry Omelette*]

For each omelette use 3 sliced strawberries that have been marinated in 1 tablespoon Kirsch and 1 tablespoon sugar. Lay strawberries down center of cooked omelette and then fold and finish according to basic recipe. Do not flame but serve with Sabayon sauce (next page). (Make sauce and then the omelettes.)

OMELETTE AUX PÊCHES

[*Peach Omelette*]

Marinate 1 sliced peach in 2 tablespoons Kirsch and 2 tablespoons sugar. Make omelettes. Lay peach slices down the middle and then fold and finish according to basic recipe. Sufficient peach slices for about 4 omelettes. Flame and serve, or serve with Sabayon sauce (next page).

SABAYON

[Frothy Wine Sauce]

When wine is substituted for milk in the Crème à l'Anglaise, and the quantities are reduced, a Sabayon sauce is the result. In Italy, homeland of the Sabayon, the wine used is Marsala and the name is Zabaione. In France white wine is ordinarily used and the sauce flavored with Kirsch.

RECIPE NO. 1

6 tablespoons sugar	3 egg yolks
Dash of salt	6 tablespoons white wine

3 tablespoons Kirsch

Put sugar, salt, yolks and white wine into top part of a double boiler. If using a chafing dish, use the water bath. Heat water in bottom part, but do not let water boil and do not let the part with the egg yolks touch the water. Beat mixture over simmering water with a hand whip or electric hand mixer. Whip until tripled in volume. Add Kirsch. Spoon over French-fried fruit or other desserts.

NOTES: To serve cold, remove from heat and continue to whip until custard is cool. Pour into goblets, cover with transparent wrap and refrigerate. Serve ice cold.

I think the following Sabayon recipe is a better one to use if the sauce is to be served cold. Try them both.

Sabayons can be cooked over low heat in a heavy enamel-coated iron saucepan.

RECIPE NO. 2

6 tablespoons sugar	2 egg yolks
Dash of salt	¼ cup white wine
1 whole egg	2 tablespoons Kirsch

Put sugar, salt, whole egg, yolks, and wine into top part of double boiler. If using a chafing dish, use the water bath. Heat water in bottom part, but do not let water boil and do not let the top part touch the water. Beat with a hand whisk or hand mixer until mixture is tripled in volume. When it is starting to go down in volume, add the Kirsch, remove from the heat, and beat until cool. Pour into tall goblets, cover with transparent wrap and refrigerate until very cold. Serve with crisp cookies. This sauce may also be served hot with cooked fruit.

Gâteaux,
Gâteaux Secs
et Glaces de Sucre

[Cakes, Cookies and Icings]

"Paris is a woman's town, with flowers in her hair," or so wrote American poet Henry Van Dyke. In the realm of food, the feminine spirit of Paris is nowhere better expressed than through the plain cakes that become fashionable ladies.

Through the two basic cakes—Pâte à Génoise and Pain de Gênes, we will introduce you to the most gorgeous ladies of the cake world. Pâte à Génoise gives us such gracious ladies as Charlotte Portugaise and the ever-famous gâteau sec called Madeleine. Through Pain de Gênes, we meet the crisp Sylvia and create Mirror cookies in which these luscious ladies reflect themselves.

Learn to know the ladies of the cake world, their cooky offspring, and their frosting adornments. But without their adornments they are "plain Janes." With French frostings and American cakes we have the best of two cake worlds.

GÂTEAUX
[*Moist Cakes*]

Batter cakes and pastries are both called *gâteaux* in French culinary language. Creations big and little, crisp and soft, shortened and unshortened all fall within this category.

But in American cooking a *cake* is always made with batter, is customarily shaped in rounds, loaves, or squares, and is either layered or unlayered. Pastry is used for making dessert pies, cobblers, and tarts and is not confused with cake.

In an effort to bridge the gap in culinary thinking between this side of the Atlantic and the other, I have sought to organize French cake and pastry making along American lines. First, French gâteaux are fitted into American dessert categories and each is assigned a chapter to itself.

In this chapter I try to point out the many fashionable French cakes and cookies that originate from the two basic cake recipes. Notice in particular how simple it is to adjust these basic cake recipes to produce a kaleidoscope of sweet desserts.

PÂTE À GÉNOISE
[*Yellow Cake*]

Génoise cake is not velvety-rich and light like our American type of cake. The basic cake contains no butter and no baking powder. It depends upon eggs for its lightness and, therefore, tends to be somewhat heavy and coarse in texture. It is usually given moisture through the use of a butter-cream frosting, cream sauce, or a syrup. Seldom is this cake enjoyed for itself, but it is fundamental to other desserts.

Melted butter	½ cup sugar
3 whole eggs	1 cup sifted cake flour
Dash salt	½ teaspoon vanilla

1. Prepare cake pan. Use a 6-cup charlotte mold; two 7-inch round pans 1½ inches high; one 9-inch round pan 2 inches high; or one 8-inch square pan 2 inches high. Brush all surfaces with melted butter. Set pan in freezer and then coat again with melted butter. Do not refrigerate after the second coating.

2. Put eggs and salt in metal bowl. Mix together and then add the sugar. Set bowl on an asbestos mat over very low heat. Warm and beat until mixture is

about three times the original volume. (Bowl should never get too hot to hold in your hand.) Use an electric hand mixer or balloon whisk. When mixture is thick enough to write your name in the batter, remove it from the heat and continue to beat until it is cool.

3. With a wooden spatula or spoon, fold in the flour and vanilla. Pour into prepared cake pan, filling it ⅔ full. Tap bottom of pan on counter to settle the batter. Bake in 375-degree oven for about 30 minutes, or until done.

4. Remove cake from oven. Cool on wire rack for about 5 minutes and then place rack over the top of the pan and invert, letting the cake drop out. Cool cake completely. If cake is to be cut into layers, refrigerate it for at least 2 hours. (Cold cakes are easier to cut.) Frost, or turn into one of the following desserts. This is a small cake, designed to make other desserts. Plain, it will serve no more than 8.

VARIATIONS

PÂTE À GÉNOISE AU BEURRE
[*Génoise Butter Cake*]

When the Génoise cake is to be used with fruits, it is normally enriched with melted butter. Fold ⅛ pound cooled, melted butter into the egg-sugar mixture alternately with the flour in Pâte à Génoise recipe.

GÂTEAU MOKA
[*Génoise Mocha Cake*]

Make Pâte à Génoise and bake in a 6-cup charlotte mold. While cake bakes, prepare Moka Crème au Beurre frosting (p. 335). When cake is done, remove it immediately from the pan. Cool and then refrigerate to get cold. Slice cold cake horizontally into ⅛-inch slices. Put slices on a cooky sheet. Coat with frosting. Refrigerate until cool. Stack iced slices, putting the cake back together with the top of the cake on the bottom, icing side up. In other words, largest round on the bottom. Press layers together and then coat with remaining Moka Crème. Refrigerate overnight. If not used, freeze, and then wrap. When it is to be served, unwrap the cake, and then let it thaw in the refrigerator. Serves 10.

GÂTEAU MOKA ARLEQUIN
[*Marbled Mocha Cake*]

Make Pâte à Génoise and bake in charlotte mold. Tear cake into pieces. Coat charlotte mold with Crème au Beurre frosting (p. 335). Add a layer of torn cake, then a layer of butter cream. Repeat layers until mold is full. Pack tight. There must be no air pockets. Cover with transparent wrap and refrigerate overnight, or at least 8 hours. Dip mold into warm water, invert on serving plate. Smooth frosting and refrigerate to set frosting. Decorate with rosettes of remaining frosting. Cut into wedges and serve. Serves 10.

CHARLOTTE PORTUGAISE
[*Hat-shaped Cake*]

And why should this particular dessert be called a Charlotte? Perhaps because Charlotte, who was the French-sponsored Empress of Mexico about the time of the American Civil War, took great pleasure in wearing fancy hats. Even yet, a charlotte in France is a chapeau adorned with flowers and birds.

That indispensable item of French cookery, the charlotte mold, seems to be modeled after the hat, and the most decorative of charlotte dishes are still garnished with pastry or sugar birds and ornaments.

Pâte à Génoise recipe	1 teaspoon grated orange zest
Crème à l'Anglaise	4 egg whites
3 tablespoons Kirsch	1 cup sugar
Confectioners' sugar	

1. Prepare Génoise cake batter. Bake it in a 6-cup charlotte mold or similar container. Line bottom of pan with waxed paper and coat with butter. Fill pan ¾ full. (The deeper the dough in a pan, the less it rises.) Bake in 375-degree oven for about 30 minutes, or until done. Cake leaves the sides of the pan when done.

(*continued*)

2. Make Crème Anglaise while cake bakes. Flavor with Kirsch and zest of orange. Cool, and then cover and refrigerate. When cake is done, cool in pan for 5 minutes and then turn out on wire cake rack to finish cooling. Wrap in transparent wrap. Refrigerate several hours.

3. Cut cold cake into six round slices. Put the top slice top down on serving plate. Moisten with Crème Anglaise, but don't dissolve cake. Add next slice, coat with sauce and then repeat the coating of the slices until all are used. The cake is now restacked and the bottom has become the top. Refrigerate until ready to serve.

4. Whip egg whites. When big bubbles give way to little ones, add 2 table-spoons sugar and continue to beat until stiff. Gradually add remainder of sugar. Beat until very stiff. Give cake a thick (¼-inch) frosting of meringue. With a spatula make waves around the outside. Put remainder of meringue into a pastry bag (see p. 359 for making a bag of waxed paper) with ½-inch plain nozzle.

5. Create meringue birds on top of cake. Make the body of the bird by squeezing out a large teardrop. The wings are small teardrops on each side, the head another teardrop attached to the body and tapering into a beak. Make eyes of cooky decorations or chocolate shot.

6. Once birds are made, hold a star nozzle over the round nozzle and make a rippled ribbon of meringue around the top and bottom edge of the cake. Dust cake with sieved confectioners' sugar. Wipe sugar from edge of plate. Put ice cubes into a pan large enough to hold the plate. Set plate with cake on the ice (this will prevent the possibility of the plate cracking). Put into a preheated 450-degree oven. Lightly brown meringue and then serve. Serves 8.

NOTE: Meringue may be sprinkled with sliced toasted almonds and con-fectioners' sugar and then browned.

ANANAS BOURDALOUE

[*Pineapple Butter Cake*]

Melted butter for mold	Pâte à Génoise au Beurre recipe

Sauce

6 tablespoons sugar	3 eggs
¼ teaspoon salt	1 cup milk
½ cup ground almonds	Chunk of butter
4 tablespoons flour	3 tablespoons Kirsch

Syrup

1 cup pineapple juice	2 tablespoons Kirsch
4 tablespoons sugar	

Glaze

4 tablespoons apricot preserves	2 tablespoons Kirsch

Decorations

3 pineapple slices	Chopped toasted almonds
Angelica	

1. Butter a 6-cup savarin or ring mold. Chill it, and then give it a coating of melted butter. Make Génoise butter cake (p. 316). Pour into savarin mold, filling it to ½ inch from the top. Bake in 375-degree oven for about 30 minutes or until done. Invert on cake rack and let cool.

2. While cake bakes, make sauce. Put 6 tablespoons sugar, salt, ground almonds, and flour into a saucepan. Add eggs and enough milk to make a paste, then stir in remainder of milk. Cook over low heat until thick. Remove from heat. Add butter and 3 tablespoons Kirsch. Cool, and then refrigerate.

3. To make syrup heat pineapple juice, 2 tablespoons Kirsch, and 4 table-spoons sugar. Once mixture is boiling remove from heat. To make the glaze, heat preserves and 2 tablespoons Kirsch. Mash through a strainer.

4. Cut cool cake into two layers. Put top half on serving plate, cut side up. Soak with pineapple syrup. Put cut side of the bottom half on top, making the cake whole again, so the bottom is the top of the cake. Soak with pineapple syrup.

5. Cut the pineapple rings into three very thin slices, making nine. Drape these over the curved top of the cake. Brush cake and slices with apricot glaze. Fill center with sauce. Sprinkle sauce with chopped almonds and decorate cake with pieces of green angelica. Serves 8.

NOTE: Angelica is an aromatic plant native to the Alps and many parts of Europe. The tender leaf-stalks are candied and sold as a confectionery and for use as a decorative garnish of desserts. It is usually bought where candied fruits are sold.

GÂTEAU AUX FRAISES

[*Strawberry Shortcake*]

Pâte à Génoise au Beurre recipe   2 tablespoons Kirsch
2 quarts fresh strawberries   Red food coloring
1 cup sugar   Confectioners' sugar

1 cup whipping cream, whipped

1. Make Génoise batter (p. 315), and bake it in a 9-inch-round or 8-inch-square cake pan. When done, remove from pan, cool, and refrigerate until ready to use.

2. Wash and hull berries. Reserve enough whole berries to stand over both layers of the cake. Put remaining berries into a bowl and crush. Add sugar, Kirsch and a few drops of red coloring to give the juice color. Put whole berries on a plate. Sprinkle with confectioners' sugar.

3. When ready to serve, cut the cake horizontally through the middle, making two layers. Put the top layer down on a serving plate with the cut side up. Spoon half the crushed berries over it. Stand half the whole berries over this layer. Place the bottom layer, cut side up, on top of the erect berries. Coat this layer with crushed berries and then stand whole berries over the top. Pour any remaining juice of the berries over the cake.

4. Put whipped cream into a pastry bag with star nozzle. Decorate base of cake and then squeeze stars of cream among the berries on top. Serves 10.

GÉNOISE AUX FRUITS

[*Fruit Cake*]

¼ cup raisins   ½ cup rum
½ cup mixed, diced candied fruits   ½ teaspoon baking powder
Boiling water   Pâte à Génoise au Beurre recipe

1 tablespoon cake flour

1. Put raisins and candied fruits into a small bowl. Pour boiling water over them and let soak until water is cool. Drain and then squeeze water from fruits with your hand. Add rum to fruits and let soak while making the cake.

2. Sift the baking powder with the flour in the Génoise recipe and then proceed to make the cake (p. 316). When batter is made, squeeze fruits from rum, put them into a plastic bag, sprinkle with about 1 tablespoon flour, and shake the bag to coat the fruits. Mix floured fruits into the batter.

3. Fill a greased and floured 9 × 5 × 3-inch bread pan ¾ full of batter. If there is extra batter, make cookies (see below). Bake cake in 325-degree oven for about 1 hour, or until cake leaves sides of pan and tests done. Cool on wire cake rack for 5 minutes and then turn cake out of pan onto rack.

PALAIS DE DAMES
[*Fruit Cookies*]

Add 1 tablespoon each shredded candied lemon and of orange peel to preceding recipe. Drop dough by spoonfuls on buttered and floured cooky sheets, and bake in a 350-degree oven for about 10 minutes, or until edges are browned and cookies test done. Make cookies small in size. Cool cookies on wire cake racks.

MADELEINES
[*Génoise Cookies*]

These cookies are variants on the Génoise butter cake batter. The ingredients are somewhat different, but the technique is essentially the same.

Clarified butter to coat pans	Dash of salt
1½ sticks butter (¾ cup)	¾ cup sugar
¼ teaspoon baking powder	1 teaspoon grated lemon rind
1½ cups sifted cake flour	½ teaspoon vanilla
4 whole eggs	Confectioners' sugar

1. Coat Madeleine cooky pans with melted, clarified butter. Refrigerate and then give a second coating of butter. Melt the 1½ sticks butter in a small skillet. Let it cool, but do not let it solidify.

2. Stir baking powder into the flour. Put eggs, salt, and sugar into a metal bowl. Beat and warm over very low heat as in the basic Génoise recipe. When mixture is thick and tripled in volume, remove from heat and continue to beat until cool.

3. Stir in lemon rind and vanilla. Alternately fold in the melted butter and the flour mixture. When mixed, fill each Madeleine shell with about a tablespoon of batter. Bake in 400-degree oven for about 10 minutes, or until browned.

4. When cookies are done, remove from pans and cool on wire racks. Sift confectioners' sugar over tops and then brush off the surplus sugar. Makes about 3 dozen.

NOTES: Wash and coat pans again with butter before adding the next batch of batter. This is necessary to prevent cookies from sticking.

Madeleine pans are shallow muffin pans in a fluted design. They look like shells.

BISCUIT ROULÉ

[*Sponge Cake*]

When the eggs in the Génoise recipe are separated and the whites beaten stiff and added, a Biscuit Roulé to make jelly roll, ladyfingers and sponge cakes is the result.

6 tablespoons sugar	½ teaspoon vanilla
3 egg yolks	3 egg whites
Dash of salt	3 tablespoons sugar
¾ cup sifted cake flour	Confectioners' sugar

1. Butter a 12 × 14 cooky sheet. Cover with waxed paper. Turn the paper over, putting the buttered side up. Coat again with butter. Sprinkle with flour and then shake off the surplus flour.

2. Beat 6 tablespoons sugar, yolks, and salt together until light, fluffy, and very thick (about 10 minutes with electric mixer). Gradually and carefully fold in flour and vanilla.

3. Beat whites until big bubbles give way to tiny ones and then start adding the 3 tablespoons sugar. Continue to beat until very stiff. Stir a "gob" of whites into the yolk mixture and then carefully fold in the remaining whites.

4. Pour batter onto floured paper. Spread into a ½-inch-thick rectangle. Bake in a 325-degree oven for about 15 minutes, or until done.

5. Sprinkle linen towel with confectioners' sugar. When cake is done, turn pan and cake upside down on towel. Pull waxed paper from the pan and then remove the paper from the cake. Cut all four crisp sides off the cake.

6. Roll the towel and cake up the long way in jelly-roll fashion, the towel inside the cake, and let the cake cool in this rolled condition. Once it is cool, unroll, remove the towel, and fill with Crème au Beurre (p. 335), jelly, whipped cream, or something of your choice. Roll back up (without the towel) and place cut side down on long serving dish or board. Sprinkle with confectioners' sugar. Serves 8.

VARIATIONS

BÛCHE DE NOËL

[*Christmas Log*]

Make Biscuit Roulé. Fill and frost the log with Crème au Beurre au Moka (p. 335). With a fork or knife, mark the icing to resemble the bark of a log, and then decorate with shaved chocolate curls. Ornament with chopped green pistachio nuts to resemble moss. Do not frost the ends of the cake; the rolled ends should remind you of the rings of the tree. The decorations on this Christmas log can be as fancy as you would like to make them. Miniature toadstools and leaves can be made from Glace Royale (p. 341), as well as holly berries, leaves, and mistletoe.

BISCUITS À LA CUILLER

[*Ladyfingers*]

Make Biscuit Roulé. Put the batter into a pastry bag with ½-inch nozzle. Squeeze out 4-inch-long ladyfingers onto greased and floured waxed paper. Sprinkle them heavily with confectioners' sugar. Bake in 325-degree oven until lightly browned. Cool pan on rack and then remove ladyfingers from the paper.

CHARLOTTE MALAKOFF

[*Molded Almond-Butter Cream*]

Malakoff is also a charlotte with a Russian name. It is unlike the famous à la Russe in that it is not made with a Bavarois. In some respects its butter-almond base makes it a richer dessert than the Russe.

Recipe of ladyfingers	½ teaspoon vanilla
¼ pound butter	3 tablespoons Kirsch
¾ cup sugar	1 cup whipping cream
Dash of salt	3 tablespoons confectioners' sugar
1¼ cups ground almonds	Whipped cream for decorating

1. Make ladyfingers (see preceding recipe).

2. Cream butter, sugar, salt, and almonds together in large mixing bowl. Beat until light and fluffy and sugar is no longer granular. Add vanilla and Kirsch. Continue to beat.

3. Whip cream. When stiff, add confectioners' sugar. Fold into creamed mixture.

4. Put circle of waxed paper into bottom of 5-cup charlotte mold. Do not oil. Cut off one end of each ladyfinger. Taper sides toward the cut end so that ladyfingers will fit tightly around the mold. No cream should peak through the fingers.

5. Fill with Malakoff mixture. Refrigerate for at least 8 hours, or until set. Cut off ladyfingers even with the filling. Put serving plate over top of mold. Invert and mold will drop out. Remove paper and cover top of mold with rosettes of whipped cream. Cut in wedges to serve.

GÂTEAUX SECS
[Dry Almond Cakes]

With the addition of ground almonds to the moist Pâte à Génoise au Beurre, we create a dry Pain de Gênes which gives nutlike flavor and crispness to cakes and cookies. From this batter we make the famous Tile cookies, Leaves, Cigarettes and Mirrors.

Then when we drop the yolks, butter, and flour from the recipe we come up with the delightfully crisp and unusual Sylvia cake. And finally, when the nuts are removed from the egg whites, we are left with a basic meringue recipe from which to create the famous Vacherin. And this is how a cuisine is built —from one stage to the other.

PAIN DE GÊNES
[Meringue-Almond Cake]

The basic Pain de Gênes is a plain cake respected for its keeping qualities. Normally, it is not frosted, but its chocolate variation is improved with a coating of Glace au Chocolat.

¼ pound butter	½ cup flour
¾ cup sugar	¼ teaspoon salt
1 cup ground almonds (4-ounce package)	3 eggs

1 tablespoon Kirsch, or 1 teaspoon vanilla

1. Put butter and half the sugar (guess at it) into mixer bowl. Beat until light and fluffy. While this beats, mix together the remaining sugar, almonds, flour and salt.

2. Add eggs, one at a time, to the butter-sugar mixture. Beat well after each addition. Add the flavoring, then add the almond-flour-sugar mixture. Mix and then pour into a buttered and floured 9-inch round cake pan. Prepare pan before starting cake. Bake in a 350-degree oven for about 30 minutes.

3. When done, cool cake in pan for about 10 minutes, then remove and place on a cake rack. Serve plain, or frost. Serves 8.

PAIN DE GÊNES AU CHOCOLAT

[*Chocolate Meringue-Almond Cake*]

To the Pain de Gênes recipe add 3 (1-ounce) squares melted bitter or semisweet chocolate when the almond-sugar mixture is added. Separate the eggs. Add the yolks and flavoring to the mixture and beat one minute. Whip whites stiff, adding 2 tablespoons of sugar as they become stiff. Stir a "gob" into the chocolate batter. Fold in the balance of the whites. Pour into prepared 8-inch pan (chocolate, being heavy, does not rise as much as the plain cake). Bake and finish as in above recipe. Frost with Glace au Beurre or with Glace au Chocolat (pp. 338–339).

NOTE: *To melt chocolate* place chocolate on a small plate and set into a pilot-heated oven for several hours. With planning, it will be ready to use when needed. Or place in top part of a double boiler and melt over hot, but not boiling, water.

With slight changes in quantity, or additions, to the basic Pain de Gênes many a delightful cooky can be created.

TUILES AUX AMANDES NO. 1

[*Tile Cookies*]

These cookies are curved to resemble the red tiles on the roofs of France.

¼ pound butter	¼ teaspoon salt
1 cup sliced almonds	6 tablespoons flour
1½ cups ground almonds	8 egg whites
1¼ cups sugar	Extra egg white to glaze

Confectioners' sugar

1. Preheat oven to 400 degrees. Melt butter and clarify (see p. 599). Coat cooky sheets with clarified butter. Chill pans and then brush again with butter, but in the opposite direction.

2. Put sliced and ground almonds in bowl. Add sugar, salt, and flour, and mix. Beat egg whites to a froth. Add dry ingredients and 3 tablespoons clarified butter to the whites.

3. Put batter onto greased cooky sheets by the teaspoonful. With fork beat extra egg white to a froth. Using the fork, dip it in egg white and then press cooky down onto the sheet. Treat each cooky in the same way. Sprinkle with confectioners' sugar. Use tea strainer (see step 6 of Sylvia recipe, p. 331).

4. Bake in 400-degree oven until lightly browned. Wrap a sheet of waxed paper around a rolling pin. When cookies are done, remove them from the oven, lift from pan with a spatula and drape over the covered rolling pin. Remove when cool to make room for the next ones. Makes about 6 dozen, depending upon the size.

TUILES AUX AMANDES NO. 2

[*Tiles, Leaves, or Other Shapes*]

Clarified butter	6 tablespoons flour
1 cup ground almonds	¼ teaspoon salt
½ cup plus 2 tablespoons sugar	3 egg whites, or ½ cup

2 tablespoons Cognac

1. Brush cooky sheets lengthwise with clarified butter. Chill pans and brush again in the opposite direction, or across the pan.

2. Put ground almonds, sugar, flour, and salt in mixing bowl. Add un-beaten egg whites and Cognac. Mix well, using a wooden spatula or spoon.

3. To make cookies, use a bought metal leaf stencil, or make stencils from a shirt cardboard. Cut out shapes that look like 4-inch round balloons. The neck of the balloon becomes the handle. On the balloon part draw a diamond, square, circle, or any other feasible design. Cut these out and you have a cooky stencil. (See illustration above.)

4. Put the stencil, whether the metal leaf or the cardboard cutout, down on the cooky sheet. Fill the hole with the cooky batter, making it ¹⁄₁₆ inch thick. Lift off the stencil by the handle and make more.

5. Bake in a 400-degree oven until edges are brown. Lift cookies from the cooky sheet while they are still hot. If cookies are to be filled with Crème Saint Honoré (p. 307), or Crème au Beurre (p. 335), shape them around metal, or wooden pastry cones to look like small ice-cream cones. Let cool and slip them off. If cookies cool too much to shape, reheat them in the oven, but don't cook them.

6. If cookies are to be coated with melted chocolate, cool them on wire cake racks and then coat the smooth bottom side. Place them chocolate side up and let chocolate harden before serving the cookies. Makes about 4 dozen.

NOTE: *To melt chocolate,* place chocolate in a bought foil custard cup (discard when through and there is no clean-up job), cover with foil and place in a 170-degree oven until chocolate is completely soft. Stir and use.

CIGARETTES
[*Cigarettes*]

¼ pound butter, plus a chunk	3 egg whites, or ½ cup
¾ cup sugar	¼ teaspoon salt
½ cup ground almonds (bought)	2 teaspoons grated lemon peel
½ cup flour	½ teaspoon vanilla

1. Melt butter and clarify. Coat cooky sheets with butter. Chill and then coat a second time in the opposite direction. Carefully toast the remaining clarified butter and set aside. Do not let it burn.

2. Put sugar, almonds, and flour into a bowl. Mix together. Beat whites and salt to a foamy froth. Add dry ingredients and beat. Add the rest of the toasted butter (should be about 6 tablespoons; if not, add more to make it so). Add lemon peel and vanilla. Mix well.

3. Put batter into pastry bag with ¼-inch nozzle. Make 1-inch cookies on cooky sheets. Cookies will spread to about 3 inches. Bake in a 400-degree oven until lightly browned. When done, remove from oven.

4. Lift one cooky off at a time and turn upside down on counter. Place a clean steel (one that sharpens knives) or handle of a wooden spoon, on one edge of the cooky. Roll up tight and then press down to seal the cooky into a roll. Push off the steel and make the next one in the same fashion. These go very fast once the technique is mastered. If cookies cool, reheat them in the oven. Serve plain, or fill with Crème Chantilly (p. 332) or Crème au Beurre (p. 335), piped into the cookies with a pastry tube. Makes about 6 dozen.

MIROIRS
[*Mirrors*]

Crème d'Amandes

Butter and flour for coating cooky sheets	6 tablespoons sugar
⅛ pound butter	¾ cup ground almonds (bought)
	1 whole egg

1 tablespoon rum

Apricot Glaze

¼ cup apricot preserves	2 tablespoons sugar

2 tablespoons water

Tuiles aux Amandes No. 3 (another variation)

10 tablespoons sugar	½ teaspoon salt
1¼ cups ground almonds (bought)	Chopped almonds
4 egg whites	Confectioners' sugar

Mirror Glaze

1 cup confectioners' sugar	2 tablespoons rum

1. Preheat oven to 400 degrees. Butter and flour cooky sheets. Make Crème d'Amandes. Cream ⅛ pound butter in mixer bowl. Mix sugar and ground almonds together and then add to the butter. Add egg and rum. Beat well and set aside ready to use.

2. To make glaze, boil preserves, sugar, and water for a minute, then mash through a strainer ready to use.

3. Make Tuiles aux Amandes. Sift sugar and ground almonds together. Beat whites and salt until very stiff. Remove beaters and fold sugar-almond mixture into beaten whites. Put mixture into pastry bag with ¼-inch round nozzle. Squeeze 1-inch slightly hollow ovals onto prepared cooky sheets—just like making zeros, but let insides of the ovals barely bump together. Sprinkle ovals with chopped almonds.

4. Fill centers of zero cookies, to the top, with the Crème d'Amandes mixture. Sprinkle both filling and cooky with confectioners' sugar. (If you put confectioners' sugar into a small tea strainer, then hold the strainer over each cooky and stir the sugar at the bottom of the strainer with a chopstick or skewer, the sugar will sprinkle onto the cooky and not onto the cooky sheet.) Bake in 400-

degree oven until brown. Take cookies from oven when done. Increase oven heat to 500. Brush almond centers with apricot glaze.

5. Make a glaze, of frosting consistency, from the confectioners' sugar and rum. (This is called a "mock fondant.") Put about ¼ teaspoon on top of the apricot glaze. Set cookies into a 500-degree oven just long enough to melt the rum glaze. Take from oven and cool cookies on wire racks. Makes about 8 dozen. Cookies improve with age.

VACHERIN POMPADOUR

[*Timbale of Almond Cookies*]

This recipe is further proof of the logical system of French cuisine. To know the basic recipes is to be able to create fancy foods.

Caramel Syrup	Crème au Beurre or Crème Chantilly
Mock Pistachio Nuts	Glace à la Vanille
Tuiles aux Amandes No. 2	Strawberries

1. Put ingredients for Caramel Syrup (p. 342) on to cook. This will be used like glue to hold the dessert together, so it must be ready when it is needed. If it is done before the Vacherin is ready for "gluing," simply set it into cold water to stop its cooking, then set back on the warm turned-off burner. If it hardens, reheat to melt it and then use, but don't cook it more. Make the Mock Pistachio Nuts (p. 608). Try to keep these as a staple in your pantry.

2. Make Tuiles aux Amandes No. 2 (p. 326). Spread a ⅟₁₆-inch layer of batter on one buttered cooky sheet to the size of 8 by 16 inches. Bake according to Tuiles recipe. On a second buttered cooky sheet make 1 round cooky 5 inches in diameter and then use remainder of batter to make 2-inch round cookies. Shape these in a round cardboard stencil (see Tuiles recipe) and bake according to Tuiles recipe.

3. Cut a sheet of waxed paper to fit around a 2½-size fruit can, and with a ½-inch overlap. When the long, flat cooky is brown, take from the oven. Place waxed paper on cooky and with a sharp knife, trim off the surplus cooky. Place the unopened can of fruit (you need the weight) on the waxed paper and roll the cooky and waxed paper up around the can. Press the can down on the over-lap, and let the cooky cool around the can to give it a cylindrical shape.

4. Take cookies from oven when done. Put the big round cooky on wire rack to cool. Shape the smaller cookies around a metal cone to give them ice-cream-cone shapes. See Tuiles recipe for specifics. Let cones cool.

5. Now we are ready to use the caramel glue. Reheat it if it has cooled.

(continued)

Put the large round cooky on a serving plate. Remove can from rolled cooky. Separate overlapped ends and drip syrup down between the overlap. Press tight to seal. Coat one open end of the cylinder with caramel glue. Set it evenly on the big round cooky, thus creating a Vacherin.

6. Dip the top edge of each cone cooky in syrup and then in chopped green nuts. Coat one side of the cone with caramel glue and then stick these around the top of the Vacherin even with the top. If there are enough, put a circle of cones around the bottom, otherwise coat base with caramel glue and press green nuts into the syrup. Let the Vacherin set to harden the glue.

7. When ready to serve, fill cones with Crème au Beurre (p. 335) or with Crème Chantilly (p. 332). Fill the cylinder with Glace à la Vanille or Crème Chantilly and strawberries.

NOTE: This dessert is beautiful. It takes time, but it is easy, since every part can be made in advance and assembled almost at the moment of serving.

SYLVIA
[Crisp Almond Cake]

2 (4-ounce) packages ground almonds, or 2 cups	½ teaspoon salt
2 cups sugar	8 egg whites
	Crème au Beurre au Moka

1. Butter and flour two cooky sheets. Using an 8-inch lid, a compass, or a piece of string 4 inches long tied between two wooden picks, make 4 perfect 8-inch circles in the flour.

2. Sift almonds with half the sugar, or 1 cup. Add salt to whites and beat. When big bubbles turn into tiny ones and whites begin to stiffen, start adding the remaining cup of sugar while continuing to beat. Beat until very stiff and creamy, then remove the beaters and fold in almond-sugar mixture with a rubber spatula.

3. Put batter into a pastry bag with ½-inch round nozzle. Squeeze batter onto floured cooky sheet about ½ inch thick. Begin at the center of each marked circle and coil batter around and around to fill the circles. Make 4 large circles and then finish the batter by making small circles of cookies around the big layers on the cooky sheet.

4. Bake in a 275-degree oven for about 1 hour, or until cakes are lightly browned and quite dry. While cakes bake, make the Crème au Beurre au Moka (p. 335). Chill. When cakes are done, set the pans on cake racks. Cool cakes on the pans and then lift them off with a spatula. Crush the small cookies into crumbs ready to use.

5. Coat three layers with the butter cream and then stack one on top of the other. The top layer may be covered with Glace au Beurre icing (p. 339), or sprinkled with confectioners' sugar. Frost before placing on the cake.

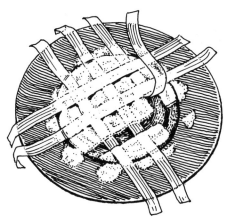

6. If using sugar, lay ½-inch-wide strips of waxed paper over the top layer at ½-inch intervals in a diamond or square pattern. Sift sugar over cake and strips. To give an even coating of sugar, put a tablespoon of sugar into a fine tea strainer and then stir the sugar around with a teaspoon and sieve it onto the cake. Carefully lift off the strips, leaving a pattern of sugar. Place top layer on cake. Gently press layers together. Coat sides of cake with Crème au Beurre au Moka. Press crushed cooky pieces around base of cake. Refrigerate at least 8 hours, or overnight, to harden the Crème au Beurre.

7. To serve, cut with a very sharp, thin-bladed knife. Cut into wedge-shaped pieces. Serves 10.

PÂTE À MERINGUE
[*Meringue*]

When the ground almonds are left out of the Sylvia, the Pâte à Meringue is the result. The basic recipe for making all meringues is usually a ratio of ¼ cup sugar to each egg white. When other ingredients are added to the meringue, then the ratio may or may not change.

8 large egg whites	**½ teaspoon salt**
1 drop blue food coloring (optional)	**½ teaspoon cream of tartar**
	2 cups sugar

1. Put whites, coloring (bluing makes whites whiter, just as with clothes), and salt into large mixing bowl. (Be sure bowl is free of fat. Scour it with cleanser to be certain.) Start beating whites and salt on low speed of hand

mixer (or use a balloon whisk in a copper bowl if you have them). Beat about 2 minutes. Add cream of tartar and then increase speed to medium. When big bubbles give way to tiny ones, add about 3 tablespoons of the sugar and then beat on high speed until stiff.

2. Once eggs are creamy and stiff, gradually add remaining sugar. Beat until sugar is dissolved. Taste to see if there are grains of sugar. If so, continue to beat until they dissolve. Once sugar is dissolved and whites are very stiff, use in the following recipes.

NOTE: When making meringue for a pie, reduce the recipe to 3 or 4 egg whites, but keep the ratio of ¼ cup sugar to each white.

VARIATIONS
MERINGUES À LA CHANTILLY
[Meringues with Whipped Cream]

Butter and flour two cooky sheets. Make meringue. Put the mixture into a pastry bag with ½-inch nozzle. Squeeze mixture onto prepared cooky sheets in oval mounds, or to resemble half a hard-cooked egg when cut in half lengthwise. Sprinkle meringues with sugar and then with confectioners' sugar. Let stand about 1 hour (providing it is a dry day). Sprinkle a second time with confectioners' sugar. Let stand a few minutes and then blow the sugar off the pan so it doesn't burn. Now lightly sprinkle meringues with water. This forms pearls on top of the meringues as they bake and they are very pretty. Put them into a 225-degree oven. Bake about 1 hour, or until dried out. Do not let them brown at all. When done, and completely dried out, cool, and then store in an air-tight container and put in a dry place.

At the moment of serving make Crème Chantilly (below). Coat bottom of one meringue with whipped cream. Stick another meringue onto the crème. Make as many as you need, then put the remainder of the crème into a pastry bag with a star nozzle. Pipe whipped cream around where the two meringues are joined. Serve with ice cream, strawberries, raspberries, or something else of your choice.

CRÈME CHANTILLY
[Whipped Cream]

Whip 1 cup whipping cream until stiff, then add 1 tablespoon confectioners' sugar and ½ teaspoon vanilla. Beat until very stiff, but not until it turns to butter. It should be creamy and stiff.

VACHERIN

[*Meringue Timbale*]

1. Butter and flour two cooky sheets. With a pan lid, or a compass, mark four 8-inch circles in the flour. Make Pâte à Meringue (p. 331).

2. Put meringue into a pastry bag with ½-inch nozzle. Squeeze out 1-inch-thick meringue rings on the marked circles on the cooky sheets. Fill one ring completely with egg white from pouch in zig-zag fashion. Bake these in a 225-degree oven for about one hour, or until completely dried out. Do not let them brown at all. Set remaining meringue in a cool place, or refrigerate. (If meringue has been properly whipped, it will not "weep" in an hour.)

3. When rings are done, take from oven. Let cool on pans and then lift each from the cooky sheet with a spatula. Wash one cooky sheet and dry. On it place a square of foil. Put the solid layer of meringue on the foil. Pipe raw meringue around the edge. Put a ring on top. Coat it with meringue and add the second ring. Coat it and then add the third ring. Continue until all rings have been added. The smaller the rings the higher a Vacherin can be built. For 8-inch size, 3 rings plus the bottom layer is about high enough, but you could add one more ring. Bake the stacked rings until the new meringue is dried out, or about another 40 minutes.

4. When dry, take from oven and cool. Prepare a half recipe of meringue (4 whites and 1 cup of sugar plus salt). Coat the outside with meringue just as you would frost a cake. Once it has been frosted, put remaining meringue into pastry bag with star nozzle. Decorate with swirls and fancy designs of meringue. Bake a third time to dry out this new layer of meringue. If there is meringue left, make three fancy S-shaped meringues on the cooky sheet and two tapering plumes. These stand on top of the filled Vacherin.

5. To serve, fill at the time of serving with assorted ice-cream balls, whipped cream, and fresh strawberries or with whipped cream and red raspberries. If you have made the S and plume meringues, lean the three S-shaped meringues together on top of the filling, stick the two plumes together with a bit of meringue or whipped cream, and stand them in the center of the S-shaped pieces. Meringues can be made days in advance so long as they are kept dry. I store them in my pilot-heated oven. Meringues can only improve with drying out.

GLACES DE SUCRE
[*Icings*]

The icings of France are among the best in the world. They are simple to make and always successful. You will notice that Fondant icing can be made in advance and then reheated when ready to use. Glace Royale can be made in advance and stored in an air-tight container ready to use. There are many icing tricks in this section that you can apply to our American cakes—even the commercial varieties—to make them exotic.

MERINGUES À L'ITALIENNE
[*Seven-minute Frosting*]

1 cup granulated sugar	3 large egg whites
½ cup cold water	Dash of salt
½ teaspoon white corn syrup	¼ teaspoon lemon juice
1 teaspoon vanilla	

1. Put sugar, water, and syrup into a small pan. Stir-cook until sugar is dissolved and mixture starts to boil. At that point stop stirring and let it simmer until it reaches 242 degrees or until a few drops in cold water make a firm-soft ball.

2. When this syrup is about ready to be used, put egg whites into a bowl. Add salt and lemon juice and whip stiff but not dry. If whites are ready for use before syrup is done, add 2 tablespoons confectioners' sugar, which will help to stabilize them. Continue to beat them on low speed. If syrup is ready before the whites, which is better, set the pan into cold water to stop its cooking and then reheat when ready to use.

3. Gradually pour hot syrup over the stiff whites. Beat them until cool. Flavor with vanilla or other flavoring, and then frost the cake.

MERINGUES À L'ITALIENNE AU BEURRE
[*Meringue Butter Cream*]

Cream ½ pound butter, but do not let it melt. When meringue is completely cold, beat the butter into the meringue and then use as frosting. If it seems thin, set the bowl in ice water to firm the butter. Flavor with vanilla. If icing separates, set it in and out of warm water while continuing to beat. This recipe is temperamental; if the butter is added too fast, it may curdle.

MERINGUES À L'ITALIENNE AU CAFÉ

[*Coffee-flavored Meringue*]

Stir 4 teaspoons instant coffee into the sugar, then add the water and syrup and make a syrup. Then proceed to make the basic meringue, or au Beurre.

CRÈME AU BEURRE AU SIROP

[*Butter-cream Frosting*]

This delicious frosting is made just like Meringues à l'Italienne au Beurre, except yolks are used in place of the whites. It is rich and creamy and you will want to eat it by the spoonfuls.

1 cup granulated sugar	Dash of salt
½ cup cold water	5 egg yolks
½ teaspoon white corn syrup	1 teaspoon vanilla
2½ sticks butter, or 1¼ cups	

1. Cook sugar, water, and syrup to 242 degrees or until a few drops in water make a firm-soft ball.

2. While this boils, add salt to yolks in small mixer bowl. Start beating when syrup reaches 230 degrees. Beat until light and fluffy. It is not possible to overwhip yolks.

3. Gradually pour hot syrup into yolks while continuing to beat. (Electric mixers are great for this.) Add vanilla. Continue to beat until frosting is completely cool and bowl is cold. (This can be speeded up by setting bowl in ice water and beating.)

4. Cream butter and then add to cooled frosting. Spread over cake or use as filling. If frosting seems soft, refrigerate and butter will firm the frosting.

VARIATION

CRÈME AU BEURRE AU MOKA

[*Mocha Butter Cream*]

Add 4 teaspoons instant coffee to the sugar, water, and syrup mixture and then proceed with the master recipe. (If available, use instant espresso; it gives better flavor.)

SOUFFLÉ GLACÉ
[*Frozen Soufflé*]

When whipping cream is substituted for the butter in the Crème au Beurre the basis of a very rich frozen dessert is created. It may be used to make bombes, or be frozen in a soufflé dish. It is called a Soufflé Glacé because it looks like a frozen soufflé.

**Recipe of Crème au Beurre au Sirop   2 cups whipping cream
1 teaspoon vanilla, 1 tablespoon Kirsch or Rum**

1. Make a collar for a 3-cup soufflé dish. Measure the circumference of the dish with a piece of string or tape measure. Tear off a piece of waxed paper two inches longer than the dish measures. Fold it lengthwise in thirds. Butter the dish and the side of the collar that will be on the inside. Fasten collar around the dish with freezer tape or pins. Refrigerate prepared dish.

2. Make Crème au Beurre recipe (p. 335), but *omit* the butter. Beat until syrup and yolks are cool. Remove beaters and refrigerate to get cold. When cold, beat the whipping cream to very stiff. Add vanilla, or other flavoring, then fold into the cold syrup and yolk mixture. (Be sure yolk mixture is cold, otherwise the whipped cream will revert to cream and there is no way to harden it, as there is with the butter cream. If mixture gets too cold, let it sit at room temperature for a while and then combine with the whipped cream.)

3. Pour mixture into prepared soufflé dish. (The smaller the dish, the higher the filling will be in the collar.) Freeze for at least 8 hours, or overnight. When ready to serve, carefully remove the collar. Set dish on a napkin and then on a serving plate. This dish looks like a soufflé because it has "risen" above the dish.

VARIATIONS
SOUFFLÉ GLACÉ À L'ANANAS
[*Frozen Pineapple Dessert*]

Buy a ripe pineapple. Leave the green spiny tops attached to the pineapple and cut off the top, about 1 inch down on the fruit, at a point where the sides go straight. Cut meat from the skin of the pineapple, leaving the outside shell. Put a 3-inch-wide collar around the pineapple and butter the collar. Wrap, and refrigerate the top.

Cut the pineapple fruit from the hard center core. Discard the core. Grind the fruit through a food chopper, or blend in a blender. Put fruit into a strainer to drain. Blot juice from pineapple shell with paper towels. Sprinkle inside of shell with Kirsch. Put drained fruit into a bowl and sprinkle with 2 tablespoons Kirsch.

Make Soufflé Glacé. Flavor with Kirsch. When cool, add drained pineapple and mix. Fill the pineapple shell to the top of the paper collar. (If some mixture is left, fill fluted tart pans, freeze and then unmold and use them to decorate the serving platter.) Enclose pineapple in a plastic food bag. Freeze at least 8 hours. When ready to serve, remove collar and pipe whipped-cream rosettes around top of pineapple where the fruit and filling meet. Set on long serving platter. Cut spiny top lengthwise in half. Trim off the fruit in a semi-circle so that the tops will fit around the bottom of the curved pineapple. Put a row of whipped-cream rosettes on the joining curves.

SOUFFLÉ GLACÉ AU CITRON

[Frozen Lemon Dessert]

To the Soufflé Glacé recipe add 2 tablespoons grated lemon rind and ½ teaspoon lemon flavoring. Pour into a collar-topped, 3-cup soufflé dish. Cover and freeze 8 hours, or overnight. When ready to serve, remove the collar and decorate with rosettes of whipped cream and either grated lemon peel or strips of peel tied in knots.

SOUFFLÉ GLACÉ AUX FRAISES

[Frozen Strawberry Dessert]

Make Soufflé Glacé. Mash 2 cups ripe strawberries, drain and then sprinkle with Kirsch. Stir into the cold soufflé. Pour into a collar-topped 4-cup soufflé dish. Cover and freeze at least 8 hours. Remove collar, decorate with rosettes of whipped cream and whole berries.

SOUFFLÉ GLACÉ GUILLAUME II
[Frozen Chocolate-shot Soufflé]

Make Soufflé Glacé. Flavor with 2 tablespoons rum and ½ cup chocolate shot (cooky decorations). Mix well. Put into a collar-topped, 3-cup soufflé dish. Cover and freeze at least 8 hours. Remove collar and decorate with whipped cream and chocolate curls.

SOUFFLÉ GLACÉ MOKA
[*Frozen Coffee Dessert*]

Boil 4 teaspoons instant coffee with the sugar-water in the Crème au Beurre recipe (p. 335). Then proceed to make the Soufflé Glacé. Freeze in a 3-cup, collar-topped soufflé dish at least 8 hours. Remove collar, and decorate with whipped cream and candy coffee beans (available in fancy candy shops).

GLAÇAGE
[*Glaze Icings*]

Glaçage might well be defined as the varnish for a cake, or for its frosting. When cakes are being glazed they are first brushed with a paint brush to remove the crumbs, then put on a wire cake rack which is set on a cooky sheet. The glaze is then poured over the cake. The weight of the glaze spreads it evenly over the surface and down the sides. The cooky sheet catches the glaze; then, once the glaze is set, the glaze is scooped up from the cooky sheet, put into a glass jar, covered and refrigerated. When needed, it is rewarmed and used. If there is a trick to a glaze, it is having it at the proper consistency so that it will behave.

GLACE AU CHOCOLAT NO. 1
[*Chocolate Glaze*]

⅛ pound butter	3 tablespoons white corn syrup
1 tablespoon Cognac, or other liqueur	1 teaspoon instant coffee
2 tablespoons water	Dash salt
4 ounces German sweet chocolate	

1. Bring butter, Cognac, water, syrup, coffee, and salt to a boil. Remove from heat. Add chocolate, cover saucepan, and let stand 5 minutes.

2. Once chocolate has softened, stir-cool until glaze thickens to the proper consistency, which is about like whipping cream but a little thicker. You may set the pan in cool water to hasten the cooling. If it gets too hard, reheat and proceed again.

3. Put the cake on a rack then on a cooky sheet. Pour *all* of the glaze onto the middle of the cake and it will run off, provided your cake does not sink in the middle. Have ready a spatula in a glass of hot water just in case you need to

help the glaze run down the sides. A wet, hot spatula will not do too much damage to the glaze. Let glaze set for about 2 hours before cutting the cake.

4. Once set, slide the cake off the rack—down the wires, not across, using the wires as runners. If you have a fancy cake rack, one designed just for glazing cakes, be sure to use it and then you need not move the cake, which too often damages the glaze. Glaze sufficient for one 2-layer cake.

GLACE AU CHOCOLAT NO. 2
[*Chocolate Glaze*]

2 ounces German sweet chocolate   Chunk of butter (about 2
(½ the bar)   tablespoons)
1 tablespoon Cognac, or other liqueur

Put all ingredients into a small enamel-coated pan or skillet. Warm over very low heat. Stir-cook and cream ingredients together. Do not melt butter or chocolate, just let it soften together. Take the pan on and off the low heat as you stir. This is an easy, quick glaze for all cakes. Sufficient for a 1-layer cake.

GLACE AU BEURRE
[*White Glaze*]

1 tablespoon Cognac, or other liqueur   Chunk butter (about 2 tablespoons)
1 tablespoon water   1 cup sifted confectioners' sugar
Food coloring of your choice

Heat Cognac, water, and butter over low heat until butter melts. Add confectioners' sugar. Stir until creamy. If it seems stiff, add 1 teaspoon of very hot water, stir, and add more if it needs it. Use plain or make any color you wish, but not blue. Blue is not a natural food color and is not a complement to food. Sufficient for a 1-layer cake. See step 3 in Glace au Chocolat No. 1 for coating techniques.

NOTE: This does not make a glassy glaze like the chocolate, but it is a pouring glaze and a nice one to cover cakes with before pouring over a chocolate glaze. Be sure to let the butter glaze set before adding the chocolate glaze.

GLACE AU FONDANT
[*Shiny Icing*]

2½ cups sugar   1 cup cold water
1 tablespoon white corn syrup

1. Put sugar, water, and syrup into heavy pan. Stir-cook until starting to boil. Stop stirring. Cook to about 238 degrees, or to a firm-soft-ball stage. Wrap wet paper towel around a fork and use to keep sides of pan wiped free of sugar crystals as the syrup cooks.

2. When syrup is done, pour onto a dampened marble slab, porcelain table or cooky sheet. Let cool until film collects over top but the Fondant is still very warm to the touch (about 110 degrees). There is no way to measure its heat, but a pilot-lighted oven is usually about 100 degrees.

3. Work Fondant with a heavy metal putty knife or similar tool. The French have a special shovel, about 4 inches wide, for this job, but a good putty knife works just as well. Work Fondant until it is pure white and creamy. If it seems too dry, sprinkle with a bit of water and continue to work. (It is better to err on the side of overcooking since you can always add a bit of water to prevent its getting hard before it is creamed. If it is undercooked, it must be cooked more to make it right.) Fondant should have the consistency of a well-worked putty. Put into a jar and cover tight with a lid. It will not harden as long as it is kept tightly covered. Refrigerate until ready to use. It will keep indefinitely.

4. When ready to use, put required amount into a small pan, add 1 table-spoon water or Kirsch, and heat. Add food coloring if you want Fondant colored, and add a flavoring to go with the color. The *trick* to Fondant is to get it on cakes evenly.

5. To accomplish this, put the cake on a wire rack. Set rack on a clean sheet of foil, or on a cooky sheet. Pour the Fondant directly from the pan onto the center of the cake and let the Fondant spread itself over the cake. The Fondant should be liquid enough to run and thick enough to cover the cake as it does so. When icing a big cake, heat the whole batch of Fondant to be sure the cake gets completely covered. There is really no good way to complete the icing of a partially covered cake, although a knife dipped into hot water works fairly well.

6. Collect the Fondant that drains from the cake onto the foil and put it back into the jar to use another time. Try to avoid crumbs in the Fondant. If the cake has been brushed before the Fondant is poured onto the cake, it remains free of crumbs. Let Fondant set, and then decorate with Glace Royale (p. 341) or colored Fondant.

NOTE: A simple Fondant may be made by mixing 1 cup confectioners' sugar with ¼ teaspoon lemon juice and about 1 teaspoon boiling water, or sufficient to make a thin paste. This Fondant should also be poured, not spooned. It may also be tinted with food colors. This is a convenient frosting to use when making petits fours from leftover cake, but is impractical for large cakes.

To draw a spider-web design: Make a pastry tube of foil or freezer paper (p. 359). Fill with melted chocolate. Pour white Fondant over a round layer cake. Then, quickly, before the Fondant sets, make a spiral of chocolate over the top and then take a pointed knife and pull it from the center out through the frostings. Make 8 marks from the center out. Then, beginning at the outside edge of the cake make 8 marks toward the center and you will have a spider-web pattern in the icings. To make a spider-web of color, use Fondant dyed with food coloring. To make a spider-web pattern on an oblong cake, put chocolate lines lengthwise down a white frosted cake and at 2-inch intervals. Pull the point of a knife across these lines every 2 inches and in the opposite direction.

GLACE ROYALE

[*Decorating Icing*]

1 egg white   2½ cups (about) sifted confectioners' sugar
1 teaspoon lemon juice

1. Put egg white into bowl. Start to beat and gradually add the sugar. Add lemon juice after 1 cup of sugar has been added. Use sufficient sugar to make a thick, soft paste. Size of egg white will determine how much sugar it will absorb.

2. Put small amounts of icing into separate dishes. Make different colors. Make cones of foil or waxed paper (see p. 359), but make them small. Put the different colors into the cones and fold over the tops, making them airtight. As long as the icing is enclosed, it does not harden. Once on a cake it gets very hard and does not run, providing the consistency is right.

3. Use icing to write names, to make lines and designs as well as leaves and flowers. Cut the tips from the cones for line work. For leaves, cut an upside-down "V" (∧) in the point of the cone, or slip metal nozzles of your choice over the cones and tape in place. Leaves and rosettes can be made on waxed paper and then, when hard, stored in airtight containers. When ready to use, peel off the paper and place on cake.

SIROP
[Syrups]

To a cuisine that builds cakes and pastries into dessert skyscrapers, the syrups are essential as culinary cement.

SIROP AU CARAMEL
[Caramel Syrup]

1 cup granulated sugar	½ cup cold water

½ teaspoon white corn syrup

Put ingredients into small heavy pan. Stir-cook until sugar dissolves and then stop stirring. Simmer to 310 degrees or to hard-crack stage, when sugar turns golden, and a few drops turn hard when dropped into cold water. Set pan into cold water to stop its cooking. Use to stick foods together. When syrup thickens, heat to rewarm, but do not cook.

VARIATIONS
SUCRE FILÉ
[Spun Sugar]

Add a pinch of cream of tartar to the Sirop au Caramel recipe. Boil to about 325 degrees or until syrup is brown and cracks when dropped into cold water. Set in cold water to stop its cooking and then immediately remove. Oil 2 chopsticks, or use handles of 2 wooden spoons. Put chopsticks on counter, projecting out from counter as far as possible. Weight them down; I put mine between my marble slab and the counter. Use books or devise something better. Place them about 12 inches apart.

Cover the floor and base of the counter with newspapers. Dip a whisk, or whatever it is you use, into the hot syrup and then quickly sling the syrup back and forth between the oiled chopsticks, thus spinning sugar threads. Remove the threads as they collect and shape them into nests, brooms, or whatever your imagination dictates.

The perfect gadget to dip into the syrup is a whisk that has been cut in half. The more points the sugar can drip from the better. I drove about 20 small nails into the back of a wooden spoon and it works quite well, but thin long nails would be even better. French pâtissière chefs use a sawed-off whisk.

PRALINE

[*Praline*]

Toast about 1½ cups finely chopped almonds in a 300-degree oven. Combine ⅛ teaspoon soda and ½ teaspoon vanilla in a spoon, ready to use. Make Sirop au Caramel (p. 342), and let it caramelize to a brown (about 325 degrees, but not all candy thermometers go that high, so judge by the color). Do not let it burn, or it will become bitter. Add the hot nuts, stir, and heat to a boil. Add vanilla and soda. Remove from heat, mix well, and pour onto oiled marble or an oiled cooky sheet. When cold, break into pieces; then crush in a mortar with pestle, in a blender, or in a food chopper. Use crushed praline in sauces, frostings, whipped cream, or on ice cream. Keep in an airtight container in a dry place to prevent its becoming sticky.

Praline on cake tops. If cake is 8 inches in diameter, pour 1/16 inch hot praline into an oiled pie tin that measures 8 inches across the bottom. While praline is still hot, cut it into wedges from the center out and to within 1 inch of the outside. Then, when it is just cool enough to hold its shape, with a knife lift the point of each wedge and curl it back over itself toward the 1-inch border. If the praline is too hot the curls will not hold. The only trick to this is doing it when the praline is cool enough. Test one point. If it doesn't hold, spread back in pan; if too cool it will break, in which case set the pan over low heat and warm it. Once praline is curled, let it get completely cold and then place on top of the cake. Fill the center with Crème au Beurre au Moka (p. 335). These may be made in advance. Store in a pilot-heated oven or other dry place.

Praline cups. Pour praline onto oiled marble, cooky sheet, or porcelain table top. Let it cool a bit, but while still hot take a large ball of it and put it into a small oiled dariole mold (the shape of a demitasse cup). Hold the mold in a towel, and with an oiled chopstick or handle of a wooden spoon force the praline to take the shape of the mold. Then remove from mold. Roll a small piece of praline into a ⅛-inch rope and attach to the cup for the handle. Make as many as you intend to serve. Saucers can be shaped by pressing the hot praline onto the underneath side of an oiled demitasse saucer. Remove, set the cup in the saucer and fill with Crème au Beurre au Moka (p. 335). These are fun to make, but they take work. One eats the cup and saucer too.

XVI

Pâte

[Pastry Doughs]

The pastries of France are many. They are used as serving dishes for non-sweet foods and as the base of sweet desserts.

Pâte Feuilletée, the puff pastry that makes Napoleons, is likewise essential to a vol-au-vent, or crust casserole, used to contain such elegant foods as sweetbreads and truffled sole. Feuilletée dough also makes tart shells, cakes, and cookies.

Pâte Brisée is used as a wrap for ham and beef fillets. It also makes timbales, a type of crust casserole in which sauced foods are presented. When sugar is added to the Brisée dough it becomes Pâte Sucrée. In this sweetened form it is used for tart and pie shells as well as for cookies.

Pâte à Chou, or cream-puff dough, is used as the base for main dishes and for desserts. This dough is the foundation for such famous desserts as Croquembouche, Paris-Brest, and La Religieuse, as well as potatoes Dauphine.

Crêpe and Cassolette are batter doughs. Crêpe may be stuffed with a lobster soufflé and served as a main course, or with a Grand Marnier soufflé and served for a dessert. The Cassolette is used as a container in which to present vegetables; and when the batter is sweetened, it becomes a crisp cup in which to serve ice cream, mousse, or Bavarois.

In what follows the master recipe is given for each pastry, and then it is followed by its nonsweet and sweet family of related recipes.

PÂTE FEUILLETÉE
[*Puff Pastry*]

Feuilletée, or puff pastry, must be delicate, flaky, and crisp. The flour-and-water mixture is handled lightly. The butter is worked in water to wash it of impurities and to make it waxy. When the consistency and temperature of both dough and butter are the same, it is then easy to incorporate the butter into the dough. Trapping the butter in layers within the dough is what gives the crust its many layers.

2½ cups all-purpose flour	1½ cups ice water (about)
½ cup cake flour	½ teaspoon salt

½ pound butter

1. Put flours onto a cold marble slab or cold bread board or into a chilled mixer bowl. Measure 1¼ cups water and to it add 4 ice cubes. Make a hole in the flour and add the salt. Start adding the water and mix to a dough. Knead until dough is smooth and satiny. Handle as little as is necessary. If using a mixer, simply add the water to the flour-and-salt mixture and mix to a dough. When a ball forms in the bowl, remove dough from the mixer to a floured surface and knead a few times and refrigerate. The mixer does a better job than hot hands.

2. Wash butter in cold water until waxy and impurities are washed from it. Drain off the water and work the butter with a rubber spatula to extract all of the water. Wrap the butter in foil and refrigerate.

3. When dough and butter are both chilled, put butter on a floured surface, sprinkle with flour, cover with transparent wrap, and with a rolling pin flatten butter to a ¼-inch square. Fold the butter in thirds, as though it were the pastry. Flatten again with the rolling pin. This works the butter (hands are too hot to do this job). Fold in thirds, making an oblong of butter.

4. Roll chilled dough into a ¼-inch-thick large round circle, as for a pie crust. Place oblong of worked butter in the center. Dampen edges of the dough with cold water. Fold bottom up, sides over, and the top down. Press edges into the dough and completely seal in the butter (just like sealing an envelope). Give dough one turn to the right. Now press the top and bottom ends with the rolling pin. Roll dough from the ends toward the middle, and then the middle out, but not across the ends. To do so might push the trapped air from the dough. Roll into a strip about ¼ inch thick, making the length 3 times the width, that is, 18 x 6 or 24 x 8.

5. Turn the bottom third up over the middle of the dough and the top third down over the two layers of dough. Turn dough to the right, thus putting

folded sides on the right and left with the open sides at the top and bottom. Again press top and bottom with rolling pin and roll again from each end to the middle and then from the middle out. Roll to ¼-inch thickness and then fold dough in thirds, always bottom up, and top down. Wrap in transparent wrap, put on a plate and refrigerate for about 20 minutes and then give the dough two more turns. Chill again for 20 minutes.

6. To this point the dough may be chilled for 20 minutes or left for as long as 24 hours. When ready to use, give the dough its final 2 turns. If the dough is left for any length of time it must be warmed to room temperature before it is pliable enough to be rolled. To roll it when it is too cold would cause the dough to crack and the trapped air to escape.

7. Roll dough into the desired width and length as indicated in the particular recipe.

COOKY VARIATIONS

Feuilletée trimmings turn into cookies. Remember you have very carefully rolled and folded the dough to make many layers. Therefore try to keep the trimmings in layers rather than wadding them all up into a ball of dough. Press the raw cut sides together and then roll and fold into the following cookies. Refrigerate, and bake after puff pastry recipe is done.

These cookies may also be made from a whole recipe of puff pastry. When they are, make them larger.

PALMIERS

[Palm Tree Cookies]

Put the trimmings from the dough onto a sugar-coated surface. Push the cut edges together and then sprinkle with sugar. Roll into a strip, fold in thirds and turn. Sprinkle with sugar and roll again into a strip. Sugar. Fold each end not quite to the middle. Sugar the top. Then fold the folded edges to the middle, making each side 4 layers high. Now fold down the middle, putting one side over the other to make a strip 8 layers high. Cut into ½-inch slices. Place these folded cookies on a dampened cooky sheet. Pull the folded ends slightly out, which gives them room to expand. Bake in a 350-degree oven until bottoms are caramelized and tops brown, or about 15 minutes. These can be made large-size from a batch of dough or small-size from the trimmings.

PAPILLONS
[Butterfly Cookies]

Push trimmings from dough together. Sprinkle with sugar, roll, fold in thirds, turn, and fold. Cut strips 2 inches wide and the length of the dough. Sprinkle each with sugar and stack 4 layers high. With a rolling pin, or the side of your hand, press the 2-inch-wide layers together right down the middle, making a groove. Cut across the depressed line into ½-inch-wide cookies. Pick up ends and give a half twist at the middle of the dough. Lay these, cut side down, on a damp cooky sheet. Bake at 350 degrees for about 15 minutes. As they bake, the layers open to look like butterflies.

SACRISTAINS
[Twist Cookies]

Push trimmings together. Roll on a sugared surface into a strip. Fold in thirds, turn, and roll again into a strip 6 inches wide. Brush dough with mixture of 1 egg yolk and 1 tablespoon water. Sprinkle with chopped almonds and then with granulated sugar. Cut dough into ½-inch-wide strips. Pick up each strip and give it 2 twists. Place on damp cooky sheet, pressing each end into a dampened area to make it stick so it will keep its twist as it bakes. Bake about 15 minutes at 350 degrees or until crisp and brown.

GALETTE DES ROIS
[Cake of the Kings]

Galette des Rois is a puff pastry cake as traditional for Epiphany, or the Twelfth Night celebration, as is plum pudding for Christmas. Hidden within each cake is a small treasure. He who gets the treasure in his piece of cake is king for the day. Paris pastry shops sell a gold or silver crown with each cake.

In and around Paris feuilletée pastry is the traditional dough used to make these cakes. In the provinces to the south and west a brioche dough is used and the cake is baked in the shape of a crown.

1. Prepare Feuilletée dough (p. 345). Give it four turns and it is ready to use. On the fourth turn roll the dough to about ¾-inch thickness. Cut out a 9-inch circle, cutting on the slant or bias (see instructions in Vol-au-Vent recipe, p. 351).

2. With a spatula lift up an edge of the dough and then pick up the dough by placing your hands on the top and bottom, avoiding the cut edges. Put dough upside down (smaller side down) on dampened cooky sheet. Place a

kidney bean under the dough and press down on top to push it into the dough. With the back of a knife, push the slanted dough in at 1-inch intervals (see step 4, p. 352).

3. Brush the top surface with a mixture of 1 egg yolk and 2 tablespoons water. Avoid letting it run down the sides. With a pointed knife make designs over the top through the egg coating and into the dough. Do not cross the cuts; that would drag yolk mixture over the cut surfaces.

4. Refrigerate 20 minutes and then bake in a 450-degree oven for 15 minutes. Reduce heat to 350 degrees. Bake another 30 minutes. Sprinkle with confectioners' sugar, increase heat to 450 degrees, and set cake on upper rack to glaze. When done, cool on cake rack. Cut in wedges to serve. He who gets the bean is king.

MILLE-FEUILLE

[*Thousand-layer Pastry or Napoleons*]

1. Make Feuilletée dough (p. 345). After the second turn, while the dough chills, prepare Crème Pâtissière for the filling (p. 306). Refrigerate sauce so it will be cold when ready to use.

2. Give the dough its required six turns. On the sixth and final turn of the dough, roll it into a ¼-inch-thick oblong, about 12 x 18 inches.

3. Sprinkle a cooky sheet with cold water. Roll the dough up around the rolling pin and then unroll on the dampened cooky sheet. Roll the dough out once it is on the pan.

4. With a sharp chopping knife make 2 diagonal cuts the long way of the dough to create three 4-inch-wide strips of dough. With the back of a small pointed knife push all edges in at intervals of 1 inch. With a table fork, stick the dough all over, but not on the edges. Refrigerate 15 minutes and then bake in a preheated 450-degree oven for 20 minutes. Reduce heat to 350 degrees and bake another 15 minutes. If bottom gets too brown, slide another cooky sheet under the pan, or use a sheet of foil.

5. When strips are done, slide them off pan to a wire rack to cool. Mix 1 cup confectioners' sugar, ¼ teaspoon lemon juice, and about 4 teaspoons hot water to make a thin paste. Spread this mixture over one of the strips of pastry.

6. With a very sharp knife cut the strips of pastry across into six 3-inch-wide pieces. A few hours before they are to be served, coat 2 cut pieces with the chilled Crème Pâtissière, stack one on top of the other, and top with an iced piece. Refrigerate until ready to serve.

NOTE: Fondant icing may be used in place of the simple one given and a web of chocolate streamed over the icing (p. 341); or they may simply be sprinkled with confectioners' sugar.

PITHIVIERS

[*Filled Galette*]

Recipe of Feuilletée dough	½ teaspoon vanilla
6 tablespoons butter (¾ of a stick)	1 tablespoon rum
½ cup sugar	1 egg yolk
1 cup ground almonds	2 tablespoons water
1 whole egg	Confectioners' sugar

1. Make Feuilletée dough (p. 345). Give it 2 turns and then refrigerate. Make the filling. Put butter and sugar in mixer bowl. Cream until light and fluffy. Add the ground almonds. Beat in whole egg, beating well after adding it. Add vanilla and rum. Chill the filling until ready to use, but do not let it harden.

2. Give Feuilletée dough a third turn. On the fourth turn, roll the dough into a strip about 8 inches wide, ¼ inch thick, and as long as it will go and still retain these dimensions. Cut the dough in half crosswise. Trim the sides at an angle. (See Vol-au-Vent instructions, p. 352, for cutting on the bias.)

3. Put ½ of the dough upside down on a dampened cooky sheet. Be careful not to touch the cut edges with your warm hands. Put the cream filling over the dough to within 1 inch of the edges. Brush this border with cold water. Turn the second half upside down over the filling. Press the edges together to seal in the filling.

4. With the back of a knife push the dough in about ¼ inch all the way around the cake at 1-inch intervals. Mix the egg yolk and water together. Brush the top surface with the mixture, being careful it does not run down the sides.

5. With a pointed knife make attractive cuts in the dough in an orderly fashion. Do not intersect the cuts, or the yolk mixture will be pulled over the raw dough. Remove the dough from the knife before making the next cut. Punch a small hole in the middle of the top crust and down into the filling so the steam can escape as the cake bakes.

6. Refrigerate 20 minutes and then bake in a 450-degree oven for 15 minutes. Reduce heat to 350 degrees and bake 30 minutes. Sprinkle with confectioners' sugar. Increase heat to 450 degrees and bake on an upper rack for about 15 minutes to glaze the cake. Cool cake on a wire rack.

NOTE: Cake may be made round. When it is, make spiral cuts from the center out to the edge. Serves 10.

TARTE AUX CERISES

[Cherry Tart]

Tart shells are normally made from puff pastry when they are to be filled with fresh fruits. They are made from Pâte Sucrée when they are filled with canned fruits.

Recipe of Feuilletée dough	Sugar
1 egg yolk	½ cup currant jelly
Water	2 tablespoons sugar
2 pounds Bing cherries, pitted	2 tablespoons Kirsch

1. Give dough (p. 345) four turns. On fourth turn, roll it ¼ inch thick, 9 inches wide, and as long as it will go and still retain these dimensions. Cut off a 9-inch piece, or square of 9 inches. Cut the sides on an angle (see p. 352). Lift, avoiding hitting the cut sides, and place upside down on a dampened cooky sheet. Brush a 1-inch border of the dough with water. Cut ½-inch strips from the dough and place around all 4 sides to build a small wall of dough. Press into the bottom crust. With the back of a knife, push the dough in at 1-inch intervals. Mix yolk and 2 tablespoons of water together. Carefully coat the ½-inch border of dough. Do not let yolk mixture run down the cut sides.

2. Arrange the pitted cherries in neat, tight rows over the top of the dough within the border of dough. Sprinkle cherries with sugar, enough to sweeten them. (Eat a cherry to see how sour they are.) Chill 20 minutes in refrigerator. Bake tart in a preheated 425-degree oven for about 20 minutes. Reduce heat to 350 degrees and bake another 15 minutes, or until brown, puffed, and done. Heat jelly, 2 tablespoons of water, and 2 tablespoons sugar to a boil. Add Kirsch and cool. Spoon over the tart while it is hot to glaze the cherries. Cool tart on wire rack. Cut into squares and serve.

TARTE AUX POMMES

[Apple Tart]

Recipe of Feuilletée dough	Piece of vanilla bean (1-inch)
9 apples	1 tablespoon lemon juice
½ cup white wine	1 egg yolk
½ cup sugar	Water
Dash of salt	Sugar
Chunk of butter	½ cup apple jelly
Piece of cinnamon stick	2 tablespoons Kirsch

1. Make Feuilletée (p. 345). Give two turns and then chill. Peel and core 5 of the apples. Cut into quarters and put into a pan. Add wine, ½ cup sugar, salt, butter, cinnamon, and vanilla bean. Cover and simmer until tender. Add more wine, if necessary, as they cook. Do not let them caramelize.

2. When apples are done, remove cinnamon stick and vanilla bean. Purée through a food mill. Use a coarse disc. Add lemon juice, cool, and then refrigerate. (Filling must be cold before putting it on the pastry.)

3. When puréed apples are cool, give final third and fourth turns to the pastry. On the fourth turn roll pastry into a long strip ¼ inch thick and about 7 inches wide. Cut strip in half crosswise. Place dough pieces on a dampened cooky sheet. Trim the other 3 sides of each piece of dough to make them straight and even. Sides of puff pastry must be cut to make them puff. Then with the back of a knife, push the edges in at 1-inch intervals to make a border to hold the apples.

4. Mix yolk and 2 tablespoons of water. Brush flat surface of dough with mixture, but avoid the cut edges. Spread the puréed apples over the egg-coated dough and to within ¼ inch of the edge. Peel and core 4 or 5 apples, depending upon their size, and cut them into thin slices. Lay slices across the puréed apple filling, the narrow way, in neat rows.

5. Sprinkle apples with sugar. Chill in refrigerator for 20 minutes. Bake in a preheated 425-degree oven for about 20 minutes. Reduce heat to 350 degrees and bake another 15 minutes, or until dough is crisp and brown. Boil apple jelly, Kirsch, and 1 tablespoon water. Cool the mixture and then glaze apple slices while they are still hot. Cool tart on a wire rack.

NOTE: You can make your own apple jelly just by boiling the peelings, cores, some sugar and a bit of water. Strain and flavor with Kirsch.

VOL-AU-VENT
[*Flaky Pastry Timbale*]

1. Make Feuilletée (p. 345). On the sixth and final turn, roll the pastry into an 8 x 16-inch strip and about ½ inch thick, or a little less than ½ inch.

2. Invert a 7- or 8-inch plate on the dough. Then with a sharp paring knife cut out a circle from the dough on a 45-degree angle, making the edge of the circle slanted. Make 2 circles the same size and slanted in the same way.

3. Brush a cooky sheet with cold water. With a spatula lift 1 circle of the dough. Put your fingers on the flat surfaces, being careful not to touch the cut edges with your hot hands. (At the place it is touched, rising is retarded.) Turn this circle of dough over, and put the narrow side down on the cooky sheet. Brush a 2-inch border of the pastry with cold water.

(continued)

4. Cut a 5- or 6-inch circle from the center of the second piece of pastry, leaving a 2-inch ring of dough. (Make a Galette des Rois [p. 347] from the 5- or 6-inch circle.) Do not cut small circle out on the slant, but straight up and down. Carefully lift the ring of dough, turn it over and put the narrow side down on the dampened pastry. Gently press ring to lower layer. With the back of a knife push the slanted edges in at 1-inch intervals and to a depth of ¼ inch all the way around the outside of the two layers of dough. Puff pastry shrinks as it cooks. If it is cut on the bias the top will shrink back to be about the same size as the base and the Vol-au-Vent will be straight up and down. Also, when cut on the bias, heat strikes the edges and the Vol-au-Vent puffs higher. When baked, the edges are scalloped.

5. With a small sharp knife cut a circle just through the top surface of the bottom layer of dough to match the hole in the top layer. This will become the lid for the Vol-au-Vent once it is baked.

6. Mix together 1 egg yolk and 2 tablespoons cold water. With a very soft small paint brush (I use a camel's-hair art brush) coat the circle down in the hole and the flat top surface with the egg mixture (called *dorure* in French). Do not hit any of the cut surfaces with the egg mixture or the Vol-au-Vent will not rise at those spots. With a very sharp knife, make attractive marks in the future lid down in the hole and around the ring of dough.

7. Chill for 20 minutes, then bake in a preheated 450-degree oven for about 15 minutes. Reduce heat to 400 degrees and bake another 15 minutes. Now coat all surfaces with egg mixture and bake another 20 minutes at 350 degrees. (Egg mixture makes pastry brown and glazed.) When it is done, carefully lift off cooky sheet to a wire rack. Cut the circle of dough out of the center and lift out. Scrape the uncooked layers of dough from it and the Vol-au-Vent. Cool Vol-au-Vent. Use, or store in a cool, dry place ready to use. Its life is that of the butter and after that it will become rancid. Vol-au-Vents are normally filled with something expensive, such as Sweetbreads Financière (p. 176).

PÂTE À FONCER
[*Short Doughs*]

The word "Foncer" means "to put a bottom under." In French cooking we use both the Feuilletée and the short doughs Brisée and Sucrée as a foundation for other foods.

Brisée, or the Foncer Ordinaire, is the dough we use in cuisine cookery, such as in the making of Quiche Paysanne, while Sucrée dough, or Foncer Fine, is used in desserts, such as tarts.

The difference between ordinaire and fine Foncer is the addition of sugar, egg yolk, and crème fraîche to the fine pâte, or Pâte Sucrée. Both doughs are mixed quickly, handled very little, and always refrigerated for several hours or overnight before they are rolled and used. As these doughs rest, the flour starch combines with the moisture, which mellows the dough and makes it easy to handle. Cold doughs absorb less flour; consequently, recipe ingredients remain unchanged and products of better quality result. However, doughs should not be too cold to roll.

PÂTE BRISÉE
[*Nonsweet Short Pastry*]

Pâte Brisée is nothing more than pie crust dough made with eggs and butter. Eggs give strength and rich color to the dough, which makes it perfect for timbales and crusts.

Timbale cases are simple to make and elegant to serve. The form in which they are baked is a bottomless mold, made in 2 parts and held together by pins. A cooky sheet is used as the bottom for the mold. When the crust is done, the pins are removed, the sides taken off, and the crust browned. The sides of the mold are dented into designs which leave their imprint on the crust. Timbales can be made days in advance of use. The filling for these fancy crust casseroles is usually as elegant as the timbale itself.

2 cups sifted all-purpose flour	1 teaspoon sugar
½ cup sifted cake flour	¾ cup butter, pliable but cool
½ teaspoon salt	1 egg
Ice water	

1. Sift together flours, salt, and sugar. Put on marble or into large mixing bowl. Make a hole in the center. Add butter and cut into flour with a pastry blender, mixer, or your fingers. Blend in the egg, and sufficient water to make a firm dough.

2. Once dough is made, do not knead it, but, with the heel of your hand, push the dough out, little bits at a time, away from you. Do this twice, and then shape into a ball, wrap in foil, and refrigerate for several hours, or overnight. The dough loses its elasticity upon standing. When ready to use, roll on a lightly floured surface to thickness called for in the particular recipe. Sufficient for 1 timbale, 2 (8-inch) pie shells, or 12 tarts.

NOTE: Double the recipe for crust in which you plan to wrap large pieces of meat.

TIMBALES

[*Crust Casseroles*]

1. Make Pâte Brisée. Refrigerate dough several hours. Roll dough into a 10-inch circle. Roll the edges somewhat thinner than the center. Flour the top surface and then fold the dough in half. Put your fist into the fold. Carefully work the dough out into a deep or oblong pocket, depending on the shape of the timbale mold being used. Trace the shape of the timbale, if not round, on waxed paper, and use for lid pattern. Round timbales come with a dome lid.

2. Once the fold is rounded into a pocket, sprinkle inside of pocket with flour and roll the folded dough to an even thickness. Set timbale mold on a cooky sheet. Brush interior of the mold and the cooky sheet with oil. Put the pocket of dough in the timbale mold. Carefully fit and press the dough into the form, making the bottom flat on the cooky sheet. The dough will take the form of the mold.

3. Cut the dough off around the top ½ inch above the edge of the mold. Dampen the underneath side of the ½ inch of dough. Fold dough under, damp sides together, and crimp with thumb and finger in a fancy design. Prick bottom of dough with a table fork. Roll the trimmings of dough together. Cut out a lid of dough from pattern to fit the top of the timbale. Place on oiled cooky sheet. Decorate the lid with fancy pastry cutouts. Make a knob with which to lift it from the timbale (see p. 191).

4. Cut 2-inch strips of foil or waxed paper. Fit and overlap them down the sides of the dough and over the bottom. Then from a square of foil make a pouch and fit into the foil-lined dough. Fill the pouch with dried beans, lentils, or rice to hold the dough in place. Bake in a 425-degree oven for about 30 minutes, or until crust is brown. The lid will be done before the timbale. Coat it after about 10 minutes with mixture of 1 egg yolk and 2 tablespoons water, brown, and then remove from the oven when done.

5. After 30 minutes remove timbale from the oven. Spoon out some of the beans and then lift out the pouch. Remove the foil or waxed-paper strips

and unpin the mold. (Save the beans to use again, or use them in cooking.) The easiest way to remove the pins is to turn the hot timbale mold on its side, then, while holding with a pot holder, pull out the pins. Once pins are out, turn the mold upside down, on its crimped edge, and carefully push the crust from around the rim and remove each side. Then in this upside-down position, coat with yolk mixture and bake 20 minutes at 350 degrees. Then carefully turn right side up and brush both inside and out with egg mixture. Bake another 15 minutes at 350 degrees. When done, cool on wire cake rack. Use, or store in a cool, dry place until needed.

6. Fill timbales with sauced foods *just* before serving and cover with pastry lid. Use such foods as fillets or suprêmes of chicken in sauce (p. 148), sweetbreads (p. 176), or creamed mushrooms.

TARTES

[*Pie Crusts*]

Make tarts from Brisée dough (p. 353) when filling the crusts with non-sweet foods, and from Sucrée dough (p. 356) when they are to be filled with sweet dessert fillings. If dough is too cold, let it stand at room temperature until warm enough to roll without breaking.

1. Roll dough to less than ⅛-inch thick. Lightly coat pie pan with butter, then wipe surplus butter from pan with paper towel, thus leaving a film of butter on the surface. Roll pastry around the rolling pin and then unroll over the pan. Fit dough into the pan. Trim crust ¼ inch larger than the edge of the pan.

2. Crimp the edge of the dough between thumb and first finger. Prick dough on bottom in about 8 places with the point of a knife.

3. Line the dough with a circle of foil or waxed paper big enough to come up the sides of the dough. Cut the edge of the circle in about 6 places to make it fit. Fill with navy beans to hold the dough in place as it bakes. It is not necessary to line Sucrée dough, only Brisée.

4. Bake in a preheated 450-degree oven, on lowest shelf, for about 15 minutes. Take from oven, lift out paper and beans. Return tart to the oven for 5 minutes to dry. (Save beans to use again.) The crust is partially baked, which some recipes call for, such as the Quiche Paysanne.

5. If the crust is to be completely baked, return it to a 400-degree oven and bake until brown. Once it is brown remove from the oven, slide the shell from the pan onto a cooky sheet, coat with a mixture of 1 yolk and 2 tablespoons of water and return the shell to the oven to get golden brown and crisp. Cool crust on wire rack. Use, or store in a cool, dry place.

PÂTE SUCRÉE
[*Sweet Short Pastry*]

Pâte Brisée becomes Pâte Sucrée with the addition of sugar, and is used as the crust in dessert tarts. The more sugar that is added, the crisper becomes the dough when it is baked. The quantities, *by weight, not volume,* of sugar and butter are about the same in Pâte Sucrée. As the sugar is increased, so is the butter.

¾ cup butter, softened	2 cups sifted all-purpose flour
½ cup sugar, plus 2 tablespoons	1 egg yolk
(or 10 tablespoons)	1 egg
½ teaspoon salt	2 tablespoons crème fraîche or
1 cup sifted cake flour	whipping cream

1. Cream butter, sugar, and salt together in electric mixer until light and fluffy. Sift flours together.

2. Stir yolk, egg, and crème into butter mixture. Add flours and mix. Do not beat, just blend. (Add 1 tablespoon cold water if dough seems too stiff.) Put dough on lightly floured surface. Push the dough out twice with the heel of your hand and then shape into a ball, wrap, and refrigerate several hours or overnight. When ready to use, roll on lightly floured surface. Recipe will make about 12 tartelettes or 1 (10-inch) tart and a few cookies.

TARTELETTES
[*Tart Shells*]

Cutting dough to fit tart pans is tricky. If the pans are round, use a tape measure, and measure the outside across the bottom of the pan from edge to edge, then make a circle of that diameter and use it as a pattern to cut out the dough. If the pans are diamond shaped, you can make a pattern by shaping foil around the outside of the pan, then cutting it out and using. Bake shells according to instructions for making Tartes (p. 355).

TARTELETTES AUX CERISES
[*Cherry Tarts*]

12 tart shells	1 (no. 2) can pitted cherries in syrup
Crème Pâtissière	¼ cup sugar
2 tablespoons Grand Marnier	½ cup Kirsch

1. Make tart shells from Sucrée dough (p. 356) and bake completely. Make Crème Pâtissière (p. 306). Pour crème into a bowl, cover, and cool. When cool, pour Grand Marnier over the top, cover tight and refrigerate overnight or for several hours.

2. Drain cherries. Put them into a nonmetal bowl or a glass jar. Add sugar and Kirsch. Let them marinate overnight or for several hours in the refrigerator.

3. To finish tarts, pour cherries into a sieve. Let liquids drain into a bowl. Stir Grand Marnier into the Crème Pâtissière. If the sauce seems too thick, add some of the Kirsch juice from the cherries. The cream sauce should be thick enough to support the cherries.

4. Fill tart shells with sauce and then arrange the drained cherries over the top. Refrigerate, if not served immediately. They should not stand too long, or they might get soggy. Filling for 6 or 8 tarts, depending upon size of tarts. Freeze the extra tart shells and use later.

VARIATIONS

TARTELETTES AUX ABRICOTS
[*Apricot Tarts*]

Make the tart shells round and from Sucrée dough. Use canned whole apricots. (They have better flavor than halved apricots.) Carefully remove the pits. Fill tart shells with Crème Pâtissière and top each with an apricot. Decorate base of apricot with stars of whipped cream.

TARTELETTES AUX ANANAS
[*Pineapple Tarts*]

Make round shells from Sucrée dough. Cut canned pineapple slices horizontally in half, making them half their original thickness, or even thinner if possible. Then cut the whole slices into halves. Soak in Kirsch for several hours. Fill tart shells with Crème Pâtissière. Drain pineapple slices and then overlap them on the cream filling in the tart shells.

TARTELETTES AUX PÊCHES
[*Peach Tarts*]

Use sliced canned peaches in place of the pineapple slices.

TARTELETTES AUX POIRES
[*Pear Tarts*]

Use canned pear halves. Marinate in Kirsch, then, when ready to use, paint a "blush" on each pear half with diluted red food coloring. Cut the halves across into thin slices. With a spatula lift the sliced pear half and place on cream-filled tart.

PÂTE À CHOU
[*Cream-puff Dough*]

Pâte à Chou is a soft batter-type pastry dough. It is the foundation for simple cream puffs to be filled with whipped cream or it makes lavish and exciting structures as well buttressed as Notre Dame.

La Religieuse, with its elongated chocolate-coated éclairs, reminds one of the flowing black robes of the nuns for which the pastry was named.

Croquembouche is a pyramid of small cream puffs, called profiteroles, held together with a mortar of caramelized sugar. Translated, "Croquembouche" means "here's a real cake to wrap your mouth around."

And, finally, if all else fails you in the dessert line, get on the track of Paris-Brest. This big wheel of a cake is as important to French cuisine as the railway line is to the two cities it connects.

1 cup water	1 cup sifted all-purpose flour, less
¼ pound butter, plus 2 tablespoons	2 tablespoons
½ teaspoon salt	¼ cup sifted cake flour
2 teaspoons sugar	4 eggs

1. Put water, butter, salt, and sugar into a saucepan. Bring to a boil. Sift flours together. Remove saucepan from heat. Stir flours in all at once. Beat with a wooden spoon until the dough collects in a ball at the center of the pan. Set pan back over very low heat to warm the dough.

2. Take pan from heat. Add 2 eggs. Beat at least several minutes if beating dough by hand, or use hand mixer. (This mixing can be done with a mixer, but warm the bowl before putting the dough into it. The heat of the dough must be sufficient to bind the eggs.) Add the third egg, beat well. Add the fourth egg and beat. The dough should be stiff without being heavy. Dough is ready to use in one of the following recipes.

CHOUX À LA CRÈME

[*Cream Puffs*]

1. Make Pâte à Chou dough. Put dough into a pastry bag with a ½-inch round nozzle, or make a pouch from foil (see Note). Fill the pastry bag with the dough.

2. Brush cooky sheets with melted butter. Squeeze mounds of dough 2 inches in diameter and about 1½ inches high onto cooky sheets, spacing them about 3 inches apart. Make about 12.

3. Mix 1 yolk and 2 tablespoons water. Coat the puffs with the egg mixture but do not let it run onto the cooky sheet.

4. Bake in 400-degree oven for 30 minutes. Brush again with egg mixture. Reduce heat to 350 degrees and bake 10 minutes. Stick each puff with an ice pick or wooden pick to let the steam escape. Bake another 10 minutes, or until brown and dried out. Cool on wire racks.

5. When ready to serve, carefully cut and break off the top halves. Remove any uncooked soft dough. Fill with cold Crème Pâtissière à la Vanille (p. 306). Replace tops. Put powdered sugar into a sieve and then sift over the tops of the cream puffs.

NOTE: *Waxed-paper pastry bag.* Tear off about 2 feet of waxed paper. Fold lengthwise in half. Take one end and fold at right angles to the open long side. Hold, and wrap the other end around, making a cone. With a pin, stick through all layers to fasten. Fill with the choux paste. Fold the high side of the cone over the dough and then fold tight with the short side. Now cut the pointed end off to make a ½-inch opening. (Make several pouches at one time so they will be ready to use.) The advantage of a paper pouch is it can be thrown away when you are through using it. Foil may be used as well.

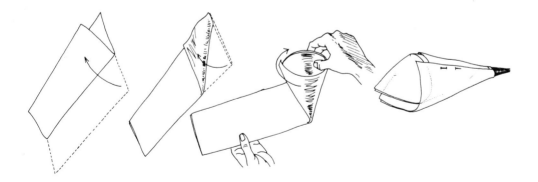

VARIATIONS ON CREAM PUFF FILLINGS

Choux au Café: fill with coffee-flavored Crème Saint-Honoré (p. 307).
Choux à la Chantilly: fill with Crème Chantilly (p. 332).
Choux au Chocolat: fill with Chocolate Crème Pâtissière (p. 306).

PROFITEROLES
[*Little Cream Puffs*]

1. Squeeze Pâte à Chou dough from pastry bag onto greased cooky sheets in mounds the size of a walnut. (All puffs double in size.) Recipe makes about 6 dozen.

2. Coat with mixture of 1 egg yolk and 2 tablespoons water. Bake about 15 minutes at 400 degrees and then at 350 degrees until crisp and brown. Stick with a wooden pick so steam can escape. Cool on racks when done.

3. To fill these, find a crack in the shell, then make an incision with the point of a knife and squirt the filling into the profiterole from a pastry bag with a small nozzle. (To use a nozzle with a foil pastry bag, cut the tip from the foil cone before filling and then drop the nozzle into the opening. Tape foil and nozzle together to keep filling from oozing out as the bag is squeezed. (Remember to cut off the nozzle before discarding the bag.)

4. Fill with Chocolate Crème Pâtissière (p. 306) and then coat the tops with melted chocolate (p. 327) or Chocolate Glace (p. 339).

PETITES PROFITEROLES
[*Tiny Cream Puffs for Soup*]

Make dots of dough about ¼ inch round. Use a paper bag (p. 359) with a ¼-inch opening. Make as many as are needed, then cut the opening in the bag bigger and make the remainder of the dough into cream puffs. Do not try to coat the tiny puffs with egg mixture. Bake at 350 degrees for about 10 minutes, or until crisp and brown. It is possible to fill these with a savory stuffing. Use a pastry bag and very small metal nozzle. Make a cut in the bottom and force filling into profiteroles with metal nozzle. (Paper pastry bags are not strong enough for this job.)

CROQUEMBOUCHE
[*Cream-Puff Tree*]

Recipe of Pâte à Chou   **Recipe of Crème Saint-Honoré**

Caramel Syrup

½ cup cold water   1 cup sugar
½ teaspoon white corn syrup

1. Make Pâte à Chou (p. 358). Shape dough into Profiteroles and bake according to recipe (p. 360). Cool puffs. Make Crème Saint-Honoré (p. 307). Fill profiteroles.

2. When ready to build the cake tree make the syrup. Boil water, sugar, and syrup to a hard-crack stage, or 310 degrees on a thermometer. When it reaches this stage take pan from heat. Set into cold water to stop its cooking and then remove. The syrup must remain hot.

3. Dip the top of a filled profiterole into the syrup. Let syrup run down one side. Place that side down on a serving plate. Make a bottom ring of about 12 profiteroles. Treat each profiterole in the same manner. Reheat the syrup when it gets cool and starts to thicken, but don't cook it.

4. Set the next ring of dipped profiteroles back about ½ inch on top of the bottom ring, filling in the spaces between the first ring of profiteroles. The dipped puffs stick to the preceding ring. (If they don't, it's because the syrup was not cooked to the crack stage, in which case cook it some more.)

5. In the building of this Christmas-tree-shaped cake make the bottom layer 12 profiteroles, then 11, 10, 8, 7, 6, 4, 2, and 1. As the top is reached, the space in the circle gets less. Until you become skilled at making these you will always have profiteroles left over, but that is better than not having enough to finish to the top. Recipe of Pâte à Chou makes about 72 profiteroles, and it takes but 61 to make the tree. Croquembouche will serve about 12.

PARIS-BREST
[*Cream-puff Cake*]

1. Make Pâte à Chou dough (p. 358). Put dough into pastry bag with ½-inch opening. (See Pâte à Chou recipe for instructions to make paper bag.)

2. Butter a cooky sheet and then dust with flour. Shake off surplus flour. With an 8-inch saucepan lid stamp a ring in the floured surface.

3. Squeeze dough around the circle, making it slightly flat on top. Then, beginning on the opposite side from where you ended, squeeze another layer

(continued)

of dough on top of the first ring of dough. In other words, the dough is two rings high.

4. Squeeze the remaining dough in the pastry bag onto the cooky sheet, making about 6 small cream puffs, or profiteroles.

5. Brush dough with mixture of 1 egg yolk and 2 tablespoons water. With a fork, draw lines around on top of the cake and then sprinkle the top with shredded almonds.

6. Bake in a preheated 400-degree oven for about 25 minutes. Reduce heat to 350 degrees. Bake another 20 minutes or until brown and crisp. Cool on cake rack. Make Crème Saint-Honoré (p. 307) while cake bakes.

7. When ready to serve, cut horizontally in half. Lift off the top ring. Place bottom half on serving plate. Remove any soft dough. Fill with Crème Saint-Honoré.

8. Cut the small cream puffs in half. Set them into the cream sauce cut side up. Fill them with Crème Saint-Honoré. Place the top back on. Sieve confectioners' sugar over the top. Put remaining Crème Saint-Honoré into a pastry bag with a star nozzle. Fill in the spaces between top and bottom with rosettes of Saint-Honoré. Refrigerate until ready to serve. Serves 8.

ÉCLAIRS AU CHOCOLAT
[Chocolate Éclairs]

1. Make Pâte à Chou dough (p. 358). Put dough into a pastry bag, or make bag of paper. See Choux à la Crème recipe (p. 359) for instructions.

2. Squeeze dough onto greased cooky sheet in 4-inch-long éclairs ¾ inch thick. To make the dough thick with a ½-inch nozzle, move the bag slowly as you squeeze the dough from it.

3. Coat top surface of éclairs with mixture of 1 egg yolk and 2 tablespoons water. Be careful none runs onto the cooky sheet or it will become dark. With a fork make marks through the egg-coated dough the long way of the éclairs. Recipe makes about a dozen éclairs.

4. Bake in a preheated 425-degree oven for 20 minutes. Stick each éclair (find a crack in the éclair so the hole doesn't show) with an ice pick or wooden pick. Reduce heat to 350 degrees. Bake another 10 minutes, or until éclairs are crisp and brown. Cool on wire racks.

5. When ready to serve, carefully cut along one side. Fill with Chocolate Crème Pâtissière and coat with chocolate icing (pp. 338–339).

NOTE: Filling and icing always match in flavor. To change them is to change the name of the éclair: *Éclairs au Café* are coffee flavored; *Éclairs à la Vanille* are vanilla flavored.

LA RELIGIEUSE

[*Éclair Cake of the Nuns*]

This cake is one of the most beautiful of all French desserts. It has many parts—so many even that the pâtissière shops of France make them in miniature. These facsimiles are made by stacking a profiterole on top of a cream puff and then running ribbons of icing up the profiterole.

This recipe with its many parts illustrates more than any other the French system of cooking and "to know the system, is to be able to create food."

The parts are easy; the creation of the cake, fun. In all, six basic recipes (Pâte Brisée, Pâte à Chou, Crème au Beurre, Crème Saint-Honoré, Glace, and Caramel Syrup) are used.

Make the parts and then assemble the cake. At the end of the main recipe a short cut is given to make a big La Religieuse.

Part 1. Make a 6-inch tart shell from Pâte Brisée dough (p. 353). The tart shell must have straight sides. Do not make it in a pie pan; the slanting sides will not support the weight of the cake. Use a flan ring or make a ring from a 20-inch sheet of foil. Fold the foil the long way several times into a 1-inch strip and then make a 6-inch ring from it. Pin the ends together, grease it, set on a cooky sheet and line with dough. Bake crisp, and then cool ready to use. Leave foil collar on crust for support. Remove when ready to serve.

Part 2. Squeeze 9 tapering éclairs (like candles) from Pâte à Chou dough (p. 358) onto a buttered and floured cooky sheet. Make them about 8 inches long. Coat, mark, and bake according to éclair recipe (p. 362). Make two ½-

(*continued*)

inch-thick doughnut-shaped rings, one approximately 4 inches and one 2 inches in diameter, and make one medium-sized cream puff. These will be used to finish off the top of La Religieuse.

Part 3. When tapered éclairs are cool, trim off each pointed tip on the tapered end, making them all the same length, with a flat surface on which the doughnut rings will be set. Fill éclairs and cream puff with Crème au Beurre (p. 335). Do not fill the rings. Ice all parts with Chocolate Glace No. 1 (p. 338). Let icing set.

Part 4. Make Crème Saint-Honoré (p. 307). Refrigerate until ready to use. Cook caramel syrup (see Croquembouche recipe, p. 361).

Part 5. If you have pistachio nuts, chop some ready to use. If not, make Mock Pistachio Nuts (p. 608).

Part 6. To assemble cake. Put tart shell on serving dish. Set a Rhine wine bottle or soda bottle into the empty pie shell. Dip bottom of each filled éclair into the hot caramel syrup. Stand each éclair on the rim of the shell, letting the éclairs lean against the bottle. When all éclairs are stuck to crust, carefully pull the bottle out, letting éclairs come together at the top.

Fill the interior, where the bottle was, with the chilled Crème Saint-Honoré. Spoon some hot syrup onto the tips of the éclairs. Set the 4-inch ring on the syrup. Set the second ring on top of the first and then crown the whole with the cream puff. Dip the second ring and cream puff into caramel before adding.

Heat the remaining caramel syrup with 1 tablespoon water. Bring to a boil. Brush the hot syrup on the outside of the pie shell and then immediately press chopped green nuts on the sticky syrup.

Put whipped cream, or remaining Crème au Beurre if there is sufficient, into a pastry bag with star nozzle. Fill in the cracks between the éclairs, around the bottom and the top. Make the bottom decorations heavier than the top. Chill until ready to serve. Serves 8 or 9.

SHORT-CUT METHOD

Part 1. Buy a small round coffeecake and substitute it for the tart shell.

Part 2. Make the tapering éclairs and rings. Fill them with Crème Pâtissière. Coat them with a simple chocolate frosting (p. 339).

To assemble the cake. Insert wooden picks halfway into the bottom of each éclair. Stand a bottle on the coffeecake. Stick the éclairs into the cake, leaning them against the bottle. Remove bottle, letting éclairs come together at the top. Fill interior, where bottle was, with Crème Saint-Honoré. Stick the rings on the top with frosting. Fill crevices with whipped cream. Coat the outside of the coffeecake with nuts if you wish.

PÂTE À CRÊPES
[*Crêpe*]

Contrary to what you may have always thought, Crêpes Suzette should not be flamed—not if their filling is the traditional butter cream. To flame them with this filling would be to melt the butter. Crêpes flambées, the ones that are flamed, are sprinkled with sugar, doused with liqueurs and set ablaze. The aristocrat of all crêpes is the pannequet. This noble dessert of France is made by stuffing crêpe with Grand Marnier soufflé. Once baked it is then caramelized and served.

CRÊPE
[*Pancakes*]

¾ cup sifted all-purpose flour
¼ cup sifted cake flour
½ teaspoon salt
1 tablespoon sugar
2 whole eggs

3 egg yolks
1 cup milk
½ cup cream
2 tablespoons Cognac
1 tablespoon Grand Marnier

¼ pound butter, melted

1. Sift the two flours into a mixing bowl. Add salt, sugar, eggs, and yolks. Stir with a whisk while adding milk to make a thin batter the consistency of light cream. Add cream, Cognac, and Grand Marnier. Let batter age for at least two hours.

2. Melt ¼ pound butter in a small skillet. When ready to fry crêpes, stir 3 tablespoons melted butter into the batter. Heat a 6-inch crêpe skillet. Pour some of the melted butter into it. Tip and turn the skillet to coat bottom and sides with butter. Then pour the butter back into the pan of melted butter.

3. Add about 3 tablespoons pancake batter to the hot skillet. Tip skillet and coat with batter. Cook about 1 minute. Flip crêpe over by tossing it in the air, or carefully turn with a spatula. Cook second side about 30 seconds and then place on a plate to cool. Repeat process, coating skillet each time with melted butter. Crêpe should be rich, thin, and pliable. Makes about 24 crêpes.

VARIATIONS

CRÊPES FLAMBÉES

[*Flamed Pancakes*]

Sprinkle each crêpe with sugar. Fold in half and then into quarters. Arrange on platter. Sprinkle heavily with granulated sugar. Set under broiler to glaze. Heat ½ cup rum and 2 tablespoons Cognac. Pour over crêpes and ignite. (Keep at arms' length.) Serve flaming.

CRÊPES SUZETTE

[*Crêpes with Suzette Sauce*]

In a small mixer bowl blend ¼ pound butter, grated zest from 1 orange, 1½ cups confectioners' sugar, 2 teaspoons thawed concentrated frozen orange juice, and ¼ cup Grand Marnier. (It will separate, but beat hard and it will become smooth; but if not, do not worry.) Refrigerate ready to use. Make crêpes. After crêpes are fried and cool, dot each with the creamed butter mixture. Fold in half and then in fourths. Put on well-buttered metal platter. When ready to serve, sprinkle with Grand Marnier and granulated sugar. Warm over high heat and serve. Three or four per serving.

NOTE: These should not be flamed because the butter will melt and run out of the crêpes when they are set afire—but you may, if you wish—most people do!

PANNEQUETS SOUFFLÉS

[*Souffléed Pancakes*]

Prepare recipe of crêpes. Make Soufflé au Grand Marnier (p. 310). Add whites and fill crêpes before serving dinner. Put about 3 tablespoons soufflé mixture through the middle of each crêpe. Fold the sides up over the filling. Place the folded side of each crêpe down on a buttered heat-proof platter, side by side. When ready to serve, bake in a preheated 425-degree oven for about 10 minutes, or until hot and puffed. Sprinkle with granulated sugar and Grand Marnier. Serve hot.

PÂTE À CASSOLETTE
[*Pastry Cups*]

A special cassolette form is necessary to make these. It is available at specialty shops, is inexpensive, and is easy to work with.

1 cup sifted flour	¼ teaspoon salt
1 whole egg	1 cup milk
1 egg yolk	Vegetable oil for deep fat-frying

1. Put flour, egg, yolk, and salt into a small mixing bowl. Blend with a whisk or hand beater, while adding the milk. Do not whip the mixture, just mix.

2. Heat about 3 inches of oil to 380 degrees. Place cassolette iron in the oil to get hot. When hot, drain oil from iron and dunk iron into the batter to ¼ inch of the top of the iron. (Hot iron sears batter to it.) Then place the batter-coated iron back into the hot oil. Submerge to the bottom of the pan. Let brown.

3. When cup is brown, tip the form upside down to drain oil from it and to keep cassolette from sliding off the form. Push cup off the iron and drain on paper towels. Reheat iron, dip again in batter, and brown in hot oil. Repeat until all batter cups are made. Makes about 48.

NOTE: For ice-cream cones, add 1 tablespoon sugar to the recipe. Or, you can make cassolettes with half the batter, then add 2 teaspoons sugar and use remainder of batter for dessert cups. Use these sweet cups to hold ice cream, fruit, or a mousse. Fill at the time of serving. Store unfilled cups in a pilot-heated oven. Will keep about 2 weeks and then they become rancid.

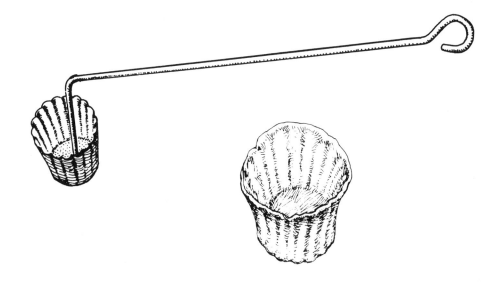

XVII

Pâtes Levées
[Yeast Doughs]

The French housewife does not normally make bread at home. The small restaurants ordinarily do not bake on the premises. Breads are bought from the neighborhood bakeshop. Therefore, practically no bread recipes come to us from the homes or the chefs of France. The men who work in the bakeries are all members of the bakers' guild. Their secrets of dough making are passed on to apprentice bakers and do not become common knowledge.

I learned some techniques of handling dough while in France, but nothing about bread making. So desperate was I to learn to make French bread that I offered my services to our neighborhood bakeshop for nothing. I was refused on the grounds that it was not possible for "Madame" to become a guild member. I was, however, allowed to sit at a respectful distance and watch; but I could ask no questions nor could I interfere with the baking process. After a short time of sitting I departed.

I learned about "leaven" and the problems of flour. Our hard-wheat flour has so much more gluten than the soft-wheat flour of France that I have yet, after hundreds of attempts, to make a "real" loaf of Paris-type bread in this country. The bread recipes that follow are good and have an excellent crisp crust, but they are not the *pain ordinaire* of Paris about which we dream. But even the Frenchman outside Paris also dreams of Paris bread, since the bakers in the provinces are not privy to the secrets of the Paris guild.

You will notice that a blend of cake flour (soft-wheat) and of all-purpose flour (hard-wheat) is used in most of the dough recipes. A combination of flours seems to give an approximation of French flour, and the results are somewhat better. It is also possible to use nothing but all-purpose and unbleached flour, but do not use cake flour alone.

Both sweet and nonsweet yeast doughs are included in this chapter. They are grouped together because of their family relationship. Notice that the basic Brioche recipe becomes a dessert Savarin with minor changes in the amounts of sugar and the addition of milk. The Savarin becomes a Pâte à Frire with the omission of the butter. Baking, like cooking, follows a system.

PAIN ORDINAIRE NO. 1

[*French Bread*]

1 cup warm water

1 (⅗ ounce) package compressed
    or (¼ ounce) dry yeast

1 tablespoon sugar

1½ teaspoons salt

2 tablespoons soft butter

3 cups all-purpose flour

¾ cup cake flour

Glaze

1 egg white   2 tablespoons cold water

1 teaspoon salt

1. Run hot tap water into mixing bowl to warm it. Drain, and then put 1 cup warm water and the yeast into the bowl. Mix and let stand 5 minutes. Stir in sugar, salt, and butter.

2. Sift flours together. Add 2 cups flour. Beat for 2 minutes with electric mixer, or 4 minutes by hand. Then add 1¼ cups of flour. Mix well, then put onto floured surface. Let rest 10 minutes and then knead until smooth and elastic and dough fights back as it is worked. The dough should not stick to the counter or to your hands. It will take about ½ cup of flour for the kneading.

3. Grease a bowl, add dough, turn upside down to grease both top and bottom. Cover and let rise in a warm place. Pilot-heated ovens are about 100 degrees. Bread should rise at 85. Prop open the oven door if you use the pilot-heated oven. When dough is doubled in volume, put out onto a floured counter. Poke down lengthwise, cover, and let rest 30 minutes. Cut into thirds lengthwise of the dough. Shape each piece into a long loaf with your hands, or roll each into a rectangle and then roll up tight, like a jelly roll. Seal edge into the dough and taper ends. (Hand-shaped bread is lighter, but the loaves are not as pretty.)

4. Place on greased and cornmeal-coated cooky sheet. Combine glaze ingredients, brush loaves with mixture, then cut ¼ inch diagonal gashes across the top about every 2 inches and let the loaves double in size.

(*continued*)

5. Put a big flat pan of boiling water on the floor of a preheated 450-degree oven. Bake bread 15 minutes, brush again with glaze and reduce heat to 400 degrees and bake another 15 minutes, or until done. To test for doneness, tap the bread with a wooden spoon; if the sound is a hollow one, the bread is done; if not, bake another 5 minutes and test again. Makes 3 loaves.

6. Bread may be frozen. Then, when it is needed, put frozen into a 350-degree oven for about 20 minutes. This bread is improved with a second baking.

PAIN ORDINAIRE NO. 2

[*French Bread*]

1½ cups warm water or potato water	1 teaspoon sugar
2 (¼ ounce) packages dry, or 2 (⅗ ounce) packages compressed yeast	1½ tablespoons melted butter
	4 cups all-purpose flour
	1 cup cake flour
	2 egg whites, beaten to a froth

2 teaspoons salt

Glaze

1 egg white	2 tablespoons water

1 teaspoon salt

1. Run hot water into mixing bowl to warm it. Pour out, then put 1½ cups warm water and yeast into bowl. (Use warmer water for dry yeast than for compressed yeast. Potato water gives better flavor.) When yeast is dissolved, add sugar and butter. Let rest 10 minutes. Sift flours together. Add half the flour. Mix well. Add the beaten egg whites.

2. Stir in salt and add remainder of the flour. Mix until stiff. Put onto floured counter and knead for at least 10 minutes, or until dough is smooth and elastic and no longer sticks to hands and counter.

3. Put into greased bowl. Turn dough over to grease both sides. Let it rise 10 minutes. Make 10 cuts through dough with a sharp knife. Let rise. Repeat this cutting process through the dough every 10 minutes for 1 hour.

4. At the end of an hour turn dough out onto floured counter. Cut into three pieces. Roll each into a ¼-inch rectangle, then roll up, stretching dough as you roll. Pinch edges into the dough to seal the loaf, and taper ends. Place on greased and cornmeal-coated cooky sheet. (Loaves may be shaped with your hands if you wish.)

5. Mix glaze ingredients. Brush loaves with mixture. With a sharp knife make ¼-inch-deep diagonal cuts every 2 inches across the top of each loaf. Let rise until at least doubled in bulk, or about 2 hours.

6. Put a large flat pan of boiling water onto the floor of a 450-degree oven. Add risen bread and bake about 20 minutes. Brush again with glaze. Bake another 15 minutes at 400 degrees, or until done. Cool on wire racks. Makes 3 loaves.

PAIN ORDINAIRE NO. 3

[*French Bread*]

Sponge

1 (⅗-ounce) cake yeast	1 tablespoon sugar
¼ cup warm water	1½ teaspoons salt
¼ cup milk	½ cup cold water
Piece of butter	2¼ cups sifted all-purpose flour

Bread

½ cup milk	1 (⅗-ounce) cake compressed
2 tablespoons butter	yeast or 2 packages dry yeast
2 tablespoons sugar	3 tablespoons sponge
1½ teaspoons salt	4 cups sifted all-purpose flour
1 cup cold water	1 cup cake flour
¼ cup warm water	Butter and cornmeal to coat pans

Glaze

1 egg white	2 tablespoons cold water
1 teaspoon salt	

(continued)

1. *To make the sponge,* dissolve yeast in ¼ cup warm water. (I find compressed yeast makes better bread than dry yeast and is better when it is dissolved in water rather than milk.) Scald milk and then add butter, sugar, and salt. Stir until sugar and salt are dissolved and butter is melted. Add cold water. When liquids are lukewarm, stir in dissolved yeast.

2. Put 2¼ cups flour into small mixing bowl. Make hole in center. Pour in liquids. Mix well. Cover with transparent wrap. Set in a warm place and let rise and ferment for at least 12 hours, or overnight. It is then ready to use in the making of bread and rolls. Sufficient for about 6 batches of bread. Keep refrigerated between bakings.

3. *To make the bread.* Scald milk. Add butter, sugar, and salt. Stir to dissolve sugar and salt. Add 1 cup water. In ¼ cup warm water, dissolve yeast. Add to mixture and then add 3 tablespoons sponge. Sift flours together. Put 4½ cups flour into bowl. Make a hole in the center of the flour. Add the liquids. Mix well, but do not knead. Put into a greased bowl. Let it double. Grease a cooky sheet with butter and sprinkle with cornmeal.

4. When dough has doubled in bulk, turn out onto floured surface. Use remaining ½ cup flour. Cut dough into four or six pieces, depending upon size of loaf you prefer. Let rest 10 minutes, then shape into loaves, or cut into small pieces and make rolls. Place loaves on cooky sheet. Combine glaze ingredients. Brush loaves, then make ¼-inch-deep diagonal cuts every 2 inches over the top of the loaves. Let double in size in a warm place.

5. Put into 450-degree oven and bake for about 20 minutes. Brush again with glaze. Reduce heat to 400 degrees. Bake another 10 minutes, or until done. Cool bread on racks. Makes about 4 or 6 loaves.

CROISSANTS

[*Flaky Rolls or Crescents*]

1 (⅗-ounce) cake yeast	½ teaspoon salt
2 tablespoons water	1½ cups all-purpose flour
2 teaspoons sugar	1½ sticks butter (¾ cup)
½ cup cake flour	1 egg yolk
¾ cup warm milk	2 tablespoons cold water

1. Soften yeast in 2 tablespoons water with 1 teaspoon sugar. When dissolved, add the ½ cup cake flour. Mix to a dough. Work with your hands to make a smooth ball. It will have the texture of putty. Cut a 1-inch deep cross in the top. Pour the warm milk into a 4-cup measuring cup, or similar container. Drop the yeast-dough ball into the warm milk, cross up. (This is a quick leaven.) The dough ball will rise to the surface of the milk after about 10 minutes. Let it rise and ferment for about 30 minutes, or until doubled in size.

2. Stir remaining teaspoon sugar and the salt into the milk around the dough ball. Put the all-purpose flour into a bowl. Make a well in the flour, then add the milk and yeast ball. Mix to a soft dough. Turn out onto well-floured marble slab or counter. Knead dough on floured surface until satinlike and smooth. Put into floured bowl (not oiled). Sprinkle top with flour, cover with damp towel, set in a warm place, but not over 85 degrees, and let rise until double in size.

3. Knead butter in cold water. Shape into a 4-inch square. Let it stand in cold water until ready to use.

4. Once dough has risen to twice its size, put onto floured counter, sprinkle with flour and roll to about an 18-inch circle. Blot butter with paper towels. Lay butter on a floured surface, cover with piece of transparent wrap, and with rolling pin flatten to a ¼-inch-thick square.

5. Place butter in center of circle of dough. Fold the bottom of the dough up, the sides over, and the top down to cover the butter. With rolling pin press edges into the dough to seal in the butter. Roll dough into a long strip, approximately 18 × 8 inches. With the 8-inch end toward you, fold the bottom third up over the middle and the top down over the two layers. This rolling and folding is called a turn. Give dough ¼ turn to the right. Press open ends together with rolling pin. Roll again into a strip 18 × 8 and fold as before. Encase folded dough in transparent wrap and refrigerate for 20 minutes.

6. Take dough from refrigerator. Roll and fold a third time. On the fourth rolling of the dough, roll into an oblong about 18 × 10 inches and about ¼ inch thick. Cut the dough down the middle the long way, making two strips. Cut each strip into 6 or 7 triangles. Sprinkle two cooky sheets with water.

7. Consider the center cut and the outside edges of the dough as bases of the triangles. Roll each triangle of dough from the base with your right hand and, holding the point of the triangle, stretch the dough as you roll it. This will pull the dough thinner and make it easier to shape into a crescent. Place rolls on dampened cooky sheet, point down, and curve into a crescent shape. Press the ends to the cooky sheet.

8. Mix yolk and 2 tablespoons water. Carefully brush the top surface of each roll with egg mixture, but *do not* brush the cut edges with the egg mixture or they will not rise. Let rolls rise uncovered for 3 to 4 hours, or until more than doubled in size. Preheat oven to 500 degrees. Bake rolls in the middle of the oven, one pan at a time, for about 10 minutes. Coat again with yolk mixture and bake another 2-3 minutes. When they are done, remove from cooky sheets and cool on wire racks. When cool, they may be frozen in plastic bags ready to heat and eat. When ready to use, thaw and reheat in 350-degree oven for about 7 minutes, or until hot. Makes about a dozen. Serve plain or iced.

NOTE: Roll the imperfect end pieces together. Roll on sugared surface, fold and turn again and make a few small Palmiers (see recipe, p. 346).

ICING FOR CROISSANTS

4 tablespoons apricot jam	1 tablespoon water
2 tablespoons Kirsch or water	1 teaspoon rum
1 tablespoon corn syrup	1 teaspoon lemon juice

Confectioners' sugar

1. Boil jam and Kirsch for one minute. With a paint brush, coat hot croissants with the jam mixture.

2. Bring syrup and 1 tablespoon water to a boil. Remove from heat. Add rum and lemon juice. Stir in about ½ cup confectioners' sugar, or sufficient to make a thin paste. Spread over jam-coated croissants. Serve immediately while still warm.

NOTE: If croissants are to be frozen, do not ice until after they have thawed and been reheated.

BRIOCHES

[*Crusty Buns*]

1 (⅗-ounce) cake yeast	2 tablespoons sugar
2 tablespoons warm water	1 teaspoon salt
1 teaspoon sugar	4 eggs
½ cup sifted cake flour	1½ sticks butter (¾ cup)
Warm water	1 egg yolk
2 cups sifted all-purpose flour	1 tablespoon water

1 tablespoon milk

1. Dissolve yeast in 2 tablespoons water. Stir in 1 teaspoon sugar and ½ cup cake flour, or a little more. The dough should be thick enough to be handled like putty and should not stick to your hands. Shape into a ball and then cut a 1-inch deep cross in the top with kitchen scissors or a knife.

2. Half fill a 4-cup measuring cup or similar container with warm water. (Warm the cup first with hot water or the cup will cool the water.) Drop dough ball, cross side up, into the water. It will rise to the top after a few minutes. Let it ferment for about 5 minutes. Do not let it start to dissolve into the water. (In hot weather use it as soon as it rises to the top of the water.)

(*continued*)

3. Put 2 cups flour into large mixer bowl. Add 2 tablespoons sugar, salt, eggs, and yeast ball. Beat for about 5 minutes. Dough will be rather soft.

4. Wash butter in cold water. Squeeze and work the impurities out of the butter and into the water. Butter should be creamy and not hard. Let drain on plate and blot with paper towels; then cream the butter.

5. Add butter to the dough in about 6 portions. Blend after each addition. When all butter is blended into the dough, stop beating. (Note: When ready to incorporate the butter, I put the dough into the blender container and add the butter in 3 pieces. This is a better technique, but it does dirty both the mixer and blender. It also takes great skill to keep the dough pushed from the sides of the blender so it mixes and doesn't just whirl. When I learned to make Brioche and Savarin doughs, I had to beat them with my hand so that I could feel their texture and consistency. There were no electrical appliances available.)

6. Put dough into a lightly oiled large clean bowl. Cover with a damp (not wet) towel. Cover tight with foil or transparent wrap. Refrigerate overnight, and for no longer than 24 hours.

7. When ready to bake, put dough onto cold floured surface. (Marble is best.) Quickly mold dough into a long roll. Cut into 12 pieces and then mold into ovals, or egg-shapes. Handle butter doughs deftly and quickly—hands are hot. Cover pieces of dough with transparent wrap and let rest 10 minutes. Coat individual 3-inch (across the top) fluted brioche molds or muffin pans with vegetable oil.

8. Roll each egg-shaped piece of dough into a duck-pin shape: fat on one end, tapered on the other. Shape with your hand.

9. Put big end into mold. At the point where the dough begins to taper, place your fingers and thumb around the dough. Push your fingers down into the center of the dough pushing the tapering top into the body of the Brioche. This becomes the topknot of the Brioche. Place molds on a cooky sheet.

10. Mix together yolk, 1 tablespoon water, and milk. Dampen (don't wet) surfaces with mixture, but *do not* let it run into the crack around the topknot, or down into the molds. (I use an artist's sable-hair brush for this kind of delicate coating. French chefs use a goose feather brush. Although this brush may be difficult to find outside of New York, you can order one from H. Roth & Son, 1577 First Avenue, New York, New York 10028.) Let Brioche rise to double in size. Bake in a preheated 450-degree oven, on an upper-middle rack of the oven, for about 15 minutes. Coat again with yolk mixture (you don't have to be so careful this time) and bake another 5 minutes.

11. When Brioches are done, immediately remove from pans and place on wire cake racks. Serve hot, or let cool and freeze. When ready to serve, thaw and then reheat in a 350-degree oven. Serve plain as breakfast or dinner rolls.

VARIATIONS

To make a big Brioche. Cut the dough in half. Roll one half into a round ball, cover, and let rest 10 minutes. (Cut the other half into 6 individual pieces and make small Brioche.) Place big ball of dough in a 6-inch (across the top) oiled, fluted Brioche mold or other mold. Fill the container a little over half full. Take a small Brioche piece of dough in your fingers, force your fingers into the center of the big ball of dough, and down to the center of it. Deposit the small Brioche in the center. This becomes the topknot for the big Brioche. Coat with egg mixture, avoiding the cracks. With kitchen scissors make 4 cuts in the big dough ball around the topknot. (Not necessary for small Brioche.) Let double in bulk. Bake in a preheated 450-degree oven on a lower-middle rack of the oven for 15 minutes. Coat again with yolk mixture and reduce heat to 350 degrees. Bake another 15 minutes. Remove from pan when done and place on wire cake rack. (To leave hot breads in the pan will cause them to "sweat" and the crisp crust will be lost.)

Coat large Brioche with icing (p. 374) or spread with just the apricot glaze and sprinkle with sliced almonds and crushed lumps of sugar. Cool and serve plain, or slice and serve with a Sabayon sauce (p. 313) for dessert.

Stuffed Brioche. Cut Brioche (large or small) at the point where the fluted ridges stop. With a fork, remove the soft dough from both the top and the bottom parts, leaving only the shell. Pack top and bottom with pâté (p. 416). Put Brioche back together. Wrap and refrigerate. Slice and serve as a first course.

To use interiors of Brioche. Make a Crème Saint-Honoré (p. 307). Oil a fancy mold. Pour a layer of sauce into it. Add a layer of Brioche interiors. Sprinkle them with Grand Marnier and then add another layer of sauce and then Brioche. Repeat these layers until all Brioche pieces are used. Refrigerate until set. Dip mold in warm water and invert on serving plate. Serve with a fresh strawberry sauce or Sabayon (p. 313) for dessert.

SAVARIN
[*Yeast Cake*]

1½ cups sifted all-purpose flour	*Syrup*:
½ cup sifted cake flour	1 cup water
1 (⅗-ounce) cake yeast	¾ cup sugar
¼ cup warm milk	3 tablespoons rum
1 teaspoon salt	½ cup apricot preserves
2 tablespoons sugar	2 tablespoons water
3 whole eggs	1 tablespoon rum
Melted butter	Candied red cherries
¼ pound butter	Candied green angelica

1. Sift flours into large mixer bowl. Make a well in the flour. Break yeast into the well. Add the warm milk. Stir yeast with the milk until dissolved and then stir in enough flour to make a soft ball of dough. Cover bowl and let yeast rise about 15 minutes. (This is a leaven.)

2. Add salt, 2 tablespoons sugar, and eggs to the well with the yeast ball. Blend together in mixer bowl on low speed. This should be a soft dough, softer than the Brioche dough. Add more milk if necessary to keep the dough soft. Beat about 10 minutes.

3. Coat a Savarin ring mold (9 inches across the top, with a 4-inch opening) with melted butter. Set in freezer to harden butter, then coat again and refrigerate to harden butter.

4. Wash ¼ pound butter in cold water, then work on a plate until creamy and thick like sour cream. Beat butter into the dough in small amounts. Do not beat once all the butter has been incorporated into the dough. Spoon dough into the buttered mold, filling it about half full. Set in a warm place to rise and double in size.

5. When dough has doubled, place in preheated 500-degree oven. Reduce heat immediately to 350 degrees. The hot oven sears the top of the dough and keeps it from rising over the top of the pan. Bake about 20 minutes, or until cake tester comes out clean.

6. Oil the wires of a cake rack. Invert cake on rack when done. Remove pan. While cake bakes, prepare syrup: Heat 1 cup water and ¾ cup sugar to dissolve sugar. Set rack with cake over a large bowl to catch the syrup that runs off the cake. Spoon syrup over hot cake many times. When syrup cools, reheat it. Soak the cake, but do not dissolve it. Cake must remain firm to the touch, not soggy, yet moist with syrup.

7. Once cake is soaked, spoon 3 tablespoons rum over cake and then spoon syrup over again to force the rum throughout the cake. When cake is cool, carefully slide it down the oiled wires and onto serving plate. Use the wires as runners to transport the cake to the plate.

8. Bring apricot preserves and 2 tablespoons of water to a boil. Stir in 1 tablespoon rum. Using a paint brush, glaze Savarin with mixture. Decorate the top with cherries. Cut green angelica (p. 319) into diamond-shaped pieces and stick into cake on each side of the cherries. Glaze with apricot mixture. Serve plain, or fill center with Crème Saint-Honoré (p. 307).

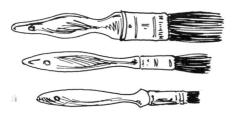

VARIATIONS

BABA AU RHUM

[*Miniature Rum Cakes*]

Soak 2 tablespoons each of currants and seedless Sultana raisins in 3 table-spoons rum while making the cake. Drain, and dust with flour. Put fruits in a plastic bag, add flour and shake. (Flour helps them cling to the dough so they will not settle to the bottom of the mold.) Stir floured fruits into the Savarin recipe and then spoon into twice-buttered individual Baba molds, filling them half full. Set molds on a cooky sheet. Let rise until doubled in bulk, then put into 450-degree oven and bake for about 12 minutes. Turn out on wire rack. Soak with syrup, then rum from fruits, and glaze with apricot mixture as in the Savarin.

KUGELHOPF

[*Alsatian Yeast Cake*]

Pour Baba Rhum mixture into a twice-buttered Turk's-head or Kugelhopf mold, filling half full. Let rise until doubled in bulk. Set into preheated 450-degree oven and immediately reduce heat to 350 degrees. Bake about 40 minutes, or until cake tester or wooden pick comes out clean when inserted into the middle of the cake. Turn out onto wire rack. Sprinkle heavily with confectioners' sugar, or simple butter frosting (p. 339), while cake is still hot.

PÂTE À FRIRE

[*Yeast French-frying Batter*]

1 cup flour	1 tablespoon sugar
1 (⅗-ounce) cake compressed yeast	2 egg yolks
	½ cup warm milk
2 tablespoons warm water	2 egg whites, beaten stiff
½ teaspoon salt	Oil for French-frying

1. Put flour into mixer bowl. Make a hole in the middle. Put crumbled yeast into the hole. Add water. Stir yeast and water together to dissolve yeast. Don't worry if some flour mixes into it. When yeast is dissolved, add salt, sugar, and yolks. Beat together in mixer on low speed while adding milk. Mixture should be like a thick custard. Beat for about 5 minutes.

2. Remove beaters and let batter rise for about one half hour, and no longer than one hour.

3. When ready to use, stir in about ¾ of the beaten egg whites. (Discard remaining whites.) Use batter on foods, or drop batter from a teaspoon into oil heated to 380 degrees. These will turn over by themselves. Done when brown. Drain on paper towels. Sprinkle with sugar. Serve plain, or with Sabayon sauce (p. 313).

VARIATION

BEIGNETS DE FRUITS

[*French-fried Fresh Fruits*]

Peel whole apples and pears. Slice across the fruit, making circles. With the hole from a doughnut cutter, or a knife, cut the seeds and center from each slice, making fruit doughnuts. Lay fruits in a shallow pan. Sprinkle with sugar, ¼ teaspoon Fruit Fresh (p. 605), and then with Kirsch. Let soak 15 minutes. Make a Sabayon sauce (p. 313). Drain fruit and blot on paper towels. Put on a clean, dry plate. Pour over sufficient Pâte à Frire batter to coat each piece. Drop into 380-degree oil and French-fry until brown. (Do not crowd the pan and cool the fat, or fruits will be soggy.) Serve with Sabayon sauce. Fry batter that is left and then sprinkle with sugar and eat as doughnut balls.

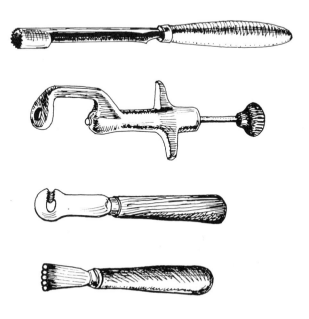

XVIII

Buffet Froid
[*Cold Buffet*]

The summary of this book is contained in this chapter. For the cold buffet is nothing more than a synopsis of the French luncheon and dinner menus. Once you understand the system of French cuisine, you will be able to create many picturesque and novel cold foods through the use of basic recipes found elsewhere in this book.

The skillful cook can take cold cooked foods, incorporate them with cold sauces, and decorate them with fancy food cutouts to create culinary masterpieces for display on a sumptuous board.

A well-appointed cold buffet should include a selection from each category of food: eggs, seafood, poultry, meat, pâtés, pickled vegetables, salads, and sweets. And, in addition to cold cooked foods, the buffet usually has an assortment of cheeses, fresh fruits, breads, toast, crackers, and such extras as pickled herrings, anchovies, sardines, olives, oysters on the half shell when in season, and caviar. The cold buffet has no limits. It is designed to evoke satisfying visual and gustatory responses.

Before we go into the preparation of the recipes for the cold buffet, let us discuss their decorations. Always use edible foods for decorating foods, and never paper frills or doilies, not even on the serving dish.

To create decorations for cold foods takes patience and imagination. But nothing is more rewarding to a cook than a beautiful cold buffet—especially when the food pictures being displayed are one's own creations. Decorations for cold foods are created from vegetables, fruits, and eggs.

The carrot has numerous possibilities. Once cooked, it is easily cut into jonquils, mimosa, tulips, and daisies. A small circle of carrot is often added to flowers of other foods to make a bright center. A slice of cooked carrot can be carved into the shape of a flower pot and dyed to look like a clay pot. Green onion tops, cucumbers, and green peppers simulate stems and leaves. Radishes convert into fan flowers, roses, and tulips. Lemon and orange peelings roll into yellow and orange roses, which may be dyed into red roses. Hard-cooked eggs can be turned into lilies-of-the-valley, daisies and yellow mimosa, and while still hot, they may be shaped into shiny pears and apples and dyed yellow and red.

Try to make your miniature vegetable flowers exact copies of real flowers, both in shape and in color.

HOW TO DECORATE COLD FOODS

To make decorations stick, put the little food pieces into cooled, liquid gelée (p. 387) and then, using the tip of a paring knife, lift them out and place them where you want them on the food. Have your design in mind before placing the gelée-dipped food, since to move it would leave its "foodprint" in the Chaud-Froid. Once the food is decorated, brush decorations and the food with cooled gelée, refrigerate until set, and then give the food a second coat of liquid gelée. Use an artist's paint brush number 8, or feather brush (p. 375) so that the design will not slip under the weight of the brush and the gelée. This final coating of gelée will keep the decorations from drying out and give the food a showcase appearance.

HOW TO MAKE DECORATIONS

I. *Carrots* (cooked) make:

Flower Pots. Cut a ¹⁄₁₆-inch-thick lengthwise slice from a cooked carrot. Then cut out a flower pot from the widest part of the slice. Put carrot pot into brown coloring (see p. 3) and a bit of water. Bring to a boil, then lift out the carrot pot when it has turned the color of clay. Blot on paper towels. Place pot down flat on the food to be decorated. Run green onion stems out of the pot and top the stems with assorted food flowers.

Jonquils. Cut a ½-inch piece from the bottom of a cooked carrot. Trim it to a cylinder about ¼ inch in diameter. Hollow out the center with the point of a knife, then taper the outside down to

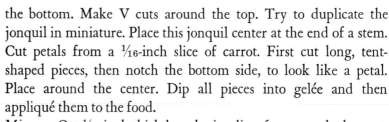

the bottom. Make V cuts around the top. Try to duplicate the jonquil in miniature. Place this jonquil center at the end of a stem. Cut petals from a ¹⁄₁₆-inch slice of carrot. First cut long, tent-shaped pieces, then notch the bottom side, to look like a petal. Place around the center. Dip all pieces into gelée and then appliqué them to the food.

Mimosa. Cut ¹⁄₁₆-inch-thick lengthwise slices from a cooked carrot. Then, with a small (¹⁄₁₆-inch) round pastry tube, stamp out circles from the slice. Let them collect in the tube and then turn them out and separate. These are tiny. Use a wooden pick to separate them and to dot them up a thin, curving, green-onion-top stem.

Tulips. With a ¼-inch pastry tube, cut circles from a lengthwise slice of cooked carrot. Then make two V cuts from one side to make the circle tuliplike.

Yellow Daisies. With a knife or small elongated oval cutter, cut long petals from a ¹⁄₁₆-inch-thick lengthwise slice of cooked carrot. Arrange the petals in daisy fashion around a center of carrot. To make a black-eyed Susan, cut off the tip of a black olive and place it in the center. To make the center look more real, dip the olive tip in gelée and sprinkle with sieved hard-cooked egg yolk.

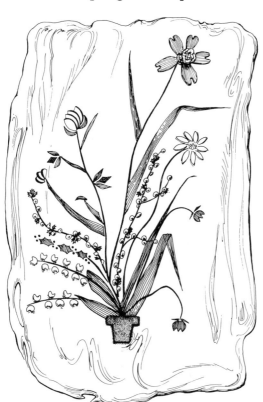

NOTE: Carrots are usually cut in lengthwise slices so that the whole decoration can be cut from the same part of the carrot slice; thus the whole flower is the same color. The center of the lengthwise slice is darker than the outside, so cut petals from the center for a daisy and stamp out mimosa from the outside lighter part. Thus you can have shades of yellow for various flowers. To cut carrots across into coinlike slices will result in petals of two shades of yellow with a light streak in the center, which is not as pretty as a solid color. Use a vegetable slicer to cut the cooked carrot so that the slice will be uniform in thickness.

II. *Cucumbers* make:

Leaves. With a vegetable peeler, remove the green skin of the cucumber in wide strips. Place a strip on a cutting board and with a sharp knife cut into ¼-inch-wide strips, then cut diagonally into diamond-shaped pieces. Use these diamonds as leaves or put two together on the end of a stem and let them hold a piece of red radish and thus create a rosebud. Or, using a sharp knife, cut out leaf shapes and place up a stem.

Stems. From a strip of cucumber skin, cut a very thin strip, less than ⅟₂₅ inch thick, and then taper these at the top to nothing so that they are fine and delicate. Use cucumber stems for lilies-of-the-valley. In general I think green-onion and leek tops make better stems and they are easier to shape than the stiff cucumber peel, but you may have a cucumber on hand and not a green onion.

III. *Leeks and Green-Onion Tops* make:

Leaves and Stems. The tops of these two vegetables are hollow. With a sharp knife, split them open. Once they are open, drop them into boiling water and then immediately lift them out and put into cold water. (Blanching makes them greener.) Lay the opened tops on a paper towel. With a dull knife, gently push the cooked mush from the inside, being careful not to destroy the outside. Cut tops into stems or into the shape of leaf needed. These tops make nice long leaves for jonquils or tulips. On some leaves fold the top down, to make them droop as real leaves often do.

IV. *Peppers* make:

Holly. Cut green peppers into quarters. Remove seeds and cut some of the meat from the shiny green outside. With a sharp knife cut out holly leaves. Then cut tiny circles, using a ⅟₁₆-inch pastry tube, from a red pepper, or from the skin of a radish. Place these red berries between the leaves of holly. Holly decorations are nice to use at Christmastime.

Poinsettia. Cut elongated petals from a shiny red pepper and place around a center of sieved hard-cooked egg yolk. Make leaves from green peppers.

V. *Radishes* make:

Fan flowers. Cut the end off a radish and discard. Then, beginning at the outside of the radish, cut paper-thin wedge half slices to the center of the radish. Let the knife shave off the half slices at the center. Overlap these, like a fan, to create petals of red and white. If the fan shape is continued you can create a beautiful red and white mum. Be sure the half slices taper to nothing at the center of the radish so that they can overlap.

Roses. With a very sharp knife cut the peeling, beginning at the tip, into a spiral no wider than ⅛ inch. Once it has been removed, wrap it around itself, dunk into gelée and let it set. Place at the top of a wavy green stem and add leaves made from green onions or leeks (p. 383).

Tulips. Cut the red skin from a radish, then cut out circles with a ¼-inch pastry tube. Notch one side with two V cuts and set at the top of a stem.

VI. *Truffles* make:

Designs. Cut canned truffles into 1/16-inch slices. With a knife, or with small truffle cutters (they come 6 or 12 to a set and are nothing more than miniature cooky cutters) cut out designs to decorate food. Dice the trimmings and pieces left from the slices, and use to decorate the edge of the food, or sprinkle over peeled cherry tomatoes. Do not waste truffle trimmings. If you do not have truffle cutters, you can make some. Remove the erasers from several pencils, then with pliers shape the metal tops into diamonds, squares, or other shapes. Leave one pencil top round. Dip tops into boiling water to sterilize, and then they are ready to use. Extract the truffle pieces from the pencil top with a needle.

VII. *Lemons* make:

Small yellow roses. Cut very thin and very narrow spiral strips from a lemon, beginning at one end. Cut about 3 inches long and then roll up in spiral fashion to make miniature roses. Dip these into gelée and let them set. Stick lemon roses onto foods at the end of a green stem and attach leaves. Also create some small lemon buds and surround them with pieces of green pepper.

Large yellow roses to decorate a serving dish are made in the same way, only use the whole skin, cutting it in spiral fashion from one end to the other, and cutting into the meat of the fruit. Roll these big lemon roses up and set into a bed of parsley. For variety, the fruit and inside skin can be painted with a weak solution of green food coloring. The yellow skin will not turn color because of the oil it contains.

VIII. *Oranges* make:

Small and large orange roses. Make like lemon yellow roses.

Red roses. Cut the outside orange skin from a thick-skinned orange. Then cut the thick white part from the fruit in a continuous ½-inch spiral strip. Cut into the fruit so that there is a layer of orange fruit attached to the white skin. Do not let the skin break.

Once it has been removed from the orange, curl the white spiral of inside skin within the palm of your hand, making the outside first and ending in the middle. Fasten the center end with ¼ of a wooden pick.

Mix 1 small (⅜-ounce) bottle of red food coloring with ½ cup cold water. Put into small bowl (just large enough to hold the rose). Add the white skin rose and let it dye red. Once it is dyed, remove it, drain, and blot on paper towels. Fill center with parsley sprigs and sprinkle with a bit of sieved egg yolk. Make a small nest of transparent wrap and set rose into it. We do this for two reasons. It will support the rose in the position you want, and it keeps the red rose from dyeing the food it leans against. Do not let the wrap show. Use parsley or watercress to hide it. Watercress wilts more quickly than parsley.

IX. *Hard-Cooked Eggs* make:

Daisies. Cut thin slices of white, then cut elongated oval petals. Arrange at the end of a cucumber stem and add a center of yellow hard-cooked egg.

Lilies-of-the-valley. Cut 1/16-inch slices of egg white. Then cut out 1/8-inch circles, using a pastry tube of that size, or the round metal end of a pencil. With the point of a very sharp knife cut two V shapes from each circle. Place these bells on a stem, the Vs down, just as the lily grows. Make broad leaves up around the stem from leek or onion tops. These show off nicely on the pink flesh of a cooked, skinned trout.

Mimosa. Mash a cooked egg yolk through a fine sieve and then add enough mayonnaise to make a paste. Put mixture into a small waxed-paper cone (see p. 359 for details). Cut the end tip from the cone and put small dots, or periods, up a long green wavy onion stem. Dot the stem with tiny, curly pieces of parsley.

Fruits. Cook eggs 11 minutes after cold water comes to a boil (see p. 56 for details). Lift eggs from hot water with a spoon. Crack the shell all over and carefully peel under cold running water.

Once it has been peeled, shape the hot egg, under cold running water, into a pear or apple. To make a pear, gently squeeze your thumb and index fingers around the smaller half of the egg. Hold the egg in this shape under cold water, while pushing in the bottom with your other index finger. Hold under cold running water, or in ice water, until the egg sets in this shape.

To mold apples, place your middle finger on fat end of the egg, your thumb on the other, and press. The egg gets pushed into a fat apple. Hold under cold running water until it sets.

Add 1/2 teaspoon yellow or 1 teaspoon red food coloring to 1/2 cup cold water, or enough to cover the egg. Dye the pear yellow, the apple red. Once they have been colored, stand on paper towels to drain. Insert a piece of parsley stem in the top and add two watercress leaves, or leaves from a shiny house plant. In the bottom of the fruits insert a whole clove, with the round bud removed.

NOTE: Select a long egg for making pears, a fat one for apples.

COATINGS FOR COLD FOODS

The two coating sauces used to glaze cold foods are Gelée and Chaud-Froid.

Gelée is a gelatin-thickened consommé. It varnishes foods to keep them from drying out, and it is used as the glue for sticking decorations onto Chaud-Froid.

Chaud-froid is a gelatin-thickened Béchamel or Mayonnaise. It is a kind of white enamel used to paint foods that are to be decorated. Once decorated these Chaud-Froid foods get a coating of Gelée.

GELÉE
[*Jellied Consommé or Aspic*]

Gelée, since it holds foods together, must be stiffer than the ordinary cold jellied consommé which is contained by a serving cup.

2 packages unflavored gelatin	½ teaspoon dry tarragon leaves
½ cup cold water	1 carrot, minced
4 egg whites	1 small leek or 2 green onions
4½ cups cold chicken stock	2 tablespoons chopped parsley
1 teaspoon salt	(guess at it)
Freshly-ground pepper to taste	2 tablespoons Port

1 tablespoon Cognac

1. Put gelatin, cold water, and egg whites into saucepan. Beat to a froth. Add cold chicken stock, salt, pepper, tarragon, and carrot. Clean leek (p. 607) and slice thin, using 2 inches of the green tops. Add leek and parsley.

2. Stir-cook over medium heat until starting to boil. Immediately reduce heat to a simmer and stop stirring. Under no conditions let this boil or the impurities will boil back into the consommé as fast as they collect. Simmer for about 15 minutes.

3. Rinse a clean linen cloth in cold water. Line a strainer with the cloth and set over a porcelain or crockery bowl. When gelée is done, carefully pour liquid through a hole in the cooked egg whites, being careful not to disturb the coagulated whites, and into the cloth-lined strainer. Cool gelée, then add Port and Cognac.

4. If gelée is to be used immediately, pour some into a small stainless-steel pan or bowl. (Thin metal cools faster than enamel or crockery, and it can be heated if necessary.) Set bowl into a dish filled with ice cubes and water. Stir

with a paint brush until it starts to thicken. At that point remove from the ice and paint the foods being coated. If the gelée becomes too thick, heat to melt it and then cool again in ice water. Using the gelée at the right moment is tricky, but very quickly learned.

NOTE: To be sure gelée will be the firmness you want, pour about ½ inch into a small metal pan and set into the freezer compartment. It should set as soon as it is cold. If not firm enough, soak a teaspoon of gelatin, then heat with ½ cup of consommé and pour into the batch. Test again.

How much gelatin was extracted originally from the bones and meat when the stock was cooked will determine how much extra gelatin is needed to set gelée. The only sure way to know is to test a small amount and then adjust the batch accordingly. But do not add so much gelatin that the gelée becomes like rubber.

VARIATIONS
GELÉE DE PERSIL
[Parsleyed Aspic]

Add 3 tablespoons minced parsley to 2 cups liquid gelée. Use to line a mold, or pour into shallow pan, refrigerate until set, then chop, or cut into fancy designs.

GARNITURES À LA GELÉE
[Gelée Garnishings]

To make *cut designs* pour gelée into a square pan to a depth of ¼ inch. Cover tightly with foil and refrigerate until quite firm, overnight if possible. When ready to use, dip pan into warm water and invert on foil. Cut into 2-inch strips and then cut triangles from the strips. Or dip small cooky cutters into cold water and stamp out gelée patterns. Make any design you want from the gelée. Use them to decorate platters.

To *chop gelée* sprinkle a sheet of foil with cold water. Add strips of gelée, sprinkle lightly with cold water, and chop with a knife, making pieces coarse or fine, as you wish. Water keeps gelée from sticking to the knife.

To make *fine lines* of gelée put finely chopped gelée into a cold pastry bag with small star nozzle. Refrigerate until cold. Then squeeze the bag to pipe lines of gelée onto decorated foods. This is used mainly on poultry.

To *coat a mold* with gelée, fill it full and refrigerate. The gelée will become firm from the sides toward the middle. When set to about 1 inch from the sides, spoon out the syrupy gelée and then refrigerate until the sides are very firm. If you find the sides are too thick, dip a tablespoon into very hot water and cut out the gelée to the thickness you want. Set the mold in ice water while you work on it. Or let the mold get firm, then, with a hot spoon, cut out center.

GELÉES DIVERSES
[Foods with Gelée]

OEUFS POCHÉS EN GELÉE
[Poached Eggs in Gelatin]

Gelée	Vegetable decorations
Poached eggs, 1 per person	Boiled ham

1. Make gelée (p. 387) ready to use. Poach eggs (p. 56). Cook 4 minutes, not 3, for they will not be reheated. Put eggs into cold water ready to use.

2. Pour ⅛-inch layer of gelée into oval or round ramekins deep enough to hold an egg. Refrigerate to set the gelée.

3. Now decorate the set gelée in each ramekin. Make each one different. Add another layer of gelée and refrigerate. Remove eggs from water. Blot on towel and trim the egg white to make it tidy. Place the smoothest side of the egg down in the ramekin and fill with gelée to ¼ inch of the top. Refrigerate until set.

4. Cut a piece of ham to fit the ramekin. Lay this over the gelée and egg and cover with more gelée. Refrigerate again.

5. When ready to serve, dip ramekins into warm water. Run knife around top of each and invert on small, cold plates. Serve 1 per person. These take time, though they are not difficult and are fun to make. Serve for Sunday brunch on a hot day.

OEUFS FARCIS
[Stuffed Eggs]

Shell and cut top and bottom from hard-cooked eggs. Remove yolks, leaving a cylinder of white. Mash yolks through a sieve and then blend with Moutarde Mayonnaise (p. 407) to make a paste. Stuff into the white cylinders, filling them full. There will not be sufficient filling for all the cylinders. When cylinders are filled, stand on a plate. Cut flat anchovies into about 4 strips each. Wrap a strip near the top and bottom of the cylinders like barrel hoops. Glaze top of yolk stuffing with gelée and sprinkle with minced parsley. (Note: 8 eggs will normally make 6 stuffed eggs.)

VARIATIONS

OEUFS FARCIS AUX ANCHOIS

[*Stuffed Eggs with Anchovies*]

Make Oeufs Farcis. Top the filling with a rolled anchovy.

OEUFS FARCIS AU CAVIAR

[*Stuffed Eggs with Caviar*]

Cut hard-cooked eggs in half. Mash yolks through a sieve and blend with plain Mayonnaise. Fill egg-white halves even. Cover yolk mixture with black caviar. Coat the cooked white edge with Mayonnaise and sprinkle with minced parsley and finely minced onion. Spoon gelée over caviar.

HOMARDS ET CREVETTES (Hors-d'oeuvres)

[*Lobster and Shrimp*]

Cook lobster (p. 82) and shrimp (p. 83). Cool and chill. Shell lobster and cut into bite-sized pieces. Shell shrimp if necessary and remove black vein. Add 4 tablespoons liquid gelée to Seafood Mayonnaise (p. 407) and refrigerate for about 2 hours. The gelée thickens the sauce slightly, and it is less likely to drip off the seafoods when they are dunked. Guests spear lobster and shrimp with wooden picks and dunk into the sauce.

ASPIC DE HOMARD

[*Lobster in Mold*]

Cook lobster (p. 82). Hard-cook 4 eggs (p. 56). Remove claw and tail meat. Cut tail into ⅛-inch slices. Make gelée (p. 387). Pour about ¼ inch of gelée into a 2- or 3-cup mold with fluted sides. Refrigerate until set, then arrange slices of truffle with slices of lobster over the gelée. Cover with gelée and refrigerate. Make the next layer with slices of hard-cooked eggs and lobster. Cover with gelée and refrigerate until set. Add layers until all lobster is used. Unmold on serving plate and decorate the plate with chopped gelée. Serve with Seafood Mayonnaise (p. 407).

HOMARD EN GELÉE
[*Lobster in Gelatin*]

1 (2½-pound) lobster, cooked   Gelée
3 pounds cooked shrimp   Seafood Mayonnaise

Truffles

1. Cook lobster (p. 82) and shelled shrimp (p. 83). (Or buy them ready cooked, but what you cook will be better.) Cool and refrigerate.

2. Make gelée (p. 387) and chill ready to use. Mix Seafood Mayonnaise (p. 407). Cut truffles into fancy designs, or use black olives as a substitute for truffles.

3. When lobster is cold, remove the tail meat, keeping the shell intact. Cut the skin from the underneath side, or the belly of the lobster. Use kitchen scissors and cut down each side next to the shell. Beginning at the tail, carefully pull out the meat, keeping the orange skin on the meat.

4. Cut the tail meat into ¼-inch slices. With a wooden pick remove the vein from each piece.

5. Place the whole lobster, minus the tail meat, right side up on a large platter. Stretch lobster out long and then prop him up in the front, under the body, with transparent wrap. Do not let the wrap show. He must be on an incline, as on a sliding board.

6. Overlap the lobster slices, placing the biggest ones up on the body, and then continuing them down the tail. Coat each slice with syrupy gelée. Refrigerate. Dip fancy-cut pieces of truffle into gelée and then place on the spots in the meat where the vein was removed. Coat again with gelée. Remove any gelée that has run onto the platter.

7. Fill platter around each side of the lobster with cold cooked shrimp. Pull the tiny legs out and let them rest on the shrimp. It will look as if the lobster is walking on a bed of shrimp. Into the big claws set a footed crystal dish filled with Seafood Mayonnaise. Let the claws hold the stem of the dish. Tie the feelers into a knot. Tuck parsley in around the body of the lobster to look like sea moss. Stand small glasses of wooden picks on each side of the lobster and let the shrimp hide the glasses. Guests spear and dunk their own shrimp and lobster meat. Serves many. (Remember to eat the meat from the claws when the party is over.)

SALADE DE HOMARD
[*Lobster Salad*]

Coat bottom of a fancy 3-cup fluted mold with ¼ inch of gelée. Refrigerate. Lay slices of truffles and lobster alternately on the gelée, around the bottom of the mold. Cover with gelée and refrigerate. Dice remaining pieces of the meat from the tail and claws. Add ½ cup minced celery, 2 minced hard-cooked eggs and about ½ cup Seafood Mayonnaise (p. 407), or enough to make it a salad consistency. Season with salt and pepper. Add 4 tablespoons liquid gelée and mix well. Spoon lobster salad into the center of the mold, keeping it about ½ inch from the sides. Fill the mold with gelée, cover, and refrigerate at least 8 hours, or overnight.

When ready to serve, unmold the lobster salad and surround with chopped parsley-flavored gelée (p. 388).

TRUITE EN GELÉE
[*Glazed Trout*]

3 trout, no larger than 1 pound each	Gelée Decorations

1. Poach trout according to recipe (p. 107). Make gelée (p. 387). When trout are done, set pan under cold running water and let cold water displace the hot. Leave under cold running water until trout are cool and can be lifted from the water. Place on a cake rack to drain, then skin and decorate.

2. Cut trout along the gills, down the back, across the tail, and down the belly. Remove fins and peel off the skin from the top side. Do not skin the underneath side. Once they have been skinned, cover with wrap and refrigerate until very cold. Then set cake rack on cooky sheet.

3. Decorate trout. Coat the skinned side with gelée and then decorate with lilies-of-the-valley, white daisies, or something else. Put the decorations onto a plate and pour over them about ¼ cup gelée. Lift the pieces out of the gelée with the point of a knife and stick onto the coated trout and the pieces will hold in place. (This technique is easier than dipping each piece individually into gelée.) Decorate each fish. Be sure to give the trout an artificial eye (small round of carrot, radish, or egg white); then you won't feel he is looking at you.

4. Once trout are decorated, coat twice with gelée, refrigerating between coatings so the gelée will set. When ready to serve, lift trout from cake rack with two pancake turners and place on long serving platter. Outline the gills with small sprigs of parsley. Serve with a Mayonnaise sauce (pp. 405–407).

POULET EN GELÉE

[*Chicken in Aspic*]

1 (6-pound) roasting chicken or capon	Gelée
Salt and pepper to taste	Fresh tarragon leaves for decorating
Fresh tarragon, or dried	Cold Béarnaise sauce
Chunk of butter	2 tablespoons whipped cream
	1 egg white, beaten stiff

1. Clean chicken. Remove giblets and make some stock to use at a later date. Season cavity with salt and pepper. Stuff with branches of fresh tarragon, or sprinkle the cavity with about 1 tablespoon dried tarragon. Add a chunk of butter. Truss and roast according to roast chicken recipe (p. 126).

2. When done, cool, cover, and refrigerate overnight. Remove the breast meat from each side in one piece. Remove skin. Cut into ¼-inch slices and place back on the breastbone. Make it neat.

3. Coat chicken with gelée. If you have fresh tarragon, dip perfect leaves into boiling water, then in cold water and blot dry. Dip them into gelée and arrange over the breast and legs of the chicken. Coat again with gelée. Refrigerate until ready to serve. Lift coated chicken to a clean platter and surround with chopped gelée.

4. Make Béarnaise sauce (p. 24). When the sauce is finished set into cold water and stir until cool. Then stir in about 2 tablespoons whipped cream and half a stiffly beaten egg white. (You can't beat less than 1 egg white, so use only half and discard the rest.) (Whip cream and beat egg white before making the Béarnaise sauce.) Pour sauce into the dish in which it will be served. Cover with wrap and refrigerate. Serve with cold sliced chicken.

GALANTINE DE VOLAILLE

[*Chicken Pâté in Aspic*]

1 (3–4 pound) chicken	2 onions, diced
Water	4 sprigs parsley
2 carrots, diced	Celery leaves from 1 branch

1 teaspoon salt

Meat Strips

1 (¼-inch-thick) slice veal, about ½ pound	1 bay leaf
	1 clove garlic, minced
1 (¼-inch-thick) slice baked ham, about ½ pound	2 shallots, minced
	¼ teaspoon dried thyme
½-pound piece salt pork	3 tablespoons Madeira

1 tablespoon Cognac

Pork Sausage

½ clove garlic, mashed	2 pounds ground pork
½ teaspoon salt	2 minced shallots
Freshly ground pepper	Gelée

1. The skin from the chicken must be removed in one piece and hopefully be free of cuts since it will be used as a casing to hold the meat stuffings. The traditional method is to cut down the back, through the skin, then follow the bones and remove both meat and skin from the carcass. Then the meat is cut from the skin and all too often the skin is also cut. Therefore, I offer you another way.

2. Put the chicken on its back. Beginning at the neck, run your hand down inside, between the skin and the flesh. Stay close to the meat, and work your way down the chicken. The skin actually separates itself easily from the meat. Once the skin is loose from the body of the bird, cut the wings off at the second joint, leaving the big joint attached to the breast meat.

3. Now set the bird up on its haunches, push the skin down, then lift the bird up and pull off the skin, wrong side out, just as you would pull off a pillowcase.

4. Now that the skin is off, cut it open down the back and lay it, outside down, on a double thickness of cheesecloth, or on an old napkin, or something similar that is clean. The cloth should be boilable, without holes, and big enough to enclose the chicken roll.

5. Cut breast meat from the carcass. Remove the little fillet and strip out the tendon (p. 146). Put into a nonmetal shallow dish. Cut the breast meat into

¼-inch strips. Add to dish. Cut rest of meat from the chicken's carcass. Remove the tendons from the dark meat. Put the dark meat and other tidbits into a small bowl and set aside.

6. Put the carcass of the bird into a large kettle. Add about 2 quarts water, carrots, onions, parsley, celery leaves, and salt. Simmer to make stock.

7. Cut veal and ham slices into ¼-inch strips. Add to chicken breast strips. Cut 3 (⅛-inch-thick) slices from salt pork, then cut the slices into ⅛-inch strips. Add to chicken strips.

8. Tuck bay leaf in under meats in dish. Sprinkle strips with garlic, shallots, thyme, Madeira and Cognac. Cover with transparent wrap and let marinate about 2 hours.

9. To make the sausage: Mash garlic in a wooden bowl. Add salt and pepper and continue to mash. Add ground pork and shallots. Mix well. Let stand about 1 hour, or until the meat strips are ready to use. When they are, pour liquids from strips into sausage and mix.

10. To make the galantine, layer the ingredients in the skin in neat designs so that, when the cooked galantine is cut into slices, the pattern of foods will be interesting. In the middle fourth of the skin place a ¼-inch layer of sausage and to within 1 inch of the neck and tail ends. Alternate strips of ham, chicken, and salt pork over sausage. Cover with layer of sausage. Add a layer of veal, ham, and chicken strips, then sausage, and continue to repeat these layers until about 5 layers high. End with sausage and completely enclose the sides with sausage. You will not use all of the meat strips or sausage, because the skin will not be big enough to hold it all.

11. Once the meat strips and sausage are shaped into a square meat loaf on the skin, press the meats tightly together. Pull one side of the skin over the top, and then overlap the other side. Fold the ends up, just like making a package. Now bring one side of the napkin up over the meat roll and fold the other side around tight. With string tie one open end tightly against the roll. Then, with your hands, take hold of the other open end, and squeeze the cloth tightly up to the meat roll. Tie close to the meat, then tie around the roll in three other places so it will keep its shape.

12. Remove the carcass from the stock. Add the chicken roll and push down under the liquid. Add canned stock if necessary. The roll must be submerged. Simmer about 2 hours. Make gelée and have ready to use.

13. When roll is done, lift out with cloth ends (do not stick with a fork), cool 15 minutes, then remove strings and napkin. Put into a sheet of foil and roll the foil around it tightly. Trim off ends of foil to leave ends open. Put into a plastic bag, close bag, and place in a pan. Run cold water into the pan to cool the roll. When cool, remove from bag. Wrap tightly and completely in foil.

(continued)

Remember the meat contracts as it cools. The traditional method is to place the roll between two plates and put a rock on top to press the roll. I like the roll to be round, not flat, and I find foil easier to come by than rocks, hence the foil method.

14. When ready to serve, slice 1 inch from an end and lay it aside. Cut the galantine into ⅛-inch slices and down to about 3 inches of the end. Lean the rounded side of the 1-inch piece against the cut side of the 3-inch end. It is a prop for the slices. Now arrange the slices against it in the order in which they were sliced. Let about ½ inch of the top of each slice show.

15. Decorate the 3-inch base and the ½-inch top of each slice with fancy-cut truffles, egg white, or radish, and then coat with gelée. The 3-inch base can be decorated with potted vegetable flowers (pp. 381–386), but keep the decorations on the slices simple.

NOTE: Minced truffles can be sprinkled over the layers of raw meat as the galantine is made. When they are, omit the truffle decorations on the cooked roll and simply coat with gelée.

Use the dark meat of the chicken, the remaining veal, ham, salt pork and sausage to make a Pâté à la Maison (see p. 416).

CANARD À LA MONTMORENCY
[*Duck with Red Cherries*]

1 duck (about 6 pounds)	2 cups red wine (Bordeaux)
Salt and pepper	1 cup sugar
1½ pounds fresh Bing cherries, pitted	Gelée
	Food coloring

Chicken-liver Pâté

1. Clean duck. Cook giblets to make a stock, but do not use the giblets themselves for their taste tends to be strong. Salt and pepper the cavity of the duck and truss according to instructions on p. 125. Roast according to chart (p. 126).

2. Cool duck when it is done, cover, and refrigerate overnight. Do not overcook the duck—the French eat them rare, which is better than overcooked.

3. Put pitted cherries, wine, and sugar into a pan and bring to a boil. Immediately drain cherries. Save juice and use to make a gelatin dessert. Leave cherries in sieve to drip. Make gelée (p. 387). Color a rich red-brown with red and brown food coloring (p. 3).

4. Pick out the nice big cherries to decorate the duck. How many it will take will depend on the size of the cherries and the size of the duck. Pick out

more than you'll need to decorate. Put remaining cherries into small, round timbale molds and fill with gelée. Cover and refrigerate until set.

5. Make Chicken-liver Pâté (p. 416). When pâté is finished, add 3 table-spoons gelée, pour into a bowl, cover, and refrigerate until very cold. Beat with a hand mixer to make it light and then refrigerate again, or overnight.

6. To finish Duck Montmorency: Cut circle around duck at the top of the legs and just below the breast meat. Remove the whole breast meat from each side and lay aside. With kitchen scissors, cut out the breast bone in one piece from the lower part of the duck. Leave the legs, thighs, and wings at-tached to the lower part. Trim the rib bones and the breast bone neat. Put crumpled foil into cavity to support the breast bone.

7. Turn the trimmed breast bone upside down and place in the lower part of the duck. The cavity of the breast bone is up. Fill this hollow breast bone with Chicken-liver Pâté and shape the pâté to look like the duck breast.

8. Now carefully cut the breast meat (do not skin), diagonally across, into ⅛-inch slices. Lay slices back in place over the pâté. Press into the pâté. Refrigerate for about 1 hour, or until quite cold. Coat with syrupy gelée. Re-frigerate.

9. Put the choice cherries into a shallow dish. Add 1 cup gelée and re-frigerate. When gelée just starts to set, cherries may be placed on duck, and they will stay in place. Take duck from refrigerator.

10. Beginning at the base of the wishbone, lay a triangle of cherries up to the top of the wishbone and then run a row of cherries down the breast bone to the cavity. Coat with gelée. Refrigerate. When cold and set, give the duck 2 more coats of gelée. Refrigerate between coatings.

11. When ready to serve, chop gelée fine (p. 388). Put into pastry bag with small round nozzle. Squeeze gelée into the cracks in the sliced breast. Chopped gelée glistens like jewels.

12. Unmold cherries in cups and place on platter to decorate. Refrigerate. Put chopped gelée between the mounds of cherries. Refrigerate and serve very cold.

NOTE: It is not necessary to cover foods that will be served within 6–8 hours. When foods are finished the day before, cover them with a tent of foil. Make sure the covering does not touch the gelée, or it will be damaged.

BOEUF À LA MODE EN GELÉE
[*Beef in Gelatin*]

Boeuf à la Mode	**Gelée**

1. Prepare recipe of Boeuf à la Mode (p. 216). Make gelée (p. 387). Lift meat from sauce when it is done. Place on platter to cool, wrap tight, and refrigerate overnight. (Freeze sauce for later use.) Lift vegetables from sauce and put them into small timbale molds. Fill molds with gelée, cover, and refrigerate.

2. The next day cut a 1-inch slice from the meat, then cut in ⅛-inch slices down to a 3-inch base. (Always leave a piece of meat to lean the slices against.) Put the base on serving platter. Lean the 1-inch piece of meat against the 3-inch base, cut side out, and then arrange the slices against this. Put the first slices against the base and end with the nice center slices.

3. Coat meat slices with gelée, refrigerate, and then give two more coatings. Surround meat with chopped gelée (p. 388). Unmold vegetable cups and place on chopped gelée. Cover and refrigerate until ready to serve.

VARIATION
FILET DE BOEUF FROID EN GELÉE
[*Cold Beef in Gelatin*]

Use leftover roast fillet. Put the piece of roast into a dish, or bowl, slightly larger than the piece of meat. Pour over Port-flavored gelée (p. 387), cover, and refrigerate until set. Remove from dish, slice, and serve. Decorate platter with chopped gelée and bunches of watercress. Serve with Mustard Mayonnaise (p. 407).

FILET DE BOEUF ARKANGEL
[*Fillet with Vegetable Garnish*]

Roasted fillet of beef	6 artichoke bottoms, fresh or
Gelée	canned
Salade Russe	3 hard-cooked eggs
Cucumber salad	3 tomatoes

1. Roast fillet according to recipe (p. 211). Refrigerate overnight. Next day make gelée (p. 387), and make salads (p. 411). Cook artichokes, or buy the canned bottoms ready to use. Hard-cook the eggs and refrigerate.

2. To assemble the dish: Slice the rare-roasted fillet. Arrange the slices neatly on the serving platter, the last slices becoming the first ones (see above,

step 2). Fill artichoke bottoms with Salade Russe. Cut the tomatoes in half, remove seeds and pulp, and fill with cucumber salad. Peel, then cut eggs lengthwise in half in serrated fashion. (With a small paring knife make joining V cuts all the way around the egg and to the center.) Alternate eggs, filled artichoke bottoms and tomato halves around the fillet. Coat with gelée. Refrigerate, and coat again. Refrigerate. Add chopped gelée (p. 388) between the decorations, cover, and refrigerate until ready to serve.

JAMBON PERSILLÉ
[*Ham in Parsley Gelée*]

3 cups cooked ground ham	2 tablespoons minced parsley
1 cup gelée	1 teaspoon grated lemon rind
1 tablespoon Grand Marnier	1 tablespoon minced chives

Chopped parsleyed gelée

Mix all ingredients, down to the chopped parsleyed gelée (p. 388). Rinse a 3-cup fancy mold with cold water. Add ham mixture, cover and refrigerate overnight. Unmold, decorate platter with chopped parsleyed gelée. Serve with toast points.

NOTE: To serve as a first course, mold in individual timbales, or tart pans. Then unmold and place on a bed of chopped gelée and decorate with parsley. Serve one per person.

CHAUD-FROID
[*Jellied White Sauce*]

Chaud-Froid means hot-cold. The sauce is made from a hot Béchamel, gelatin is added, it is cooled and then used to paint foods. Its white glaze makes a perfect background on which to display food decorations.

1 tablespoon unflavored gelatin	Celery tops from 3 branches
½ cup sherry	⅛ pound butter
2 cups milk	4 tablespoons flour
2 sliced shallots	½ teaspoon salt
3 sprigs parsley	½ teaspoon sugar

½ cup whipping cream

1. Soak gelatin in sherry. Put 1 cup milk into a pan. Add shallots, parsley, and celery tops. Bring to a boil and then remove from heat, cover, and let stand.

2. Melt butter in skillet. Add flour, salt, and sugar. Stir-cook for about 2

(continued)

minutes. Remove from heat. Add remaining cup of cold milk and the whipping cream. Strain the hot milk into the skillet. Heat and stir until thickened.

3. When thick, add soaked gelatin and stir until dissolved. Set pan in ice water. Stir until mixture starts to set and then use to coat cold cooked foods. Use in the same way as gelée. That is, cool in ice water until ready to set, then coat foods. If it sets, reheat and chill again to the proper consistency, then use.

CHAUD-FROIDS DIVERS
[Foods with Chaud-Froid]

CHAUD-FROID DE SAUMON
[Salmon in Jellied White Sauce]

1 (6-8-pound) whole salmon	Chaud-Froid
Carrots	Decorations
Gelée	Dill Sauce

1. Bake salmon a day in advance according to recipe (p. 101). Fill cavity of salmon with whole, long carrots. Put the narrow ends of the carrots down, the fat top ends up toward the head. Carrots just keep the fish in shape; they will not be eaten. Fill cavity tight and then sew with kitchen needle and string. Put ball of foil into the mouth to prop it open and cover fins with foil. Place fish on a large sheet of foil. Curve the salmon into a swimming position. Prop in this shape with foil and then bake in a 425-degree oven for about 1½ hours, or until done.

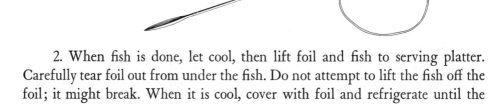

2. When fish is done, let cool, then lift foil and fish to serving platter. Carefully tear foil out from under the fish. Do not attempt to lift the fish off the foil; it might break. When it is cool, cover with foil and refrigerate until the next day.

3. Make gelée (p. 387) and Chaud-Froid (p. 399) and have ready to use. Cut decorations from vegetables (pp. 381–386). Take salmon from refrigerator, remove dorsal fins and skin salmon from gills to tail.

4. Coat the pink meat of the salmon with Chaud-Froid. A fine 2-inch paint brush is best for this job. Be sure the Chaud-Froid flows on, or the surface will not be smooth. Refrigerate, and then give another coating of Chaud-Froid. The pink flesh should not show through the coating. Refrigerate.

5. When Chaud-Froid has set, begin decorating the salmon. Plan your design, then put the cutout decorations on a large plate and add ½ cup liquid gelée. Lift vegetables with the tip of a pointed knife and place on the fish where you want them. (You can arrange your flower design in the liquid gelée and lift the pieces, one by one, and place them on the salmon.) Decorate the eyes.

6. Once decorations are on salmon, refrigerate to set decorations. Then, carefully, with an artist's sable-hair brush, or soft brush, paint the decorations and fish with gelée. Refrigerate until set. Coat again, refrigerate, and coat again. Do not cover salmon if it is to be served in the evening. If it is to be held until the next day, then, using foil, make a big tent over the salmon and close it tight to keep it from drying out. (Do not let the foil touch the Chaud-Froid, or it will be damaged.)

7. When ready to serve, clean the edge of the serving platter. (Platter is easier to clean once coatings are completely cold.) Remove foil from mouth of fish and insert an olive or radish rose. Add sprigs of parsley around the jaws.

8. To carve fish, cut down the back, and then with two forks, begin at the tail and flake off chunks of salmon onto the platter. Serve with a Dill or Fines Herbes Mayonnaise (pp. 406, 407).

NOTE: Mayonnaise Chaud-Froid (p. 406) may be used in place of the Béchamel Chaud-Froid. Large trout may be substituted for the salmon.

VARIATION

FILETS DE SOLES FROIDS

[*Sole Fillets in White Sauce*]

Poach sole or other fish fillets or steaks (p. 111). Lift from court bouillon when done and place in shallow dish. Combine 1 cup milk and 4 tablespoons sherry. Pour over fillets and let them cool. When cool, lift from liquid and place on a wire cake rack to drain. Make recipe of Chaud-Froid, using the milk and sherry in which the fillets have soaked for 1 of the cups of milk in the Chaud-Froid recipe. Give 2 coatings of Chaud-Froid. Refrigerate; then decorate fillets and glaze with gelée. Refrigerate, glaze again and refrigerate.

CHAUD-FROID DE POULET À LA GELÉE

[*Chicken in Jellied White Sauce*]

1 (5–6-pound) roasting chicken	1 celery branch, sliced
or capon	Parsley sprigs
2 carrots, cut in chunks	Chaud-Froid
2 leeks, cleaned and sliced	Gelée
1 onion, sliced	Truffles

1. Cook chicken the day before it is to be served. Remove giblets and tie chicken (p. 125). Put into a large kettle. Cover with water. Add giblets, carrots, leeks, onion, celery, and parsley. Bring to a boil. Reduce heat, cover, and simmer 1½ hours. Remove from heat and let stand, uncovered, for 1 hour.

2. Lift chicken from liquid to platter. (Stick long fork into cavity of chicken, put wooden spoon under chicken and lift out.) Cool completely, cover, and refrigerate overnight. Next day make Chaud-Froid (p. 399) and gelée (p. 387). Cool and have ready to use. Cut 1 truffle into thin, round slices. Remove trussing string and skin from chicken.

3. Put cold skinned chicken on wire cake rack. Set rack with chicken over plate to catch the Chaud-Froid. Coat with Chaud-Froid. Chill. Dip truffle slices into liquid gelée. Spot them over the chicken. Refrigerate. Coat chicken and truffles with Chaud-Froid and refrigerate. Give chicken 2 coatings of gelée. Slide chicken onto serving platter. Decorate platter with chopped gelée (p. 388) and minced truffles.

VARIATIONS

POULARDE LAMBERTYE

[*Chicken Stuffed with Pâté in Chaud-Froid*]

Poach chicken or capon as in the Chaud-Froid de Poulet recipe. Treat cold chicken like duck in Canard à la Montmorency (p. 396), beginning with step 5 and continuing through step 8. Coat twice with Chaud-Froid and then give 2 coatings of gelée. Omit the cherries. Garnish platter with chopped gelée.

SUPRÊMES DE VOLAILLE FROIDS

[*Suprêmes of Chicken in Chaud-Froid*]

See p. 146 about suprêmes and then make them like Filets de Soles Froids (p. 401).

CHAUD-FROID DE JAMBON

[Jellied Ham in White Sauce]

1 (6-pound) deboned, precooked　　　　Chaud-Froid
　　ham　　　　　　　　　　　　　　　Gelée

Decorations

1. Have butcher slice the ham and tie it back in shape. Bake in a 325-degree oven for about 2 hours. Cool when done and refrigerate overnight.

2. Next day make Chaud-Froid (p. 399) and gelée (p. 387). Cut decorations from vegetables (pp. 381–386). Make decorations and put into liquid gelée. When appropriate, make decorations seasonal. Create poinsettias and holly for Christmas; make spring flowers for Easter; and at New Year's carve bells, horns, and musical notes and write "Happy New Year." To do this, pick out the letters from alphabet noodles and cook them in water dyed with food coloring. When alphabets are barely done, lift out, and blot on paper towels ready to use. Do not put in gelée, or they will dye the gelée. Once these are arranged on the Chaud-Froid-coated ham, make a parsley frame around the New Year's greeting. It is wise to cook 2 of each letter; often they break.

3. Place cold ham on serving platter. Remove strings. Coat twice with Chaud-Froid. Lift food decorations from the liquid gelée and arrange on the ham. Refrigerate and then give Chaud-Froid and decorations 2 coats of gelée. Garnish serving platter with chopped gelée (p. 388).

VARIATION

JAMBON GLACÉ REINE PÉDAUQUE

[Ham with Pâté in Jellied White Sauce]

Cook ham as in above recipe and refrigerate overnight. Make 2 recipes of Chicken-liver Pâté (p. 416). Remove strings from the cold ham. Coat as many ham slices as the pâté will cover, and put them back in shape on the serving platter. Press slices together. Coat with Chaud-Froid, decorate with vegetable flowers (pp. 381–386), and glaze with gelée. Decorate platter with triangles of gelée (p. 388). Top each triangle with a rosette of pâté. Reserve 1 cup pâté for this.

MOUSSE DE JAMBON
[*Ham Mousse*]

Recipe of gelée	3 cups diced ham
1 tablespoon gelatin	¼ cup Madeira
¼ cup cold water	1 tablespoon Cognac
½ recipe of Chaud-Froid	1 cup whipping cream, whipped
2 tablespoons horseradish	3 tablespoons confectioners' sugar
½ teaspoon salt	2 tablespoons Grand Marnier

Minced truffle or parsley

1. Make gelée (p. 387) and have ready to use. Soak gelatin in cold water. Make ½ recipe of Chaud-Froid (p. 399). Add soaked gelatin to hot Chaud-Froid and stir until dissolved. Put the Chaud-Froid, horseradish, salt, ham, Madeira, and Cognac into blender container. Whirl to blend. If you have no blender, grind meat through a food chopper and blend into the other ingredients. Refrigerate ham mixture until cold, but do not let it set.

2. Whip cream to very stiff. Add sugar, then fold into the ham mixture. Add Grand Marnier. Mix well and refrigerate.

3. Pour a ¼-inch layer of gelée into the bottom of a 4-cup ring mold. Sprinkle with 1 minced truffle or 2 tablespoons minced parsley. Refrigerate until firm. Pack mold with ham mixture and coat with liquid gelée. Cover and refrigerate 8 hours, or overnight.

4. When ready to serve, run knife around the top of the mold, dip mold into warm water, put plate over top and invert. Fill the center of the ring with peeled cherry tomatoes.

NOTE: When molds do not drop out the first time it is usually because you take too long and the mold cools. Do not increase the heat of the water, just work faster. A knife run down the side of the mold will often break the suction and let the mold drop out. Lift one edge of the inverted mold carefully from the plate and slide a table knife down the side of the pan. When you hear it starting to let go, withdraw the knife and put the mold back down on the plate.

ASSAISONNEMENTS
[*Salad Dressings*]

Cold dressings appear in two basic forms: Mayonnaise, and Oil and Vinegar. The various methods of making Mayonnaise and the offspring sauces used chiefly on hot foods appear in Chapter III, "Sauces." For convenience, we repeat the basic Mayonnaise recipe here and list additional offspring sauces used chiefly with cold foods.

Mayonnaise plays a big role in French hors d'oeuvres that precede the meal, but is seldom served on the dinner salad. The salad that accompanies dinner is usually dressed with oil and vinegar. Lemon juice or white wine may be substituted for vinegar, but there is no satisfactory substitute for olive oil. Connoisseurs of olive oil are almost as rabid as wine experts as to the region and vintage of the oil.

The basic Oil and Vinegar dressing may be doubled, tripled, or what you will, but keep the proportions constant: 1 of *wine* vinegar (made from grapes) to 3 of olive oil. If, however, you are using *cider* vinegar (made from apples and hence stronger), increase the ratio to 4 of oil to 1 of vinegar.

Garlic is as essential to Oil and Vinegar dressings as suspenders are to British trousers. So don't try to omit garlic. We are heartily in accord with Sydney Smith's admonition:

> Let garlic atoms lurk within the bowl
> And half-suspected, animate the whole!

MAYONNAISE

3 egg yolks	⅛ teaspoon white pepper
2 tablespoons vinegar	1½ cups oil
½ teaspoon salt	Juice of ½ lemon
1 tablespoon boiling water	

1. Have all ingredients at room temperature. For a better sauce remove the hard piece, or core, that clings to each egg yolk. Beat yolks together and then add vinegar, salt, and pepper. Use whisk, hand beater, or mixer.

2. Add oil by drops, then in a fine stream. Periodically stop adding oil and blend mixture. Use hand mixer on high speed, regular mixer on medium. After ½ cup oil has been added the mixture is thin, but then it starts to thicken with the addition of more oil and will be heavy when finished.

3. After all oil has been added, stir in lemon juice, and then boiling water, which will keep mixture from separating. Pour into a jar and refrigerate. Makes about 1 pint.

NOTE: We recommend making Mayonnaise in a blender. If you do, mix on *low* speed and use 1 scant cup of oil. More oil will clog the blender. Add 2 tablespoons boiling water.

VARIATIONS
ANETH MAYONNAISE
[*Dill Mayonnaise*]

2 cups Mayonnaise
4 tablespoons fresh dill, or 2
   tablespoons dried dill weed

½ cup crème fraîche or sour cream
2 tablespoons sherry
Green food coloring

Mix all ingredients. Add sufficient green coloring to give Mayonnaise a soft avocado color. Careful; too much will give a soft blue. Pour into serving dish, cover, and refrigerate overnight. Makes 2½ cups.

BOUQUET GARNI MAYONNAISE
[*Herbal Mayonnaise*]

2 cups Mayonnaise
1 whole bay leaf
½ teaspoon dried thyme

1 tablespoon minced fresh parsley
2 tablespoons crème fraîche
2 tablespoons sherry

Put Mayonnaise into bowl. Add remainder of ingredients, mix, cover, and let age at least 4 hours before using. Remove bay leaf and discard it at the end of 4 hours. Makes 2 cups.

CHAUD-FROID MAYONNAISE
[*Mayonnaise Glaze for Cold Foods*]

1 tablespoon gelatin
¼ cup cold water

2 tablespoons whipping cream
3 cups Mayonnaise

1. Soak gelatin in cold water in small pan. When gelatin has absorbed the water, warm over very low heat to dissolve the gelatin.

2. Add cream, warm, and then stir in Mayonnaise. (Have Mayonnaise at room temperature.) Use on fish and chicken suprêmes (pp. 401–402).

NOTES: Chaud-Froid Mayonnaise may be used in place of Béchamel Chaud-Froid. It is somewhat harder to use than the Béchamel Chaud-Froid because it is tricky to reheat if it sets. Its flavor, however, is often preferred to that of the Béchamel.

If Chaud-Froid Mayonnaise is lumpy, or becomes partially set, place the pan in a bowl of warm water. Stir while lifting the pan in and out of the water. Just a bit of heat will usually return the Mayonnaise to a smooth consistency. Then, if you wish to hasten the cooling process, use cold water, but no ice.

FINES HERBES MAYONNAISE
[*Seasoned Mayonnaise*]

2 hard-cooked egg whites
2 sliced shallots
1 teaspoon Dijon-type mustard
1 tablespoon washed capers
1 cup Mayonnaise
6 sprigs parsley
1 tablespoon dried tarragon, or
 fresh

1 teaspoon dried sweet basil, or
 fresh
1 teaspoon lemon juice
1 tablespoon freshly-grated fennel
 root, or of Pernod liqueur, or
 sherry
½ teaspoon sugar
⅛ teaspoon pepper

2 tablespoons crème fraîche

Put egg whites, shallots, mustard, and capers into blender container. Whirl on "chop" speed. Add half the Mayonnaise and remainder of ingredients down to the crème. Whirl to blend. Add remainder of Mayonnaise and crème. Blend. Pour into dish, cover, and refrigerate until very cold and set. Makes about 1½ cups. Use within 1 week.

MOUTARDE MAYONNAISE
[*Mustard Mayonnaise*]

2 tablespoons Dijon-type mustard   2 cups Mayonnaise
2 tablespoons sherry

Combine ingredients and mix well. Age overnight in refrigerator; then it is ready to use. Do not substitute our American-type mustards in this recipe. Makes 2 cups.

NOTE: If you have no Dijon mustard, blend 1 teaspoon dry mustard into the egg yolks before making Mayonnaise and then proceed to make the Mayonnaise, using recipe p. 405. Finish with sherry.

MAYONNAISE AUX FRUITS DE MER
[*Seafood Mayonnaise*]

2 cups Mayonnaise
½ cup catsup

2 tablespoons fresh lime juice
2 tablespoons horseradish, drained

1 tablespoon sherry

Mix all ingredients together. Refrigerate for at least 2 hours before serving. Makes about 2½ cups.

SAUCE SIMPLE DE SALADE
[*Oil and Vinegar Dressing*]

½ clove garlic   Freshly-ground black pepper
¼ teaspoon salt   6 tablespoons olive oil
                2 tablespoons wine vinegar

1. Mash garlic in salad bowl with spoon. Crush to a pulp. Add salt and pepper to give traction, and continue to mash the garlic.

2. Measure the oil and then the vinegar, using the salad spoon as the measure. Stir to blend. Dressing for a salad for 6.

VARIATIONS
CURRIE
[*Curry*]

Add 1 teaspoon (or more) of curry powder to the bowl along with the salt and pepper. Gradually add the oil, working curry powder to a paste, then add remainder of oil and the vinegar. Mix well. Serve on salad greens. Especially good with roast meats and fowl.

MOUTARDE
[*Mustard*]

Substitute dry mustard for the curry powder in the above recipe. Use as a dressing for watercress or Bibb lettuce.

VINAIGRETTE
[*Oil and Vinegar with Minced Parsley*]

To the basic Oil and Vinegar dressing add about 3 tablespoons minced parsley. Use on salad greens, sliced cooked vegetables, or thinly-sliced fresh, unpeeled tomatoes.

SALADES
[*Salads*]

SALADE VERTE
[*Green Salad*]

In French cuisine the salad is usually served as a separate course, and it is usually green. We have many varieties of lettuce and other greens to enliven the salad bowl. These include romaine, escarole, curly endive, Bibb, oak leaf, Boston, iceberg or head, and leaf lettuce; also Chinese cabbage, spinach, dandelion greens, and almost any other leafy green vegetable. Use one, or use an assortment, but keep the salad bowl green. Allow about 1 cup broken greens per serving. Guess at it, don't measure.

Wash the greens and then thoroughly dry them. Oil dressings will not cling to wet greens. Make the dressing in the salad bowl, then no flavor is lost. When the dressing is finished, cross the salad fork and spoon over the dressing and then add the greens, letting the fork and spoon hold the greens up out of the dressing. Cover the greens with a damp towel (not wet) and let stand at room temperature, but no longer than 2 hours or the greens may begin to wilt. Toss when ready to serve. Salads should be served cool, but not icy cold. When greens are refrigerator cold, they *hang heavy* with oil and lack both flavor and bouquet.

LAITUE
[*Lettuces*]

Break or tear dry, clean leaves into the salad bowl. If you cut them with a knife, the cut edges turn rusty. Also broken pieces are prettier than sharp-cut pieces. Serve with a simple Oil and Vinegar dressing (p. 408).

CRESSON

[Watercress]

When watercress is plentiful, treat the family to this great delicacy. Allow 1 small bunch per serving. Wash the cress and dry on a cloth towel. Break off the tough lower stems and leaves. (Turn them into a watercress potage, p. 49.) Put the *heads* in the salad bowl with a Moutarde dressing (p. 408). Good with roast pork or poultry.

ENDIVE

[Belgian Endive]

These innocent little stalks contradict everything I've said about the making of salads. They are white in color (blanched) because they have been grown without light. They are cut into the salad bowl and not torn. Allow about 8 stalks for 6 servings. At the moment of serving, slice the stalks into ½-inch thick discs, across the stalks, and add to a parsley-loaded Vinaigrette dressing (p. 408). Toss and serve. The bitter tang of this salad is something you will like. Like olives, it is an acquired taste; and once acquired, its taste will haunt you in early spring when endive becomes plentiful.

SALADE DE LÉGUMES

[Cold Vegetable Salads]

Cold cooked vegetables may be served with a Mayonnaise, or Oil and Vinegar dressing. Cook the vegetable according to its basic recipe, cool, refrigerate, and serve cold with Mayonnaise, or at room temperature with Oil and Vinegar. In France, these salads are normally served as a part of *les hors d'oeuvres variés* before the noontime meal. Leftover cooked vegetables take well to the hors d'oeuvres treatment. Here are a few examples from each vegetable group.

Artichauts (Artichokes). Slice artichoke *bottoms* and add to Vinaigrette, or serve with Fines Herbes Mayonnaise.

Cut artichoke *hearts* into fourths and marinate in Vinaigrette, or toss in a thinned Dill Mayonnaise. Dilute the Mayonnaise with 2 tablespoons cream and 1 of sherry.

Cook whole, leaf-trimmed artichokes, cool, then lift out the inside cone of leaves, exposing the downy choke. With a spoon, cut out the choke, leaving the artichoke bottom and outside petals attached to it. Serve whole artichoke with a small dish of Vinaigrette. Or serve with Moutarde Mayonnaise, turning the cone, from the inside of the artichoke, upside down and putting back into the artichoke once choke is removed. Fill the cone with the Mayonnaise and serve.

Asperges (Asparagus). Use cooked green asparagus or canned white spears. Serve with Vinaigrette or Fines Herbes Mayonnaise.

Brocolis (Broccoli). Serve icy cold with Fines Herbes Mayonnaise.

Carottes (Carrots). Cook carrots as in à la Vichy (p. 229). Drain when done and run cold water into pan to stop the cooking process. Drain again and blot on paper towels. Put into shallow serving dish and spoon Vinaigrette dressing over them.

Champignons (Mushrooms). Cook according to Carved Mushroom recipe (p. 281), cool, then marinate in Vinaigrette dressing. May also be served in Bouquet Garni Mayonnaise and sprinkled with minced parsley.

Concombres (Cucumbers). Use raw cucumbers. Peel, then slice in half lengthwise. With a melon baller scoop out the seeds. (In English-type cucumbers with very few seeds this is not necessary.) Cut cucumbers into $\frac{1}{16}$-inch slices. Toss with Vinaigrette dressing, or with Bouquet Garni Mayonnaise. Garnish with minced red onions.

Haricots Verts (Green Beans). Cook whole small beans. Serve in Vinaigrette dressing, spoon over Fines Herbes Mayonnaise or let guests dunk whole beans into a bowl of mayonnaise.

Pommes de Terre (Potatoes). Slice whole boiled potatoes and arrange them in a flat glass dish. Spoon over Vinaigrette dressing and let marinate. Or dice the potatoes, toss with plain Mayonnaise and place in a flat dish. Garnish with red onion rings. Grind fresh pepper over the top.

Salade de Tomates (Tomato). Cut out stem end from small fresh tomatoes. Do not peel. Stand tomato up, stem end on plate; slice vertically, in $\frac{1}{8}$-inch slices. Once it has been sliced, push the tomato over, thus separating slices in an overlapping fashion. Spoon a parsley-loaded Vinaigrette dressing over the sliced tomato. If you happen to like Mayonnaise with tomatoes, help yourself.

Salade Russe (Mixed Vegetables). Combine peas, and diced cooked carrots, potatoes, green beans, and turnips with Mayonnaise. Serve in a glass dish and sprinkle with parsley.

Barquettes de Légumes (Tart Shells Filled with Vegetables). Make pastry boats from Brisée recipe (p. 353). Fill with Salade Russe mixture.

NOTE: Any mayonnaise-type hors d'oeuvres may be presented à la Barquettes, or in tart shells.

(*continued*)

Cornets de Jambon (Ham Cornucopias). Cut 4-inch-square boiled ham slices a little more than ⅟₁₆-inch thick. Cut cater-cornered into 2 triangles. Bring A of the diagonal cut in illustration to point (C). Wrap B of the diagonal cut around the ham, making a cone. Glue with bit of Mayonnaise Chaud-Froid. Fill with Salade Russe made with a Mayonnaise Chaud-Froid (p. 406). Refrigerate at least 2 hours, then serve.

MARINADES CUITES
[*Cooked Marinades*]

In addition to the regular cold sauces (which could be called marinades), there are several cooked marinades, among them the famous à la Grecque and Mireille. These two sauces turn cooked vegetables into tasty pickles. A cold buffet normally displays an assortment of cold, spicy vegetables as a contrast to the meat and fish dishes.

CHAMPIGNONS À LA GRECQUE
[*Mushrooms in Marinade*]

1 pound large white mushrooms

Sauce

2 shallots, chopped fine	2 whole cloves
1 cup white wine	Juice of ½ lemon
1 fresh tomato, peeled and diced	½ cup chicken bouillon
2 cloves garlic, minced	2 tablespoons olive oil
3 sprigs parsley	½ teaspoon salt
Pinch of dried thyme	⅛ teaspoon pepper
½ bay leaf	1 tablespoon sugar

¼ cup Madeira

1. Wash mushrooms. Cut stems off even with the caps. Cut caps into quarters. Put quartered caps and the remainder of ingredients into an enamel-coated pan or skillet. Bring to a boil. Once boiling, lift out mushrooms and put into a Pyrex mixing bowl. Boil liquids hard. Reduce them to about 1 cup.

2. Pour liquid over mushrooms, cool, and put into a quart glass jar. Cover with lid and refrigerate. Age at least 24 hours before serving. Makes about 3 cups.

ARTICHAUTS À LA GRECQUE
[*Artichokes in Marinade*]

Cut 8 cooked fresh artichoke bottoms (p. 263) or 2 cans artichoke bottoms into eighths. Substitute for the mushrooms in the above à la Grecque recipe. Do no lift them out, but cook in the sauce until it reduces to the desired consistency.

CÉLERIS À LA GRECQUE
[*Celery in Marinade*]

Cook celery according to basic recipe (p. 251). Cut hearts in half lengthwise and substitute for the mushrooms in the sauce. Cook until sauce is reduced to desired consistency.

OIGNONS À LA GRECQUE
[*Onions in Marinade*]

Blanch small boiling onions according to the basic recipe (p. 231). Substitute for the mushrooms in the sauce. Cook onions in the sauce until it is reduced to the desired consistency.

ARTICHAUTS À LA MIREILLE
[*Artichokes in Tomato Sauce*]

6 artichokes

1 lemon, cut in half

Sauce

½ cup olive oil	Bouquet garni
1 cup white wine	⅛ teaspoon thyme
Juice of ½ lemon	Top part of 1 celery branch
¼ teaspoon salt	3 medium-sized onions
¼ teaspoon freshly-ground pepper	2 large tomatoes, or 2 cups canned,
½ cup chicken stock	peeled, plum tomatoes
1 tablespoon tomato paste	2 tablespoons Madeira

Chopped parsley

1. Wash and peel artichokes, as in Fonds d'Artichauts (p. 263), but do *not* cut the cone off the top of the artichoke bottom. Rub each artichoke with lemon juice and put into lemon-flavored water while peeling rest of artichokes. Then put peeled artichokes into a nonmetal pan. Add sauce ingredients down to the onions. Simmer 30 minutes.

2. Peel onions and slice. Separate into rings. Add to sauce and bring to a boil. Peel tomatoes, dice, and add to pan. Cook about 20 minutes. Liquid should be reduced to a thick sauce. Stir in Madeira. Put artichokes in serving dish and pour sauce over. Discard bouquet garni and celery tops.

3. Cool, cover and marinate overnight. Remove from the refrigerator 6 hours before serving. These are heavy with oil and if served cold the oil does not drain from them. Sprinkle with chopped parsley and present on the buffet table. Guests remove the cone and the choke for themselves.

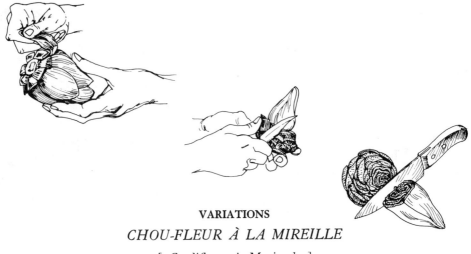

VARIATIONS
CHOU-FLEUR À LA MIREILLE
[*Cauliflower in Marinade*]

Break 1-pound head of cauliflower into flowerets. Peel the stems and blanch (p. 266). Prepare the sauce from the Artichauts à la Mireille. Cook sauce 30 minutes, then add the blanched cauliflower. Cook 10 minutes. Cool and refrigerate. Warm to room temperature before serving so that the oil will drain from the vegetable.

OIGNONS À LA MIREILLE
[*Onions in Marinade*]

Peel boiling onions and blanch (p. 231). Prepare Mireille sauce. Cook sauce 15 minutes then add the blanched onions and simmer 30 minutes. Cool, then refrigerate. Serve at room temperature.

See also the Aubergines à la Mireille recipe (p. 269).

PÂTÉS ET TERRINES
[*Molded Ground Meats*]

This special group of cold foods depends on no sauce, but derives its subtle flavors from a blend of ground meat or meats, fat, herbs, spices, and liqueurs. And, like most blended creations, these are best when allowed to age. Among these famous meat mixtures the uncooked, strength-giving Steak Tartare is one of the most popular.

PÂTÉ DE CAMPAGNE
[*Country Sausage*]

1 (¼-inch-thick) slice boiled ham, about ½ pound	¼ teaspoon thyme
1 (¼-inch-thick) slice veal, about ½ pound	2 tablespoons Madeira
	2 tablespoons Cognac
½ pound salt pork	2 pounds lean ground pork
1 shallot, minced	1 teaspoon salt
1 bay leaf	⅛ teaspoon pepper
	Sliced bacon

1. Cut ham slice into ¼-inch strips. Trim veal edges and remove any fat. Cut into ¼-inch strips. Cut salt pork into ⅛-inch-thick slices and then cut into ⅛-inch strips.

2. Put shallot, bay leaf, thyme, Madeira, and Cognac into a flat dish. Add the meat strips and marinate 6 hours, or overnight. Mix pork, salt, and pepper. Refrigerate both.

3. When ready to make pâté, line a 4-cup mold (or make 2 small molds) with bacon slices. Drain liquid from meat strips into the sausage. Mix. Put layer of sausage into bacon-lined mold. Add a layer of meat strips, then a layer of sausage. Repeat layers until all meats and sausage are used, ending with sausage.

4. Cover top of mold with bacon slices. Cut the slices to fit. Press down firmly in the mold. Cover tightly with foil, and set mold into a water bath. Bake in a 325-degree oven for 2 hours.

5. When done, take from oven, set mold into a pie pan to catch the fat, and weight the pâté down in the mold. Use a quart jar or other container filled with water and closed tight, or wrap a brick in foil and use, or improvise something else. The pâté must be pressed while warm. When cool, refrigerate with weight. When cold, turn out of mold and scrape off the congealed fat. Save fat to cook with—it has good flavor.

6. Slice the pâté thin and serve with pickles.

VARIATION

PÂTÉ MAISON

[*Sausage of the House*]

Use fresh ingredients or those left over from a Chicken Galantine (p. 394) to make this pâté. Line a mold or casserole with slices of bacon. Add a layer of sausage. Top with ham, salt pork, and veal. Then a layer of sausage and a layer of dark meat of chicken. Fill mold, ending with sausage. Cover with foil and set in a water bath. Bake in a 325-degree oven for about 2 hours. Remove when done, weight down, cool, and then refrigerate. Slice pâté thin and serve with pickles.

PÂTÉ DE FOIE DE VOLAILLE

[*Chicken-liver Pâté*]

2 pounds chicken livers	1½ sticks softened unsalted butter
1 clove garlic, minced	(¾ cup)
1 small onion, minced	1 tablespoon Cognac
1 teaspoon dry sweet basil	1 tablespoon Madeira
¼ pound unsalted butter	1 tablespoon cream sherry
½ teaspoon salt	Melted clarified butter
⅛ teaspoon pepper	3 truffles, minced
1 teaspoon anchovy paste	Watercress

1. Make pâté the day before it is to be served. Cut livers apart. Remove fat and white tissue. Be sure bile sack is removed (it is green and is attached between the two halves). Sauté livers, garlic, onion, and basil in ¼ pound butter for about 7 minutes. Do not overcook.

2. Lift livers to a plate and cool to room temperature. Freeze pan liquids to use at a later time. (When needed add ½ cup crème fraîche, or whipping cream, heat, and then thicken with beurre manié. Flavor with Madeira and Cognac and serve with grilled or roasted chicken. Call the dish Poulet à la Docteur à la Crème.)

3. Put livers into blender container. Add salt, pepper, anchovy paste, and the 1½ sticks softened butter. Pour Cognac, Madeira, and sherry into container. Whirl to blend. With a rubber spatula keep the mixture pushed from one side of the blender so that air can get to the bottom. Heavy mixtures in a blender must breathe or the blades will just whirl and not mix. Blend. Taste mixture and adjust seasonings. Try to make this pâté taste like the real goose-liver pâté.

4. Coat a 3-cup fancy mold with clarified butter. Put in freezer to harden. Coat again. Fill with pâté mixture. If there is pâté left, make some small pâtés. Cover tight with transparent wrap and refrigerate overnight.

5. Next day remove from refrigerator. Dip mold into warm water. Dry, set plate over mold and invert. If molded pâté does not drop out, run a knife into the edge of the mold to break the suction. Pâté should then drop out. If not, dip again in warm water. Once it is unmolded, with a paint brush coat pâté with cool, clarified butter. Refrigerate until butter hardens. Add minced truffles to the butter. Lift truffles from the butter with the brush and spread over the buttered pâté. Refrigerate.

6. When you are ready to serve the pâté, dip pancake turner into hot water, dry, then slip under pâté and lift to serving plate. Let pâté stand at room temperature for about 1 hour before serving. Decorate plate with watercress and serve with toast points or soda crackers.

VARIATION

PÂTÉ DE FOIE AUX TRUFFES

[*Truffled Liver Pâté*]

Make pâté according to above recipe. Add the 3 minced truffles to the pâté mixture and then pour into the mold.

NOTE: Meat pâtés can be baked in a crust, but I think they are better when not given this treatment. To be good they must be fat, and, as the fat cooks, the pâté shrinks. In the shrinking process there develops a gap between the meat and the crust. This hollow is often filled with gelée—but there is no way to scrape off the fat, for it is cooked into the crust. Also there is no way to press the pâté and make the meat firm and easy to slice. Therefore, I say pâtés are better when not served *en croûte*.

BIFTECK À LA TARTARE

[*Ground Raw Steak*]

3 pounds round steak, ground

1 teaspoon Fruit Fresh (ascorbic acid)

2 teaspoons salt

¼ teaspoon freshly-ground pepper

4 flat white onions, diced

3 flat white onions, minced

¾ pound unsalted butter, clarified

Flat anchovies

Capers (large Spanish variety, if available)

1. Trim all fat and white tissue from round steak. If you have a careful butcher, one who will understand that no pork must be in the meat since it is to be eaten raw, then let him grind it for you. Otherwise grind it yourself. Grind it only 1 time, for it should be coarse.

2. Buy the meat and immediately take it home. Put into a bowl and stir in Fruit Fresh (p. 605), to keep the meat from turning dark. It is best to buy the meat the day it is to be used, but it will hold 1 day with the addition of the ascorbic acid and not turn dark. Finish when ready to serve.

3. Mix in the salt and pepper. Put 3 minced onions into the middle of the meat. Heat the clarified butter and toast it to a nut brown. Do not burn. Pour the hot butter over the minced onions. Mix meat, onions, and butter together.

4. Place meat on white platter and shape into a meat loaf. Drain anchovies. Place them on paper towels. Cut each anchovy into 4 strips. Weave these into a latticework pattern over the top of the loaf. Into each diamond place a large whole caper.

5. Put 4 diced onions into a bowl. Add ice cubes and cover with cold water. Let stand 15 minutes, or longer. Discard cubes and drain onions in sieve. Blot with paper towels. (Washed onions are less strong.) Surround base of loaf with onions. Serve with hot, buttered toast points. Serves many.

NOTE: With individual portions of Steak Tartare, a raw egg yolk is often served on top and the individual mixes the yolk with the meat as he eats. But *never* should yolks be combined with ground meat in advance of eating. They change the flavor, color, and texture and create an undesirable stickiness.

THE MARRIAGE OF
FOOD AND WINE

by George Rezek

In Heaven, where marriages are made, there exists a special bureau for the matching of wine and food. According to the rules of this bureau, certain wines are thought to be most compatible with particular foods—the orthodox viewpoint. But, as things normally go in Heaven, it is clearly understood that what sometimes appear to be mismatchings turn out to be inspired combinations. Therefore, we feel that one should ordinarily follow the conventions in mating wine with food, while remaining fully aware of the fact that an unlikely twosome could, under the proper conditions, turn out to be a blissful duo.

It is very difficult to match wine and food perfectly. To begin with, not all wines are universally available. In Bordeaux one hardly ever enjoys a Burgundy, and the Burgundians rarely list a Bordeaux wine on their menus. The shops of Paris have all the wines of France but very few foreign wines. In this country we should have them all, but in fact only a few of our major cities come close to this high standard. Here or abroad the wine drinker has to know what is available in his own community and must work constantly to keep his own cellar well stocked.

The German wines, unlike those of the more amorous Latin countries, are not especially reared for marriage with food. All the highest-quality German wines, the "selected" or Auslese types particularly, are best when drunk

Dr. George Rezek is a Chevalier du Tastevin, Sir Bacchus of the Wine and Food Society of Chicago, and Chairman of the North American Committee of the International Wine and Food Society. It is from his fine wine cellar that such vintage wines as those that accompany the first classical menu (p. 431) have been selected.—*A.L.*

alone. Only the dry white wines of the Rhine and Moselle regions mate naturally with main-course dishes, primarily with fish, chicken, and veal. Most German dry wines, because they are so light and delicate, are overpowered by highly seasoned dishes or rich sauces. The great sweet German wines, like the Sauternes of France, are at their best when served with desserts and fresh berries.

Like the girl who is looking for a husband, you may have to be happy with the prospects that are around. In practice this means that you should know what wines are readily available before planning your menu. In other words, fit your food to the wine rather than trying to find wines that will fit your food. It is a simple fact of life that your choice of food is more variable than your choice of wines.

Economic considerations are also important to a successful marriage. If money is no problem, buy the best wine that is available as long as it fits with your food. It would be utterly foolish to match an expensive Burgundy with a simple sausage when a young, pétillant Beaujolais would be more suitable. If money matters, as it usually does, you should unblushingly hunt for the best in-expensive wine in the shop. Care and persistence will usually turn up a variety of acceptable prospects in any community. Make a game out of the search, and it will become as exciting as hunting a spouse.

GROUND RULES

Simple dinners with one main course may be served with one wine throughout. Slightly more involved dinners and complicated banquets require a progression of appropriate wines.

For dinners at which several wines are served there are a few guidelines to follow. Avoid, if possible, hard liquors. Precede dinner with a dry champagne, white wine, apéritif, or sherry.

Champagne classifications are: Brut (the driest), Extra Dry, Dry, Sec, and Demi-Sec or Doux (which has seldom been made since the Tsars). The last two are very sweet and usually served with desserts.

If sherry is your choice, its classifications are: Manzanilla (the driest), Fino (very dry), and Amontillado (dry). The sweet sherries are Amoroso (quite sweet), often called "milk sherry"; Olorosos (a dry sweet); cream sherry; and brown (very thick and syrupy sweet).

White wines, generally speaking, go best with light-colored foods and red wines with dark foods. But even this simple rule must be broken as circumstances require. Most fish are served with white wine. But all fish heavy in fat may be served with light red wines if there are other courses to follow. You might well serve a fatty fish with a fine white Burgundy, such as a Montrachet, but then you would be confronted by the problem of what could possibly follow such a great white wine.

This dilemma highlights the general problem of progression in wines. As a rule the lighter wines precede the heavier ones as you escalate to a climax. For example, when serving white wines with the soup and fish courses serve the lighter wine with the soup and the heavier one with the fish. When serving more than one red wine during a meal, let the ladylike clarets precede the masculine Burgundies.

Age is likewise a matter of concern in marriages and wine. Assume that you will serve nothing but clarets. The traditional way is to start with the youngest and work up to the oldest—deference to age! But such a scheme also has its pitfalls. Imagine a vigorous 1947 being followed by a tired 1924 and then by a robust 1953. It would be better to serve the 1924 with its fading charm at the beginning, followed by the hearty 1953 and then the superb 1947. While no rules really pertain strictly in this area of wine selection, it might be helpful to say that I have found that the clarets of fifty or more years of age are not as robust or stalwart as their young or middle-aged sisters and should therefore precede them on the table.

VINTAGES

What is all this talk about vintages and why are they so important?

A vintage wine is basically a wine of a particular year. Nonvintage wines are ordinarily a blend from several years. In addition to these, there are the condemned years. The weather in those censured years did not permit the grapes to reach full maturity, and the resulting wines did not reach excellent quality.

Vintage wines usually cost more than blended wines and both cost more than wines from condemned years. To get the most for your money, investigate the nonvintage wines and those of the condemned years carefully. They can be excellent.

The connoisseur who pays little attention to price and wants the best vintages he can find takes a number of points into consideration.

It does not necessarily follow that the older the vintage the more mature the wine. Weather conditions at the time when the grape was growing and the length of the primary fermentation period are essential factors in assessing maturity. A hot summer usually produces wines high in sugar and tannin content, and those wines will take a long time to mature. A long period of primary fermentation produces a wine high in tannin that will also take a long time to mature. Late-maturing wines last longer in the cellar than those which reach their zenith early.

Vintage wines always have an uncertain life expectancy. Bordeaux wines of 1945 were expected to reach their peak in 1957, but it is now thought that they will be mature only in 1977. The 1948 wines are still harsh and they need about five more years before they come into their own. As a contrast, the 1946 wines matured at an early age and are now beyond their prime. At the moment we should be drinking all the 1947 and 1949 wines available because they will never be better.

WINE SERVICE

White wines should be served chilled, but never ice cold—45 to 50 degrees is the best temperature. If you chill the glasses, the wine does not have to be so cold.

Light red wines are best when served cool, or at around 60 degrees. Heavy red wines are best when served at room temperature—or at around 75 degrees. The bottles of red wine should be opened and allowed to breathe for about 2 hours before being served. White wines do not need to be aerated as much, but do improve with breathing.

Normal estimates *per person* for wine:

> Apéritif—⅓ bottle Champagne
> Soup course—⅛ bottle
> Fish course—⅙ bottle
> Meat course—⅙ bottle
> Cheese course—⅛ bottle
> Dessert—1/12 bottle of sweet wine

Since the recipes in this book are designed for 6, we suggest 1 bottle for each course and 2 bottles for the apéritif. Note that wine is normally not served with the salad course. The vinegar in the salad dressing is not compatible with wine.

Glasses for all wines should be crystal clear, colorless, and unadorned with etching. The wine must be seen to be fully appreciated.

The shape of the glass is as vital as the shape of a girl. While girls may be narrow and slim, the wine glass should be rounded to resemble a tulip.

The bowls of the red-wine glasses should be slightly larger than those of white-wine glasses. Red-wine glasses have shorter stems than white-wine glasses.

The longer stem on the white-wine glass insures that your hot hand will not warm the chilled wine; therefore, lift the glass by its stem and not by the bowl when drinking from it.

Champagne glasses are of two basic types: saucer and tulip-shaped chalice. Saucer glasses allow the bubbles to escape too rapidly and encourage the Champagne to go flat. The tulip-shaped chalice holds the bubbles in the champagne and is generally preferred by connoisseurs. Hollow-stemmed glasses are to be avoided for they help to dissipate the bubbles and are a nuisance to clean.

Wine glasses of all types should be filled not more than half full, then the bouquet collects above the wine and below the rim of the glass. The bouquet is to be enjoyed as one drinks the wine.

PROGRESSION OF WINES

Apéritif. Champagne, any dry white wine, Vermouth, apéritif wines, dry sherry, or dry Madeira

Soup. White wine with consommé and potages or, with one of the heavy soups, a light red wine.

Fish. Usually a dry white wine, but there are exceptions. When the number of guests is small, the little white wine that accompanied the soup can be served.

Fowl. White or red wines depending upon how the fowl was prepared. Chicken cooked in red wine calls for a red wine, but when cooked in a cream sauce calls for a heavy white wine. Game calls for a red wine.

Meat. Beef and lamb normally call for a red wine such as a Bordeaux, Burgundy, or Rhône. Veal calls for a lighter red and may also be served with a heavy white wine, depending upon how it is made.

Cheese. Usually a heavy red wine.

Dessert. With fruit serve a sweet Sauterne, Madeira, sherry, barsac, Port, or one of the famous Moselle wines. For pastry-type desserts, semi-dry sweet wines such as demi-sec or extra-dry Champagne are preferred.

Coffee. Cognac, Armagnac, Marc, or liqueur such as Grand Marnier, Benedictine, Kirsch, Anisette, etc.

*The following charts are arranged, for the most part, according to avail-
ability in this country.*

WHITE WINE CHART

BURGUNDY WINES	BORDEAUX WINES

Première Classe (Expensive)

BURGUNDY WINES	BORDEAUX WINES
Montrachet	Château Haut-Brion Blanc
Chevalier Montrachet	Pavillon Château Margaux Blanc
Bâtard Montrachet	Château Carbonnieux
Genevrières Meursault	Château Laville Haut-Brion
Perrières Meursault	Domaine de Chevalier
Corton-Charlemagne	Château Olivier
Musigny Blanc	Château La Tour Aliéné
Clos de Vougeot Blanc	Dessert Wines:
Bienvenue Bâtard Montrachet	*Sauternes and Barsacs*
Chablis Grand Cru	Château d'Yquem (premier grand cru)
Chablis Premier Cru	Château Guiraud
	Château La Tour-Blanche
	Château Lafaurie-Peyraguey
	Château de Rayne-Vigneau
	Château Rabaud
	Château Haut Peyraguey
	Château Coutet
	Château Climens
	Château de Suduiraut
	Château Rieussec
	German Eiswein and the many sweet German wines that come from late pickings carry on the label the designations: Trockenbeerenauslese, Beerenauslese, and Auslese

Deuxième Classe (Moderate)

BURGUNDY WINES	BORDEAUX WINES
	Dessert Wines:
Pouilly-Fumé (Loire)	*Sauternes and Barsacs*
Pouilly-Fuissé (Burgundy)	Château d'Arche
Château Grillet (Condrieu)	Château Filhot
Chablis	Château Lamothe
Pommard Blanc	Château Myrat
Chassagne-Montrachet	Château Doisy-Védrines
Puligny-Montrachet	Château Doisy-Daëne

WHITE WINE CHART

BURGANDY WINES	BORDEAUX WINES

Dessert Wines:

Chablis Les Preuses   Château Suau
Meursault   Château Broustet
    Château Caillou
    Château Nairac
    Château de Malle
    Château Romer

Troisième Classe (Inexpensive)
Other Nationalities:

Muscadet (Loire)   *German*
Saumur (Loire)   Niersteiner
Vouvray (Loire)   Hochheimer
Sancerre (Loire)   Rauenthaler
Montlouis (Loire)   Liebfraumilch
Rully Blanc (Loire)   Steinwein
Hermitage Blanc   Schwarz Katz
Beaujolais Blanc   Nacktarsch
    Piesporter Goldtroepfchen
    Erdener Treppchen
Hungarian
    Villány Pécs
Italian
    Soave
    Frascati
    Lacrima Christi
Portuguese
    Vinho Verde Branco
Spanish
    Allella
    Valdepeñas Blanco
    Rioja Blanco

RED WINE CHART ❧

BURGUNDY WINES	BORDEAUX WINES

Première Classe (Expensive)

Romanée-Conti	Château Lafite-Rothschild
Romanée-Conti La Tâche	Château Latour
Richebourg	Château Margaux
Clos des Lambrays	Château Haut-Brion
Musigny	Château Mouton-Rothschild
Clos de Vougeot	Château Cheval Blanc
Clos de Bèze	Château Ausone
Les Bonnes Mares	Château Petrus
Grand Echézeaux	Château Montrose
Romanée-St.-Vivant	Château Gruaud-Larose
Echézeaux	Château Cos d'Estournel
Nuits-Saint-Georges	Château Léoville Poyferré
Corton	Château Ducru-Beaucaillou
Chambertin	Château Lascombes
Mazoyères-Chambertin	
Charmes	
Clos de Tart	
Clos de la Roche	
Clos Saint-Denis	
Malconsorts	
Volnay	

Deuxième Classe (Moderate)

Pommard	Château Cantenac-Brown
Clos Arlot	Château Kirwan
Les Corvées	Château d'Issan
Clos Maréchale	Château Palmer
Bourgeois	Château Lagrange
Artisans	Château Giscours
Pomerol	Château Branaire-Ducru
Santenay	Château Talbot
Montrachet Rouge	Château Beychevelle
Savigny-les-Beaune	Château Pontet-Canet
Volnay les Santenots	Château Batailley
Beaune	Château Bel Air
Clos-des-Mouches	Château Cantemerle

RED WINE CHART

BURGANDY WINES	BORDEAUX WINES
Les Grèves	Château Figeac
Aloxe-Corton	Château Yon
Côte Rôtie	Château Yon Figeac
	Château La Pointe
	Château La Fleur Pétrus
	Château La Croix
	Château La Fleur
	Château l'Évangile
	Château Gazin
	Vieux Château Certan
	Château Fanning Lafontaine
	Italian:
	Valpolicella
	Chianti Reserve

Troisième Classe (*Inexpensive*)

Chinon (Loire)
Bourgueil (Loire)
Beaujolais Group
  Mâcon
  Beaujolais
  Moulin-à-Vent
  Morgon
  Juliénas
  Brouilly
  Fleurie
Mercurey
Givry
Hermitage
Châteauneuf-du-Pape
Rully Rouge

Regional Wines
  Médoc
  Ferrière
  Marquis de Termes
  Saint-Pierre
  Saint-Julien
  Saint-Estèphe
  Margaux
  Saint-Émilion

Other Nationalities:
Hungarian
  Villány Pécs
  Egri Bikaver
Italian
  Bardolino
  Barolo
  Chianti
  Freisa
Portuguese
  Vinho Verde Tinto
Spanish
  Valdepeñas Tinto
  Rioja Tinto

AMERICAN WINES

American wines have their own charm. The vines that produce our wines were all imported originally from Europe and belong to the famed Vitis vinifera species of grapes. Though the vines are the same, our soil and climate produce a grape of different flavor.

American wines are known by their varietal and their generic names. The varietal wine is named after the grape that it is produced from, such as Cabernet Sauvignon, Zinfandel, Pinot Noir, Gamay, etc. By law, in California, a wine can be called after a particular grape if only 51 percent or more of the wine is produced from that grape. A varietal wine characteristically possesses the aroma, flavor, and distinctive color of the grape whose name it bears. Usually a varietal wine is superior to a generic wine, but not necessarily so.

Generic wines usually have a name of European origin, such as Claret, Burgundy, etc. American vintners who try to reproduce famous European types of wine usually use a generic name to help the consumer identify the wine.

Some American wines are created from a careful blending of choice grapes. Blended wines can be of very high quality and many believe that the blended wines, if properly handled, will have a great future. Normally the blended wines, unlike the varietals, cannot be traced by taste to a specific grape.

American champagnes carry the same designations as their French counterparts and the better ones are fermented by the French Méthode Champenois.

AMERICAN RED WINES

VARIETAL NAMES	GENERIC NAMES
Claret Types	
Cabernet Sauvignon	Claret
Zinfandel	
Burgundy Types	
Pinot Noir	Burgundy
Gamay Beaujolais	
Gamay	
Red Pinot	
Red Italian Types	
Grignolino	Vino Rosso
Barbera	Chianti

AMERICAN WHITE WINES

Sauterne Types	
Semillon	Sauterne
Sauvignon Blanc	Sweet Sauterne
	Haut Sauterne
	Dry Sauterne
Burgundy Types	
Chardonnay (Pinot)	Chablis
Pinot Blanc	
Folle Blanche	
White Pinot	
Rhine Types	Rhine Wine
White Riesling (Johannisberger)	
Traminer (Gewürztraminer)	
Sylvaner	
Riesling	
Grey Riesling	

MENUS

The perfect menu is a faultless balance of taste, texture, and color. Each course complements what has gone before and subtly prepares the palate for what is to follow. When a white sauce accompanies the first course, a dark sauce attends the meat. When orange sauce gives zest to the duck, an orange mousse for dessert upsets the menu balance.

The foods, like the wines, follow a distinct pattern in the French classical menu. The meal begins with the lighter and more delicate courses and vintages, and crescendos to the richer foods and heavier wines. It tapers off with salad to cleanse the palate, cheese to soothe the stomach, fruit to refresh the weary taste buds, and sweets to complete the fulfillment.

But a well-planned menu is only the beginning. Once it has been designed, the dishes included must be cooked to perfection and served with wines so carefully selected that each wine is a complement to the others, as well as to the foods. And the wine should never dominate the food. To be able to match wines with foods takes a great knowledge of wines. Over the years I have created a few meals of distinction. The menu for one of my most successful dinners immediately follows. It is the most nearly perfect of all I have made and it is the only one in which the vintage years are given for the wines.

Unless otherwise stated, "Salade" means a green salad with simple Oil and Vinegar dressing and "Pain Ordinaire" means homemade bread. All dishes listed in the menus will be found in the pages of this book.

MENUS CLASSIQUES

[*For 6 People*]

Apéritif: Dom Pérignon Champagne, 1961

Consommé à la Royale
Wine: Sancerre, 1964

Bisque de Crevettes aux Quenelles*
Wine: Montrachet, 1959

Ris de Veau Braisés sous Cloche
Wine: Château-Margaux, 1949
Premier Grand Cru Classé

Tournedos Belle Hélène
Wine: Corton, 1947

Pommes de Terre Gaufrettes

Salade

Fromage de Brie
Wine: Chambertin, 1949

Pain Ordinaire

Fruits

Gâteau Moka
Wine: Trittenheimer Mosel Eiswein, 1961

Espresso   Cigares

Cognac: Delamain et Bras d'Or

* Reduce Bisque de Crevette by a fourth, then thicken to
a sauce consistency with beurre manié, add quenelles,
and serve in shells.

MENUS CLASSIQUES

[For 6 People]

Potage Cressonnière

Filets de Soles à la Normande
Wine: Pouilly-Fuissé

Carré d'Agneau Grillé
Wine: Nuits-Saint-Georges

Pommes de Terre Château

Tomates Sautées à la Provençale

Salade

Fromage
Wine: Chambertin

Orange à la Cyrano
Wine: Château d'Yquem

Café   Cognac

Potage Crème de Champignons

Grenouilles à la Provençale
Wine: Savigny-les-Beaune

Poulet Sauté Fédora
Wine: Côte Rôtie

Pommes de Terre Anna

Asperges à la Polonaise

Salade

Fromage
Wine: Clos de Tart

Omelette Soufflée
Wine: Château Suau

Café   Cognac

MENUS CLASSIQUES

[*For 6 People*]

Consommé aux Quenelles

Fruits de Mer
Wine: Chablis

Paupiettes de Veau
Wine: Clos Maréchale

Pommes de Terre Château

Choux Brocolis au Beurre Noisette

Salade

Fromage
Wine: Chambertin

Mousse au Chocolat No. 2
Wine: Château Climens

Café   Cognac

Potage d'Épinards

Filets de Soles Farcis
Wine: Meursault

Poularde à l'Asturienne
Wine: Château Beychevelle

Pommes de Terre à la Parisienne

Salade

Fromage
Wine: Pommard

Marquise Alice
Wine: Château Guiraud

Café   Cognac

MENUS CLASSIQUES

[For 6 People]

Potage Crème de Crécy

Champignons-Quenelles sous Cloche
Wine: Bâtard Montrachet

Ris de Veau Braisé à la Sauce Madère
Wine: Artisans

Pommes de Terre Bouillies

Haricots Verts à la Polonaise

Salade d'Endive
Sauce Vinaigrette

Fromage
Wine: Richebourg

Fraises
Sauce Sabayon
Wine: Château Rieussec

Café   Cognac

Bisque de Crevettes
Wine: Hermitage Blanc

Tournedos à l'Ambassade
Wine: Valpolicella

Pommes Frites Pont-Neuf

Salade

Fromage
Wine: Santenay

Crème Renversée
Wine: Château de Malle

Café   Cognac

MENUS CLASSIQUES

[*For 6 People*]

Potage Cultivateur

Huîtres à la Florentine
Wine: Chablis Les Preuses

Canard à l'Orange
Wine: Saint-Émilion

Pommes de Terre Fondantes

Salade de Cresson
Sauce Moutarde

Fromage
Wine: Châteauneuf-du-Pape

Mousse au Café
Wine: Château Lamothe

Café   Cognac

Consommé aux Truffes

Foies de Volaille au Madère
Wine: Beaujolais

Turbot Bouilli à la Mère Martin
Wine: Montrachet

Pommes de Terre Gaufrettes

Haricots Verts Amandine

Salade
Sauce Vinaigrette

Fromage
Wine: Bourgeois

Soufflé au Grand Marnier
Wine: Château Romer

Café

MENUS CLASSIQUES

[*For 6 People*]

Consommé Demidoff

Escargots à la Bourguignonne
Wine: Bâtard Montrachet

Tournedos au Poivre
Wine: Châteauneuf-du-Pape

Paniers de Pommes de Terre Gaufrettes

Petits Pois à la Française

Salade
Sauce Vinaigrette

Fromage
Wine: Echézeaux

Pêches Melba
Wine: Château Rabaud

Café   Cognac

Champignons à la Grecque

Potage Dubarry

Suprêmes de Volaille Sauté Fédora
Wine: Hermitage Blanc

Carottes Glacées

Pain d'Épinards

Salade

Fromage
Wine: Les Corvées

Tartelettes aux Cerises
Wine: Château Crutet

Café

MEAL PLAN

To serve the above dinner to six people without help takes more than magic. It takes planning and organization. Therefore, write out a plan—it is easier than trying to remember. Here is how I would organize the last menu.

Two days before the dinner
   1. Do all of the shopping.
   2. Check crystal, dishes, silver, and linens to be sure all are clean and ready.
   3. Wash greens for the salad. Wrap in linen towel and refrigerate.
   4. Make salad dressing. Pour into glass jar, cover, but do not refrigerate. The oil will congeal if you do.
   5. Make Champignons à la Grecque. Cool and refrigerate in a glass jar. They should be aged.

Day before
   1. Make potage. Cool, cover, and refrigerate. Finish when served.
   2. Make tart shells.
   3. Cook Crème Pâtissière for tarts. Cool, pour into a nonmetal dish, cover, and refrigerate.
   4. Put cherries to soak in sugar and Kirsch. Cover and refrigerate.
   5. Wash spinach, cook, cool, chop, and refrigerate.
   6. Make cream sauce for spinach mold. Cool and refrigerate.
   7. Clean the dining room if you plan to do so; then the dust can settle and you can dust again before setting the table the next day.

Day of the dinner
   1. Guests are invited for 7:00, so plan to serve at 7:30.
   2. Pick up the house, then begin at noon on the dinner.
   3. Set the table. Be sure to use serving plates.
   4. Refrigerate the white wines.
   5. Pour potage into saucepan ready to heat. Keep covered.
   6. Combine liaison of yolks and crème for the potage. Cover and set aside ready to use. Place garnish with it.
   7. Take cheeses from refrigerator so they will be at room temperature when served.
   8. At 4 o'clock cook the carrots. When done remove from heat, cool by setting the pan in cold water, then cover and set aside. Prepare coffee, ready for perking or however you make coffee.

(continued)

9. While carrots cook put tart shells on dessert plates ready to fill.

10. Unwrap cheeses, arrange on serving plate, cover with transparent wrap and they are ready to serve. Put cheese plates beside the cheese in an unneeded spot.

11. Open wines. They must "breathe," before being served.

12. Take spinach and sauce from refrigerator. Butter mold and collar.

13. Make the Suprême sauce. Cover and set aside. Sauté the chicken. Place pieces on ovenproof serving platter. Finish sauce, then pour over the chicken. Cover with foil and set in cold water to cool. Mince some parsley, and wrap in a damp paper towel ready to use.

By 5:30 dinner is ready to finish and serve. Relax for 20 minutes, dress, and at 6:20 go back to the kitchen.

1. Heat oven to 325 degrees.

2. Heat water in an oven-proof pan for the water bath for the spinach mold.

3. Combine spinach, remainder of ingredients, and its cream sauce. Beat whites and fold into the spinach mixture. Pour into prepared charlotte mold, or similar container. Set into water bath and then put into the oven by 6:30.

4. If you are serving iced drinks, put ice cubes into ice bucket. Get out glasses, etc. If serving Champagne, put glasses in refrigerator to chill.

5. Put salad greens into salad bowl and cover with damp towel in which they were wrapped. Set dressing beside salad bowl.

6. At 7:00 put chicken into oven and put potage on low heat to warm. Put dinner plates into a second oven to warm, or place in hot water. Dry before using. Greet guests and offer drinks. At 7:15 put French bread into oven to warm.

7. At 7:20 put carrots on to heat.

8. At 7:25 spoon cold mushrooms onto bread-and-butter plates and place on serving plates at the table. Cut the bread and put into serving basket. Place on table.

9. By 7:30 the potage, carrots, and chicken should be ready to simmer. If not increase the heat and then reduce it to simmer. Everything must be hot, but nothing must burn.

10. Put soup plates out ready to fill and place ladle beside them. Light candles. Announce dinner and enjoy the meal. There is nothing you can do now but eat.

11. Clear plates and stack as they come from the table.

12. Add some hot soup to the yolk and crème mixture. Mix and then stir into the soup. Turn up heat, but do not let it boil. When hot, ladle into

soup plates. Garnish and serve. Check the chicken and carrots to be sure they will be hot. Eat soup and clear table when through.

13. Take chicken from oven. Arrange carrots around the edge of the platter and sprinkle chicken with minced parsley. Place on a mat on the table. Get the hot plates.

14. Set the spinach mold, wrapped in a napkin, on a plate and place on the table. Serve the dinner, eat, and clear the table. Pour cherries into a sieve to drain.

15. Pour dressing over greens and toss salad in the kitchen. Serve at the table on salad plates. Put coffee on to perk, or reheat if you have made the coffee in advance. Clear table.

16. Give guests cheese plates and let them make their own selection of cheeses. Serve some slices of unpeeled apple or pear with the cheese if you wish.

17. Clear table.

18. Fill tart shells with cold Crème Pâtissière and top with drained cherries. Serve.

19. Coffee, cigars, and Cognac in the living room.

NOTE: Have your husband, or a guest, be responsible for serving the wines.

MENUS DE BUFFET CHAUD
[*For 10 or 20 People*]

Buffet foods are designed to serve more than six. Usually guests do not sit down at a dinner table to eat. But if your dining area and table are large enough to give everybody elbow room, and you have enough comfortable chairs, have your guests sit down. Do not crowd guests around a dining table or perch them on foldup chairs. They would be happier sitting in the living room and eating "à la plat." Also do not invite more people than you have space for in the house.

Meats for the buffet should be in bite-sized pieces since it is awkward to cut meat while balancing a plate on one's lap. In other words, "fork foods."

The following menus are designed to serve ten, or more. The entrée, or main course, may be successfully doubled, but the quality will be better maintained if you simply make two or three separate batches at the same time. Also it is easier to prepare foods in small lots than in large quantities.

For ten guests I would make two recipes of each main food listed on each menu. For twenty I would make three separate pots of food with a recipe and a half in each pot. And I would never serve hot French foods to more than twenty. Most of the dessert recipes will serve ten, except for the mousse and

Bavarois. Make as many separate batches as you need, and do not double the recipes.

Once the hot foods are cooked, cool them, and then put them into casseroles ready to reheat in the oven. Most of these menus can be made a day in advance. Have foods at room temperature and then put into a 325-degree oven for 1 hour before serving.

Never double a rice recipe. Its weight will mat the grains together as it cooks. Make separate batches, then, when done, rinse in cold water, drain, and put the batches of rice into a large *flat* casserole. The weight of cooked rice would also mat it together if all batches were put into a deep casserole. Cover casserole with foil, but leave two ends open so the steam can escape as it is reheated. Put into a 325-degree oven 1 hour before serving.

Place the two hot foods on either side of a stack of plates on the buffet. Place the napkins and forks at the end of the buffet so that they are the last things to pick up, and not the first.

Suggest that guests make a separate course of salad and cheese. Have salad plates for this course. Put the wines and appropriate glasses on a sideboard and let guests serve themselves, or appoint "a husband." Serve a red wine with cheese. It may be the same red wine served with the main dish.

MENUS DE BUFFET
[For 10 or 20 People]

Blanquette de Veau
Wine: Hermitage Blanc

Riz au Blanc

Brocolis Froids
Fines Herbes Mayonnaise

Fromage
Wine: Beaune

Pain Ordinaire

Paris-Brest

Café

Choucroute Garni
Wine: Steinwein or Beer

Salade de Tomates
Sauce Vinaigrette

Fromage
Wine: Côte Rôtie

Pain Ordinaire

Éclairs au Chocolat

Café

Agneau Navarin
Wine: Pommard

Riz Pilaf

Salade

Fromage

Pain Ordinaire

Savarin

Café

MENUS DE BUFFET

[For 10 or 20 People]

Boeuf Bourguignonne
Wine: Montrachet Rouge

Pommes de Terre Bouillies

Salade d'Endive
Sauce Vinaigrette

Fromage

Pain Ordinaire

Bavarois à l'Orange*

Café

* Make as many separate batches as you need.

Cassoulet
Wine: Châteauneuf-du-Pape

Salade de Tomates
Sauce Vinaigrette

Fromage

Pain Ordinaire

Mousse au Chocolat No. 2*

Café

* Make as many batches as you need. Mold in individual servings.

Suprêmes* de Volaille Sauté Bazard
Wine: Moulin-à-Vent

Pommes de Terre Bouillies

Salade

Fromage

Pain Ordinaire

Tartelettes aux Abricots

Café

* Cut suprêmes into fillet-sized pieces.

MENUS DE BUFFET

[*For 10 or 20 People*]

Jambon à la Morvandelle
Wine: Volnay-les-Santenots

Riz Pilaf

Salade
Sauce Vinaigrette

Fromage

Pain Ordinaire

Orange à la Cyrano*

Café

Crevettes au Currie
Wine: Fleurie

Riz au Blanc

Salade de Cresson
Sauce Moutarde

Fromage

Pain Ordinaire

Sylvia

Café

Bifteck au Vin Rouge
Wine: Bardolino

Pommes Frites Pont-Neuf

Salade de Tomates
Sauce Vinaigrette

Fromage

Pain Ordinaire

Choux à la Crème

Café

SOUPER INTIME

[For 6 People]

Intimate small suppers are one of the joys of our Sunday evenings. Here are examples of what I mean.

Soupe à l'Oignon
Wine: Sancerre

Quiche Lorraine

Salade

Fromage
Wine: Moulin-à-Vent

Pain Ordinaire

Tarte aux Pommes

Café

Bisque de Crevettes aux Quenelles
Wine: Puligny-Montrachet

Salade

Fromage
Wine: Château Kirwan

Pain Ordinaire

Crêpes Flambées

Café

La Petite Marmite
Wine: Beaujolais

Salade

Fromage

Pain Ordinaire

Tartelettes aux Cerises

Café

SOUPER INTIME

[For 6 People]

Crevettes à l'Armoricaine
Wine: Meursault

Brocolis Froids
Fines Herbes Mayonnaise

Fromage
Wine: Château Talbot

Pain Ordinaire

Poires Melba

Café

Potage Portugais

Omelette aux Foies de Volaille
Wine: Brouilly

Salade

Fromage

Pain Ordinaire

Charlotte Malakoff

Café

Bouillabaisse
Wine: Clos Saint-Denis

Salade de Cresson
Sauce Mòutarde

Fromage

Pain Ordinaire

Pâte à Cassolette
avec
Glace au Café

Café

SOUPER INTIME

[For 6 People]

Poulet en Croûte*
Wine: Les Grèves

Brocolis Froids
Fines Herbes Mayonnaise

Fromage

Pain Ordinaire

Charlotte Glacée au Chocolat

Café

* Use deboned chicken breasts cut
into fillets for the Poulet en Croûte.

Quenelles d'Huîtres
Wine: Montrachet

Salade

Fromage
Wine: Château Palmer

Pain Ordinaire

Bavarois à l'Orange

Café

Foies de Volaille au Madère
avec
Croustades
Wine: Château Baleau

Salade d'Endive
Sauce Vinaigrette

Fromage

Pain Ordinaire

Ananas Bourdaloue

Café

SOUPER INTIME

[For 6 People]

Ris de Veau Braisé à la Sauce Madère
Wine: Pomerol

Salade

Fromage

Pain Ordinaire

Crème Renversée

Café

⚜

Omelette

Pissaladière Tartelettes*
Wine: Chianti Reserve

Asperges Blancs (canned)
Sauce Vinaigrette

Fromage

Pain Ordinaire

Charlotte Glacée aux Noix

Café

* Make in tart size and serve with the omelette.

BUFFET FROID

About twice a year, on a Sunday, we invite many friends for cocktails and buffet. A professional bartender makes drinks and once the party gets under way we have only to enjoy ourselves.

Foods are cooked the day before, but finished and decorated the day of the party. A lace tablecloth covers the dining table and all foods are placed on it at party time. Small plates stand at attention on each end of the table, but there are no forks. Foods are eaten on picks, crackers, breads, toast, or with fingers. There are plenty of napkins around and in sight.

Parties of this type are easy and fun. Everyone seemingly enjoys himself and no one leaves. Therefore, be prepared to make omelettes, toast, and coffee for those who linger late.

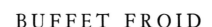

BUFFET FROID

[*For 50 People*]

Homard en Gelée
Mayonnaise aux Fruits de Mer

Galantine de Volaille

Chaud-Froid de Jambon

Pâté de Foie de Volaille

Bifteck à la Tartare

Haricots Verts Vinaigrette

Fromages Assortis

Olives   Cornichons

Crackers   Toast   Breads

BUFFET FROID
[For 50 People]

Boeuf à la Mode en Gelée

Chaud-Froid de Saumon
Aneth Mayonnaise

Pâté à la Maison

Jambon Persillé

Champignons à la Grecque

Pâté de Foie de Volaille

Bifteck à la Tartare

Fromages Assortis

Olives   Cornichons   Chou-fleur à la Mireille

Crackers   Toast   Breads

BUFFET FROID
[For 30 People]

Crevettes
Mayonnaise aux Fruits de Mer

Mousse de Jambon

Pâté de Foie de Volaille

Oeufs Farcis

Pâté de Campagne

Fromages Assortis

Olives   Cornichons

Crackers   Toast   Breads

PROVINCIAL MENUS
AND RECIPES

Every Frenchman is convinced that he is personally not very interested in *haute cuisine*. It is too tiring, hard on the liver, overpriced, and ostentatious. He will earnestly reassure you that the "true Frenchman" values nothing more than simplicity in food and wine. He really prizes the excellent preparation of a simple casserole far more than an elegant and elaborate sauce. If your patience lasts, he will then confide in you that the best dishes are really those of the provinces—especially the one in which he was born and brought up. And all of this talk usually occurs over an elaborate Parisian meal.

The provinces of France are really much more different from one another than are our states. Each one has its distinctive memories, cherished legends, and treasured customs. But no legend is clung to more tenaciously than a fervent belief in the superiority of the local cooking.

Viewed from the outside, the provincial foods of France exhibit many similarities as well as deep differences. Casserole foods—or the meal-in-a-dish—are universal favorites in rural areas. This preference is probably related to the old ways of village life. Until recent times the baker had the only oven in the village. On their way to the fields, the housewives deposited their casseroles in the baker's oven to cook. At noon they picked up their casseroles, bought their bread, and hurried home. A quick trip to the cellar followed to find butter, cheese, fruit, and wine (or cider). By the time the men wandered home, they were greeted by an abundant hot meal that was the delight and high point of the entire day. This happy way of life, with variations, persists even today in small villages of rural France.

Some of the provincial cities are, like Paris, highly reputed for their cuisine, especially Lyons. Most of them have food specialties that are known everywhere in France—the *hams* of Bayonne, the *ducks* of Rouen, and the *macaroons* of Nancy. Certain regional products are highly regarded both at home and throughout the gastronomic world—the *truffles* of Périgord, the *foie gras* of Alsace, and the *sheep cheese* of Roquefort. Many provincial dishes that emigrated to Paris still retain their identifying local names— *quiche lorraine, choucroute à l'alsacienne,* and *salade niçoise.* Other rural dishes appear in Paris in various guises and under different names. The soup or stew called *pot-au-feu* in the south becomes *hochepot* in the north; when Paris chefs clarified the broth and carefully cut the vegetables, it became the *petite marmite* of *haute cuisine.* The fish stew called *chaudrée* or *pochouse* in the country became a *matelot* in Paris.

The provincial menus and recipes which follow are typical and authentic and I have tried to select those foods that would appeal most to American palates. In the accompanying text, I have set out the "hows and whys" of country cooking. Local wines, or other beverages, are suggested with each menu. If they are not available, substitute a similar wine from the wine charts in the chapter on wines. And while it is customary in the provinces to drink just one local wine throughout the entire meal, I have suggested more than one on some menus.

Here is a sampling of what is available in French country foods. As you enjoy these everyday menus of the provinces, you will come to appreciate more fully how rich and varied the food heritage is that France has prepared for itself and the world outside.

ALSACE

Memories of long and expensive Franco-German wars are evoked by the name Alsace. Culturally more German than French, the Alsatians regard Parisians as "foreigners" from the heart of the country. The Parisians think of Alsace as the land of sauerkraut, sausages, goose liver, dumplings, soft pretzels, and beer.

Located between the Rhine River and the Vosges Mountains, Alsace is separated geographically as well as gastronomically from the the rest of France. The steep Alsatian slopes of the Vosges are covered with excellent vineyards that produce the grapes for Riesling wines. From the Rhine itself come the salmon that give to Alsace a fine fish course to eat in company with its superb white wines.

The food of Alsace, like that of Germany, is typically rich and heavy. Most dishes are cooked in fat rather than butter, except in the restaurants of Strasbourg. Cheeses, except for Munster, are not common. A relatively heavy meal usually ends with a fruit tart smothered with custard. Alsace is rich in everything and its cooks make the most of this bounty.

MENU

Suprêmes de Volaille à la Strasbourgeoise
[*Chicken Breasts in Pâté Sauce*]
Wine: Riesling, Traminer, or Guebwiller

Nouilles à l'Alsacienne
[*Alsatian Noodles*]

Salade

Fromage de Munster
[*Munster Cheese*]

La Tarte Alsacienne
[*Apple-Custard Tart*]

SUPRÊMES DE VOLAILLE À LA STRASBOURGEOISE

[*Chicken Breasts in Pâté Sauce*]

3 whole breasts of chicken
⅛ pound butter, chicken fat, or
    lard
3 tablespoons Cognac
Salt

3 (2⅝-ounce) cans pâté de foie
    gras with truffles
1 cup crème fraîche, or whip-
    ping cream, approximately
1 whole truffle, julienne cut

Minced chervil or parsley

1. Debone chicken breasts, remove the skin, and cut in half, making 6 suprêmes. Remove the fillet and take out the tough white tendon (see p. 146).

2. Sauté the suprêmes in butter for about 3 minutes on each side. Do not let them brown. Add the little fillets and cook about 1 minute on each side, or until the meat turns white. Pour the Cognac over them, heat, and set aflame. When the flame dies, sprinkle with salt, cover, and set off the heat.

3. Put 2 cans of pâté into an enameled skillet. Mash it and add enough crème to make a paste. Stir-cook to blend and then add the balance of the crème. If it looks as though it were going to separate, add a pinch of soda, which may stop it from doing so.

4. Spoon about ½ cup of juice from the suprêmes into the sauce. Mix, and then add the suprêmes, but no more juice. Set lid ajar. Simmer for about 10 minutes. Taste and adjust the seasonings. To adjust the flavor of a sauce use a bit of sugar and some Madeira as well as salt and pepper. Cut the remaining can of pâté into cubes.

(continued)

5. Lift the suprêmes to a hot platter. Add the cubed pâté and cut truffles to the sauce. Heat, and then pour over the suprêmes. Sprinkle with chervil and serve. This is a rich and delicate dish.

NOTE: If using oval cans of pâté, square off two of the 3 cans, mash the trimmings, and cube squared-off pâté.

NOUILLES À L'ALSACIENNE

[*Alsatian Noodles*]

3 quarts water	½ pound noodles
1 tablespoon salt	Bread crumbs

¼ pound butter, melted

1. Bring water and salt to a boil in a large kettle. Break noodles into 2-inch lengths. Add to kettle and boil until tender.

2. If you have some French bread that is dried out, turn it into crumbs, or use whatever bread you have on hand.

3. When noodles are done, drain, and pour onto a buttered oven-proof platter. Sprinkle with crumbs and spoon melted butter over noodles. Broil for a few minutes to brown the crumbs. Serve with any main dish that has a sauce. The noodles will have good texture and tend to be dry.

LA TARTE ALSACIENNE

[*Apple-Custard Tart*]

Crust

¼ pound butter, softened	2 tablespoons confectioner's
2 cups sifted flour	sugar
	½ teaspoon salt

4 tablespoons whipping cream

Filling

6 Jonathan apples (approx.)	Dash salt
1 teaspoon Fruit Fresh	¼ teaspoon cinnamon
¼ cup sugar	2 tablespoons flour

Topping

¼ cup sugar	2 tablespoons flour
Dash salt	½ cup whipping cream

1 teaspoon lemon juice

1. Put crust ingredients into a mixing bowl. Blend together. Put onto a floured board. Knead into a ball. Cut dough in half, making one piece slightly larger. Refrigerate the smaller piece to use at another time, or freeze it. Roll the larger piece into a circle to fit a 9-inch pie pan or plate.

2. Grease and flour the pie pan and then line with the rolled pastry. Crimp the edges of the crust between your thumb and finger. Preheat oven to 425 degrees.

3. Peel apples and drop them whole into water with Fruit Fresh (see p. 605). When all apples are peeled, blot each on paper towels and slice them off the core and into a bowl. Mix together the filling ingredients, sugar, salt, cinnamon and flour. Sprinkle over the sliced apples, toss, and arrange apples in the pie crust. If the apples are large it may take only 4 to fill the crust; if small, maybe 8. Do not fill the crust too full—just to the top of the pan; the apples will shrink as they cook. Bake on the lowest shelf of the oven for 15 minutes.

4. Combine the topping ingredients of sugar, salt, and flour. Add just enough cream to make a paste and then add rest of cream and the lemon juice. Pour over the apples and reduce the heat to 360 degrees. Put pie on middle shelf and bake about 25 minutes, or until the pie is brown and the custard set. Cool pie for 10 minutes on wire rack. Serve plain, or with crème fraîche and sugar.

NOTE: If using a Pyrex or enameled-iron pie dish, reduce oven temperatures by 25 degrees. Heavy pans, once hot, hold the heat. Or, reduce the cooking times by about one-fifth.

ANJOU

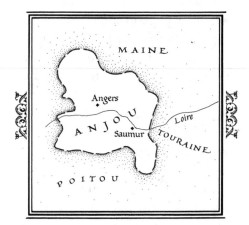

In the center of a land of milk and honey sits Angers, the historic capital of Anjou. Its cuisine is closely related to that of neighboring Touraine, but it is more distinctive and much closer to the soil.

Anjou, in contrast to the Touraine, is wine country first and foremost. Its light and sparkling wine demands agreeable and tempting foods. To eat in the Anjou style is to find a complete harmony between wine and food.

The light white wines of Saumur as well as the charming rosés and the fruity Muscadets of the rest of the region require foods that complement their flowery bouquet and pleasant tang. It would never do to serve a roast of beef with these heady and delicate wines. They call for fish, game, poultry, veal, or pork. The fish of the Loire are usually served in the famous beurre blanc, Anjou's supreme gift to the sauces of France.

The simple fruits and vegetables of Anjou become elegant when served in company with a fine fish. Homely cabbages take on an aristocratic air when they appear as part of an attractive menu. And the strawberries of this bountiful land go so well with its wines that it seems they were made expressly for each other.

MENU

Brochet au Beurre Blanc
[*Pike with Butter Sauce*]

Wine: Muscadet

Pommes de Terre Bouillies
[*Simple Boiled Potatoes*]

Chouée
[*Buttered Green Cabbage*]

Pain Ordinaire
[*French Bread*]

Fraises aux Crémets d'Angers
[*Molded Cream with Strawberries*]

Wine: Saumur (sparkling)

BROCHET AU BEURRE BLANC

[*Pike with Butter Sauce*]

Poaching liquid

3 cups water

1 cup white wine or vermouth

¼ cup wine vinegar

1 teaspoon sugar

1 carrot, diced

1 onion, sliced

½ teaspoon salt

6 peppercorns

1 bay leaf

6 sprigs parsley

1 branch celery, chunked

Fish

1 (2–3 pound) pike or striped sea bass

Butter sauce

6 shallots, minced (about 3 tablespoons)

1 cup Vouvray, or other white wine

¼ teaspoon salt

Dash white pepper

½ teaspoon sugar

½ pound creamed butter (keep it cool)

1. Put all of the poaching liquid ingredients into an enameled pan. Simmer for about 1 hour. Strain out the vegetables and discard. Cool the liquids.

(continued)

2. Wrap the fish in cheesecloth. Put it into a fish poacher, or long pan, and add the cooled liquids. Bring to a boil and then simmer about 25 minutes. Allow 10 minutes for every inch the fish is thick. If you guess its diameter to be 3 inches, poach the fish for 30 minutes, or a little less.

3. Put shallots, Vouvray, salt, pepper, and sugar into a small enameled saucepan. Boil liquids, reducing them to about 3 tablespoons. Remove from heat and set aside.

4. Lift fish from liquids when done, using the cheesecloth to do so, and place cloth and fish on a hot platter. Roll the fish out of the cheesecloth, and position it attractively on the platter. Skin the fish. Lay the wet cheesecloth over the fish and put it into a 225-degree oven to keep warm. Finish the beurre blanc sauce.

5. Reheat the sauce and then remove from the heat. Stir in a chunk of butter and add another piece immediately to cool the sauce. Now whisk in the butter, piece by piece. The sauce will become creamy, white, and thickened. Whether you will need all the butter will depend upon how much liquid was left in the saucepan. Serve the sauce in a small dish. Add boiled potatoes (p. 236) to fish platter and decorate with bunches of parsley, and tomato, and lemon wedges—although decorating foods is not a country custom.

CHOUÉE

[*Buttered Green Cabbage*]

1 (1 pound) head green cabbage	Salted water
	⅛ pound butter, melted

Freshly ground pepper

1. Cut cabbage in half. Lay cut side down on cutting board and cut into fine shreds, or cut fine on a slicer. Avoid the fat ribs in the cabbage leaves. Use only the green leafy parts.

2. Separate the shreds and drop them into boiling, salted water. Cook about 5 minutes, or until tender. Lift out of the water with a slotted spoon and place in serving dish. Pour melted butter over the cabbage, toss, and then grind pepper over it.

NOTE: For a change, sprinkle with grated Gruyère cheese.

FRAISES AUX CRÉMETS D'ANGERS

[*Molded Cream with Strawberries*]

1 (8-ounce) package cream
  cheese
2 tablespoons whipping cream
1 (8-ounce) carton whipping
  cream
Dash salt

2 egg whites
Strawberries for six
2 teaspoons lemon juice
2 cups crème fraîche, or
  sour cream
Confectioners' sugar

1. Have cream cheese at room temperature. Whip it, adding the 2 tablespoons of cream. Beat until light and then set aside.

2. Whip the cream until stiff and creamy and set aside. Add salt to egg whites and beat until stiff and creamy. Do not over-beat.

3. With a whisk, or hand beater on low speed, mix about ¼ of the whipped cream into the cream cheese to lighten it. Blend well. Add whites to the remaining whipped cream and blend with a rubber spatula.

4. Add ¼ of the whipped egg-cream mixture to the cream cheese. Blend together and then add another ¼, blend, and then add the rest. Try to keep all mixtures light and blend them together carefully. Avoid letting them lose their lightness.

5. Rinse a double layer of cheesecloth in cold water, then line a large, cone-shaped strainer with the damp cloth. Stand strainer in a 4-cup measuring cup (liquids will drain from the mixture into the cup). Fill the cheesecloth with the whipped mixture and fold cheesecloth over the top. Refrigerate overnight and until needed.

6. When ready to serve, wash the strawberries and dry on paper towels. Stir lemon juice into crème. Pour into a serving dish. Sift confectioners' sugar into a bowl.

7. Peel back the cheesecloth from the crémets and invert the mixture onto a chilled, shallow, serving dish. Remove the cheesecloth. Surround with berries.

8. To serve, spoon crémets onto serving plate, add berries and a spoonful of crème. Sprinkle crémets with lots of sugar. Guests dunk berries into more sugar and eat them with the crémets and crème. This is a very light and delicious dessert.

NOTE: There are special porcelain molds with holes right in the porcelain that can be used to mold crémets and other desserts, and are called Coeur à la Crème Molds, or Faisselle. But the cheesecloth technique works well and is easier to unmold.

ARTOIS

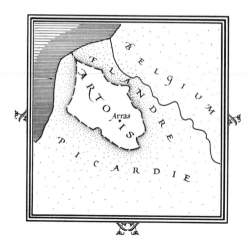

The homeland of the artesian well, Artois lies in the flatlands of northern France where streams flow sluggishly and cooking is dull. Located between Flanders and Picardy, it lies north and west of the wine belt. The natives of Artois, like their closest neighbors, are drinkers of beer and great eaters of the heavy and sweet-sour foods that seem to go with it.

Arras, its main city, was the first French center of weaving in wool and a great producer of superb Renaissance tapestries. Textile and other industries have ever since set the simple life style of Artois. Repeated invasions by foreign troops from Burgundy, France, and Spain also kept Artois from developing a distinctive cuisine.

A part of France only since 1640, Artois enjoys a style of cooking which is guileless and filling and almost utterly unrelated to the wine-based cuisine of the areas to the south. Essentially Artois eats the foods of Picardy and Flanders with a few admixtures from as far north as Belgium and Holland.

The revolutionary hero Robespierre was born in Arras. Small wonder that he was reputedly so virtuous and abstemious. With the frugal meals of Artois, there was little temptation to be otherwise.

MENU

Lapin à l'Artesienne
[*Rabbit Stew*]

To drink: Hard Cider

Les Pommes de Terre Dunkerque
[*French-Fried Boiled Potatoes*]
Salade de Chou Rouge (p. 574)
[*Sweet-Sour Red Cabbage Salad*]

Crêpes des Pays Miniers
[*Country Pancakes*]

LAPIN À L'ARTESIENNE

[*Rabbit Stew*]

Rabbit tastes very much like chicken and can be cooked by any of the chicken recipes in this book that uses wine. Rabbit is tougher than chicken, and so it is best when braised. Allow the same amount of rabbit to serve six as you would of chicken. The following has a mild sweet-sour flavor.

½ cup flour
1 teaspoon salt
Freshly ground pepper
1 (6–8-pound) rabbit, cleaned, or 4–5 pounds frozen, cut-up rabbit, thawed
¼ pound butter
2 tablespoons peanut oil
3 small onions, quartered
12 juniper berries
2 cloves garlic, minced
2 branches celery, cut into 4 pieces
2 bay leaves
6 sprigs parsley
¼ teaspoon dried thyme
2 (12-ounce) cans of beer
3 tablespoons vinegar
1 pound small mushrooms
1 tablespoon dry mustard
2 teaspoons sugar
4 tablespoons Cognac
1 egg yolk
½ cup crème fraîche, or whipping cream
2 teaspoons lemon juice
2 tablespoons minced parsley

1. Combine flour, salt, and pepper in a plastic or paper bag. Add rabbit pieces and coat with flour.

2. Heat butter and oil in a large skillet. Add the rabbit and brown. Add onions and ingredients down through the vinegar. When it starts to boil, cover, reduce heat, and simmer 1½ hours.

3. Cut stems from mushrooms even with the caps. Wash. (Save stems for

PROVINCIAL MENUS AND RECIPES

soup or stock.) Add caps to skillet and cook another hour. With a fork, stick the thigh of the rabbit to see if it is tender. When it is, discard the bay leaves, parsley, and celery. Pick out the juniper berries if you wish. Combine mustard and sugar. Add Cognac to make a paste. Add to the skillet. Mix well, taste, and adjust the seasonings; it may need salt.

4. Lift rabbit pieces to a serving platter. If sauce seems thin, thicken it with beurre manié (p. 2). Combine yolk, crème, and lemon juice. Stir into sauce. Heat, but do not boil. When thickened, pour over rabbit on platter. Sprinkle with minced parsley, and add potatoes to the platter.

NOTE: Plain boiled potatoes are equally good with this dish. If you cannot get rabbit, substitute chicken thighs, but remove the skin, and cook about 1 hour.

LES POMMES DE TERRE DUNKERQUE

[*French-Fried Boiled Potatoes*]

6 medium-sized potatoes	Oil for French-frying
Salted water	Fine, dry bread crumbs

1. Peel potatoes. Put whole potatoes into cold, salted water. Bring to a boil and cook until done. Do not overcook. Potatoes must be firm, yet done. Have the oil heated to 330 degrees and ready to use.

2. When potatoes are done, drain and roll in bread crumbs. French-fry until brown and crusty, or about 7 minutes.

CRÊPES DES PAYS MINIERS

[*Country Pancakes*]

1 teaspoon dry yeast	1 cup milk
1 tablespoon very warm water	2 egg yolks
1 cup flour	2 egg whites
1 tablespoon confectioners' sugar	1 tablespoon Calvados
¼ teaspoon salt	Clarified butter
1 tablespoon butter	Sugar

Butter

1. Put yeast into small dish. Add very warm tap water. Stir to dissolve. Put flour, sugar, and salt into large mixer bowl. Put butter into milk and warm. Separate eggs. Add yolks to flour mixture. Put whites into small mixer bowl. Beat until stiff.

2. Using the same beaters (do not wash), mix flour, and yolks and gradually pour in warm milk. Add Calvados. Mix into a batter. Fold in the egg whites. Mix well. Cover and let rise until doubled in quantity.

3. Stir down dough. Fry pancakes in clarified butter, browning both sides. Serve sprinkled with sugar and top with a pat of butter. Makes about 24 three-inch pancakes.

AUVERGNE

Like Japan, the Auvergne is a land of extinct volcanoes surrounded by high basaltic plateaus where mineral waters seem to spring from the earth. Unlike Japan, it is far from the sea and the people are engaged mostly in stock-raising and dairying in the upper regions and in agriculture in the rich plains and fertile valleys. Its people, like the Japanese, are tough, sharp traders, and very thrifty.

Auvergne is a land where the garlic is never hidden or whispered about. The famous soups, lamb roasts, and pâtés of the region are quite frankly dependent upon garlic for their special appeal. The dominant fat of the area is the lard of pig and goose, both of which readily purvey the reek of garlic to whatever they are put with.

Local wines of average quality for everyday drinking abound in the Auvergne. The Chanturgne red wine is the best of its vintages. In the spring the forests of Auvergne produce a bountiful harvest of morel mushrooms like those treasured in Indiana and Illinois. Among its most distinctive products are the cheeses of Cantal and the *Bleu d'Auvergne*. Each is made of cow's milk and each associates extremely well with the dark wines of the region and the succulent but heavy dishes.

MENU

Potage d'Auvergne
[*Lentil-Potato Soup*]

Daube de Mouton à la Chanturgne
[*Lamb in Red Wine*]

Wine: Chanturgne or Bourgueil

Salade d'Auvergne
[*Lettuce with Bleu Cheese Dressing*]

Pain de Campagne aux Noix
[*Country Nut Bread*]

Crème aux Pommes
[*Apple Custard*]

Sabayon No. 3
[*Frothy White Sauce*]

POTAGE D'AUVERGNE

[*Lentil-Potato Soup*]

This soup has excellent flavor and will remind you of the simple everyday soups served in small restaurants throughout France. It is an unattractive muddy color, and the dark bread slices add nothing but more brown. Therefore, I suggest using split peas, a specialty of Le Puy, instead of lentils for a fresh and appetizing soup. Garnish with brown croutons rather than slices of dark bread.

½ cup green split peas, or brown lentils

3 potatoes, diced

2 large onions, diced

2 carrots, diced

2 cloves garlic, minced

⅛ teaspoon thyme

Salt and pepper to season

6 cups water

Chunk butter, or 3 tablespoons bacon fat

Toasted dark bread (pumpernickel) slices, or croutons

Minced parsley

Soak peas or lentils about 1 hour. Drain, rinse, and put into a large kettle. Add balance of ingredients down to the butter. Bring to a boil and simmer about 1 hour, or until foods are tender. Grind through a food mill and pour into a tureen. Add a chunk of butter, stir, and serve over toasted bread and sprinkle with parsley.

DAUBE DE MOUTON À LA CHANTURGNE

[*Lamb in Red Wine*]

3 cups dry red wine

2 cloves garlic, minced

1 large onion, sliced

1 bay leaf

¼ teaspoon thyme, or 1 branch

4 sprigs parsley

3 pounds cubed, lean lamb

4 (⅛-inch-thick) slices salt pork, diced

3 tablespoons flour

1 teaspoon salt

1 teaspoon sugar

¼ teaspoon pepper

8 carrots, peeled and chunked

2 tomatoes, peeled and diced, or ¾ cup plum tomatoes, crushed

6 small, whole, peeled potatoes

Minced parsley

1. Put wine, garlic, onions, and herbs into a non-metal bowl. Add cubed lamb, cover, and refrigerate overnight, or for 8 hours.

2. Brown diced salt pork in a flame-proof casserole, or skillet. Spoon off all but about ¼ cup of fat. Add flour. Stir-cook about 1 minute. Drain marinade from lamb into casserole. Stir-cook until thickened. Add salt, sugar, and pepper.

3. Add lamb, carrots, and tomatoes. Bring to a boil. Cover and braise in a 325-degree oven for about 2 hours. After 1 hour, discard bay leaf, parsley, and the thyme branch if used. Add the potatoes, pushing them down into the sauce. If liquids seem thin, set lid ajar so that they will evaporate and thicken during the remaining hour. If liquids are of proper consistency, cover and cook another hour. Taste and adjust seasonings. Sprinkle with parsley and serve with crusty French bread (p. 530).

SALADE D'AUVERGNE

[*Lettuce with Bleu Cheese Dressing*]

The Bleu cheese of this area is famous, and so it is only natural that here one finds a Bleu cheese dressing served on salad. This fact, no doubt, will disillusion many of us who have always thought this dressing to be an American contribution to the world of food.

1 clove garlic

⅛ teaspoon salt

Freshly ground pepper

2 tablespoons white vinegar, or
wine vinegar

½ teaspoon grated lemon rind

1 teaspoon Madeira

½ cup mayonnaise

¼ cup whipping cream,
approximately

¼ cup Bleu cheese

¼ cup sour cream

½ teaspoon chervil

½ teaspoon crushed tarragon
leaves

Head lettuce to serve 6

Minced parsley and paprika

1. Mash garlic to a pulp in a salad bowl. Add salt (remember the cheese is salty), pepper, and vinegar. Continue to mash the garlic. Add lemon rind, Madeira, and mayonnaise.

2. Put whipping cream into a measuring cup. Add Bleu cheese to the cream until the cream measures ½ cup; thus you will have ¼ cup of Bleu cheese. Pour cream off the cheese and into the salad bowl. Mix well. Add the sour cream to the bowl and blend. Stir in chervil and tarragon. (Tarragon is the perfect complement to Bleu cheese. Be sure to add it.)

3. Break the Bleu cheese into small pieces and add to the dressing, or mash it into a paste and then blend into the dressing. Whirl in a blender if you want the dressing to be smooth. Add more whipping cream to thin to the right consistency, which is about like a thin mayonnaise.

4. Cut a head of lettuce, beginning at the top and slicing across, into thin slices. Place each slice on a salad plate and spoon dressing over it. Add a bit of minced parsley and a dash of paprika to make the salad more attractive.

PAIN DE CAMPAGNE AUX NOIX

[*Country Nut Bread*]

1 (⅝- or 0.6-ounce) cake yeast

6 tablespoons warm water

4 cups all-purpose flour

½ cup cake flour

1 teaspoon salt

1 tablespoon sugar

1 cup warm milk

1 cup chopped walnuts

¼ pound butter, softened

Cornmeal

Melted butter

1. Dissolve yeast in warm water. Put the flours into a large mixer bowl. Make a well in the center of the flour. Add the salt, sugar, milk, and dissolved yeast. Mix into a dough. Add the nuts and ¼-pound butter. If dough seems too stiff, add a bit of warm water.

(continued)

2. Turn onto a floured board. Knead until dough fights back. Cover with a towel and then transparent wrap to keep out the air. Let double for at least 2 hours. Knock down the dough and knead for about 5 minutes.

3. Sprinkle cooky sheet with cornmeal. Shape dough into a firm ball. Place on cornmeal. Coat with melted butter. Let rise for about 40 minutes. Preheat oven to 450 degrees. Slash the bread down the middle and about ¼ inch deep. Coat again with melted butter. Put a pan of boiling water on the floor of the oven. Reduce oven to 400 degrees. Bake bread for 20 minutes. Reduce heat to 325 degrees. Remove pan of water and bake bread another 40 minutes. Spray or coat with water twice during the last 20 minutes of baking. Cool on a cake rack, slice, and serve.

CRÈME AUX POMMES

[*Apple Custard*]

⅛ pound butter

8 Jonathan apples, peeled and
  sliced

⅛ teaspoon salt

3 tablespoons cornstarch

¼ teaspoon cinnamon

1-¼ cups sugar

2 eggs

6 yolks

¼ cup whipping cream

1 teaspoon lemon juice

2 tablespoons Kirsch

½ teaspoon vanilla

Butter and flour

1. Melt butter in saucepan. Add apples and salt. Cover and simmer until apples are soft and done. Grind through a food mill and into a bowl. Put back into saucepan.

2. Mix together cornstarch, cinnamon, and sugar. Blend into apples. Stir-cook until thickened and so juices are transparent. Remove from heat.

3. With a whisk beat together eggs and yolks until they are somewhat light. Stir in cream, lemon juice, Kirsch, and vanilla. Pour into apples and mix well.

4. Butter and flour an 8-inch square cake pan. Fill with apple mixture. Bake in a preheated 325-degree oven for 1 hour. Reduce heat to 300 degrees and bake another hour, or until brown and done.

5. When it is done, set on cake rack to cool. Run knife around edge of mold. Place plate over top and invert. Serve at room temperature with sabayon, or cover the dessert, refrigerate, and serve cold the next day with the hot sauce.

SABAYON NO. 3

[Frothy White Sauce]

5 tablespoons sugar	3 yolks
⅛ teaspoon salt	2 tablespoons white wine
1 egg	2 tablespoons Grand Marnier

2 tablespoons Kirsch

1. Put everything but Kirsch into top part of a double boiler. Put water (about 1 inch) into bottom part of double boiler. Be sure top part does not touch the water.

2. Beat with hand mixer on low speed while water comes to a boil. As mixture gets warm and begins to inflate, increase the speed of the mixer. It will take about 15 minutes of heating and beating to make the sauce. Mixture will triple in volume.

3. Remove from heat, add Kirsch, and pour into a serving dish. Do not scrape the sides of the boiler. Some yolk usually cooks onto the sides. Just let the sauce pour out and gently help it along. Good with any dessert that needs a sauce.

BÉARN, PAYS BASQUE

[Béarn and the Basque Country]

In the southwestern corner of France, bordering on Spain, live the Basques, who speak their own language, and the Béarnese, who speak French. While its people are divided by language and mountains, the cuisine of the Pyrenean provinces unites them into a gastronomic entity.

The Basques of France particularly enjoy the fish of sea and stream. But they have also learned from their neighbors an appreciation for the famous *garbure* and *poule au pot* of Béarn. *Garbure* is a sumptuous vegetable and meat soup that is served thick and steaming hot. Many of the local inhabitants, after finishing a bowlful, add a little red wine to the empty bowl, swish it around and drink it. Should any one object to this vulgarism, the offender replies: "His Eminence, the Bishop of X, likes it this way." Whether you decide to add wine or not, you will find the *garbure* a meal in itself.

The other renowned specialties of the region are associated with the city of Bayonne: sweet lemons (cedrat), hams, and chocolates. Jewish refugees from Spain reportedly brought the art of chocolate making to France in the sixteenth century. At the beginning chocolate was valued mainly for its medicinal properties. The addition of sugar to the chocolate made it into a confection and a drink that became popular at the court of Louis XIV.

With all these gastronomic achievements to their credit, it is no wonder that the cooks of Béarn are sometimes credited with inventing *sauce béarnaise*. It is much more likely, however, that this famous and delectable butter sauce was created in Paris around 1600 to honor King Henry IV, a native son of Béarn. Royal and delicate as this sauce may be, it is safe to bet that in Paris Henry must occasionally have longed for the hearty *garbure* of home.

MENU

Garbure Béarnaise
[*Vegetable Stew with Ham*]

Wine: Red Portet or Rosé de Béarn

Pain Ordinaire
[*French Bread*]

Salade

Pots de Crème au Chocolat
[*Chocolate Custard*]

Wine: Jurançon or Monbazillac

GARBURE BÉARNAISE

[*Vegetable Stew with Ham*]

This dish is a bunch of vegetables stewed together to make a porridge-like soup so thick that a spoon can stand up in it.

½ pound dry lima beans	4 cloves garlic, minced
½ pound dry white beans	3 potatoes, cut into ½-inch slices
1 (2-pound) smoked butt or ham shank (3–4 pounds)	3 slices bacon
2 quarts water	2 tablespoons minced parsley
2 cloves	⅛ teaspoon thyme
2 whole onions	¼ teaspoon basil and marjoram
4 carrots, chopped	Salt and pepper
2 turnips, chopped	2 bay leaves
1 rutabaga, chopped	2 dried red-hot peppers (small)
2 leeks, sliced	1 (1-pound) head green cabbage, shredded fine

6 slices rye bread, toasted

1. Soak lima and white beans separately for about 4 hours. About 1 hour before beans are to be cooked, start the *garbure*.

2. Put ham into a large kettle with the water. Stick the cloves into 1 onion. Add to kettle. Dice the remaining onion into the kettle. Add carrots, turnips, rutabaga, leeks, garlic and potatoes. Simmer 1 hour.

3. On one slice of bacon put the parsley and thyme. Lay second slice of bacon on top and add the basil, marjoram, lots of pepper, and about ½ teaspoon of salt. Add third slice of bacon. Put through a food grinder, using the

finest blade. Add to kettle. Put a piece of bread through the grinder to force out the remaining bacon and add this to the kettle.

4. Drain, rinse, and cook beans separately in salted water until tender. Wash and drain. Add the cooked beans to the garbure kettle. Add bay leaves and hot peppers. Cover and simmer about ½ hour. Remove the clove-studded onion, bay leaves, and hot peppers. Taste and adjust seasonings.

5. Add shredded cabbage, cover, and simmer about 30 minutes. Taste again and adjust seasonings. Remove ham. Cut meat from bones and put meat back into kettle. If you have made *rillettes* (p. 592) spread some of this potted pork on each slice of bread and place in soup plates. Spoon garbure over bread and serve.

After this rather heavy mass of vegetables, real mountain-folk food, you will enjoy a sliced orange sprinkled with Grand Marnier and sugar for dessert. But we are in the chocolate area and so I must give you a chocolate dessert too.

POTS DE CRÈME AU CHOCOLAT

[*Chocolate Custard*]

4 ounces German sweet chocolate	⅛ teaspoon salt
1 cup whipping cream	8 small egg yolks
2 tablespoons sugar	1 teaspoon vanilla

1. Put chocolate on a plate and into a pilot-heated oven to soften. This will take about one hour. Or soften chocolate by putting it into the top part of a double boiler and setting the top into the bottom part filled with very hot tap water. Cover and let chocolate soften.

2. Heat the cream, sugar, and salt to a simmer. Cool to lukewarm.

3. Beat yolks in mixer bowl until very thick. Add softened chocolate and warm cream. Pour into top part of double boiler and set over hot water. Be sure top part does not touch the water. Stir-cook until thick. Add vanilla and pour into pots de crème containers, demitasse cups, small goblets, or a serving dish. Cover with transparent wrap and refrigerate overnight, or for about 8 hours. Serve plain, or topped with whipped cream. Makes 6 small servings.

MENU

Poule au Pot d'Henri IV
[*Stuffed Chicken with Pot-au-feu*]
Wine: Madiran or Pacherenc du Vic-Bilh
Pain Ordinaire
[*French Bread*]
Salade
Crème aux Pommes
[*Apple-Crumb Custard*]
Wine: Jurançon or Monbazillac

POULE AU POT D'HENRI IV

[*Stuffed Chicken with Pot-au-feu*]

This is the famous chicken King Henry IV referred to when he said, "I wish that, every Sunday, my peasants of France may have *la poule au pot.*" This is indeed a king-sized meal!

Pot-au-feu

1 (3-pound) beef pot roast	3 leeks
2 pounds marrow bones	2 teaspoons salt
Neck and giblets from chicken	Freshly ground pepper
4 cups chicken stock	1 teaspoon sugar
1 cup white wine	8 carrots, chunked

6 turnips, quartered

Chicken

1 (5–6-pound) roasting chicken, or capon	2 eggs
¾ pound lean pork	2 teaspoons salt
½ pound lean veal	⅛ teaspoon pepper
3 slices bacon	1 tablespoon Cognac
1 tablespoon minced parsley	1 tablespoon Madeira
1 onion, minced	¼ cup olive oil
1 clove garlic, minced	1 carrot, diced
	1 onion, diced

2 cups chicken stock

Sauce

2 egg yolks	3 tablespoons flour
½ cup whipping cream	Cooking liquids
1 teaspoon lemon juice	Salt and pepper to season
Chunk butter	Beurre manié

(*continued*)

1. Put pot roast, bones, chicken neck and giblets, stock, and wine into a large kettle. Clean leeks (p. 607), tie into a bundle, add. Bring to a boil and then reduce the heat to a simmer. Remove the scum as it collects on top of the liquids and discard.

2. Make stuffing for chicken. Cut pork and veal into fine cubes. Cut bacon into very thin strips. Put these foods into a large mixing bowl. Add parsley, minced onions, garlic, eggs, salt, pepper, Cognac, and Madeira. Mix with a fork.

3. Stuff into the chicken. Sew opening closed with a kitchen needle and thread (p. 608). Tie legs to the tail. Tuck wings behind the neck. Sew in place, or tie.

4. Heat oil in an enameled casserole, or kettle. Brown the chicken on all sides. Use wooden spoons to turn the chicken. Spoon the oil from the pan. Add the carrots and diced onions and push down under the chicken. Add the chicken stock. Bring to a boil, reduce heat, cover, and simmer for at least 2 hours, or until done.

5. To the pot roast add the salt, pepper, and sugar after 1 hour of cooking. Cook another hour and add the carrots and turnips. Cook another hour, or until both meat and chicken are done.

6. When they are done, place the chicken on a large platter, remove strings, and surround with pieces of pot roast and the vegetables. Set into a 200-degree oven to keep warm.

7. Make the sauce. Combine the yolks, cream, and lemon juice and set aside. Melt butter in a skillet. Stir in the flour and cook a minute. Ladle 3 cups of liquids from the kettles and into a 4-cup measuring cup. Add to the skillet and stir-cook until thickened. Remove from the heat. Add a cup of warm liquids to the egg-cream mixture. Mix well and stir back into the skillet. Taste and adjust seasonings and thickness with beurre manié. Pour into a sauce dish. Spoon the sauce over the chicken and stuffing as it is served. Beef and vegetables are served plain. Serve in flat soup plates.

CRÈME AUX POMMES

[Apple-Crumb Custard]

6 large Jonathan apples, or 8 small
¼ pound butter
2 tablespoons Cognac
2 tablespoons Kirsch
½ cup sugar
Grated rind of 1 lemon
½ teaspoon cinnamon, or to flavor

Dash nutmeg
¼ pound butter, melted
Bread crumbs, lots
4 egg yolks
4 tablespoons whipping cream
½ teaspoon salt
Butter

1. Peel and core apples. Slice them into a saucepan with ¼ pound butter. Cook until tender. It makes no difference whether the apples fall apart or remain in slices.

2. When apples are tender, add Cognac, Kirsch, sugar, rind, and spices. Mix and cool.

3. Pour half the melted butter into an 8-inch pie plate, or pan. Coat sides too and sprinkle with crumbs. Let crumbs soak up the butter and add more crumbs until there is a dry layer.

4. Beat the yolks with the cream and salt. Stir into the apples. Pour into the crumb crust. Sprinkle again with lots of crumbs and pour over the remaining melted butter. Dot with more butter. Bake in a 325-degree oven for about 1¼ hours. Cool 15 minutes in pan. Run knife around sides of pan and then invert onto serving plate. Serve plain, or with sour cream that has been flavored with lemon juice. Serve brown sugar on the side for those who might like it with the sour cream. This is a delicious dessert, but must be served warm. It is no good the next day.

LE BORDELAIS

[*The Bordeaux Country*]

The city of Bordeaux is the commercial and cultural center of Guyenne, a large province in southwest France crossed by the Dordogne River in the north and the Garonne in the south. The two rivers come together at Bordeaux and so in a sense do the truffles from Périgueux to the north and the early vegetables from Montauban to the south. The wines on which the international fame of Bordeaux rests come from all its neighboring areas. Montaigne, who was for a while mayor of Bordeaux, was said to have had trouble with his digestion when he traveled far away from his native region.

Many Bordeaux dishes, like its wines, have become a part of international dining. A few specialties, however, remain exclusive to Guyenne. These rustic dishes feature the regional lamb, poultry, and game. In Bordeaux they often appear on menus along with dishes considered more urban, such as the delicate *écrevisses à la bordelaise*.

No matter what you eat from this region, it must be accompanied by its unequaled wines. The only problem in the Bordeaux country is to know which wine to select from the riches at hand. With country food, select a simple wine with body. With dessert, use a sauterne or one of the lesser sweet wines.

MENU

Tourin Bordelais
[*Creamy Onion Soup*]

Foie Gras aux Raisins
[*Chicken Livers with Grapes*]

Wine: Château Faubernet

Entrecôte à la Bordelaise
[*Steak with Bordelaise Sauce*]

Wine: Château La Commanderie or Cissac

Pain de Campagne
[*French Bread*]

Salade

Poires à la Bordelaise
[*Pears with Almond Cream*]

Wine: Château Suau

TOURIN BORDELAIS

[*Creamy Onion Soup*]

In the Bordeaux area onion soup includes garlic. Also, it is a cream of onion soup and therefore differs strikingly from the bouillon-like onion soup of Paris.

4 tablespoons bacon drippings	Salt and pepper to season
4 large onions, chopped	3 egg yolks
2 cloves garlic, minced	½ cup crème fraîche, or whipping
2 tablespoons flour	cream
2 cups chicken broth	1 teaspoon lemon juice
2 cups water	Butter

6 slices French bread, toasted

1. Put bacon fat into a large saucepan. Add onions and garlic. Stir-cook until transparent and soft. Do not let mixture brown. Stir in flour. Cook 1 minute or so. Add broth and water. Stir until it comes to a boil. Season with salt and pepper. Cover and simmer 30 minutes with lid set ajar.

2. Beat together yolks, crème, and lemon juice. Remove soup from heat.

(*continued*)

Gradually add 1 cup of soup to yolk mixture. Stir back into the soup. Do not boil. Dot with bits of butter and blend them into the soup.

3. Put toasted bread into soup bowls, or into a tureen, pour the soup over it, and serve.

FOIE GRAS AUX RAISINS

[*Chicken Livers with Grapes*]

Foie gras means fat goose or duck livers, and is not to be confused with pâté. Since these livers are not easy to find in the United States, chicken livers will substitute here quite acceptably.

⅛ pound butter	½ cup white Bordeaux wine
1 pound chicken livers	(Barsac if possible)
½ teaspoon anchovy paste	¼ cup chicken stock
1 clove garlic, minced	2 tablespoons Cognac
Salt and pepper to season	1 cup white seedless grapes
1 small tomato	Minced parsley
¼ teaspoon sugar	French bread, sliced

1. Preheat oven to 300 degrees. Melt butter in a shallow enameled *au gratin* dish or casserole. Cut chicken livers apart, remove the fat, and check to see that no bile sac is present. Add the livers, anchovy paste, and garlic to the melted butter. Stir with a wooden spoon until the livers are completely coated with butter. Remove from the heat and sprinkle with salt and pepper. Cover with foil and bake for about 10 minutes.

2. Peel, core, and remove seeds from the tomato. Chop fine and put on a plate ready to use. Remove livers from oven and lift them from the pan to a plate. To the pan juices add the chopped tomato, sugar, wine, and stock. Bring to a boil on top of the range. Reduce liquids by one-third, and then add the livers, Cognac, and grapes. Toss together. Cover and put back into the oven for 10 minutes.

3. To serve, sprinkle with parsley and spoon onto slices of French bread. Serves 4 as a main course, or 6 as a first course.

ENTRECÔTE À LA BORDELAISE

[*Steak with Bordelaise Sauce*]

6 delmonico or strip steaks

Sauce

1 cup red Bordeaux wine	⅛ teaspoon thyme
6 shallots, minced	1 cup chicken stock
¼ teaspoon salt	6 teaspoons chopped beef marrow
Freshly ground pepper	½ teaspoon lemon juice
¼ teaspoon sugar	Chunk butter
1 bay leaf	Minced parsley

1. Make sauce. Put wine, shallots, salt, pepper, sugar, bay leaf, and thyme into an enameled saucepan. Boil to reduce liquids to half. Add stock and boil again, reducing liquids to less than half, or until slightly thickened.

2. Strain sauce into a small bowl. Rinse out pan, dry it, and pour liquids back into it. Combine marrow and lemon juice. Add to sauce. At this point broil the steaks. When steaks are almost done, heat the sauce to a boil and then remove from the heat.

3. Cut butter into 4 pieces. Blend one piece at a time into the sauce. Serve a spoonful of sauce on each steak and sprinkle with parsley.

NOTE: Marrow is the soft material one finds in the round bone of a round steak, as well as in other bones. Marrow is a delicate, choice morsel of food. Buy marrow bones from the butcher, remove the marrow, chop and use.

POIRES À LA BORDELAISE

[*Pears with Almond Cream*]

2 cups red Bordeaux wine	¼ cup sugar
1 (1-inch) stick cinnamon	Dash salt

3 ripe pears

Almond cream

½ cup sugar	2 tablespoons butter (guess at it)
6 tablespoons flour	1 (2-inch) piece vanilla bean, or 2
¼ teaspoon salt	teaspoons vanilla
¼ cup ground almonds	2 tablespoons pear liqueur or
6 egg yolks	Kirsch
1½ cups whole milk	Sweetened whipped cream to decorate
¼ cup crème fraîche or whipping cream	

(continued)

1. Put wine, cinnamon, sugar, and salt into an enameled pan just large enough to hold the pears. Bring to a boil.

2. Cut pears in half. Peel and core. Add to the hot wine. Reduce heat. Simmer about 15 minutes, or until pears are translucent. Ripeness of the pears will determine the cooking time. When done, remove from heat and let pears stand in the hot liquid for about 10 minutes. Lift out. Cool liquid. Return pears to liquid, cover, and refrigerate.

3. Make almond cream. Put sugar, flour, salt, and almonds into a saucepan. Stir together with a whisk. Add yolks and enough milk to make a paste. Add remainder of milk, crème, butter, and vanilla bean. Set pan on an asbestos mat over medium-low heat. Stir-cook until thickened. This hot sauce is done when it is about as thick as a cold pudding.

4. Remove from heat, discard vanilla bean, or add vanilla if bean has not been used. Set pan into cold water. Stir sauce until cool. Add liqueur. Pour into a glass serving dish. Cover with transparent wrap and refrigerate.

5. When the sauce has set and the pears are cold, finish the dessert by combining them. Lift pears from the wine, blot on paper towels, and lay pears, stem end to the center, on top of the sauce. Pipe sweetened whipped cream around the pears, filling in spaces. Refrigerate until serving time.

BRETAGNE

[*Brittany*]

A peninsula that stretches farther out into the Atlantic than any other part of France, Brittany is surrounded on three sides by salt water. Even in its central region of gentle hills and swift streams, one is never far from the sea and its influences.

The Bretons, like their Celtic cousins of Great Britain, are seafarers. Like the Portuguese, they still sail to the Banks of Newfoundland to fish for cod. Along their own shores they cultivate oysters of several varieties and trap lobsters, both the *homard* and the *langouste*. From the rivers of Brittany come trout, shad, salmon, pike, and eels.

While it is not surprising that the sea provides a rich harvest of fish and shellfish, it comes as something of a shock to find that sheep are raised on meadows where the earth is still salty from the tides. The salt-meadow mutton from the island of Ushant off the tip of Brittany is the pride of the province. On the mainland sheep are raised in meadows fertilized with seaweed. Typically the internally salted meat is served *à la Bretonne* with locally produced white beans.

The Bretons, who finally gave up their political independence to France only in 1532, still retain their independent ways. They are inclined to disdain wine and to prefer cider. They make pancakes in every unusual, as well as usual manner imaginable, and are certainly the progenitors of the pancake house. They cultivate ducklings and pigs and have their own way of preparing them for the table. Simplicity and independence are the words which best describe both the Breton and his cooking.

MENU

Les Coquilles à la Nantaise
[*Scallops with Onions*]

Le Gigot à la Bretonne
[*Lamb with White Beans*]

To drink: Hard cider or Sancerre

Salade

Crêpes à la Fromage
[*Cheese Pancakes*]

LES COQUILLES À LA NANTAISE

[*Scallops with Onions*]

1 large, or two medium-sized
   onions, chopped
1 bay leaf
3 sprigs parsley
1 branch thyme, or omit
⅛ pound butter
2 cloves garlic, minced
½ teaspoon salt

Freshly ground pepper
1 pound sea scallops
½ cup white wine, or vermouth
¼ pound butter
4 slices firm-type bread
Parsley (lots)
Fine dry bread crumbs
Butter

1. Put onions, bay leaf, parsley, and thyme branch into skillet with ⅛ pound of butter. Sauté 20 minutes without browning. Add garlic, salt, and pepper. Cook 10 minutes. Lift out herbs and discard.

2. Cut scallops in half, making 2 scallops from each. Put into an enameled saucepan. Add wine. Poach scallops about 2 minutes. Add onion mixture to scallops and simmer 10 minutes. Remove from heat. Cut ¼ pound butter into 4 pieces. Add a piece at a time and stir until absorbed.

3. Cut crusts from bread, discard, and cut bread into cubes. Stir into the scallops. Let soak.

4. Remove buds from parsley stems to make ¾ cup. Put into a mortar and mash to a pulp with a pestle. The parsley buds must be totally destroyed and almost a liquid. Stir into the scallops. Mix well. Butter 6 coquille shells, or small au gratin dishes. Spoon mixture into shells. Sprinkle heavily with dry crumbs. Put a small pat of butter on top. Broil 4 to 5 inches from heat for about 10 minutes, or until browned and hot.

LE GIGOT À LA BRETONNE

[*Lamb with White Beans*]

1 pound dried white beans (flageolets)	½ teaspoon soda
	7 small, whole onions
1 (6-pound) leg of lamb, approximately	1 clove
	1 bay leaf
3 cloves garlic	6 sprigs parsley
Butter	⅛ teaspoon thyme, or 1 branch
Salt and pepper	3 shallots, minced
Water	1 large, fresh tomato

1. Soak beans about 4 hours in cold water. To soak beans too long (overnight) causes them to split in half and the hulls to float off.

2. Trim the tight, dry skin off the lamb if the butcher has not done so. Cut 2 garlic cloves in half. Insert these into the meat along the bone. Coat lamb with butter and season with salt and pepper. Roast on a spit, or in a 425 degree oven for 20 minutes and then at 325 degrees for about 2 hours. Lamb should be pink, not well-done.

3. Drain beans and cover with fresh cold water. Add the soda, bring to a boil and cook for 20 minutes. Drain, rinse the beans in cold water and remove any hulls. Add cold water to cover by 2 inches. Insert clove into 1 onion. Add to pot along with the remaining 6 onions. Add bay leaf, parsley, and thyme. Tie in a bundle if using branch thyme (bouquet garni).

4. Mince the third garlic clove and add to the pan. Add 2 teaspoons salt and bring to a boil. Reduce heat and simmer about 1½ hours, or until beans are tender. Eat a bean to test for doneness. Remove the 6 onions after 20 minutes of cooking. Set aside to use later. When beans are done, run hot tap water into the pan (to separate the beans), discard the herbs, and then lift the beans from the water. Put beans on serving platter.

5. Put a chunk of butter into a skillet. Add the shallots and cook 3 minutes. Add the cooked onions. Peel the tomato, remove seeds, and mash with a fork and then add to the skillet. Sauté these vegetables about 20 minutes, or until liquids are creamy. Add beans, stir and remove from heat.

6. When lamb is done, put onto oven-proof serving platter and into a 225 degree oven to keep warm. Add juice from roasting pan (not the fat) to the vegetables. Mix well, heat, and then spoon around the lamb. Put platter back into oven and heat at 325 degrees for 20 minutes to blend flavors. Slice lamb and serve with the beans.

VARIATIONS ON COOKED WHITE BEANS

SALADE DES FLAGEOLETS

[*Bean Salad*]

3 tablespoons olive oil
1 tablespoon wine vinegar
¼ teaspoon salt
Dash pepper

1 onion, thinly sliced
½ clove garlic, minced
1 teaspoon dried chervil or fresh
    parsley

2 cups cooked, cold beans

Combine ingredients down to the beans. Mix well and let age overnight. Add the beans, toss, and age for about 8 hours. These beans are normally served in an assortment of hors d'oeuvres, or they may be served on a lettuce leaf as a first course.

FLAGEOLETS À L'ANGLAISE

[*Beans English Style*]

To two cups of hot, cooked beans add a chunk of butter, salt, and pepper. Toss and serve sprinkled with minced parsley.

FLAGEOLETS AU VELOUTÉ

[*Creamed Beans*]

½ cup crème fraîche, or whipping
    cream
1 teaspoon flour

1 egg yolk
Dash nutmeg
2 cups cooked flageolets

Minced parsley

Put crème into saucepan. Stir in flour to make a paste, and be sure there are no lumps. Beat in yolk and nutmeg. Add beans and warm over very low heat, or use a double boiler. Mixture must not boil. When hot, serve sprinkled with parsley.

CRÊPES À LA FROMAGE

[*Cheese Pancakes*]

4 egg whites
4 egg yolks
½ teaspoon salt
5 tablespoons flour
1 (8 ounce) package cream cheese,
    at room temperature

3 tablespoons crème fraîche, or sour
    cream
Clarified butter
Softened butter
Sugar

1. Beat whites until stiff yet creamy. Then with the same beaters (don't wash them) beat the yolks until light. Add salt, flour, and cream cheese. Blend well and then add the crème.

2. Fold in the beaten whites. Mix well. Melt a piece of clarified butter in a skillet. When it is hot, spoon batter into skillet to make 3-inch pancakes. Brown both sides. These pancakes do not develop little holes on top to tell you when they are ready to be turned. Just guess and turn them.

3. When pancakes are done, put one on a plate, spread with soft butter, and sprinkle with sugar. Put second pancake on top of first, spread with butter and sugar, and then do the same to a third pancake. Serve hot with more sugar.

Variations. Combine 2 tablespoons Calvados and 1 of Grand Marnier. Spoon about 1½ teaspoons over the stacked pancakes and set aflame at the table. Or, flame the pancakes, let them cool, wrap, and refrigerate. They are delicious served cold and can be made ahead of time. When cold they may be cut like a layer cake. To make a pancake layer cake, make the pancakes about 6 inches in size, then butter and sugar each layer. These pancakes have endless possibilities.

BURGUNDY

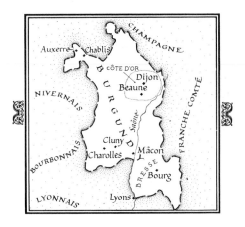

Jean Anthelme Brillat-Savarin (1775–1826), the great gastronome, is claimed by Burgundy. He became involved in the French Revolution and was banished from France under Robespierre's Reign of Terror. During the years from 1794 to 1797, as a refugee in America, he sadly missed the wines and foods of home. His exile from France taught him how important fine dining is in the enjoyment of life. Upon returning to his native France he wrote *The Physiology of Taste,* which was published just before his death.

Since Savarin's time very little that is new or different has been written about the foods of France. This is perhaps understandable for it is virtually impossible to write about the foods and wines of France without belaboring the obvious, especially in Burgundy.

Burgundy, unlike Bordeaux, has an abundance of fine food. In the south around Mâcon the wines are fruity and the food heavy. This is the region of Beaujolais wine and the best Charollais beef. In the center around Dijon the full-bodied and elegant red wines of the Côte d'Or provide the background for a rich, varied, and sophisticated menu that gourmets everywhere dream about. In the north around Auxerre lies the Chablis country. The presence of this finished white wine and the proximity of the Île-de-France region combine to encourage a simple cuisine. When taken as a whole, Burgundy probably provides more varieties of good eating than any other province of France.

To help you enjoy life in the traditional Burgundian fashion, not one, but three menus characteristic of the region follow.

MENU

Fonds d'Artichauts Farcis à la Hollandaise
[*Stuffed Artichoke Hearts with Hollandaise Sauce*]

Wine: Pouligny-Montrachet

Entrecôte à la Marchand de Vin
[*Steaks with Wine Sauce*]

Wine: Fixin or Gevrey-Chambertin

Salade de Tomate
[*Tomato Salad*]

Pain Ordinaire
[*French Bread*]

Poires Maxim
[*Pear Sabayon-Bavarian*]

Wine: White Sparkling Burgundy

FONDS D'ARTICHAUTS FARCIS À LA HOLLANDAISE

[*Stuffed Artichoke Hearts with Hollandaise Sauce*]

6 artichokes	Salt and pepper to season
2 cups minced mushrooms	1 teaspoon minced parsley
Chunk butter	Soft, coarse bread crumbs

Melted butter

1. Cut, trim, and cook artichokes (see p. 261). While artichokes cook, sauté mushrooms in a chunk of butter. Season with salt and pepper. Add parsley, stir, and taste. Tear about 2 slices of bread into small pieces. Let dry until artichokes are done.

2. When artichokes are done, turn upside down to drain. When cool enough to handle, remove the leaves from each artichoke. With a fork push off the edible kernel from the end of each leaf. Do this on a plate. It is not hard, but it takes time. Add this artichoke meat to the mushrooms and mix. Adjust seasonings.

3. Remove the cone and choke from each artichoke and discard (see pp. 261–62). Fill artichoke bottoms with mushroom mixture. Mound the filling high. Sprinkle with crumbs and drizzle with melted butter. Bake in a 500 degree oven for about 15 minutes. Serve with Hollandaise sauce (p. 21) as a first course, or as a vegetable course with broiled fish.

ENTRECÔTE À LA MARCHAND DE VIN

[*Steaks with Wine Sauce*]

The sauce here is nothing more than a Beurre Blanc, but made with red wine. It probably ought to be called Beurre Rouge.

6 delmonico or strip steaks, about 1-inch thick

Marchand de Vin Sauce

2 tablespoons minced shallots	Dash salt
1 cup red Burgundy wine	¼ teaspoon sugar
⅛ teaspoon freshly ground pepper	¼ pound butter, cool, but not cold
1 tablespoon minced parsley	

1. Have steaks at room temperature. Combine shallots and wine. Boil until reduced to about 3 tablespoons.

2. Broil steaks to desired doneness (see chart p. 220). While steaks cook, finish the sauce.

3. To the reduced wine and shallots add pepper, salt, and sugar. Bring to a boil. Add juice from steaks, if there is some, but not the fat. If no juice, add 1 teaspoon of Madeira and 1 tablespoon beef stock. Bring to a boil and then remove from heat.

4. Whisk in the butter in small amounts. Blend each piece before adding the next one. The sauce will thicken and become creamy. It should absorb all of the butter, maybe more, depending upon the reduction of the liquids. Add parsley, taste and adjust seasonings, spoon onto each steak, and serve.

NOTE: How much more sugar is needed in the sauce will depend upon the quality of the wine used. Sugar takes the edge off immature wine.

SALADE DE TOMATE

[*Tomato Salad*]

6 ripe tomatoes

Mustard Dressing

1 clove garlic	2 tablespoons wine vinegar
½ teaspoon salt	1 teaspoon Dijon-type mustard
Freshly ground black pepper	3 tablespoons minced parsley
6 tablespoons olive oil	1 teaspoon dried chervil

1. Do not peel the tomatoes, but remove cores. Stand each tomato on a salad plate. Cut vertically into thin slices and then push the slices over so that they lean one against the other.

2. Put garlic in the salad bowl, mash to a pulp with wooden spoon, and then discard the pulp. Add salt, pepper, oil, and vinegar. Mix well together. Stir in mustard, parsley, and chervil. Spoon over the tomatoes just before serving.

POIRES MAXIM

[*Pear Sabayon-Bavarian*]

Sabayon-Bavarian

1 envelope gelatin	3 yolks
3 tablespoons cold water	¼ cup Grand Marnier
6 tablespoons sugar	2 tablespoons Kirsch
Dash salt	½ pint whipping cream (1 cup)
1 whole egg	2 tablespoons confectioners' sugar

½ teaspoon vanilla

Pears

1 cup sugar	½ teaspoon Fruit Fresh
1 cup water	1 inch piece vanilla bean

3 fresh pears

Garnish

Whipped cream	Chopped pistachio nuts

1. Soak gelatin in cold water. Put sugar, salt, egg, yolks, and Grand Marnier into top part of a double boiler. Heat and beat with a whisk, or hand mixer, until mixture triples in volume. When it starts to go down, add the soaked gelatin. Beat until gelatin is dissolved and then add Kirsch. Remove from heat, set into ice water, beat, and cool until it starts to set.

2. Whip the cream. When it is almost stiff, add confectioners' sugar and vanilla. Beat until stiff. Stir into the cold sabayon-Bavarian when it starts to thicken and set. Pour into a glass serving dish, cover with transparent wrap, and refrigerate.

3. Boil together sugar, water, Fruit Fresh, and vanilla bean. Stir until sugar dissolves. Peel pears and remove cores. Add to the syrup. Simmer until tender. Remove from syrup, drain, and place on a plate to cool. Cover and refrigerate until icy cold.

4. When ready to serve, place the pears, core side down, on top of the firm sabayon-Bavarian. Put the whipped cream into a pastry bag with a star nozzle. Pipe the cream around each pear, filling the space completely, and then sprinkle with pistachio nuts. Cover and refrigerate until the moment of serving.

MENU

Le Cochon de Lait Farci
[*Stuffed Suckling Pig*]

Wine: Moulin-à-Vent or Pommard

Nouilles
[*Noodles*]

Salade au Cresson
[*Watercress Salad*]

Charlotte aux Pommes
[*Apple Pudding*]

Crème à l'Anglaise
[*Cream Sauce*]

LE COCHON DE LAIT FARCI

[*Stuffed Suckling Pig*]

1 (12–15-pound) suckling pig	½ cup white wine
½ cup Sultana raisins	1 cup minced celery
Boiling water	2 carrots, shredded fine
Cognac	2 cups minced mushrooms
Salt and pepper	½ cup minced parsley
1 pound chicken livers, diced	2 tablespoons Madeira
1 pound calf's liver, diced	2 egg yolks, or more
Butter	1 whole egg
1 large onion, diced	3 carrots, quartered
4 shallots, minced	3 onions, sliced
1 clove garlic, minced	2 cloves garlic, sliced
4 slices bacon, diced	Olive oil
½ pound sausage meat	2 cups white wine

Spiced crabapple and parsley

Sauce

2 shallots, minced	1 cup chicken stock
Butter	Soaked raisins and their liquids
2 tablespoons flour	½ teaspoon sugar
1 cup white wine	Pan liquids

1. Small pigs are difficult to come by. Be sure the pig will fit into your oven. A 12- to 15-pound pig is about as small as a piglet comes, and while he

may weigh less than a 20-pound turkey, he is not the same shape. Therefore, do consider the length of the pig and the size of your oven before purchasing the pig.

2. The day before cooking the pig, prepare the raisins. Pour boiling water over raisins and let them soak for 1 hour. Drain and cover with Cognac. Let them marinate at room temperature overnight.

3. Splash the interior of the pig with Cognac and season with salt and pepper. Let marinate while making the stuffing.

4. Sauté both diced livers in a large chunk of butter for about 5 minutes. Put into a bowl. Sauté onions, shallots, and garlic in more butter and add to the bowl. Fry the diced bacon. Lift bacon from fat to the bowl. Discard fat. Sauté sausage meat, mashing it as it fries. Add ½ cup white wine and bring to a boil. Simmer 10 minutes. Add to bowl. Add celery, carrots, mushrooms, parsley, ¼ cup Cognac, and Madeira. Mix well. Preheat oven to 500 degrees.

5. Squeeze Cognac from half the raisins. Add to stuffing and mix. Add yolks, egg, 1 teaspoon salt, and pepper. Mix and then fry a teaspoonful in some butter and see if the stuffing will hold together when it is fried. Taste the fried cake and adjust seasonings. If it does not hold together, add another yolk or an egg (your decision—yolk will make it heavier, an egg will make it heavier and lighter). Test again. Stuffing is soft and liquid, but will firm as it fries, or roasts.

6. Lay pig on its back. Add the stuffing. It will probably not fill the pig, depending upon its size, but it will give good flavor and is delicious to eat. Sew opening closed with a kitchen needle and string. Remove rack from broiler pan. Cover pan with heavy duty foil, extending the foil over the edges of the pan. Grease the foil. Place quartered carrots, sliced onions, and garlic on foil.

7. Place piglet on this bed of vegetables, belly-side down. Tuck the front feet back under the pig. Stretch out the back feet (if your oven can take it, otherwise tuck them under the pig too). With a sharp knife make small cuts in the skin so that the fat can cook out of the pig. Brush entire surface of pig with olive oil. Wrap a piece of foil around the tail and shape it into an attractive position. Wrap the ears with foil and in an upright position. Put a ball of foil into the pig's mouth to hold it open. A spiced crabapple will replace the foil once the pig is cooked. Pour 2 cups of wine into foil.

8. Put piglet into a 500 degree oven for 10 minutes. Reduce heat to 350 degrees and roast 25 minutes per pound, or 5 to 6 hours for a 12-pound pig. Brush every 30 minutes with oil. For the last two hours of roasting remove foil from ears and tail. Coat with oil and let these parts brown. Reduce temperature to 325 degrees.

9. An hour before pig is done, make the sauce. Sauté shallots in a chunk

of butter until soft. Add flour. Stir-cook 2 minutes. Add wine and stock and stir until thickened. Set lid ajar and simmer over very low heat for 1 hour. When pig is about done, add the remaining raisins, their Cognac, and sugar. Bring to a boil, reduce heat, and simmer 15 minutes. Now turn your attention to the pig.

10. When pig is done, spoon liquids and fat from the foil into a bowl before moving the pig. Lift piglet from broiler, using the foil as a hammock to transport the pig to a very large platter. Tear out the foil from underneath the pig and discard the cooked vegetables.

11. Remove ball of foil from the mouth and insert a spiced crabapple, or a bunch of parsley. If the eyes bother you, they will others too. Insert a wooden pick into stuffed olives and then insert the pick into the eyes. Tie a string around the neck and tuck parsley sprigs under the string to make a lei. The pig is now ready to present at the table.

12. Spoon juice from the fat (juice goes to the bottom). Tip pan to one side so that a well of liquids forms on one side of the pan. Push a ladle down through the fat and into the juice, fill it with juice and then lift up through the fat. Add about 4 tablespoons of juice to the sauce. Taste and adjust seasonings. Serve separately with the piglet.

TO SERVE: Cut down through the middle of the rack of chops and the stuffing. Carve toward the hindquarters, serving them first, and then carve the forelegs. Carving is a bit tricky, but only because we do not carve as many pigs as we do chickens. Serve stuffing too.

NOTE: The stuffing may be used to stuff poultry or game. Reduce the quantities accordingly.

NOUILLES
[*Noodles*]

2 cups flour   2 eggs
½ teaspoon salt   2 egg whites

Warm water to make a dough

1. Put flour and salt into mixer bowl. Make a well in the center. Add eggs and whites. Turn on mixer and gradually add water to make a smooth dough.

2. Knead a few minutes. Cover with transparent wrap and let dough rest for about 2 hours. Be sure dough is covered so that it will not dry out.

3. Make 2 pieces from the dough by squeezing it in half with your hand. Lay 1 piece aside and cover well. Roll each piece very thin, sprinkle with flour, and then roll it up and cut into the widths you want noodles to be—¼ inch,

⅛ inch, or 2 inches. If you make an assortment of widths, keep them separate. Put cut noodles on a kitchen towel to dry. If not used within a day or two, let them dry completely and then store until needed.

4. Cook in lots of boiling, salted water for about 10 minutes, or until done. Drain, butter, and serve. Use in casserole dishes, or other recipes.

NOTE: To make green noodles, substitute ¼ cup cooked, pureed spinach for the water.

SALADE AU CRESSON
[*Watercress Salad*]

Watercress for six

Dressing

½ clove garlic	½ teaspoon Dijon-type mustard
½ teaspoon salt	3 tablespoons olive oil
Dash sugar	2 teaspoons wine vinegar
Freshly ground pepper	Lettuce leaves

1. Break heavy, tough stems from watercress and discard. Wash, dry, and wrap in a terry towel. Refrigerate overnight.

2. Mash garlic in salad bowl. Add salt, sugar, and pepper and continue to mash. Add mustard, oil, and vinegar. Blend.

3. Put a lettuce leaf on each salad plate (will help to extend the watercress). Toss watercress in the dressing and spoon onto lettuce. Serve.

CHARLOTTE AUX POMMES
[*Apple Pudding*]

¼ pound butter	1 teaspoon vanilla
8 Jonathan apples	Firm-type bread
1 cup sugar, approximately	Melted, clarified butter

1. Melt butter in a sauce pan. Peel apples and slice from the core and into the pan. Cover and cook until soft. Add sugar (amount will depend upon the tartness of the apples) and cook until dissolved and moisture evaporated. Stir in vanilla.

2. Cut crusts from several slices of bread. Turn a 5-cup charlotte mold upside down. Cut triangles from the trimmed bread to fit the bottom of the mold. Now turn the mold rightside up. Dip triangles into melted butter and wedge them into the bottom of the mold. With a small round cutter, like the

hole of a doughnut cutter, cut the points off the bread (they do not fit well) and then cut a round from a slice of bread, dip into butter, and drop into the center of the bread triangles.

3. Cut strips 1½ by 4 inches from trimmed bread slices. Dip these, one side only, into the melted butter and place buttered side to the mold in over-lapping fashion around the inside. Overlap slices by about ⅜ of an inch.

4. Into this bread-lined mold, spoon the cooked apples. Bake in a 350 degree oven for about 30 minutes. Reduce heat to 325 degrees and bake another 20 minutes. Cool and refrigerate overnight or about 4 hours. Make sauce now and chill, or make it the day before. When ready to serve, invert the dessert into a shallow serving dish. Pour a moat of cream sauce around the dessert. Cut into wedges and serve at the table along with the sauce. Serve remaining sauce on the side.

CRÈME À L'ANGLAISE

[Cream Sauce]

2 cups milk	¼ cup crème fraîche, or whipping
6 egg yolks	cream
¾ cup sugar	2 tablespoons Grand Marnier
½ teaspoon salt	1 tablespoon Kirsch

1. Scald the milk. Beat yolks, sugar, and salt together in small mixer bowl. Gradually beat in the hot milk, then pour back into the pan the milk was in.

2. Set pan on an asbestos mat and cook over direct heat, or cook the sauce in a double boiler. It must not get too hot, and it must not boil. Stir-cook over very low heat until the sauce thickens. The foam on top will disappear as the sauce becomes cooked. Also there is a color change.

3. Remove from heat when done. Set pan into cold water. Stir until cool. Add crème, Grand Marnier, and Kirsch. Strain sauce into a serving dish, cover, and refrigerate. Serve cold.

NOTE: It is better to strain the sauce because some egg white always clings to the yolks and gets cooked in the sauce. If this is not strained out, there will be small lumps in the sauce.

MENU

Potée Bourguignonne
[*Hearty Meat Soup*]

Wine: Chablis or Rully

Salade

Pain Ordinaire
[*French Bread*]

Crème Frit
[*French-Fried Cream Custard*]

POTÉE BOURGUIGNONNE

[*Hearty Meat Soup*]

Almost every province has its potée. Some omit the meats and use just vegetables. The potée of Burgundy is as famous as the potée of Auvergne. The Auvergne potée follows the same recipe, with the addition of ½ pound of cooked white beans.

1 (4-pound) ham shank	6 sprigs parsley
1 salted chine of pork	⅛ teaspoon thyme, or 1 branch
6 slices lean bacon, diced	Salt and pepper to season
2 quarts water	6 carrots, chunked
2 cups white wine (Burgundy)	4 turnips, quartered
2 cloves garlic, minced	6 medium-sized potatoes
3 onions	1 green cabbage (about 1 pound)
2 cloves	1 pound cervelat sausage, or
3 leeks	German-type frankfurters
2 bay leaves	

1. Put ham, chine of pork, and bacon into a large kettle with water and wine. Add the garlic. Stick the cloves into 1 onion. Add onions. Wash and tie leeks (see p. 607). Add to kettle, then add bay leaves, parsley, thyme, salt, and pepper. Simmer 2 hours. Discard bay leaves, parsley, thyme branch, and leeks. Skim foam from top of liquids and discard.

2. Add carrots, turnips, and potatoes. Cook another hour. Cut cabbage into 6 wedges. Add to the kettle. Cook 20 minutes. Remove the ham to a platter and add the cervelat, or frankfurters. Cook another 15 minutes.

3. Slice the ham. Serve meats, vegetables, and broth in flat soup plates with plenty of French bread, or broth may be served as soup and then the meats and vegetables served as the main course.

CRÈME FRIT

[*French-Fried Cream Custard*]

1 egg	2 tablespoons Grand Marnier
2 yolks	1 tablespoon Kirsch
6 tablespoons confectioners' sugar	Oil for French-frying
6 tablespoons flour	1 egg white
½ cup half-and-half cream	Flour

Fine bread crumbs

1. Put egg and yolks into a heavy saucepan (or cook this recipe in a double boiler), and beat together. Mix together sugar and flour and then stir into the eggs. Beat and then add the cream. Stir-cook over very low heat until very thick. Add the Grand Marnier and Kirsch.

2. Remove from heat, pour into a buttered, square pan so that depth of custard will be about 1 inch. (You can always make a container smaller than it is just by buttering a double thickness of foil and pushing it up against the mixture in the pan to hold the mixture where you want it.) Butter a sheet of foil and lay over the top of the custard and cover tight. Refrigerate overnight.

3. Heat oil to between 350 and 360 degrees (not more). Put egg white on a dinner plate and beat to a froth, using a table fork. Put about ¼ cup flour on a separate plate and crumbs on another plate.

4. Remove the cold custard from the refrigerator and take off the foil. Spoon about a tablespoon of custard into the flour. Coat and shape, using a table knife and your fingers, into a square, or a cylinder shape. Then, with the knife, lift it to the frothy whites. Completely coat and then lift to the crumbs. Roll and shape again. Lift to a plate and let dry while shaping and coating the rest of the custard. The custard is soft and somewhat difficult to mold.

5. Fry a few at a time in the heated oil. When they are brown, lift out and drain on paper towels. Serve one or two per person. Serve plain, or with sour cream flavored with lemon juice and sprinkled with sugar.

NOTE: Refrigerate and eat cold any that are left. They are delicious.

CHAMPAGNE

The centrally located and open flatlands of Champagne made it historically into a land of trade and tension. It has been a major European battlefield
from the time of Attila the Hun in the fifth century through the First World
War. In times of intervening peace its towns held fairs which brought together merchants and bankers from all over western Europe.

The white wine of western Champagne has been a favored beverage of
prince and commoner since Roman times. In the seventeenth century Dom
Perignon discovered a process by which the natural wine of the region could
be transformed into bubbly Champagne. Unfortunately, he did not invent any
dishes to go with it.

Champagne is one of the few wines that is best when drunk before or
after the meal. It does not go particularly well with any course; so it goes
equally well with all. In cooking, the bubbly loses all the charge that was
put into it at so great an expense.

The cuisine of the Champagne country is limited and not distinctive.
Chicken, trout, and other local products are often cooked in Champagne. But
in the menu that follows, the favorite simple dishes of the region appear. You
may serve Champagne with them, but I would suggest instead a sparkling
white Burgundy.

MENU

Pieds de Porc Sainte-Menehould
[*Braised-Broiled Pig's Feet*]

Vinaigre à l'Echalote
[*Vinegar Sauce*]

Ragoût d'Agneau
[*Lamb in Sauce*]

Wine: Sparkling White Burgundy or Bouzy

Salade au Lard
[*Lettuce with Bacon*]

Pain Ordinaire
[*French Bread*]

Poires au Sucre
[*Caramelized Pears*]

PIEDS DE PORC SAINTE-MENEHOULD

[*Braised-Broiled Pig's Feet*]

Pig's feet are like tripe—you either like them, or you do not, there is no halfway about it. They are enjoyed for their texture and the flavor brewed into them in the braising process. French pig's feet are so small that the bones too become soft and one eats the whole "trotter." Our pig's feet are large and one must contend with bones. Give them a try; they are less expensive than Chinese shark's fins and have about the same gelatinous quality.

6 pig's feet	1 bay leaf
2 onions	½ teaspoon thyme
2 whole cloves	6 sprigs parsley
2 cups chicken stock	1 teaspoon salt
2 cups white wine	Freshly ground pepper
1 carrot	Fine dry bread crumbs
1 garlic, cut in half	Melted butter

1. One normally buys pig's feet cut in half lengthwise. But if they are not cut, ask your butcher to do this for you. Then, with string, tie the two halves together in three or four places. Put the feet into a large kettle. Stick the cloves into 1 onion. Add onions and balance of ingredients, down to the pepper. Bring to a boil, reduce heat to a simmer, cover, and cook about 3 hours. Do not let it boil.

2. When they are done, carefully lift the feet from the broth. Place them on a greased broiling pan. Cut strings from each foot and lay them flat side down on the broiler. Grind pepper over them and sprinkle with a bit of salt and lots of crumbs. Drizzle melted butter over the crumbs. Broil about 20 minutes. This is not easy. Have the pan as far as possible from the heat and regulate the heat so that the crumbs do not burn. Drizzle with butter every 5 minutes or so. The crumbs must be crisp and brown to give contrast to the gelatinous gristle of the feet.

3. When done, put onto a platter large enough to hold them flat. Cool, cover, and refrigerate. The feet are full of gelatin. Serve them cold with Vinegar Sauce (which is also great on raw oysters or clams).

VINAIGRE À L'ECHALOTE

[*Vinegar Sauce*]

3 tablespoons minced shallots	½ teaspoon sugar
3 tablespoons white vinegar	Dash salt
3 tablespoons water	⅛ teaspoon freshly ground pepper
1 tablespoon Madeira	2 cloves garlic, cut in half

3 tablespoons minced parsley

Combine the ingredients in a glass, or plastic container. Let age several hours and then serve with the pig's feet. Discard the garlic if you wish.

NOTE: Any leftover sauce is delicious stirred into mayonnaise and spooned over a salad of grapefruit and avocado slices. Use about 1 tablespoon to ½ cup mayonnaise.

RAGOÛT D'AGNEAU

[*Lamb in Sauce*]

3 pounds lamb stew meat	6 sprigs parsley
Chunk butter	2 bay leaves
2 tablespoons peanut oil	1 large branch thyme, or ¼ teaspoon
2 onions, diced	1½ teaspoons salt
2 tablespoons minced shallots	½ teaspoon sugar
2 cups chicken broth	Freshly ground pepper
2 cups white wine	8 small potatoes
½ cup Madeira	12 mushrooms

Minced parsley

(*continued*)

1. Trim lamb of fat and cut into 1-inch pieces. Brown lamb in butter and oil. Add onions and shallots. Add broth, wine, and Madeira. Bring to a boil. Remove from heat. Add parsley sprigs, bay leaves, thyme, salt, sugar, and pepper. Cover and put into a 325-degree oven. Braise 1¼ hours. Check liquids. If reduced too much, add ½ cup broth.

2. Peel potatoes. Put into cold water and bring to a boil. Cook 20 minutes, or until done. Drain and add to the casserole, tucking them down into the meat and covering with meat pieces. Cut stems from mushrooms even with the caps. Wash and add to casserole. Reduce heat to 300 degrees. Braise another 40 minutes after adding the vegetables. Taste and adjust seasonings. Sauce should be reduced by more than half and the meat pieces shiny and brown. Sauce should be the proper thickness, but if it isn't, thicken with beurre manié (p. 2). Sprinkle with minced parsley and serve.

SALADE AU LARD

[*Lettuce with Bacon*]

6 slices lean bacon	½ teaspoon sugar
Lettuce for six	Freshly ground pepper
1 onion, diced	3 tablespoons vinegar
½ teaspoon salt	6 tablespoons whipping cream

1. Cut bacon into ½-inch pieces. Stir-fry until crisp and the fat is rendered. Observe how much fat is in skillet. If more than 5 tablespoons, spoon some out, leaving approximately 5 tablespoons in the pan. Set aside until ready to serve the salad.

2. Break up the lettuce into small pieces and put into a wooden salad bowl. Put the diced onions on top of the lettuce.

3. When ready to serve the salad, season with salt, sugar, and pepper. Reheat the bacon and fat. Measure the vinegar into a glass so that it can be added all at once. Have a skillet lid in one hand. Pour the vinegar into the hot bacon fat and cover with the lid. It pops a lot. Lift off the heat and pour over the onions and lettuce. Turn the hot skillet upside down over the lettuce in the salad bowl. Leave for a minute or so. Remove, add cream and toss. Taste and adjust the seasonings. Serve.

POIRES AU SUCRE

[*Caramelized Pears*]

⅛ pound butter

6 tablespoons sugar

4 pears

½ cup whipping cream

Dash salt

½ teaspoon vanilla

2 tablespoons Kirsch

1. Melt half the butter in an 8-inch pie pan, or one just large enough to hold the pears flat. Size of pears will determine size of pan. Sprinkle pan with half the sugar.

2. Cut pears in half. Peel and core. Lay pears, cut side down, into the pie pan. Sprinkle with remaining sugar and top each pear with a piece of butter. Bake about 20 minutes in a 475-degree oven.

3. Combine cream, salt, vanilla, and Kirsch. Pour over pears. Bake about 20 minutes, or until slightly thickened. Remove, cool on a cake rack, but serve slightly warm.

DAUPHINÉ, SAVOIE

From the Rhone valley eastward the land rises quickly to the Alpine heights of Dauphiné and Haute Savoie, two provinces which separate France from Italy and Switzerland. From the fortress town of Nyons in the south to the waters of Évian in the north, the mountains make life rugged and austere. While a few of the gastronomic specialties of lowland Dauphiné have climbed to mountain cities like Grenoble and to famous spas and ski resorts, the ordinary Alpine fare is heavy, crude, often coarse and tasteless, and very monotonous.

Still, as in any part of the world, nature provides a few foods that are distinctive and excellent in quality. The walnuts, chestnuts, plums, pears, and apples of this Alpine region are among the finest of their kind produced in France. Mountain potatoes are firm and tasty, carrots are crisp and sweet. Fish from cold mountain streams and lakes compete with small game and birds for the tender ministrations of fine cooks. Cheese in many forms, the soft Rablochon and the hard Swiss types, is eaten at any hour of the day. The hard cheeses appear in many gratin dishes to which they add taste, bouquet, and texture. Cream is lavishly used.

Fine white wines, like Le Chablais, are produced in Savoie. They make excellent companions to simple fish and game dishes. In Dauphiné good *vins du pays* come from the valley of the Isère. The mountain people of France also enjoy a happy variety of beverages: cherry brandy (*Kirsch*), vermouth, cider, and beer. Near Grenoble they make the famous after-dinner liqueur called Chartreuse, now an international favorite. But what is perhaps most important to foreigners in France is the tasteless, clear water that is bottled in Évian and sent to every hamlet. Americans, when in France, often spend more money for this water than for wine. Because it is tasteless, Évian is the only water that can appropriately be served with the meal. Most Frenchmen drink water, usually of the bottled mineral variety, only between meals or when ill.

MENU

Potage Crème de Tomate
[*Cream of Tomato Soup*]

Truite Saumonée
[*Salmon Trout*]

Wine: Tavel Rosé

Pommes de Terre Dauphinoise
[*Potatoes au Gratin*]

Pain Ordinaire
[*French Bread*]

Salade

Fromage de Rablochon avec Fruit
[*Rablochon Cheese with Fruit*]

Wine: Côte Rôtie

Truffettes Dauphinoise
[*Chocolate Truffles*]

POTAGE CRÈME DE TOMATE

[*Cream of Tomato Soup*]

4 shallots, minced	¼ teaspoon soda
2 garlics, minced	3 cups whipping cream
Butter	2 cups milk
4 tablespoons flour	1 teaspoon salt
8 canned plum tomatoes, or	1 tablespoon sugar
2½ cups	Freshly ground pepper

Croutons

1. Sauté shallots and garlic in a chunk of butter for about 3 minutes. Do not brown. Add flour. Stir-cook another minute.

2. Add tomatoes and soda. Stir-cook until hot. Add cream, milk, salt, sugar, and pepper. Bring just to a boil. Grind through a food mill and into a clean pan. Heat to hot. Remove, and swirl-in a large piece of butter. Taste and adjust seasonings. Pour into tureen and serve with garlic-flavored croutons.

NOTE: Can also be used as a cream sauce on breaded veal, chicken, croquettes, or fried eggplant or zucchini.

(*continued*)

Garlic-flavored croutons. Put a chunk of butter into a skillet. Crush 2 cloves of garlic through a garlic press and into the skillet. Heat to melt butter and to release the garlic flavor into the butter. Cut crusts from about 4 slices of firm type bread (French bread is best). Cut into cubes. Add to skillet and fry cubes until browned on all sides and dried out. Try to keep these on hand. Frozen they keep indefinitely. If frozen, reheat in a skillet before using, or in an oven.

TRUITE SAUMONÉE

[*Salmon Trout*]

1 (3–4 pound) salmon trout	Freshly ground pepper
1 cup water	2 canned plum tomatoes
2 cups white wine	2 cups minced mushrooms
3 sprigs parsley	Chunk butter
1 bay leaf	2 tablespoons flour
1 small onion, minced very fine	Pinch of soda
Juice of ½ lemon	3 tablespoons crème fraîche, or
½ teaspoon salt	whipping cream
½ teaspoon sugar	3 tablespoons Madeira

Parsley

1. Wash trout. Let stand in cold water 10 minutes and then drain. Wrap in cheesecloth.

2. Put all ingredients, down to the tomatoes into a fish poacher, or long shallow pan that will hold the fish. Simmer ingredients about 20 minutes, then discard the parsley and bay leaf.

3. Crush tomatoes with a fork. Discard seeds and hard stem ends. Add tomatoes and mushrooms to liquids. Place cheesecloth-wrapped fish in pan. Cover and poach fish over low heat for about 30 minutes. Allow 10 minutes of cooking for every inch the fish is thick. If fish is 3 inches thick, allow 30 minutes. Preheat oven to 250 degrees.

4. Melt butter in a medium-sized saucepan. Stir in flour and cook 1 minute. Remove from heat.

5. When fish is done, lift it out, using several layers of paper towels to hold the cheesecloth ends. Unwrap fish and deposit it in an upright position on serving platter. Carefully remove skin and the dorsal fin. Lay a sheet of foil over the fish (not tight) and place in oven to keep warm.

6. Poaching liquids should now measure about 1½ cups (guess at it). If there is more, boil hard to reduce the amount. Pour liquids into the butter-flour mixture. Heat-stir until thickened. Add soda and stir in crème. (Soda

prevents curdling when crème is combined with tomatoes.) Add Madeira. Heat, taste, and adjust seasonings. Adjust thickness of sauce with beurre manié (p. 2) if necessary. Glaze fish with sauce and pour balance of sauce around fish. Decorate platter with bunches of parsley. Serve.

POMMES DE TERRE DAUPHINOISE

[*Potatoes au Gratin*]

7 medium-sized red potatoes	1 small clove garlic
Clarified butter, or lard	Light cream
Salt, pepper, and nutmeg	Butter

1. Peel potatoes and slice paper thin. Coat a shallow casserole, or gratin dish with clarified butter. (Be sure casserole will hold the potatoes.) Arrange potato slices in overlapping fashion in layers. Sprinkle each layer with salt, pepper, and nutmeg. Repeat layers until all potatoes are used.

2. Mash a small clove of garlic in a salad bowl with the spoon. Discard the pulp. Add 1 cup of cream, stir, and then pour over potatoes. Add cream to cover slices. Dot with butter. Bring to a boil on top of the range. Loosely cover with foil and bake in a 275-degree oven for about 2 hours. Check after 1½ hours. If liquids have not evaporated, remove the foil. Liquids should be completely absorbed by the potatoes and the potatoes browned and moist. Serve from the casserole.

TRUFFETTES DAUPHINOISE

[*Chocolate Truffles*]

4 ounces bittersweet or German	½ teaspoon vanilla
sweet chocolate	Dash salt
1 tablespoon cream	¼ cup cocoa
1 tablespoon rum or Cognac	2 tablespoons confectioners'
1 egg yolk	sugar
⅛ pound butter	¼ teaspoon cinnamon

1. Put chocolate, cream, and rum into top part of a double boiler. Into lower part of boiler put about 1 inch of hot tap water. Set top part into lower part (be sure it does not touch water), cover and bring water to a boil. Turn off heat and let stand until chocolate has softened. Reheat water if necessary to melt chocolate.

2. When chocolate is soft, add yolk. Stir into chocolate mixture and heat

until chocolate begins to stiffen. Remove top part of boiler. Beat in the butter, vanilla, and salt. If salted butter has been used, omit the salt.

3. Butter a small, shallow dish and spoon chocolate mixture into it. Cover with buttered foil and refrigerate.

4. Combine cocoa, confectioners' sugar, and cinnamon. When chocolate hardens, or sets, cut it into squares. Butter your fingers and mold the squares into small irregular balls that resemble truffles. Coat the chocolate truffles with the cocoa mixture. Cover and store in refrigerator, but serve truffles at room temperature. Makes about 3 dozen.

Suggestions. Put ¼ inch of chocolate mixture between two pecan halves and coat the chocolate mixture, between the nuts, with cocoa.

The chocolate mixture may also be used, as soon as it is made, to ice cookies or cake. Put the cake into the refrigerator to set the icing. Frosting will set on the surface, but be creamy underneath—a beautiful finish for cakes.

MENU FOR FOUR

Fondue de Fromage
[*Cheese Fondue*]

Gratin d'Écrevisses
[*Shrimp au Gratin*]

Wine: Château Grillet or Hermitage Blanc

Riz au Persil
[*Parsleyed Rice*]

Cardons â la Crème
[*Creamed Cardoons*]

Salade

Fraises au Grand Marnier
[*Strawberries with Grand Marnier*]

Gâteau de Savoie
[*Sponge Cake*]

Wine: Seyssel

FONDUE DE FROMAGE

[*Cheese Fondue*]

1 teaspoon cornstarch	½ pound Gruyère cheese, cubed
2 teaspoons Kirsch	¼ teaspoon salt
1 clove garlic, cut in half	Dash cayenne pepper
1 cup white wine	3 tablespoons Kirsch

French bread pieces for 4

1. Combine cornstarch and 2 teaspoons of Kirsch in a tablespoon ready to use. Rub a small enameled saucepan with the cut side of the garlic. Mash, and then discard garlic. Add the wine, cheese, salt, and pepper. Stir-cook over very low heat with a wooden spoon. The cheese must dissolve into the wine as the whole is heated and stirred. If the heat is too high the cheese will become elastic, like rubber.

2. When the cheese and wine have become a creamy blend, add just enough cornstarch solution to bind the mixture. Stir in the 3 tablespoons of Kirsch. Add a bit more cornstarch if mixture seems thin. Cornstarch stabilizes the fondue and helps to keep it creamy.

3. Pour into a fondue server or chafing dish, or set the enameled saucepan over a candle warmer. One eats the fondue by spearing a piece of bread and dipping it into the liquid cheese.

GRATIN D'ÉCREVISSES

[*Shrimp au Gratin*]

Chunk butter	½ teaspoon sugar
2 shallots, minced	Beurre manié
Dash cayenne pepper	½ cup milk
1½ pounds shrimp (24 to the pound)	1 tablespoon Madeira
3 tablespoons Cognac	½ cup crème fraîche, or whipping cream
1 cup dry white wine	3 egg yolks
¼ teaspoon salt	1 teaspoon lemon juice

Bread crumbs

1. Sauté shallots in butter until soft. Do not brown. Add cayenne and shrimp. Stir-cook until shrimp begin to turn pink. Add Cognac and set aflame. Add wine and salt. Bring to a boil, lift from heat, cover and let stand 3 minutes.

(continued)

2. Lift shrimp from liquids. Add sugar and boil liquids, reducing them by half. Thicken with beurre manié (p. 2). Lift pan from heat. Combine milk, Madeira, crème, yolks, and lemon juice. Mix well and then stir into pan. Stir-cook over very low heat until thickened. Do not boil. Add shrimp, heat, and pour into gratin dish, or shallow casserole. Sprinkle with crumbs. Brown under broiler and serve with parsleyed rice (p. 279). Make rice before cooking the shrimp, but add parsley to rice just before serving. Serves 4. If serving as a first course, spoon shrimp into shells, sprinkle with crumbs, broil, and serve to 6.

CARDONS À LA CRÈME

[*Creamed Cardoons*]

The cardoon is a relative of the artichoke without its edible flower, but grows like celery, only much taller. Cardoons are available in Italian and specialty grocery stores.

1 bunch of cardoon	½ teaspoon salt
½ lemon	Freshly ground pepper
Water	Dash nutmeg
2 teaspoons Fruit Fresh	¼ teaspoon sugar
Salt to season water	1 cup milk
Butter	½ cup crème fraîche, or
2 tablespoons flour, plus 1	whipping cream
teaspoon	1 tablespoon minced parsley

¼ teaspoon dried chervil

1. Discard tough outer stalks of the cardoon. Break off the tender, inside ones. With a potato peeler, peel the ribs, or strings, off the stalks, just like peeling celery.

2. Cardoons turn dark (like artichokes) when cut; to prevent this, rub the cut side of a lemon over the branches as soon as they are peeled. Cut into 2-inch lengths and put into water to which has been added Fruit Fresh (ascorbic acid, p. 605). When enough stalks have been cleaned and cut to serve 4, lift them from the water and bring the water to a boil. Add salt to season the water and then add the cardoons. Simmer for about 1 hour, or until tender.

3. When done, drain. Melt chunk of butter in a skillet. Add cardoons and sauté for 5 minutes. Put into a dish. Stir flour into butter. Add salt, pepper, nutmeg, and sugar. Stir in milk and crème. Stir-cook until thickened. Taste and adjust seasonings.

4. Add cardoons, parsley, and chervil. Heat. Pour into serving dish, dot with butter, and serve.

NOTE: I would serve this as a separate vegetable course after the shrimp, since the shrimp dish has a sauce.

FRAISES AU GRAND MARNIER

[*Strawberries with Grand Marnier*]

6 large strawberries per person	1 tablespoon sugar

1 tablespoon Grand Marnier per person

1. Wash berries and remove stems. Slice berries into ⅛-inch slices. Place the perfect center slices in a petal design around the edge of a bread-and-butter-sized plate. Arrange the end slices from the berries in the center. Cover with transparent wrap and refrigerate.

2. When ready to serve, sprinkle with sugar and spoon Grand Marnier over each serving. Serve with cake.

NOTE: Thinly sliced oranges may be substituted for the berries.

GÂTEAU DE SAVOIE

[*Sponge Cake*]

Clarified butter, or lard	1 teaspoon vanilla
Sugar and flour for pan	1 tablespoon Kirsch
6 large egg yolks	6 large egg whites
½ teaspoon salt	¼ teaspoon salt
1 cup sugar	2 tablespoons sugar

1½ cups sifted cake flour

1. Preheat oven to 300 degrees. Use a 9-inch angel food cake pan with removable bottom. Coat pan with clarified butter, or lard, sprinkle with sugar, and then with flour.

2. Put yolks into small bowl of electric mixer. Beat until light. Add ½ teaspoon salt and 1 cup sugar. Beat for about 5 minutes, or until very light and somewhat stiff. Add vanilla and Kirsch and continue to beat.

3. Beat whites with ¼ teaspoon salt until they start to stiffen. Gradually add 2 tablespoons of sugar and beat until creamy and stiff.

4. On low speed, or by hand, mix flour into yolk mixture alternately with ¼ of the beaten whites. Remove bowl from mixer. Fold balance of whites into batter with a rubber spatula. Pour into prepared cake pan, filling

it ⅔ full, approximately. If there is batter left, make a small cake. Bake in preheated oven for about 1 hour, or until done.

5. When it is done, remove from oven, stick the neck of a club soda bottle into the tube of the cake pan, and invert so that the cake is held upside-down on the bottle. Let cake hang this way until cool and then remove from pan. Run a knife around inside of pan and around tube. Lift cake from pan by the tube and then cut cake from bottom of the tube part. Invert onto a cake plate. Serve plain, or sprinkle with confectioners' sugar. Serves 10 or 12.

FLANDRE

[*Flanders*]

In its food preferences French Flanders is closer to neighboring Belgium than to France. It is the only part of the country where the herring, salted or smoked, is the favorite of all classes.

Valenciennes, located on the Escaut River, which empties into the sea at Antwerp, is, like many Belgian towns, famous for its lace. Like other Flemings the workers of this thriving industrial city delight in game, especially wild rabbit, cooked with prunes or grapes. They are also ravenous eaters of hearty stews and quaffers of beer in quantity.

The *hochepot* (hotchpotch in English) of Flanders is a thick soup whose ingredients are so numerous as to boggle the imagination. Every person in most of the north Atlantic countries has his own favorite combination of things to put into it, but pig's ears and tails and bread crumbs are essential. Since these extremities of the pig do not appeal to most, I have chosen a hearty beer stew. It will give you a taste of what it feels like to be a Fleming. And don't forget the beer!

MENU

Carbonade Flamande
[*Beer Stew*]

To drink: Beer

Pommes de Terre Bouillies
[*Boiled Potatoes*]

Salade Chaude à la Flamande
[*Hot Lettuce Salad*]

Pain Ordinaire
[*French Bread*]

Galopins
[*Bread Pancakes*]

CARBONADE FLAMANDE

[*Beer Stew*]

3 pounds lean chuck beef, cubed
½ cup flour
2 teaspoons salt
¼ teaspoon pepper
4 tablespoons peanut oil
1 clove garlic, minced
1 bay leaf

3 tablespoons tomato puree
1 tablespoon sugar
⅛ teaspoon thyme
6 sprigs parsley, chopped
2 cans beer
3 large onions, peeled and
    quartered

14 carrots (approx.), peeled and chunked

1. Be sure meat is lean. Trim any tough skin from the pieces. Combine flour, salt, and pepper in a plastic or paper bag. Add the meat pieces and shake to coat them with flour.

2. Put oil into a large kettle. Heat, and then add the meat. Brown meat on all sides. Add the ingredients through the beer and bring to a boil. As soon as it boils, reduce the heat to a simmer. Cook about 1½ hours. Remove the bay leaf.

3. While stew cooks, prepare the onions and carrots. Add them and cook another hour. Taste and adjust the seasonings. Thicken the sauce with beurre manié (p. 2) if it seems too thin. Serve with boiled potatoes (p. 236).

SALADE CHAUDE À LA FLAMANDE

[*Hot Lettuce Salad*]

½ head lettuce, or enough
    to serve 6
2 whole eggs
4 tablespoons cold water
2 tablespoons vinegar

1 small onion, minced
Salt
Freshly ground pepper
Dash sugar
¼ pound butter, softened, yet cool

1. Break lettuce into bite-sized pieces into a salad bowl.
2. Put eggs into top part of a double-boiler. Whisk together. Add water, vinegar, and onions. Heat-stir over simmering water until thickened. This will take about 10 minutes. (If you have a small enameled saucepan, this sauce can be made directly over very low heat in just a few minutes. Make it first in a double-boiler and then you will know what you're aiming at and what your problems might be.)
3. Remove top part of boiler, add salt, pepper, and sugar. Whisk in the butter, piece by piece, adding the next piece after the previous one has been absorbed. Pour sauce over the lettuce, toss, and serve.

NOTE: This is a country Hollandaise sauce and a very easy method of preparation. Try it on vegetables, broiled or poached fish, and chicken.

LES GALOPINS

[*Bread Pancakes*]

This is one of the best ways I know to use old bread. There is no exact recipe. One must adjust the quantities to the amount of bread. However, the following formula will give you something to go by. These are very light and end up tasting like fried custard.

1½ cups milk
6 slices of bread or 6-inch piece
    of French bread
2 eggs

¼ teaspoon vanilla
Dash salt
⅛ pound butter
Sugar

1. Bring milk to a boil. Take from heat. Add the bread and let soak 10 minutes. Mash with a fork and then beat with a whisk. Beat eggs, vanilla, and salt together until light. Add to the bread mixture. Beat. The mixture should have the consistency of pancake batter—a little on the moist side. Adjust thickness with more bread or milk.
2. Heat a skillet. Add a piece of butter. Spoon batter into the skillet to

make pancakes. Brown both sides. Serve topped with more butter and sprinkle with sugar.

NOTE: These are best made with French bread. The cornmeal on the bottom crust gives a great flavor to the pancakes.

Galopin soufflé. To the recipe add 3 tablespoons of sugar and mix. Butter 6 (3-inch) porcelain soufflé dishes and sprinkle them with sugar. Fill half full. Bake 30 minutes in a 325-degree oven, then increase heat to 375-degrees and bake another 10 minutes. Invert each onto individual serving plates, sprinkle with sugar, and serve with crème fraîche, cream, or a cold Crème à l'Anglaise (p. 494). Make the Anglaise the day before and have it cold.

FRANCHE-COMTÉ

A hilly area in the gap between the Jura and Vosges mountains, the Franche-Comté (name derived from the area's once having been a "Free-County" of Burgundy) sits astride one of the major commercial and military routes of central Europe. Because of its strategic location near the spot where Germany, Switzerland, and France meet, it was perennially invaded throughout history and only finally became a part of France in 1678. In the Middle Ages and thereafter, the powers of Europe also sought to control it to exploit and market its extensive salt deposits.

The Franche-Comté is first and foremost an agricultural region with stock-raising and dairying being among its leading enterprises. While it has an abundance of native produce, Franche-Comté is also surrounded on all sides by neighbors noted for their excellent foods and wines. The plain of Bresse, a part of Franche-Comté, has the reputation throughout France of raising the finest chickens anywhere.

The fish and crayfish of the Jura streams and rivers are the most distinctive of the natural products. Pork, fresh or smoked, is its best domesticated meat. Hard cheeses of the Gruyère type are numerous, but more interesting for consumption at the end of the meal are its Bleu cheeses. The soft cheese called *Vacherin* is now generally available throughout the world.

The wines of the Jura district are not generally as well known as they should be. Its Arbois wines were appreciated by the Romans and today its rosés are among the best produced anywhere. South of the Arbois area, the white wine region begins. Its most unusual vintages are yellow wines, especially those produced at Château Chalon. These are sweet dessert wines comparable to the sauternes of the Bordeaux region and to the *Eiswein* of the Rhine vineyards.

MENU

Soupe aux Écrevisses
[*Shrimp Soup*]

Carré de Porc aux Herbes
[*Roast Loin of Pork with Herbs*]

Wine: The straw-colored Arbois or Côte-de-Mouchard

La Râpée
[*Creamed Potato Pancake*]

Salade

Pain Ordinaire
[*French Bread*]

Pommes Renversées
[*Baked Caramelized Apple Pudding*]

Sauce à la Crème
[*Cream Sauce*]

Wine: Château Chalon

SOUPE AUX ÉCREVISSES

[*Shrimp Soup*]

1 leek, sliced	2 cups water
2 onions, diced	2 tablespoons Cognac
1 small clove garlic, minced	Salt to season
1 carrot, diced	20 large shrimps in the shell
Chunk butter	1 egg yolk
2 tablespoons flour	1 cup whipping cream
1 bay leaf	1 teaspoon lemon juice
1 tablespoon minced parsley	2 tablespoons Madeira
Dash thyme	2 tablespoons butter
1 cup white wine	6 slices toasted French bread
1 cup clam juice (bottled)	Garlic cloves

1. Sauté leeks (see p. 607 for cleaning them), onions, garlic, and carrots in butter until lightly browned. Stir in flour. Add bay leaf, parsley, and thyme. Add wine, clam juice, water, Cognac, and salt. Add the shrimp and bring to a boil. Turn off heat and let stand about 8 minutes. Remove shrimp. Shell

when cool enough to handle. Put the shells back into the pot (not the shrimp). Simmer about 30 minutes.

2. Remove the black vein from the shrimp and cut them into ¼-inch pieces. Strain the liquids into a clean pan. Discard shells and vegetables.

3. Combine yolk, cream, and lemon juice. Add some of the hot liquids to this mixture and then stir back into the soup. Add the shrimp. Then heat, but do not boil. Add Madeira and 2 tablespoons of butter. Taste, and adjust.

4. Rub toasted bread with cut garlic, place a slice in each soup cup, and spoon the soup over it. Serve.

CARRÉ DE PORC AUX HERBES

[*Roast Loin of Pork with Herbs*]

1 (4-pound) pork loin	½ cup olive oil
4 teaspoons sage leaves	2 carrots
½ teaspoon thyme	4 plum tomatoes (canned)
3 bay leaves	2 cups white wine
1 onion, minced	6 whole potatoes
Salt and pepper to season	Beurre manié

1. Have butcher cut through the backbone of the pork to separate bone from meat, but not entirely; the bone must be hinged to the meat.

2. Open the backbone from the meat and into this "hinged area" place 3 teaspoons sage, the thyme, bay leaves, and minced onion. Sprinkle with salt and pepper. Close bone to meat.

3. With a small paring knife, make pockets in the fat of the meat. Into these pockets, stuff 1 teaspoon of sage. Tie the roast in several places to secure the hinged backbone.

4. Put roast into a plastic bag. Add the olive oil. Close the bag and squeeze the meat in the bag to coat it completely with oil. Marinate in the bag overnight in the refrigerator, or for at least 8 hours. Remove from the refrigerator 2 hours before roasting.

5. When ready to roast the meat, quarter the carrots lengthwise. Lay them in a shallow roasting pan. Crush tomatoes with a fork. Add to the pan. Set roast, bone side down, on top of the vegetables. Pour the olive oil from the bag into the pan and add the wine. Roast in a 325-degree oven for about 2½ hours, or until a meat thermometer registers 185 degrees.

6. Peel potatoes. Cook them in salted water until done. Add to the roasting pan the last hour of cooking. Turn after 30 minutes so that they become totally brown.

7. When meat is done, remove strings and backbone and discard. Place

roast on serving platter. Add potatoes to platter and keep warm in the turned-off oven.

8. Discard carrots and skim fat from juices. Thicken juices with beurre manié (see p. 2). Taste and adjust seasonings. Serve sauce separately.

LA RÂPÉE
[*Creamed Potato Pancake*]

4 medium-sized potatoes	4 tablespoons clarified butter, or
1 small onion, minced fine	lard
Salt and pepper to season	½ cup whipping cream, or more
	Melted butter

1. Peel potatoes and shred on grater, or coarse disc of electric shredder. There should be about 3 cups of shredded potatoes. Add onions to potatoes and mix well. Season with salt and pepper.

2. Heat butter in an 8-inch skillet. When it is hot, add potatoes. Reduce heat and let them brown on the bottom. When they have browned, add the cream and simmer until cream evaporates. Brush top with melted butter, or dot with butter, and set under a broiler to brown the top. Serve from the pan.

POMMES RENVERSÉES
[*Baked Caramelized Apple Pudding*]

6 apples	1 teaspoon vanilla
Chunk butter	2 tablespoons water
Sugar	2 egg yolks
Salt	4 egg whites

1. Put apples into a saucepan with the butter. Cover and simmer about 20 minutes. Add ½ cup sugar and ¼ teaspoon salt. Cook until thick and dry. Remove from heat. Pour into a food mill and let juice and butter drain from the apples. Discard liquids. Grind through the food mill and into a bowl. Add vanilla and mix. Preheat oven to 310 degrees.

2. Put ¼ cup sugar and water into a 6-cup charlotte mold, or an enameled soufflé dish. Boil in the pan and caramelize the sugar. When dark brown, lift from heat and twist pan around to coat sides. Set pan into cold water to harden the caramel.

3. Add yolks to apples and mix well. Add ¼ teaspoon salt to whites in mixer bowl and beat until they start to stiffen. Gradually add ¼ cup of

sugar and beat until creamy and stiff. Fold into the apples. Pour into caramelized mold, filling it ¾ full.

4. Set mold into a hot water bath. Bake 1¼ hours. When mold is done, remove from oven, set on a cake rack, and cool for 30 minutes. Mold will settle as it cools.

5. To serve, run knife around top and then down to the bottom of the mold. Place serving dish over top and invert. Surround with sauce and serve. Make the cream sauce while the soufflé bakes.

SAUCE À LA CRÈME
[*Cream Sauce*]

¼ cup sugar

1 egg

2 yolks

⅛ teaspoon salt

½ cup whipping cream

1 teaspoon vanilla

1. Put sugar, egg, yolks, and salt into top part of a double boiler. Set into bottom part of double boiler and be sure water does not touch the top part. Heat and beat. Use a whisk or hand beater. Mixture will triple in volume. Let it get very hot. Heat the cream to hot.

2. When mixture is hot and thick, gradually add the cream and continue to beat. Cook a few minutes. Remove from heat, add vanilla, and mix. Pour around apple mold, or serve with any dessert that needs a sauce.

MENU

Crème de Foie de Poularde Moulée
[*Chicken Liver Custard*]

Sauce d'Écrevisses
[*Shrimp Sauce*]

Wine: Pouilly Fuissé, or Beaujolais Blanc

Poularde à la Crème
[*Chicken in Cream Sauce*]

Wine: Chassagne-Montrachet, or Meursault

Pommes de Terre Grillées
[*Grilled Potatoes*]

Salade

Pâtes aux Poires Brillat-Savarin
[*Pear Bread*]

CRÈME DE FOIE DE POULARDE MOULÉE

[*Chicken Liver Custard*]

This dish is one of the true wonders of the food world.

Oil

½ pound chicken livers

1 clove garlic, quartered

1 (½-inch) pat of butter,
softened

2 tablespoons concentrated
chicken stock

¼ cup milk

2 large eggs

2 large egg yolks

½ teaspoon salt

Freshly ground pepper

1. Coat with oil a 4-cup charlotte mold, or similar small round mold with straight sides. Line bottom of mold with a circle of waxed paper. Turn paper over so that the greased side is up. Put water into a foil pan and heat for the water bath. Preheat oven to 325 degrees.

2. Check livers to be sure bile sac is removed. Cut fat and tissue from the livers. Be sure there are no hearts or gizzard pieces.

3. Put livers into blender container, or grind through finest blade of a meat grinder. Squeeze ¼ garlic through a garlic press. With a knife scrape the pulp and juice off the press and into container. Add butter and stock. Whirl on mix speed and then on blend.

4. Add milk. Blend to make a thin puree. Add eggs, yolks, salt, and pepper. Blend. Pour into prepared mold. Mixture will fill mold about half full. Cover mold tightly with a sheet of foil. Set in hot water bath and then into oven.

5. Bake 1¼ hours on middle shelf. Turn off heat and leave in the oven for 10 minutes. Do not remove foil until cooking time is up. Make sauce half an hour before mold is done.

6. To serve, remove foil from mold and run knife around edge of mold and down to the bottom. Place serving dish over top and invert. Remove waxed paper from the bottom and pour shrimp sauce around the mold. Serve as a first course with French bread.

SAUCE D'ÉCREVISSES

[*Shrimp Sauce*]

½ pound frozen raw, cleaned
    shrimp (12 to the pound)
Chunk butter
1 cup minced mushrooms
2 tablespoons flour
¼ cup whipping cream

¾ cup milk
½ teaspoon salt
¼ teaspoon sugar
Dash pepper
Dash cayenne
1 teaspoon fresh lemon juice

1 tablespoon Cognac

1. Thaw shrimp. Cut into very small pieces. (Large shrimp are not as strong-tasting as the small ones.)

2. Melt butter in skillet. Add mushrooms. Sauté about 1 minute. Add flour and cook-stir about 1 minute. Add cream, milk, salt, sugar, pepper, and cayenne. Stir-cook until thickened. Do not add the shrimp until the mold is ready to be served.

3. When mold should be done, add the shrimp and stir-cook for 2 minutes, or until shrimp turn white. Add lemon juice and Cognac. If sauce is too thick, add a bit of milk and Cognac. Serve.

POULARDE À LA CRÈME

[*Chicken in Cream Sauce*]

2 (3–4 pound) chickens, cut up
Salt and pepper to season
Butter
2 tablespoons peanut oil
½ cup dry white wine
½ cup chicken stock
6 small onions, leave whole
3 sprigs parsley
1 bay leaf

6 carrots
1 leek, leave whole
2 cups sliced mushrooms
3 egg yolks
1 cup crème fraîche, or
    whipping cream
2 teaspoons lemon juice
Salt and pepper to season
Dash of sugar

Minced parsley

1. Use only the meaty pieces of the chickens. (Cook the bony pieces to make broth and then remove the meat from the bones and make some chicken salad, or combine with some crab or shrimp in a cream sauce and serve on rice for another meal.)

2. Sprinkle chicken pieces with salt and pepper to season. Heat ⅛ pound butter and oil in a skillet. Add chicken and lightly brown. Add wine, stock,

onions, parsley sprigs and bay leaf. Peel carrots. Cut across the middle in half. Add lower halves to skillet and cut the top halves in half lengthwise. Add to skillet. Clean the leek (p. 607), and add to skillet. Cover and simmer about 1 hour or until chicken is tender.

3. Lift chicken pieces to a platter. Discard leek and herbs. Arrange carrots and onions around chicken. Set into 300-degree oven to keep warm. Add mushrooms and boil to reduce liquids to about ¼ cup.

4. Combine yolks, crème, and lemon juice. Add salt and pepper to season. Add a dash of sugar. Remove skillet from heat and stir yolk mixture into the skillet. Stir-cook over very low heat until thickened. Stir in a chunk of butter. Glaze chicken with sauce, sprinkle with parsley, and serve. Serve balance of sauce separately.

POMMES DE TERRE GRILLÉES

[*Grilled Potatoes*]

6 medium-sized red potatoes	Melted butter
Salted water	Pepper

1. Boil potatoes in their skins in salted water for 25 minutes or until done. Drain, cut in half lengthwise, and make a cut down the middle, but not through the skin.

2. Put potato halves onto broiler rack. Spoon melted butter over potatoes and grind pepper over each half. Broil until brown. Arrange on platter with chicken.

PÂTES AUX POIRES BRILLAT-SAVARIN

[*Pear Bread*]

Dough

1 cup milk	1 teaspoon salt
¼ pound butter	1 (⅝- or 0.6-ounce) yeast cake
6 tablespoons sugar	2 eggs, beaten
4 cups flour	

Filling

2 ripe pears	¼ cup crème fraîche, or
Kirsch	sour cream
2 tablespoons sugar	1 egg yolk
Melted butter	

Sauce

¼ cup whipping cream	1 egg yolk

1. Put milk, butter, sugar, and salt into a saucepan. Heat to melt the butter. Remove and cool to lukewarm. Crumble the yeast into the liquids. Stir until dissolved. Add beaten eggs and mix. Pour liquids into flour. Mix and then knead on floured board. Put into floured bowl, sprinkle with flour, cover, and let rise until doubled in bulk.

2. Put dough onto counter. Make three equal-sized pieces. Do this by pinching the dough into three pieces, which tends to form the dough into balls. Let rest.

3. Peel, core, and dice 2 pears (or 3, depending upon their size and whether or not you want to make 3 loaves of pear bread) into a small bowl. Sprinkle with Kirsch. Combine sugar, crème, and yolk. Mix well and toss with pears.

4. Roll, or press, 1 piece of dough into an oblong, making the middle thicker than the edges. Spoon some pear mixture onto center of dough. Pull the dough up around the pears and pinch together to seal.

5. Butter a 9-by-4-by-3-inch bread pan. Put bread loaf into pan. Make a chimney of foil for the cake: Tear a sheet of foil 6 inches long. Fold cut edges to the middle and then fold in half, making 4 layers. Roll this around handle of a wooden spoon. Coat foil with oil and slide chimney off handle. Then with the handle of the spoon make a hole in the seam of the loaf, in the middle. Insert the foil chimney.

6. From a second piece of dough tear a piece about the size of a tennis ball. Divide it in half. Roll each piece into a rope about 18 inches long. Twist the two together at one end and pinch the twisted end to one end of the loaf. Twist the two ropes together and cover the seam on top of the loaf. Twist dough around the chimney and proceed to the other end of the loaf. Cover the end seams with small ropes of dough. Brush loaf with melted butter and let rise until doubled.

7. Make 2 cakes with pears, another with apples, or turn the third piece of dough into dinner rolls. For rolls, flatten the dough into a circle, about 1/4 inch thick, coat with melted butter, and cut the circle into 12 pie-shaped pieces. Roll these up, from the wide outside edge to the point. Place point down on a buttered cooky sheet. Coat with melted butter and let rise until doubled in size.

8. Bake fruit loaves in a 400-degree oven for 5 minutes. Reduce heat to 350 degrees and bake about 25 minutes. Combine sauce ingredients. Remove the foil chimney and insert a small funnel. Pour the sauce into the funnel and tip the loaf of bread from one end to the other so that the sauce can distribute itself. Put back into the oven and bake another 15 minutes. Cool in pan for 10 minutes. Remove loaf and cool on a wire rack. Slice and serve.

9. Bake rolls in a 375-degree oven for about 20 minutes. Serve, or freeze until needed.

GASCOGNE

[*Gascony*]

A part of France only since 1607, Gascony was called Aquitania by the Romans. Geographically, like all of Gaul, it divides into three parts. The swampy and sandy region of Landes covered with scrub pine faces the Atlantic. To the south are the majestic Pyrenees, Béarn and the Basque country. At the center is the hilly Armagnac country between the Adour and Garonne rivers.

The Gascons are a hearty people who are portrayed in literature and on the stage as swashbucklers constantly

> Bragging of crests and pedigrees—
> And all most noble through and through.
> [E. A. Church, *Gasconade,* Stanza I]

Whether their claims to nobility are authentic or not, the Gascons can honestly boast of a heroic and hardy cuisine. Goose grease rather than butter or oil is the common cooking fat of the region. Most appreciated are the hams of the Landes which are eaten raw (cured) like the ham of Parma. The *bec-fins* birds are held by the beak and the rest popped into the mouth. The Gascons make many of their dishes with corn meal, because they were among the first, and bravest, of the Europeans to grow maize and eat it.

The Armagnac district produces the famous brandy of the same name. Many of its foods, especially game and poultry, are naturally cooked with Armagnac.

After their hearty meat dishes, the Gascons ordinarily enjoy a simple salad of one frizzy green or another. Desserts are simple and are always followed by a glass of the local liqueur. It is therefore not surprising that the Gascons easily fall into the jovial habit of post-prandial boasting.

MENU

Poulet de Saint-Astier
[*Chicken Stew*]

Wine: Madiran or Château Olivier

Pommes de Terre Bouillies
[*Boiled Potatoes*]

Salade
[*Frizzy-Green Salad*]

Pain Ordinaire
[*French Bread*]

Chocolat à la Bayonne
[*Chocolate Cream Mold*]

Wine: Monbazillac

POULET DE SAINT-ASTIER

[*Chicken Stew*]

12 chicken thighs
Salt and pepper to season
Olive oil
2 tablespoons Armagnac, or
　Cognac
1 onion, diced
1 clove garlic, minced
1 green pepper, cut in strips

2 cups sliced mushrooms
1 cup diced, smoked ham (or
　Canadian bacon)
6 whole canned plum tomatoes
1 cup white wine
2 tablespoons Madeira
2 tablespoons Armagnac, or
　Cognac

1 tablespoon minced parsley

1. Sprinkle chicken thighs with salt and pepper to season. Sauté in olive oil until browned. Add Armagnac and set ablaze.

2. Add onions, garlic, green peppers, mushrooms, and ham. Mash plum tomatoes with a fork and discard the hard stem area. Add wine, cover, and simmer 1 hour, or until chicken is tender. Add Madeira and Armagnac and cook 10 minutes with the lid off. Lift chicken to a hot platter, and skim fat from liquids. If sauce seems thin, boil hard to reduce it, or thicken with a bit of beurre manié. Spoon sauce over chicken and serve sprinkled with parsley. Serve with boiled potatoes (p. 236).

SALADE

[*Frizzy-Green Salad*]

1 clove garlic	1 tablespoon wine vinegar
⅛ teaspoon salt	½ teaspoon sweet basil
Freshly ground pepper	Curly endive
1 slice bread	Romaine
4 tablespoons olive oil	Leaf lettuce

1. Mash garlic in salad bowl with salad spoon. Add salt and pepper and continue to mash.

2. Cut crusts from bread slice. Tear bread into small pieces. Mash half of the bread into the mashed garlic. Add oil, vinegar and basil to the bowl. Mix together. Let stand for an hour or so to age.

3. Add greens to serve 6. Sprinkle with remaining bread pieces. Toss and serve.

CHOCOLAT À LA BAYONNE

[*Chocolate Cream Mold*]

This is one of the richest and best chocolate desserts I know.

½ cup light cream	2 tablespoons Cognac
6 tablespoons sugar	½ pound sweet butter
½ teaspoon salt	3 whole eggs
1 (4-ounce) bar German sweet chocolate	½ teaspoon vanilla
	Butter
1 (1-ounce) square bitter chocolate	Vanilla wafer or graham cracker crumbs

1. Put water into bottom part of a double boiler. Bring to a simmer and be sure the water does not touch the bottom of the top part. Let the top part heat.

2. Put cream, sugar, and salt into a saucepan. Stir-cook until sugar dissolves and cream is hot. Turn off heat.

3. Put chocolate (both) and Cognac into a small enameled pan. Bring to a boil, remove, cover, and set into a pilot heated oven, or into very hot water. Let chocolate soften. Do not stir.

4. Take butter from the refrigerator. Cut it into pats. Put butter into a mixer bowl and beat until it is fluffy and white. This will take about 15 minutes. The butter must be cold when it is beaten, or it tends to melt and not whip.

5. Put eggs into a bowl and beat with a whisk. Mix well, but do not whip to a froth. Gradually pour in the hot cream and continue to mix. Pour this into the hot double boiler. Stir-cook with a wooden spoon until mixture thickens to the consistency of whipping cream. Stir-cool in cold water, and then in ice water. Strain sauce into a clean pan. Add the vanilla.

6. When the butter is whipped and the cream sauce is cold, combine the recipe. Stir chocolate and Cognac together. Cool slightly, quickly blend half of the chocolate into the butter, and add the rest before the chocolate hardens. Mix well. Scrape down sides of the bowl. Very slowly pour the very cold custard into the chocolate-butter mixture while beating. The mixture will become creamy and smooth in about 5 minutes of constant beating.

7. Butter an oblong mold (I use a 2-cup pâté mold) and sprinkle with crumbs. Spoon mixture into mold. Smooth the top, cover with more crumbs, cover with transparent wrap and refrigerate.

8. To serve, dip the mold into warm water, dry it off and then invert the mold onto a serving plate. Cut into slices and serve with crisp cookies. Cigarette cookies (p. 327) are perfect with this dessert. Make them in advance, freeze, and serve them frozen.

NOTE: For a refreshing treat, mix 1 teaspoon of peppermint flavoring into the cream when it is finished and then pour into the mold.

This dessert can be frozen. Refrigerate it over night and then the next day unmold onto foil, wrap, and freeze. Slice and serve in its frozen state.

ÎLE-DE-FRANCE

The name Île-de-France first came into use in the fifteenth century when the kings of France spread their authority from this original "island" to the other parts of the nation we now know as France. Paris is, of course, at the center of this fertile basin, where the Marne and Oise rivers join the Seine. In Paris the regional foods of all of France have met and merged into the great recipes and menus constituting what is internationally known as *haute cuisine*. Many traditional dishes have thus lost their provincial identity, particularly those originating in the Île-de-France itself.

One of the few specialties of the province that does not appear elsewhere on the gastronomic map of France is *friture,* especially French-fried potatoes. These are called *Pommes Frites Pont Neuf,* a name that conjures up the very heart of riverine Paris.

The Île-de-France, apart from Paris, is a rolling countryside with beautiful forests and sparkling streams. Its vegetables, fruits, fish, game, and cheeses were proudly served in the past at the vast tables spread in the many royal and noble châteaus of the region. While it is impossible to separate the Île-de-France from Paris, it is certainly worthwhile to put a few of the esteemed products of the region into a menu that you might be more likely to encounter in the area north of Paris than in the "City of Lights" itself.

MENU

Friture de l'Île de France
[*French-Fried Fish*]

Wine: Suresnes, or Meursault

Sauce Gaillarde
[*Seasoned Mayonnaise*]

Haricots Verts au Lard
[*Green Beans with Bacon*]

Baguettes de Campagne
[*French Country Bread*]

Poires et Fromage de Brie
[*Pears with Brie Cheese*]

Wine: Château Margaux or Pontet-Canet

FRITURE DE L'ÎLE DE FRANCE
[*French-Fried Fish*]

Smelts, perch, or other fish fillets	1 cup flour
	1½ cups ice-cold beer, approx.
Peanut oil for frying	Parsley sprigs, lots
Lemon wedges	

1. Clean smelts and dry on paper towels. If using fillets, cut them into about 4 lengthwise pieces. Make them about the size of a smelt.

2. Heat oil to 340 degrees. Put the flour into a mixing bowl. With a whisk stir in the beer. Beat out the lumps. Dip fish into the batter and then put into the hot oil. Fish are done when they are brown and crisp. Drain on paper towels.

3. Dip parsley sprigs into the batter and fry. Serve with the fish along with lemon wedges and the following sauce. Normally in French cooking the parsley is simply dropped into the fat and cooked, and you may prefer it that way.

NOTE: To keep fish hot, place wire cake racks on a cooky sheet and put the cooked fish on the racks after they are cooked and then into a 325-degree oven. French-fried foods must be placed on racks so that the heat can circulate around them and keep them crisp. These fish are better with the oven treatment than they are served directly from the oil—they are crisper when the batter has dried out a bit.

SAUCE GAILLARDE

[*Seasoned Mayonnaise*]

1½ cups mayonnaise	½ teaspoon dried chervil
1 shallot, minced	1 tablespoon minced parsley
1 teaspoon minced onions	1 teaspoon sugar
4 teaspoons whipping cream	1 teaspoon Dijon-type mustard
1 teaspoon lemon juice	1 teaspoon Madeira

1 teaspoon Calvados or brandy

Mix all ingredients together. Age several hours, or overnight. Serve with any French-fried meat, poultry, seafood, or vegetable.

HARICOTS VERTS AU LARD

[*Green Beans with Bacon*]

1½ pounds green beans	Freshly ground pepper
2 teaspoons salt	½ teaspoon sugar
2 quarts water	2 tablespoons vinegar
6 slices lean bacon, diced	Pinch baking soda
1 onion, diced	3 tablespoons crème fraîche, or
	whipping cream

1. String the beans. Cut into 1-inch lengths. Drop into boiling salted water. Cook about 8 minutes, or until tender. Eat a bean to test. Keep them green and crisp—yet done. When done, drain and run cold water on them to stop their cooking. Drain again and set aside.

2. Sauté the bacon until crisp. Spoon all but 5 tablespoons of fat from the skillet. Set aside until ready to serve.

3. When ready to serve, drop the cooked beans into boiling, salted water to reheat. Drain and leave in the pan. Heat the cooked bacon and fat. Add onions, pepper, sugar, and vinegar to the beans. Pour over the bacon. Heat for about 5 minutes. Add the soda (soda retards curdling) and then the crème. Heat and toss. Taste and adjust seasonings and then serve.

BAGUETTES DE CAMPAGNE

[*French Country Bread*]

The French homemaker never makes bread at home. She buys it fresh each day from the local baker in her area. And you may be sure French bakers do not spend seven hours making a batch of bread. Nor do they have special equipment. What they do have are large ovens, often clay lined, and with steam piped into them. These conditions we cannot duplicate in our homes, nor could the French homemaker.

But we can make a loaf of French bread in our everyday kitchens that looks and tastes like the real French bread we all remember. What you do need is a gun-type plastic spray bottle that can be filled with water so that the oven and bread can be sprayed often. This is excellent French bread—do make it. It is even better when frozen and reheated.

Starter

1 (⅝- or 0.6-ounce) cake of yeast　　　1½ cups warm water
1½ cups all-purpose flour

Next day

1 teaspoon dry yeast	¾ cup warm water
½ teaspoon sugar	½ teaspoon soda
2 tablespoons very warm water	Cornmeal
4 cups flour	Melted butter or lard
1 tablespoon salt	1 egg white

2 tablespoons cold water

1. Prepare the starter the night before you plan to make bread. Dissolve yeast in small amount of warm water and then add balance of water. Beat in the flour. Mix this in the bowl you will use to mix the bread. Cover tight and let ferment overnight. (If you really like sour dough, let the starter ferment for 2 or 3 days.)

2. Next morning dissolve dry yeast and sugar in very warm water (follow package instructions). Let stand until it rises. Add 1 cup of flour and the salt to the starter. Beat 2 minutes. Add another cup of flour and enough of the water to keep the dough a batter. Beat another 2 minutes.

3. Add soda to the yeast mixture. Stir and add to bowl. Add 1½ cups of flour. Beat, and if necessary add more water. The dough should be stiff, yet pliable. The consistency of the dough should be such that when the dough is pinched between the finger and thumb it does not stick. Add more flour or water to make it so. Turn out onto a floured surface and knead. Sprinkle top and underneath the dough with flour.

4. Cover the dough with a towel and then lay transparent wrap over the towel to keep out the air. The towel is less likely to stick than the wrap. Let dough double in size. Sprinkle cooky sheet with cornmeal.

5. Be sure dough has doubled when you start to work it; on the counter it is difficult to judge. It is better that the dough rises too long than not long enough. When the dough has doubled, knock the dough down, fold it in

half, flatten, and fold in half again. Do this three or four times to trap the air. Then flatten the dough into an oval pancake about 1 inch thick.

6. Now we are going to remove the outside curves of the oval, which are perfectly shaped loaves of bread. To do this, do not cut with a knife, but use a wooden cutting board, or ½-inch dowel (available at all hardware stores). Stand the board up on its side and press the board down through the dough, about 2 inches in along the long oval sides of the dough and press through to the counter. Then with a table knife cut through the pressed-down dough and separate the loaf from the dough. Make two such loaves, one from each side of the oval of dough. Pinch the cut edges together and place cut side down on the cornmeal and across two corners, leaving the diagonal middle of the pan for the longer loaves.

7. Pinch the sides of the remaining piece of dough and then press down the center with the cutting board, making two more loaves of bread. Cut apart. Pinch cut edges together. Roll and shape loaves and then place diagonally on the cornmeal-coated cooky sheet. Coat with melted butter or lard.

8. Let loaves rise, uncovered, for about 30 minutes. With a very sharp, thin knife, make 4 or 5 long cuts, lengthwise of the loaf and about ⅜ inch deep. Preheat oven to 425 degrees. Let loaves rise until cuts have flattened out and loaves have doubled.

9. Beat egg white to a froth. Add water and continue to beat until well mixed. Brush loaves with mixture and put into oven. Bake 15 minutes. Open oven door and spray bread and oven. Reduce heat to 375 degrees. Heat a large, flat pan of water. When water is boiling set into oven. Bake 10 minutes and spray again with water. Repeat in another 10 minutes. After 10 minutes remove pan of water and brush loaves with egg-white. Spray again in 10 minutes. Turn off oven heat. After 10 minutes open door halfway and let loaves dry. Take out and cool on cake racks. Eat, or freeze. To reheat frozen bread, run loaf under cold running water and place on center rack of a 350-degree oven for about 15 minutes. Remove and let cool, then cut and serve. Or, thaw bread, coat with water, and reheat at 350 degrees for 10 minutes. Frozen, reheated bread is better than when it is fresh; I do not know why.

NOTE: If you want a half loaf, just hit the frozen bread on the edge of the counter and it will break in half. Rewrap the remaining half and put back into the freezer. Leftover reheated frozen bread is no longer good by itself; it will make nothing but Galopins (p. 513), or crumbs.

POIRES ET FROMAGE DE BRIE

[*Pears with Brie Cheese*]

As Rabelais said, "creamy ripe pears and ripe Brie make the perfect wedding."

6 ripe Anjou pears   **1 ripe Brie cheese**

To ripen pears. Put pears (or any fruit) on a cool window sill where no sun hits the fruit. Turn the fruit each day until the flesh, at the stem end, gives when gently pushed. Try to use the same pear for testing; pushing damages the fruit. When the fruit is ripe, refrigerate it until needed. Like cheese, fruit should be served at room temperature (70 degrees).

To ripen Brie cheese. In late autumn buy a whole Brie, the 10- to 12-inch-in-diameter size. Ask to see the cheese out of its thin wooden box. Feel the cheese. Buy the cheese that does not give when you push it and that feels hard. (It will feel a bit hard because it will be cold, but push enough to judge that it is still firm under its coldness.) Do not buy a Brie that the clerk tells you is ready to eat—trust yourself to ripen the cheese—but if you want it to eat immediately, ask to buy a piece and then you can judge its ripeness. If there is a firm, white line through the middle of the cheese it is not ready to eat. If it is totally runny and the outside dark and dry looking the cheese is too old. Therefore, it is better to buy a "green" cheese and ripen it yourself.

Once you have the "green" cheese, leave it in its flimsy wooden box, at room temperature (70 degrees), for about 24 hours. Then refrigerate it for 24 hours. Do this 2 times. Test it each time by feeling the cheese. Remove the cheese from its box and with your thumb on the bottom and your finger on top, gently press the cheese together. As the cheese ripens you will be able to feel the softness develop toward the middle and thus determine how much green cheese still remains in the middle. Continue to ripen the cheese with warmth and cold until the cheese feels totally soft to your fingers. Train your fingers to judge the ripeness of both Brie and Camembert. Experience alone will teach you.

When the cheese is ripe, cut it into serving wedges and quickly wrap the cut edges tightly in transparent wrap so that the soft cheese does not run out of the white crust. Make the pieces of cheese the size you will want to serve. Wrap and freeze. Save one wedge to eat with French bread so that you can appreciate how good a truly ripe Brie can be. In freezing, the cheese loses flavor, but it is better to have it with a little less flavor than to have an unripe, or an old, strong Brie. Thaw the cheese, then unwrap and serve at room temperature.

Creamed Brie. When Brie is left over and becomes somewhat dry, cut the white crust from it, put into a small plastic dish, or a glass, cover with a Barsac or sauterne wine and let the cheese marinate for 24 hours. Drain off the wine (save it to cook with, or discard) and blend the cheese with an equal amount of sweet butter. Shape the mixture into a round cake, coat with fine, dry bread crumbs, wrap, and refrigerate. Serve with French bread.

LANGUEDOC, ROUSSILLON, COMTÉ DE FOIX

[*The Languedoc Area*]

The southernmost region of France, the Languedoc, stretches from the Garonne to the Rhone valley. In its western quarter, in the shadow of the Pyrenees, are the small but historically important countship of Foix and the province of Roussillon, which add dimensions of their own to the regional cooking.

Gastronomically the Languedoc is a melting pot of foreign influences. In its eastern reaches around the ancient city of Nîmes there remain both Roman amphitheaters and traces of Roman cooking. The old seaport towns and those close to the Spanish frontier owe a certain debt to the Arabs for their cuisine. In Roussillon, where Catalan is still the common language, the oil cookery of Spain still holds its own.

In the Middle Ages the Languedoc produced much of the sea salt for southern France. Montpellier, once a port city but now inland, was the center for spice distribution. Merchants from the Levant and Portugal congregated there to sell the pepper, cloves, and cinnamon of the East. The local cuisine continues to feature salted meats and exotically spiced dishes. In the hinterlands foods are heavily laced with garlic, a substitute for the spices lavishly employed in city foods.

Basically the dishes of the Languedoc are of peasant origin. *Cassoulets,* bean dishes with pork and other meats, appear in a variety of forms. Other meat, fish, and vegetable soups and stews are also favored. There are just a few local wines to accompany these hearty dishes. Among those most available outside of Languedoc are the red wines of the Corbières district.

MENU

Croquettes de Volaille
[*Chicken Croquettes*]

Sauce de Tomate aux Champignons
[*Tomato-Mushroom Sauce*]

Wine: Corbières

Salade de Capon
[*Garlic-Crouton Salad*]

Kalouga
[*Chocolate-Pudding Cake*]

CROQUETTES DE VOLAILLE

[*Chicken Croquettes*]

¼ pound butter	1 cup chopped, cooked chicken
¾ cup minced ham	3 eggs
1 cup minced mushrooms	2 tablespoons sherry
6 tablespoons flour	Peanut oil for French-frying
1½ cups light cream	½ cup flour
Salt and pepper to season	2 egg whites
Dash sugar	Fine dry bread crumbs

1. Sauté ham and mushrooms in butter for 1 minute. Add flour and stir into a paste. Add cream and stir-cook until very thick. Season with salt, pepper, and sugar. Stir in chicken.

2. Beat eggs. Add some hot sauce to eggs and mix. Gradually add eggs to the sauce. Add sherry. Heat, but do not boil. Pour into a buttered, square pan and cover with a buttered piece of foil. Refrigerate until very cold.

3. Heat oil to 360 degrees. Cut cold mixture into 1 × 2-inch bars. Roll in flour and shape into cylinders. Beat egg whites to a froth. Roll cylinders in egg whites and then roll in crumbs. Put on plate ready to fry.

4. Fry croquettes until totally browned and hot. Drain on paper towels and keep warm in a 350-degree oven. Make the tomato sauce, or another sauce, before frying the croquettes. Mushroom, curry, or Hollandaise are all good, but I prefer the tang of tomatoes.

FONDANTS DE VOLAILLE AUX AUBERGINES FRITES

[*Chicken Croquettes on Fried Eggplant*]

Slice an eggplant, peel, sprinkle with salt, and let stand 20 minutes. Wash, dry, and coat with flour. French-fry after croquettes are cooked. Place 2 croquettes on an eggplant slice and serve with the sauce.

SAUCE DE TOMATE AUX CHAMPIGNONS

[*Tomato-Mushroom Sauce*]

6 fresh tomatoes or 3 cups canned plum tomatoes	2 cloves garlic, minced
	Dash pepper
1 green pepper, minced	¼ teaspoon soda
1 onion, minced	2 tablespoons Madeira
1½ teaspoons salt	3 tablespoons minced parsley
2 teaspoons sugar	2 cups sliced mushrooms

Butter

1. Remove cores from fresh tomatoes. Dice and place in enameled skillet or saucepan. Add remaining ingredients, down to the mushrooms. Boil about 1 hour. Grind through a food mill. Put back into pan. If the sauce seems to have water in it, boil hard to reduce the sauce to a thick pulp. Sauté mushrooms in a chunk of butter. Add to the sauce.

2. Remove from heat and whisk in pieces of butter to make the sauce turn creamy. Sauce should absorb about 6 tablespoons of butter, depending upon thickness of sauce. Add the butter to the sauce after the croquettes are fried. Once butter is added to the sauce it should be served immediately.

SALADE DE CAPON

[*Garlic-Crouton Salad*]

In French capon does not mean a bird, but a sneak or a cheat. This salad is especially good with this menu and is served as an everyday salad in the Languedoc.

3 cloves garlic, cut in half	1½ tablespoons vinegar
¼ teaspoon salt	5 tablespoons olive oil
Freshly ground pepper	3 slices dry, thin-cut, bread
Dash sugar	1 tablespoon minced parsley

6 Belgium endive (or more, according to size), or Boston lettuce

(continued)

1. With salad spoon mash 4 garlic halves in the salad bowl. Add salt, pepper, and sugar. Continue to mash to a pulp. Add vinegar and oil. Mix well.

2. Put bread slices into a pilot-heated oven to become dried out, or leave out at room temperature for a day or so. Rub each side of slices with the remaining 2 halves of garlic and put aside.

3. When ready to serve the salad, add parsley to bowl. Cut the endive into ½-inch slices, or break lettuce into pieces, and add to bowl. Toss the salad. Break the bread into small pieces, sprinkle over the salad, and toss again at the table and serve.

KALOUGA

[*Chocolate-Pudding Cake*]

6 ounces German sweet chocolate	¼ cup sugar
(1½ packages)	½ teaspoon salt
2 tablespoons Cognac	¼ pound butter, softened
Butter and flour for pan	4 egg whites
4 egg yolks	¼ cup sugar
¼ cup sifted cake flour	½ teaspoon vanilla

1. Put chocolate and Cognac into small pan, cover with foil, and set into very hot tap water and heat for a few minutes. Turn off heat and let chocolate soften in the Cognac.

2. Butter a 6-cup charlotte mold and coat with flour. Hit pan on edge of sink to knock out surplus flour. Preheat oven to 425 degrees.

3. Beat yolks in small mixer bowl until thick and light. Combine cake flour, ¼ cup sugar, and salt.

4. When chocolate has softened, stir into the Cognac and start adding the butter. Stir in a piece at a time, adding the next piece once the previous one has melted into the chocolate. Stir flour-sugar mixture into the chocolate and then add to the yolks. Beat well to mix.

5. Beat whites until they start to stiffen. Gradually add sugar, then vanilla. Beat until very stiff. Stir about ¼ of the beaten whites into the batter to lighten it and then fold in the rest. Mix well. Pour into prepared pan. Bake 20 minutes, or until cake has risen to the top of the pan and the top begins to crack. Turn off oven and leave cake for 5 minutes. Remove and set on wire rack to cool. Cake will deflate back to its original size. It will be cake on the outside and pudding within.

6. When dessert is cool, run a knife around the top edge and then to the

bottom. Place serving plate over the top and invert. Serve with cream sauce (p. 519). Make the sauce a day in advance and serve it cold with the kalouga. Crème Chantilly (p. 332) is also good with it.

MENU

Tripe à la Mode de Narbonnaise
[*Tripe in Tomato Sauce*]

Wine: Château de Fontarèche, or Corbières

Artichauts Froids à la Vinaigrette
[*Artichokes with Herb Sauce*]

Pain de Campagne
[*French Bread*]

Soufflé au Confiture des Oranges
[*Orange Marmalade Soufflé*]

TRIPE À LA MODE DE NARBONNAISE

[*Tripe in Tomato Sauce*]

The tripe we buy in supermarkets has been processed, that is, precooked, and should not be cooked for the 8 to 24 hours most French cookbooks recommend. Tripe in European countries has not been processed, and long cooking is therefore necessary.

Tripe is the muscular lining of beef stomach; there are four types available. We usually find tripe from the second stomach in our markets. In buying tripe look for small holes, which indicate that the tripe will be relatively tender. Tripe with big, waffled holes will be tougher and will have to be cooked longer.

Tripe is a delicious dish, gelatinous in texture, full of flavor, and very rich. Have plenty of French bread on hand.

4 pounds tripe	2 bay leaves
1 cup olive oil	1 branch thyme, or ⅛ teaspoon
10 large cloves garlic (lots)	8 sprigs parsley
Big dash cayenne pepper	1 (40-ounce) can plum tomatoes
Freshly ground pepper (lots)	1 cup white wine
2 teaspoons salt	⅛ teaspoon baking soda
¼ teaspoon sugar	¼ cup minced parsley

Fresh basil, minced, or 1 teaspoon dried

(*continued*)

1. Wash tripe. Scrape with a knife to remove surplus fat. Cut off fat if necessary. Scrape across the honeycomb side too. Wash again. Put into cold water, bring to a boil, drain, wash, scrape, cover with cold water and bring to a boil again. Repeat this process, removing as much fat as possible. Cut tripe into ½ × 2-inch strips. Refrigerate.

2. Put olive oil into a large enameled kettle, or casserole. (Do not use aluminum.) Peel garlic cloves. Cut each into about three slices. Sauté garlic in oil until soft, but *do not let it brown*. (When garlic turns brown it also turns bitter.) Add red and black pepper, salt, sugar, bay leaves, thyme, parsley, and tomatoes. Mash tomatoes with a potato masher, or crush with a fork before adding to the kettle. Add wine and simmer for 1 hour. Add soda. Cook another hour. (Soda removes the acid taste of tomatoes and imparts no flavor.)

3. Discard parsley sprigs, bay leaves, and thyme branch if used. Add minced parsley and tripe. Bring just to a boil. Cover and put into a 250-degree oven. Braise, in the oven, for about 3 hours. Check the casserole occasionally to be sure it is not boiling. If it is, reduce the oven temperature. It is important that this dish *not boil* or the tripe will tend to become tough. (You may cook this casserole on top of the range, but oven cooking is easier when a food must not boil and must cook for a long time.)

4. When the tripe is done, sprinkle with basil, or minced parsley. Tripe must be eaten hot. If it cools, even slightly, the fat begins to coagulate and the dish is ruined. Therefore figure out a way to keep it hot while you are eating it. In France tripe is served in special pottery pots, but it is not necessary to buy these. Use onion soup casseroles, au gratin dishes, or soup bowls. Put these dishes into the oven to heat so that they will be very hot when the tripe is spooned into them. Serve in the sauce and with plenty of French bread.

NOTE: If you have glass bells, serve the tripe under glass.

ARTICHAUTS FROIDS À LA VINAIGRETTE
[*Artichokes with Herb Sauce*]

6 cooked artichokes

Sauce

3 cloves garlic	½ teaspoon salt
3 tablespoons minced shallots	Freshly ground pepper
2 tablespoons white wine vinegar	1 tablespoon minced parsley
5 tablespoons olive oil	1 teaspoon chervil
¼ teaspoon sugar	1 teaspoon marsala, or sweet sherry wine

1. Cook artichokes (p. 261). Stand them on their heads to drain, cool, cover, and refrigerate overnight.

2. Make the sauce and let it age several hours. Mash garlic in a salad bowl with wooden spoon. Discard the pulp. Add shallots, vinegar, oil, sugar, salt, pepper, parsley, chervil, and marsala. Mix well.

3. Serve each artichoke with a small dish of sauce. Guests pull off the artichoke petals, dunk into the sauce, and eat. This is a refreshing salad to serve with tripe.

PAIN DE CAMPAGNE

[*French Bread*]

2 (1-ounce) cakes yeast	1 cup warm water
1 teaspoon sugar	Cornmeal
½ cup warm water	Peanut oil, or melted butter
4 cups flour	1 egg white
2 teaspoons salt	2 tablespoons cold water

1. Dissolve yeast and sugar in ½ cup water. Put 3 cups flour and salt into mixer bowl. If you have a mixer with a dough hook, use it. Otherwise mix by hand. Make a well in the flour. Add the dissolved yeast and gradually add the 1 cup of warm water. Knead the dough with the dough hook, or by hand, until the dough is smooth and elastic. Add as much of the remaining 1 cup of flour as is needed to make a stiff dough. It will absorb about ¾ cup. Put remaining ¼ cup on counter and knead the dough for about 5 minutes. A perfect dough does not stick to your fingers and is resilient and smooth. When dough reaches this consistency place in a floured bowl and sprinkle flour over the top. Cover with a towel and a piece of foil. Let expand until more than double in size or until it falls. Sprinkle cooky sheet with cornmeal.

2. Knock dough down with your fist. Knead on counter, and let rise again. After it rises again, put onto a floured counter, knead by folding the dough in half, knead, and fold again. Do this several times. Or, hit the dough with a rolling pin to work it and then fold and knead it into an oval, flat pancake. Let rest 10 minutes. With a ½-inch dowel (buy in hardware store), press through the two long sides and about 2 inches into the dough, thus you will have two perfectly shaped loaves of bread. Put these two loaves across two corners of the cooky sheet, leaving the center for the two remaining loaves, which will be longer. Now press the dowel down through the middle of the dough, thus making two more loaves of bread. Pinch the raw edges together and place on cooky sheet. Coat loaves with oil. Preheat oven to 475 degrees.

3. Let loaves rise 20 minutes. Slash the tops lengthwise in three or four

places, cutting about ¼ inch deep. Let rise 20 minutes. Put pan of boiling water onto floor of oven. Put bread into oven and reduce heat to 375 degrees.

4. Beat the egg white until frothy. Add 2 tablespoons of cold water and beat together. When bread starts to brown, remove from oven and coat with egg-white solution. Return to oven and after 10 minutes spray, or brush with water. (A gun-type plastic spray container also available at hardware stores is great for spraying bread.) Spray bread every 7 minutes or so. Remove pan of water after 20 minutes. Bake about 40 minutes, or until done.

5. When bread is done, turn off oven, open the door, and let loaves cool 10 minutes. Remove them from the oven and place on wire racks to get cold. Freeze, or reheat and serve.

To reheat bread, spray with water and put into a preheated 350-degree oven for 10 minutes. If bread is frozen, run the frozen bread under cold tap water and heat for 15 minutes. Remove, cool to crisp the crust, and serve.

SOUFFLÉ AU CONFITURE DES ORANGES

[*Orange Marmalade Soufflé*]

½ cup sugar
½ cup flour
½ teaspoon salt
¾ cup milk
1 tablespoon butter (pat)

4 tablespoons Grand Marnier
3 tablespoons bitter orange
   marmalade (Dundee), diced
4 egg yolks
Butter and sugar for soufflé dish

5 egg whites

1. Put sugar, flour, and salt into a saucepan. Mix. Gradually add milk to make a paste and then stir in remainder of milk. Cook over low heat until it becomes very thick. Remove from heat.

2. Stir in pat of butter. Add Grand Marnier and marmalade. Mix well. Add the yolks. Cover and set aside until ready to finish the soufflé and bake it.

3. Coat a 5-cup soufflé dish, or straight-sided mold, with butter and then sprinkle with sugar. Thirty minutes before you expect to serve the souffle, finish the recipe. Preheat oven to 375 degrees.

4. Whip egg whites until creamy and stiff, but not dry. Stir a "gob" into the custard and then fold in balance of egg whites. Pour into prepared dish, smooth off the top, and push away from sides of dish (see p. 67 for details). Bake 15 minutes at 375 degrees, then increase heat to 400 degrees and bake 10 minutes. Soufflé is done when top has a slight dent in the middle which means the center is still a custard—the way a soufflé should be. Serve immediately to 4, or small servings to 6.

LORRAINE

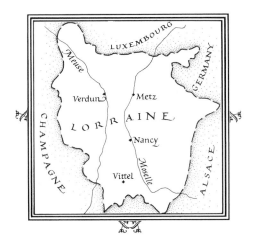

A slightly rolling plateau, Lorraine borders Alsace on the east and Champagne on the west. Two great rivers bisect it, the Meuse and, further east, the Moselle. Metz and Nancy, its two main cities, lie in the valley of the Moselle. In the south is the spa of Vittel, where the mineral water comes from that refreshes the livers of overindulgent Parisians.

Lorraine is psychologically and gastronomically much closer to Champagne and Paris than it is to Alsace and Germany. The natives of Metz speak German, but they think and eat French. Their famous *Quiche Lorraine* bears a resemblance to the onion tart of Alsace, but this classic dish really has no competitor in any other region of France.

Sweets come in profusion from Lorraine. Nancy, a city famous for its perfect central square, specializes in chewy macaroons. Verdun, a fortress of renown, supplies France with Jordan almonds. Lorraine also provides the French pantry with *Kirsch,* a liqueur derived from cherry pits, without which a sophisticated cuisine would well nigh be impossible.

MENU

Le Pâté Lorraine
[*Meat Pâté*]

Beckenoffe-Tourte Lorraine
[*Meat-Potato Casserole*]

Wine: Traminer

Salade

Le Gâteau au Chocolat de Nancy
[*Creamy Chocolate Cake*]

LE PÂTÉ LORRAINE

[*Meat Pâté*]

Stock

Bones from chicken thighs	1 teaspoon salt
1 pig's or calf's foot	1 teaspoon sugar
1 cup chicken stock	Freshly ground pepper
2 cups white wine	1 carrot, chunked
Parsley	1 onion, sliced
1 bay leaf	1 garlic, cut in half

Pâté

½ pound lean pork	2 tablespoons minced shallots,
½ pound lean veal	or onions
Salt	1 clove garlic, minced
Pepper	⅛ teaspoon dried thyme
6 chicken thighs	½ teaspoon minced parsley
3 slices fat bacon	2 tablespoons Cognac
Dash allspice	½ pound pork fat
	2 bay leaves

½ cup white wine

1. Prepare the stock. Remove meat from chicken thighs. Put bones and balance of stock ingredients into a large saucepan, or kettle. Cover and simmer for about 2 hours. Liquids should reduce by about half. Strain ingredients from liquids. Cool and remove coagulated fat from surface. What remains is nothing more than a seasoned gelée. Use it to flavor the pâté and

to give it a gelatinous quality. If pig's feet are not available, add 2 teaspoons of soaked gelatin to the hot stock.

2. Make the pâté. Cut pork and veal into very small pieces. Sprinkle with ½ teaspoon salt and some pepper. Mix well. Grind the meat from the chicken thighs and the bacon through the fine blade of a meat grinder. Put into a large mixing bowl. Add ½ teaspoon salt, dash pepper, and allspice; then the shallots, garlic, thyme, and parsley. Mix well. Add Cognac and stir. Put through grinder again.

3. Put a thin layer of pork fat on the bottom of a 3 × 8-inch terrine (bottom measurement) with a lid, or a 4-cup casserole or mold. Add a layer of the ground meats. Into the ground meat push pieces of veal and pork. Repeat these layers until ingredients are used, ending with the ground meats. Lay bay leaves on top and cover with a layer of pork fat. Pour the wine over the top. With a fork jab holes through the fat and into the pâté so that the wine can distribute itself throughout.

4. Set lid to terrine ajar and put into a 350-degree oven. Bake 1 hour. Remove from oven. Add some stock. Remove lid, reduce heat to 325 degrees, and bake another hour. Add more stock, reduce heat to 300 degrees, and bake another hour.

5. When done, cover with stock, put layers of foil on top of the pâté and put a salad dressing jar, half-filled with water, and closed tight, on top of the pâté to weigh it down. Cool the pâté in the terrine. When cool, refrigerate (with the weight on top). When it is completely cold, remove the weight. Scrape off the coagulated fat. Fill terrine with stock and refrigerate until set.

6. Pâtés are always served cool, not refrigerator cold and not at room temperature. Slice the pâté from the terrine, giving each guest some gelée and fat. Some people like this seasoned fat to spread on their French bread. Serve with pickles (p. 593) and eat within a week. Keep refrigerated.

BECKENOFFE-TOURTE LORRAINE

[*Meat-Potato Casserole*]

Beckenhoffe means to bake in a baker's oven and usually in a baking dish, or a round casserole. In Alsace this recipe is made with pork, mutton, and potatoes and has no custard sauce. In Lorraine it is called a *tourte,* which also means a round casserole or pan. Its recipe calls for pork and veal, and it has a custard but no potatoes. It is similar to other *Quiches Lorraines,* except that it has a top crust and so becomes a meat pie.

The following recipe is not a true Alsacian Beckenoffe, or a true Lorraine Tourte. It is a combination of the two dishes and was given to me by a Paris friend who came from the Alsace-Lorraine region. It is, as she said, "the way my mother made it and I don't know if it is Alsace or Lorraine." It is, to my way of thinking, better than either the Alsace or the Lorraine casseroles.

1 pound pork tenderloin	1½ cups Moselle, or white wine
1 pound lean veal	⅛ pound butter
6 red potatoes (medium size)	3 eggs
3 onions (medium size)	1½ cups whipping cream
Salt and pepper	2 tablespoons minced parsley

1. Cut all fat and tough skin from meats. Cut into ½-inch cubes. Peel potatoes and onions. Slice ready to use. Size of the potatoes and onions will determine how many you will need.

2. Arrange a layer of potatoes in the bottom of a 2-quart casserole with a lid. (If you don't know the casserole size and can't guess at it, measure water into it.) Add a layer of meats, sprinkle with salt and pepper and add a layer of onions. Repeat these layers until the meats are used, but end with onions. Add the wine and dot with butter. Cover and bake at 350 degrees for 2 hours. Do not lift the lid to check the dish. The wine, as it evaporates, gives flavor to the ingredients. To lift the lid would allow the fumes to escape. However, if you think it has cooked dry, it is better to check.

3. At the end of 2 hours the casserole should be moist but with no liquids left. (If there are liquids, remove the lid and cook another 15 minutes to volatilize them.) Take from oven, remove lid, and let casserole cool while mixing the custard. Reduce oven temperature to 325 degrees.

4. Mix the eggs with a whisk. Add the cream and parsley. Add salt and pepper to season (taste) and mix well. Pour into the casserole, filling it to the top of the onions. Do not cover. Set into the 325-degree oven and let it bake for about 20 minutes, or until the custard is set. Serve from the casserole.

LE GÂTEAU AU CHOCOLAT DE NANCY

[*Creamy Chocolate Cake*]

Butter and flour	1 tablespoon flour
¼ pound plus 2 tablespoons	Sugar
butter	4 egg yolks
½ pound semisweet chocolate	¼ teaspoon salt
1 tablespoon Cognac	½ teaspoon vanilla
1 tablespoon ground almonds	4 egg whites

1. Butter and flour a 9-inch cake pan with removable bottom. Put butter on a plate and cut into 4 pieces.

2. Put chocolate in top part of double boiler with the Cognac. Melt over warm water, but do not let top part touch the water. Remove from heat. Stir until warm. Set into cold water to hasten process. While still warm, add butter in 4 pieces. Blend each piece into the chocolate before adding the next piece.

3. Combine ground almonds, flour, and 4 tablespoons of sugar. Add to the chocolate.

4. Beat yolks with salt until light and thick. Beat in the chocolate mixture very gradually so that the mixture blends and does not separate. Add vanilla.

5. Beat whites until they start to stiffen and then gradually add 4 tablespoons of sugar and beat until stiff. On lowest speed mix whites into the chocolate batter. Pour into the prepared cake pan. Bake just 18 minutes at 425 degrees. No longer. The cake firms as it cools. Place cake on wire rack when done. When it is cool, remove from pan. Glaze with the following frosting (chocolate glaze), sprinkle with confectioners' sugar, or serve with whipped cream. The glaze is traditional.

GLACE AU CHOCOLAT DE NANCY
[*Chocolate Glaze*]

⅛ pound butter	3 tablespoons white corn syrup
1 tablespoon Kirsch	1 teaspoon instant espresso coffee
1 tablespoon Cognac	Dash salt
1 tablespoon water	4 ounces German sweet chocolate

Almond halves

1. Bring butter, liquids, syrup, instant espresso, and salt to a boil. Add chocolate, cover, and remove from heat. Let stand about 5 minutes, or until chocolate is soft. Stir until cool and thickened. Set into cold water to hasten process. If it gets too firm, reheat and cool again.

2. Put cake on wire cake rack, set on a cooky sheet, and pour all the frosting on the cake. With a rubber spatula push frosting over the sides to cover the cake completely. Work quickly or the glaze will not be smooth. This cake sinks in the middle, which is what it should do, and so you have to help the frosting down over the sides.

3. Place almond halves around the outside edge of the cake, one every inch, to create the traditional gâteau de Nancy. This cake may be frozen. Cut and serve in its frozen state.

NOTE: Save the frosting that has dripped onto the cooky sheet. Put it into a small container, cover, and refrigerate until needed. Or, spread it over crisp cookies.

LYONNAIS, BOURBONNAIS, NIVERNAIS

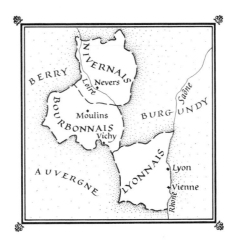

To the south and west of Burgundy lie three of the best known areas of provincial gastronomy. Fish and game dishes dominate the menus of the Bourbonnais and the Nivernais, both being lands which specialize in copious country foods. The Lyonnais, though small in area, is great in cuisine. At its center is Lyons, the traditional capital of French gastronomy.

Historically, the city of Lyons lay across the trade routes from north to south and east to west. Merchants, bankers, and churchmen from Italy met there in the sixteenth century with their French colleagues. In the fine houses of Lyons along the Rhone the cuisine of late Renaissance Italy quietly passed into France. Here it was gradually transformed into a method of menu planning and cooking that was eventually to become the basis of *haute cuisine*.

Over the years Lyons has preserved its reputation for hearty eating. But, like its neighbors of the Bourbonnais and the Nivernais, its menus are inclined to be heavy. The foods of Lyons are naturally richer and more elaborate than the simpler fare set out by its country cousins. There is, however, a tendency on the part of Lyonnais chefs to overwhelm rather than to tantalize the taste buds.

The local wines of the Nivernais and the Bourbonnais are generally light and pleasant. The Nivernais produces the superb Pouilly-sur-Loire and the Pouilly-Fumé. Both of these white wines go well with fish, poultry, and game. In the Lyonnais, with its tripe, omelettes, potatoes, and cakes, it is best to look for a sturdy red wine, usually one of the many Beaujolais wines in which the region abounds.

MENU

Les Quenelles de Brochet à la Nantua
[*Pike Dumplings with Shrimp Sauce*]
Wine: Pouilly-Fuissé or Hermitage Blanc

Salade au Cresson
[*Watercress Salad*]

Pain Ordinaire
[*French Bread*]

Mont d'Or Cheese
Wine: Château Timberlay

Flan aux Raisins
[*Grape Tart*]
Wine: Château Doisy-Védrines

LES QUENELLES DE BROCHET À LA NANTUA
[*Pike Dumplings with Shrimp Sauce*]

¼ cup milk	½ pound butter, approximately
¼ cup water	1 large egg
½ teaspoon salt	2 yolks, maybe 3
2 tablespoons butter	½ teaspoon salt
½ cup flour	White pepper to season
1 egg	Dash nutmeg
½ pound skinned and deboned	Salted water
pike meat (takes about ¾	
pound of fillets)	

1. Combine milk, water, ½ teaspoon salt, and 2 tablespoons butter in a saucepan. Bring to a boil. Remove from heat. Add the flour all at once and mix into a heavy dough. Add 1 egg and beat until it is incorporated into the dough. Pour this dough into a shallow dish, cover with buttered, transparent wrap. Cool and refrigerate.

2. The dough weighs about ½ pound, check it if you question its weight because the dough, pike meat, and butter should be about equal in weight, not measure. Skin the pike and be sure all bones are out of the fillets. Weigh the fillets once they are skinned—they will be about ½ pound. Cut fillets into

pieces. Place in blender container. Whirl to grind, or put the pike through fine blade of a food chopper. When dough, or panade, is cold put the dough into a mixing bowl. Add the ground pike and blend together.

3. Have the butter cool and creamed. Gradually add the butter to the pike mixture and blend each addition of butter before adding the next one. If using a blender, keep the mixture pulled away from the sides with a rubber spatula or it will not blend. After 1½ sticks of butter have been added, proceed with caution. The mixture will absorb just so much butter. The quality of the dough should be stiff and the butter an amalgamated part and not separated, or curdled. It is better to add too little butter than to add too much. Absorption is sudden.

4. Add the egg and blend. Add one yolk at a time and blend. The mixture may be perfect after two yolks; you can tell by the thickness of the dough. Size of the yolks is a determining factor. If, however, 2 yolks are added and the dough seems too heavy, add an egg white. Season with ½ teaspoon salt, pepper, and nutmeg. Blend. Pour into a shallow 6 × 8-inch buttered pan, cover with a buttered piece of foil, and refrigerate overnight. Make Nantua sauce before poaching quenelles.

5. Next day cut mixture into 12 pieces. Roll each piece on a lightly floured surface, shaping it into a cylinder, or what we call quenelle shape. Preheat oven to 350 degrees.

6. Butter a very large skillet. Lay quenelles into skillet as they are shaped. Have water boiling. When all quenelles are in skillet, carefully pour boiling water down the side of the pan. Completely cover with water and add 1 teaspoon of salt for each quart of water (guess at the amount). Poach quenelles 10 minutes and do not cover on this first cooking. Heat the Nantua sauce.

7. Butter a baking dish large enough to hold the quenelles in a single layer. Spoon the Nantua sauce over them. Cover tight with a sheet of foil and place in the oven. Bake for 20 minutes. These quenelles will inflate as they cook. Do not remove the foil until the quenelles are done or they will fall. Serve immediately, 2 per person.

SAUCE NANTUA

[Shrimp Sauce]

Seafood butter
¼ pound butter

6 large, cooked shrimp with shells, chopped

Sauce

2 tablespoons butter

3 tablespoons flour

½ teaspoon salt

1 cup fish stock, or ¼ cup clam juice, ½ cup white wine, and ¼ cup chicken broth

½ cup crème fraîche, or whipping cream

1 teaspoon lemon juice

2 tablespoons Cognac

2 tablespoons shrimp butter

Dash cayenne

¼ teaspoon sugar

Drop red coloring

1 tablespoon Madeira

Chunk butter

Minced truffle (optional)

1. Make seafood butter. Heat butter in a skillet. Put chopped shrimp into a blender container, or grind through a food chopper. When butter is hot, pour over shells in container and blend. Pour back into skillet, heat, and then pour back into blender container. Whirl again. Pour into a strainer set over a small bowl. Mash through as much of the shrimp mixture as possible. Discard dregs. Use what is needed of the shrimp butter and freeze the rest.

2. To make the sauce put butter into skillet and melt. Stir in the flour and salt. Add stock and crème. Stir-cook until thickened. Add lemon juice, Cognac, shrimp butter, cayenne, and sugar. This sauce should be a light orange-pink in color. Put a drop of red coloring on a plate. Dip the end of a spoon into the coloring and stir coloring into the sauce. Keep adding coloring until the desired shade is achieved. Add Madeira. Whisk small pieces of butter into sauce until you have added the equivalent of a chunk.

3. If you have a truffle, mince it fine and stir into the sauce. Have the sauce ready to reheat before poaching the quenelles.

NOTE: When you have had lobsters, save the tail shells, and little legs and turn them into lobster butter. Allow about ¼ pound of butter for shells from 2 lobsters. Freeze the butter until needed.

SALADE AU CRESSON

[*Watercress Salad*]

1 clove garlic

½ teaspoon salt

Freshly ground pepper

1 teaspoon Dijon-type mustard

1½ tablespoons wine vinegar

6 tablespoons olive oil

½ teaspoon chervil

Dash sugar

Watercress

1. Mash garlic in salad bowl with the spoon. Add salt, pepper, and mustard. Mash to a pulp. Add vinegar, oil, chervil, and sugar. Mix well. Taste and adjust.

(*continued*)

2. Wash the watercress the day before, break off the tough stems and wrap the watercress in paper towels to dry. Refrigerate until ready to use. It will take a lot of watercress to serve 6. Since the size of a bunch of watercress varies, you will have to judge the amount to purchase. The dressing is for 6.

3. Add watercress at the moment of serving, toss, and serve.

FLAN AUX RAISINS

[*Grape Tart*]

1 (9-inch) tart shell

Filling

3 cups seedless grapes (about 1½ pounds)	1 teaspoon flour
	½ teaspoon salt
3 whole eggs	1 cup sugar

1. Preheat oven to 450 degrees. Make tart shell (p. 454). Butter and flour a 9-inch tart or pie pan. Roll ⅔ of the dough into a circle to fit the pan. Line the pan. Cut off dough that hangs over the edge of the pan. Crimp the dough between thumb and finger to make the edge fancy. Stick bottom of tart shell with a fork in about six places (allows steam to escape so that bubbles will not form under the dough). Line dough with a circle of foil. Put on lowest shelf of oven and bake about 10 minutes, or until lightly browned. Remove from oven, discard foil, and set on wire rack. Reduce oven heat to 350 degrees.

2. Wash grapes. Remove stems and dry grapes on terry or paper towels. You should have about 3 cups of grapes.

3. Put eggs into small mixer bowl. Beat until well mixed and a bit light, but not whipped. Stir flour and salt into sugar. Add sugar to eggs and beat until sugar is dissolved. Add grapes. Toss together and pour into tart shell. Bake about 40 minutes, or until crust is brown as well as the top of the tart. When done, cool at least 30 minutes on a wire rack before serving. White grapes have a gooseberry flavor when cooked.

MENU

Boule de Fromage Frit
[*French-Fried Cheese Balls*]

Cuissot de Chevreuil
[*Haunch of Venison*]

Wine: Moulin-à-Vent or Clos de Tart

Pâté de Pommes de Terre
[*Fried Potato Pâté*]

Salade

Tarte Bourbonnaise
[*Country Cheesecake*]

BOULE DE FROMAGE FRIT
[*French-Fried Cheese Balls*]

1 small egg white

1 cup grated Gruyère, or Swiss
cheese (⅛ pound)

1 teaspoon minced parsley

¼ teaspoon grated onion

Dash cayenne

Peanut oil for French-frying

Flour

1 egg white, mixed to a froth

Fine bread crumbs

1. Using a whisk, beat 1 egg white to a froth. Add cheese, parsley, onion, and cayenne. Mixture should be thick and heavy. Beat well and then add more cheese if necessary. Amount of egg white will determine thickness. Heat oil to 320.

2. Shape cheese mixture into ¾-inch balls. Roll them in flour, then egg white and then crumbs. Dip again in egg white and crumbs. Place in French-fryer basket. Lower into hot oil. Fry until puffed and browned. Keep oil between 320 and 330 degrees. If the oil goes to a higher temperature the puffs are likely to pop in the oil. Drain on paper towels.

3. To serve, put two or three on individual plates and spoon tomato sauce (p. 537, omit mushrooms), or garlic sauce (p. 587) over them. Makes approximately 1 dozen. These may also be served as cocktail food, with or without the sauce.

CUISSOT DE CHEVREUIL

[*Haunch of Venison*]

1 (4–5-pound) leg of venison	1 bay leaf
2 cups red wine (Burgundy)	½ teaspoon rosemary
2 tablespoons olive oil	2 slices salt pork cut ⅛ inch thick
¼ teaspoon thyme	Salt and pepper
1 tablespoon minced parsley	3 carrots
1 onion, diced	1 onion, sliced

4 sprigs parsley

Sauce

Chunk butter	Marinade liquids
1 carrot, minced	1 teaspoon brown sugar
1 onion, minced	1 teaspoon vinegar
3 tablespoons flour	Freshly ground pepper
1 cup red wine	3 tablespoons Cognac

Butter

1. Always remove all visible fat from game. It very quickly becomes rancid. Put meat into a plastic bag. Add wine, oil, thyme, parsley, onions, bay leaf, and rosemary. Put the salt pork slices into the marinade so that they will take on flavor. Marinate in the refrigerator for 3 days.

2. Remove venison. Blot with paper towels. Rub with salt and pepper. Cut 1 slice of salt pork into ¼-inch pieces. With the point of a paring knife, make pockets all over the meat and insert pieces of salt pork. Lay the other slice on top of the roast.

3. Preheat oven to 450 degrees. Cut carrots lengthwise into quarters. Put into a roasting pan. Add sliced onion and lay parsley on top. Set venison on this bed of vegetables. Reduce heat to 325 and put venison into oven to roast for 1 hour.

4. Make sauce while venison cooks. Put butter into saucepan. Add minced carrot and onions. Sauté for about 20 minutes. Stir in flour. Cook 1 minute. Add wine, marinade liquids, sugar, vinegar, and lots of pepper. Stir-cook until thickened, then set lid ajar and let sauce simmer until roast is done, or about 1 hour.

5. When roast is done, pour 3 tablespoons of Cognac over it and set aflame. When flame dies, lift roast to serving platter. Spoon liquids from roasting pan and add to the sauce. Strain sauce into a clean pan. Heat. Taste and adjust seasonings and thicken with beurre manié (p. 2) if necessary. Swirl a piece of butter into the sauce and serve sauce separately with the roast.

NOTE: Venison, like beef, should be served medium to rare. Roast about 20 minutes per pound for rare.

PÂTÉ DE POMMES DE TERRE
[*Fried Potato Pâté*]

7 potatoes	Milk
Butter	Salt, pepper, and nutmeg
Cream	Flour

Bacon fat, or lard

1. Peel potatoes, cut into fourths, and boil until done. Drain and dry off over low heat. Turn into mashed potatoes. Make them very rich with butter and cream and then thin with a bit of milk. Do not whip in a mixer, but mash with a potato masher. Season with salt, pepper, and nutmeg.

2. Coat a bread pan with butter. Pack the potatoes into it, keeping them to one end of the pan and to the depth of the pan. Use foil to hold them to one end. Cover and refrigerate until cold and molded into a loaf. Turn the potato cake out onto a floured board and cut into six slices. Flour the slices well and fry on both sides in bacon fat or lard. Have the fat hot before adding the potato slices. (Leftover potatoes may be given the same treatment.)

TARTE BOURBONNAISE
[*Country Cheesecake*]

1 (8-ounce package) cream cheese	½ teaspoon vanilla
¼ teaspoon salt	Butter and flour for pan
2 whole eggs	Pieces of butter
2 tablespoons softened butter	Sugar
2 tablespoons flour	Crème fraîche, or sour cream

Fruit

1. Preheat oven to 325 degrees. Put ingredients, down through the vanilla into a mixer bowl. Beat until smooth, thick, and like whipped cream.

2. Give an 8-inch pie pan a heavy coating of butter and then coat with flour. Fill pan with cheese mixture. Level mixture out in the pan, but keep it away from the top edge. Mixture will push itself out as it rises. Push 6 or 8 thin pats of butter halfway down into the batter. Bake on the middle shelf for about 40 minutes.

3. When it is done, turn oven off, open the door, and let cake cool 10 minutes in the oven. Put cake on wire rack, sprinkle with sugar, and let cool. Serve, or cover and refrigerate until ready to serve.

4. This cake rises high, but will settle as it cools and create a natural recessed area on the top. Fill this space with about 2 cups of crème fraîche, or sour cream, and arrange sliced strawberries, peaches, or other fruit over the top. Sprinkle with lots of sugar; there is none in the cheesecake.

MENU

Matelote de Veau
[*Veal Stew with Red Wine*]

Wine: Fleurie or Brouilly

Pommes de Terre Bouillies
[*Boiled Potatoes*]

Pissenlit au Lard
[*Dandelion Greens with Bacon*]

Mousse aux Pommes à la Chantilly
[*Apple Mousse with Whipped Cream*]

Les Sablés
[*Shortbread*]

MATELOTE DE VEAU

[*Veal Stew with Red Wine*]

3 pounds cubed veal	Thyme branch or ⅛ teaspoon
¼ pound butter	3 sprigs parsley
2 onions, quartered	Salt and pepper
4 tablespoons flour	12 boiling onions
1 bottle red Burgundy wine	18 small mushroom caps
1 clove garlic, minced	Chunk butter
1 bay leaf	1 teaspoon sugar

2 tablespoons Madeira

1. Sauté veal in butter with the onions. Stir in flour and cook a few minutes. Add wine, garlic, bay leaf, thyme, and parsley. Set lid ajar and simmer about 1 hour. Discard bay leaf, thyme branch if used, and parsley. Add 1 teaspoon salt and season with pepper.

2. Peel the onions. Put them into cold water, bring to a boil, drain, and rinse. Brown onions and mushrooms in a chunk of butter. Add to the stew. Cook another hour, or until stew is done. Add sugar and Madeira. Stir, taste, adjust seasonings and thickness with beurre manié (p. 2). Cook potatoes (p. 236) during last hour. Serve potatoes separately, or add to the stew.

PISSENLIT AU LARD

[*Dandelion Greens with Bacon*]

Dandelion greens for six   3 slices bacon, diced
Salt, pepper, and sugar   2 tablespoons white vinegar

1. In early spring dig up dandelion plants. The tender inside leaves are the best. Cut the leaves from the roots, discard the tough outside ones, and then wash well those you select to eat. Drain and dry. Place in salad bowl. Sprinkle with salt, pepper, and a dash of sugar.

2. Fry bacon crisp. Turn off heat. Measure vinegar into a cup. Have a lid in one hand and with the other hand pour the vinegar into the hot skillet. Cover and let it pop. If it does not pop, heat again.

3. Pour the very hot liquids over the dandelion greens. Invert the skillet over the greens, which will help to wilt the dandelions. Toss and serve.

MOUSSE AUX POMMES À LA CHANTILLY

[*Apple Foam*]

8 Jonathan apples, or enough to   2 tablespoons Kirsch
   make 2 cups cooked apples   ½ teaspoon vanilla
Dash salt   Lady fingers
1 cup white wine   1 cup whipping cream
4 teaspoons unflavored gelatin   Dash salt
5 tablespoons cold water   2 tablespoons confectioners' sugar
1 cup sugar, or to sweeten apples   ¼ teaspoon vanilla
         2 tablespoons Kirsch

1. Peel, core, and slice apples into saucepan. Add salt and wine. Cover and cook until mushy and very well done. Put mixer bowl and beaters into freezer or refrigerator.

2. Soak gelatin in water until soft. When apples are done, add sugar and cook 10 minutes. Grind through a food mill. Add gelatin to the hot apples. Stir until dissolved. Add 2 tablespoons of Kirsch and ½ teaspoon vanilla. Cool mixture and refrigerate until starting to set.

3. Line the bottom of a 6-cup charlotte mold with waxed paper. Do not butter the mold. Line the sides of the mold with lady fingers. If bought lady fingers are used, separate them in half and put the round side to the mold.

4. When apple mixture is cold and starting to set, put mixture into cold mixing bowl and beat until fluffy and the mixture turns white and thick. It

may take 15 minutes. Pour into the lined mold. Cover and refrigerate at least 8 hours, or overnight.

5. When ready to serve, invert mold onto a shallow serving dish and remove the waxed paper.

6. Whip the cream to which has been added a dash of salt. When it is whipped add the confectioners' sugar and flavor with ¼ teaspoon vanilla and 2 tablespoons of Kirsch. Put some whipped cream into a pouch with a star nozzle and squeeze stars of cream over the top of the apple mold. Serve balance of whipped cream separately. Cut into wedges to serve.

LES SABLÉS

[Shortbread Cookies]

2 hard-cooked egg yolks	1 teaspoon grated orange rind
1 cup flour	¼ pound butter, softened
¼ cup sugar	¼ teaspoon salt

1. Cook eggs (p. 56) and cool. Preheat oven to 450 degrees. Put flour in mixer bowl. Add sugar, rind, butter and salt. Sieve the yolks into these ingredients. Mix into a dough. Chill dough 1 hour.

2. Sprinkle work area with flour. Place dough on flour and sprinkle top of dough with more flour. Roll dough ⅛ inch thick. Cut into 4-inch cookies with a fluted cutter. Score cookies in criss-cross lines with a fork dipped first into flour. Cut cookies into fourths.

3. Moisten a cooky sheet with water (use plastic spray bottle if you have one). Lift cookies off work area with a spatula and place on damp cooky sheet. Bake about 8 minutes on middle shelf of oven, or until lightly browned. Remove from cooky sheet and place on wire racks to cool. Makes about 24 cookies.

NOTE: The dough is very fragile and delicate to work. Resist the temptation to add more flour.

MARCHE, LIMOUSIN

West of the Auvergne mountains is Limousin. It is separated from the Marche by the Vienne River. While the Marche and the Limousin are divided by geography and history, they are united gastronomically because they both enjoy the same produce and identical food specialties.

The chief city of the Marche is Guéret, a town of ten thousand inhabitants which is the marketing center of the entire region. It supplies agricultural produce both to Aubusson, the tapestry town, and to Limoges, the porcelain town. Whatever is left over eventually finds its way to the bustling markets of Paris.

Pork, beef, fish, and game (especially hares) rank highest among the meat products of the region. These are often served *à la Limousin,* a designation that ordinarily indicates an accompaniment of red cabbage braised with chestnuts, cèpes, morels, or other local products.

As in many rural areas, the menu is studded with dishes in which food grains predominate. Soups are heavy with rye and buckwheat. Meats and pâtés are stuffed with cereals and embellished with mushrooms of many types. Fruit tarts are among the best of the desserts.

The wines of the area are undistinguished, the most unusual being the "gray wines" of the Vienne valley. The natives enjoy these simple wines best when they are served with the marzipan, macaroons, meringues, pancakes, and other sweets prepared by the local bakers and housewives.

MENU

Potage Crème de Champignons
[*Cream of Mushroom Soup*]

Wine: Saumur

Faisan en Barbouille
[*Pheasant in Casserole*]

Wine: Red Rochecorbon

Pommes de Terre Bouillies
[*Boiled Potatoes*]

Pain Ordinaire
[*French Bread*]

Salade

Clafouti du Limousin
[*Cherry Cake*]

POTAGE CRÈME DE CHAMPIGNONS

[*Cream of Mushroom Soup*]

2 leeks, sliced

2 yellow onions, sliced

¼ pound butter

1 pound mushrooms, sliced

4 tablespoons flour

2 cups chicken stock

3 cups half-and-half cream

2 teaspoons salt

1 tablespoon sugar

⅛ teaspoon white pepper

1 cup crème fraîche, or whipping cream

Mushrooms and parsley to garnish

1. Clean leeks (p. 607). Slice into saucepan along with onions and butter. Cover and simmer 30 minutes. Add mushrooms and cook 10 minutes. Stir in flour. Cook a few minutes.

2. Add stock, half-and-half cream, salt, sugar, and pepper. Stir-cook until slightly thickened. Grind through a food mill. Pour back into saucepan and keep warm. Stir in crème or whipping cream when ready to serve. Heat and then pour into a tureen. Garnish with sliced raw mushrooms and some minced parsley.

FAISAN EN BARBOUILLE

[*Pheasant in Casserole*]

One pheasant will normally serve 3 people; this is why we usually buy pheasants by the brace (2).

Cooked chestnuts	2 bay leaves
2 pheasants (approx. 5 pounds)	3 sprigs parsley
Butter	2 cloves garlic, minced
2 tablespoons vegetable oil	1 teaspoon salt
¼ cup Armagnac, or Cognac	Freshly ground pepper
4 carrots, diced	2 cups red wine
2 onions, diced	12 small boiling onions
3 tablespoons flour	18 mushrooms
⅛ teaspoon thyme	2 (¼-inch) slices salt pork, diced

1 truffle, sliced

1. Prepare chestnuts (p. 273), or use canned ones. Cut pheasants into pieces as you would a chicken. Sauté pieces in a chunk of butter and oil until lightly browned. Pour Armagnac over them and set aflame. When flame dies, remove pheasant from skillet.

2. Add carrots and onions to skillet and sauté until browned. Stir in the flour and cook 1 minute. Add thyme. Tie bay leaves and parsley into a bundle (bouquet garni) and add to skillet. Add garlic, salt, and pepper. Pour in wine and stir until sauce thickens. Add onions and return pheasant to the skillet. Set lid ajar and simmer about 40 minutes.

3. Cut stems off even with mushroom caps and wash. Add mushrooms and cooked chestnuts. Sauté diced salt pork in a piece of butter. Add to skillet. Simmer 30 minutes, or until pheasant is tender. Prepare recipe of boiled potatoes (p. 236). When pheasant is done, taste and adjust seasonings and thickness of sauce with beurre manié (p. 2). Arrange pheasant on platter. Add onions, mushrooms, and whole boiled potatoes. Spoon sauce over pheasant and garnish with slices of truffle.

CLAFOUTI DU LIMOUSIN

[*Cherry Cake*]

Limousin claims this dessert as its invention—but so do the good cooks of Berry. Whose creation it was originally I do not know, except to say that the cooks of Berry in preparing it insist upon using the cherries of Poligny, a small market village specializing in the fruits of the Jura Mountains. The original recipe cooks the dough as pancakes, while in Touraine it is baked in pastry, thus a cherry tart. I prefer the pancake or tart to the Limousin way, but here is the Limousin cake.

1¼ cups sweet black cherries	3 tablespoons flour
Butter and flour	¾ cup whipping cream
3 whole eggs	½ teaspoon vanilla
4 tablespoons confectioners' sugar	1 tablespoon Kirsch
½ teaspoon salt	Sugar

1. If using fresh cherries, pit them without tearing the meat. If using canned cherries, drain them well and then squeeze out the juice. Butter and flour a 9-inch quiche dish, solid-bottomed tart pan, pie pan, or square cake pan. Preheat oven to 325 degrees.

2. Put eggs into mixing bowl. Whisk them together as for an omelette. Mix together confectioners' sugar, salt, and flour. Blend into the eggs. Add cream, vanilla, and Kirsch.

3. Pour half the custard into the prepared pan. Add the cherries and balance of custard. Bake in preheated oven for approximately 40 minutes, or until puffed and brown.

4. When done, remove from oven and sprinkle with lots of sugar. Set on wire cake rack to cool for 20 minutes. Cake settles as it cools. Cut into wedges and serve.

NOTE: Use a very sharp knife to cut this cake so that you cut through the cherries and do not mash them into the custard-like cake.

NORMANDIE

The river Seine winds its way from Paris to Rouen and thence to the sea through one of the finest agricultural regions of France. Along the highways stretching from Paris to the seaports of Normandy huge trucks loaded with seafoods, fish, butter, and cheese make daily runs into the capital.

The Normans, who were originally sea raiders from Scandinavia, settled down in this maritime region of northern France in the tenth century. There, despite being involved in the numerous wars between England and France, they developed a way of life that is still distinctive. Like their northern forefathers the Normans of France are seafarers, fishermen, dairymen, and great trenchermen.

While the grape does not grow in Normandy, the apple does. The typical Norman rarely drinks wine. He prefers cider with his meals and warms himself with the apple liqueur called Calvados.

The dishes of Normandy are typically rich, for almost everything is cooked in cream or a special fat called *graisse normande*. Its cheeses, especially Camembert and *petit-suisse* cream cheese, enjoy fine international reputations. Omelettes are also favored in this region, especially the one prepared at the Hotel Mère Poularde at marvelous Mont-Saint-Michel. But perhaps the best recommendation for the food of Normandy is the fact that so much of it is eaten in Paris.

MENU

Champignons Moulés aux Crevettes
[*Mushroom Molds with Shrimp Sauce*]

Côte de Veau à la Crème
[*Veal in Cream Sauce*]

To drink: Hard Cider or Rosé d'Anjou

Petits Pois à la Normandie
[*Creamed Peas*]

Salade

Pain Ordinaire
[*French Bread*]

Omelette Fourée aux Pommes Dite à la Normandie
[*Apple Upside-Down Pancake*]

Calvados (Apple Brandy)

CHAMPIGNONS MOULÉS AUX CREVETTES

[*Mushroom Molds with Shrimp Sauce*]

Mushroom molds

Clarified butter

4 large eggs

Salt

2 teaspoons cornstarch

½ cup whipping cream

1 cup chicken stock

½ teaspoon paprika

Dash nutmeg

2 cups minced mushrooms
(about ½ pound)

1 tablespoon minced parsley

Shrimp sauce

Chunk butter

2 cups raw shrimp, cut-up

1 tablespoon minced shallots

3 tablespoons Calvados

3 tablespoons flour

Dash nutmeg

½ teaspoon sugar

¼ teaspoon salt, or to season

2 cups light cream

¼ cup Madeira

Minced parsley

1. Bake in individual, straight-sided molds and in a water bath. Give 6 individual (6-ounce) soufflé dishes or timbales a heavy coating of melted, clarified butter. Line bottom of each timbale with a round of waxed paper,

letting the paper extend up the sides by ⅟₁₆ of an inch or so. Press these rounds into the dishes. Coat paper with melted butter. Refrigerate dishes and coat again before filling them.

2. Preheat oven to 350 degrees. Put about 1-inch of water into a pan large enough to hold the molds. Bring water to a boil.

3. Break eggs into mixer bowl. Add ½ teaspoon salt. Put cornstarch into a small saucepan. Stir in enough cream to make a paste. Add balance of cream, stock, ¼ teaspoon salt, paprika, and nutmeg.

4. Wash mushrooms. Cut stems off at caps, slice thin, and then chop very fine. Add to saucepan. Heat-stir until thickened.

5. Beat eggs together but do not make them light. Add the hot mushroom mixture by spoonfuls. Add parsley.

6. Take molds from refrigerator. Coat again with melted butter. Stir mushroom mixture and then ladle into the prepared molds. Mushrooms, being light, come to the top. Be sure each mold has its share of mushrooms and liquids. Mixture will not rise during baking.

7. Set molds into water bath and place in preheated oven. Bake 30 minutes, or until done. Test as you do custard, by inserting a table knife into the center. If it comes out clean, the mold is done. If it doesn't, bake another 5 minutes and test again.

8. Ten minutes before timbales are done, make the sauce. Melt butter in a skillet. Cut the shrimp across into ¼- to ½-inch pieces. Add shrimp and shallots to skillet. Sauté about 1 minute. Add Calvados and set aflame. (Stand back; this really burns.)

9. When flame dies, stir in flour. Stir-cook 1 minute or so and then add nutmeg, sugar, salt, cream, and Madeira. Stir-cook until thickened. Taste and adjust seasonings. Set lid ajar and put skillet on asbestos mat over low heat to keep warm.

10. Unmold the timbales. This is not easy. Run the point of a knife around the top edge of the custard and then run the knife around the sides and down to the bottom. Do this very carefully. Invert each mold onto serving plates. Shake the mold and the custard should drop out. If it doesn't, carefully insert a table knife under one edge of the waxed paper, while inverted, and the custard should drop out. Peel off the round of waxed paper. Spoon sauce over the top, sprinkle with minced parsley, and serve as a first course to 6, or make 4 larger molds and serve as a main dish along with salad and dessert for a light supper.

NOTE: This is a beautiful dish. It ends up with a mushroom layer on the bottom, then a mushroom-flavored custard layer, and the creamy shrimp on top.

CÔTE DE VEAU À LA CRÈME

[*Veal in Cream Sauce*]

1½ pounds thin veal slices, or
  steaks
3 cups sliced mushrooms
4 apples
Butter
1 teaspoon sugar

Salt and pepper
3 tablespoons Calvados
1¼ cups whipping cream
2 egg yolks
2 teaspoons lemon juice
Parsley

1. Have the butcher cut thin slices of veal from a rump roast, or buy veal steaks. If you get steaks, separate the muscles in them and cut the muscles, or the slices, into 2-inch pieces. Pound each one thin with a wooden kitchen mallet, or the bottom of a pan. Set aside ready to use.

2. Wash mushrooms and slice enough for 3 cupfuls. Sauté in a chunk of butter. While mushrooms cook, peel and slice apples. Put sautéed mushrooms onto a plate. Add more butter to the skillet. Add the apple slices and fry. When they are soft, sprinkle with sugar. Let them caramelize.

3. While apples cook, sauté the veal in a large skillet in butter. When each side has been lightly browned, veal should be done. Sprinkle with salt and pepper. Add Calvados and carefully set aflame. When flame dies, add apples, mushrooms, and ¾ cup of cream. Bring to a boil.

4. Combine remaining ½ cup of cream, yolks, and lemon juice. Stir some hot cream into the mixture and then stir back into the skillet. Heat until it thickens, but do not let it boil. Taste and adjust seasonings.

5. Put veal onto hot platter and pour sauce over it. Decorate platter with parsley. Serve with waffled potatoes (p. 240), that have been made earlier.

PETITS POIS À LA NORMANDIE

[*Creamed Peas*]

2 cups frozen peas, or 2
  (10-ounce) packages
2 yolks

1¼ cups whipping cream
¼ teaspoon salt
Pepper and nutmeg to season

1. Cook peas in salted water until tender. Drain, and dry over low heat.

2. Combine yolks, cream, and seasonings. Pour over peas. Gradually heat and stir until thickened. Do not boil. Taste and adjust the seasonings. If the sauce seems too thick, add a bit more cream; if too thin, adjust with beurre manié (p. 2).

OMELETTE FOURÉE AUX POMMES DITE À LA NORMANDIE

[*Apple Upside-Down Pancake*]

3 apples	4 tablespoons sugar
Chunk butter	¼ teaspoon vanilla
Dash salt	Dash cinnamon

1 tablespoon Calvados or Cognac

Batter

3 tablespoons unsifted flour	2 egg whites
¼ teaspoon baking powder	Sugar
Dash salt	1 teaspoon lemon juice
3 tablespoons milk	1 cup crème fraîche, or sour cream
2 egg yolks	¼ cup whipping cream

1. Peel apples. Cut them from their cores in wedge-shaped slices. Put a chunk of butter into a 10-inch iron, enamel, or ovenware skillet that is also flame-proof. Add apple slices and sauté about 15 minutes, or until soft. Sprinkle with salt and 4 tablespoons of sugar. Remove from heat. Add vanilla and cinnamon to the Calvados. Pour over the apples. Stir and set aside to cool.

2. Preheat oven to 400 degrees. Fifteen minutes before serving the dessert, mix the batter. Put flour, baking powder, and salt into a small mixing bowl. Pour milk into a measuring cup, add the yolks to it, and beat together.

3. Beat the whites until they start to stiffen. Gradually add 2 tablespoons of sugar and beat until stiff.

4. Stir the milk-yolk combination into the flour. Beat out the lumps. Stir in the stiffly beaten egg whites. Mix well. Pour over the cooled apples in the skillet. Sprinkle with sugar and bake about 12 minutes, or until lightly browned and puffed to the top of the skillet.

5. Stir lemon juice into the crème. Dilute it with whipping cream. Pour into a serving dish. When the pancake is done, remove it from the oven and invert it onto a serving plate. The apples are on top and the cake on the bottom. (It will fall, like a soufflé.) Sprinkle apples with a lot of sugar, cut the pancake into wedges, and serve with the sour cream. Should serve 6, but 3 will eat the whole pancake.

ORLÉANAIS

[*The Orléans Country*]

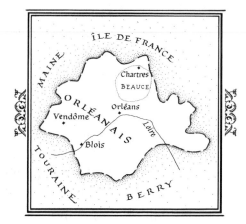

Located on both sides of the middle Loire River, the chief cities of this region are Orléans, Chartres, and Blois. The Château of Blois, built during the sixteenth century was one of the great gastronomic centers of royal France and famous particularly for its game specialties.

The countryside surrounding Orléans, at the heart of this province, is noted for its fine produce. Its beef and poultry are highly prized in neighboring Paris and Tours. The asparagus from Vendôme, to the east of Orléans, is in demand throughout France when it is in season.

My favorite town in this region is Chartres, most famous for its magnificent Gothic cathedral with its two spires, stained glass, and sculptures. The road from Paris to Chartres takes one through the gardenland of France, the fertile fields on either side extending as far as the eye can see. Once I have renewed my acquaintance with the cathedral, I can hardly wait to visit one of Chartres' famous restaurants. I remember once eating a hen fixed in the simple style of Beauce. On another occasion I had pike, spiced with saffron raised just to the east of Chartres.

There are no regional wines of quality, and so you might accompany the following menu with a simple red wine from the Loire.

MENU

Boeuf Braisé à la Beauceronne
[*Beef Casserole*]

Wine: Bourgueil (Loire)

Salade d'Asperges Blanc
[*Asparagus Salad*]

Pain de Mie
[*French Sandwich Bread*]

Tarte des Demoiselles Tatin
[*Carmelized Apple Tart*]

Wine: Monmousseau

BOEUF BRAISÉ À LA BEAUCERONNE
[*Beef Casserole*]

Lean bacon slices

6 red potatoes, approximately

3 onions, sliced thin

Salt and pepper

¼ teaspoon dried basil

1 tablespoon minced parsley

1 (2-pound) slice round steak
  cut ½-inch thick

¼ teaspoon thyme

1 bay leaf

White wine, about ¾ cup

Chicken consommé, about ¾ cup

⅛ pound butter

Minced parsley

1. Line the bottom of a large casserole with slices of bacon. Peel potatoes and slice paper thin. Put a layer of potatoes on top of the bacon. Add a layer of onion slices. Season with salt and pepper. Sprinkle with basil and parsley.

2. Cut steak into serving-sized pieces. Add to casserole. Sprinkle with thyme. Add another layer of onions and then potatoes. Sprinkle again with salt and pepper. Lay bay leaf on top. Add wine and consommé in equal proportions to cover the vegetables. Dot with butter. Bring to a boil on top of the range, remove, cover, and braise in a 325-degree oven for about 1 hour. Reduce heat to 300 degrees and braise another 1½ hours. Discard bay leaf, sprinkle with parsley, and serve from the casserole.

SALADE D'ASPERGES BLANC

[*Asparagus Salad*]

Herbed Dressing

½ clove garlic

¼ teaspoon salt

Freshly ground pepper

1 teaspoon minced shallots

1½ tablespoons wine vinegar

6 tablespoons olive oil

1 teaspoon minced parsley

¼ teaspoon chervil

Boston or Bibb lettuce leaves

Canned white asparagus

1. Mash garlic in salad bowl. Add balance of ingredients, down to the lettuce. Mix well. Let it age for several hours.

2. Put lettuce leaves on salad plates. Add about 3 stalks of asparagus and spoon dressing over the salad. Serve.

PAIN DE MIE

[*French Sandwich Bread*]

1 (⅝- or 0.6-ounce) cake yeast

¼ cup warm water

4 cups flour

½ cup cake flour

4 tablespoons sugar

1 teaspoon salt

¼ pound butter, softened

2 eggs, beaten light

¾ cup warm water, approximately

Melted butter

1. Dissolve yeast in ¼ cup warm water. Put flours, sugar, and salt into large mixer bowl. Mix. Add yeast, butter, and eggs. Beat with mixer, or by hand, while adding enough warm water to make a firm-soft dough. The trick to this bread is the consistency of the dough. When it is mixed, push dough down from sides of the bowl, coat sides of bowl with butter and brush top of the bread. Cover and let rise in a warm place until it has doubled in size.

2. Punch down dough and knead on a lightly floured board for a minute or so. Divide dough in half. Shape into two loaves and place in two 5 × 3 × 4-inch greased bread pans. Coat loaves with melted butter. Grease two sheets of foil. Place these over the top of each pan. Tie tight with a string. Let dough rise until almost touching the foil. Preheat oven to 375 degrees. Bake 30 minutes. Reduce heat to 325 degrees and bake 20 minutes longer.

3. When done, remove from oven. Take foil off pans and turn loaves out onto wire racks to cool.

NOTE: In France straight-sided bread pans with metal lids are used to make this bread. These pans are available in specialty shops, but a regular bread pan and foil work well, except that the sides of the bread will be slanted and the top somewhat rounded. You may also bake these without the foil.

TARTE DES DEMOISELLES TATIN

[*Caramelized Apple Tart*]

History records that this particular dish was unwittingly created by the Tatin Sisters, restaurateurs of Lamotte-Beuvron. It seems they put this tart into the oven and then rushed off to church forgetting about it. Upon returning to their restaurant, they were forced to serve the ruined tart to their hungry church-going clientele. They foisted it off as a new upside-down caramelized tart.

Most recipes direct you to put melted butter and sugar into a deep pan, or casserole, add apple slices, more melted butter, and sugar, and top with a crust and bake. I find this method unpredictable as to caramelization, and so offer you the following adapted recipe. Try making it both ways.

Pie crust	½ cup sugar
½ cup sugar	Dash salt
¼ cup water	1 tablespoon flour
Apples, 6 to 8 depending upon size	½ teaspoon cinnamon
	Melted butter

1. Make pie crust (p. 454). Use a round 8 inch metal pan about 2 inches deep, a pie pan, a square cake pan, or a similar container. Put sugar and water into pan. Heat-stir to dissolve the sugar and then caramelize the sugar to a medium brown. Remove from heat.

2. Peel and core apples. If the apples are small, cut them into quarters; if large, into eighths. Place these, cut side down, on the burnt sugar. Fill pan to the top. Preheat oven to 375 degrees.

3. Combine sugar, salt, flour, and cinnamon. Sprinkle mixture over apples and spoon lots of melted butter over the whole. Roll crust ⅛ inch thick. Lay crust over the top of the apple slices. Press dough down on edge of pan. Cut designs in the crust to allow steam to escape.

4. Bake tart for about 30 minutes. When done, remove, let stand about 20 minutes, and then invert onto a serving plate. Serve with crème fraîche and sugar. Serve hot, or warm, but never refrigerator cold.

PICARDIE

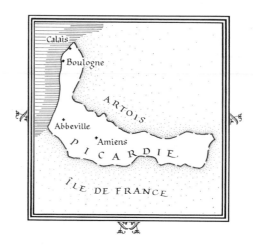

A land of sandy farms and inland lakes, Picardy slopes to the sea. Boulogne, its port, is the first fishing city of France. Its other towns are primarily industrial centers divided one from the other by sand dunes on whose sparse grass big sheep graze hungrily to produce wool and mutton.

Essentially this is a land of home cooking and family meals in both the country and the cities. In the seaports the fare is fish soup accompanied by great schooners of beer. Inland the rural family dines on salty mutton or fresh pork with leek tarts and a salty cheese called Marolles.

In Amiens, the traditional capital, the urbanites' favorite is duck pâté, which they wash down with local cider. One of the dishes of Picardy enjoyed everywhere is a red cabbage salad that helps to lighten meals and refresh the palate.

MENU

Caqhuse
[*Pork-Onion Casserole*]

To drink: Hard Cider

Pain Ordinaire
[*French Bread*]

Salade de Chou Rouge
[*Sweet-Sour Red Cabbage Salad*]

Poires à la Crème Pâtissière
[*Pears with Cream Sauce*]

CAQHUSE

[*Pork-Onion Casserole*]

2 pounds pork tenderloin	1 tablespoon brown sugar
6 onions	1 bay leaf
¼ pound butter	⅛ teaspoon thyme
2 (12-ounce) cans beer,	1 tablespoon minced parsley
approximately	Salt

Freshly ground pepper

1. Cut tenderloins into ¼-inch-thick slices. Clean onions and slice ⅛ inch thick.

2. Sauté pork slices in butter until brown. Put on a plate. Add onions and brown. Put on another plate. Pour 1 cup of beer into the skillet (guess at it). Stir, add sugar, bay leaf, thyme, and parsley. Bring to a boil and then turn off heat.

3. Put a layer of onions into a 2-quart casserole with a lid. Add a layer of pork slices. Season with salt and pepper. Repeat these layers, ending with onions. Pour liquids and herbs from the skillet into the casserole. Press meat down into the casserole. Add beer to cover the top of the onions. Cover and bake in a 325-degree oven for about 2 hours.

To serve. Put a slice of toasted French bread into a soup plate. Top with broth and meat. Provide additional French bread on the side.

SALADE DE CHOU ROUGE

[*Sweet-Sour Red Cabbage Salad*]

1 (1 pound) head red cabbage	2 tablespoons olive oil
4 tablespoons sugar	½ teaspoon salt
2 tablespoons cider vinegar	Freshly ground pepper to season

1. Cut cabbage in half. Shred very fine on a slicer, or by hand.

2. Put sugar, vinegar, oil, salt, and pepper into a non-metal bowl. Stir to dissolve sugar. Add cabbage. Toss, cover, refrigerate, and let marinate for at least 8 hours. Overnight if you wish. Toss occasionally.

3. Put into a bowl and serve as is done in Picardy, or spoon it into dark green Bibb lettuce leaves and serve as individual salads.

POIRES À LA CRÈME PÂTISSIÈRE

[*Pears in Cream Sauce*]

Sugar	Grand Marnier
¼ cup flour	2 tablespoons Kirsch
Salt	3 fresh pears
4 egg yolks	1 teaspoon Fruit Fresh
2 cups whole milk	Butter

1. Combine ½ cup sugar, flour, and ½ teaspoon salt in a saucepan. Mix together with a whisk. Add yolks and milk to make a paste. Add balance of milk. Stir-cook over very low heat until thick. Remove from heat. Add 3 tablespoons Grand Marnier and Kirsch.

2. Set into cold water. Stir until cool. Pour into a serving dish and cover with transparent wrap. Refrigerate over night, or until very cold. If the sauce seems too thick, dilute it with a bit of cream and Kirsch.

3. Peel pears and remove cores. Put into water with Fruit Fresh (ascorbic acid) which will keep pears from turning dark. Just before serving dinner, sauté the pears in a chunk of butter. Cook one side, sprinkle with salt and 2 tablespoons of sugar and turn. Sprinkle again with salt and sugar. Cook about 5 minutes per side. Set aside.

4. When ready to serve the dessert, heat the pears. Add 3 tablespoons Grand Marnier and set ablaze. Cook until the flame dies. Serve in individual fruit dishes and top with a spoonful of the cold sauce. Heat of the half pear will thin the sauce, so do not thin the sauce too much when you make it. Chopped green pistachio nuts are nice sprinkled over the sauce, but then the dish takes on Paris airs. Let guests help themselves to more sauce.

POITOU, BERRY

The names of these two provinces are synonymous with simple and satisfying foods and wines. Both have superb raw materials. Cattle, sheep, and pigs are excellent in flavor, and poultry of every description is raised—especially ducks for their foie gras. All sorts of other foods are available, from shellfish to goat's milk, but the rustic dishes of these provinces suffer from comparison with the elegant cuisine of the neighboring Île-de-France and Touraine.

Poitou is famous for its vegetables, especially onions, cauliflowers, and green cabbages. Most of its best specialities are vegetable dishes, particularly a hash of vegetables to which bacon, cream, and eggs are added. Poitevine dishes like this one are ordinarily cooked at a low heat for a long time. Its meat and fish dishes, aside from ordinary stews, frighten off strangers, for much use is made of those parts of the animal euphemistically referred to as "variety meats" in this country. More often than not the dishes also include the head as well as a few tails and ears.

Berry is undisputedly the producer of the best sheep raised in France. But the countryman of Berry prefers rich soups to roasted or braised meats. Compounded of potatoes and salt pork, soup is eaten at every meal, including breakfast. For guests the Berrichon cook will often prepare a hearty dish of lamb and beans and serve it with a local variety of Sancerre wine. And as a special treat one might even be offered the dessert called *Citrouillat,* or pumpkin pie!

MENU

Filets de Boeuf à la Poitou
[Fillets with Chicken Liver Pâté]

Wine: Château Lagrange or La Commanderie

Pommes de Terre à l'Angoumois
[Potato-Cabbage Casserole]

Petits Pois de Cérons
[Peas with Pork]

Pain Perdu
[French Toast]

FILETS DE BOEUF À LA POITOU

[Fillets with Chicken Liver Pâté]

12 (¼-inch thick) tenderloin
    fillets
½ pound chicken livers
Clarified butter
1 teaspoon anchovy paste
1 bay leaf
¼ teaspoon sugar
½ teaspoon salt
Dash thyme

Freshly ground pepper
¼ cup chicken broth
2 tablespoons crème fraîche, or
    whipping cream
2 tablespoons Madeira
1 cup sliced mushrooms
Chunk butter
2 tablespoons Cognac
Minced chives or green onion tops

1. The easiest way to get fillets cut the way you want them is to buy a whole, or tail half of a tenderloin and cut them yourself. Freeze what is not used in this recipe.

2. Cut livers apart so that they will cook evenly. Check each liver to be sure the green bile sac has been removed. Sauté livers in a chunk of clarified butter with anchovy paste, bay leaf, sugar, salt, thyme, and pepper. Stir-cook about 4 minutes. Discard bay leaf.

3. Put livers into blender container. Add chicken broth, crème and Madeira. Blend to a puree. Sauté mushrooms in a chunk of butter. Add liver sauce. Heat.

4. Sauté beef slices in clarified butter for about 1 minute on each side. Keep the beef rare. Pour Cognac over the meat and set aflame. When flame dies, add the liver sauce. Heat to a boil and then lift fillets to a platter. Glaze with the sauce and sprinkle with chives.

NOTE: The trick of this dish is to keep the beef rare. Pack any meat and sauce that is left into a small dish, refrigerate, and serve as a pâté. It is delicious when cold.

POMMES DE TERRE À L'ANGOUMOIS
[*Potato-Cabbage Casserole*]

½ head green cabbage, shredded	Freshly ground pepper
Butter	Salt
3 slices lean bacon, diced and fried	1 clove garlic, crushed
4 red potatoes	Chicken stock

Grated Gruyère cheese

1. Sauté cabbage in butter for a few minutes. Keep the cabbage crisp. Put cabbage into a buttered 8 × 6 × 2-inch baking dish. Fry bacon crisp.

2. Peel potatoes. Cut into ⅛-inch slices. Put a layer of potatoes over the cabbage. Sprinkle with pepper. Add a bit of salt, providing the stock is not salted. Sprinkle potatoes with bacon bits. (Just one layer of potatoes.)

3. Crush garlic through a press, or mash in a salad bowl with the spoon. Add 1 cup of stock to the salad bowl, or crush the garlic into the stock. Stir and pour over the potatoes. Add more stock to cover the potato slices. Sprinkle with cheese. Cover dish tight with foil. Bake in a 350-degree oven for 30 minutes. Reduce heat to 325 degrees and bake about 1 hour. Liquids should be evaporated. If not, remove foil and cook until liquids are gone, and the potatoes browned. Serve from the casserole, using a pancake turner.

PETITS POIS DE CÉRONS
[*Peas with Pork*]

2 (10-ounce) packages of frozen peas	1 bay leaf
	3 sprigs parsley
½ pound lean pork	⅛ teaspoon thyme
Chunk butter	⅛ teaspoon chervil
12 boiling onions	1 teaspoon sugar
2 teaspoons flour	1 teaspoon salt
1 head Boston lettuce, shredded	½ cup water

1. Thaw peas. Cut pork into small pieces. Fry pork in butter with the onions until lightly browned. Add flour and stir.

2. Add peas and balance of ingredients. Cover and simmer 30 minutes. Discard bay leaf and parsley. Taste and adjust seasonings.

PAIN PERDU

[*French Toast*]

½ cup milk	6 slices firm-type bread
5 tablespoons sugar	2 small eggs
⅛ teaspoon salt	Flour
¼ teaspoon vanilla	Clarified butter (at least ¼ pound)
3 tablespoons Grand Marnier	Sugar and butter

1. Heat milk to very warm. Remove from heat. Add sugar, salt, vanilla, and Grand Marnier. Stir to dissolve sugar and salt.

2. Place bread (leave crusts on) in one layer in a shallow foil pan, or similar container. Spoon 2 tablespoons of milk mixture onto each slice and then pour the rest in around the slices. Let soak at least 10 minutes and no longer than 20.

3. Put eggs into mixing bowl. Beat with a whisk until light and well mixed. Put flour onto a dinner plate.

4. Heat a large, heavy skillet. When it is hot, add about 2 tablespoons of butter and let it melt. Dip soaked bread into eggs and then coat with flour. Fry. When first side is brown, turn. Sprinkle the browned side with sugar. Put on serving platter, top each slice with a pat of butter, and serve with sugar.

MENU

Agneau Farci
[*Stuffed Lamb*]

Wine: Sancerre, or Chavignol

Pommes de Terre à la Berrichonne
[*Herbed Potatoes*]

Salade

Matafan
[*Skillet Cake*]

AGNEAU FARCI

[*Stuffed Lamb*]

1 (5–6 pound) leg, or butt end of a leg of lamb

Stuffing

2 cups minced mushrooms	½ teaspoon rosemary, crushed
2 tablespoons olive oil	1 teaspoon minced parsley
1 clove garlic, minced	2 teaspoons cornstarch
½ teaspoon dried fennel, crushed	2 egg whites

Salt and pepper to season

1. Debone the lamb (or have your butcher do it). Trim off some of the fat. Cut some of the meat from the inside of the leg so that the thickness of the meat is about the same throughout. Use trimmed off meat to make curried lamb or ground lamb patties, or if the meat can be cut into cubes, make stew for two. Use within a day or so, or freeze.

2. Combine the stuffing ingredients and any bits of meat that have been scraped from the bones. Spread over the deboned lamb, and fold meat over stuffing to make a rolled roast. Tie in several places. The mixture will ooze out, so put a sheet of foil over both ends and down the seam, but not over the top. Tie foil in place. Put foil side down into roasting pan.

3. Roast in a 425-degree oven for 30 minutes and then reduce heat to 325 degrees and cook about 2 hours, or 155 degrees on a meat thermometer for medium, 165 degrees for medium to well-done. (A thermometer is hard to use on this piece of meat because of the stuffing.) When it is done, remove roast from oven and let rest 15 minutes. Remove string and foil. Garnish platter with potatoes and parsley and serve.

POMMES DE TERRE À LA BERRICHONNE

[*Herbed Potatoes*]

3 slices lean bacon, diced	4 sprigs parsley
Piece butter	Thyme branch, or dash of thyme
1 onion, diced	Dash of sugar
6 potatoes	1 bay leaf
Chicken stock	Salt and pepper to season

Minced parsley

1. Put diced bacon into cold water and bring to a boil to blanch the bacon. Drain. Put into a 9-inch skillet with the butter and onions. Stir-fry until bacon is rendered and is somewhat crisp. Spoon off fat.

(*continued*)

2. Peel potatoes. Cut into fourths and then across into eighths. Carve each piece into an olive shape. (Boil trimmings in water and then add cream and some butter and make a small dish of soup for lunch.) Add the carved potatoes to the skillet. Sauté until lightly browned. Add stock to cover potatoes. Add parsley, thyme, sugar, and bay leaf. Season. Cover and simmer until done, or about 30 minutes. Liquids should have reduced and become thick. If not, remove lid and boil. Discard parsley sprigs, bay leaf, and thyme branch if used. Sprinkle potatoes with minced parsley and place around the lamb.

MATAFAN
[Skillet Cake]

1 cup flour	2 eggs
½ cup sugar plus 2 tablespoons	⅓ cup milk
¼ teaspoon salt	Clarified butter

1. Mix together flour, sugar, and salt in a medium-sized bowl. Put eggs into mixer bowl and beat until light. Add milk to eggs and mix. Pour into the dry ingredients and mix well.

2. Melt about 2 tablespoons clarified butter in a 6- to 7-inch enameled or iron skillet. Add half the batter. Reduce heat to very low, or set skillet on a mat. Lay a sheet of foil over the skillet and cook pancake about 5 minutes. Do not let it burn.

3. Put a piece of clarified butter on a fork and run it around the inside of the skillet. Run a knife around the sides and then with a pancake turner, turn the pancake over. The top should still be soft, but not runny. Brown and cook the second side for about 3 minutes. Lift out and make the second cake.

4. Put on a plate, spread with jam, or jelly, or sprinkle with sugar. Cut into wedges to serve.

NOTE: Do not make the cake larger than 6 or 7 inches or it will be difficult to turn. I think these taste better fried in small cakes, like pancakes, but small cakes are less authentic.

PROVENCE, NICE

In its customs, especially cooking, Provence resembles Italy, its eastern neighbor. The coastal region from the Rhone to the Alps was the most important Roman *provincia* (hence its name) outside of Italy from the second century B.C. During much of the fourteenth century the popes were in "Babylonian captivity" at Avignon, now a great center for the distribution of Rhone wines. Petrarch, the contemporary poet, wrote that "the princes of the church value the wine of Provence." This is hardly surprising, since they had close at hand the distinguished vintages of the Côtes du Rhone. In addition to these there are today other local wines of the Côtes de Provence. They are grown north of the coastal mountains, the whites by far surpassing the reds and rosés. One of the most popular red wines of the region, the Châteauneuf-du-Pape, recalls in its name the period when the popes enjoyed "protective custody" in one of the finest food and wine regions of France.

As in most Mediterranean areas, olive oil, garlic, and tomatoes are the hallmarks of Provençal cooking. The Provençals cherish the olive for its unequaled oil and its many useful by-products. Garlic has but one important virtue, the taste and texture it adds to other foods. The sunny, tolerant Provençals happily add it to almost everything without apology. But it should be remembered that the garlic of the south, like the temperature, is relatively mild. The tomato, an American product, has been eaten by the Mediterranean peoples only since 1600 (the northern Europeans took much longer to accept it). Today it is a staple in Provençal sauces, soups, and salads as well as a vegetable in its own right.

Visitors to the Riviera often hesitate to leave the protected dining rooms of their international hotels, but for those adventurous few willing to strike out on their own, the hinterlands of Provence provide worthwhile tours of culinary exploration.

MENU

Daube de Boeuf à la Provençale
[*Beef Stew Mediterranean Style*]

Wine: Châteauneuf-du-Pape or Hermitage

Piments Doux à la Vinaigrette
[*Grilled Sweet Red Pepper Salad*]

Pain Ordinaire
[*French Bread*]

Tarte aux Citrons
[*Lemon Pie*]

La Liqueur de Lait
[*Golden-Milk Liqueur*]

DAUBE DE BOEUF À LA PROVENÇALE

[*Beef Stew Mediterranean Style*]

6 slices bacon	6 cloves garlic, minced fine
Salt and pepper	Minced parsley, lots
	3 pounds lean chuck beef in the piece

Marinade

2 cups white wine, approximately	¼ cup olive oil
	3 tablespoons Cognac

For braising

3 slices bacon	½ pound pork shoulder, diced
4 carrots	1 cup Italian black olives
4 large onions	2 bay leaves
½ pound mushrooms, sliced	6 sprigs parsley
6 whole, canned plum tomatoes	1 branch thyme, or ⅛ teaspoon

1. Lay 6 bacon slices on a large cutting board. Sprinkle with salt, pepper, garlic, and parsley.

2. Cut 6 pieces of meat from the chuck that are about 2 by 3 inches in size. Lay each piece, lengthwise, on the bacon slices. Fold bacon around the meat and tie like a package. Place in a non-metal flat dish. Cut remainder of beef into chunks. Add to dish. Pour marinade of wine, oil, and Cognac into the dish. Let the meat marinate 3 hours.

3. Put 3 bacon slices into the bottom of a casserole. Peel carrots. Cut on the diagonal into ⅛-inch thick slices. Put on top of the bacon. Peel onions. Cut into ⅛-inch-thick slices and separate into rings.

4. Put the beef packages on top of the carrots and the pieces of beef around the packages of meat. Add the onion rings and mushrooms. With a fork, mash the tomatoes, discarding the tough stem end. Add tomatoes to casserole. Add pieces of pork shoulder and tuck olives down into the tomatoes. Add bay leaves, parsley, and thyme. Add the marinade liquids. Bring to a boil on top of the range. Cover with foil and press the casserole lid into the foil to close the casserole tight. Braise in a 350-degree oven for 15 minutes. Reduce heat to 300 degrees and cook another 2½ hours.

5. Discard bay leaves, parsley, and thyme branch if used. Put meat packages on serving platter. Remove strings without damaging the packages. Place the packages along center of platter. Put meat pieces and vegetables around them. Skim fat from surface of liquids and discard. Spoon sauce over the meat. Add boiled potatoes to the serving platter if you wish and serve with French bread. This sauce is great for "dunking."

PIMENTS DOUX À LA VINAIGRETTE

[*Grilled Sweet Red Pepper Salad*]

4 large red bell peppers	½ teaspoon sugar
3 cloves garlic	½ teaspoon dried chervil
¼ teaspoon salt	½ cup olive oil (no substitutes)
2 tablespoons wine vinegar	

1. Wash peppers and dry them. Place over charcoal, under broiler, or on a cal-rod grill. Char and cook the peppers on all sides. Rotate the peppers by their stems.

2. When peppers are charred and cooked, lift them, one at a time, to a plate. Pull off charred outside skin and discard. Cut peppers in half. Remove seeds and membrane and discard. Cut the half-peppers again in half. Put the quartered peppers, and their liquids into a non-metal container.

3. Mash garlic to a pulp. Add salt, sugar, and chervil and continue to crush. Add oil and vinegar. Mix well. Spoon over the peppers. Let marinate at room temperature for several hours.

4. If peppers are not used the same day, pour a layer of olive oil over the top and refrigerate. Eat within a week. To keep indefinitely, freeze. Always bring to room temperature before serving.

TARTE AUX CITRONS

[*Creamy Lemon Pie*]

Pie shell

¼ pound butter

2 cups flour

2 tablespoons confectioners' sugar

½ teaspoon salt

4 tablespoons whipping cream

Butter and flour for pan

Filling

2 cups milk

¾ cup sugar

½ cup flour

2 whole eggs

3 egg yolks

½ teaspoon salt

Grated rind from 1 lemon

6 tablespoons lemon juice (about

1½ lemons)

2 tablespoons butter, or a piece

¼ cup Kirsch

Meringue

Sugar

1 tablespoon cornstarch

½ cup water

3 egg whites

⅛ teaspoon salt

½ teaspoon vanilla

½ teaspoon lemon flavoring

1. Preheat oven to 450 degrees. Put butter into mixer bowl to soften. Add flour, sugar, and salt. Blend until mixture looks like fine crumbs. Add cream and beat until mixture becomes a putty-like dough.

2. Put dough on a lightly floured counter. With the heel of your hand, push bits of dough off the ball of dough; then collect dough into a ball and push out again. Collect again into a ball of dough. Cut dough in half, making one piece slightly larger. Wrap smaller piece, refrigerate, or freeze to use later.

3. Butter and flour a 9-inch pie pan. Shape dough into a round. Roll dough into a 10½-inch circle, or to fit the pie pan. When dough has been rolled, place rolling pin on one edge of circle and roll dough around the rolling pin. Place rolling pin so that the open edge of the dough is on one edge of the pie pan. Unroll the dough over the pan. Push dough down into the pan and trim off what hangs over the edge. Crimp edges of dough between thumb and finger in a fancy design.

4. With a table fork, stab the bottom of the pie crust in about six places. This allows the air under the crust to escape. Cut a 10-inch circle of foil. Place foil in pie crust and push down tight over the dough. Bake in 450-degree oven for 10 minutes. Remove foil and bake another 10 minutes, or until nicely browned. Remove. Set on a wire rack to cool. Make filling when pie shell is cool.

5. Heat milk to a simmer. Put sugar and flour into small mixer bowl. Mix together. Add eggs, yolks, and salt. Beat on low speed while adding the hot milk. Mix well.

6. Pour mixture into top part of a double boiler. Grate rind from 1 lemon into mixture. Squeeze lemon juice and add 6 tablespoons of it to mixture. Cook in double boiler until custard thickens. Remove from heat. Add butter and Kirsch. Set boiler top into cold water and stir custard until cool. Set aside while making the meringue. Preheat oven to 325 degrees.

7. Combine 2 tablespoons sugar and cornstarch in a small pan. Stir in cold water. Stir-cook over low heat until thickened and clear. Cool mixture by setting into cold water.

8. Put whites into mixer bowl. Add salt and beat until whites start to get stiff. Add flavorings, sprinkle in 6 tablespoons sugar, and add the cooled cornstarch mixture. Beat until mixture is stiff yet creamy. *Do not* overbeat.

9. Pour custard into baked pie shell. Cover with meringue. Be sure the meringue touches the crust at all points around the pie. Bake for about 20 minutes, or until brown. Do not cook meringue at a temperature higher than 325 degrees or the meringue will become tough. Cool pie on a wire rack for an hour or so before serving. Do not refrigerate. Serve at room temperature.

LA LIQUEUR DE LAIT

[*Golden Milk Liqueur*]

1¼ cups milk	Rind from ¼ orange, cut in strips
1 cup sugar	½ lemon, sliced thin
1½ cups Cognac	1 (3-inch) piece vanilla bean

1. Put all ingredients into a glass fruit jar. Split the vanilla bean in half, lengthwise, before adding it to the jar. In winter set the jar on a windowsill where it will be cool. In summer it will have to go into the refrigerator. Stir every day for about 15 days, or 20 days if refrigerated. The mixture will become curdled and unattractive.

2. Filter the mixture. Use Chemex coffee filters. Stand about four cones in glasses and divide the liqueur among them. Let the clotted brew turn into teardrops of gold. Store in a crystal decanter and serve in small quantities. To make different flavored liqueurs, such as cinnamon or herb, simply add cinnamon bark or herbs to the milk and Cognac and let it age together. Makes about 1 pint and has a proof of 41.4.

MENU

La Bourride
[*Fish Stew*]
with
Aïoli à la Provence
[*Garlic Sauce*]
or
Sauce Rouilleuse
[*Red Garlic Mayonnaise*]

Wine: Blanc de Cassis, or Bandol Blanc

Salade Niçoise
[*Niçoise Salad*]

Quartiers d'Orange Glacés
[*Caramelized Orange Sections*]

Café Brûlot
[*Flaming Coffee*]

LA BOURRIDE

[*Fish Stew*]

Stock

1 pound fish bones and heads	10 whole peppercorns
1 onion, sliced	6 sprigs parsley
1 carrot, sliced	1 bay leaf
1 teaspoon salt	6 cups cold water

Sauce

3 cloves garlic, minced	6 fresh tomatoes, peeled and sliced, or 8 canned plum tomatoes, mashed
3 leeks, cleaned and sliced (white part only)	
3 onions, chopped	2 bay leaves
1 branch celery, sliced	⅛ teaspoon thyme
1 teaspoon salt	Pepper
4 medium-sized potatoes	Toasted bread rounds
2 pounds assorted white fish (cod, grouper, flounder, whiting)	

1. Put stock ingredients into large kettle. Simmer (uncovered) 1 hour. Strain off liquids and discard bones and vegetables. (If it is not possible to buy fish bones in your area, add 1 cup of white wine and 1 cup of clam juice to 4 cups of water and proceed.)

2. Put strained liquids into a large, shallow, enameled serving casserole. Add garlic, leeks (see p. 607), onions, celery, and salt. Boil 10 minutes. Peel the potatoes, cut into ½-inch slices, and add a layer of potatoes to the liquids and vegetables. Simmer 20 minutes.

3. Cut fish into serving-sized pieces. Add to casserole. Lay slices of tomatoes on fish. Add bay leaves, sprinkle with thyme, and pepper. Set lid ajar and simmer 20 minutes. Serve from casserole.

4. Put a toast round into each flat soup plate. Spoon fish, vegetables, and liquids over toast. Serve with a garlic sauce. Two recipes follow.

AÏOLI À LA PROVENCE
[*Garlic Sauce*]

The quantity of garlic used in this recipe in Provence is about five times what I have used. Add more if you wish.

1 slice firm-type bread	¾ to 1 cup olive oil
Milk	Salt and pepper to season
6 large cloves garlic	2 teaspoons lemon juice
3 egg yolks	1 tablespoon boiling water

1. Remove crusts from bread. Tear into small pieces and soak in milk.

2. If you have a blender, use it to make this sauce. If not, use a salad bowl and spoon. Crush garlic cloves through a garlic press, if you have one, and into the blender container, or mash in a salad bowl and add to the blender. Add egg yolks. Squeeze milk from bread and add bread to blender. Whirl.

3. Gradually pour oil into blender with speed set on "mix." Sauce made in the blender will absorb ¾ cup of oil—in salad bowl, about 1 cup. Season with salt, pepper, and lemon juice. Mix, add water, mix and pour into a small bowl. Cover and have ready to serve.

4. Serve with fish stews, bouillabaisse, cold poached fish, or green vegetables. Let guests serve themselves, garlic sauces are a personal thing.

NOTE: If this sauce should curdle, mash a clove of garlic in the salad bowl, blend in 1 egg yolk, and then gradually add the curdled sauce to the yolk mixture. The sauce will be even better if this happens.

SAUCE ROUILLEUSE

[*Red Garlic Mayonnaise*]

This sauce is especially for bouillabaisse, but it is also good with other fish stews.

4 cloves garlic
¼ teaspoon red pepper
¼ teaspoon paprika
¼ teaspoon salt
2 egg yolks

½ cup olive oil
1 teaspoon lemon juice
2 tablespoons hot liquids from
    stew or bouillabaisse

Mash garlic in wooden salad bowl with spoon. Add pepper, paprika, salt, and yolks. Mix well. Gradually add oil to make a mayonnaise. When thick, add lemon juice and liquids to thin mixture to the consistency of a sauce. Guests spoon what they want into their plate of stew, mix, and eat.

SALADE NIÇOISE

[*Niçoise Salad*]

This salad is a meal in itself when served with French bread and a rich dessert. It is also a good accompaniment to a meal, such as fish stew that needs a vegetable and a salad. Omit the tuna when the salad accompanies fish or meat meals, and if potatoes appear on the menu, omit them too. There are as many ways to make this salad as there are cooks in Nice. It is comparable to our "Chef's salad," that is to say, a salad created by the cook to go with the meal.

Lettuce to line the bowl
3 tomatoes, peeled and quartered
1 cup cooked, cut green beans
2 small, cooked red potatoes, diced
3 hard-cooked eggs, quartered
1 onion, thinly sliced

1 green pepper, sliced in thin rounds
12 small, Italian black olives
1 small can white tuna (optional)
Minced fresh chervil (lots), or
    parsley

Dressing

1 large clove garlic
6 anchovy fillets
¼ teaspoon salt
Freshly ground pepper

Dash sugar
1 teaspoon dried chervil
¼ teaspoon basil
1 tablespoon vinegar

7 tablespoons olive oil

1. In making this salad one tries to arrange the vegetables in the salad bowl as attractively as possible. The dressing is then poured over the "pretty as a picture" salad and it is then destroyed in tossing.

2. Begin the salad by lining the bowl with crisp leaves of lettuce and then arrange the vegetables in circles, in pie-shaped wedges like a wheel, or in bunches of the same thing.

3. Make the dressing. Mash garlic in mortar with pestle. Add anchovies, salt, pepper, sugar, chervil, and basil. Continue to mash. Add vinegar and oil. Mix well. Let age several hours. Spoon over the salad, toss at the table, and serve.

QUARTIERS D'ORANGE GLACÉS

[*Caramelized Orange Sections*]

6 navel oranges	Dash salt
2 cups sugar	3 tablespoons Grand Marnier
1 cup water	1 tablespoon Cognac

1. Cut orange skin (no white) from thick-skinned oranges. Use a very sharp knife for this job. Cut the thin skin into julienne strips. Put into a saucepan and cover with cold water. Bring to a boil, simmer 5 minutes, drain, add cold water, and drain again. (Boiling blanches the skin and removes the bitterness.)

2. Carefully peel the white membrane from the orange sections without tearing into the meat of the orange. Break the oranges into their natural sections.

3. Bring sugar, water, and salt to a boil. Cook 2 minutes. Add about 12 sections. (If oranges are large, use only 4 oranges and not 6.) Cook 5 minutes. Lift from syrup and arrange sections in wagon wheel fashion on plates. Cook the remaining sections. Cook enough orange sections to make 6 servings, or as many as you need.

4. When sections are cooked and on the plates, add the blanched rinds to the syrup. Cook about 5 minutes, or until skins turn a very dark orange. Remove syrup from heat. Add Grand Marnier and Cognac. Stir well and distribute candied peel over orange sections. Spoon syrup over each plate, cool, cover, and then refrigerate. Serve very cold with Sablé cookies (p. 558).

CAFÉ BRÛLOT

[*Flaming Coffee*]

This is nothing more than Italian Cafe Diablo!

4 cups regular coffee	4 whole cloves
4 cups Italian espresso	Sugar
20 Italian coffee beans	Peel from 1 lemon and 1 orange
10 Juniper berries, or ¼ cup gin	Dash salt
1 (3-inch) cinnamon stick	½ cup Cognac

¼ cup Grand Marnier

1. Put coffees into Italian diablo coffee maker (see note below), or into an enameled saucepan. Add beans, berries, cinnamon, cloves, and 1 cup of sugar. Peel fruits in one continuous spiral piece. Add these to the pan. Add salt and let simmer uncovered for about 1 hour. The liquids should then be reduced by one-third.

2. Add about ¼ cup more of sugar. Stir, taste, and decide whether to add more sugar. The brew should be very sweet and spicy. When the taste seems right, heat the Cognac and Grand Marnier to warm, and ignite it. Lift the hot lemon rind from the brew and pour the flaming liqueurs down the spiral, letting the flames fall into the coffee.

NOTE: If you do not have the fancy diablo coffee maker, just brew the mixture in an enameled pan in the kitchen, strain it into a coffee pot, and serve in demitasse cups. One may also serve cinnamon sticks instead of spoons to stir the coffee.

LA TOURAINE

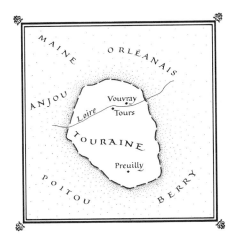

The Touraine, a Loire province comprising Tours and its environs, was the birthplace of Rabelais, Descartes, and Balzac and is the setting for some of the most beautiful châteaus of France. Like the Île-de-France, the province of Paris, it is a garden land of fertile farms, orchards, and vineyards. In cooking it has but few unique specialties because its traditional dishes have become essential components of *haute cuisine*. Just a few dishes remain distinctively local, notably the potted pork of Tours, the shad of the Loire, and the roast pork with prunes of Preuilly.

Vouvray is the best known wine of the Touraine. It is never a great wine with a great year, but it is an honest, natural wine with an earthy flavor and a sparkling look. It is one of the few French wines apart from Champagne that can be drunk alone either before or after the meal.

Over the centuries the Touraine has spawned a cultural and a gastronomic elite. To join their company try the following menu with plenty of Vouvray.

MENU

Rillettes
[*Potted Pork*]

Cornichons
[*Pickles*]

Fricassée de Volaille
[*Chicken-Vouvray Casserole*]

Wine: Vouvray

Pain Ordinaire
[*French Bread*]

Salade

Gâteau aux Noix
[*Walnut Cake*]

RILLETTES

[*Potted Pork*]

1 pound lean pork, cut into strips	Dash nutmeg
¾ pound pork fat, diced	1 branch thyme or ⅛ teaspoon
¾ pound country-style bacon, diced	1 bay leaf
½ teaspoon salt	2 shallots, cut in half
Lots of freshly ground pepper	1 clove
	6 sprigs parsley

¾ cup water

1. Put pork strips, fat, and bacon into a mixing bowl. Add salt, pepper, and nutmeg. Toss together and put into an enameled casserole. Add thyme branch and bay leaf to top of mixture. Put shallots in where you can find them. Tie a string around the clove so that it can be removed. Add sprigs of parsley and water. Bring to a boil on top of the range, cover, and put into a 300-degree oven. Braise for about 4 hours. Remove clove after 1 hour.

2. Water will evaporate and the meat should brown just a little. If it is browning too fast, reduce heat to 275 degrees. When it is done, discard thyme branch, bay leaf, shallots, and parsley. Spoon meat into a strainer and let fat drip from it. Reserve the fat. Using two forks, pull the meat into small shreds. Do not grind it. Put the torn meat into small earthen containers, custard cups, or small soufflé dishes. Press down, but do not pack, and set containers aside.

When the meat has cooled, fill the containers with the fat drained from the *rillettes*.

3. Refrigerate to harden the fat. If any meat sticks up through the fat, add more liquid fat, or melted lard. The containers must be made airtight with a deep layer of fat over the top and no air pockets in the meat. When the fat has hardened, cover tightly and keep refrigerated. *Rillettes* will keep for months, provided they are covered in fat and are airtight.

4. Serve cool but not ice cold, as a first course or with cocktails. Homemade French bread is a must, as are pickles of some kind.

CORNICHONS

[*Pickles*]

This recipe is not from France, but from my French great-grandmother. The women in the family have added mustard seeds sometimes and on other occasions dill seeds. They also used fresh onions and their own dilled pickles. I like them plain and prefer to use dehydrated onions, but do whatever you want with them. This is one of my most used recipes and I am never without these pickles.

1 gallon of dill pickles   Sugar
Dehydrated onions

Make or buy dill pickles. Garlic pickles are the best. Slice pickles *paper thin,* discarding the ends. Put about 1 inch of slices into a Mason-type quart jar (never a metal container), and sprinkle with about 3 tablespoons of sugar and 1 teaspoon of onions. (If container is broader than a Mason jar, increase sugar and onions on each layer.) Repeat layers, packing the slices to the top of the jar. End with sugar and press down to make the sugar wet. Do not add any liquids. Sugar will become liquid. Put the pickles into the refrigerator to age. They will be ready to eat in about 2 weeks. During these 2 weeks, occasionally press the pickles down in the jar. They must be covered with liquid. If there seems to be no liquid, add more sugar and press down on the slices. Keep pickles refrigerated to preserve them. Makes about 2 quarts of packed pickle slices.

FRICASSÉE DE VOLAILLE

[*Chicken-Vouvray Casserole*]

2 (3-pound) fryers, cut up
Salt and pepper
2 slices bacon, diced
12 boiling onions, or 2 big onions,
 quartered
12 mushrooms
¼ pound butter
2 tablespoons flour
6 sprigs parsley

3 cups Vouvray wine (1 bottle)
½ cup chicken stock
1 tablespoon sugar
1 small clove garlic
3 egg yolks
½ cup crème fraîche or whipping
 cream
1 teaspoon lemon juice
Heart-shaped croutons

1. Use only breasts, legs, and thighs of chickens. Cut breasts in half. (Boil remaining pieces of chicken and the giblets to make stock. Use the meat from these pieces to make salad.) Salt and pepper the chicken. Let stand. Fry bacon until slightly crisp.

2. Peel onions. Cut stems from the mushrooms even with the caps. (Add stems to stock pot.) Wash caps.

3. Melt butter in a large skillet. Put chicken into skillet, skin side down, and brown both sides. Add bacon, onions, and mushrooms when chicken is turned.

4. When chicken is brown, stir flour into the fat in the skillet. Cook 1 minute. Fold parsley into a bundle and tie with string. Add to skillet. Add wine, stock, and sugar. Crush garlic clove with the flat side of a knife, and add it to the liquids.

5. Bring liquids to a boil, set lid ajar, and simmer about 1½ hours. After an hour lift the crushed garlic clove from the liquids and discard. Put yolks, crème, and lemon juice into a small bowl ready to use.

6. When chicken is done, put it on a serving platter. Discard parsley bundle. With slotted spoon lift onions and mushrooms to chicken platter. Put platter into a 250-degree oven to keep warm. Liquids should have reduced to about 2 cups; if they have not, boil the sauce hard for a few minutes to attain this quantity.

7. Whisk together yolks, crème, and lemon juice. Spoon some of the hot sauce into the mixture, stir well, and then quickly stir the whole mixture into the sauce in the pan. Heat, but do not boil. Yolks should thicken the sauce, but if it doesn't, add a bit of beurre manié (p. 2) and heat. Spoon some of the sauce over the chicken to glaze it. Serve balance of sauce separately. Decorate platter with heart-shaped croutons.

Heart-shaped croutons. With a heart-shaped cooky cutter, stamp out hearts from slices of bread. Fry these in melted butter until they are crisp and brown on both sides. Place them in a 250-degree oven to dry. Make in advance of using.

GÂTEAU AUX NOIX
[*Walnut Cake*]

Butter and flour to coat pan	1 cup coarsely ground walnuts
1½ cups sugar	1 cup ground almonds
1 egg	¾ cup cornstarch
6 yolks	1 teaspoon vanilla
½ teaspoon salt	6 egg whites

¼ teaspoon salt

Frosting

2 cups whipping cream	1 teaspoon vanilla
4 tablespoons confectioners' sugar	Chopped walnuts

1. Butter and flour an angel food cake pan. Put sugar, egg, yolks, and ½ teaspoon salt into a mixer bowl. Blend together until sugar is dissolved. Mix together walnuts, almonds, and cornstarch. Blend them into the sugar-egg mixture. Add vanilla. Preheat oven to 325 degrees.

2. Put egg whites and salt into a mixer bowl. Beat until stiff and creamy. Beat a "gob" of this into the egg-sugar mixture to lighten it. Fold the remaining whites into the mixture. Pour into prepared cake pan. Bake for about 60 minutes, or until done. When it is done, cool in pan on cake rack. When cool, cover and refrigerate until the next day.

3. Remove cake from pan. Using a long, sharp knife cut cake into 3 layers. (If this seems difficult, tie a string around the cake in two places, where you wish to cut, and then slice above or below the string, using the string as a guide line.)

4. Whip cream until stiff and creamy. Add sugar and vanilla. Beat until very stiff, yet creamy. Spread between the layers. (Be sure to put layers back in the same position as they were before the cake was cut.) Coat the top layer and sprinkle with chopped walnuts. Refrigerate until ready to serve. Serves 12–16.

NOTE: Cake settles as it cools, so don't worry about it.

Conversion Tables

Standard American measuring cups and spoons are used to measure recipe ingredients in this book. Most recipes are written in quarter measurements, or in multiples of 2 ounces.

American measuring spoons are calibrated as follows: 1/8, 1/4, 1/2, 1 teaspoon and 1 tablespoon.

3 teaspoons = 1 tablespoon or 1/2 fluid oz.	1 Am. teaspoon = 1 Brit. or French teaspoon
16 tablespoons = 1 cup or 8 fluid oz.	1 Am. tablespoon = 1 Brit. or French dessertspoon
4 cups = 1 quart or 32 fluid oz.	4 Am. teaspoons = 1 Brit. or French tablespoon
4 quarts = 1 gallon or 128 fluid oz.	5 Am. cups = 1 Brit. quart or 40 fluid oz.

LIQUID MEASUREMENTS

American 8 oz. measuring cup	British 20 oz. measuring jug	French and Continental liter measure
1/4 cup (2 fl. oz.)	1/3 c. −3 dessertspoons	1/20 liter
1/2 cup (4 fl. oz.)	1/3 c. +1 dessertspoon	1/10 liter
3/4 cup (6 fl. oz.)	2/3 c. −1 dessertspoon	1/8 liter +3 dessertspoons
1 cup (8 fl. oz.)	3/4 c. +1/2 dessertspoon	1/4 liter −1 dessertspoon
2 cups (16 fl. oz.)	1 1/2 c. +1 dessertspoon	1/2 liter −4 teaspoons

DRY AND SOLID FOOD MEASUREMENTS

Food	American Measure	Ounces	Grams	Food	American Measure	Ounces	Grams
Almonds, ground	1 cup	4	113	Salt	1 tsp.	1/16	6
Butter	1/2 cup	4	114		1 Tbsp.	3/16	18
Flour:				Sugar:			
All-purpose, unsifted	1 cup	4.2	122	Conf., unsifted	1 cup	4	113.4
All-purpose, sifted	1 cup	3.8	114	Conf., sifted	1 cup	2 3/4	80
				Granulated	1 cup	7	201.6
All-purpose, sifted	4 cups	16	454	Vanilla	1 tsp.	1/16	5.4
Cake, sifted	1 cup	3.1	91				
Milk, whole	1 cup	8	243	Whipping cream	1 cup	8	238
Rice	2 1/2 cups	16	454				

TEMPERATURES

Liquids			Ovens		
	Fahrenheit	Centigrade	Fahrenheit	British "Regulo" (Fahrenheit)	Centigrade
Water:			Slow (250°–275°)	#1/4, #1/2, (241°–265°)	Doux (121°–135°)
Freezing	32°	0°			
Boiling	212°	100°			
Simmer	175°–200°	80°–93°	Moderate (300°–325°)	#1, #2, #3 (290°–335°)	Moyen (150°–165°)
Sugar syrup:					
Soft ball	234°–238°	112°–114°	Medium (350°–375°)	#4, #5 (360°–380°)	Assez chaud (175°–190°)
Firm ball	240°–242°	115°–117°			
Hard ball	248°–250°	120°–121°			
Hard-crack	300°–325°	149°–163°	Hot (400°–425°)	#6, #7 (405°–425°)	Chaud (205°–218°)
Fat:					
Deep frying	310°–330°	155°–165°	Very hot (450°–500°)	#8, #9 (445°–470°)	Très chaud (232°–260°)
	340°–360°	171°–182°			
	370°–390°	188°–199°			

To convert Fahrenheit temperatures to Centigrade: subtract 32, multiply by 5, and divide by 9. To convert from Centigrade to Fahrenheit work the reverse: multiply by 9, divide by 5, and add 32.

Food Equivalents and Substitutes

Baking powder: 1 teaspoon equivalent to 1/3 teaspoon baking soda plus 1/2 teaspoon cream of tartar.

Cake flour: 1 cup sifted cake flour equals 1 cup sifted all-purpose flour less 3 tablespoons, or 91 grams.

Gelatin: 1/4 oz. package, or 1 tablespoon powdered unflavored gelatin, is equal to 3 (4 in. by 6 in.) sheets of gelatin.

INFORMATION

Most cookbooks have separate chapters on such items as definitions, equipment, and measurements. In such an organization the cook must know at what category to look for the answer to a question. Believing that such an arrangement is awkward to use, I have put the terms, or words, that may not be known to you into this one section.

Procedures that apply to particular recipes appear in the recipes where they are needed. For example, the cure for curdled mayonnaise appears in the mayonnaise section and not in some remote part of the book.

Special equipment is not listed because I believe it is not necessary to have great numbers of fancy utensils or machines to cook, or to use this book. When specific implements are suggested, adequate improvisation is also given. For example, a way to broil snails without the special snail pans is given with the snail recipes.

Here then, in one chapter, I offer you the answers to the questions that might arise as you cook from this book. You will find listed here, *in alphabetical order,* the terms and names that are used in many of the recipes as well as explanations of how to make some of the essentials for French cooking.

ARROWROOT. See THICKENING AGENTS.

BAIN-MARIE. A top-of-the-range water bath. The water in it should not be hotter than the food that is placed in it to keep warm or hot.

BAKE. See COOKING METHODS.

BEURRE MANIÉ. A thickening agent of flour and butter. See recipe, p. 2.

BLANCH. According to Webster means to bleach. In food terminology it means to change the particular food by precooking it in boiling water or oil.

Boiling water method No. 1. To peel peaches, tomatoes, and other fragile fruits, dunk the ripe fruit into boiling water to a count of 15; then remove the fruit from the boiling water and dunk it into cold water to stop the cooking process. Then the skin peels from the fruit without damage.

Boiling water method No. 2. This method is used to make green vegetables greener. Submerge the vegetable in boiling salted water for the time designated in the recipe, then remove, cool off in cold water, and finish cooking according to the given recipe.

This method is also used to blanch vegetables when they are to be frozen, but omit the salt.

Cold-water method. Foods are placed in cold water, brought to a boil, cooked the specified time, drained, and cooled in cold water. Use this method to remove the salt from green olives, Smithfield hams, bacon, and smoked tongues. Also:

Almonds and *walnuts* are blanched by this method to loosen their skin and make it easy to remove, leaving white nuts.

Chestnuts are cooked by this method to remove their exterior shell and the interior brown skin, leaving golden chestnuts.

Sweetbreads and *brains* are given the cold-water blanching treatment, after all blood clots have been removed, to firm the meat and make it whiter.

Hot-oil method. Precook or blanch French-fried potatoes in hot oil to evaporate the moisture in them and to cook them inside. Then let them cool and, at the moment of serving, give them a final cooking in very hot oil to make them crisp and brown.

BOUILLON. See LIQUIDS IN COOKING.

BOUQUET GARNI. A combination of 3 herbs: bay leaf, thyme and parsley. French laurier is not as strong as our bay leaves. Some spice houses import laurier leaves. Buy them when you can. The French also have dried thyme on the branch, which is superior to dried thyme leaves. To my knowledge no one imports it.

To make a bouquet garni. Take a bay leaf, lay it on about 3 or 4 sprigs of parsley (in France one would also add a small branch of thyme), and wrap the stems and leaves of the parsley around the bay leaf and tie the bundle together with a string. Since we cannot buy thyme on the branch, add about ⅛ teaspoon thyme to the pot.

This little bundle of herbs is added directly to the cooking liquid. When it has released sufficient bouquet to the food, it is lifted out by its string and discarded before it imparts too much flavor, thus giving a bitter taste to the sauce.

BRAISE. See COOKING METHODS.

BREAD. Throughout the book we use firm-type sliced or unsliced bread.

Croustades are nothing more than hollowed-out, thick bread slices. *To make them:* Cut a 2-inch slice of bread. Trim off crusts. Cut a cube in the center of the slice, leaving a ½-inch wall of bread on the sides. With a fork carefully tear out the center cube, leaving the bottom ½-inch thick. Put the croustades on a cooky sheet and toast in a 325-degree oven until dried out and browned. These may be made in advance and kept on hand in a metal container. Be sure they are completely dried out, or they will become moldy.

Croutons are small dried-out cubes of bread. *To make them:* Cut crusts from sliced bread. Butter both sides of the slice, then cut into ¼- or ½-inch cubes, depending upon the size desired. Fry-toss in hot skillet until browned on all sides. When brown put on cooky sheet and place in 300-degree oven for about 20 minutes, or until dry.

Fried bread. Butter a slice of bread on both sides and then fry in a skillet, browning both sides.

Toast points. Trim crusts, then toast or fry a buttered slice of bread. Cut diagonally into fourths.

BROIL. See COOKING METHODS.

BROWN COLORING. See recipe, p. 3.

BUTTER. Throughout this book only unsalted butter is used, and for three reasons:

    a. Salt toughens protein;

    b. It is easier to control the saltiness of a dish if the butter has no salt; and

    c. The salt settles to the bottom as do other impurities in the butter, and it tends to burn before the butter is hot.

If using salted butter to prepare the recipes, adjust the salt accordingly.

Clarified butter is butter with the impurities removed. Melt the butter over low heat, then remove from the heat and tilt the pan to one side to create a well of liquid butter. Skim the foam from the top and discard. Ladle the pure golden butter off the milky residues that have settled to the bottom of the pan.

Plastic-bottle clarification of butter: Put melted butter into a plastic bottle with a nozzle (available in dime stores and at hardware dealers or from your beauty operator). Then stand the bottle upside down in a cup and let the impurities settle into the nozzle. This will take about 5 minutes. Once milky impurities are in the nozzle, squeeze them out and discard. The color of the liquid in the nozzle changes from milky-white to yellow when down to the pure butter. There will be about a tablespoon of impurities in ¼ pound of butter.

Measuring butter.

Piece of butter	= about 1 tablespoon
Chunk of butter	= about 2 tablespoons
⅛ pound	= about 4 tablespoons
¼ pound	= about 8 tablespoons, or ½ cup
½ pound	= 1 cup

CARROTS, CHOPPED. See CHOPPED, DICED, OR MINCED FOODS.

CAPERS. These are the flower buds of the caper bush which grows along the Mediterranean coast and in India. We buy them pickled to use in sauces and dressings. When old, they become soft and impossible to use. Check the bottle before buying. If the liquid is cloudy and the capers without shape, don't buy them.

Washed capers are those that have been rinsed in clear cold water to remove their salty flavor. Put them into a small tea strainer and submerge them in ice water. Cold water also has a tendency to plump them. Blot on paper towels before using.

CHOPPED, DICED, OR MINCED FOODS:

Chopped	= ¼-inch cubes
Diced	= ⅛-inch cubes
Minced	= ¹⁄₁₆-inch cubes

Carrots. Rather than peeling carrots from top to bottom, do the lower half first then turn carrot upside down and peel the top half, or vice versa. In this way fingernails and polish are not damaged.

Once a carrot is peeled, trim off top and bottom. Slice in half the long way and place cut side down on chopping board. Cut in horizontal slices, if carrot is thick; then cut in strips the length of the carrot and then cut across these two cuts into pieces of the size desired.

Garlic. Place an unpeeled clove of garlic on a cutting board. Cut in half the long way, from root to top. Put cut side down on cutting board. Cut off the root end and the top. Lay blade of knife on the rounded surface and press to flatten and mash the garlic. The skin will usually stick to the blade of the knife. If not, lift it off and discard. Thus garlic is peeled and mashed at the same time. Now cut across the garlic to obtain pieces of the desired size.

Garlic should always be mashed and then cut across its fibers. When so treated it seems to disintegrate into the sauce as it is cooked. If cut into pieces, it tends to remain in those pieces when cooked. It is the pieces of garlic that are unpleasant and bitter and that give garlic its bad reputation.

Nuts. Put nuts on cutting board. Take a large chopping knife; with the left hand hold the point firm and in one spot on the board. With the right hand on the handle, swivel the blade and chop the nuts. Using the knife, push the nuts to the center each time after chopping through them and chop through them again. Chop until they are the texture desired.

Nuts are better cut by hand than in a chopper or blender, although such contrivances may be used. A machine tends to mash the nuts and release the oil from them. The knife cuts clean, leaving the oil within the nut pieces.

Onions. Slice onions in half, lengthwise. Cut the roots and tops from them. Lift off the outside layer of skin. (If an onion is peeled in this fashion, you will never cry. It is the tearing off of the onion skin that causes tears.) Put the onion, cut side down, on a chopping board. Slice down, cutting perpendicular to the root; then make horizontal slices from the rounded top to the cut side. Now slice, making the onion minced, diced, or chopped. Use a chopping knife. Put your fingernails midway on the onion, then bend your knuckles forward against the blade of the knife. The knuckles guide the blade and move back as the onion is cut. The fingernails are always back about ½ inch from the area being cut and the knuckles are against the blade, about ½ inch from the cutting edge of the knife as it comes up to make the next cut. When using this method of cutting, one can chop, talk, and not even look while slicing. The knuckles are in command, knowing at all times where the blade is cutting.

Parsley. Pull the stems of the parsley between your thumb and forefinger, thus collecting the curly parsley leaves on one side of your finger and thumb and the stems on the other. Holding these tight, place them on the cutting board and with a sharp knife cut the leaves very fine.

Once parsley is chopped, place in a paper towel and twist moisture and juice from parsley. Dried in this fashion parsley can be sprinkled. If it is not used immediately, leave twisted in the towel to keep it fresh.

CLARIFIED BUTTER. See BUTTER.

CLAY CASSEROLES. See EQUIPMENT.

COATING PANS:

1. Using a paint brush, coat the pan with melted butter, refrigerate, and then coat again.
2. Or coat pan with melted butter. Cut a piece of waxed paper to fit the bottom. Place in bottom of the pan and coat paper with butter.
3. Or coat pan with butter, then add sifted flour and shake the pan to coat the butter completely with flour.

COLLAR. See step 1, p. 336.

CONSOMME. The name given to clarified stock (p. 41). In all clear soups use consommé and *not* stock.

COOKING METHODS. For more detail read Chapter II.

Bake. Cook by dry heat, usually in the oven. We bake fish, cakes, pies, casseroles, etc.

Braise. Cook in seasoned liquids.

Broil. Cook under direct heat.

French-fry. Cook foods in hot fat deep enough to float the food.

Grill. Cook over direct heat.

Poach. Cook food in deep liquids just below the boiling point, a condition called a "simmer."

Roast. Cook by dry heat, usually in the oven. The term normally applies to meats and fowl.

Sauté. Cook foods quickly in very little hot fat.

COOK-STIR. Stir continuously as the food cooks or sauce thickens.

COOK-TOSS. Lift the skillet or pan from the heat and toss the foods within it into the air to turn them over.

COPPER PANS. See EQUIPMENT.

COQUILLES (shells). See SHELLS.

CORNSTARCH. See THICKENING AGENTS.

CRÈME FRAÎCHE. This is a thick sweet-sour cream commonly used in France and throughout this book. Such a product cannot be bought, but it can easily be made at home. If there is a secret to French cuisine, I think it is to be found in crème fraîche. See recipe p. 3.

CROUSTADES. See BREAD.

CROUTONS. See BREAD.

DECORATE. Make foods look pretty through the use of edible foods.

DEGLAZE. A method of rinsing the pan in which foods, usually meats or seafoods, have been cooked. Add a chunk of butter or a little wine or other liquid to the pan. Then heat to release the pan flavors and to volatilize the alcohol if wine is used. The liquid is then poured over the cooked food. If a separate sauce is to be served with the food, rinse the pan with Madeira, sherry, or Cognac and add to the sauce. Do not use butter.

DEGREASE. This means to skim the fat from the pan as it rises to the surface, as you might skim cream from milk. It is no problem to ladle it off the top of the liquid. If the fat is butter, put it into water, heat, cool and then refrigerate. The impurities will settle into the water and the butter will harden on the surface of the water. Once it is hard, lift off the butter and use again in cooking. It is now clarified butter.

DORURE. To coat pastry and breads with a mixture of egg and water. Use yolk and water for pastry, and egg white and water for breads.

DRY OFF. After liquids have been drained from the pan, set the pan back over high heat to evaporate the remaining moisture and dry off the food. Do not let the food scorch on the bottom of the pan. After the foods have been dried, they may be buttered or added to a sauce.

DRY WINES. See pp. 419–429, "The Marriage of Food and Wine." See also LIQUIDS IN COOKING.

DUXELLES. A mixture of onions and mushrooms. See recipe p. 286.

ENAMEL-COATED IRON PANS. See EQUIPMENT.

EQUIPMENT. All equipment used in this book is available on the American market.

Clay Casseroles. These containers will cause any food cooked in them to taste of clay unless they are treated. To prepare them for use rub the entire casserole and the lid, inside and out, with cloves of cut garlic. Put the cut garlic into a piece of foil and press hard against the pot, extracting the juice from the clove and rubbing it into the casserole. After rubbing with garlic, fill with water and add some diced celery, carrots, onions, parsley, and any other vegetable that will impart good flavor.

Set the casserole on a cooky sheet and bake in a 350-degree oven for about 3 hours. At the end of that time, discard the liquid and vegetables and wash casserole in clear hot water.

Remember, clay casseroles are porous and will absorb flavors. Therefore, wash, rinse, and dry in one operation and do not let them soak in soapy water. If you do, they will give a soapy taste to the foods next cooked in them. Even after it is seasoned, occasionally submerge the casserole and the lid in a large kettle of seasoned water and boil for a half hour.

Copper pans from Europe are impractical in an American kitchen. They have been designed for use over very low heat. Our ranges are just too hot, and the flame too close to the bottom of the pan. Invariably the tin lining from the sides of the pan will melt down the sides and into the bottom of the pan. If you have tin-lined copper pans, use an asbestos pad between the pan and the burner when cooking with them.

Enamel-Coated Iron pans. These are perhaps the best all-purpose cooking utensils. They come in all sizes and in many colors. Their one disadvantage is that they chip, therefore requiring some care in handling. Do not run cold water into a hot pan and do not stack in the sink. Some pans have a "raw" rim on the bottom (not coated with enamel) and such pans will leave a rust ring in a porcelain sink.

Iron Skillets and Kettles. Black iron containers will discolor foods containing acids (wines, tomatoes). They are fine for fat cooking.

To season iron containers before using. Put a tablespoon of vegetable oil (or other unsalted fat) into the pan. With paper towels wipe the receptacle inside and out with oil. (Never wash iron with water before it is cured.) Now fill with about one inch of oil, set on a cooky sheet, and put into a 325-degree oven. Let it heat for several hours. During that time brush the sides often with the oil. At the end of the time, discard the oil, as it will have taken on a metallic flavor. Wipe the pan with paper towels and it is ready to use. Store in a plastic bag to keep clean.

Seasoned skillets may be washed after they are used, but never soak them in soapy water. Wash, rinse, and dry in one operation. To keep foods from sticking, periodically coat skillet with oil and heat on stove.

Mortar and Pestle. These are small, deep, wooden, marble, or porcelain bowls with mashers (the pestles) of the same material. The bottom of the bowl is rounded to fit the bottom of the pestle and makes for easy mashing of foods.

Planks. Cooking on wooden boards is a very ancient custom. Before use, they must be seasoned. With a paint brush (see p. 609), brush the entire surface with vegetable oil (but not olive oil), then wipe with paper towels. Thus the plank is washed in oil, not water. Brush again with oil, set on a cooky sheet and put into a cold oven. Heat oven to 300 degrees and bake plank for 20 minutes. Coat again with oil and bake at 325 degrees for 10 minutes; then coat again and bake 10 minutes at 350 degrees. Remove from oven, cool, and store in a plastic bag, ready to use.

FINISH. To add a final food, or foods, to the dish before it is served. Finishing foods include butter, egg yolks, crème fraîche, whipping cream, wines and liqueurs. After a dish has been "finished," it may be heated but never boiled.

FLAVORING LIQUEURS. See LIQUIDS IN COOKING.

FLAVORING WINES. See LIQUIDS IN COOKING.

FLOUR. See THICKENING AGENTS.

FOND DE CUISINE. Basic stock. See recipe, p. 4.

FREEZING STAPLES. Beurre Manié, see p. 2. Consommé, see p. 41. Roux, see p. 613. Stock, see recipe p. 4. Tomato paste, see p. 613. Truffles, see p. 613.

FRENCH-FRY. See Chapter II, "Methods of Cooking."

FRESHLY-GROUND PEPPER. See PEPPER.

FRIED BREAD. See BREAD.

FRUIT FRESH. This is a form of ascorbic acid. It prevents foods from turning dark and is without taste. Fruits such as peaches, pears, avocados, and bananas will not turn dark when treated with this preparation. It is available at drugstores and is put out by Merck Chemical Co. Make it a staple of your pantry shelf.

GARLIC. See CHOPPED, DICED, OR MINCED FOODS. *Mashed to nothing* means to crush garlic in a mortar and pestle (see EQUIPMENT) to absolutely nothing but mush and liquid. Salt and pepper are usually added to give traction and to help in the mashing process. Lacking a mortar and pestle use a wooden salad bowl and wooden spoon.

GARNISH. In French cooking the garnish is usually a part of the total recipe and is often more complicated than the dish itself.

The garnish frequently gives its name to the recipe and tells the diner what to expect. For example:

> à la provençale—with tomatoes, parsley, and garlic
> à la Rossini—with foie gras and truffles
> financière—with quenelles, truffles, cocks' combs, etc.
> Dubarry—with cauliflower
> Florentine—with spinach

GELÉE. Consommé with gelatin added to make it jell. Used as a coating for cold foods. See p. 387.

GRILL. See Chapter II, "Methods of Cooking."

INVERT. Turn food in a container upside down. Usually applies to jellied foods and cakes. To do this without having the food fall out, place the serving dish over the top of the filled container, then, holding the two tightly together, turn them over, letting the contents drop out onto the serving plate. If food does not drop out, lift up an edge of the pan and insert a knife between the contents and the container to let the air into the container and to break the suction. If this does not work, turn plate and container right side up, remove plate, and again dip container in warm water if it contains jellied food. Repeat process and the food will drop out. Do not lift an inverted container from a plate; the contents might, at the moment of lifting, decide to let go of the container. Always turn plate and container together.

IRON SKILLETS AND KETTLES. See EQUIPMENT.

LARDING NEEDLES. See NEEDLES.

LEAVEN. An ingredient that causes lightness, or fermentation. Baking powder, yeast, soda (when used with sour milk), beer, soda water, and egg whites are all leavens. Of course, air itself, when incorporated into foods (puff pastry), becomes a leaven.

LEEKS. These are the fat cousins of skinny green onions. They grow in cinder-like earth and trap gritty particles within their white stalks.

To clean leeks. Cut off tops as you would on green onions, then insert your knife at a point 1 to 2 inches below the green and split up through the tops. Usually you can see the black dirt under the white skin of the leek. It is at this point that you split the leeks. Insert the knife twice, cutting in half one way, then the other, dividing the upper part of the leek into fourths.

Once they have been quartered swish tops through cold water and wash out all the grit. Cut off roots and use the rest.

LIAISON. See THICKENING AGENTS.

LIQUIDS IN COOKING. Water has no flavor. Therefore, whenever possible cook with stock, wine, vermouth, or beer. If using water, season it with butter, sugar, and salt when cooking vegetables, or add a few vegetables such as onions and parsley to give the water flavor when cooking foods other than vegetables.

Dry wines, ranging from 10 to 13 percent alcohol, are used in sauces and meat dishes. The long cooking process volatilizes the alcohol from the wine, leaving nothing but bouquet and flavor. Wine helps to tenderize less tender cuts of meat. Unless otherwise stated, the recipes in this book have been made with moderately-priced red or white imported Bordeaux wines.

Flavoring Liqueurs range from 80 to 100 proof and are used chiefly in desserts. These include Kirsch, Grand Marnier, Cognac, rum, Anisette, Chartreuse, Benedictine, and others. The higher the proof the better the liqueur is for flaming desserts.

Flavoring wines range from 30 to 35 proof. These wines should be added to the hot food at the time the food is taken from the heat, just as you would add vanilla. The warmth of the food volatilizes some of the alcohol. Madeira and sherry are used to flavor hot sauces; Port is used for flavoring cold sauces and gelées.

Stock. Homemade beef or chicken stock is best for making soups and sauces. If canned stock is used, improve its flavor by simmering it for about 20 minutes with a chopped carrot, onion, some parsley, and shredded lettuce leaves. Strain and use.

Bouillon cubes are a poor substitute for stock or canned stock. They have strong flavor and are usually very salty. (Seasonings must be limited when they are used. They are not used in the recipes in this book.)

The words *stock, broth,* and *bouillon* are interchangeable names for the same thing, namely, the liquid obtained by cooking meat, bones, and vegetables together. Throughout this book we will use the word *stock* to mean this unclarified liquid. See p. 4 for stock recipe. When stock is clarified it becomes consommé (see p. 41).

MARROW, BEEF. The center from the round bone of a round steak.

MOCK PISTACHIO NUTS. Coarsely chop almonds to make 1 cup. Put into a jar. Mix about 2 drops green food coloring with ½ teaspoon water. Pour into the jar and cover with a lid. Shake to color nuts. Pour onto cooky sheet. Toast in 300-degree oven for about 20 minutes.

Sugared. Sprinkle damp nuts with granulated sugar and then toast. All nuts can be sugared in the same way. That is, sprinkle with water and with sugar and then toast in a 300-degree oven. Always sprinkle nuts with water before toasting them.

MORTAR AND PESTLE.   See EQUIPMENT.

MUSHROOMS, CARVED. See p. 281.

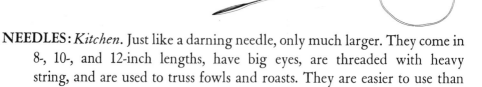

NEEDLES: *Kitchen.* Just like a darning needle, only much larger. They come in 8-, 10-, and 12-inch lengths, have big eyes, are threaded with heavy string, and are used to truss fowls and roasts. They are easier to use than skewers.

Larding. These needles are of two kinds and have no eyes. One of them is a long, hollow, pointed, tapered needle. A strip of fat is forced into the hollow end of the needle and then the needle is pulled through the meat while you hold on to the end of the strip of fat. The other type of needle is a semicircle of steel, similar to a steel used to sharpen knives. This needle is pushed all the way through the meat, then strips of fat are laid into the trough of steel and then the steel is turned over and pulled back out, threading the meat with fat. Hold on to the end of the fat as the needle is pulled out.

NUTS, CHOPPED. See CHOPPED, DICED, etc.

ONIONS, CHOPPED. See CHOPPED, DICED, etc.

PAINT BRUSHES. The small, inexpensive paint brushes found in hardware stores are indispensable in the kitchen. Use them in place of the broom-like pastry brushes. Sterilize before using, then wash as you do pots and pans.

PANADE. A cooked mixture of butter, water, and flour. It is used to give body to delicate mixtures, such as quenelles. When eggs are added, it becomes a pâte à choux.

PARSLEY, CHOPPED. See CHOPPED, DICED, etc.

PEPPER. *Freshly-ground black pepper* is used in all recipes that call for pepper. To get it one puts whole peppercorns into a pepper-mill and grinds them as needed. Pre-ground pepper may be substituted.

White pepper is used in light sauces for two reasons. First, black pepper makes the sauce appear dirt-speckled, and secondly, white pepper is not as strong as black pepper. Since white sauces are milder creations than dark sauces, they do not require harsh spices.

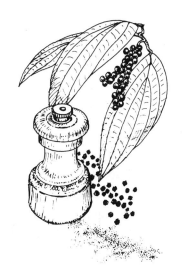

PÉRIGUEUX. With diced truffles.

PÉRIGOURDINE. With round slices of truffles.

PLANKS. See EQUIPMENT.

PLASTIC BOTTLES. See BUTTER.

POACH. See Chapter II, "Methods of Cooking."

PROFITEROLES. Miniature cream puffs. See p. 360 for recipe.

REDUCE. Means to boil liquids to reduce their volume and concentrate their flavor.

REST. Means to let meats stand a few minutes after they are roasted. As meat is cooked the muscles contract, squeezing the juice toward the center. When roasts and fowl are removed from heat the meat relaxes and absorbs the juices back into the meat. The bigger the roast the longer it should rest, the smaller the less time.

ROAST. See Chapter II, "Methods of Cooking."

ROUX. See THICKENING AGENTS.

SAFFRON. Iodine in flavor, this spice is derived from the dried stigmas of the purple autumn crocus. The blossoms are picked by hand and then stripped of their 3 orange-red stigmas. Reportedly it takes some 70,000 blossoms to yield one pound of saffron, or over 4,000 for every ounce. It is the most expensive of all our cooking spices.

How to use: Add the saffron shreds directly to the liquids when the liquid will be strained; when not strained, the shreds are first soaked in hot water, then boiled, and this flavored liquid is added to the sauce and the shreds discarded. Saffron also comes in powdered form, but I prefer to use the whole stigmas.

SAUCE INFORMATION. Cold liquids added to hot flour-and-butter roux will always make a smooth sauce. Cold liquids cool the pan and let roux and liquids heat and thicken at the same time; thus they can be stirred and blended as fast as they thicken.

When hot liquids are added to hot roux, it is not possible to blend them as fast as they thicken. Always add cold, or cool, liquids to hot butter-and-flour mixtures to insure a velvety sauce.

Coloring sauces. Brown coloring is necessary for the coloring of sauces. It cannot be bought, but see recipe p. 3.

SAUTÉ.   See Chapter II, "Methods of Cooking."

SEASONING INFORMATION. Cooked foods when served cold lose flavor in the cooling process. Therefore, always increase the amount of seasonings when foods are to be served cold.

The colder the food the more seasonings required. For instance, ice-cream custard before it is frozen will be almost too sweet to the taste and too strong in flavor. Yet, when frozen, it will taste perfect.

Sugar brings out the flavor in nonsweet dishes, just as salt brings out the flavor in sweet foods. Start using sugar in sauces and vegetables, just as you use salt in cakes and pies.

Taste all foods before they are served and adjust the seasonings to your taste—they have to satisfy someone and it should be you!

Water should always be seasoned if used in cooking. Vegetables frozen or bought fresh lose their oil and sweetness in freezing or in the weeks they have spent traveling to your kitchen. Put back these natural flavors by adding a chunk of butter and a teaspoon of sugar to the salt-flavored water in which these vegetables are cooked.

SHALLOTS. These are as essential to French cooking as crème fraîche. They are a part of the onion tribe and have a mellow garlic-onion flavor. They grow in clusters like garlic. If your market does not have them they may be ordered from Shallot Distributors, Vineland, New Jersey.

When a recipe calls for 2 shallots, it is the whole shallot, and not the individual cloves that make up the shallot, that is required, or about 3 tablespoons minced shallots.

SHELLS. Both coquille and pearl shells may be bought at better fish markets across the country. The coquille is the scallop shell; the pearl shell comes from the mussel. They are attractive containers in which to cook individual servings. Department stores charge more for these shells than do fish markets.

SIMMER. Cook in liquid heated to just below the boiling point, about 210 degrees. The water works and bubbles underneath the surface, but bubbles do not break on the surface of the water. Usually the liquid is brought to the boil, then the heat is reduced to maintain the simmer.

SOUBISE.   An onion mixture used as a stuffing or in sauces. Recipe p. 235.

STOCK.   See LIQUIDS IN COOKING.

SUPRÊME.   Name given a deboned half breast of chicken. Also a white sauce.

SWIRL. Means to rotate a pan of sauce in a circular motion to incorporate a chunk of butter into the sauce as the butter melts.

THICKENING AGENTS. Rules such as "2 tablespoons flour will thicken 1 cup of liquid" are but approximations. A great deal depends upon the thickness of the liquid being thickened. For instance, heavy cream will take less thickening than thin consommé. Adjust the thickness of sauces with beurre manié or roux after the sauce is cooked and before it is finished and ready to serve.

Arrowroot. Use to thicken fruit sauces and in fruit tarts. One tablespoon arrowroot has the thickening power of 3 tablespoons flour. Arrowroot is not used to any extent in meat sauces. If overcooked or reheated it has a tendency to break down and lose its thickening power; so the sauce goes thin. Therefore, I do not use or recommend it for meat sauces.

Beurre manié is an uncooked thickening agent of butter and flour. It is used to adjust the thickness of sauces (see recipe p. 2).

Cornstarch. Corn is not widely produced in France; therefore, cornstarch is seldom used as a thickening agent in French cooking. Like arrowroot, if overheated or reheated it has a tendency to break down and lose its thickening power. The sauce then goes thin. When used to thicken meat sauces it must be incorporated at the last minute and the dish served immediately. It works best as a thickener for sweet acid fruit desserts.

Flour. Throughout the book all references to "flour" are to all-purpose flour unless otherwise stated. Do not substitute instant flour for "flour." If the flour is to be sifted, the recipe will so state. If cake flour is needed, the recipe will so indicate.

Liaison. A mixture of 3 tablespoons crème fraîche and 2 egg yolks. Always this ratio unless otherwise stated.

A liaison gives the finishing touch to potage and sauces. It mellows all ingredients and binds the whole together. A liaison is to soups and sauces what aging is to wine.

Always stir about 1 cup of the hot liquid into the liaison and then pour this mixture back into the whole. After the addition of the liaison, the liquids are heated, but are *not* allowed to boil for they might curdle.

Roux is a cooked thickening agent of butter and flour. It is made by sautéing 4 tablespoons flour in ⅛ pound butter for about 3 minutes. Do not let it brown or burn. As the flour cooks in the butter, the starch cells absorb the butter. Then, when added to hot liquids, the butter melts and the cells release their starch and thicken the liquid.

If the flour is cooked too fast, or over high heat, the cells get seared on the outside and cannot release their starch content to the sauce being thickened. When this happens the tendency is to add more and more roux and then the sauce gets loaded with flour, will not clear itself, refuses to become glossy, and the seared cells give a bitter taste to the sauce.

So, very carefully poach the flour and butter. Once mixture is cooked, put into a jar, cover, and refrigerate or freeze, depending upon how fast it will be used. Its life is equal to the life of the fat.

Roux may be frozen in individual portions of 1 tablespoon; then its life is indefinite. One tablespoon will thicken about ¾ cup liquid.

Roux may be made various shades of brown, matching the color of the sauce to which it will be added. However, the possibility of scorching the flour is great; having 2 or 3 colors of roux on hand is a nuisance; therefore, I make only the light roux and adjust the color of the sauce accordingly with brown food coloring (p. 3).

NOTE: I find beurre manié simpler to make and easier to use than roux.

TOAST POINTS. See BREAD.

TOMATO PASTE. This is used in many recipes. Once a can is opened, freeze the remainder of it in tablespoon-size portions ready to use. When it is needed, simply drop the frozen paste into the hot sauce and let it melt.

TRUFFLES. Expensive underground fungi. We use them as we do mushrooms, but not so frequently because of their cost. One 2-ounce can contains four or five truffles, depending upon their size. Use what is called for in the recipe, then freeze the remaining truffles in individual packages. Freeze what little juice there is with the truffles, or use it in the sauce you are making. Frozen truffles will keep indefinitely.

WATER BATH. A pan of boiling water into which is set a casserole of food, and then placed in the oven to bake. It is kind of an oven double boiler.
Bain-marie is a top-of-the-range water bath (p. 597).

WHITE PEPPER. See PEPPER.

ZEST. The outer skin of the orange and lemon. With a potato peeler, or very sharp knife, remove only the colored layer from the fruit, leaving the white layer attached to the fruit. This layer of colored skin should be as thin as paper and with no white. When grating zest directly from the fruit be very careful not to grate too deeply into the fruit.

INDEX

Definitions and explanations of technical cooking terms
may be found in the Information section, pp. 597–614.

*Recipes are designed to serve six,
unless otherwise stated.*

FL

ART

PIC

ÎLE
FRA

NORMANDIE

Seine

Paris

MAINE

ORLÉANAIS

BRETAGNE

ANJOU

TOURAINE

Loire

BERRY

B

POITOU

MARCHE

SAINT ONGE
&
ANGOUMOIS

LIMOUSIN

PÉRIGORD

Dordogne

A

BORDELAIS

GUYENN

&

Garonne

GASCOGNE

LA

BASQUE

BÉARN

PYRÉNÉES

COMTÉ DE FOIX

S
P
A
I
N